D0081002

Tap into **engagement**

MindTap empowers you to produce your best work—consistently.

MindTap is designed to help you master the material. Interactive videos, animations, and activities create a learning path designed by your instructor to guide you through the course and focus on what's important.

MindTap delivers real-world activities and assignments

that will help you in your academic life as well as your career.

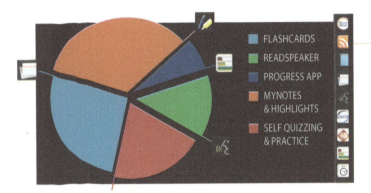

MindTap helps you stay organized and efficient

by giving you the study tools to master the material.

MindTap empowers and motivates

with information that shows where you stand at all times—both individually and compared to the highest performers in class.

"MindTap was very useful – it was easy to follow and everything was right there."
— Student, San Jose State University

"I'm definitely more engaged because of MindTap."
— Student, University of Central Florida

"MindTap puts practice questions in a format that works well for me."
— Student, Franciscan University of Steubenville

Tap into more info at: **www.cengage.com/mindtap**

Engaged with you.
www.cengage.com

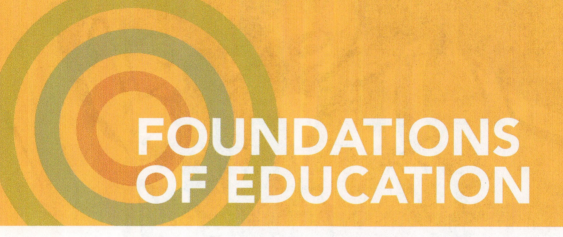

FOUNDATIONS
OF EDUCATION

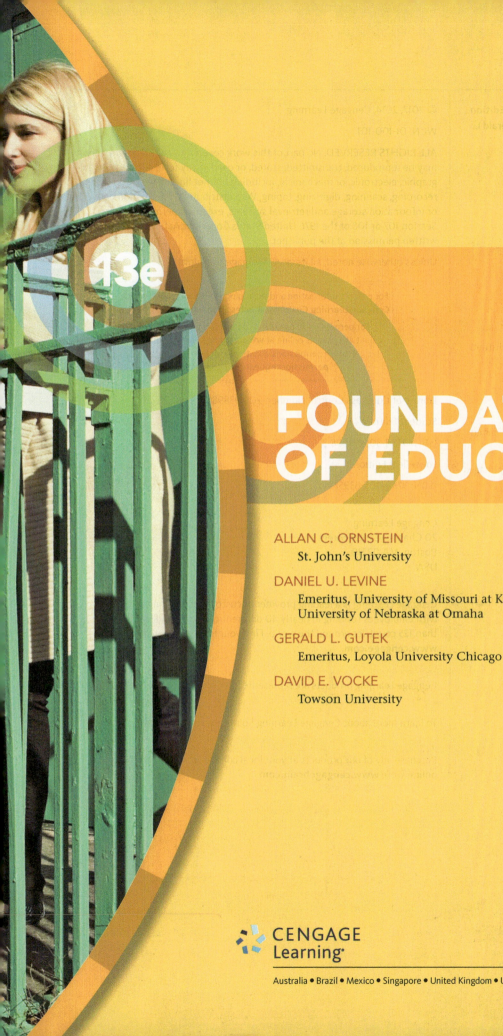

13e

FOUNDATIONS OF EDUCATION

ALLAN C. ORNSTEIN
St. John's University

DANIEL U. LEVINE
Emeritus, University of Missouri at Kansas City and
University of Nebraska at Omaha

GERALD L. GUTEK
Emeritus, Loyola University Chicago

DAVID E. VOCKE
Towson University

CENGAGE
Learning·

Australia • Brazil • Mexico • Singapore • United Kingdom • United States

CENGAGE
Learning

***Foundations of Education*, Thirteenth Edition**
Allan C. Ornstein, Daniel U. Levine, Gerald L. Gutek, and David E. Vocke

Product Director: Marta Lee-Perriard

Product Manager: Mark Kerr

Content Developer: Kassi Radomski

Product Assistant: Valerie Kraus

Marketing Manager: Christine Sosa

Content Project Manager: Samen Iqbal

Art Director: Andrei Pasternak

Manufacturing Planner: Doug Bertke

Intellectual Property Analyst: Jennifer Nonenmacher

Intellectual Property Project Manager: Brittani Morgan

Photo Researcher: Ranjith Rajaram

Text Researcher: Manjula Subramanian

Copy Editor: Julie McNamee

Production Service: Lori Hazzard, MPS Limited

Cover and Text Designer: Jennifer Wahi

Cover Image credit: Image Source/Getty Images

Compositor: MPS Limited

For product information and technology assistance, contact us at
Cengage Learning Customer & Sales Support, 1-800-354-9706.
For permission to use material from this text or product,
submit all requests online at **www.cengage.com/permissions.**
Further permissions questions can be e-mailed to
permissionrequest@cengage.com.

Library of Congress Control Number: 2015938980

Student Edition:

ISBN: 978-1-305-50098-3

Loose-leaf Edition:

ISBN: 978-1-305-63958-4

Cengage Learning
20 Channel Center Street
Boston, MA 02210
USA

Cengage Learning is a leading provider of customized learning solutions with employees residing in nearly 40 different countries and sales in more than 125 countries around the world. Find your local representative at **www.cengage.com.**

Cengage Learning products are represented in Canada by Nelson Education, Ltd.

To learn more about Cengage Learning Solutions, visit **www.cengage.com.**

Purchase any of our products at your local college store or at our preferred online store **www.cengagebrain.com.**

Printed in Mexico
Print Number: 15   Print Year: 2022

BRIEF CONTENTS

CONTENTS

PART 3

POLITICAL, ECONOMIC, AND LEGAL FOUNDATIONS 199

PART 4

SOCIAL FOUNDATIONS 286

PREFACE

We are dedicated to the professional preparation of educators. To achieve this goal, we provide quality content, technology, and services to ensure that new teachers are prepared for the realities of the classroom. Our aim is to connect preservice to practice to foster teachers' lifelong career success.

Goals of This Edition

As *Foundations of Education* enters its thirteenth edition, three goals continued to be central in revising and updating the book:

Goal #1: Include contemporary and substantive subject matter   To meet this goal, we have worked to refine and update the following themes that recur throughout the book:

- **Diversity:** We continue to place emphasis, throughout this revision, on addressing educational issues involving or influenced by cultural diversity.
- **Standards and accountability:** We have added new information to several chapters that addresses the growing emphasis on holding students, teachers, and schools accountable for performing at levels specified by local, state, and national standards.
- **Technology:** We have systematically placed emphasis on the growing role of technology in education. This emphasis includes sections on the history of technology in education, the place of technology in school reform, the expanding reach of new technological literacies such as social networking, and the effects of digital technologies on children.
- **Developing your own history, autobiography, and philosophy of education:** This edition, especially Part Two, Historical and Philosophical Foundations, emphasizes the relevance of reflecting on and writing your history of education, your own educational autobiography, and your own philosophy of education to your professional development as an educator.

NEW and updated content covered in the thirteenth edition includes the following:

Chapter 1: New information on the status of certification and licensing; quality of preparation programs; efforts to improve teacher qualifications and functioning; evaluating current and future teachers based on student achievement; Excellent Educators for All Initiative; criticism of VAM and observation data; elimination of Race to the Top in 2015; waivers from NCLB; Council on Accreditation of Educator Preparation (CAEP); US Department of Education Regulations and Rating Systems; and implications and prospects for future teachers.

Chapter 2: Enhanced discussion of knowledge base for beginning teachers and the Council for the Accreditation of Teacher Education; and updated information on alternative certification programs; teacher prestige and status; state efforts to limit collective bargaining; focus on performance pay based on value-added measures; teacher organization efforts to challenge recent reform efforts; private school demographics; and PTA's efforts to lobby Congress.

Chapter 3: Emphasis on the development of literacy, a written script, and schools; educational implications of the transition of human groups from nomadic to agricultural settlements, and the importance of place (living space) and time (the development of calendars in plotting seasons).

Chapter 4: New information on mentoring used as a strategy to connect pioneers in education teaching and learning.

Chapter 5: Discussion of relating the history of American education to constructing a personal educational autobiography and history; commentary on the importance of location in a place in Native American education; examples of how some teachers used the one-room country school for innovations in instruction; and an illustration of how educational history provides the context for educational issues such as the Common Core State Standards.

Chapter 6: Emphasis on constructing a personal educational philosophy.

Chapter 7: Updated information on school superintendents, principals, and central office staff and their changing roles; updated information on parent and community involvement; new discussion of the Obama administration's policy changes to NCLB; and updates on the adoption of Common Core State Standards by many states.

Chapter 8: Updated school finance statistics from the most up-to-date sources and updated information on taxes that generate revenues for state and local governments; new information on vouchers as a funding source for education, efforts from the Obama administration to fund education reform efforts, and the impact of recent economic times on school budgets and the response of school districts; and updated information on needed school infrastructure repairs.

Chapter 9: New information on the erosion of tenure; teacher exemplars; personal behavior, Internet use, and dress codes; cyberbullying and other electronic misdeeds; disparagement of school or staff; gaining access to prohibited materials; restraining and secluding disabled students; zero tolerance and its effects on schools; and the legal muddle regarding government regulation and support of nonpublic schools.

Chapter 10: New material on poverty, marriage, and parenting problems; establishing a productive classroom culture; and the possible negative effects of social media and the Internet.

Chapter 11: New discussion of issues in measuring and interpreting socioeconomic mobility and aiming to reclaim the promise of equal opportunity for all students.

Chapter 12: New information on current, promising examples of comprehensive ecological intervention; status of NCLB and movement toward waivers; and culturally responsive teaching.

Chapter 13: New discussion of the Common Core Curriculum Standard's influence on curriculum development; and the influence of Partnership for Assessment of College and Career Ready Standards and the Smarter Balance assessment on curriculum.

Chapter 14: A revised look at the history of the influence of values in the curriculum; discussion of the changes in the textbook market, focusing on the digital market; new sections on Social and Emotional Learning (SEL), blended learning and flipped classrooms, pre-K education, and career and technology education; and updated information on direct instruction, twenty-first century skills, virtual schools, the importance of the arts, and Education of English Language Learners.

Chapter 15: Updated information concerning US Teachers in the Teaching and Learning International Survey (TALIS); US achievement among young adults; and sex differences in achievement in the United States and internationally.

Chapter 16: New information on technology and school reform; research on technology achievement effects; full-time virtual schools; flipped classrooms; gaming to learn; and the status of big city school districts.

Other important topics that continue to receive particular emphasis in the thirteenth edition include professional development, the history of education in China, legal protections regarding assaults on teachers and students, problems with and prospects for federal legislation, school choice and charter schools, curriculum and testing standards, promising instructional innovations and interventions, approaches for helping students from low-income families and for equalizing educational opportunity, and international achievement patterns. Unique to this text, you'll find that footnotes not only point to up-to-date sources but also lend themselves to helping students explore topics that particularly interest them. The wide range of sources cited also provides students with access to a wealth of resources for future study of educational issues.

Goal #2: Increase the effectiveness of the text for student learning and provide material that instructors need when preparing their students for teaching careers
Foundations of Education, Thirteenth Edition, includes many special features designed to help students easily understand and master the material in the text and provide professors with the tools to create in-depth and lively classroom discussions.

- **NEW Learning objectives** at the beginning of each chapter are linked directly to major sections in the chapter, so students and instructors clearly understand expected outcomes.
- **NEW Key Terms** defined in the margins make it easy for students to access definitions and review terms in the chapter.
- **Timelines** are included in the history and philosophy chapters in Part Two to mark milestones in education.
- **Focus Questions** appear at the end of each major section and are designed to help students reinforce their comprehension by connecting the concepts discussed in the book to their own personal situations.
- **From Preservice to Practice** helps students both apply and think critically about concepts discussed in each chapter. In this boxed feature, students read vignettes that describe situations in which new teachers might find themselves and answer case questions that encourage critical and applied thinking about how they might best respond in each situation.
- **Topical Overviews,** found in every chapter of the text, summarize and compare key topics, giving students a concise tool for reviewing important chapter concepts.
- **Technology @ School** features keep students up to date on relevant developments regarding educational technology and provide access to websites that will be valuable resources as they progress through their teaching careers. Some examples of this feature include Helping Students Develop Media Literacy (Chapter 10) and Safety Issues and Social Media (Chapter 14).
- **Taking Issue** features present controversial issues in the field of education, offering arguments on both sides of a question so that students can understand why the topic is important and how it affects contemporary schools. These features address issues such as alternative certification, Common Core Standards, merit pay, magnet schools, teacher objectivity, and high-stakes exams for graduation. Instructors may want to use these features as the basis for class discussion or essay assignments.
- In addition, **end-of-chapter features** include **summary lists** that facilitate understanding and analysis of content, and annotated lists of selected **print and electronic resources for further learning** that may be of special interest to readers.
- An **extensive glossary** at the end of the book defines important terms and concepts.

Goal #3: Draw on the Internet and other electronic media to enhance learning Our updating has drawn, to a considerable extent, on resources available on the Internet. Students may explore areas of personal interest by scrutinizing digital versions of many sources we cite—including news sources such as the *New York Times* and *Education Week* and journal sources such as the *American School Board Journal* and *Educational Leadership*. In general, most of our citations are available to students on the Internet or can be accessed easily by searching with university library resources such as EBSCO Academic Search Premier. On controversial issues, we encourage use of sites that represent a variety of viewpoints.

Organization

The text consists of sixteen chapters divided into the following six parts:

- **Part One (Understanding the Teaching Profession)** considers the climate in which teachers work today and its impact on teaching. Changes in the job market and in the status of the profession and issues such as teacher empowerment, professional learning communities, and alternative certification are treated in some detail.
- The four chapters in **Part Two (Historical and Philosophical Foundations)** provide historical and philosophical contexts for understanding current educational practices and trends by examining the events and ideas that have influenced the development of education in the United States. These chapters provide a historical and philosophical perspective needed by professionals in education, encourage students to develop a philosophical understanding early in the course, and establish a knowledge base that will help them comprehend and think critically about the discussion of the contemporary foundations that occur later in the text.
- **Part Three (Political, Economic, and Legal Foundations)** presents an overview of the organization, governance, and administration of elementary and secondary education; the financing of public education; and the legal aspects of education.
- **Part Four (Social Foundations)** examines the relationships between society and the schools that society has established to serve its needs. The three chapters in this part discuss culture and socialization; the complex relationship among social class, race, and educational achievement; and the various programs aimed at providing equal educational opportunities for all students.
- **Part Five (Curricular Foundations)** examines the ways in which changes in societies have led to changes in educational goals, curriculum, and instructional methods. Throughout these chapters, we explicitly point out how the particular philosophical ideas discussed in Chapter 4 are linked to goals, standards, curriculum, and other facets of contemporary education. This section concludes with a look at emerging curriculum trends.
- **Part Six (Effective Education: International and American Perspectives)** provides a comparative look at schools and their development throughout the world and an in-depth analysis of current efforts to improve school effectiveness in the United States.

Teaching and Learning Supplements

- **MindTap™: The Personal Learning Experience.** MindTap for Ornstein et al., *Foundations of Education*, Thirteenth Edition, represents a new approach to teaching and learning. A highly personalized, fully customizable learning platform with an integrated eportfolio, MindTap helps students elevate thinking by guiding them to do the following:
  - Know, remember, and understand concepts critical to becoming a great teacher.
  - Apply concepts, create curriculum and tools, and demonstrate performance and competency in key areas in the course, including national and state education standards.

- Prepare artifacts for the portfolio and eventual state licensure to launch a successful teaching career.
- Develop the habits to become a reflective practitioner.

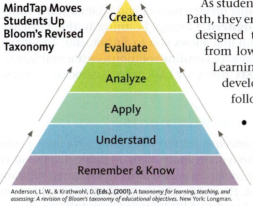

MindTap Moves Students Up Bloom's Revised Taxonomy

Create
Evaluate
Analyze
Apply
Understand
Remember & Know

Anderson, L. W., & Krathwohl, D. **(Eds.). (2001).** *A taxonomy for learning, teaching, and assessing: A revision of Bloom's taxonomy of educational objectives.* New York: Longman.

As students move through each chapter's Learning Path, they engage in a scaffolded learning experience, designed to move them up Bloom's Taxonomy, from lower- to higher-order thinking skills. The Learning Path enables preservice students to develop these skills and gain confidence in the following ways:

- Engaging them with chapter topics and activating their prior knowledge by watching and answering questions about authentic videos of teachers teaching and children learning in real classrooms.
- Checking their comprehension and understanding through Did You Get It? assessments, with varied question types that are autograded for instant feedback.
- Applying concepts through mini-case scenarios—students analyze typical teaching and learning situations, and then create a reasoned response to the issues presented in the scenario.
- Reflecting about and justifying the choices they made within the teaching scenario problem.

MindTap helps instructors facilitate better outcomes by evaluating how future teachers plan and teach lessons in ways that make content clear and help diverse students learn, assessing the effectiveness of their teaching practice, and adjusting teaching as needed. MindTap enables instructors to facilitate better outcomes in the following ways:

- Making grades visible in real time through the Student Progress App so students and instructors always have access to current standings in the class
- Using the Outcome Library to embed national education standards and align them to student learning activities, and also allowing instructors to add their state's standards or any other desired outcome
- Allowing instructors to generate reports on students' performance with the click of a mouse against any standards or outcomes that are in their MindTap course
- Giving instructors the ability to assess students on state standards or other local outcomes by editing existing or creating their own MindTap activities, and then by aligning those activities to any state or other outcomes that the instructor has added to the MindTap Outcome Library

MindTap for Ornstein et al., *Foundations of Education,* Thirteenth Edition, helps instructors easily set their course because it integrates into the existing Learning Management System and saves instructors time by allowing them to fully customize any aspect of the learning path. Instructors can change the order of the student learning activities, hide activities they don't want for the course, and—most importantly—create custom assessments and add any standards, outcomes, or content they do want (for example, YouTube videos, Google docs). Learn more at www.cengage.com/mindtap.

- **Online Instructor's Manual with Test Bank.** The online Instructor's Manual that accompanies this book contains information to assist the instructor in designing the course, including sample syllabi, discussion questions, teaching and learning activities, field experiences, learning objectives, and additional online resources. For assessment support, the updated test bank includes

true/false, multiple-choice, matching, short-answer, and essay questions for each chapter.
- **Microsoft PowerPoint® Lecture Slides.** These vibrant PowerPoint lecture slides for each chapter assist you with your lecture by providing concept coverage using images, figures, and tables directly from the textbook.
- **Cognero.** Cengage Learning Testing Powered by Cognero is a flexible online system that allows you to author, edit, and manage test bank content from multiple Cengage Learning solutions; create multiple test versions in an instant; and deliver tests from your LMS, your classroom, or wherever you want.

Acknowledgments

The thirteenth edition would not have been possible without contributions and feedback from many individuals. In particular, David Vocke, Professor of Education at Towson University, planned and implemented substantial revisions in Chapters 2, 7, 8, 13, and 14. His outstanding contributions to this volume are in themselves a testimonial to the breadth of his knowledge and the acuity of his insight as an educator dedicated to improving professional preparation. Gerald Gutek, Professor Emeritus of Education and History at Loyola University of Chicago, has also made an outstanding contribution to the book as the author of Chapters 3, 4, 5, and 6, which he thoroughly revised and updated for this edition.

A number of reviewers made useful suggestions and provided thoughtful reactions that guided us in every edition. We thank the following individuals for their conscientiousness and for their contributions to the content of this edition:

Cara Barth-Fagan, *State Fair Community College*
Mona Bryant-Shanklin, *Norfolk State University*
LaShundia Carson, *Alcorn State University*
Cheresa Clemons, *North Carolina Central University*
Arnetta Crosby, *Alcorn State University*
Kadene Drummer, *Stone Child College*
Rebecca Fredrickson, *Texas Woman's University*
Sheila Ingle, *Gardner-Webb University*
Karen Martin-Jones, *Bennett College*
Rodney McConnell, *Texas A&M Corpus Christi*

Belete Mebratu, *Medaille College*
Veronica Ogata, *Kapi'olani Community College*
Chukwunyere Okezie, *Marygrove College*
Priscilla Palmer, *Richland Community College*
Beth Sanders-Rabinowitz, *Atlantic Cape Community College*
Deborah Tulloch, *College of Saint Elizabeth*
Mary Ware, *SUNY Cortland*
Murlene Watwood, *LeTourneau University*
Amy Williamson, *Angelo State University*
Julia Zoino-Jeannetti, *Framingham State University*

In addition, we thank the numerous reviewers who have contributed to prior editions.

We also want to acknowledge and express appreciation to content developer Kassi Radomski for her assistance. Other important contributions were made by Mark Kerr, product manager; Chris Sosa, senior marketing manager; Samen Iqbal, senior content project manager; and Lori Hazzard, project manager.

CHAPTER 1

MOTIVATION, PREPARATION, AND CONDITIONS FOR THE ENTERING TEACHER

LEARNING OBJECTIVES

1-1 Identify the usual reasons for becoming a teacher, and determine how your reasons compare.

1-2 Summarize the salaries and benefits teachers earn.

1-3 Explain how teachers are certified.

1-4 Discuss the current trends in teacher education.

1-5 Describe the findings of research on testing of teachers' abilities and the controversy surrounding it.

1-6 Describe what teachers find satisfying and dissatisfying about their work.

1-7 Summarize some of the recent efforts to improve teacher workforce quality and functioning.

David Kennedy/AGE Fotostock

This chapter was revised by Daniel U. Levine.

YOU PROBABLY HAVE BEEN WONDERING whether teaching is the right career for you and whether you will be entering a profession with good opportunities for personal and professional growth. Even if your goal has long been to teach, you might be wondering about the difficulties and rewards of the field you have chosen or are considering. Is your desire to be a teacher strong enough to withstand the challenges you are likely to meet? What can you expect to encounter in your preparation program, and what lies ahead after you become a teacher? This chapter (and subsequent chapters) will examine such topics, including motivations for becoming a teacher, teacher supply and demand, pay scales, career preparation, and efforts to improve the teaching workforce and to give teachers more decision-making power.

1-1 CHOOSING A CAREER IN TEACHING

The path to becoming a teacher begins when you choose teaching as a career. In this section, we'll review some motives for choosing a teaching career and the challenges that accompany this choice. We'll also examine the growing concern that too few minority college students are becoming teachers.

1-1a Motivations for Choosing Teaching

We have many motives, both idealistic and practical, for choosing a career in teaching. Often, a person's reasons for wanting to teach stem from his or her *personal philosophy of education,* a topic we will revisit throughout this book. If you are thinking of entering the teaching profession, ask yourself why. Your motives may include (1) love of children, (2) desire to impart knowledge, (3) interest in and excitement about teaching, and (4) desire to perform a valuable service to society.

One study asked future teachers to state their reasons for selecting the teaching profession. Of the respondents, 90 percent cited "helping children grow and learn" as a reason. Next highest was "seems to be a challenging field" (63 percent), followed closely by "like work conditions" (54 percent), "inspired by favorite teachers" (53 percent), and "sense of vocation and honor of teaching" (52 percent). These reasons also were cited in several other recent studies. Some of these studies further found that admiration for one's elementary and secondary teachers often shapes decisions to become a teacher.[1] This chapter's From Preservice to Practice box also looks at the reasons people decide to become teachers.

1-1b The Challenge of Teaching All Students

You probably are strongly motivated to perform effectively when you anticipate becoming a teacher, but you are likely to encounter some difficulties in achieving this goal after you actually begin teaching. As we point out in this section and in subsequent chapters, numerous jobs will be open in schools, but many of them will require teaching disadvantaged students who live in difficult circumstances with which you may be unfamiliar.

Many of these jobs will involve working with special-education populations, students who are just learning English, and/or distinctive racial or ethnic minority groups with whom you may have had little contact. You probably will be well prepared to teach subject matter in your chosen field, but many of the students you are assigned may be performing poorly in reading comprehension and will need much help to improve their understanding and to learn how to learn.

[1]"Report Looks at Keeping Gen Y Teachers in the Profession," 2011 posting by the American Federation of Teachers, available at **www.aft.org**; Bob Kizlik, "'Why I Chose Teaching as a Career' Statement," 2014 posting by Adprima, available at **www.adprima.com/wannateach .htm**; and Marie Cameron and Susan Lovett, "Sustaining the Commitment and Realizing the Potential of Highly Promising Teachers," *Teachers and Teaching* (February 2015).

FROM PRESERVICE TO PRACTICE

CONSIDERATIONS

"Are each of you certain that you want to enter the teaching profession?" Professor Johnson asked. "Remember, the challenges of the profession often become stressors. About half of the teachers who enter the profession leave within a few years. So, tell me why you want to become a teacher, Jennifer."

"My grandmother was a teacher, and my mother is a teacher. Both of them have told me how rewarding the career can be. I like children. I've loved my experiences with children in summer camps, so now I'm choosing elementary school teaching."

"I want to coach and teach," said Mark. "Some of the best times in my life have been when I played basketball or tennis. The coaches made it their business to see that I followed their discipline and that I paid attention to academics, too. These experiences taught me new values and new disciplines and gave me a vision for what I want to do with my life. I want to work at the high school level."

"I don't have any great yearning to teach," said Caitlin. "I have to support myself after I graduate—my parents made it plain that I'm on my own financially after next year. I want to be an artist, and I think I can do that if at first I support myself by teaching. There are several galleries in the area, and if I could

get a job teaching junior or senior high, maybe I could get some work shown locally, earn a few commissions, and be on my way."

"I know I won't get rich," said Peter, "but there is something compelling about watching the 'aha' experience in a student's face. I've taught swimming and diving during the summers. When a skill finally clicks in, the triumph of that young boy or girl makes it all worthwhile. I want to teach physical education in an elementary school."

Professor Johnson replied, "Each of you seems to have considered this choice for some time. I will share a few other reasons mentioned by other students. Teaching is one profession you can use to travel the world. International schools and foreign private schools search regularly for people such as you. Teaching English as a second language has given many a free ticket to China, Japan, and Korea. Or you can teach as a missionary in church schools.

"Another primary consideration is that state retirement systems usually provide fairly secure long-term benefits. That kind of security can be hard to find in the business world today.

"As a follow-up to this discussion, write a reflection paper about the discussion and your reasons for choosing education. Bring it to class next week."

CASE QUESTIONS

1. Why is it important that preservice teachers reflect on their motivations for selecting the teaching profession?

2. Why are you choosing the teaching profession?

3. Geographically, where do you think you might want to teach? Why? What are the projected job opportunities in that area at the time you finish your education?

Despite the difficulties inherent or implicit in these kinds of situations, you will be expected to help make sure that *all* students perform at an adequate level in accordance with national and state laws, particularly the federal No Child Left Behind Act (NCLB). Although historically relatively few schools and classrooms have had significant numbers of hard-to-teach students in which most of them are performing adequately, the number has been growing in recent years. We devote attention to these schools and classrooms in subsequent material dealing with effective teaching and with unusually effective schools.

1-1c Teaching Force Diversity: A Growing Concern

Although the US school population is becoming increasingly diverse, the teaching force has not kept pace. For example, African American, Asian American, and Hispanic American students make up more than 50 percent of the public-school student population, but the proportion of elementary and secondary teachers from these minority groups is generally estimated at less than 20 percent. Although the number of minority public-school teachers has about doubled in the past twenty years, the number of minority students has increased about 75 percent, thus maintaining a wide shortfall in minority teachers. The disparity is particularly acute in the largest urban districts, where minority students in some locations comprise more than 90 percent of enrollment.

This underrepresentation of minority groups in the teaching force is expected to become even more severe in the future. Currently, only about 10 percent of teacher-education majors are African American or Hispanic; yet members of these minority groups are predicted to constitute a still higher percentage of elementary and secondary students in the near future. In recent years, the shortage of Asian American teachers has also become an important problem. Asian Americans now constitute about 5 percent of the population of K–12 students, but they account for less than 2 percent of the teaching force.[2]

Increasing teaching force diversity to better reflect the student population is widely viewed as an important goal. For one thing, teachers from a cultural or ethnic minority group generally are in a better position than are nonminority teachers to serve as positive role models for minority students. In many cases, minority teachers also may have a better understanding of minority students' expectations and learning styles (see Chapter 11, Social Class, Race, and School Achievement, and Chapter 12, Providing Equal Educational Opportunity), particularly if minority teachers working with low-income students grew up in working-class homes themselves. For example, Lisa Delpit and other analysts have pointed out that many African American teachers may be less prone than nonminority teachers to mistakenly assume that black students will respond well to a teacher who is friendly in the classroom. In addition, teachers from Asian American, Latino, and other minority groups are in demand for working with students who have limited English skills.[3]

Officials of the American Association of Colleges for Teacher Education (AACTE) have stated that data on the low proportion of minority teachers constitute a "devastating" crisis. Along with other organizations, the AACTE has proposed and helped initiate legislation for various new programs to increase the number of minority teachers, including increasing financial aid for prospective minority teachers, enhancing recruitment of minority candidates, and initiating precollegiate programs to attract minority students.[4]

FOCUS What do you think might make teaching a more attractive career option for today's college students, both minority and nonminority? If you are a member of a minority group, what attracts you to teaching? How will you prepare to work with students who may have a different ethnic or socioeconomic background from your own?

1-2 SUPPLY/DEMAND AND SALARIES

supply and demand Market conditions that affect salaries such that pay decreases when there is a large supply of teachers and rises when supply is low and teachers are in high demand.

Will you find work as a teacher? How much money will you earn? These two questions are related, following the economic principle of **supply and demand**. When teacher supply exceeds demand, salaries tend to decline. Conversely, high demand and low supply tend to increase salaries. As discussed in the chapter on The Teaching Profession, supply and demand also affects the social status and prestige accorded to a particular occupation.

1-2a Job Opportunities

In the 1960s and 1970s, a falling birth rate resulted in a teacher surplus. As college students and teacher educators recognized the substantial oversupply, enrollment in teacher-education programs decreased. The percentage of college freshmen interested in becoming

---

[2]Ulrich Bolser, "Teacher Diversity Revisited," May 4, 2014, posting by the Center for American Progress, available at **www.americanprogress.org**; Maisie McAdoo, "The New US Teacher—Not What She Used to Be," October 2, 2014, posting by the United Federation of Teachers, available at **www.uft.org**; and Melissa Sanchez, "To Boost Teacher Diversity, State Scraps Limits on Basic Skills Test-Taking," *Catalyst Chicago*, March 12, 2014, available at **www.catalyst -chicago.org**.

[3]Lisa D. Delpit, "The Silenced Dialogue," *Harvard Educational Review* (August 1988), pp. 280–298; and "Review of 'Other People's Children' by Lisa Delpit," May 26, 2014, posting by Rhapsody in Books, available at **www.rhapsodyinbooks.wordpress.com**.

[4]Esther J. Cepeda, "The Need to Keep Minority Teachers," *Statesman Journal*, June 30, 2014; and Anna Egalite and Brian Kisida, "The Benefits of Minority Teachers in the Classroom," March 6, 2015, posting by *Real Clear Education*, available at **www.realcleareducation.com**.

TABLE 1.1	Public- and Private-School Kindergarten through Grade 12 Enrollments, 1992 to 2022 (in Millions)			
	Total	**Public**	**Private**	**Private as Percentage of Total**
1992	48.5	42.8	5.7	11.8
2000	53.4	47.2	6.2	11.6
2022 (projected)	57.9	53.0	4.9	8.0

Note: Data include most kindergarten and some prekindergarten students. Projected sum differs from 100 percent due to rounding.

Source: William J. Hussar and Tabitha M. Bailey, *Projections of Education Statistics to 2022* (Washington, DC: US Government Printing Office, 2014), Table 1.

teachers declined from 23 percent in 1968 to 5 percent in 1982. Since then, the trend has reversed. The percentage of college students interested in teaching rose by nearly 100 percent during the late 1980s and 1990s and has remained relatively high, although it has declined by about 10 percent in recent years. In addition, many community colleges are now participating in teacher preparation, and economic recession appears to be encouraging more individuals to apply for entry into preparation programs for teachers.[5]

Analysts predict many candidates in upcoming years but also many teaching jobs. Several million new teachers will be needed in the next decade for the following reasons:[6]

- When the post–World War II baby boom generation began to produce its own children, a mini baby boom developed. Most of those children now attend K–12 schools. In addition, many immigrant families have entered the United States in recent years. As a result, school enrollment has been increasing (see Table 1.1).
- A significant proportion of the current teaching force will reach retirement age in the coming decade.
- Educational reformers are attempting to reduce class size, expand preschool education, place greater emphasis on science and mathematics, and introduce other changes that require more teachers.
- Higher standards for becoming a teacher are limiting the supply.
- New charter schools are being established in many locations.
- Employed teachers continue to leave the classroom and/or the profession at a substantial rate.

Other educators, however, insist that the chances are slim of a widespread shortage of teachers in the upcoming decade. For one thing, recent shortages have mainly involved large urban districts and specialized fields such as math and science; many districts have reported no general shortage of potential teachers. In addition, it may be that fewer teachers are leaving the profession than in earlier years, and increased enrollment of students may be leveling off. Improved salaries may also bring ex-teachers back to the schools and attract people who trained as teachers but did not enter the profession.[7]

---

[5]Stephen Sawchuck, "Steep Drops Seen in Teacher-Prep Enrollment Numbers," *Education Week*, October 22, 2014.

[6]Richard Ingersoll, Lisa Merrill, and Daniel Stuckey, *Seven Trends* (Philadelphia: Consortium for Policy Research in Education, 2014).

[7] Robert Hanna and Kaitlin Pennington, "Despite Reports to the Contrary, New Teachers Are Staying in Their Jobs Longer," January 8, 2015, posting by the Center for American Progress, available at **www.americanprogress.org**.

Given the arguments on each side of the issue, it is difficult to determine whether major teacher shortages will be widespread in the next decade. However, shortages certainly will continue to exist in special-needs fields such as education of students with disabilities, remedial education, bilingual education, science and mathematics, and foreign languages. Teachers also will be needed to staff new and existing charter schools. In addition, teachers will remain in short supply in many rural areas and in some city and suburban communities that register significant population growth, particularly in the South and Southwest.[8]

Opportunities in Nonpublic Schools   Prospective teachers may find numerous job opportunities in nonpublic schools during the next decade. As Table 1.1 shows, private schools enroll about 8 percent of the nation's elementary and secondary students. Like the public schools, many private schools are upgrading their instructional programs, often by hiring more teachers who specialize in such areas as science, math, computers, educating children with disabilities, and bilingual education.

In the past three decades, Catholic school enrollment has declined, but many other nonpublic schools have been established. Enrollment has increased most in the independent (nonreligious) sector and in schools sponsored by evangelical and fundamentalist church groups. Moreover, many Catholic schools have been increasing the percentage of lay teachers on their faculties, and this trend is likely to continue. Furthermore, some Catholic schools have been or are being converted to charter schools with increased staffing by personnel who are not part of the church hierarchy.[9]

Regardless of whether a large teacher shortage does or does not develop in the next ten years, astute prospective teachers will take certain steps to enhance their opportunities for rewarding employment. Some of these are outlined in Overview 1.1.

1-2b Pay Scales and Trends

Traditionally, teachers have received relatively low salaries. In 1963, for example, the average teacher salary in current dollars was less than $36,000. By 2005, this figure had risen to more than $52,000. Today, experienced teachers in wealthy school districts frequently earn $80,000 to $100,000. Moreover, teachers have opportunities to supplement their income by supervising after-school programs, athletics, drama, and other extracurricular activities. Some teachers advance to administrative positions with annual salaries of well over $100,000. In addition, keep in mind that public-school teachers usually take advantage of benefits (such as pensions and health insurance) that are excellent compared to those of workers in other professions.[10]

Teaching pay varies considerably among and within states. Figure 1.1 shows the range of variation. Average overall salaries in the three highest-paying states (California, Connecticut, and New York) were much higher than those in the three lowest-paying states (Mississippi, Oklahoma, and South Dakota). Of course, we must take into account comparative living costs. It is much more expensive to live in New York, for example, than to live in the northern plains states. Salaries differ widely within states, too, where average state pay scales are high. Salary schedules in wealthy suburban districts generally are substantially higher than those in most other school districts.

---

[8]Caro Clarke, "Demand for Special Education Teachers," February 7, 2014, posting by USC Rossier; and Alexandria Neason, "Half of Teachers Leave the Job after Five Years," *The Hechinger Report*, July 18, 2014, available at **www.hechingerreport.org.**

[9]Kelly Medinger, "The New Shepherd of Catholic Education," October 2, 2014, posting by the Knott Foundation, available at **www.knottfoundation.org**.

[10] 2012–2013 Average Starting Teacher Salaries by State (Washington, DC: National Education Association, 2014).

OVERVIEW 1.1

WAYS TO IMPROVE YOUR EMPLOYMENT PROSPECTS

Advance Preparation

Check your state's certification requirements and follow them correctly.

Acquire adjunct skills that make you multidimensional, ready to assist in activities such as coaching or supervising the student newspaper.

Maintain an up-to-date file listing all your professional activities, accomplishments, and awards.

Keep well-organized notes on what you learn from classroom observations.

Begin a journal specifically related to teaching concerns. Use it to reflect on what you see and hear and to develop your own ideas.

Scouting and Planning

Collect information on school districts that have vacant positions. Possible sources of information include your career planning or placement office and the state education department's office of teacher employment. Look into computerized job banks operated by professional organizations or available elsewhere on the Internet.

Visit, call, or write to school districts in which you are particularly interested.

Plan your application strategy in advance.

Assembling Materials

Prepare a neat, accurate, clear résumé.

Prepare a professional portfolio that includes lesson plans, peer critiques, descriptions of relevant experience, supervisors' evaluations, and, if possible, a video of your teaching.

Ask your career planning or placement office for advice on other materials to include with the credentials you will submit.

Applying for a Job

Begin applying for teaching jobs as soon as possible.

Apply for several vacancies at once.

Preparing for an Interview

Take time to clarify your philosophy of education and learning. Know what you believe, and be able to explain it.

Be prepared for other interview questions as well. In particular, anticipate questions that deal with classroom management, lesson design, and your employment history.

Learn as much as you can about the school district before the interview, for instance, its organization, its levels of teaching positions, its types of schools, and its use of technology.

FOCUS　What salary do you expect to earn in your first teaching position?

The greatest variation in salaries relates to years of experience and education. Teachers with more experience and more education earn more than those with less of either. Table 1.2 shows the range based on years of experience and additional education in a typical salary schedule for the public schools of Metropolitan Nashville. The salary schedule provides $41,257 for a first-year teacher with a standard certificate and $70,953 for a teacher with a doctorate and twenty-five years of experience. Although numbers change from district to district and state to state, the wide difference between upper and lower pay levels is fairly common.

1-3　STATUS OF CERTIFICATION

During the US colonial period and well into the early nineteenth century, anyone who wanted to become a teacher usually obtained approval from a local minister or a board of trustees associated with a religious institution. A high school or college diploma was considered unnecessary. If you could read, write, spell, and demonstrate good moral character, you could teach school. By the 1820s, future teachers had begun attending normal schools (discussed in Chapter 5, Historical Development of American Education), although formal certification remained unnecessary. Eventually, the

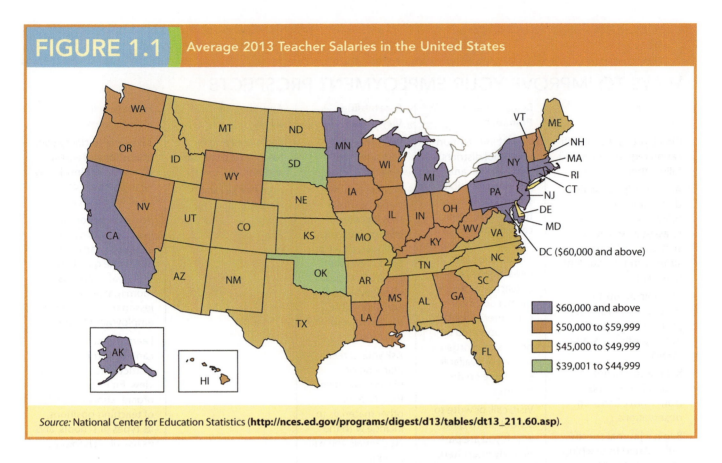

FIGURE 1.1 | Average 2013 Teacher Salaries in the United States

Legend:
- $60,000 and above
- $50,000 to $59,999
- $45,000 to $49,999
- $39,001 to $44,999

DC ($60,000 and above)

Source: National Center for Education Statistics (**http://nces.ed.gov/programs/digest/d13/tables/dt13_211.60.asp**).

normal schools became teacher colleges, and most of the teacher colleges are now diversified colleges and universities. Today, all public-school teachers must be certified or licensed. Except for some alternative certification or temporary certification programs, all states require a bachelor's degree or five years of college work for an individual to enter into teaching.

Prospective teachers who want to teach in a US public school must be certified by the state in their chosen subject areas and grade levels. At one time, most states granted this **certification** based on documentation that the candidate possessed appropriate professional preparation and good moral character. (The terms "licensed" and "licensure" are often used synonymously with "certified" and "certification" for an individual candidate. By way of contrast, "accreditation" usually refers to official approval of a preparation program.) However, increasing public dissatisfaction with the quality of education led to changes in certification practices. States generally now require that a candidate for certification pass a subject-matter test, a pedagogy exam, and, in many

certification State government review and approval that permits a teaching candidate to teach.

TABLE 1.2 | Selected Steps in the Salary Schedule for Metropolitan Nashville Public Schools in 2015

	Bachelor's Degree	Master's Degree	Doctorate
First year	$41,257	$42,167	$47,586
Tenth year	45,028	49,121	57,308
Twenty-fifth year	54,664	60,122	70,953

Note: All teachers must earn an advanced certificate within ten years of initial state certification.
Source: National Council on Teacher Quality

cases, a basic-skills test and a background check. A small number of states require elementary teachers to pass a test on how to teach reading. State governments also require satisfactory completion of a teacher-preparation program, as well as a clinical experience such as student teaching.[11]

Variation in Requirements   Specific requirements for an individual to obtain a teaching certificate vary widely from state to state. The resulting variance in teacher-preparation programs leads to problems in determining the actual preparedness of entering teachers. The required semester hours in general education (that is, arts and sciences) for a secondary certificate varies nationwide from about thirty hours to about seventy-five hours. The minimum hours required in professional teacher-education courses and the number of semester or quarter hours needed to teach an academic subject also vary in accordance with state requirements. Add to this the fact that courses with the same title may have drastically different content from one institution to another, and you'll see why state and institutional requirements, even when taken together, do not guarantee that teachers have studied a uniform set of skills and concepts.

Reciprocity of Teacher Certificates   Differences in certification/requirements between states have also traditionally inhibited the movement of teachers throughout the country. If you were certified to teach in New York, for example, you might not meet the requirements for teaching in Illinois. Organizations concerned with educational quality generally criticized this lack of reciprocity among states. Many educators argued that easing interstate movement of teachers would help (1) balance teacher supply and demand, (2) improve opportunities for teachers, (3) reduce inbreeding and provincialism in local school systems, and (4) increase morale among teachers.

Reciprocity compacts of varying success were established between some states as early as 1900. In recent years, regional agreements have developed that recognize preparation requirements across states. Most states have signed interstate contracts in which they agree to issue comparable certificates to teachers who have completed a state-approved program at an institution accredited by the region covered in the contract. In addition, various organizations are developing nationwide approaches to improve teachers' geographic mobility.

alternative certification Teacher certification obtained without completing a traditional teacher-education program at a school or college of education.

Alternative Certification   Most states have introduced **alternative certification** programs, partly to attract talented candidates to teaching and partly in reaction to current or anticipated shortages in teaching fields such as science and math. These programs help prospective teachers pursue certification without following the traditional preparation path at schools and colleges of education. A New Jersey program, for example, seeks to attract "talented persons who did not study education in college." Nationwide, hundreds of thousands of teachers have been licensed through alternative certification programs. Many new teachers within this group pursue teaching careers after leaving the armed forces.[12]

Critiques of Alternative Certification   Alternative certification programs promote intense supervision and compressed formal course work during the first few years of teaching assignment. Such programs almost always require professional development activities and courses while learning to teach. Several systematic examinations of

---

[11]Elizabeth A. Kaye, ed., *Requirements for Certification of Teachers, Counselors, Librarians, Administrators for Elementary and Secondary Schools*, 79th ed., 2014–2015 (Chicago: University of Chicago Press, 2014); and Julie Rowland, "Trends in Teacher Certification," January 2015 posting by the Education Commission of the States, available at **www.ecs.org**.

[12]"The Pros and Cons of Alternative Teacher Certification," March 16, 2012, posting by Certification Map, available at **www.certificationmap.com**; and Morgan Smith, "Efforts to Raise Teacher Certification Standards Falter," *Texas Tribune*, August 22, 2014, available at **www.texastribune.com**.

alternative certification programs have provided encouraging indications that some attract well-educated individuals and may be meeting their goal of intense supervision. However, there appears to be great variation in both requirements and outputs among the many programs being implemented, and some assessments have raised questions. For example, data on several alternative certification programs indicate that many participants received little or none of the training or supervision that school districts were supposed to provide. In several cases, participants acquired large debts and were unable to find teaching jobs afterward. In addition, mentoring for alternatively certified teachers can place a heavy burden on school districts.[13]

Teach for America   Probably the best-known alternative certification program is a national effort called Teach for America (TFA). Designed to attract recent graduates from colleges at which students have high achievement scores, TFA has spent tens of millions of dollars to recruit potential teachers, train them intensively for five weeks, and place them in school districts with severe urban problems. Some initial reports were promising. For example, in some years, more than one-quarter of the participants were minority individuals, and many of the secondary-school participants had much-needed skills in math or science. Tens of thousands of teachers have been trained, and many are still teaching or hold other jobs in school districts. Several studies have reported promising results regarding the contributions of TFA participants. But other studies indicated that many of these potential new teachers were frustrated by conditions in difficult schools and/or withdrew before completing their teaching assignments. Some analysts believe that TFA has led occasionally to districts firing experienced teachers in order to hire less-costly new teachers.[14]

Despite the growing popularity of alternative certification programs, most teachers attend more traditional teacher-education programs. The Taking Issue box presents some arguments for and against alternative certification programs.

Teacher Residency   The Teacher Residency approach lies somewhere between the traditional route to certification and alternative certification. On the one hand, this approach recruits motivated but untrained candidates, as do many alternative programs. On the other hand, it places candidates in at least a full-year residency under the supervision of experienced teachers, where they have time and help to begin or complete a master's degree approaching the depth frequently found in traditional preparation programs. Carried out cooperatively by school districts and institutions of higher education, a Teacher Residency program can help districts obtain new teachers who are able to function successfully in difficult situations. Furthermore, the program can help universities or colleges meet their obligations to prepare and place outstanding teachers in difficult schools.[15]

[13] Jill Constantine et al., "An Evaluation of Teachers Trained Through Different Routes to Certification," 2009 report prepared for the Institute of Education Sciences, available at **www.ed.gov**; Llyod Bentsen IV and Megan Simons, "Lessons from Teach for America," July 24, 2014, posting from the National Center for Policy Analysis, available at **www.ncpa.org**; and Julian Vasquez Heilig and Su J. Jez, "Teach for America: A Return to the Evidence," *NEPC Policy Brief*, January 7, 2014, available at **www.nepc.colorado.edu**.

[14] Ildiko Laczko-Kerr and David C. Berliner, "The Effectiveness of 'Teach for America' and Other Under-Certified Teachers on Student Academic Achievement," *Education Policy Analysis Archives,* September 6, 2003, available at **http://epaa.asu.edu**; Alexandra Hootnick, "Teachers Are Losing Their Jobs But Teach for America's Expanding. What's Wrong with That?" *The Hechinger Report*, April 21, 2014, available at **www.hechingerreport.org**; and Katie Osgood, "An Open Letter to Teach for America Recruits," *Rethinking Schools* (Spring 2014), available at **www.rethinkingschools.org**.

[15] Liz Bowie, "Baltimore Is Using a Residency Program to Keep New Teachers," August 25, 2014, posting by Governing the States and Localities, available at **www.governing.com**; and Ron Thorpe, "Residency: Can It Transform Teaching the Way It Did Medicine?" *Phi Delta Kappan* (September 2014).

TAKING ISSUE

ALTERNATIVE CERTIFICATION

Many states have introduced alternative certification programs that bypass traditional teacher-education requirements. In general, these programs help orient college graduates to the teaching experience. They then place graduates in full-time teaching positions, where they receive training that leads to certification while they learn about teaching and education.

Question

Should we encourage alternative certification programs that bypass traditional teacher-education requirements? (Think about this question as you read the following PRO and CON arguments. What is *your* response to this issue?)

Arguments PRO

1. Learning to teach on the job can provide better opportunities to determine what does and doesn't work in the actual world and to talk with, observe, and emulate successful teachers.

2. Professional studies integrated with full-time teaching are likely to be more meaningful and practical than studies presented in largely theoretical college courses.

3. Alternative programs, which avoid years of study for certification, can attract teacher candidates to shortage areas such as mathematics, science, and bilingual education.

4. Alternative programs help attract minority teachers, retired persons with special skills in technical subjects, and other candidates who can make important contributions in improving the education system.

5. Competing alternative programs will stimulate colleges and universities to improve their teacher-training programs.

Arguments CON

1. Learning to teach on the job frequently proves unsuccessful because many participants find the immediate demands overwhelming and fail to develop and hone their skills adequately.

2. Initial data on several alternative certification programs show that, in practice, school districts either lack sufficient resources to provide professional studies for participants or have other priorities.

3. These programs offer short-term relief only. Many participants realize they are unsuited for or not interested in the work and withdraw during or soon after the first year.

4. Alternative certification reinforces inequity in education because it often places inexperienced persons at inner-city schools, which have high turnover and the most need for well-trained and experienced faculty.

5. Competing alternative programs may distract colleges and universities from offering training that develops the understanding and skills of reflective teachers over several years of study.

Among the first Teacher Residency programs were three established in Boston, Chicago, and Denver, respectively. Early research has indicated that graduates are performing at a high level, and retention rates in teaching are unusually strong. In addition, implementers and researchers are identifying the program components and elements that help make residencies most successful. Substantial funds for Teacher Residency programs have been made available through the Higher Education Opportunity Act, and numerous institutions are planning or exploring how to participate in establishing these programs.[16]

Assessment of Certification Practices   Tamara Hiler and Stephanie Johnson reviewed the wide variety of approaches and arrangements for preparing individuals to obtain teaching certificates/licenses and reached the following conclusions as detailed in a report circulated by the Education of Commission of the States:[17]

---

[16]"Building Effective Teacher Residencies," November 12, 2014, posting by Urban Teacher Residency United, available at **www.utrunited.org/blog/entry /building-effective-teacher-residencies-a-new-research-report-from-urban-tea**.

[17]Quotes are from Tamara Hiler and Stephanie Johnson, "Creating a Consistent and Rigorous Teacher Licensing Process," November 20, 2014, posting by Third Way Publishing, available at **www.ecs.org**.

- Given the nearly 600 different teacher licensure exams in use, teachers "in various states are held to grossly different standards of rigor in the teacher certification process."
- The standard for teacher licensure exams is "set shockingly low—with almost every state granting licenses to teachers who score as low as the 16th percentile."
- The current framework should be replaced with one that "lays out a consistent set of entry requirements, demands a high bar for entry, and allows teachers to readily take their skills across state lines."

As you shall see later in this chapter, many efforts are underway to bring about improvements in certification/licensure arrangements and processes, along with related reforms in teacher-preparation practices and programs.

FOCUS What are the certification requirements in the state where you want to teach? How can you find out? How might you prepare yourself for geographic mobility during your teaching career?

1-4 TRENDS IN PRESERVICE EDUCATION

In recent years, major developments in preservice teacher education have included increased emphasis on producing "reflective" teachers; growing use of computers and other technology; requirements that future teachers learn about methods for teaching students with disabilities and other special populations; programs to prepare teaching candidates for the diverse cultural and ethnic settings of contemporary US schools; and more rigorous requirements for entry into and exit from teacher education.

1-4a Reflective Teaching

reflective teaching A style of teaching that emphasizes reflective inquiry and self-awareness.

In accordance with a recent emphasis on improving students' thinking and comprehension skills, many institutions emphasize **reflective teaching** as a central theme in teacher education. Reflective teachers frequently observe and think about the results of their teaching and adjust their methods accordingly. Closely related terms such as *inquiry-oriented teacher education, expert decision making,* and *higher-order self-reflection* also describe this concept. Hundreds of schools of education have reorganized their programs to prepare reflective teachers, but the programs are diverse and show little agreement on what reflective teaching should mean.[18]

1-4b Computer and Technology Use

Most likely, your teacher-education program offers you some training and access to a computer lab. National surveys of teacher-education programs indicate that nearly all have established computer or technology laboratories. These laboratories encompass a wide variety of activities and objectives, such as orienting future teachers in computer use, introducing hardware and software developed for elementary and secondary schools, and strengthening interest and capability in technology for lesson design or delivery. Many institutions have begun to emphasize the use of technology and electronic media to help teachers advance their students' critical thinking, social and civic development, and digital and visual literacy. Usually, one purpose of this aspect of teacher education is to reduce the possibility that future teachers will become overwhelmed when encountering students who are acquainted with and even adept at the latest technologies.[19]

---

[18]Johan Luttenberg and Theo Bergen, "Teacher Reflection," *Teachers and Teaching* (October 2008), pp. 543–566; Lana M. Danielson, "Fostering Reflection," *Educational Leadership* (February 2009); and Meagan C. Arrastia et.al, "The Nature of Elementary Preservice Teachers' Reflection During an Early Field Experience," *Reflective Practice* (April 2014).

[19]Phyllis K. Adcock, "Evolution of Teaching and Learning through Technology," *Delta Kappa Gamma Bulletin* (Summer 2008), pp. 37–41; and Robin L. Flanigan, "Teacher Colleges Seek to Shift to Digital Age," *Education Week*, January 29, 2014.

1-4c Requirements for Teaching Students with Disabilities

Many states and teacher-training institutions now require that all future teachers receive some preparation in working with students who have significant disabilities. As a teacher, you will likely have students with special needs in your classes. The law demands that students with disabilities be *mainstreamed* in regular classes as much as is possible and feasible, and the growing trend is toward full *inclusion* of disabled students no matter how extensive their special needs. (See Chapter 12, Providing Equal Educational Opportunity, for information about mainstreaming, inclusion, and related topics.) As a consequence, most teachers can expect certain responsibilities for working with students with special needs. Typical teacher-training requirements involve the following:[20]

● Cooperative, interdisciplinary efforts in which both higher-education faculty and knowledgeable field educators help future teachers learn approaches to working with students with disabilities
● Requirements in many states that all future teachers complete one or more courses in education for students with special needs and/or that existing courses incorporate substantial amounts of material on the subject

1-4d Preparation for Teaching in Diverse Settings

Increasing enrollment of racial and ethnic minority students in US schools is prompting programs to prepare future teachers by adding components to help candidates function successfully in diverse settings. Similar efforts are underway in teacher licensing. For example, the Praxis III teacher performance assessment approach, developed by the Educational Testing Service (ETS), specifies that a candidate for a teaching license should be able to demonstrate a "comprehensive understanding" of why it is important to become familiar with students' background knowledge and experiences.[21]

1-4e Quality of Preparation Programs

It is difficult, if not impossible, to characterize the overall adequacy and effectiveness of the myriad teacher-preparation programs in the United States. They range from very large to tiny, from relatively well funded to financially skimpy, and from brand new to nearly a century old. Moreover, they all offer widely varying definitions of what it means to be the quality teachers they are trying to produce. Nevertheless, analysts have been trying to evaluate them.

"Teaching at Risk"   For example, a group of business and civic leaders called The Teaching Commission examined various aspects of teacher quality and issued a major report titled "Teaching at Risk." Regarding a perceived need to reinvent teacher-preparation programs, the Commission assigned a grade of C for effort and a grade of D for results. Among other findings, it concluded that too many teachers have too little knowledge of mathematics, science, and other subjects they are teaching; that

---

[20]Tamara J. Arthaud et al., "Developing Collaboration Skills in Pre-Service Teachers," *Teacher Education and Special Education* (Winter 2007), pp. 1–12; and Bethany M. Hamilton-Jones and Cynthia O. Vail, "Preparing Special Educators for Collaboration in the Classroom," *International Journal of Special Education*, v. 29 no.1, 2014.

[21]Nancy L. Commins and Ofelia B. Miramontes, "Addressing Linguistic Diversity from the Outset," *Journal of Teacher Education* (May/June 2006), pp. 240–246; and Emmeline Zhao, "Raising the Bar for Teacher Colleges," October 28, 2014, posting by the Education Writers Association, available at **www.ewa.org**.

alternative certification programs are not adequately providing skilled teachers where needs are greatest; and that the training of future teachers "adds far too little value" to their skills and capabilities.[22]

Education Schools Project   An organization named the Education Schools Project similarly released the results of a five-year study of teacher-education programs. Its "Educating School Teachers" report concluded that as many as one-quarter to one-third do an excellent job, but that most future teachers are being prepared in programs that too often have inadequate curricula, low standards, and faculty out of touch with the schools. The report included recommendations (among others) that "failing" schools of education should be closed, "quality" programs should be expanded, scholarships should be provided to attract the "best and brightest" into teaching, and quality control should be strengthened.[23]

National Council on Teacher Quality   Assessments of teacher-preparation programs also have been conducted by the National Council on Teacher Quality (NCTQ). The Council collects information on candidate selection and graduate exit policies and practices, course offerings and syllabi, clinical observation and student teaching arrangements, provision of mentoring, and related matters. Its 2014 report stated that the "country is finally waking up to the critical importance of improving teacher-preparation quality." It also reported that of the 1,612 programs for which it collected data, only 107 were classified in its highest category of quality. Many educators, some of them highly respected leaders in teacher education, were publicly critical of the Council's data collection methods and analysis.[24]

FOCUS What trends listed here especially describe your teacher-education program? Do any of the trends describe directions in which you *wish* your program would head?

1-5 PROSPECTIVE TEACHERS: ABILITIES AND TESTING

In recent years, much discussion has centered on improving the quality of the teaching workforce, particularly on improving the abilities of prospective teachers and on testing their competence for teaching. Discussions of the quality of the teaching workforce frequently focus on ability scores derived from standardized tests such as the Scholastic Assessment Test (SAT) and the American College Test (ACT). Among potential teachers, such test scores declined in the 1970s, as they did for students majoring in business and numerous other subjects. For example, between 1973 and 1981, the average SAT verbal score of college students intending to teach fell from 418 to 397. Since 1982, however, test scores of college students who say they intend to become teachers have appreciably increased and generally resemble those of students majoring in business, psychology, and the health professions. Data also show that the SAT percentile rank of new teachers increased from the 45th percentile in 1993–94 to the 50th percentile in 2008–09. In addition, some recent studies have found that teachers' average test scores are about the same as those of other college-educated adults.[25]

---

[22]Louis V. Gerstner, Jr., et al., *Teaching at Risk: Progress and Potholes* (New York: The Teaching Commission, 2006).

[23]Arthur Levine, *Educating School Teachers* (Washington, DC: Education Schools Project, 2006), available at **www.edschools.org**. See also Lyndsey Layton, "Education Department Moves to Regulate Teacher Education Programs," *Washington Post*, November 25, 2014, available at **www.washingtonpost.com**.

[24]Julie Greenberg, Kate Walsh, and Arthur McKee, *2014 Teacher Prep Review* (Washington, DC: National Council on Teacher Quality, 2014), available at **www.nctq.org**; Linda Darling-Hammond, "Why the NCTQ Teacher Prep Ratings Are Nonsense," *Washington Post*, June 18, 2013, available at **www.washingtonpost.com**; and Chris Kardish, "States Are Strengthening Teacher Preparation Laws," June 25, 2014, posting by Governing the States and Localities, available at **www.governing.com**.

[25]Drew H. Gitomer, *Teacher Quality in a Changing Policy Landscape* (Princeton, N.J.: Educational Testing Service, 2007), available at **www.ets.org**; and Dan Goldhaber and Joe Walch, "Gains in Teacher Quality," *Education Next* (Winter 2014), available at **www.educationnext.org**.

basic-skills testing Testing that examines preservice teachers' basic skills with respect to subjects such as reading, mathematics, and communications.

1-5a Testing Teachers

Some efforts to improve the teaching force focus on **basic-skills testing** of preservice teachers, new teachers, and sometimes experienced teachers. Drawing on the argument that teachers whose scores are low in reading, mathematics, communications, and/or professional knowledge probably are ineffective in their teaching, many states have introduced requirements that prospective teachers pass some form of minimum skills test in reading and language, math, subject-area specialty, and professional knowledge. More than forty states now use the Praxis test developed by the Educational Testing Service for this purpose. To become a certified teacher, you likely will need to pass a series of Praxis exams.[26]

1-5b Criticisms of Testing

Testing of prospective and current teachers remains a controversial topic. Many political leaders see testing as one of the few feasible steps they can take to improve public confidence in the teaching force. Opponents argue that the process unjustifiably excludes people who do poorly on paper-and-pencil tests. Many opponents believe that existing tests are biased against minorities and other candidates not from the cultural mainstream. Critics also cite data indicating that scores on standardized tests taken by future teachers correlate poorly with subsequent on-the-job measures of teaching effectiveness.[27]

1-5c Proponents of Testing

Proponents of basic-skills testing generally counter that all or nearly all teachers must be able to demonstrate that they can function at least at the seventh- or eighth-grade level in reading, writing, and math—the minimum level currently specified on some tests—to perform effectively in their jobs. Many proponents also argue that research has provided enough information to justify minimum standards and to allow for the creation of more valid exams.[28] In any case, testing remains highly popular, and you should make sure that your teacher-preparation program and general studies help you prepare to pass any exams that you must take.

1-5d Controversies over Basic-Skills Testing

Controversy regarding basic-skills testing of prospective teachers became nationally prominent in 1998 after Massachusetts administered its first statewide test for this purpose. Thirty percent of the candidates failed the reading and writing test, and 63 percent of candidates for mathematics certification failed the subject-matter test in their field. The chairman of the state board of education stated that "the real story … is that so many prospective public school teachers failed a test that a bright 10th grader could pass without difficulty" and that "no responsible person would subject anyone's children, much less his own, to teachers who had failed these topics." Subsequently, legislators and educators in Massachusetts and elsewhere initiated ongoing debates and arguments concerning appropriate test-performance levels for entering and exiting teacher-preparation programs and for obtaining and retaining teaching certificates and licenses.

FOCUS Are teachers in your state required to pass a test? If yes, what are the requirements? What are the passing and failing rates in your state and at your institution?

---

[26]Chris O'Neal, "Improving Teacher Quality," 2008 essay prepared for Edutopia, available at **www.edutopia.org**; and "The Praxis Series Information Bulletin 2014–2015," 2015 posting by the Educational Testing Service, available at **www.ets.org**.

[27]Ayres G. D'Costa, "The Impact of Courts on Teacher Competence Testing," *Theory into Practice* (Spring 1993), pp. 104–112; and Adrienne Hu, "The Accountability of Teacher Preparation Programs," 2014 posting by Michigan State University College of Education.

[28]Donald Boyd et al., "The Effect of Certification and Preparation on Teacher Quality," *The Future of Children* (Spring 2007), available at **www.futureofchildren.org**; and Beth Hawkins, "Are Minnesota's Teacher-Prep Programs Leaving Too Many Graduates Unprepared?" *Minnpost*, April 3, 2014, available at **www.minnpost.com**.

In recent years, focus has shifted somewhat toward introducing tests assessing real-world skills, such as New York's requirement to submit a video showing the candidate working successfully in a classroom with a group of students.[29]

1-6   JOB SATISFACTION AND DISSATISFACTION

Are people who become teachers generally satisfied with their work? Job conditions strongly affect satisfaction, and, as you'll see in this section, job conditions are changing in response to many calls for educational reform. Several of these changes seem likely to improve teachers' job satisfaction.

In polls conducted for the Metropolitan Life Insurance Company, teachers have been asked, "All in all, how satisfied would you say you are with teaching as a career?" Most of the respondents have answered either "very satisfied" or "somewhat satisfied." About half have reported that they were more enthusiastic about teaching than when they began their careers. Furthermore, the percentage of satisfied teachers has increased from 40 percent in 1984 to more than 80 percent in recent years. Similar results have been documented in several other recent polls. Additional information about teacher satisfaction is provided in Chapter 2, The Teaching Profession.[30]

1-6a Reasons for Dissatisfaction

Many teachers do, however, report dissatisfaction with their work. Nationwide surveys show that significant percentages believe they have insufficient time for counseling students, planning lessons, and other instructional functions. Other complaints include ambiguity in supervisors' expectations; unresponsive administrators; decrepit facilities; obligations to participate in staff development perceived as irrelevant or ineffective; inadequate salaries; lack of supplies and equipment; forced concentration on teaching low-level skills; extensive paperwork and record keeping; and insufficient input on organizational decisions. Perceived overemphasis on pedestrian instruction as well as low-level tests as part of responses to No Child Left Behind legislation (see Chapter 12, Providing Equal Educational Opportunity, in this book) has become an important aspect of teacher dissatisfaction in recent years.[31]

1-6b State and District Standards and Teacher Stress

Teaching is a difficult profession that usually involves significant stress. In recent years, the introduction of state and district standards for student performance has substantially increased this stress. Standards are often accompanied by accountability mechanisms involving standardized testing and publication of achievement scores for schools and, sometimes, individual classrooms. All states now require some degree of uniform testing in all school districts. Many of these tests carry high stakes, such as whether students pass from one grade to another, become eligible to graduate, or must attend summer school, as well as whether or not schools may be closed or intensely scrutinized because of low test scores.

Teaching to the Test   With such consequences, many teachers feel severe pressure to improve their students' test scores. This reaction is particularly prevalent at low-performing

---

[29]John Silber, "Those Who Can't Teach," *New York Times*, July 7, 1998. See also Larry H. Ludlow, "Teacher Test Accountability," *Education Policy Analysis Archives*, February 22, 2001, available at **http://epaa.asu.edu**; "Reports Blast Teacher Tests," June 26, 2007, posting by Fair Test, available at **www.fairtest.org**; and John Hildebrand, "New Teacher Candidates Facing Demanding Rules for Certification," *Newsday*, March 12, 2014, available at **www.newsday.com**.

[30]*The MetLife Survey of the American Teacher*, 2012 (New York: Metropolitan Life, 2013, available at **www.metlife.com**; James M. Crotty, "Report Finds Rising Job Satisfaction and Autonomy Among Teachers," *Forbes*, January 30, 2014, available at **www.forbes.com**; and Terry Stoops, "Data Do Not Reflect Claims of Teacher Dissatisfaction," *Carolina Journal*, February 4, 2014, available at **www.carolinajournal.com**.

[31]Melissa Lazarin, "Testing Overload in America's Schools," October 16, 2014, posting by the Center for American Progress, available at **www.americanprogress.org**.

TECHNOLOGY @ SCHOOL

AN INTERNET RESOURCE FOR PROSPECTIVE TEACHERS

The "Survival Guide for New Teachers" (available on the US Department of Education's website) offers a "collection of reflections by award-winning first-year teachers." Sections in this document advise you on how to work with veteran teachers, parents, and principals. The following is an excerpt from the introductory message:

What Does "Sink or Swim" Mean?

To start with, first-year teachers are still liable to be assigned the most challenging courses—the ones with a heavy developmental emphasis and students who need additional expertise to teach. Moreover, many new teachers receive little more than a quick orientation on school policies and procedures before they start their jobs. And there is often no time in the day—or week, for that matter—allotted for sitting down with colleagues to discuss pedagogical methods, daily dilemmas like time and classroom management, and coping strategies ….

Fortunately, some promising new initiatives are already under way. For example, 100 percent of the graduates of a program for first-year teachers from Texas A&M University-Corpus Christi, Texas, have stayed on the job after five years of teaching.

Meanwhile, the statewide retention rate is about 50 percent after five years, according to the university.

Texas's Induction Year Program is designed to provide support and instruction to first-year teachers while getting them started toward master's-level professional development. The program focuses on practical issues such as classroom management, communication skills, and discipline. Also, faculty members regularly visit participants' classrooms to evaluate the teacher's performance.

In addition to university teacher-preparation programs, school districts are doing more to make first-year teaching a success. Districts from Wilmington, Delaware, to Columbus, Ohio, to Omaha, Nebraska, have instituted induction programs for new teachers that include mentoring, peer assistance, and other forms of guidance and support.

You will also find headings for links to state departments of education. In addition to digesting the information and suggestions provided in these documents, you can discuss their meaning and implications with other prospective teachers or familiarize yourself with information on certification and assistance possibilities in your own or other states.

schools, but it also occurs even at some high-performing schools in locations where states or districts set high requirements for improved performance every year. Faculty in many schools wind up devoting much of the school year to preparing for tests and to emphasizing test-preparation materials in obtaining and using teaching resources, practices known collectively as "teaching to the test." As we point out elsewhere in this book, this situation has raised controversial questions as to whether the standards movement facilitates or impedes improvements in student performance, as teachers narrow their instructional focus to the tested skills. Although some teachers report finding ways to provide engaging, quality instruction within frameworks that require continuous attention to the many learning objectives specified on state and district tests, even these teachers typically experience high-level stress as they learn to function effectively within such frameworks.[32]

FOCUS Do you think your favorite teachers in high school were satisfied with their jobs? What do you think may have caused them occasional dissatisfaction?

Coping with Stress   As you have seen, teaching has its difficult moments. Research also indicates that elementary and secondary teaching has become more stressful in recent years. In response, many professional organizations and school districts offer courses or workshops emphasizing coping techniques and other stress-reduction approaches.

Counselors point out that exercise, rest, hobbies, good nutrition, meditation or other relaxation techniques, vacations, and efficient scheduling of personal affairs can help individuals cope with high-stress jobs. You may also reduce stress if you participate in professional renewal activities or support groups, separate your job from your home life, and keep an open-minded attitude toward change. First-year teachers experience unique stress as they enter new teaching jobs. For this reason, professional organizations, school districts, and even the US Department of Education offer supportive programs. The Technology @ School box in this chapter describes one such effort.

---

[32]Stuart S. Yeh, "Limiting the Unintended Consequences of High-Stakes Testing," *Educational Policy Analysis Archives,* October 28, 2005, available at **http://epaa.asu.edu**; "Testing the Joy Out of Education," *American Teacher* (October 2008), available at **www.aft.org**; Michigan State University, "High-Stakes Testing, Lack of Voice Driving Teachers Out," *Science Daily,* September 9, 2014, available at **www.sciencedaily.com**; and Amanda A. Fairbanks, "Will Test-Based Teacher Evaluations Derail the Common Core?" *The Hechinger Report,* January 8, 2015, available at **www.hechingerreport.org**.

1-7 EFFORTS TO IMPROVE TEACHER QUALIFICATIONS AND FUNCTIONING

As we have stated in preceding sections, most teachers are motivated by a desire to work with young people and to enter a challenging and honorable field. Most are satisfied with most aspects of their jobs. Some dissatisfaction arises, however, mostly with various nonteaching considerations and with the demands imposed by the contemporary movement to raise students' achievement. As discussed next, nationwide efforts have been under way to address some of the conditions that teachers find difficult and to reform schools by improving teachers' qualifications and functioning.

1-7a The No Child Left Behind Act

No Child Left Behind Act (NCLB) The federal Elementary and Secondary Education Act passed in 2001, which requires states and school districts that receive federal funding to show adequate yearly progress, as measured by standardized tests of students in grades 3–8 and in high school, and to provide all students with "highly qualified" teachers.

In 2001, teacher-quality-improvement activities became an integral part of the national school reform movement with passage of the **No Child Left Behind Act (NCLB)**. We will discuss major components of NCLB dealing with student achievement elsewhere, particularly in Chapter 12, Providing Equal Educational Opportunity. Here we review the key sections dealing with requirements that teachers in school districts receiving federal funding must be "highly qualified."

Requirements in these sections were explained in a 2004 US Department of Education document (see "A Toolkit for Teachers," available at the US Department of Education website). The document notes that the NCLB "represents a sweeping overhaul of federal efforts to support elementary and secondary education" and "sets the goal of having every child making the grade on state-defined education standards by the end of the 2013–14 school year." As part of the overhaul, NCLB "outlines the minimum qualifications needed by teachers and paraprofessionals who work on any facet of classroom instruction. It requires that states develop plans to achieve the goal that all teachers of core academic subjects be highly qualified."[33]

highly qualified teacher An aspect of the No Child Left Behind Act, which specifies that teachers should have (1) a bachelor's degree; (2) full state certification and licensure as defined by the state; and (3) demonstrated competency as defined by the state in each core academic subject he or she teaches.

Three Requirements   Under NCLB, a **"highly qualified teacher"** must have (1) a bachelor's degree, (2) full state certification and licensure as defined by the state, and (3) "demonstrated competency as defined by the state in each core academic subject he or she teaches."

Defining Competency   New elementary teachers can demonstrate competency by "passing a rigorous state test on subject knowledge and teaching skills in reading or language arts, writing, mathematics and other areas of the basic elementary school curriculum." New middle- and high-school teachers can demonstrate competency "either by passing a rigorous state test in each subject they teach, or by holding an academic major or course work equivalent to an academic major, an advanced degree or advanced certification or credentials." Those already employed as teachers at any level can demonstrate competency by meeting the requirements for new teachers or by meeting a state-defined "high, objective, uniform state standard of evaluation (HOUSSE)." States have defined and established their HOUSSE standards for competency among current teachers. Many are using point systems that allow teachers to count a combination of years of successful classroom experience, participation in high-quality professional development that evaluates what the teacher has learned, service on curriculum development teams, and other activities related to developing knowledge in an academic area.

---

[33]*A Toolkit for Teachers* (Washington, DC: US Department of Education, 2004); Bonnie Billingley, "'Highly Qualified' Teachers," January 1, 2014, posting by Teaching LD, available at **www.teachingld.org/questions/11**; and "NCLB:20 Frequently Asked Questions about Highly Qualified Teacher Requirements," undated posting by Teaching Community, available at **www.teaching.monster.com/benefits/articles/1826**.

Range of Developments   Developments with respect to implementation of NCLB teacher-quality goals have included the following:[34]

- The federal government has been distributing millions of dollars for activities such as devising and implementing alternative certification programs for teachers and administrators, establishing teacher merit-pay programs, providing bonus pay for teaching in high-need subjects and high-poverty schools, testing teachers in their subjects, and forming a Teacher Assistance Corps to help states carry out their quality-improvement initiatives.
- In 2006, Secretary of Education Margaret Spellings issued a report on teacher quality in which she provided data on state efforts to comply with NCLB. She acknowledged that states had approached but not been able to meet the goal of providing a highly qualified teacher in every classroom, and that minimum scores for passing tests to obtain a teacher's certificate in most states were low. The situation appears not to have changed very much in the intervening years.
- Much controversy has arisen regarding state progress toward ensuring highly qualified teachers in all classrooms. For example, although many states have reported that more than 90 percent of courses are taught by highly qualified teachers, some observers have cited various data indicating that numerous teachers teaching science, math, and other specialty subjects were working "out-of-field," that is, teaching in areas where they had not demonstrated competency. These observers have concluded that either the state data were incorrect or criteria for defining "highly qualified" had been set very low, or both.

Many organizations and individuals have expressed impatience and/or skepticism regarding NCLB implementation regarding teacher quality. For example, the Education Trust has criticized the federal government for doing little to ensure that teachers in urban schools are becoming truly qualified to raise the achievement of low-income students and minority students. Observers also point out that many rural districts face insuperable difficulties in meeting NCLB requirements for highly qualified teachers. To address these and related issues, the American Recovery and Reinvestment Act of 2009 (that is, the federal government's economic stimulus plan) required that states must stipulate they are making progress toward appointing experienced teachers to difficult schools before being eligible to receive part of the Recovery Act's $5 billion in educational incentive grants.

By 2009, more than 95 percent of teachers were highly qualified, as classified by the standards in their states. In addition, about half the states were funding induction and/or mentoring programs for new teachers. But it should be kept in mind that the meaning of "highly qualified" and the scope and effectiveness of supports for new teachers vary widely between and within states. In addition, most analysts believe that major problems still generally exist with respect to providing highly qualified teachers in high-poverty urban districts and in certain teaching areas such as special education and instruction for English language learners.

1-7b Evaluating Current and Future Teachers Based on Student Achievement

Despite the lack of consensus regarding the status and influence of NCLB and HOUSSE, nearly all state governments have initiated activities to improve the quality and effectiveness of teachers. Most states have stiffened entrance and exit requirements for teacher education, and/or expanded testing of new teachers. And, as described next, states and the federal government are participating in the Excellent Educators for All

---

[34]Mary M. Kennedy, "Sorting Out Teacher Quality," *Phi Delta Kappan* (September 2008), pp. 59–63; and "The Highly Qualified Teacher Limbo," July 29, 2014, posting by Ecology of Education, available at **www.ecologyofeducation.net/wsite**.

Initiative, Race to the Top, and other new programs and activities to reduce the incidence of ineffective teachers, particularly at high-poverty schools, and most states have introduced requirements that teachers be evaluated partly in terms of their students' performance.

Excellent Educators for All Initiative   Introduced by the US Department of Education in 2014, this initiative is intended to support states and school districts in their efforts to bolster teacher quality and effectiveness at low-performing, high-poverty schools. Secretary of Education Arne Duncan explained that "we must work together to enhance and invigorate our focus on how to better recruit, support, and retain effective teachers and principals for all students, especially the kids who need them most." The Initiative contains three major components. The first is to "create new comprehensive educator equity plans that put in place locally developed solutions to ensure every student has effective educators." The second is to establish an Educator Equity Support Network that will "work to develop model plans, share promising practices, [and] provide communities of practice... to discuss challenges and share lessons learned." The third component, titled "Educator Equity Profiles," is designed partly to publish profiles that will "help states identify gaps in access to quality teaching for low-income and minority students" and will publicize successful districts and schools.[35]

Race to the Top (RTTT) A federal program that between 2009 and 2015 provided competitive grants to support educational innovations and reforms in states and districts.

Race to the Top (RTTT)   Following widespread recognition that implementation of the NCLB Act had been generating negative outcomes (described in Chapter 12, Providing Equal Educational Opportunity), the federal government introduced the **Race to the Top (RTTT)** program. RTTT has been described in Department of Education publications as an "invitation for ... [states to use] best ideas on raising standards to prepare all students for college and careers, investing in America's teachers and school leaders, turning around the lowest-performing schools, and using data to inform support for educators and decision making." Many government officials recognized that teachers seldom were evaluated in terms of their students' performance. They also knew that well over 90 percent of teachers in most districts were assessed as satisfactory, even if their students were failing miserably. In response, grants awarded for the purpose of improving teacher quality require funded states to do the following:[36]

- Link data on students' achievement level and growth in performance to their teachers.
- Relate this information to the in-state programs that prepare teachers.
- Publicly report these and other data on program effectiveness for each preparation program in the state.

Seeking funding from RTTT and spurred by the desire to obtain NCLB waivers (see the waiver discussion later in this section) as well as public demands for better student performance and international research emphasizing the importance of effective teachers, most state governments have moved to carry out the teacher quality activities specified earlier. In many states, teacher evaluations now are based on increasingly rigorous, frequent, and sophisticated observation of classroom teaching, with additional meaningful support provided for low-scoring teachers. For the minority of

---

[35]Leila Meyer, "ED Launches Excellent Educators for All Initiative," *The Journal*, July 8, 2014, available at **www.thejournal.com**; and "New Initiative to Provide All Students Access to Great Educators," July 7, 2014, posting by the US Department of Education, available at **www.ed.gov**.
[36]Chad Aldis, "Next-Generation Teacher Evaluations," *Ohio Gadfly Daily*, November 3, 2014, available at **www.edexcellence.net**; "Principals' Group Latest to Criticize 'Value Added' for Teacher Evaluations," December 5, 2014, posting by *Education Next*, available at **www .educationnext.org**; "Setting the Pace," March 2014 posting by The White House and the US Department of Education; Valerie Strauss, "Statisticians Slam Popular Teacher Evaluation Method," *Washington Post*, April 13, 2014, available at **www.washingtonpost.com**; and Mike Rose, "School Reform Fails the Test," *American Scholar* (Winter 2015).

teachers with students in grades and subjects (for example, reading, math) included in state assessments, evaluations of these teachers in some districts make significant use of so-called Value-Added Measurement (VAM) of their students' achievement gain or loss during the academic year. In some cases, observational information on teachers' performance and students' standardized test scores now constitute half or more of some teachers' annual evaluation ratings.

Criticism of VAM and Observation Data   However, some leading analysts have been vocal in their criticism of these developments. Many researchers and statisticians believe that VAM does not provide valid data useful in making decisions about teacher effectiveness, and they question the usefulness of observational data as currently collected in reaching conclusions about any teacher's job performance. They also point out that in many or most districts, teachers are still categorized in terms allowing only for either satisfactory or unsatisfactory, with only a small number placed in the unsatisfactory category.

Elimination of Race to the Top in 2015   Following many criticisms and much dissatisfaction regarding RTTT policies and requirements, the US Congress did not continue the program as part of ESEA/NCLB reauthorization in 2015. However, some of the goals and policies that characterized RTTT may well be pursued by the federal government and state governments in the future.

Waivers from NCLB   As the 2014 deadline approached requiring that all students be proficient on state tests, states faced the prospect that many or even most of their schools would be classified as not making "adequate yearly progress," and then would be responsible for providing large amounts of financial and other support, for replacing most or all faculty at some or many schools, and/or for seeking other drastic solutions. (NCLB requirements are described at some length in Chapter 12, Providing Equal Educational Opportunity.) Most states have sought and received waivers from these NCLB requirements by participating in RTTT or similar activities. Thus, more than forty states now require that teachers be evaluated at least partly in terms of data on their performance.[37]

Council for the Accreditation of Educator Preparation (CAEP)   The Council was formed in 2013 by a consolidation of the National Council for Accreditation of Teacher Education (NCATE) and the Teacher Education Accreditation Council (TEAC). The CAEP is now the sole national accreditor of teacher-education programs. It has introduced new standards requiring that teacher-training programs have students with a collective grade point average of at least 3.0, as well as college admissions test scores above the national average by 2017 and in the top third by 2020. Mary Brabeck, chair of CAEP's board, and a colleague have stated that the Council "will evaluate programs on what teacher-candidates can do and how effectively they can teach, as demonstrated though reliable assessments, including classroom observations and students' standardized-test scores."[38]

US Department of Education Regulations and Rating Systems   In 2015, the Department of Education established new regulations requiring state governments to be more rigorous in rating teacher-education programs according to whether their graduates find jobs in their subject field, how long they stay in those jobs, and the performance on standardized tests and other measures of the students taught by their graduates. If a program is deemed "low-performing" or "at risk" for two consecutive years, it will not

---

[37]Matthew P. Steinberg and Lauren SarTain, "Does Better Observation Make Better Teachers?" *Education Next* (Winter 2015), available at **www.educationnext.org**.
[38]Mary Brabeck and Frank C. Worrell, "Best Practices for Evaluating Teacher Ed. Programs," *Education Week*, November 4, 2014.

receive TEACH grants that provide up to $4,000 per year to participants who agree to work in high-need fields or in struggling schools for at least four years. However, states will not be required to publish report cards with such information until 2019.[39]

1-7c Implications and Prospects for Future Teachers

As political leaders and the general public have become seriously concerned with alleged poor student performance, attention increasingly has focused on education, and there has been good news regarding teachers' prospects. Governments at all levels are acting to improve teacher recruitment and preparation, working conditions, and professional responsibility. Individuals dedicated to helping young people learn and grow in school should have considerable opportunities to realize their ambitions. In years to come, the teaching profession should continue to experience a renewed excitement and an even greater sense that the work is of vital importance to American society.

The most recent developments have signaled a growing recognition of the importance of elementary and secondary schools, and the central role of well-prepared teachers in educating the nation's students. Efforts have been inaugurated to improve the recruitment and preparation of future teachers, their opportunities for learning from capable mentors, and their chances for obtaining a rewarding and stable professional position.

No one can say for sure how these developments will affect each individual candidate for a teaching certificate. For some, improved opportunities will be increasingly evident; for others, major hurdles and even disappointments will have to be overcome. For example, many new teachers will find exciting jobs at improving urban schools, innovative schools with advanced technology, or schools with collaborative staff who provide excellent advice and assistance. Many others will encounter difficult circumstances such as decreased financial aid at their college or university, problems involving the accreditation of their home institutions, or declining reputations and resources at the school districts that hire them. We hope that your experience turns out to be overwhelmingly positive.

FOCUS Which of the reform efforts described here would you most like to see in a school district in which you wanted to teach? Which of the reforms do you think might cause teachers dissatisfaction or stress? Why?

SUMMING UP

1. Although we see many reasons for entering the teaching profession, research indicates that most teachers do so to help young children and to provide a service to society.

2. Many educators are focusing on ways to increase diversity in the teaching workforce to better reflect the student population.

3. Demand for new teachers will likely continue.

4. Teacher salaries have improved in recent years.

5. Requirements for teacher certification or licensure vary from state to state and among institutions of higher learning.

6. Trends in teacher education include a growing emphasis on developing reflective teachers. Teachers also are increasingly prepared to use up-to-date technology, to work with students who have special needs, and to teach in widely diverse settings.

7. Although admitting that it is not possible to generalize about the myriad teacher-preparation programs, several major reports have concluded that many programs are not doing an adequate job in training future teachers.

8. Most teachers are satisfied with most aspects of their jobs, despite some dissatisfaction with starting salaries and certain other aspects of the profession.

9. Concern is widespread over the quality of the teaching workforce and teacher preparation. Significant reports and legislation dealing with student performance have helped generate a variety of efforts and programs to improve teacher quality and functioning.

---

[39]Louis Freedberg, "Impact of Teacher Rules Unclear," *EdSource*, December 2, 2014, available at **www.edsource.org**; and Lydia Wheeler, "Federal Incentive Program for Teachers 'Not Working' Study Finds," January 13, 2015, posting by The Hill, available at **www.thehill.com**.

SUGGESTED RESOURCES

INTERNET

The federal government maintains various sites on the Internet. Many topics in this chapter (and in this book) can be explored at the US Department of Education website and the Institute of Education Sciences website. Various professional organizations, such as the Association for Supervision and Curriculum Development and Phi Delta Kappa also sponsor relevant sites.

Updated reports and developments regarding topics in this chapter are described in The Hechinger Report website.

The *Teacher Quality Bulletin* newsletter is a publication available by e-mail or online from the Teacher Quality Clearinghouse.

PUBLICATIONS

Goldstein, Dana. *The Teacher Wars*. New York: Doubleday, 2014. *Subtitled "A History of America's Most Embattled Profession," this volume includes material on teacher preparation and on new teachers.*

Herndon, Joseph. *The Way It Spozed to Be*. New York: Bantam, 1968. *A classic when it was published, this book, which describes the satisfactions and difficulties of teaching in the inner city, remains relevant in the new millennium.*

Journal of Teacher Education. American Association of Colleges for Teacher Education. *Regularly provides information and analysis regarding important issues in preservice and in-service education.*

CHAPTER **2**

InTASC INTASC
STANDARDS
ADDRESSED IN
THIS CHAPTER

9 Professional Learning and
   Ethical Practice
10 Leadership and Collaboration

THE TEACHING PROFESSION

LEARNING OBJECTIVES

2-1 Explain how teaching lags behind full-fledged professions in the four areas highlighted in this section.

2-2 Examine the trends that suggest teaching is moving toward a full-fledged profession.

2-3 Determine the goals and benefits of the two primary professional organizations, the specialized professional organizations, and the other professional organizations discussed in this section.

Jim West/AGE Fotostock

This chapter was revised by Dr. David E. Vocke, Towson University.

UNTIL THE TWENTIETH CENTURY, teachers received relatively little preparation and had little say in the terms of their employment. Formal teacher training consisted of one or two years at a normal school or teacher's college, and after they were employed in a local school, teachers had to follow strict rules and regulations that monitored their behavior outside school. Unorganized and isolated from one another in small schools and districts, teachers could be summarily dismissed by a local board of education. Many were told they could not teach material that a community member might find objectionable.

Times have changed. Today, teachers strive to be professionals with expert knowledge concerning instruction, content, and assessment in their particular fields. In addition, most belong to teacher organizations and have gained greater rights to be judged on their classroom performance rather than on their behavior outside school. In schools today, they are likely to participate in decision making about work conditions. In many cases, they are forging stronger links with school administrators, university researchers, government officials, and the communities they serve. The first part of this chapter describes ways in which teachers are striving for full professional status, and the second part discusses the teacher organizations that have grown in power and prominence.

2-1 IS TEACHING A PROFESSION?

profession An occupation that rates high in prestige and requires extensive formal education and mastery of a defined body of knowledge beyond the grasp of laypersons.

The question of whether or not teaching is a true profession has been debated for decades. Some have tried to identify the ideal characteristics of professions, and by rating teachers on these items, determine whether teaching is a profession. The following are characteristics of a full **profession**, based on the works of noted authorities during the latter half of the twentieth century.[1]

1. A sense of public service; a lifetime commitment to career
2. A defined body of knowledge and skills beyond that grasped by laypeople
3. A lengthy period of specialized training
4. Control over licensing standards and/or entry requirements
5. Autonomy in making decisions about selected spheres of work
6. An acceptance of responsibility for judgments made and acts performed related to services rendered; a set of performance standards
7. A self-governing organization composed of members of the profession
8. Professional associations and/or elite groups to provide recognition for individual achievements
9. A code of ethics that signals an overriding commitment to the welfare of the client
10. High prestige and economic standing

Critics claim that teaching is not a profession in the fullest sense because it lacks some of the previously listed characteristics, but it may be viewed as a "semi-profession" or the "not-quite-profession" in the process of achieving these characteristics. Several sociologists contend that nursing and social work, like teaching, are also semi-professions.[2]

---

[1]Ronald G. Corwin, *Sociology of Education* (New York: Appleton-Century-Crofts, 1965); Robert B. Howsam et al., *Educating a Profession* (Washington, DC: American Association of Colleges for Teacher Education, 1976); Susan J. Rosenholtz, *Teachers' Workplace: The Social Organization of Schools* (New York: Longman, 1989); and A. Lin Goodwin, "Response to Section II: What's Needed Now: Professional Development Schools and the Professionalization of Teaching" in *Yearbook of the National Society for the Study of Education* (New York: Teachers College, Columbia University, 2011).

[2]Amitai Etzioni, *The Semiprofessions and Their Organizations: Teachers, Nurses, and Social Workers* (New York: Free Press, 1969), p. v; Linda Darling-Hammond and A. L. Goodwin, "Progress Toward Professionalism in Teaching," in G. Cawelti, ed., *Association for Supervision and Curriculum Development 1993 Yearbook* (pp. 19–52) (Alexandria, VA: ASCD, 1993); and Richard Ingersoll and David Perda, "The Status of Teaching as a Profession," in Jeanne H. Ballantine and Joan Z. Spade, eds., *Schools and Society: A Sociological Approach to Education* (Thousand Oaks, CA: Sage Publication, 2008).

In particular, teaching seems to lag behind professions such as law and medicine in four important areas: (1) a defined body of knowledge and skills beyond that grasped by laypeople, (2) control over licensing standards and/or entry requirements, (3) autonomy in making decisions about selected work spheres, and (4) high prestige and economic standing. In the following sections, we explore these four aspects of teaching.

2-1a A Defined Body of Knowledge

All professions have a monopoly on certain knowledge that separates their members from the general public and allows them to exercise control over the vocation. Members of the profession establish their expertise by mastering this defined body of knowledge, and they protect the public from untrained amateurs by denying membership to those who have not mastered it. In the past, it was difficult to argue that "education" or "teaching" had established an agreed-upon, specialized body of knowledge.[3] Nor has teaching been guided by the extensive rules of procedure and established methodologies found in professions such as medicine or engineering. As a result, too many people, especially the public and politicians, talk about education as if they were experts—the cause of many conflicting and sometimes negative conversations. Some detractors even claim that teaching skills are innate rather than learned.[4]

What some contend is a still developing body of knowledge allows teacher-education course content to vary from state to state and even among teacher-training institutions. Today, teacher preparation usually consists of three major components: (1) liberal (or general) education, (2) specialized subject-field education—the student's major or minor, and (3) professional education. Almost all educators agree that preparing good teachers rests on these three components. Arguments arise, however, over the relative emphasis that each component should receive. How much course work, for example, should the education program require from liberal-education courses versus specialized subject field courses and professional education courses? Viewpoints also differ concerning the extent to which clinical experience, which involves actual practice in school settings, should be incorporated in professional education programs. Thus, teacher-education programs may differ among various colleges and universities.[5]

In the 1960s, James Koerner and James Bryant Conant described the issue in highly critical books, and their criticism from several decades ago can still be heard today. Koerner argued that by requiring too many education courses—as many as sixty hours at some teacher colleges—and by making these courses too "soft," colleges of education were producing teachers versed in pedagogy at the expense of academic content.[6] In 2002, then-Secretary of Education Rod Paige echoed this criticism and called for a de-emphasis on education course work in the preparation of teachers. Critics today

[3]John Loughran, "Is Teaching a Discipline?" *Teacher and Teaching: Theory and Practice* (April 2009), pp. 189–203; and Darrel Drury, "The Professionalization of Teaching—What NEA Surveys Tell Us about a Common Knowledge Base," *Education Week* (June 30, 2011).

[4]Valeri R. Helterbran, "Professionalism: Teachers Taking the Reins," *Clearing House* (January 2008), pp. 123–127; F. Murray, "The Role of Teacher Education Courses in Teaching by Second Nature," in M. Cochran-Smith, S. Feiman-Nemser, and J. McIntyre, eds. *Handbook of Research on Teacher Education,* 3rd ed. (New York: Routledge/Taylor and Francis, 2008), pp. 1228–1246; and Trip Gabriel, "Teachers Wonder, Why the Heapings of Scorn?" *New York Times*, March 3, 2011, p. A1.

[5]Arthur Levine, "Are Schools of Education in Urgent Need of Reform?" *Trusteeship* (January 2007), p. 40; and National Council for Accreditation of Teacher, Education, "Transforming Teacher Education through Clinical Practice: A National Strategy to Prepare Effective Teachers," Report of the Blue Ribbon Panel on Clinical Preparation and Partnerships for Improved Student Learning, *National Council for Accreditation of Teacher Education* (November 1, 2010): ERIC, EBSCO*host* (accessed September 23, 2011).

[6]James D. Koerner, *The Miseducation of American Teachers* (Boston: Houghton Mifflin, 1963); James Bryant Conant, *The Education of American Teachers* (New York: McGraw-Hill, 1963); and George Will, "Ed Schools vs. Education," *Newsweek*, January 16, 2006.

continue to advocate for a reduction in required education courses and challenge the notion that teacher-preparation programs provide a knowledge base that equips novice teachers with the expertise to be professional educators.[7]

There are education scholars who contend the knowledge base for beginning teachers does exist and can be incorporated into teacher-education curricula.[8] Additionally, educators have worked to incorporate a developing professional knowledge base into a set of national performance standards that are now being used to hold teacher-education institutions accountable. The **Council for the Accreditation of Educator Preparation (CAEP)** has adopted standards that determine which teacher-education programs comply with national standards in the preparation of teaching candidates and specialists about to enter the classroom. These new accrediting standards will require documentation evidence of teacher-preparation program graduates' teaching skills and impact on PK–12 student learning.[9] Prior to the formation of CAEP, the National Council for the Accreditation of Teacher Education (NCATE) and the Teacher Education Accreditation Council (TEAC) were the accrediting agencies for teacher-education programs. By the standards NCATE and TEAC used (predecessors to the new CAEP standards), only 791 of the 1,624 educator-preparation providers (49 percent) were accredited.[10] Going forward, with one accrediting body, CAEP, implementing and monitoring compliance with standards widely believed to be more rigorous than earlier ones, the theory is that teacher preparation programs will be more professional in educating teachers for the real world classrooms.[11]

2-1b Controlling Requirements for Entry and Licensing

Whereas most professions have uniform requirements for entry and licensing, teaching historically has lacked such requirements because each of the fifty states sets its own certification requirements, which vary from state to state. As indicated in Chapter 1, Motivation, Preparation, and Conditions for the Entering Teacher, prospective teachers in most states are required to pass minimum competency tests in reading, writing, and math; graduate from an approved teacher-education program; complete an internship experience; and possess a bachelor's degree. Furthermore, over the past quarter of a century, National Board Certification has been implemented through the independent National Board for Professional Teaching Standards (NBPTS) for the purpose of awarding additional teaching certification to master teachers beyond initial state certification. You might want to research the qualifications and testing required for certification in your state to compare with others nearby.

If teacher certification is to verify professional skills and knowledge, it is unfortunate that some reports suggest a significant number of secondary-school teachers appear to be teaching out of license—in other words, outside their certified areas of expertise. This is a problem in the core academic subjects—English, social studies,

Council for the Accreditation of Educator Preparation (CAEP)
The national accrediting body for educator preparation programs that utilizes peer review and evidence-based accreditation.

---

[7]Linda Darling-Hammond, "Teacher Education and the American Future," *Journal of Teacher Education* (January 2010), pp. 35–47; A. Lin Goodwin, "Response to Section II: What's Needed Now: Professional Development Schools and the Professionalization of Teaching" in *Yearbook of the National Society for the Study of Education* (New York: Teachers College, Columbia University, 2011); and Jal Mehta, "Teachers: Will We Ever Learn," *The New York Times* (April 12, 2013).

[8]Linda Darling-Hammond and John Bransford, eds., *Preparing Teacher for a Changing World*, (San Francisco: Jossey-Bass, 2005).

[9]"AACTE Celebrates Approval of New Professional Accreditation Standards" (September 3, 2013) at **http://aacte.org/news-room/press-releases-statements/154-aacte-celebrates -approval** (January 6, 2015).

[10]"Council for the Accreditation of Educator Preparation, *Annual Report to the Public, the States, Policymakers, and the Education Profession,* (Washington, DC: Council for the Accreditation of Educator Preparation, 2013).

[11]"AACTE Celebrates Approval of New Professional Accreditation Standards" (September 3, 2013) at **http://aacte.org/news-room/press-releases-statements/154-aacte-celebrates -approval** (January 6, 2015).

science, and mathematics—where, in 2012–2013, 4.3 percent of classes at the high school level were taught by an out-of-field teacher. The problem is more pronounced in high-poverty high schools, where 5.4 percent of core classes were taught by an out-of-field teacher.[12]

The further development of professional preparation is clouded by the trend toward alternative certification, discussed in Chapter 1, Motivation, Preparation, and Conditions for the Entering Teacher. This process—by which teachers are recruited from the ranks of experienced college graduates seeking second careers—is intended to be an expedited route to eliminate teacher shortages in certain subject areas such as mathematics, science, and special education or to upgrade the quality of new teachers. In most such programs, participants are placed directly in classrooms without prior field experiences or internships. In a 2013 report, it was noted that 11 percent of all prospective teachers were enrolled in alternative programs.[13] Alternative certification is often praised as practical and innovative by critics of traditional programs. Most teacher-preparation organizations, on the other hand, see alternative certification as a threat to the profession. New research suggests that new teachers who have little training in pedagogical skills have attrition rates that are higher than traditionally certified teachers.[14]

Whatever teachers might think about differing requirements for certification, they traditionally have had little to say in these matters. However, teacher organizations are lobbying state legislatures, departments of education, **professional practice boards**, and independent organizations to implement rigorous licensure standards for entry into the teaching profession. The more input teachers have—that is, the more control they exercise over their own licensing procedures—the more teaching will be recognized as a full profession.

professional practice boards A state or national commission that permits educators to set professional standards and minimal requirements of competency.

2-1c Autonomy in Determining Spheres of Work

In a profession, every member of the group, but no outsider, is assumed to be qualified to make professional judgments on the nature of the work involved. In fact, control by laypeople is considered the natural enemy of a profession; it limits a professional's power and opens the door to outside interference. Professionals usually establish rules and customs that give them exclusive jurisdiction over their area of competence and their relationships with clients; professional autonomy is characterized by a high degree of self-determination.

---

[12]Daniel C. Humphrey and Marjorie E. Wechsler, "Insights into Alternative Certification: Initial Findings from a National Study," *Teachers College Record* (March 2007), pp. 483–530; Sarah Almy and Christina Theokas, *Not Prepared for Class: High-Poverty Schools Continue to Have Fewer In-Field Teachers* (Washington, DC: The Education Trust, November 2010); and *A Summary of Highly Qualified Teacher Data for School Year 2012–2013* (August 2014) at **www2.ed.gov/programs /teacherqual/resources.html** (April 21, 2015).

[13]Melanie Shaw, "The Impact of Alternative Teacher Certification Programs on Teacher Shortages," *International Journal of Learning* (July 2008), pp. 89–97; Jennifer Locraft Cuddapah and Anika Spratley Burtin, "What All Novices Need," *Educational Leadership* (May 2012), pp. 66–69; and Council for the Accreditation of Educator Preparation, *Annual Report to the Public, the States, Policymakers, and the Education Profession,* (Washington, DC: Council for the Accreditation of Educator Preparation, 2013).

[14]Linda Darling-Hammond, "Teacher Education and the American Future," *Journal of Teacher Education* (January 2010), pp. 35–47; Richard Ingersoll, Lisa Merrill, and Henry May, "What Are the Effects of Teacher Education and Preparation on Beginning Math and Science Teacher Attrition," a paper presented at the Annual Meeting of AERA, April 8–11, 2011; Stephen Sawchuk, "Higher Education Groups Oppose Teacher-Training Bill," *Education Week* (July 26, 2011) at **http://blogs.edweek.org/edweek/teacherbeat/2011/07/higher_ed_groups_line_up _again.html;** and Richard Ingersoll, Lisa Merrill, and Henry May. *What are the effects of teacher education and preparation on beginning teacher attrition? Research Report (#RR-82).* (Philadelphia: Consortium for Policy Research in Education, University of Pennsylvania, 2014).

Teachers, in contrast, have traditionally had little input in critical decision making regarding many aspects of their working conditions. Such decisions include the topics to be covered in the curriculum or the textbooks selected for courses they teach. Many times, school officials often hire outside "experts" with little teaching experience to help them select books, write grant proposals, or resolve local school–community issues. Most often, school reform initiatives come from government officials, philanthropists, business leaders, and special interest groups rather than from teachers. Some contend that the accountability measures first established through the federal NCLB mandates and now through assessing the Common Core State Standards have undermined teachers' autonomy, thus negatively impacting the quality of teaching and the teaching profession.[15]

2-1d High Prestige and Economic Standing

occupational prestige The special status accorded to certain occupations and not to others.

Occupational prestige refers to the esteem a particular society bestows on an occupation. Do you consider teaching a high-prestige occupation? Occupations rate high in prestige if they are generally perceived as making an especially valuable contribution to society. Occupations that require a high level of education or skill and little manual or physical labor also tend to be prestigious. On these aspects of social status, the job of elementary or secondary teacher historically has ranked relatively high.

Perhaps the best-known studies of occupational prestige have been those conducted by the National Opinion Research Center (NORC), beginning in 1947. In these studies of more than 500 occupations, the highest average score for a major occupation was 82 for physicians and surgeons, and the lowest was 9 for shoe shiners. Elementary-school teachers were rated at 60, and secondary-school teachers at 63—both above the ninetieth percentile.[16] In a 2014 Harris Poll, 60 percent of respondents indicated that teaching was a job with more prestige rather than less prestige; doctors were at the top of the scale with 88 percent, and real estate agents were at the bottom of the rankings at 27 percent (see Figure 2.1). It is interesting to note that teaching has dropped five places on the ranking since the poll was published in 2009.[17]

One reason teachers have maintained or even increased their favorable rating on surveys of occupational prestige is that their average education level has risen greatly over the past century. Another reason for the continued favorable rating might be the complex nature of teaching. Brian Rowan, comparing teachers' work with other occupations, found that work complexity related directly to occupational prestige. Teaching, more complex than 75 percent of all other occupations, ranked quite high in prestige. The complexity of teachers' work is manifested in their need to apply principles of logical or scientific thinking to define problems, collect data, establish facts, and draw conclusions. To be a teacher, you must be highly proficient in language

[15]Celine Coggins and P. K. Diffenbaugh, "Teachers with Drive," *Educational Leadership* (October 2013), pp. 42–45; and Luman E. G. Strong and Roland K Yoshida, "Teachers' Autonomy in Today's Education Climate: Current Perceptions from an Acceptable Instrument," *Educational Studies* (March 2014), pp. 123–145.

[16]C. C. North and Paul K. Hatt, "Jobs and Occupation: A Popular Evaluation," *Opinion News*, (September 1, 1947), pp. 3–13; Robert W. Hodge, Paul M. Siegel, and Peter H. Rossi, "Occupational Prestige in the United States, 1925–63," *American Journal of Sociology* (November 1964), pp. 286–302; and Donald J. Treiman, *Occupational Prestige in Comparative Perspective* (New York: Academic Press, 1977).

[17]"Firefighters, Scientists and Doctors Seen as Most Prestigious Occupations," *The Harris Poll* (Harris Interactive, Inc., August 4, 2009) at **www.harrisinteractive.com/vault/Harris -Interactive-Poll-Research-Pres-Occupations-2009-08.pdf;** and "Doctors, Military Officers, Firefighters, and Scientists Seen as Among America's Most Prestigious Occupations," *The Harris Poll* (Harris Interactive, Inc., September 10, 2014) at **www.harrisinteractive.com /vault/Harris%20Poll%2085%20-%20Prestigious%20Occupations_9.10.2014.pdf**.

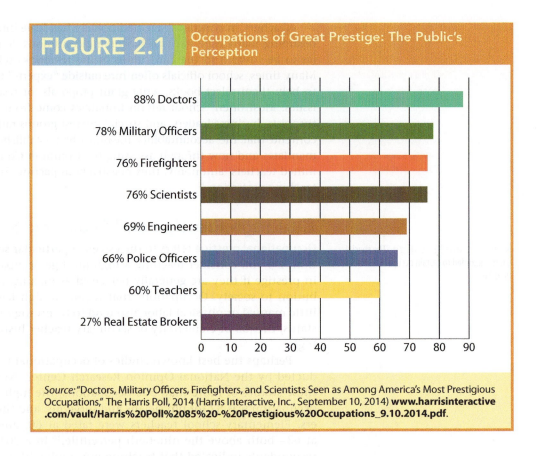

FIGURE 2.1 | Occupations of Great Prestige: The Public's Perception

- 88% Doctors
- 78% Military Officers
- 76% Firefighters
- 76% Scientists
- 69% Engineers
- 66% Police Officers
- 60% Teachers
- 27% Real Estate Brokers

0 10 20 30 40 50 60 70 80 90

Source: "Doctors, Military Officers, Firefighters, and Scientists Seen as Among America's Most Prestigious Occupations," The Harris Poll, 2014 (Harris Interactive, Inc., September 10, 2014) **www.harrisinteractive .com/vault/Harris%20Poll%2085%20-%20Prestigious%20Occupations_9.10.2014.pdf**.

(reading, writing, and speaking), and, most of all, you must work effectively with many kinds of people—children, adolescents, parents, colleagues, and superiors. Additional studies remind us that the work of teachers is multidimensional. However, society accords higher prestige (and, of course, higher pay) to professionals such as physicians, lawyers, and engineers, mainly because they must deal with information generally regarded as more abstract (complex) and because these fields currently require more rigorous academic preparation and licensure.[18]

Although teachers' salaries since 1930 have increased more than those of the average manufacturing-industry worker (as discussed in the previous chapter), teacher pay remains lower, and the gap has grown recently, than that of the comparable college graduate, such as an architect, registered nurse, accountant, or occupational therapist.[19] In a 2014 study, researchers found that the average weekly pay of public-school teachers was nearly 13.2 percent below that of similar nonteacher, college-educated workers, and "[a]n analysis of trends in weekly earnings shows that public-school teachers in 2006 earned 15 percent lower weekly earnings than comparable workers[.]"[20] Education officials and researchers have suggested that substantially raising the salaries of teachers may be the way to enhance the profession's prestige and thus

[18]Brian Rowan, "Comparing Teachers' Work with Work in Other Occupations," *Educational Researcher* (1994), pp. 4–17; and Anthony Milanowski, *Using Occupational Characteristics Information for O*NET to Identify Occupations for Compensation Comparisons with K–12 Teaching* (Madison, WI: Wisconsin Center for Education Research, June 2008).

[19]Steven L. Denlinger, "A Look at the Problem of Teacher Deficits," *Clearing House* (January– February 2002), pp. 116–117; and Sylvia A. Allegretto, Sean P. Corcoran, and Lawrence Mishel, *How Does Teacher Pay Compare*? (Washington, DC: Economic Policy Institute, 2004).

[20]John M. Krieg, "Book Review—How Does Teacher Pay Compare?" *Economics of Education Review* (2007), pp. 265–266; and Sylvia A. Allegretto, *Teacher Pay Penalty* (November 20, 2014) at **www .epi.org/publication/teacher-pay-penalty/**.

FOCUS Which of the preceding areas of professionalism—defined body of knowledge, control of licensing and entry, autonomy in decision making, or high prestige and economic standing—is most important to your personal definition of a profession? Is it important to you that teaching seems to lag behind other professions in these areas? Why or why not?

attract better-qualified candidates to teaching. Secretary of Education Arne Duncan indicated that society should look at teaching as it does the professions of law, medicine, and engineering.[21] It is interesting to note that the results of the 2008 *MetLife Survey of the American Teacher* found that 62 percent of teachers polled were "very satisfied" with their careers, a twenty-year high, but only 16 percent agreed "strongly" that teaching allowed them the opportunity to earn a decent salary. In the most recent survey, only 38 percent of teachers in 2012 indicated they were "very satisfied."[22]

To its credit, the educational reform movement of the 1980s and 1990s put teachers in the limelight and brought pressure on school districts to increase salaries. Unfortunately, the gains of the past two decades of the twentieth century have not been sustained during the first decade and a half of the twenty-first.

2-2   TRENDS TOWARD PROFESSIONALISM

collective bargaining A procedure for reaching agreements and resolving disagreements between employers and employees through negotiation.

Although teaching, as we have seen, may not yet be considered fully professionalized, certain trends have helped it move in that direction. **Collective bargaining**, for example, has been a tool to enhance teachers' capacity to make decisions about their classroom work. Let's look at a few aspects of a long-range trend toward professionalizing teaching.

2-2a The Scope of Collective Bargaining

In the United States today, more than 65 percent of teachers have their representatives formally bargain with their employers, the school board. In as many as thirty-four states and Washington, DC, school districts are legally required to bargain with teachers, while in eleven states, collective bargaining is permissible. Five states prohibit teachers from collective bargaining by statute. The extent and nature of collective bargaining varies from negotiations conducted in the absence of a law allowing or forbidding it, to full-scale contract bargaining backed by the right to strike.[23] In contrast, the private-school sector generally has no collective bargaining.

In some ways, collective bargaining may be considered a nonprofessional or even antiprofessional activity. In law, medicine, or the ministry, for example, few professionals work in organizations in which collective bargaining determines employment terms. Collective bargaining, however, can significantly improve teaching professionalism by giving teachers greater authority to influence their work conditions and their effectiveness as teachers in the classroom.

2-2b Collective Bargaining under Attack

Today, collective bargaining is under attack in a number of states based on the assumption that the agreements sacrifice the education needs of students to the union's desire to support its members. Wisconsin, Idaho, Tennessee, Indiana, and Washington, DC are among the jurisdictions that have had legislation introduced to limit the scope of

[21]Stephen Paine, *What the US Can Learn for the World's Most Successful Education Reform Efforts* (New York: McGraw-Hill Research Foundation March 2011); and Kelly Ni, "Education Head Wants Prestige for Teachers," *Epoch Times* (July 30, 2011).

[22]MetLife, Inc., *The MetLife Survey of the American Teacher: Expectations and Experiences* (2008) at **www.eric.ed.gov/PDFS/ED504457.pdf**; and MetLife, Inc., *The MetLife Survey of the American Teacher: Challenges for School Leadership* (2013) at **www.metlife.com/assets/cao /foundation/MetLife-Teacher-Survey-2012.pdf**.

[23]Stephen Sawchuk, "States Eye Curbs on Collective Bargaining by Teachers," *Education Week* (February 9, 2011), pp. 1–20; and, Barry T. Hirsch, David A. Macpherson, and Jon V. Winters, *Teacher Salaries, Collective Bargaining Laws, and Union Coverage*, paper presented as the American Economic Association Meetings, San Diego (January 6, 2013).

collective bargaining. Teacher evaluation, salary schedules, layoffs, and tenure are but a few of the issues that some state lawmakers and governors have included in bargaining prohibitions.[24] Movements toward school reform, school restructuring, and teacher empowerment, where collective bargaining remains intact, can give teachers more professional autonomy, union strength, and higher salaries in exchange for greater accountability and reduced adversarial bargaining. Continuing in this vein, collective bargaining can reduce resistance to various reform efforts, thus resolving conflicts between school boards and teachers and potentially raising the overall status of the profession.[25]

Educators are unlikely to achieve complete autonomy in setting professional practice standards, but their role has increased. Today, a majority of states have professional standards boards that regulate the education profession, but they vary in the powers they possess. Among their responsibilities may be the authority to issue, renew, suspend, and revoke certificates for teachers and administrators. In eleven states, these boards act in an advisory capacity; in four states, their decisions are reviewed by the particular state's board of education; while in thirteen states, they have the power to make independent decisions.[26]

National Board for Professional Teaching Standards (NBPTS) A national nonprofit organization that issues certificates to teachers who meet its standards for professional ability and knowledge.

The concept of rigorous licensure standards and independent professional practice boards has been endorsed by the American Federation of Teachers (AFT) and the National Education Association (NEA), which together represent the vast majority of teachers in the United States. In 1987, the Carnegie Task Force on Teaching as a Profession was instrumental in the founding of the **National Board for Professional Teaching Standards (NBPTS)**. Today, many educators see the NBPTS as a professional board implementing meaningful standards that lead to the awarding of advanced teacher certification that goes beyond state certification. Both major teacher organization presidents sit on the NBPTS board of directors, and a majority of the board members are from the teaching profession.[27] Currently, the NBPTS has granted national certification to more than 110,000 master teachers, teachers who have demonstrated the skills of an expert by passing a series of rigorous assessments, in twenty-five certificate fields.[28] Although NBPTS certification is voluntary and cannot be required as a condition of hiring, many state boards of education, local school boards, and superintendents have developed incentives to encourage teachers to seek national certification.[29] For more information on national board standards and certification areas, see the NBPTS website.

2-2c Mediated Entry

mediated entry The practice of inducting persons into a profession through carefully supervised stages.

Mediated entry refers to the practice of inducting people into a profession through carefully supervised stages that help them learn how to apply professional knowledge successfully in working environments. For example, aspiring physicians serve one

---

[24]Daniel M. Rosenthal, "What Education Reformers Should Do about Collective Bargaining," *Phi Delta Kappan* (February 2014), pp. 58–62; and Clifford B. Donn, Rache E. Donn, Loyd Goldberg, and Brenda J. Kirby, "Teacher Working Conditions With and Without Collective Bargaining." *Nevada Law Journal* (April 1, 2014), p. 496.

[25]Susan Black, "Bargaining: It's in Your Best Interest," *American School Board Journal* (April 2008), pp. 52–53; and Mark Paige, "Applying the 'Paradox' Theory: A Law and Policy Analysis of Collective Bargaining Rights and Teacher Evaluation Reform from Selected States," *Brigham Young University Education and Law Journal* (January, 2013), pp. 21–43.

[26]NASDTEC, *2009 Status of Educator Standards Boards*, (Whitinsville, MA: National Association of State Directors of Teacher Education and Certification, June 2010).

[27]Albert Shanker, "Quality Assurance: What Must Be Done to Strengthen the Teaching Profession," *Phi Delta Kappan* (November 1996), pp. 220–224; and see "National Board for Professional Teaching Standards" at **www.nbpts.org/board-directors** (January 14, 2015).

[28]See "National Board Certification," **www.boardcertifiedteachers.org/certificate-areas** (January 14, 2015).

[29]Rick Allen, "National Board Certified Teachers: Putting in the Time, Energy, and Money to Improve Teaching," *Education Update* (2010), pp. 1–5; and see "Value for Teachers" at **www .boardcertifiedteachers.org** (January 14, 2015).

or more years as interns and then as residents before being considered full-fledged professionals.

Dan Lortie's classic study of the teacher's job from a sociological perspective concluded that teaching ranks between occupations characterized by casual entry and those that place difficult demands on would-be members. For example, secretarial knowledge and skills are significantly less demanding than those of a medical doctor.[30] Too often, novice teachers report learning to teach in isolation through trial and error in the classroom. They also report that the beginning years of teaching can be a period of anxiety, frustration, and fear—even of trauma. Perhaps as a result, teaching has a higher attrition rate than other professions.[31] Although almost any occupation or profession produces problems and anxieties at first, a more systematic induction program would likely lessen the high attrition rate of beginning teachers.

In recent years, more colleges and universities have been using professional development schools (PDSs) as clinical settings where aspiring teachers gain more extended and intensive classroom experiences before beginning their student teaching (internships). This multisemester approach—in actual classrooms, under the guidance of experienced teachers and university professors—provides a more methodical **induction** into the teaching profession. Thus, there is better retention of new teachers as they begin their careers.[32]

The teaching profession now recognizes the need to develop a period of induction and transition into teaching, especially given that approximately 45 percent of new teachers leave the profession by the end of year five. As a result of this realization, the number of beginning teachers participating in induction programs has increased from 50 percent in 1990 to 91 percent in 2008, and, while thirty-three states have induction policies, twenty-two states and numerous local school districts fund more systematic efforts to transition into the profession.[33] This growing effort to support induction programs addresses beginning teachers' primary concern that leads them to abandon the profession: the lack of adequate support. Studies suggest that there is wide variety in the continuum of services provided in induction programs, but the more multifaceted a program is, the more success there tends to be in counteracting the "sink-or-swim" approach to induction. Comprehensive programs that include mentoring by experienced teachers, shared planning time, new teacher seminars, and extra classroom assistance are more likely to lead to increased teacher learning and thus better retention and increased student learning.[34] Overall, the trend toward more carefully mediated entry is likely to continue; major teacher unions and several education reform groups support it, as does federal legislation.[35]

induction Providing a supportive environment for novice teachers so they may experience a more methodical entry into the teaching profession.

[30]Dan C. Lortie, *Schoolteacher: A Sociological Study* (Chicago: University of Chicago Press, 1975).

[31]Richard M. Ingersoll, "Beginning Teacher Induction: What the Data Tell Us," *Phi Delta Kappan* (May 2012), pp. 47–51.

[32]Sharon Castle, "Do Professional Development Schools (PDS) Make a Difference?" *Journal of Teacher Education* (January/February 2006), pp. 65–80; and Nancy I. Latham and W. Paul Vogt, "Do Professional Development Schools Reduce Teacher Attrition?" *Journal of Teacher Education* (March/April 2007), pp. 153–167.

[33]Joan Gujarati, "A Comprehensive Induction System: A Key to the Retention of Highly Qualified Teachers," *Educational Forum* (April 2012), pp. 218–223; and Richard M. Ingersoll, "Beginning Teacher Induction: What the Data Tell Us," *Phi Delta Kappan* (May 2012), pp. 47–51.

[34]Sheryn Waterman and Ye He, "Effects of Mentoring Programs on New Teacher Retention: A Literature Review," *Mentoring & Tutoring: Partnership in Learning* (May 2011), pp. 139–156; and Seok Kang and David Berliner, "Characteristics of Teacher Induction Programs and Turnover Rates of Beginning Teachers," *The Teacher Educator* (October 2012), pp. 269–282.

[35]Kathy Wiebke and Joe Bardin, "New Teacher Support," *Journal of Staff Development* (Winter 2009), pp. 34–38; NEA, "Ensuring Every Child a Quality Teacher: Full Statement" (n.d.) at **www.nea.org/home/12549.htm** (January 12, 2015); and Stephen Sawchuk, "Teacher Induction Found to Raise Student Scores," *Education Week* (March 23, 2012).

2-2d Professional Development

Your teacher training does not end when you begin teaching full time. Teaching demands rigorous and continuous training, which is often referred to as **professional development**. Effective professional development should develop a teacher's knowledge and skills with the goal of improving student achievement. To stay up to date in their preparation and to acquire new classroom skills, teachers are expected to participate in various forms of workshops, local or national conferences, college courses, or online courses. In most states, completion of a master's degree, either in a content field or in professional education course work, is a mandated form of professional development required to maintain one's certification.[36]

The ultimate goal of professional development is to improve teaching and learning. A number of recent studies examining professional development trends in the United States conclude that teachers find value in professional development that incorporates active learning, collaborative problem solving, and communities of practice tied to school improvement efforts. Those staff-development efforts that are "one-shot" presentations had little effect on student achievement. These findings coincide with international comparisons of professional-development efforts in top-performing industrialized nations and the United States. In the countries that perform well on international achievement tests, teachers spend significantly more time collaborating on ways of improving classroom instruction than teachers in the United States. Teachers are using this research to make the case for more sustained, cohesive professional-development training.[37]

Both the NEA and the AFT support the concept of staff development as integral to a teacher's professional growth. The AFT has developed its Professional Development Program to encourage teachers "to improve their practice and their students' performance by becoming users of research."[38] The NEA has developed the NEA Academy, a repository for online courses that have been peer-reviewed for content and rigor. Teachers are encouraged to collaborate with colleagues in taking the courses to develop a community of learners.[39] As the Technology @ School box describes, teachers have numerous opportunities to use the Internet for professional development.

New varieties of professional development programs are giving teachers a major voice in decisions that affect their professional careers. These programs also help to establish the concept that teaching, like other full-fledged professions, requires lengthy and ongoing training.

2-2e Performance Pay

In recent years, school reformers have been questioning the effectiveness of the single salary schedule to compensate teachers and are advocating for a form of **merit pay** (a supplement to a teacher's base salary to reward superior performance) that will change the way teachers are paid. Today, the primary form of merit pay is known as pay for performance or **performance pay**; such a proposal includes a Value-Added Measurement (VAM) where teacher pay is based on students' progress on standardized tests. When students make academic gains, the teacher is rewarded. Proponents contend

---

[36]Laura Desimone, "A Primer on Effective Professional Development," *Must Reads from Kappan* (Summer 2010–2011), pp. 28–31.

[37]Sarah D. Sparks, "Survey: Teachers Worldwide Seek More Opportunities for Collaboration," *Education Week's Blogs* (June 25, 2014); and Patricia Rice Doran, "Professional Development for Teachers of Culturally and Linguistically Diverse Learners: Teachers' Experiences and Perceptions," *Global Education Journal* (October 2014), pp. 62–80.

[38]AFT, "The AFT Professional Development Program for Educators," at **www.aft.org /education/well-prepared-and-supported-school-staff/aft-professional -development-program** (January 2015).

[39]Steven Sawchuk, "The Online Option," *Education Week: Spotlight on Reinventing Professional Development* (October 1, 2009); and NEA Academy at **www.neaacademy.org/index.html** (January 12, 2015).

TECHNOLOGY @ SCHOOL

PROFESSIONAL DEVELOPMENT OPPORTUNITIES ON THE INTERNET

Whether you are preparing to teach, you are experiencing your first year in the classroom, or you are a veteran teacher, professional growth and development are critical to your teaching success. The Internet provides a rich array of technology resources for novice and veteran teachers to assist in their development as effective classroom teachers.

New teachers especially need assistance with job search information. Teachers-Teachers.com is a free teacher-recruitment service that provides candidates with the opportunity to complete online applications and cover letters for openings that are posted on the site that match their preferences. Teachers.net also has a "Jobs for Teachers" page on its site.

A site that has consistently provided useful resources for teachers is Kathy Schrock's Guide to Everything, where you will find a wide range of Internet resources, such as assessments and rubrics, resources for teaching with iPads, and articles for creating a more active classroom.

Beginning and veteran teachers can find Internet resources in just about any subject area at a variety of websites, and each site is likely to have links to additional web resources. Scholastic Inc. sponsors a website for teachers, which includes a series of articles with insightful advice for surviving the first year of teaching, in addition to useful classroom materials for the beginning teacher.

Although thousands of sites address the professional-development needs of educators, a few are typical of the comprehensive reach these sites have. The New Teacher Survival Guide website includes information on using cutting-edge technology and provides access to new teacher blogs. PBS LearningMedia provides links to standards-based curriculum resources as well as professional-development activities. Edutopia contains "diverse and innovative media resources" that are easily accessible, and the video library is impressive. Education World includes pages on technology integration and lifestyle issues.

Finally, all of the sites feature teachers' blogs, Twitter, or Facebook pages that are designed to provide advice to the new teacher as well as the opportunity to pose questions about specific problems in forum discussions.

that such incentive systems are necessary to improve overall teacher quality by motivating classroom teachers and encouraging high-quality people to enter and stay in the profession.[40] Although polls show 82 percent of the public supports the concept of using teacher performance to determine salaries or bonuses, 61 percent oppose using student performance on standardized tests as a factor.[41]

Teachers have historically expressed reservations about such plans. Some argue that teachers' work is complicated and difficult to measure and that linking assessments to individual teachers is fraught with inaccuracies. Teachers and their professional organizations feel more comfortable with multiple factors comprising their evaluations, including observations, contributions outside of the classroom, and professional learning activities. Where merit plans have been implemented, according to some reports, teachers have often believed that the wrong people were selected for preferential pay. Some observers fear that such rewards go to relatively few teachers at the expense of many others and threaten unity and collegiality among educators.[42] The need, critics say, is to involve teachers in the design and implementation of a compensation-reform plan that focuses on helping teachers become more successful in the classroom.[43] The Taking Issue box presents some arguments for and against merit pay.

---

[40]Gene V. Glass and David C. Berliner, "Chipping Away: Reforms That Don't Make a Difference," *Educational Leadership* (Summer 2014), pp. 28–33.

[41]Al Ramirez, "Merit Pay Misfires," *Educational Leadership* (December 2010), pp. 58–55; and William Bushaw and Valerie J. Calderon, "Americans Put Teacher Quality on Center Stage: The 46th Annual Phi Delta Kappa/Gallup Poll of the Public's Attitudes toward the Public Schools: Part II," *Phi Delta Kappan* (September 2014), pp. 49–61.

[42]John Rosales, "Pay Based on Test Scores," (n.d.) at **www.nea.org/home/36780.htm** (January 14, 2015); and Motoko Rich, "Middle-Class Pay Elusive for Teachers, Report Says," *The New York Times* (December 3, 2014).

[43]Nora Carr, "The Pay-for-Performance Pitfall," *American School Board Journal* (February 2008), pp. 38–39; and Gary W. Ritter and Nathan C. Jensen, "The Delicate Task of Developing an Attractive Merit Pay Plan for Teachers," *Phi Delta Kappan* (May 2010), pp. 32–37.

TAKING ISSUE

Read the following brief introduction, as well as the Question and the pros and cons list that follows. Then, answer the question using your own words and position.

MERIT PAY

Traditionally, teachers have earned salaries based on their years in teaching and their highest degree obtained. Recent alternative pay plans, however, offer rewards to teachers considered above average in teaching skills or increasing student achievement as measured on achievement tests.

Question

Should individual teachers receive special pay increases based on "merit"? (Think about this question as you read the PRO and CON arguments listed here. What is *your* response to this issue?)

Arguments PRO

1. Teachers whose students consistently score high on assessments must be outstanding teachers. Such teachers merit extra compensation for their work.

2. A growing body of research suggests that individual teachers can impact a student's learning. If such statistical evidence exists, teachers should be rewarded for positive student performance.

3. Performance-pay programs encourage teachers to focus on teaching the established curriculum because that is what the assessments are designed to measure. This ensures that students throughout the district are learning the same information and skills.

4. Without opportunities to earn performance pay, capable and ambitious people will choose incentive-producing careers such as business; thus, the best candidates will not be attracted to teaching, and high-quality teachers will be inclined to leave teaching.

5. Merit pay promotes excellence in teaching by acting as an incentive for teachers to improve their performance. Each teacher is encouraged to develop better teaching behaviors to increase student performance. Business and most other professions offer such motivators, so why not teaching?

Arguments CON

1. Factors related to achievement are so diverse that it is impossible to differentiate the teacher's contribution from home, social-class, and peer-group influences.

2. At this time, pay-for-performance plans only reward teachers in the core subject areas because that is what is currently being assessed. Hard work can perhaps be measured, but many creative activities do not necessarily correlate with good teaching. If creativity is a criterion, merit pay may be rewarded more for the teacher's apparent inventiveness than for students' learning.

3. If student results on mandated assessments are the primary evidence of performance, teachers will only teach to the test, thus narrowing the educational experience for students.

4. Businesses can offset extensive merit pay rewards by raising prices, but schools must rely on taxes. Taxpayers often will not or cannot support financial incentives significant enough to support a fair merit-pay system.

5. Incentive pay, by definition, goes to only a few. Such a plan penalizes equally qualified teachers who miss out for lack of enough positions. Moreover, competition for merit pay pits one teacher against another, encourages political games, and destroys the collegial cooperation essential to good education.

Question Reprise: What is Your Stand?

Reflect again on the following question by explaining *your* stand about this issue: Should individual teachers receive special pay increases based on merit or performance?

Even as arguments continue, performance-pay plans are being implemented in school districts across the United States. The Obama administration is supporting these efforts through its requirement under the Elementary and Secondary Education Act (ESEA) that state education agencies implement teacher and principal evaluation and support systems that use multiple measures of performance, including student growth on state assessments. As of 2013, forty-one states included student achievement in their teacher evaluation process.[44] Overall, the trend toward raising the ceiling on teachers' salaries and making distinctions based on merit should attract brighter students into the profession and keep good teachers from leaving classrooms for more competitive salaries in other fields because they will have the opportunity to earn higher wages.

2-2f Professional Learning Communities

Many educational reforms, as we have seen, involve a movement toward teacher empowerment—increasing teachers' participation in decisions that affect their own work and careers. One such reform is the **Professional Learning Community (PLC)**, a collaborative effort among a school's teachers and staff to improve student learning. PLCs use available school and district assessment data and student work to analyze results and establish goals for student progress. Collectively, they identify instructional strategies and best practices to incorporate into instruction in a systematic effort to enhance student achievement. Success of the PLC in enhancing student achievement depends on the commitment and persistence of the educators' collaborative effort.[45]

The assumption underlying PLCs is that teams of educators are best suited to apply their professional expertise in the areas of curriculum planning, data analysis, content knowledge, teaching skills, research, and reflection to improve classroom instruction and student learning.[46] Teachers are able to use their professional knowledge and experience in the school setting to collectively plan to change the educational environment. Dufour, a leading expert on PLCs, contends that most professions require such collaboration with colleagues, and PLCs provide a platform where teachers can collaborate in a coordinated and systematic effort to support the students they serve.[47]

The fate of PLCs requires that teachers are able to overcome the traditional school culture that fosters isolation. Teachers must be willing to take responsibility for directing their own behavior and invest the extra time necessary for an effective, collaborative PLC. To support this, school leaders must provide training in the skills necessary to make PLCs function and provide structured meeting time in the teachers' schedules.[48] Advocates of PLCs claim that teachers welcome the increased involvement because when they are implemented correctly, PLCs are the best hope for school improvement.

Critics contend that PLCs actually challenge teacher autonomy and the traditional culture of schools by requiring collaboration with others. From this perspective, teachers should be able to act on their own with regard to what works in the classroom to improve student achievement. An inordinate amount of time, they say, is devoted to analyzing data, discussing remedies, and experimenting with instructional strategies.[49]

Expanding PLCs requires patience and a willingness to work collaboratively with others in the profession. Once in practice, however, upgrades in the instructional program should improve academic achievement and further enhance teachers' professional status.

Professional Learning Community (PLC) In collaborative groups, teachers and other colleagues work together to improve instruction for their students.

FOCUS How do you believe movements toward increasing professionalism in teaching will affect you? Will you look for a position in a school that has a strong induction program for new teachers? Would you prefer a mediated-entry program similar to that in the medical profession, with intern and resident teacher levels, before you become a full-fledged professional teacher? How can you prepare yourself to effectively carry out the shared responsibilities of PLCs?

[44]Kathryn M. Doherty and Sandi Jacobs, *State of the States 2013: Connect the Dots* (Washington, DC: National Council on Teacher Quality, October 2103); and Deborah S. Delisle, Assistant Secretary, US Department of Education, correspondence to Chief State School Officers (August 21, 2014) at **www2.ed.gov/policy/eseaflex/secretary-letters/cssoltr8212014.html** (April 21, 2015).

[45]SEDL, *What Is a PLC?* (April 2007) at **www.sedl.org/pubs/sedl-letter/v19n01/what-is-a-plc.html** (April 21, 2015).

[46]Anne Kennedy, Angie Deuel, Tamara Holmlund Nelson, and David Slavit, "Requiring Collaboration or Distributing Leadership?" *Phi Delta Kappan* (May 2011), pp. 20–24; and "Study Identifies Habits of Highly Effective Professional Learning Communities," *Education Research Newsletter* (n.d.) at **www.ernweb.com/educational-research-articles/study-identifies-habits-of-highly-effective-professional-learning-communities/** (January 13, 2015).

[47]Rick Dufour, "Work Together—But Only if You Want To," *Phi Delta Kappan* (February 2011), pp. 57–61.

[48]Rebecca A. Thessin and Joshua P. Starr, "Supporting the Growth of Effective Professional Learning Communities Districtwide," *Phi Delta Kappan* (March 2011), pp. 48–54; and Learning Forward, "Standards for Professional Learning," (n.d.), at **http://learningforward.org/standards/learning-communities** (January 13, 2015).

[49]Karen Seashore Louis and Kyla Ahlstrom, "Principals as Cultural Leaders," *Phi Delta Kappan* (February 2011), pp. 52–56; and Susan McLester, "Rick & Becky Dufour: Professional Learning Communities at Work," *District Administration* (September 2012), pp. 61–70.

FROM PRESERVICE TO PRACTICE

A PROFESSIONAL LEARNING COMMUNITY

During a break in the teachers' lounge, Anna Solemini, a first-year teacher, listened to her colleagues talk about the recent state achievement data that had just been released from the district assessment office. The data indicated that test scores for the sixth and eighth graders were up in math and reading, while there was a slight dip in the scores of seventh graders on both assessments. As a new teacher, Anna knew the results were important but was unsure what she and her colleagues would do next.

During the ensuing weeks, Anna discovered the impact the scores would have on her school. At each grade level, she was aware that groups of teachers were organized into three PLCs. Each PLC was comprised of content teachers representing a given grade level. Prior to forming the PLCs, some had lobbied that they be structured according to content area, but after much deliberation, the collaborative decision was made that interdisciplinary teams at each grade level would be more reflective of the middle school philosophy and be more likely to meet the academic needs of the school's students. Members of the PLCs, teachers who took on the role of team leaders, and school administrators received extensive training in how to work effectively in such a collective endeavor.

Each PLC not only reviewed the scores from the Partnership for Assessment of Readiness for College and Careers (PARCC) assessments but also examined data from formative assessments that had been administered to students during the two previous grading cycles. One of the discoveries they made as they analyzed the data was that there had to be a realignment of literacy and math instructional objectives with the new curriculum based on the Common Core State Standards, especially at the seventh grade level. After they were satisfied that the objectives were properly aligned with the assessment, they began work on improving the instructional plan to meet the needs of individual learners. The PLCs investigated strategies designed to engage middle-level learners through a literature review and consultations with a local university professor who was affiliated with the professional-development school network. Their research and investigation led them to conclude that literacy and math skills at all three grade levels needed to be incorporated into an interdisciplinary approach to reinforce the state curriculum standards. They were able to implement the use of multiple texts and collaborative learning strategies to differentiate instruction to meet the needs of all students. Convinced they were on the right track to enhance student learning, the PLCs systematically monitored the reforms to determine if they would yield the desired results.

Anna was impressed with the efforts of the PLCs. She was proud of the way her fellow teachers and administrators collaborated to improve the educational environment of her school. She is looking forward to the possibility of becoming a member of the professional learning team so she can take a more active role in making a difference for all students in her school.

CASE QUESTIONS

1. What further information should Anna seek before trying to join the school's PLC?
2. How does the concept of the PLC support the position that teaching is a profession?
3. Why might some teachers object to serving on a PLC?
4. Would you support Anna's quest to join the PLC?

2-3 TEACHER ORGANIZATIONS

National Education Association (NEA) The largest organization that represents teachers in the United States.

American Federation of Teachers (AFT) The second largest organization that represents teachers in America.

Although today's working conditions need improvement, they sharply contrast with the restrictions teachers once endured. For example, a Wisconsin teacher's contract for 1922 prohibited a woman teacher from dating, marrying, staying out past 8 p.m., smoking, drinking, loitering in ice cream parlors, dyeing her hair, and using mascara or lipstick.[50] A critical factor in the development of teaching as a profession has been the growth of professional organizations for teachers. The **National Education Association (NEA)** and the **American Federation of Teachers (AFT)**, the two most important, have been considered rivals, competing for members, recognition, and power.

---

[50]*Chicago Tribune*, September 28, 1975, sect. 1, p. 3.

OVERVIEW 2.1

COMPARISON OF THE NATIONAL EDUCATION ASSOCIATION (NEA) AND THE AMERICAN FEDERATION OF TEACHERS (AFT)

	NEA	AFT
Total membership (2014)	3,000,000	1,600,000
President	Lily Eskelsen Garcia	Randi Weingarten
President's term	3 years (maximum 6 years per person)	2 years (no maximum)
Organizational view	Professional association	Union affiliation with AFL-CIO
Geographic strength	Suburban and rural areas	Large and medium-size cities

Overview 2.1 provides a profile of the two organizations. Although some educators believe this division produces healthy professional competition, others consider it detrimental to the teaching profession—a splitting of power and a waste of resources. Still others argue that teachers will not attain full professional status until one unified voice speaks for them. Both organizations have been active in recent years in challenging the critics, state legislators, and governors who have called for reforms that limit or eliminate teacher tenure, repeal collective bargaining, and implement evaluation systems that publicly rate teachers and schools as passing or failing. They are also working to assist members in the classroom with effective practices for implementing the Common Core State Standards and to help them with the accompanying assessments.[51]

Regardless of which teacher organization you prefer or are inclined to join, the important step is to make a commitment and to be an active member. Organizational membership will increase your own professionalism and gain you collegial relationships. Your support also helps to improve salary, working conditions, and benefits for many teachers. In addition, reading the journals, magazines, or newsletters that most professional organizations publish, as well as visiting their websites, will keep you abreast of the latest developments in the field. See the Suggested Resources section at the end of this chapter for resources provided by each organization.

2-3a National Education Association (NEA)

The NEA is a complex, multifaceted organization involved in education on many local, state, and national levels. The NEA includes teachers, education support professionals, higher education faculty and staff, and administrators at the national level. As shown in Table 2.1, in 2014, membership totaled approximately 3 million. A majority of the nation's 3.3 million public-school teachers are NEA members.[52] Primarily suburban and rural in its membership, the NEA is one of the top lobbying forces in the country. Its fifty state affiliates, along with more than 14,000 local affiliates, are among the most

---

[51]Stephen Sawchuk and Liana Heitin, "AFT, NEA Agendas Converge as External, Internal Pressures Rise," *Education Week* (August 6, 2014), pp. 1, 11.

[52]Greg Toppo, "USA's Top Teachers Union Losing Members," *USA Today* (July 3, 2012); Stephen Sawchuk, "As Membership Plummets, NEA Tries to Boost Political Clout," *Education Week* (July 18, 2012), pp. 1, 18; also see **www.nea.org/home/2580.htm** (January 14, 2015) and see **http://nces.ed.gov/programs/digest/d13/tables/dt13_209.10.asp?current=yes** (January 14, 2015).

TABLE 2.1	Membership in the NEA and AFT	
Year	**NEA Membership**	**AFT Membership**
1960	714,000	59,000
1970	1,100,000	205,000
1980	1,650,000	550,000
1990	2,050,000	750,000
1995	2,200,000	875,000
1998	2,300,000	950,000
2003	2,700,000	1,000,000
2011	3,200,000	1,500,000
2014	3,000,000	1,600,000

Source: "The AFT Soars," *The 1988–90 Report of the Officers of the American Federation of Teachers* (Washington, DC: AFT, 1990), p. 15; *NEA Handbook, 1986–87* (Washington, DC: NEA, 1986), Table 4, p. 142; *NEA Handbook, 1994–95* (Washington, DC: NEA, 1995), Table 1, p. 164; and *NEA Handbook, 1997–98,* Table 1, p. 166; also see **www.nea.org/home/1594.htm** (2009) and **www.aft.org/join/** (2011); **www.nea.org/home/2580.htm** (2015) and **www.aft.org/about** (2015).

influential state-level education lobbies.[53] The NEA offers a wide range of professional services. Individual benefits include savings on optional insurance programs, financial services, and member discounts on various services. It also publishes research memos and opinion surveys on an annual basis.[54] The NEA's major publication is a quarterly magazine, *NEA Today*. There is also a daily e-newsletter, *neaToday*.

2-3b American Federation of Teachers (AFT)

Formed in 1916, the AFT is affiliated with the American Federation of Labor and Congress of Industrial Organizations (AFL-CIO) labor union. The AFT was originally open only to classroom teachers. In 1976, however, to increase membership, the AFT targeted professional employees such as higher-education faculty, nurses, health-care professionals, government employees, and school-related personnel such as paraprofessionals and cafeteria, custodial, maintenance, and transportation workers. Membership in 2014 stood at just over 1.6 million (Table 2.1).

The AFT publishes a quarterly professional magazine, *American Educator*. Members have access to resources on the AFT website that are designed to enhance classroom teaching and learning. The AFT also provides individual benefits to members similar to those of the NEA, such as access to legal services and insurance programs. Unlike the NEA, the AFT has always required its members to join the local (3,000 affiliates), state, and national organizations simultaneously.[55]

The AFT expanded rapidly in the 1960s and 1970s when its affiliates spearheaded a dramatic increase in teacher strikes and other militant job actions. Subsequently, the AFT became the dominant teacher organization in many large urban centers where unions have traditionally flourished, where militant tactics were common, and where teachers in general have wanted a powerful organization to represent them. In rural and suburban areas, where union tactics have received less support, the NEA remains dominant.

---

[53]See **www.nea.org/home/LegislativeActionCenter.html** (January 14, 2015).

[54]See **www.neamb.com** (April 20, 2015).

[55]See "About Us" at **www.aft.org/about** (January 14, 2015); "Our Periodicals" at **www.aft.org/our-news/periodicals** (January 14, 2015).

OVERVIEW 2.2

MAJOR SPECIALIZED PROFESSIONAL ORGANIZATIONS FOR TEACHERS

Organizations That Focus on Specific Subject Matter

- American Council on the Teaching of Foreign Languages
- American School Health Association
- The Association for Career and Technical Education
- International Reading Association
- International Technology and Engineering Educators Association
- Journalism Education Association
- Music Teachers National Association
- National Art Education Association
- National Business Education Association
- National Council for the Social Studies
- National Council of Teachers of English
- National Council of Teachers of Mathematics
- National Science Teachers Association
- Society of Health and Physical Educators

Organizations That Focus on Students and General Education Issues

- American Montessori Society
- Association for Childhood Education International
- Association for Experiential Education
- Association for Middle Level Education
- Association for Supervision and Curriculum Development
- Council for Exceptional Children
- Learning Disabilities Association of America
- National Association for the Education of Young Children
- National Association for Gifted Children
- Phi Delta Kappa
- Teachers of English to Speakers of Other Languages International Association

In addition to the NEA and AFT, several hundred other educational organizations exist.[56] The US Department of Education provides an easily searchable database to find an organization that is likely to meet your needs at the Education Resource Organization Directory (EROD). In the following sections, we describe some of the basic types of organizations that could be helpful to a new teacher.

2-3c Specialized Professional Organizations

At the working level of the classroom, the professional organization that best serves teachers (and education students) usually focuses on their major field. A subject-centered professional association provides a meeting ground for teachers who share similar interests. These professional organizations customarily provide regional and national meetings and professional journals that offer current teaching tips, enumerate current issues in the discipline, and summarize current research and its relationship to practice. The first column of Overview 2.2 lists fourteen major organizations that focus on specific subject matter.

Other organizations, also national in scope, focus on the needs and rights of particular kinds of students, ensuring that these children and youth are served by well-prepared school personnel. Several such organizations are listed in the second column of Overview 2.2. These associations hold regional and national meetings and publish monthly or quarterly journals.

Still another type of organization is the professional organization whose members cut across various subjects and student types, such as the Association for Supervision and Curriculum Development (ASCD) and Phi Delta Kappa (PDK), also listed in the second column of Overview 2.2. These organizations tend to highlight general innovative

---

[56]See *Education Resource Organizations Directory* (EROD—US Department of Education) at **http://wdcrobcolp01.ed.gov/Programs/EROD**.

teaching practices, describe new trends and policies affecting the entire field of education, have a wide range of membership, and work to advance the teaching profession in general. Each organization publishes a well-respected journal: *Educational Leadership* by ASCD, and the *Phi Delta Kappan* by PDK.

2-3d Religious Education Organizations

As of 2014, in grades K–12, there are an estimated 397,000 non–public-school teachers, of whom approximately 71 percent teach in religious-affiliated schools. One of the largest religious education organizations is the National Association of Catholic School Teachers (NACST), founded in 1978. It currently comprises more than 4,000 lay teachers, mainly from large cities in the eastern United States. Few Catholic K–12 schoolteachers belong to either the NEA or the AFT.[57]

The largest and oldest Catholic education organization is the National Catholic Education Association (NCEA), comprising 150,000 Catholic educators. Most members are administrators who serve as principals, supervisors, or superintendents of their respective schools. It is estimated that currently more than 1.9 million students attend approximately 6,594 Catholic elementary and secondary schools in the United States. By comparison, 245,000 students attend Jewish-affiliated schools, and 204,000 students attend schools affiliated with the Baptist religion.[58]

2-3e Parent-Teacher Groups

parent-teacher group An organization of parents and teachers in a local school community.

Parent-teacher groups provide forums for parents and teachers to work together in creating positive learning environments in schools across the nation. As a teacher, you can take an active part in these associations and work with parents on curriculum and instructional programs, student policy, and school-community relations.

Parent-Teacher Association (PTA) A national organization of parents, teachers, and students to promote the welfare of children and youth that has affiliated local groups in school communities.

Founded in 1897, the **Parent-Teacher Association (PTA)**—the most prominent of the groups—is a loose confederation of fifty-five state congresses and more than 20,000 local units in the fifty states and the territories, with approximately 5 million members in 2014. Every PTA unit devises its own pattern of organization and service to fit its school and neighborhood. PTA membership is open to anyone interested in promoting the welfare of children and youth, working with teachers and schools, and supporting PTA goals.[59] It maintains open lines of communication through Facebook, Twitter, and its official blog, "OneVoice." *Our Children* is the official print publication of the association.[60] The PTA website also offers an online newsroom (go to the National PTA website and click on "News & Events") as a source for legislative information and current news of interest to the organization.

As the nation's largest child-advocacy organization, the National PTA is constantly assessing children's welfare to respond to changes in society and in children's needs. Recently, the National PTA lobbied Congress to "reauthorize the Elementary and

---

[57]"Number of Teachers in Elementary and Secondary Schools, and Instructional Staff in Postsecondary Degree-Granting Institutions, by Control of Institution: Selected Years, Fall 1970 through Fall 2023," *Digest of Education Statistics: 2013*, at **http://nces.ed.gov/programs /digest/d13/tables/dt13_105.40.asp?current=yes**; Steven P. Broughman and Nancy L. Swaim, *Characteristics of Private Schools in the United States: Results from the 2011–12 Private School Universe Survey (NCES 2013–316)*. US Department of Education (Washington, DC: National Center for Education Statistics, 2013); telephone conversation with Virginia Crowther, office manager–membership, National Association of Catholic School Teachers, January 5, 2015.

[58]See **www.ncea.org/about-us**; and **www.ncea.org/data-information/catholic -school-data** (January 5, 2015).

[59]Susan Ludwig, "Education Interest Groups," *Research Starters Education*: *Education Interest Groups* (June 2008), p. 1; see "Today's PTA" at **www.pta.org/about/?navItemNumber=503** (January 5, 2015).

[60]See **www.pta.org/parents/content.cfm?ItemNumber=1177&navItemNumber=574** (January 5, 2015).

OVERVIEW 2.3

PROFESSIONAL ORGANIZATIONS STUDENTS CAN JOIN

Name and Location	Membership Profile	Focus	Major Publications
National Education Association Student Program, Washington, DC	Undergraduate and graduate students (55,000), 1,100 college/university chapters	Future teachers, understanding the profession, fostering leadership, liability coverage	*Tomorrow's Teachers* (annual), NEA Student Program Facebook Page
Pi Lambda Theta, Arlington, VA	Undergraduate and graduate students, and professional educators (11,000)	International honor society, promotes professionalism	*Educational Horizons* (quarterly), PLT Facebook Page
Phi Delta Kappa, Arlington, VA	Undergraduate and graduate students, teachers, administrators, and professors (33,000)	Professional association for career educators; research; service, leadership, and teaching; issues, trends, and policies	*Phi Delta Kappan* (monthly), PDK Facebook Page
Kappa Delta Pi, Indianapolis, IN	Graduate students, undergraduate students, teachers, administrators, and professors (40,000)	International honor society, teaching, professional growth	*The Educational Forum* (quarterly), *New Teacher Advocate* (quarterly), *Kappa Delta Pi Record* (quarterly), *Educational Researcher* (monthly)
American Educational Research Association, Washington, DC	Graduate students, researchers, and faculty (25,000)	Research and its application to education	*American Educational Research Journal* (quarterly), *Review of Educational Research* (quarterly), *Educational Evaluation and Policy Analysis* (quarterly), AERA Facebook page

Sources: **www.nea.org/studentprogram** (2015); **www.pilambda.org** (2015); **www.pdkintl.org** (2015); **www.kdp.org/aboutkdp/indexphp** (2015); **www.aera.net** (2015).

FOCUS

● Which of the professional organizations listed in this chapter hold the most interest for you? Which might be useful to join later in your career?

● How can you find out more information about professional organizations that interest you?

Secondary Education Act/No Child Left Behind (ESEA-NCLB); expand access to high-quality early childhood education; improve special education through the Individuals with Disabilities Education Act (IDEA); provide adequate funding for education; support continued improvements to nutrition programs; and foster safe environments before, during, and after school."[61]

2-3f Organizations for Prospective Teachers

Students considering teaching careers may also join professional organizations. These organizations can help you answer questions; investigate the profession; form ideals of professional ethics, standards, and training; meet other students and educators at local and national meetings; and keep up with current trends in the profession.

Overview 2.3 lists professional organizations that offer specific services for student members. Ask your professors for appropriate information if you are interested in joining any of these organizations. Most of the professional organizations offer discounted student membership rates. Search the Internet for any of the organizations listed to find out more about becoming a member.

[61]See "2014 Public Policy Agenda" at **www.pta.org/advocacy/content.cfm?ItemNumber=3222** (January 5, 2015).

SUMMING UP

1. It is generally agreed that teaching, although not yet a full profession, is moving toward becoming one.
2. Collective bargaining is an integral part of the teaching profession, giving teachers greater authority to determine working conditions and their effectiveness as teachers.
3. Many education trends are raising the level of teacher professionalism. State professional practice boards and National Board Certification, for example, enable teachers to participate in setting criteria for entering the profession. Induction and professional development programs help establish the idea that teaching is a full-fledged profession requiring lengthy and continued training. Professional Learning Communities (PLCs) provide opportunities for increased salaries and more professional responsibilities designed to enhance student learning.

4. The NEA and AFT represent the majority of classroom teachers; these organizations have historically improved teachers' salaries and working conditions and have gained them a greater voice in decisions that affect teaching and learning in schools.
5. Many professional organizations are open to undergraduate students or to graduate students and teachers. All provide valuable information and services to educators at different career levels.

SUGGESTED RESOURCES

INTERNET RESOURCES

Information about many of the organizations discussed in this chapter can be found on the Internet. For example, the NEA, the AFT, and the National PTA have informative websites.

In exploring specific topics such as professional development and educational technology, there are many good sites to visit first. For professional development, try the Learning Forward website.

For educational technology, visit the website of the International Society for Technology in Education (ISTE).

For information on national board certification, consult the National Board for Professional Teaching Standards (NBPTS) site.

PUBLICATIONS

Conant, James B. *The Education of American Teachers*. New York: McGraw-Hill, 1964. *A classic text on improving teacher education and teacher professionalism.*

Darling-Hammond, Linda, and John Bransford, eds. *Preparing Teachers for a Changing World: What Teachers Should Learn and Be Able to Do*. San Francisco, CA: Jossey-Bass, 2005. *Sponsored by the National Academy of Education, this book informs teacher educators and policy makers about the most effective ways to prepare teachers who will meet the needs of the nation's schoolchildren.*

Drury, Darrel, and Justin Baer. *The American Public School Teacher: Past, Present and Future*. Boston: Harvard Education Press, 2011. *Reflects on the NEA surveys that are conducted every five years.*

Goldstein, Dana. *The Teacher Wars: A History of America's Most Embattled Profession*. New York: Doubleday, 2014. *A comprehensive look at the history of the teaching profession; covers many of the topics in this chapter.*

Grimmett, Peter P., Jon C. Young, and Claude Lessard. *Teacher Certification and the Professional Status of Teaching in North America: The New Battleground for Public Education*. Charlotte, NC: Information Age Pub., 2012. *Focuses on teacher certification and questions about who will teach, the required minimum levels of competence, and who will make those decisions.*

Hannaway, Jane, and Andrew Rotherham. *Collective Bargaining in Education: Negotiating Change in Today's Schools*. Boston: Harvard Educational Publications Group, 2006. *A well-written and fair look at the collective bargaining process and its impact on educational change.*

Hess, Frederick, M., and Michael Q. McShane, eds. *Teacher Quality 2.0: Toward a New Era in Education Reform*. Cambridge, MA: Harvard Education Press, 2014. *Examines innovations taking place in various education settings that promise to improve teacher quality.*

Kahlenberg, Richard D. *Tough Liberal: Albert Shanker and the Battles over Schools, Unions, Race, and Democracy*. New York: Columbia University Press, 2007. *This biography of the long-time AFT president, Albert Shanker, describes the recent history of the teacher's union in the United States.*

Lieberman, Ann, and Lynne Miller, eds. *Teachers in Professional Communities: Improving Teaching and Learning*. New York: Teachers College Press, 2008. *Professional communities as an approach to professional development are described, and recommendations are made for incorporating them into the school setting.*

Moe, Terry M. *Special Interest: Teachers Unions and America's Public Schools*. Washington, DC: Brookings Institution Press, 2011. *Examines teacher unions and their influence on public schools from a conservative perspective.*

Skinner, Elizabeth A., Maria Teresa Garreton, and Brian D. Schultz. *Grow Your Own Teachers: Grassroots Change for Teacher Education: Teaching for Social Justice*. New York: Teachers College Press, 2011. *Examines the school reform movement in Chicago, especially teacher-preparation efforts.*

CHAPTER **3**

THE WORLD ORIGINS OF AMERICAN EDUCATION

InTASC INTASC STANDARDS ADDRESSED IN THIS CHAPTER

2 Learning Differences

LEARNING OBJECTIVES

3-1 Discuss how preliterate societies used an oral tradition to enculture children and why it is still used in contemporary education.

3-2 Explain how Chinese educators, especially Confucius, developed an ethical system and its significance in Asian countries.

3-3 Examine how hieroglyphics led to the development of scribal schools in Ancient Egypt and why primary schools throughout the world continue to emphasize reading and writing.

3-4 Describe the concept of monotheism and how reading and studying sacred scriptures shaped Western education.

3-5 Determine how the ancient Greek ideal of the liberal arts and science shaped the course of Western higher education.

3-6 Analyze how Rome's political and economic transition from a republic to an imperial empire changed its education content and values.

3-7 Analyze the method that scholastic educators in the Middle Ages used to reconcile Christian doctrines and scriptures with the classical learning inherited from Greece and Rome.

3-8 Describe the Islamic contribution to medicine and mathematics.

3-9 Assess the Renaissance educators' ideal of the teacher as an expert and a critic of culture, literature, and art.

3-10 Discuss the Reformation's impact on the growth of schools, the increase in school attendance, and the supervision of teachers.

3-11 Analyze how the Enlightenment's emphasis on nature and science inaugurated change in educational theory and practices.

This chapter was revised by Gerald L. Gutek.

Hero Images/Getty Images

EDUCATION IS ABOUT what was (the past), what is (the present), and what might be (the future). In meeting their immediate, daily classroom challenges, teachers understandably tend to focus on the present. But today's classroom episodes soon become yesterday's past. Professional standards and teacher-education programs ask teachers to reflect on their practices. Going from the ancient to the modern, this chapter invites you to broaden your reflections and to interpret today's events in the light of previous experience. Reflection, arising in the present, illuminated by the past, can aid us to envision a better future for our students, our country, and, maybe, the world.

3-1 EDUCATION IN PRELITERATE SOCIETIES

Paleolithic period The prehistoric "old stone age," which lasted for 2.6 million years to about 10,000 BCE, when small, nomadic bands of people searched for food.

Human history began in the **Paleolithic period** (the Old Stone Age in 10,000 BCE) when small nomadic bands of people searched for food, such as edible fruits, plants, and roots, or hunted for birds, fish, and animals. Organized into simple kinship clans or tribes, preliterate people lived with the ever-present fear they might not survive. The natural environment that nourished them also threatened them. Their source of food might disappear with storms, floods, earthquakes, or droughts. Between their treks for food, they sheltered in caves or in simple dwellings fashioned from branches or animal skins. They improvised tools—clubs, spears, or pointed digging sticks. Importantly, they learned to make and use fire. By trial and error, they developed survival skills that over time became cultural patterns.

For a culture to perpetuate itself, it must be transmitted from the group's adults to its children. In the Paleolithic period before the invention of writing and reading, cultural transmission took place through a largely informal process of **enculturation** by which children learned their group's language, customs, and values. From their fathers and older men, boys learned to hunt, fish, and defend the group from enemies. From their mothers and older women, girls learned to find and prepare food and sew garments. Gender patterns that designated some activities as specifically appropriate for males and others for females had a staying power in education that persisted into the late nineteenth and early twentieth centuries.

enculturation A process of cultural transmission by which children learn their group's language, customs, and values.

The group's beliefs about the world and its mores, that is, approved behaviors, were transmitted to the young through stories, songs, and religious rituals. Tribal elders, such as priests and chiefs, transmitted the group's religious beliefs and moral values to the young so they could be preserved from generation to generation. Children learned that good actions, conforming to the group's sanctions, helped it survive; bad actions, challenging the group's beliefs and values, jeopardized its survival.

FOCUS What is an oral tradition, and how does it function in education? Have you experienced an oral tradition in your own education?

Lacking writing to record their histories, preliterate societies relied on **oral tradition**—storytelling—to transmit their heritage. Elders or priests, who were often gifted storytellers, sang or recited poems and stories that commemorated events, especially legends, about the group's past. Combining myths and history, the oral tradition constructed the group's collective memory and identity by telling of its origin, heroes, and victories. The individual's passage from childhood to adulthood was celebrated with dramatic ceremonies that incorporated dancing, music, and acting that gave the event a powerful, often supernatural, meaning. Storytelling continues to be an engaging teaching strategy today, especially in preschools and primary grades. Often adults, such as military veterans and artists from the school's community, visit classrooms to tell their stories.

oral tradition The use of the spoken, rather than the written language, to transmit the cultural heritage through songs, stories, and myths.

Neolithic Age The "new stone age" in human development characterized by the making of tools, domestication of plants and animals, and settlement in small villages, which began around 10,000 BCE.

To make life more secure, the early humans made a momentous transition as they went from hunting to growing food. Ushering in the agriculture, the **Neolithic Age** began around 10,000 BCE. Now farmers, people needed to plan their activities around the seasons of the year—to times for sowing seeds, cultivating plants, and harvesting crops. The plotting of these seasons led to the calendar. Thus, a new objective was added to education: developing and using a sense of time.

Because farmers lived where they raised their crops, nomadic life yielded to living in settlements, and then to small and later larger villages. Good farming practices generated

FROM PRESERVICE TO PRACTICE

LEARNING NATIONAL IDENTITY THROUGH PATRIOTIC PROGRAMS

In this vignette, Dr. Gutek, the chapter's author, reflects on his observation of an elementary school program.

You can reflect on and draw insights from your educational experiences, as a student and teacher. Here, I reflect on my experience of attending a program about "Freedom," presented by the first-grade class at a local public school. The program was part of the school's celebration of President's Day.

The children filed on to the stage, which displayed a large American flag, and, in unison, recited, "I pledge allegiance to the flag of the United States of America…." They then sang patriotic songs, such as "This is My Flag," "America," and "This Land is My Land." One boy, costumed as George Washington, recounted the well-known story about how he told the truth to his father

that he had chopped down the cherry tree. Another boy was dressed as Abraham Lincoln.

As a historian of education, the performance led me to reflect on its educational and cultural meaning. I thought how oral tradition and celebratory performances in schools, especially stories, songs, and symbols, construct a group's identity and values. The large flag, the songs, and the costumes all built a sense of American identity in the children. The proverbial but most likely mythical story of George Washington and the cherry tree reinforced the values of honesty and truthfulness. I thought about how significant adults, such as the music director and the teachers, had planned and orchestrated the program. I am sure that many of you have either participated in or observed a program like the one I described.

CASE QUESTIONS

1. How does this contemporary school performance resemble the oral tradition in preliterate societies?

2. How do songs and stories construct children's sense of group identity?

3. How do educational episodes, like the one just described, relate to cultural identity and cultural diversity?

4. Reflect on similar school programs in your own education, and relate them to how you think about the history of education.

surpluses that supported larger populations. No longer nomads, people learned the importance of place (geography)—designating our space from the foreigners' space.

As language users, humans created pictographs and then developed symbols from the pictographs that represented people, animals, and natural phenomena. These early beginnings of expression and communication in signs, pictographs, and then various scripts signified humanity's great cultural leap to literacy. A literate society required schools, places where children learned to read and write. The preliterate peoples' development of tools led to the training of children in skills; skill learning remains important in preschool and primary schools. Their use of an oral tradition that featured songs, stories, and drama continues to have a place in contemporary education. For a historical perspective on the development of literacy and schooling, we look at three great ancient cultures: the Chinese, the Egyptians, and the Hebrews.

3-2 EDUCATION IN THE ANCIENT CHINESE CIVILIZATION

China has 4,000 years of continuous history and is one of the world's most enduring civilizations. The Chinese empire—which achieved high pinnacles of political, social, and educational development—spanned more than forty centuries, from 2200 BCE to 1912 CE.[1] Today, modern China (the People's Republic of China—PRC) is an important contemporary world power. With more than 1.3 billion people, China's population is the largest of any country in the world. (See Overview 3.1 for key periods relating to education in China and other countries.)

Like the ancient Greeks, the Chinese, who called their empire the "Middle Kingdom," saw their culture as the center of civilization. Believing their language and

---

[1]John Keay, *China: A History* (New York: Basic Books, 2011).

culture superior to all others, they looked down on foreigners as barbarians.[2] Seeking to avoid other peoples and cultures, the Chinese attempted to shut out foreign influences.

Although they invented paper, printing, gunpowder, the propeller, the crossbow, and the cannon, the Chinese did not fully exploit these technological innovations as potential instruments of power. Eventually, imperial China's reluctance to adapt technology from other cultures isolated and weakened it and, by the nineteenth century, made it vulnerable to foreign exploitation. At the end of the twentieth and into the twenty-first century, China made a dramatic change in its attitude and embarked on a concerted policy of economic and technological modernization.

3-2a Confucian Education

Unlike the Egyptian and Judaic cultures discussed later in the chapter, Chinese philosophy focused on living here and now rather than on universal questions about the immortality of the soul. Our examination of Chinese education begins in the third century BCE, when China suffered from political turmoil. During social and political crises, an important policy question is whether education should attempt to revive the traditions of the past to restore harmony, or develop new strategies for social and economic change. In answering this question, three philosophies—Legalism, Taoism, and Confucianism—proposed different paths for education in China.

During the Ch'in dynasty, Legalism, developed by scholar Shih Huang Ti, was decreed China's official philosophy. Declaring that the emperor's edicts were to be obeyed without questions, legalists established an authoritarian government, which ruthlessly maintained order and used education to indoctrinate people in their beliefs. Fearing dissent, legalists imposed a strict censorship to repress alternative philosophies such as Taoism and Confucianism.

As a more humane alternative to Legalism, Lao Tzu, a philosopher in the sixth century BCE, developed Taoism, which continues to influence Chinese culture and education. In his *Tao Te Ching*, "The Way and Virtue," Lao Tzu began a philosophical journey to find the path to the true reality, which is often hidden by misinformation. All things, Lao Tzu claimed, come from and follow an unseen, underlying, unifying force that moves through the world. Unlike the legalists, who wanted to control others, Lao Tzu advised people to stop trying to control other people and events, go with the stream of life, and live simply and spontaneously.[3] In Taoism, education's purpose is to encourage the reflection needed to find one's true self and to take the path to truth.

When they came to power in 207 BCE, the Han emperors rejected Legalism and made Confucianism China's official philosophy. Unlike Western philosophers, Confucius (551–479 BCE) did not dwell on theological or metaphysical issues about the human being's relationship to God or the universe. He believed it was much more useful to establish the standards to maintain a harmonious ethical society than to ponder unanswerable questions. **Confucius** structured his educational philosophy on an ethical hierarchy of responsibilities that began with the emperor and flowed downward, touching everyone in society. His ideal of hierarchical relationships can be depicted as an ethical ladder on which the person standing on each rung is connected to the people standing above and below. Education's major purpose is to create and maintain a harmonious society in which everyone clearly knows her or his status, duties, and responsibilities, and the appropriate way of behaving toward others.

Confucian character education set standards for civility—polite, correct, and appropriate behavior. Endorsing the ideal of the teacher as a mentor, Confucius believed children learn to behave ethically when they have a clear model of appropriate

Confucius (551–478 BCE) Chinese philosopher, government official, and educator who devised an ethical system still observed in China and other Asian countries.

---

[2]W. Scott Mouton and Charlton M. Lewis, *China: Its History and Culture* (New York: McGraw-Hill, 2005), pp. 22–40.

[3]Chung-Yuan Chang, *Creativity and Taoism: A Study of Chinese Philosophy, Art, and Poetry* (New York: Jessica Kingsley Publishers, 2011), pp. 81–100.

behavior to emulate. Teachers need to personify this model of civility that students are to follow in school.

Taking the guesswork out of living, Confucius believed there was a correct or appropriate way to behave in every situation and that everyone should learn and follow this prescribed standard. Children should be taught these right ways to behave as a set of rituals or patterns that act out the correct procedures all people are expected to follow. The Confucian model of character formation removes the chance element from behavior presented when unexpected situations arise. Because the Confucian hierarchy defines a person as a father, mother, brother, sister, ruler, or subject, the purpose of character education is to learn how to correctly perform the appropriate behavior for one's designated role and rank. When everyone knows their role and follows its duties and responsibilities, each individual will be in harmony with the larger society. Confucius established an academy to prepare officials for China's imperial government. He wanted highly motivated students and set high admission standards for entry to his school. His curriculum included the Chinese classics, music, poetry, diplomacy, the rituals of polite behavior, and ceremonial court etiquette. Believing future officials should study the same general subjects, he established a core curriculum of selected great books such as the *Classics of Change, Of Documents, Of Poetry, Of Rites*, and the *Spring* and *Autumn Annals*.[4] These Confucian texts were prominently featured in imperial examinations from 1313 BCE to 1905 CE.

Like other effective teachers, Confucius developed a well-defined system of classroom management. He held high expectations for his students. As a mentor, he did not get too personally familiar with his students. He kept a proper distance from his students but remained approachable to them. He assessed his students' work in a positive and constructive way. His students respected their teacher as "the master." In China, teacher–student relationships, like other relationships, were well known and followed with precision. The Confucian teacher was entrusted with safeguarding and transmitting the heritage to maintain cultural continuity and social stability.[5] As Confucius said, "A man worthy of being a teacher gets to know what is new by keeping fresh in his mind what he is already familiar with."[6]

The Confucian concept of hierarchical ethical relationships places students into a series of rankings ranging from superior to inferior, which differs significantly from the American idea of equal and flexible relationships. In the Confucian system, it is more important to keep old friends than to make new ones. Making new friends might bring change that upsets the established social pattern.

In situations where relationships are equal and flexible as in the United States, individuals constantly moving from old to new relationships are continually redefining their relationships and creating new openings or boundaries for old and new friends. Character education in situations of equality carries the ethical prescriptions that we should treat each person as an equal and should respect and even value their differences from us.

In contrast, Confucian ethics esteem well-known patterns of behavior rather than flexible or fluid ones. People are accorded various levels of respect based on their age, position, status, and achievements. Character education means to learn one's place in the social network of relationships that form the community and follow the prescribed role behaviors that maintain social harmony.

---

[4]Jennifer Oldstone-Moore, *Confucianism* (Oxford and New York: Oxford University Press, 2002), pp. 35–37; and Daniel K. Gardner, *The Four Books: The Basic Teachings of the Later Confucian Tradition* (Indianapolis, IN: Hackett Publishing Co., 2007). For a biography of Confucius, see Annping Chin, *The Authentic Confucius: A Life of Thought and Politics* (New York: Oxford University Press, 2007).

[5]Bryan W. Van Norden, *Introduction to Classical Chinese Philosophy* (Indianapolis, IN: Hackett Publishing Co., 2011), pp. 18–30, 34–44.

[6]Confucius, *The Analects*, Book II, in D. C. Lau, "Introduction," *The Analects*, trans. D. C. Lau (New York: Penguin Books, 1979), p. 64. Also, see *Confucius. The Analects; The Simon Leys Translations Interpretation*, Michael Nylan, ed. (New York: W.W. Norton Co., 2014).

OVERVIEW 3.1

KEY PERIODS IN EDUCATIONAL HISTORY

Historical Group or Period	Educational Goals	Students
Preliterate societies 7000 BCE–5000 BCE	To teach group survival skills and group identity	Children in the group
China 3000 BCE–1900 CE	To prepare elite officials to govern the empire according to Confucian principles	Males of the gentry class
Egypt 3000 BCE–300 BCE	To prepare priest-scribes to administer the empire	Males of upper classes
Judaic 1200 BCE to present	To transmit Jewish religion and cultural identity	Children and adults in the group
Greek 1600 BCE–300 BCE	Athens: To cultivate civic responsibility and identification with the city-state and to develop well-rounded persons; Sparta: To train soldiers and military leaders	Male children of citizens; ages 7–20
Roman 750 BCE–450 CE	To develop civic responsibility and commitment for the republic and then empire; to train administrators and military leaders	Male children of citizens; ages 7–20
Arabic 700 CE–1350 CE	To construct commitment to Islamic beliefs; to develop expertise in mathematics, medicine, and science	Male children of upper classes; ages 7–20
Medieval 500 CE–1400 CE	To develop commitment to Christian beliefs and practices; to prepare individuals to assume roles in a hierarchical society	Male children of upper classes or those entering religious life; girls and young women entering religious communities; ages 7–20
Renaissance 1350 CE–1500 CE	To educate classical humanists in Greek and Latin literatures; to prepare courtiers to serve leaders	Male children of aristocracy and upper classes; ages 7–20
Reformation 1500 CE–1600 CE	To instill commitment to a particular religious denomination; to cultivate general literacy	Boys and girls ages 7–12 in vernacular schools; young men ages 7–12 of upper-class backgrounds in humanist schools

Instructional Methods	Curriculum	Agents	Influence on Modern Education
Informal instruction; children imitating adult skills and values	Survival skills of hunting, fishing, food gathering; stories, myths, songs, poems, dances	Parents, tribal elders, and priests	Emphasis on informal education and stories to transmit skills and values
Memorization and recitation of classic texts	Confucian classics	Government officials	Written examinations for civil service and professions
Memorizing and copying dictated texts	Religious or technical texts	Priests and scribes	Placing educational authority in a priestly elite; using education to prepare officials
Listening to, memorizing, reciting, analyzing, and debating sacred texts; reading and writing for literacy	The Torah, laws, rituals, and commentaries	Parents, priests, scribes, and rabbis	Concepts of monotheism and a covenant between God and humanity; religious observance and maintaining cultural identity.
Drill, memorization, recitation in primary schools; lecture, discussion, and dialogue in higher schools	Athens: reading, writing, arithmetic, drama, music, physical education, literature, poetry Sparta: drill, military songs, and tactics	Athens: private teachers and schools, Sophists, philosophers Sparta: military officers	Athens: the concept of the well-rounded, liberally educated person Sparta: the concept of serving the military state
Drill, memorization, and recitation in primary schools; declamation in rhetorical schools	Reading, writing, arithmetic, Laws of Twelve Tables, law, philosophy	Private schools and teachers; rhetorical schools	Using education to develop sense of civic commitment and administrative skills
Drill, memorization, and recitation in lower schools; commentary and discussion in higher schools	Reading, writing, mathematics, religious literature, scientific studies	Mosques; court schools	Arabic numerals and computation; reentry of classical Greek texts to Western educators
Drill, memorization, recitation, chanting in lower schools; textual analysis and disputation in universities and in higher schools	Reading, writing, arithmetic, liberal arts; philosophy and theology; crafts; military tactics; and chivalry	Parish, chantry, and cathedral schools; universities; apprenticeship; knighthood	Established structure, content, and organization of universities as major institutions of higher education; the transmission of liberal arts; institutionalization and preservation of knowledge
Memorization, translation, and analysis of Greek and Roman classics	Latin, Greek, classical literature, poetry, art	Classical humanist educators and schools such as the *lycée, gymnasium,* and Latin Grammar school	An emphasis on literary knowledge and style as expressed in classical literature; a two-track system of schools
Memorization, drill, indoctrination, catechetical instruction in vernacular schools; translation and analysis of classics in humanist schools	Reading, writing, arithmetic, catechism, religious beliefs and rituals; Latin and Greek; theology	Vernacular elementary schools for the masses; classical schools for the upper classes	A commitment to universal education to provide literacy to the masses; the origins of school systems with supervision to ensure doctrinal conformity; the dual-track school system based on socioeconomic class and career goals

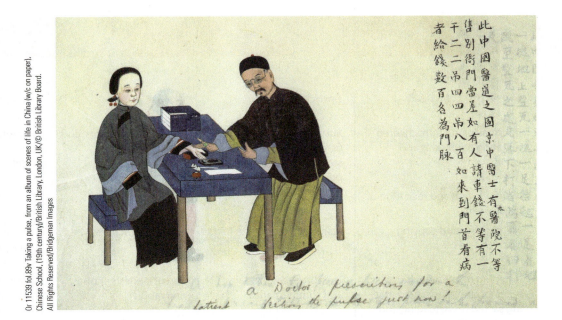

> **PHOTO 3.1** Student and teacher preparing for examinations in nineteenth century imperial China.

Confucius sought to identify and replicate the behaviors that traditionally had maintained peace, security, and tranquility in the past. Students were to learn ritualized ways of acting that they could apply to the situations they met in their lives. As you construct your educational philosophy and reflect on the purposes of education, compare and contrast Confucian and contemporary American ideals and values. How will you define civil behavior and values? Will these values reflect traditional standards or will they be open ended?

In China, teacher–student relationships followed formal hierarchical rules of approved behavior (Photo 3.1). In schools, teachers were to respect and obey the headmaster or principal; teachers were to respect their colleagues, especially older more experienced teachers; students were to respect their teachers; and students were to respect each other, with younger students respecting older ones. Each of these levels carried duties and obligations. Respect for education and teachers is important in schools in China, South Korea, Singapore, and Japan where Confucianism

TIMELINE
ANCIENT CHINA

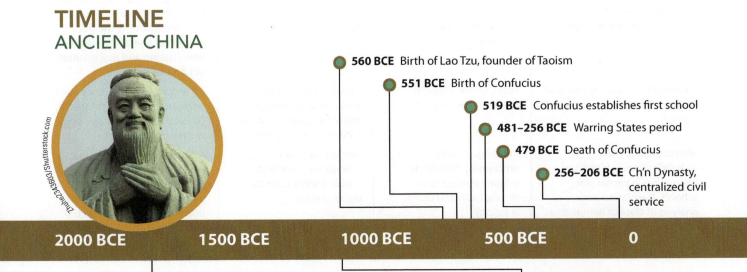

560 BCE Birth of Lao Tzu, founder of Taoism

551 BCE Birth of Confucius

519 BCE Confucius establishes first school

481–256 BCE Warring States period

479 BCE Death of Confucius

256–206 BCE Ch'n Dynasty, centralized civil service

2000 BCE   1500 BCE   1000 BCE   500 BCE   0

1776–1050 BCE Shang Dynasty: development of hierarchical society, writing, rites, and ancestor worship

1050–256 BCE Zhou Dynasty

TECHNOLOGY @ SCHOOL

CONNECTING ANCIENT CHINA TO THE HISTORY OF EDUCATION

You can research the Internet to broaden your perspectives on ancient China as well as the other civilizations and historic periods discussed in this chapter. Access the following sites to build your perspectives on China: (1) the British Museum for the geography, chronology, and arts and crafts of ancient China, and (2) the Chinese Cultural Studies site for the analects of Confucius.

pervades the culture.[7] Confucianism's diffusion from China to other Asian countries illustrates how educational ideas and processes transfer across cultures.[8]

3-2b Ancient China's Significance in World Education

Ancient Chinese education remains significant in shaping schooling in China, Taiwan, Korea, Japan, and Singapore. Learning centers on students' mastery of subjects, which is usually presented in texts, and is to be memorized rather than discussed. The teacher is to be respected, not questioned, by students and their parents as well. Practicing writing script in calligraphy classes holds its place along with the modern computer. Students strive to achieve a high academic rank in their classes. It is highly important to be admitted to schools, colleges, and universities that have a top academic ranking.[9]

Confucianism remains a powerful cultural force in the modern world, especially for Asians and for many Asian Americans. Adhering to the Confucian emphasis on family duties, parents hold themselves responsible for their children's academic achievement. Parents, especially mothers, are obligated to instill the values of perseverance, diligence, hard work, and self-discipline, which are stressed as necessary to success in school and in work. When a child's academic performance is assessed as inadequate, this not only disgraces the child but is a symptom of poor parenting that brings shame to the whole family, reaching all the way back to the ancestor.[10]

FOCUS Have family or group stories, like the oral tradition among prehistoric groups, shaped your ideas about education and schools? Did you learn specifically defined standards of behavior and manners in a way that was similar to Confucian education? Or did you learn standards of behavior in a more permissive and flexible way? In other words, how did you learn what was appropriate or inappropriate for you to do? How did you learn the "should" and "should nots" of school and society?

---

[7]For Confucianism's influence on contemporary globalization, see William Theodore de Bary, *Confucian Tradition and Global Education* (New York: Columbia University Press, 2007).

[8]Joelle Droux and Rita Hofstetter, "Going International: The History of Education Stepping beyond Borders," *Pedagogica Historica*, Vol. 50, Nos. 1 and 2 (2014), pp. 1–4.

[9]Amy Chua and Jed Rubenfeld, *The Triple Package: What Really Determines Success* (New York: Penguin Press, 2014), pp. 110, 125. Also, see Benson Tong, ed., *Asian American Children: A Historical Handbook Guide* (Westport, CN: Greenwood Press, 2004), pp. 123–129.

[10]Chua and Rubenfeld, *The Triple Package*, p. 147. Also, see Jin Li, Cultural Foundations of Learning: East and West (Cambridge, UK: Cambridge University Press, 2012), pp. 73–74, 90–92.

960–1279 CE   Song Dynasty

1295 CE   Marco Polo's *Tales of China* published in Europe

206 BCE–220 CE   Han Dynasty

1644–1911 CE   Manchu Dynasty

500 CE   1000 CE   1500 CE   2000 CE

3-3 EDUCATION IN ANCIENT EGYPT

Ancient Egypt began as a river-valley culture. Because of the Nile River's life-sustaining water, agricultural groups established small village settlements on its banks, which, over time, developed into tribal kingdoms. About 3000 BCE, these kingdoms were consolidated into a large empire ruled by an emperor, called the pharaoh.

The person and position of the pharaoh became the central focus of Egypt's social, economic, political, and—especially—religious life. Affirming the pharaoh's divine origin, the concept of a ruling deity gave stability to the Egyptian empire by endowing it with supernaturally sanctioned foundations. The concept of a king-priest gave the priestly elite high status and considerable political power. The educational system reinforced their position by making the priests the empire's cultural guardians. For much of history, priests or other religious figures have controlled formal education.

3-3a Writing, Religion, and Schooling

The Egyptians developed a writing system, known as hieroglyphics, which originated as picture representations of animals or objects. As these representations were made more abstract and symbolic, they were used to express events and situations. The Egyptians recorded their script on paper-like scrolls made from the papyrus reeds that grew on the Nile's banks. The rolled up papyrus documents could be stored conveniently in archives to be retrieved and reviewed when needed. By 2700 BCE, the Egyptians had established an extensive system of temple and court schools to train scribes, many of whom were priests, in reading and writing. As part of the temple complex, schooling began its close relationship with religion.[11] In the scribal schools, students learned to write the hieroglyphic script by copying documents on papyrus sheets. Teachers dictated to students, who copied what they heard. The goal was to reproduce a correct, exact copy of a text. Often students would chant a short passage from a text until they had memorized it and then recorded it.

Egypt, like China, needed a large civil service to collect revenues and to administer and defend its empire. After completing scribal schools, a small number of promising young males were selected to attend advanced schools to prepare for their future professions as priests, government officials, and physicians.[12] These advanced students studied mathematics, astronomy, religion, poetry, literature, medicine, and architecture.[13]

Students preparing to be priests read the texts that focused on the Egyptian preoccupation of life after death in another supernatural world. Texts such as the *Book of the Dead* provided stories, chants, and prayers that enabled the soul of the deceased to cross successfully to the other side. The higher studies also have a practical aspect that applied knowledge to life. Because wealth originated in the crops grown along the Nile, attention was given to surveying and measuring the plots of land along the River. The construction of the pyramids, temples, and massive structures required the designs of architects.

3-3b Ancient Egypt's Significance in World Education

Ancient Egypt's significance in world education is surprisingly controversial. The traditional interpretation is that Western Civilization began with the ancient Greeks.

---

[11]John Baines, *Visual and Written Culture in Ancient Egypt* (New York: Oxford University Press, 2007), pp. 117–140.

[12]Ibid.

[13]Toby Wilkinson, *The Rise and Fall of Ancient Egypt* (New York: Random House, 2013).

(Ancient Greece is discussed later in this chapter.) According to this interpretation, ancient Egyptian civilization was a highly static despotism, and its major cultural legacy was its great architectural monuments such as the pyramids. Challenging the standard interpretation, the historian Martin Bernal argues that the ancient Greeks borrowed many of their ideas about government, philosophy, the arts and sciences, and medicine from the Egyptians.[14] Furthermore, the Egyptians, living in North Africa, were an African people and the origins of Western culture were African rather than Greco-Roman. Bernal's critics contend that he has overgeneralized Egypt's influence on the Greeks.[15]

While historians debate the issue, findings indicate that Egyptian–Greek contacts, particularly at Crete, introduced Egyptian knowledge and art to the Greeks. This controversy has important educational significance. Whoever interprets the past gains the power of illuminating and shaping the present. In particular, the controversy relates to debates about an Afrocentric curriculum in schools. Did Western civilization originate in Africa or in Greece?

3-4 THE HEBRAIC EDUCATIONAL TRADITION

Judeo-Christian tradition
The Western cultural tradition that has been shaped by Judaism and Christianity.

American education, like Western culture, is deeply rooted in the **Judeo-Christian tradition**. (The sections on the Middle Ages and Reformation in this chapter discuss the Christian roots.) Here, we examine Hebraic or Judaic education, an ongoing religious and cultural tradition for the Jewish people, and an important reference point for Christians and Muslims. All three religions—Judaism, Christianity, and Islam—are monotheistic in their belief in one God, a spiritual Creator, and in their reverence for a sacred book, the Torah, the Bible, or the Koran, respectively, whose contents, for the believers, were revealed by God to prophets. With their emphasis on reading and studying sacred scriptures, all three religions emphasize literacy to read the holy book and education to learn and apply its message to life.

Early Hebraic history began when Jacob, the son of the great patriarch Abraham, united the nomadic Jewish tribes into the nation of Israel. The Jews embraced the **Abrahamic tradition**
Monotheism, the belief in one God, which originated with Abraham in Judaism and has shaped Christianity and Islam.

Abrahamic tradition of monotheism, the belief in one God, which distinguished them from the other ancient peoples who practiced polytheism, the belief in many gods. A defining event in Hebraic history occurred in 1270 BCE when Moses led the Israelites from bondage in Egypt across the desert to Judea in Palestine. The Israelites, who believed Moses had received divine revelations on Mount Sinai, developed the belief that God had chosen them to be a special people. The Mosaic revelations created a holy covenant, a religiously based and sanctioned agreement, that bound the Jews to their Creator.[16] These revelations formed an essential part of the **Torah**, Judaism's sacred scripture.

Torah The first five Books of Moses that form the foundation of Hebraic religion, culture, and education.

Hebraic education developed its literary structure when Ezra, a noted scholar and scribe in 445 BCE, collected and organized the five books of the Old Testament—Genesis, Exodus, Leviticus, Numbers, and Deuteronomy—into a written text. Education

---

[14]Martin Bernal, *Black Athena: The Afroasiatic Roots of Classical Civilization: The Fabrication of Ancient Greece 1785–1985* (New Brunswick, NJ: Rutgers University Press, 1987), pp. 2–3. Also, see Robert Bauval and Thomas Brophy, *Black Genesis: The Prehistoric Origins of Ancient Egypt* (Rochester, VT: Bear & Co., 2011). The later Greek influence on Egyptian education is discussed in Raffaella Cribiore, *Gymnastics of the Mind: Greek Education in Hellenistic and Roman Egypt* (Princeton: Princeton University Press, 2005).

[15]For a discussion of ancient Egypt's influence on Greece, access Philip Coppens, "Egypt: Origin of Greek Culture" at **www.philipcoppens.com/egyptgreece.html**.

[16]Hanan A. Alexander and Shmuel Glick, "The Judaic Tradition," in Randall Curren, ed., *A Companion to the Philosophy of Education* (Malden, MA: Blackwell Publishing, 2006), pp. 33–49.

is based on the Torah, the sacred scripture taught and studied by Jews from childhood on throughout their lives.[17]

Stressing listening, recitation, and commentary on the sacred texts and their moral prescriptions and proscriptions, the purpose of Judaic education is to inculcate the young into their culture by transmitting religious beliefs, prayers, and rituals from one generation to the next.[18]

As in most early societies, parents were responsible for their children's education and were the initial teachers. The father taught the Torah and religious observances to his children who learned to honor their father and mother, as the commandments prescribed. As Jewish society became more settled and specialized, teachers (elders, priests, and scribes) who taught in schools augmented, but did not replace, the parental role.

By the seventh century BCE, rabbis—men especially learned in scripture—emerged as teachers among the Jewish people in Israel and Babylonia. In rabbinical schools, instruction emphasized careful listening to sacred readings by the rabbi and reading, memorization, and recitation. By listening, reading, and memorizing, students were expected to internalize the lesson's meaning and message. To build group cohesion and identity, children listened to stories about important events in the history of the Hebrew people—such as their exodus from Egypt. Rituals were taught that commemorated these events.[19]

3-4a The Hebraic Significance in World Education

The Hebraic religious tradition is of special significance for the Jewish people in that it contributes to their cultural identification as a unique covenantal people of God. It has contributed to the Jewish determination to survive as a people despite persecutions, pogroms, and the Holocaust during World War II. The Jews brought the concept of monotheism into Arabic Islamic and Western Christian cultures.

---

[17]Ibid., p. 13.
[18]Ibid., p. 33.
[19]Maristella Botticini and Zvi Eckstein, *The Chosen Few: How Education Shaped Jewish History, 70-1492* (Princeton, NJ: Princeton University Press, 2012), pp. 1–2.

FOCUS Do you find emphasis on carefully listening to teachers, transmitting the cultural heritage, and instilling appropriate behavior among the purposes of contemporary American education? What is your opinion about religion's role in education? Why has the teaching of religion and religious observances been so controversial in American education? Refocus again on this question when you read Chapter 9, Legal Aspects of Education.

TIMELINE
ANCIENT EGYPT

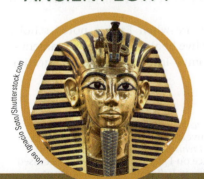

Jose Ignacio Soto/Shutterstock.com

3100 BCE Menes united Upper and Lower Egypt; Development of hieroglyphic script

2900 BCE Use of paper made from papyrus

2600 BCE Construction of great pyramids of Gaza

3600 BCE   **3200 BCE**   **2800 BCE**   **2400 BCE**   **2000 BCE**

3500 BCE Settlements in Nile River Valley

3-5 EDUCATION IN ANCIENT GREECE

Historians traditionally have asserted that Western civilization and education originated with the Greeks, a nomadic people from the Balkans, who immigrated to and settled in the peninsula and islands in the Aegean Sea that comprise modern Greece. Unlike the Chinese and Egyptians, the Greeks, who did not consolidate into a great empire, lived in small, autonomous, and independent city-states called poleis.

3-5a Homeric Culture and Education

Mycenae, a leading polis, dominated Greece from 1600 BCE until the Dorian invasions of 1200 BCE. Mycenaean society was hierarchically organized with a king at the top; warriors, courtiers, and merchants in the middle; and slaves at the bottom. Interweaving dramatic themes of love, war, courage, and pride, Homer's great epic poem, the *Iliad,* told how the Greek warriors reclaimed the beautiful wife of Menelaus, Helen, who had been carried off by Paris, the Trojan prince. Homer's sequel, the *Odyssey,* told of Odysseus, or Ulysses, King of Ithaca, who wandered for a decade after the Greek victory over Troy before returning to his native land and his wife, Penelope. Homer's epics, appearing about 850 BCE, were sources of classical Greek and Western education.[20] They illustrate the power of education as narrative storytelling to transmit and perpetuate culture.[21] Homer the poet is also Homer the teacher, who instructs his students, the young Greeks, about their culture by telling them the story of the heroic and courageous deeds of Agamemnon, Achilles, Menelaus, Odysseus, and the other Greek knights. Homer's *Iliad* and *Odyssey* provided character education by instructing generations of young Greek males on how they could become heroes by combining wisdom and prudence and courage and cunning to win glory.[22] Homer's poems served the educational purposes of (1) preserving the cultural heritage, beliefs, and values of a group by transmitting it from adults to the young; (2) providing the Greeks a sense of cultural identity rooted in their mythic historical origins as a people; (3) shaping the character and morality of the young by exposing them to heroic models; and (4) providing a context for the ongoing saga of Greek life and its extension into the future.[23]

---

[20]Scholars have long debated whether the *Iliad* and *Odyssey* were the work of one man or a compilation of the poems of many individuals over time. For our purposes, this question is still open, but for clarity in the chapter, Homer is presented as a single individual.

[21]Lillian E. Doherty, ed., *Homer's Odyssey (Oxford Readings in Classical Studies)* (New York: Oxford University Press, 2009).

[22]Robert Holmes Beck, "The Iliad: Principles and Lessons," *Educational Theory* (Spring 1986), pp. 179–195. Also, see Douglas L. Cairns, ed., *Homer's Iliad (Oxford Readings in Philosophy)* (New York: Oxford University Press, 2002).

[23]For the educational importance of Homer, see Louis Goldman, "Homer, Literacy, and Education," *Educational Theory* 39, No. 4 (Fall 1989), pp. 391–400.

1650 BCE   Scribes record *Book of the Dead*

1300 BCE   Temple at Karnak constructed

332 BCE   Alexander the Great conquers Egypt

1600 BCE	1200 BCE	800 BCE	400 BCE	0

3-5b Sparta and Athens

Two Greek city-states, Sparta and Athens, had diametrically opposed views of culture, politics, and education. Sparta deliberately chose specialized military training over liberal and humanist education. In 550 BCE, Sparta adopted the Code of Lycurgus, which required men to be soldiers and women to be the wives and mothers of soldiers.

Sparta's ruling magistrates, the ephors, appointed an education commissioner, the *paidonomos,* who supervised education in the city-state. Because every Spartan child belonged to the state, the ephors inspected every newborn male to determine if he were physically healthy enough for a future rigorous military life. Weak boys were exposed in the wilds and left to die. Until age 7, boys were raised by their families. Fathers would take their sons to veterans' clubs to familiarize them with military life. At age 7, boys went to school barracks where they were organized into packs or squads of six, led by the smartest, strongest, wiliest, and toughest among them.[24] Trained to endure pain without complaint, they were whipped to encourage a fighting spirit. Rather than condemned as vices, bullying and defending yourself against bullies so that you could bully someone else was prized. At age 18, the Spartan youth received two more years of strenuous and intensive military training. From age 20 to 30, the young man was on active army duty. Upon reaching age 30, he took a healthy wife and began his family of future soldiers.

Although educated at home by their mothers in domestic skills, Sparta's girls received physical education in running, marching, and athletic games. Allowed more freedom than her secluded Athenian counterpart, the young Spartan maiden was raised primarily to be the healthy mother of future Spartan soldiers.

3-5c Athenian Education

Athens, a large polis, had a population of more than 200,000 residents, of whom 40,000 were male citizens.[25] In 502 BCE, the Constitution of Cleisthenes, creating an assembly composed of all male citizens, made Athens a participatory democracy.[26] In contrast

---

[24]Jean-Pierre Vernant, ed., *The Greeks* (Chicago: University of Chicago Press, 1995), pp. 93–96, 105; and Nigel M. Kennell, *The Gymnasium of Virtue: Education and Culture in Ancient Sparta* (Chapel Hill: University of North Carolina Press, 1995), pp. 38, 75, 79.

[25]Mortimer Chambers, Raymond Grew, David Herlihy, Theodore K. Rabb, and Isser Woloch, *The Western Experience,* 3rd ed. (New York: Alfred A. Knopf, 1983), p. 49.

[26]Ibid., pp. 54–57.

TIMELINE
ANCIENT ISRAEL

igroupJiStockphoto.com

1020 BCE King Saul

1000 BCE King David

965 BCE First Temple in Jerusalem

1350 BCE	1200 BCE	1050 BCE	900 BCE	750 BCE

1312 BCE Exodus from Egypt

800 BCE Torah

to Sparta's military hero, the Athenian ideal was the well-rounded, liberally educated individual who was active in politics, military defense, and the general community.[27] Contrasting Athens with its rival Sparta, the great orator Pericles (490–429 BCE) stated that the Athenians' pursuit of literature, art, and philosophy did not weaken their courage but rather educated them as free individuals for life in a free city.

Unlike Sparta's singular military training, Athenian boys might attend three types of schools: that of *grammatist* who taught reading and writing; that of *citharist* who taught music, literature, and poetry; and that of the *paedotribe* who taught physical education, gymnastics, and athletics. For higher studies, men could choose the courses offered by the Sophists, rhetoricians, or philosophers.

The Athenian males did not extend their concept of democratic equality to women who lived in seclusion and were restricted to gender-determined household management and child-rearing. They could not vote, could not attend the Assembly, and did not have property rights. If girls learned to read and write, it was at home, not in schools.

The life and career of the poet Sappho (630–572 BCE) sharply contrasted with the sequestered education of the Athenian women. An early proponent of women's liberation, Sappho believed women should be educated for their own personal self-development rather than for their traditionally ascribed roles as future wives and mothers. She founded a women's school in Mytilene, on the island of Lesbos, where she taught young aristocratic women the cult rituals related to worship of Aphrodite, as well as cultural and decorative arts and skills, such as singing, dancing, playing the lyre, writing poetry, and etiquette.[28]

3-5d The Sophists

In the fifth century BCE, new wealth brought to Athens by colonial expansion generated social and educational change. The rising commercial class wanted a new kind of education that would give them social status and prepare them to exercise political power. The **Sophists,** a traveling group of teachers, designed a new kind of education to meet the needs of the rising economic class.

According to the Sophists, those who could speak persuasively and effectively would acquire prestige and power. In Athens, with its democratic institutions, those skilled in public speaking, or oratory, could persuade the assembly and courts in their favor.[29]

Sophists Members of a group of itinerant educators in ancient Greece during the period from 470 to 370 BCE who emphasized rhetoric, public speaking, and other practical skills. Their approach contrasts with that of the speculative philosophers Plato and Aristotle.

---

[27]Mogens Herman Hansen, *Polis: An Introduction to the Greek City State* (New York: Oxford University Press, 2006), pp. 33–37. Also, see David A. Teegarden, *Death to Tyrants! Ancient Greek Democracy and the Struggle against Tyranny* (Princeton, NJ: Princeton University Press, 2014); Kenneth J. Freeman, *Schools of Hellas: An Essay on the Practice and Theory of Ancient Greek Education from 600 to 300 B.C.* (Sophron Imprint, 2013).

[28]For a biographical sketch of Sappho and a reading of "The Songs of Sappho," see Madonna M. Murphy, *The History and Philosophy of Education: Voices of Educational Pioneers* (Upper Saddle River, NJ: Pearson/Merrill/Prentice Hall, 2006), pp. 17–23. Also, see Jim Powell, *The Poetry of Sappho* (New York: Oxford University Press, 2007).

[29]For "The Sophists," access **www.pbs.org/empires/thegreeks/background/30_p1.html**; also, see Robin Waterfield, *The First Philosophers: The Presocratics and the Sophists* (New York: Oxford University Press, 2009).

586 BCE Babylonian Captivity

63 BCE Roman Conquest

| 600 BCE | 450 BCE | 300 BCE | 150 BCE | 0 |

rhetoric The theory and practice of public speaking, declamation, and oratory in ancient Greece. During the Middle Ages, it tended to emphasize written discourse as well as speaking. Along with grammar and logic, rhetoric was part of the *trivium* of the liberal arts.

For the Sophists, the purpose of education was to develop their students' communication skills so they could become successful advocates and legislators. The Sophists' most important subjects were logic, grammar, and rhetoric, which developed into the liberal arts. Logic, the rules of correct argument, trained students to organize their presentations clearly, and grammar developed their powers of using language effectively. **Rhetoric,** the study of public speaking, was especially important for future orators.

The Sophists claimed they could educate their students to win public debates by teaching them how to (1) use crowd psychology to appeal emotionally to an audience; (2) organize a persuasive and convincing argument; and (3) be skillful public speakers who know what words, examples, and lines of reasoning to use to win a debate or legal trial.

Critics of the Sophists, such as Socrates and Plato, however, accused them of teaching students to argue for any side of an issue to win the case rather than being committed to the truth. The Sophists were like modern image makers who use the media to package political candidates and celebrities or to sell products to consumers. Although today's political debates take place on television rather than in the Athenian town center, the Sophists would argue that their techniques remain useful. It is still important to know one's audience, to appeal to their needs, and to use skilled persuasion to convince them. They would consider modern focus groups, public opinion polls, and negative political advertising to be useful and persuasive tools.

Protagoras (485–414 BCE) was one of the most prominent Sophists.[30] He developed an effective five-step teaching strategy in which his students (1) listened to him deliver an eloquent oration so they had a model to imitate; (2) analyzed speeches of famous orators to enlarge their repertoire of exemplary speaking styles; (3) studied logic, grammar, and rhetoric; (4) delivered practice orations, which he critiqued to provide feedback; and (5) delivered public speeches. Protagoras's method resembles present-day preservice teacher-education programs in which prospective teachers take courses in the liberal arts and professional education, practice a variety of teaching methods, and engage in clinical experience and student teaching supervised by an experienced cooperating teacher.

3-5e Socrates: Education by Self-Examination

Socrates (469–399 BCE), who believed in universal truths that are valid at all places and times, challenged the Sophists' opportunism and relativism.[31] Socrates affirmed the ethical principles that a person should strive for moral excellence, live wisely, and act rationally, which were far superior to the Sophists' promises of prestige and power. He rejected the Sophists' claim that they could transmit the truth to their students. Rather than telling students what was true and good, Socrates encouraged them to use critical self-examination and reflection to bring the universal truths present in their minds to consciousness. As a teacher, Socrates asked leading questions that stimulated students to think deeply about and reflect on the meaning of life, truth, and justice. In answering these questions, students engaged in rigorous discussion, or dialogue, in which they clarified, criticized, and reconstructed their basic concepts.[32]

Plato illustrated the use of the Socratic method in *Meno,* a dialogue between Socrates and Meno, a student of Gorgias, a prominent Sophist. When Socrates asks Meno to define virtue, he identifies particular instances of virtue such as the prudence of the judicious legislator, the love of a caring mother, and the courage of a brave soldier. Through further questioning, Socrates leads Meno to acknowledge that these

[30]Van Johannes M. Ophuijsen, *Protagoras of Abdera: The Man, His Measure* (Brill, 2013).

[31]Paul Johnson, *Socrates: A Man for Our Times* (New York: Penguin Books, 2012).

[32]Gary Alan Scott, *Plato's Socrates as Educator* (Albany: State University of New York Press, 2000), pp. 1–12.

Socratic method An educational method attributed to the Greek philosopher Socrates by which the teacher encourages the student's discovery of truth by asking leading and stimulating questions.

particular examples of virtue are really manifestations of a more general and unifying universal idea of virtue. This rigorous dialogue approach, known as the **Socratic method,** is challenging for both teachers and students.[33]

Frequenting the agora, Athens's central area, Socrates attracted young men who joined him in critically examining religious, political, and moral issues. As a social critic, Socrates made powerful enemies. Then as now, some people, especially those in positions of power, feared that critical thinking would challenge their authority and position. In 399 BCE, an Athenian jury found Socrates guilty of impiety to the gods and corrupting Athenian youth. He refused to flee to save himself and accepted his death sentence. Socrates stands out in educational history for his forthright defense of the academic freedom to think, question, and teach. He was also significant as the teacher of Plato, who later systematized many of Socrates's ideas into a coherent philosophy.

3-5f Plato: Universal and Eternal Truths and Values

Socrates's pupil Plato (427–346 BCE) followed his mentor's educational path. Plato founded the Academy, a philosophical school, in 387 BCE. He wrote philosophical dialogues about truth, virtue, and justice, as well as the *Republic* and the *Laws*, treatises on politics, law, and education.[34] Plato's philosophy, an early form of idealism, is discussed in Chapter 6, Philosophical Roots of Education.

Rejecting the Sophists' relativism, Plato argued that reality exists in an unchanging world of perfect ideas—universal concepts such as truth, goodness, justice, and beauty. What appears to our senses are but imperfect images of the universal and eternal concepts found in the Form of the Good.

Plato's "Allegory of the Cave" illustrated how we can find truth in the Form of the Good. Plato depicted prisoners in a dark cave who were chained so that they could see in only one direction. With a fire behind them, they saw only the shadows of objects that others carried before the flames. When a prisoner escapes, he climbs to the entrance of the cave. Ascending from the dark world of shadows, he sees the real world illuminated by the sun. When he reenters the cave to tell his fellow prisoners the good news, they scorn him in disbelief. In the Allegory, the sun represents the Form of the Good, the source of all that is bright, beautiful, good, and true. The difficult process of turning away from shadows to truth represents the Socratic method's process of learning by self-examination and reflection.

reminiscence The recalling or remembering of ideas that Plato asserted were latently present in the mind. Through skilled questioning, the teacher stimulates students to bring these ideas to the conscious mind.

Plato's theory of knowledge is called **reminiscence**, a process by which individuals recall the ideas present but hidden within their minds. Each human's soul, before birth, existed in a spiritual world of pure ideas. At birth, these *innate* ideas are repressed within one's subconscious mind. A person learns by rediscovering or recollecting these perfect ideas.[35]

Plato's *Republic* Plato's most systematic philosophical statement on politics and education. Using the format of dialogues, it portrays a perfect city ruled by philosopher-kings according to the principle of justice.

Plato's Ideal Society   Plato's *Republic* projected a plan for a perfect society ruled by an intellectual elite of philosopher-kings. Although Plato's utopian state was never implemented, his ideas are worth studying as an idealized version of a certain kind of society and education.[36]

---

[33]Erick Wilberding, *Teach Like Socrates: Guiding Socratic Dialogues and Discussions in the Classroom* (Waco, TX: Prufrock Press, 2014); and Matt Copeland, *Socratic Circles: Fostering Critical and Creative Thinking in Middle and High School* (Portland, ME: Stenhouse Publishers, 2005).

[34]Robin Barrow, *Plato and Education* (New York: Routledge, 2014).

[35]Gerald L. Gutek, *Historical and Philosophical Foundations of Education: A Biographical Introduction* (Columbus, OH: Merrill/Prentice Hall, 2011), pp. 37–42.

[36]William H. F, Altman, *Plato the Teacher: The Crisis of the Republic* (Lanham, MD: Lexington Books, 2012); and Plato, *Republic* (London: Folio Society, 2003).

TAKING ISSUE

Read the following brief introduction, as well as the Question and the pros and cons list that follows. Then, answer the question using *your* own words and position.

VALUES IN EDUCATION?

The ancient Greeks debated whether education should reflect universal values that were valid at all times and in all places or culturally relative values held by different peoples living at particular places and times. Socrates and Plato, who argued that truth was unchanging, debated this issue with the Sophists, who claimed that education was relative to time and circumstances. Today, heated debates are ongoing in the United States between those who want schools to instill universal moral values and others who want students to clarify their own values.

Question

Should we base moral education on universal values? (Think about this question as you read the PRO and CON arguments listed here. What is *your* response to this issue?)

Arguments PRO

1. Values, like truth, are universal and timeless. What is valuable is valid in all places and at all times. Public opinion polls do not make, nor change, what is good and beautiful.

2. Although we are members of different races, ethnic groups, and language groups, we are all members of the same human family and have universal human rights.

3. Education should search for the answer to the enduring question raised by Socrates and Plato: What is true, good, and beautiful?

4. Schools should emphasize the universal truths and values found in religion, philosophy, mathematics, literature, and science that transcend cultural differences and political boundaries.

Arguments CON

1. Values are tentative statements about what is right or wrong that are relative to various groups living in particular places at different times. What is valuable is determined by the culture of different groups in a particular society.

2. Because society is relative and changing, education needs to be flexible to adapt to social, economic, political, and technological change.

3. Education is a pragmatic means of personal and social adaptation. It should emphasize new ways of learning to prepare people to be efficient users of new technologies.

4. Schooling, based on people's needs, will differ from culture to culture and from time to time. That is why the constructivist approach and multicultural education is so useful in today's schools.

Question Reprise: What Is Your Stand?

Reflect again on the following question by explaining your stand about this issue. Should we base moral education on universal values?

The Republic's citizens were organized into three classes: (1) philosopher-kings, or intellectual rulers; (2) auxiliaries, or military defenders; and (3) workers, who produced goods and provided services. An individual's placement in a particular class was determined by an assessment of her or his intellectual ability. Similar to those who want to use IQ and aptitude tests to determine the kind of education that a person should receive, Plato's educators sorted people into ability groups and educated them on their perceived intellectual potentiality.

Once assigned to a class, individuals would be given the education or training needed to perform their specific functions. The philosopher-kings identified academically gifted children and prepared them to be the Republic's future leaders. The second class, the warriors, considered more courageous than intellectual, would receive military training to defend the Republic against its enemies. The third and largest class, the workers, who had greater physical than intellectual or military potentialities, would be trained vocationally as farmers, fishermen, and craftsmen. Plato believed that this system of educational tracking contributed to social justice in that the Republic's citizens were doing what was appropriate for them. Modern critics of tracking, or the homogenous grouping of students in schools, argue that sorting strategies, such as Plato's, reproduce the existing class situation and discourage social mobility.

Unlike most Athenian males, Plato did not believe than men were intellectually superior to women. Both men and women should receive the education that was appropriate to their intellectual abilities.[37] Women who possessed high-level cognitive powers could become philosopher-queens. Like men, women would receive the education or training appropriate to their abilities and their destined occupations.

Plato's Curriculum   Fearing that parents would pass on their ignorance and prejudices to their children, Plato wanted early childhood specialists to rear young children. Children, separated from their parents, would live in state nurseries to learn positive social and moral predispositions that inclined them to a harmonious life in the Republic.

From ages 6 to 18, children and adolescents attended state-supervised schools to study reading and writing, literature, arithmetic, choral singing, dancing, and gymnastics. Plato, who believed in censorship, thought that young people should read only officially selected and approved poems and stories that epitomized truthfulness, obedience to authorities, courage, and self-control. After mastering basic mathematics, students studied geometry and astronomy to develop higher-level abstract thinking. Gymnastics, useful for military training, included fencing, archery, javelin throwing, and horseback riding, which developed physical coordination and dexterity.

From ages 18 to 20, students pursued intensive physical and military training. At age 20, the future philosopher-kings would be selected for ten years of additional higher education in more abstract and advanced mathematics, geometry, astronomy, music, and science. At age 30, the less intellectually able in this group would become civil servants; the most intellectually gifted would continue their study of metaphysics, the philosophical search for truth. When their studies were completed, the philosopher-kings would rule the Republic. At age 50, they would become the Republic's elder statesmen.

3-5g Aristotle: Cultivation of Rationality

Plato's student Aristotle (384–322 BCE), the tutor of Alexander the Great, founded the Lyceum, a philosophical school in Athens. He wrote treatises on physics, astronomy, zoology, botany, logic, ethics, and metaphysics. His *Nicomachean Ethics* and *Politics* examined education in relation to society and government.[38] Encouraging people to avoid extremes, Aristotle's *Ethics* advised moderation.

Aristotle was a **realist** who held that reality exists objectively outside of our minds. This contrasts with the belief of his mentor, Plato, an **idealist** who thought the truth is already in our minds. While Aristotle's realism dealt with natural processes of life on earth, Plato's idealism aimed for a better and higher world above the senses. (Both idealism and realism are discussed in Chapter 6, Philosophical Roots of Education.)

For Aristotle, our knowing begins with our sensation of objects in the environment. By abstracting an object's essentials from this sensory information, we can form a general concept about the object and locate it in a class of similar objects. As rational persons, we can use this knowledge to guide our decisions and actions.

Aristotle on Education   In his *Politics*, Aristotle argues that the socially just community depends on its citizens' rationality. Education's purpose is to cultivate liberally

realism A philosophy which asserts that reality consists of an objective order of objects that, though they are external, can be known by humans through their senses and power of abstraction.

idealism A philosophy which asserts that reality is spiritual, intellectual, and nonmaterial.

---

[37]Robert S. Brumbaugh, "Plato's Ideal Curriculum and Contemporary Philosophy of Education," *Educational Theory* (Spring 1987), pp. 169–177. Also, see Dominic Scott, *Recollection and Experience: Plato's Theory of Learning and Its Successors* (New York: Cambridge University Press, 2007).

[38]Alexander Moseley, *Aristotle (Continuum Library of Educational Thought)* (London: Continuum, 2010); and Christopher Rowe and Sarah Brodie, *Aristotle: Nicomachean Ethics* (Oxford, UK: Oxford University Press, 2002).

educated, rational people who can use their reason to make decisions to govern society. Aristotle advocated the study of the liberal arts and sciences, which he believed enlarged a person's knowledge and choices. Though needed by some individuals, vocational training, limited to specific skills, did not enlarge general human choices. Contemporary liberal arts and career educators still argue over the issue of liberal versus career education. As a teacher, you may encounter similar issues when students ask you why they should learn something they believe they will never use. What is your rationale for teaching certain skills and subjects but not others? How do we know what knowledge and skills your students may need in the future?

Aristotle was a proponent of compulsory schooling. Early childhood education included play, physical activities, music, and heroic and moral stories. Children from ages 7 to 14 were to learn reading, writing, arithmetic, and proper moral habits that prepared them for the later study of the liberal arts and sciences. Their curriculum also included gymnastics and music to develop physical dexterity and emotional sensitivity. From age 15 through 21, youths were to study the liberal arts and sciences—mathematics, geometry, astronomy, grammar, literature, poetry, rhetoric, ethics, and politics. At age 21, students would proceed to more advanced subjects, such as physics, cosmology, biology, psychology, logic, and metaphysics. Aristotle, like Plato, endorsed the doctrine of education as preparation in that each lower stage of schooling was to prepare students for the next higher stage. Later, progressive educators attacked the doctrine of preparation, arguing that students should pursue their interests and solve their immediate problems. Do you think the purpose of education is to prepare for future studies or to solve the problems in one's immediate life?

Believing women were intellectually inferior to men, Aristotle was concerned only with male education. Girls were to be trained to perform the gender-specific household and child-rearing duties appropriate for their future roles as wives and mothers.

Aristotle on the School and Curriculum   As a realist, Aristotle believed the curriculum should be based on subjects that rested on the classification of objects. Early on, children were to learn that some things are like each other and other things are not like each other. Objects can be classified into minerals, plants, and animals. These three simple but basic categories lead to more specific subdivisions. For example, we can study minerals in the subjects of mineralogy and geology; plants in the subjects of botany and horticulture; animals in the subjects of zoology and ichthyology; and people in the subjects of anthropology, history, literature, and political science. Through the liberal arts and sciences, we can access and inform ourselves about these subjects and use them to make our choices and decisions.

An Aristotelian school's purpose is to develop students' rationality. As academic institutions, schools should offer a prescribed subject-matter curriculum based on academic scholarly and scientific disciplines. In their preservice preparation, teachers need to acquire expert knowledge of their subjects and learn the methods needed to motivate students and transmit this knowledge to them. Aristotle's philosophy has had great significance in Western education. Along with Christian doctrine, it became a foundation of medieval scholastic education, discussed later in this chapter, and of realism and perennialism, discussed in Chapter 6, Philosophical Roots of Education.

3-5h Isocrates: Oratory and Rhetoric

The Greek rhetorician Isocrates (436–388 BCE) is significant for his well-constructed educational theory, which, taking a middle course between the Sophists and Plato, emphasized both knowledge and rhetorical skills.[39]

---

[39]Ekaterina V. Haskins, *Logos and Power in Isocrates and Aristotle* (Columbia: University of South Carolina Press, 2004). Also, see Gerald L. Gutek, *A History of the Western Educational Experience* (Prospect Heights, IL: Waveland Press, 1995), pp. 52–54.

Isocrates identified education's primary purpose as preparing clear-thinking, rational, truthful, and honest statesmen. He held that rhetoric, the rational expression of thought, was crucial in educating leaders for the good of society. Rhetorical education should combine the arts and sciences with effective communication skills. Opposing the Sophists' emphasis on public relations skills and manipulating an audience, Isocrates wanted orators to advocate social justice. Isocrates's students, who attended his school for four years, studied rhetoric, political philosophy, history, and ethics. They analyzed and imitated model orations and practiced public speaking. Isocrates influenced the rhetorical tradition in Western education, especially the Roman educational theorist Quintilian.

3-5i The Greeks' Significance in World Education

The Greek significance in world education reaches to the present. The Athenian ideal of citizens' civic participation became a principle in American democracy. Philosophy still begins with the ideas of Socrates, Plato, and Aristotle. Questions about the liberal arts and sciences and universal truth versus cultural relativism still resonate among educators today.

3-6 EDUCATION IN ANCIENT ROME

Rome's thousand-year history stands as one of the most remarkable achievements in Western civilization. Founded as a small Latin settlement on the Italian peninsula about 750 BCE, Roman society was divided into two classes: the dominant patrician elite and the subordinate plebeians. The Senate was Rome's most powerful lawmaking body.

Early Roman education sought to instill in children, especially the sons who would inherit the family property, reverence for their ancestors and a sense of duty to family, the state, and the gods. The father, in an ancient version of homeschooling, was responsible for teaching his children the *mos maiorum,* the valued traditions of Rome's heritage. Along with prayers and rituals, he stressed the values of self-control, fear of the gods, temperance, frugality, courage, patriotism, and self-sacrifice. As Rome's future defenders, the young males learned such military skills as fencing and javelin throwing. At age 16, the youth put on the toga *virilis* to begin his adult role.

When Rome became a vast empire, its educational patterns changed. The city of Rome, the empire's capitol, with more than 500,000 inhabitants, became the classical world's greatest metropolis. The city's material grandeur reflected the achievements of Roman administration and civil engineering. A network of aqueducts carried fresh drinking and bathing water to the inhabitants and its ports, and paved roads brought food and other products to its markets.

Captives from Rome's conquests of Greece, Gaul, Spain, and Asia Minor increased its slave population. Of Italy's 7.5 million inhabitants, 3 million were slaves. While the majority of the slaves were agricultural laborers, they also worked as domestic servants, artisans, and craftsmen. In particular, educated Greek slaves were valued as tutors, teachers, and secretaries.[40]

Near the end of the fourth century BCE, a primary school, or *ludus,* appeared in Rome where boys from ages 7 through 12 learned to read and write Latin, their vernacular language. Primary schools, both ancient and modern, emphasized literacy, the ability to read and write, the students' spoken language. The teacher was called a *ludi magister* or *literator* and was usually male, either free or a slave. The school, a private, for-profit institution, enrolled a minority of boys, mainly from wealthier classes. Boys were often led to school by a slave, called *pedagogus,* preferably an educated Greek slave who could act as a tutor. The English words "pedagogue," an educator, and "pedagogy," which refers to education, come from the Latin term *pedagogus.*

---

[40]Chambers, Grew, Herlihy, Rabb, and Woloch, *The Western Experience,* pp. 132–133.

Roman boys next attended secondary level Greek grammar schools. The development of these schools related to Rome's conquest of Greece. Roman diplomats, generals, and administrators needed to know Greek as an international language. Grammar schools were established to teach the Greek language and literature, as a second language, to Rome's Latin-speaking youth. Under the direction of a grammar teacher, *grammaticus,* Roman boys from ages 11 to 16 studied Greek grammar, composition, literature, poetry, and history. The Greek grammar school led to the later development of a Latin grammar school, which taught the vernacular language, in the first century BCE.

For higher studies, upper-class Roman youths attended rhetorical schools that combined the Greek conception of liberal education and the Roman emphasis on practical politics and law. Roman rhetoric incorporated many aspects of Greek rhetoric, especially the model developed by Isocrates.

3-6a Quintilian: Master of Oratory

Marcus Fabius Quintilianus (35–95 CE), or Quintilian, was one of imperial Rome's most highly recognized rhetoricians.[41] The emperor appointed him to the first chair of Latin rhetoric.

Quintilian's *Institutio Oratoria* discussed (1) education preparatory to studying rhetoric, (2) rhetorical and educational theory, and (3) the practice of public speaking or declamation. Anticipating the modern teacher's preservice preparation, Quintilian, recognizing the importance of students' individual differences, advised that instruction be appropriate to their readiness and abilities. He urged teachers to motivate students by making lessons interesting and engaging.

Quintilian developed stage-based learning that corresponded to the patterns of human development. He recognized the importance of early childhood, the first stage from birth to age 7, in shaping later patterns of behavior. Because children construct their speech patterns on what they hear, he advised parents to select well-spoken nurses, pedagogues, and companions for their children.

---

[41]Robin Barrow, *Greek and Roman Education* (London: Duckworth Publishers, 2011). Also, see Iain Mcdougal, J. C. Yardley, and Mark Joyal, *Greek and Roman Education: A Sourcebook* (New York and London: Routledge, 2008); for a biographical sketch and an excerpt from Quintilian's *Institutio Oratoria*, see Madonna M. Murphy, *The History and Philosophy of Education: Voices of Educational Pioneers* (Upper Saddle River, NJ: Pearson/Merrill/Prentice Hall, 2006), pp. 59–66.

TIMELINE
ANCIENT GREECE

Marzolino/Shutterstock.com

404 BCE Sparta defeats Athens in Peloponnesian War

399 BCE Death of Socrates

385 BCE Plato establishes Academy

384 BCE Birth of Aristotle

| 440 BCE | 420 BCE | 400 BCE | 380 BCE |

427 BCE Birth of Plato

436 BCE Birth of Isocrates

In Quintilian's second stage of education, from age 7 to 14, the teacher was advised that the boy is using his sense experiences to form clear ideas and place them in his memory. The boy is to attend a *ludus* to learn to read and write his spoken language where he is to be instructed by a competent and ethical teacher. Instruction should be gradual and thorough, with children learning the alphabet by tracing ivory letters. Anticipating modern education, Quintilian advised having breaks for games and recess, so students could renew their energy.

Quintilian's third stage, from age 14 to 17, emphasized the liberal arts. As a proponent of Greek and Latin bilingual and bicultural education, he wanted students to study grammar, literature, history, and mythology in both languages. They also were expected to study music, geometry, astronomy, and gymnastics.

The fourth stage, from age 17 to 21, was devoted to rhetoric, which included drama, poetry, law, philosophy, public speaking, declamation, and debate.[42] Declamations—systematic speaking exercises—were especially important. When Quintilian assessed a student to be ready for public speaking, the novice orator delivered an oration to an audience in the forum that was then critiqued by his teacher. The teacher corrected the student's mistakes with a sense of authority but also with patience, tact, and consideration. Quintilian's program of rhetorical education resembled contemporary preservice teacher education. The practice oration was like supervised student teaching. The supervisor's critique of the beginning teacher's classroom skills resembles the master rhetorician's critique of the novice orator's speaking abilities.

Quintilian's ideas of rhetorical education continued on in Western history. In the medieval era, rhetoric was taught in cathedral schools and universities. It surfaced again in the Renaissance, when educators looked to the classical traditions of Greece and Rome to revive literary humanism. Rhetoric had a place in higher education at Oxford and Cambridge in England and at Harvard and Yale in the United States.

3-6b Rome's Significance in World Education

Rome's Latin language was not only important for literate and educated Romans but for later generations of European and American students, especially those attending secondary schools in the eighteenth, nineteenth, and early twentieth centuries. During this time, Latin, considered the necessary language of an educated person, was generally a requirement for entry into colleges and universities.

3-7 EDUCATION IN THE MIDDLE AGES

Historians designate the one thousand years after Rome's fall in the fifth century to America's discovery in the fifteenth century as the "Middle Ages," between the end of the Greco-Roman classical period and the beginning of the modern era. By the Middle

FOCUS Has your educational experience been speculative and abstract like the Greeks, or has it been practical and applied in the Roman sense? Has your education's purpose been to prepare you for the next phase of schooling, or did it help you deal with the problems you face in daily life?

---

[42]For a hypertext edition of Quintilian's *Institutes of Oratory,* visit **http://archive.org/stream /institutiooratoor00quin/institutiooratorio00quin-djvu.txt**.

322 BCE Death of Aristotle

| **360 BCE** | **340 BCE** | **320 BCE** | **300 BCE** |

335 BCE Aristotle founds Lyceum

347 BCE Death of Plato

Ages (the Medieval period), most Europeans were Christians. The Christian Church was organized hierarchically into local parishes with priests, regional dioceses with bishops, and a world pontiff, the Pope in Rome.

The early Church faced the issue of the relationship between Christian doctrines and classical Greek and Roman literature and philosophy. Should "pagan" (pre-Christian) authors such as Plato and Aristotle be included or purged from Western culture? If the Greek and Roman authors were judged dangerous to Christian beliefs and morals, should their books be banned or even burned? Or, should they be preserved and read?

St. Augustine (354–430 CE), the Bishop of Hippo, in North Africa, argued for the preservation of classical literature.[43] As a former teacher of rhetoric, Augustine knew the Greco-Roman classics, especially philosophy. His highly introspective memoir, *The Confessions,* told of his personal search for truth and how, through God's grace, he became a Christian. Augustine argued that the Greek and Roman literature, when illuminated by faith, could aid human understanding. The ultimate goal, however, he wrote in the *City of God,* was God's heavenly city.

3-7a Charlemagne's Revival of Learning

In what is now France and western Germany, the kingdom of the Franks arose in the eighth century. Charlemagne (768–814 CE), the most important Frankish king, was crowned by Pope Leo III as the holy Roman emperor on Christmas Day in 800 CE.[44] He engaged Alcuin (735–804 CE), an English monk, to head his palace school at Aachen. Alcuin wrote textbooks that summarized the Latin classics and the liberal arts for his students, some of whom were Charlemagne's officials.[45] Guided by Alcuin, Charlemagne required monasteries to provide schools where boys would learn to read and write in Latin and learn religious chants and psalms.

---

[43]Troy Southgate, *The Bishop of Hippo: Life and Thought of Saint Augustine* (East Sussex, UK: Black Front Press, 2014).

[44]Rosamund McKitterick, *Charlemagne: The Formation of a European Identity* (Cambridge, UK: Cambridge University Press, 2008).

[45]Douglas Dales, *Alcuin: His Life and Legacy* (Cambridge, UK: James Clarke and Co., 2012).

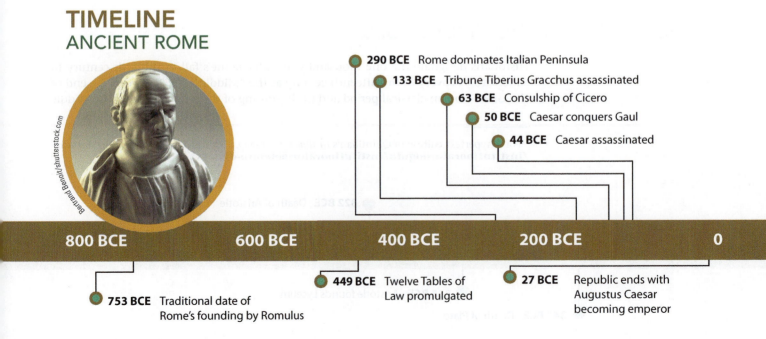

TIMELINE
ANCIENT ROME

Bertrand Benoit/shutterstock.com

290 BCE Rome dominates Italian Peninsula

133 BCE Tribune Tiberius Gracchus assassinated

63 BCE Consulship of Cicero

50 BCE Caesar conquers Gaul

44 BCE Caesar assassinated

800 BCE **600 BCE** **400 BCE** **200 BCE** **0**

753 BCE Traditional date of Rome's founding by Romulus

449 BCE Twelve Tables of Law promulgated

27 BCE Republic ends with Augustus Caesar becoming emperor

3-7b The Church and the Medieval Education

During the Middle Ages, the church established parish, chantry, monastic, and cathedral schools. Parish schools taught the ritual and music needed to celebrate the Mass, as well as reading and writing. Chantry schools, funded by endowments from wealthy patrons, trained boys to sing the responses in the Latin liturgy as members of the church choir.

Saint Benedict (c. 480–c. 583 CE) established the patterns of monastic life and education. Serving as repositories for medieval culture, monasteries maintained *scriptoria* and libraries where classical and Christian manuscripts were copied and preserved. Monastic schools trained monks either as priests or brothers in church doctrine, Latin, the rules (the *regula*) that governed their communities, and in reading, writing, and mathematics.[46]

Women's educational opportunities were limited in male-dominated medieval schools. However, some women attended convent schools, parallel institutions to the monasteries, but for girls, unmarried women, or widows. Like the monasteries, convents often had schools, libraries, and scriptoria. Convent schools taught the rules of the religious community, Latin, singing, reading and writing, and what became the "women's curriculum" of embroidery, spinning, weaving, and painting. While some girls took vows as nuns and remained in the convent's cloisters, others returned to the secular world after completing their education.

A religious superior, called an abbess or prioress, was in charge of the community of nuns. Hildegard of Bingen (1098–1179), abbess of a Benedictine convent in Germany, was a scholar, teacher, writer, and composer. She wrote *The Ways of God* and *The Book of Divine Works* to guide women's spiritual formation. She composed religious hymns and wrote medical tracts about the causes, symptoms, and cures of illnesses.[47]

Cathedral schools, established by the bishops of dioceses, offered the liberal arts and the doctrinal and liturgical studies needed by those preparing to be priests. Some of their enrollments became so large they grew into universities. The University of Bologna, in Italy, became the center for the study of law. The University of Paris

---

[46]For a thorough study of monastic life, see Janneke Raaijmakers, *The Making of the Monastic Community of Fulda, c.744–c. 900* (New York: Cambridge University Press, 2012).

[47]For a biographical sketch and an excerpt from Hildegard's writings, see Madonna M. Murphy, *The History and Philosophy of Education*, pp. 104–112. For a biography, see Fiona Maddocks, *Hildegard of Bingen: The Woman of Her Age* (New York: Doubleday/Random House, 2001). Also, see *Hildegard of Bingen: Selections from Her Writings* (New York: HarperOne, 2005).

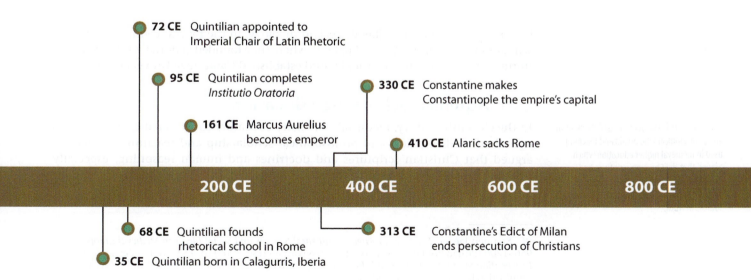

72 CE Quintilian appointed to Imperial Chair of Latin Rhetoric

95 CE Quintilian completes *Institutio Oratoria*

330 CE Constantine makes Constantinople the empire's capital

161 CE Marcus Aurelius becomes emperor

410 CE Alaric sacks Rome

200 CE   **400 CE**   **600 CE**   **800 CE**

68 CE Quintilian founds rhetorical school in Rome

313 CE Constantine's Edict of Milan ends persecution of Christians

35 CE Quintilian born in Calagurris, Iberia

OVERVIEW 3.2

MAJOR EDUCATIONAL THEORISTS TO 1600 CE

Theorist	Philosophical Orientation	View of Human Nature
Confucius 551–478 BCE (Chinese)	Developed an ethical system of hierarchical human relationships and roles; emphasized order and civility through subordination.	Human beings need a highly stable society in which they accept the duties of their station in life.
Socrates 469–399 BCE (Greek)	Social and educational iconoclast who asked basic philosophical questions about the meaning of life.	Human beings can find the truth within themselves by dialectical self-examination.
Plato 427–346 BCE (Greek)	An idealist who established the contours of Western philosophy; sociopolitical conservative.	Human beings can be classified according to their intellectual capabilities.
Aristotle 384–322 BCE (Greek)	Philosophical realist; views of society, politics, and education based on observation of natural and social phenomena.	Human beings have the power of reason to guide their decisions.
Isocrates 436–388 BCE (Greek)	Rhetorician; oratorical education in service of self and society.	Human beings have the power to use speech (discourse) to influence social and political decisions.
Quintilian 35–95 CE (Roman)	Rhetorician; oratory for personal advancement and public service.	Certain individuals with the right dispositions can be prepared as leaders through liberal and oratorical education.
Hildegard of Bingen 1098–1179 CE (German)	Medieval abbess; Christian spirituality and natural medical science.	Human beings need spiritual development and natural knowledge.
Aquinas 1225–1274 CE (Italian medieval theologian)	Christian theology and Aristotelian (realist) philosophy.	Human beings possess both a spiritual nature (soul) and a physical nature (body).
Erasmus 1465–1536 CE (Dutch Renaissance humanist)	Christian orientation; the educator as social and intellectual critic.	Human beings are capable of profound insights but also of great stupidity.
Luther 1483–1546 CE (German Protestant)	Protestant theological orientation; salvation by faith.	Human beings are saved by faith; individual conscience shaped by scripture and Reformed theology.

became renowned for the liberal arts and theology. In the twelfth century, a group of scholars migrated from Paris to England, where they founded Oxford University. In the thirteenth century, scholars from Oxford established Cambridge University.[48]

3-7c Aquinas: Scholastic Education

Scholasticism A method of theological and philosophical scholarship and teaching used in medieval higher education which argued that the Christian scriptures and doctrines, and human reasoning, especially Aristotle's philosophy, were complementary sources of truth.

In the eleventh century, medieval university educators constructed Scholasticism—a method of theological and philosophical scholarship and teaching. Scholastics argued that Christian scriptures and doctrines and human reasoning, especially Aristotle's natural philosophy, were complementary sources of truth. In their

[48]C. Stephen Jaeger, *The Envy of Angels: Cathedral Schools and Social Ideals in Medieval Europe, 950–1200* (Philadelphia: University of Pennsylvania Press, 2000), p. 153. Olaf Pedersen, *The First Universities: Studium Generale and the Origins of University Education in Europe* (Cambridge, UK: Cambridge University Press, 2009).

Orientation on Education and Curriculum	Significance
Education prepares people for their sociopolitical roles by cultivating reverence for ancestors and traditions; curriculum of ancient Chinese classics and Confucius's *Analects;* (proverbial wisdom) highly selective examinations.	Confucianism influenced Chinese, Japanese, and Korean culture and education.
Use of probing intellectual dialogue to answer enduring questions about truth, goodness, and beauty; education should cultivate moral excellence.	Socratic dialogue as a teaching method; teacher as a role model.
Reminiscence of latent ideas; music, gymnastics, geometry, astronomy, basic literary skills; philosophy for philosopher-kings.	Use of schools for sorting students according to intellectual abilities; education for universal truth and values.
Objective and scientific emphasis; basic literary skills, mathematics, natural and physical sciences, philosophy.	Emphasis on liberally educated, well-rounded person; importance of reason.
Rhetorical studies; basic literary skills; politics, history, rhetoric, declamation, public speaking.	Use of knowledge in public affairs and in political leadership; teacher education has both content and practice dimensions.
Basic literary skills; grammar, history, literature, drama, philosophy, public speaking, law.	Role of motivation in learning; recognition of individual differences.
Women should have a multidimensional education in religion, nature studies, and music.	Teacher as mentor and guide to the individual's spiritual, natural, and moral development.
Education should be based on human nature, with appropriate studies for both spiritual and physical dimensions.	Teacher as moral agent; education related to universal theological goals; synthesis of theology and philosophy; dominant philosophy in Roman Catholic schools.
Education for literary elite that stressed criticism and analysis.	Role of secondary and higher education in literary and social criticism; emphasis on critical thinking.
Elementary schools to teach reading, writing, arithmetic, religion; secondary schools to prepare leaders by offering classics, Latin, Greek, and religion; vocational training.	Emphasis on universal literacy; schools to stress religious values, vocational skills, knowledge; close relationship of religion, schooling, and the state.

teaching, Scholastics used the syllogism—deductive reasoning—to create organized bodies of knowledge.[49]

Scholastic philosophy and education reached its zenith in the *Summa Theologiae* of Saint Thomas Aquinas (1225–1274), a Dominican theologian at the University of Paris. Seeking to reconcile Christian doctrine with Aristotle's philosophy, Aquinas used both faith and reason to answer questions about God, the nature of humankind and the universe, and the relationship between God and humans.[50] For Aquinas, the ultimate human purpose is to experience eternity with God in heaven. (See Overview 3.2 for the ideas of Aquinas and other educators discussed in this chapter.)

---

[49]John W. Donohue, *St. Thomas Aquinas and Education* (New York: Random House, 1968), pp. 76–89. Also, see Vivian Boland, *St. Thomas Aquinas* (*Continuum Library of Educational Thought*) (London: Continuum, 2008).

[50]G. K. Chesterton, *St. Thomas Aquinas: "The Dumb Ox"* (Nashville, TN: Sam Torade Book Arts, 2010); Fergus Kerr, *Thomas Aquinas: A Very Short Introduction* (New York: Oxford University Press, 2009); and Francis Selman, *Aquinas 101: A Basic Introduction to the Thought of Saint Thomas Aquinas* (Notre Dame, IN: Christian Classics/Ave Maria Press, 2007).

In *de Magistro* (*Concerning the Teacher*), Aquinas portrayed the teacher's vocation as combining faith, love, and learning. Teachers need to be contemplative and reflective scholars, expert in their subjects, active and skilled instructors, and lovers of humanity. Aquinas's ideas suggest that teachers should have a vocation or a calling to teach and an in-depth knowledge of their subject matter. Aquinas called upon teachers to reflect on their teaching to find the deeper meaning of their work with students.

Aquinas's philosophy, called Thomism, has influenced education in Catholic schools, especially colleges and universities. In the United States, Catholic elementary and secondary enroll 2.1 million students, 40 percent of all private school enrollments.[51] Thomism also influenced perennialist educators such as Robert Hutchins, Jacques Maritain, and Mortimer Adler, who are discussed in Chapter 6, Philosophical Roots of Education.

3-7d The Medieval Significance to World Education

The medieval educators recorded, preserved, and transmitted knowledge by presenting it in a scholastic framework based on the Christian religion and Aristotle's philosophy. Parish, monastic, and cathedral schools and universities, under Church sponsorship and supervision, transmitted knowledge as organized subjects. The Medieval period formed a cultural bridge between Greco-Roman classical and modern education.

3-8   ISLAM AND ARABIC EDUCATION

While the Middle Ages were unfolding in Europe, the Arabs in North Africa were experiencing the Islamic religious movement.[52] Islam originated with Mohammed (569–632 CE), an Arab religious reformer and proselytizer revered by Muslims as the last and most important of God's prophets. Mohammed began his religious mission in Arabia, in Mecca, in 610 CE where he preached the need for faith, prayer, repentance, and morality. He incorporated his beliefs into Islam, a new religion, with a sacred book, the Koran, or Qur'an. Like Judaism and Christianity, **Islam**, a monotheistic

FOCUS Medieval scholastic educators sought to reconcile faith and reason as complementary sources of truth. In your own educational experience, reflect on science and religion. Have you encountered conflicts, or have these areas been complementary? Is there a conflict between religion and separation of church and state in American education?

Islam Religion founded by Mohammed (569–632 CE); currently practiced in many Middle Eastern and other countries.

---

[51]See **www.ed.gov**. Also access the National Catholic Education Association at **www.ncea.org**.
[52]Adam J. Silverstein, *Islamic History: A Very Short Introduction* (New York: Oxford University Press, 2010).

TIMELINE
ISLAM

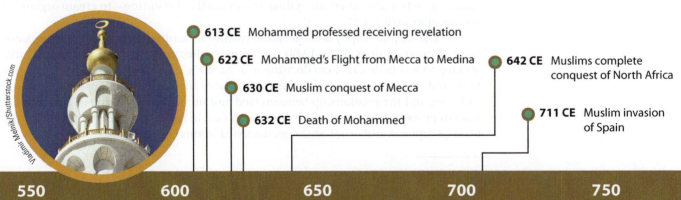

613 CE Mohammed professed receiving revelation

622 CE Mohammed's Flight from Mecca to Medina

642 CE Muslims complete conquest of North Africa

630 CE Muslim conquest of Mecca

632 CE Death of Mohammed

711 CE Muslim invasion of Spain

550   600   650   700   750

570 CE Birth of Mohammed

Vladimir Melnik/Shutterstock.com

Paul Chesley/The Image Bank/Getty Images

> PHOTO 3.2 Islamic religion and culture are widespread, and in the twenty-first century, interactions are increasing between Muslims and others throughout the world. This photograph is of students at an Islamic school in Asia.

religion, affirms the existence of one God, the creator of the universe. Written in Arabic, the Koran prescribes the pillars of faith, prayers, and religious observances such as Ramadan, a month of fasting, and the Hajj, a pilgrimage to Mecca.[53]

Today, Islam is the religious faith of one-eighth of the world's population and is the dominant religion in the Arab countries of the Middle East and North Africa. Its influence extends to Indonesia, Malaysia, and Pakistan in Asia (Photo 3.2). In addition, Muslims live in countries throughout the world.

By 661 CE, Islam had been established in Palestine, Syria, Persia, and Egypt. The cities of Baghdad, Cairo, Damascus, and Cordoba became renowned centers of Islamic culture and education. Baghdad, in particular, attracted Arab, Greek, Persian, and Jewish scholars.

Mohammed's followers extended Islamic influence through conquest and conversion. After their conquest of North Africa, the Arabs gained control of much of Spain. Here, Islamic Arabs and Christians not only struggled for power and territory but also borrowed ideas from each other. During the Moorish period, Cordoba, with a population of 500,000 people, 700 mosques, and 70 libraries, was a leading Arab cultural and educational center.[54] The Islamic, or Moorish, kingdoms of Spain persisted until 1492, when they were conquered by the armies of Christian Spain.[55]

---

[53]For Islam, access **www.encyclopedia.com/topic/Islam.aspx**.

[54]See **www.islamicity.com/mosque/ihame/Sec5.htm** (September 25, 2003), pp. 1–2.

[55]Richard Fletcher, *A Vanished World: Muslims, Christians, and Jews in Medieval Spain* (New York: Oxford University Press, 2006). Also, see Richard Fletcher, *Moorish Spain* (Berkeley, CA: University of California Press, 2006).

978 CE Muslims consolidate control of Spain

| 800 | 850 | 900 | 950 | 1000 |

Islamic scholars translated the texts of ancient Greek authors such as Aristotle, Euclid, Archimedes, and Hippocrates into Arabic. These translated works became important in Islamic education and, through contacts between Arabs and Europeans, were reintroduced into Western education.[56] In some cases, these ancient texts had been lost in the early Middle Ages. In particular, Ibn-Rushd, or Averroës (1126–1198), wrote important commentaries on Aristotle that influenced scholastic educators.

Islamic scholars contributed to astronomy, mathematics, and medicine. In mathematics, Arab scholars adopted the number system from the Indians but added the crucial number zero. This innovation made it possible to replace the cumbersome Latin system.

In the twenty-first century's global economy, there is increasing interaction between the Arabic and Islamic and European and American societies. The numbers of Muslims have increased in many European countries such as France, the United Kingdom, and Italy, as well as in the United States. Some of these interactions have been clouded by suspicion and hostility because of terrorist attacks, such as that of 9/11, and persistent tensions in the Middle East. However, abroad and in the United States, there have been positive efforts at dialogue and mutual understanding, especially through multicultural education. Today, more Americans are learning more about Arabic civilization and Islam. Many American schools and colleges now include units and courses on the Arabic language and culture.

FOCUS How have recent events brought renewed interest in Islam and Muslim peoples? What do you know about the Islamic religion and culture, and how have you learned it?

3-9 THE RENAISSANCE AND EDUCATION

The Renaissance, a transitional period between the medieval and modern ages, which began in the fourteenth century, reached its zenith in the fifteenth century. It signaled a revival of the humanist aspects of the Greek and Latin classics. Like the

[56]John Tolan, Gilles Veinstein, and Henry Laurens, *Europe and the Islamic World: A History* (Princeton, NJ: Princeton University Press, 2013).

TIMELINE
MIDDLE AGES (MEDIEVAL PERIOD)

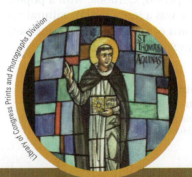

Library of Congress Prints and Photographs Division

| 500 | 600 | 700 | 800 | 900 |

910 CE Founding of Abbey at Cluny

529–534 CE Justinian I publishes Code of Civil Law

529 CE Benedict establishes monastery at Monte Casino

800 CE Charlemagne crowned Holy Roman Emperor

classical humanists The leading theory and general method of education during the Renaissance; the study of the classical Greek and Roman texts with an emphasis on their humanistic (human-centered) meaning.

medieval Scholastics, Renaissance **classical humanist** educators still looked to antiquity rather than the future but emphasized literature's earthly rather than supernatural themes.[57]

In Italy, the center of the southern Renaissance, humanists acted as critics and custodians of culture, especially in literature, art, music, and architecture. Dante, Petrarch, and Boccaccio, the great writers of their age, wrote in Italian rather than in Latin. Italian nobles established humanist schools to educate their children in revived classical learning.[58]

From their study of the Greek and Latin classics, humanist educators rediscovered models of literary excellence and style and portrayed the courtier as the ideally educated person. Wealthy aristocrats employed courtiers as counselors, secretaries, and tutors. In *The Book of the Courtier,* Baldesar Castiglione (1478–1529) wrote a guide about educating courtiers in the liberal arts and the classical literature.[59] Castiglione's courtier was to be culturally sophisticated, tactful, and diplomatic.[60]

The Renaissance humanist educators were literary critics—writers, poets, translators, and editors. As artist-teachers and cultural critics, they brought wit, charm, and satire as well as erudition to their work. They sought to educate a critically minded elite who could challenge conventional thinking and expose and correct mediocrity in literature and life. In northern Europe, humanist scholars, by critically examining medieval theological texts, prepared the path for the Protestant Reformation.

As critics, humanists wrote for an elite, like themselves, rather than a popular audience. They often kept a distance between themselves and the mass of people, distilling their conception of human nature from a carefully aged literature. As a vintage wine is used to grace an elegant dinner, humanist education was for the connoisseur rather than for the masses.

The Renaissance did not dramatically increase school attendance. Humanist preparatory and secondary schools educated children of the nobility and upper classes. Elementary schools served the commercial middle classes. Children in lower socioeconomic classes received little, if any, formal schooling.

---

[57]Charles G. Nauert, *Humanism and the Culture of Renaissance Europe* (Cambridge, UK: Cambridge University Press, 2006).

[58]Robert Black, *Humanism and Education in Medieval and Renaissance Italy: Tradition and Innovation in Latin Schools from the Twelfth to the Fifteenth Century* (Cambridge, UK: Cambridge University Press, 2007).

[59]Baldesar Castiglione, *The Book of the Courtier* (New York: Barnes and Noble Books, 2005).

[60]Peter W. R. Albury, *Castiglione's Allegory: Veiled Policy in the Book of the Courtier (1528)* (Burlington, VT: Ashgate Publishing, 2014).

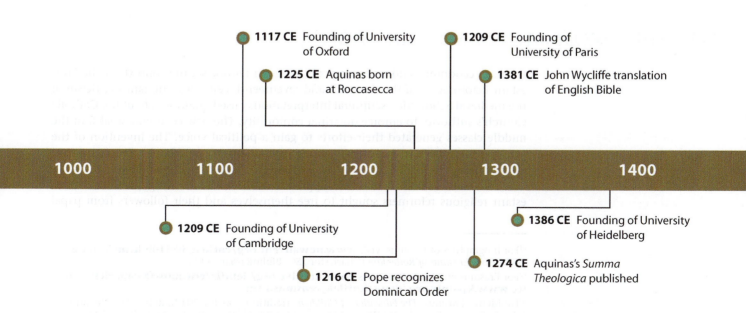

1117 CE Founding of University of Oxford

1209 CE Founding of University of Paris

1225 CE Aquinas born at Roccasecca

1381 CE John Wycliffe translation of English Bible

1000   **1100**   **1200**   **1300**   **1400**

1209 CE Founding of University of Cambridge

1386 CE Founding of University of Heidelberg

1216 CE Pope recognizes Dominican Order

1274 CE Aquinas's *Summa Theologica* published

3-9a Erasmus: Critic and Humanist

Desiderius Erasmus (1465–1536), a leading scholar, portrayed the ideal teacher as a cosmopolitan Christian humanist.[61] Ecumenical in his worldview, Erasmus emphasized the unifying features of Christianity shared by all believers rather than doctrines that divided them. Although he could be a sarcastic critic, Erasmus had a gentle view of children's education. Advising parents and teachers to be worthy cultural and ethical models for their children, Erasmus understood the importance of shaping favorable predispositions to education early in a child's life.

Erasmus believed that a cosmopolitan worldview and academic preparation in the classics were necessary for success as a humanist educator. Teachers needed to overcome narrow parochial biases and be open to divergent perspectives. As part of their preservice preparation, teachers needed to be well educated in the liberal arts, especially in the classical Greek and Latin languages and literatures, as well as in history and religion. They needed to have a world outlook.

Erasmus advised teachers to select well-written books for their students to read so they could learn to emulate the author's style. He encouraged teachers to use conversations, games, and activities to describe a book's content and explore its meaning. Erasmus developed the following method for teaching literature: (1) present the author's biography; (2) identify the book's type, or genre; (3) analyze its plot; (4) reflect on its meaning for life; and (5) study the author's writing style.[62]

Erasmus's *The Education of the Christian Prince* (1516), which expressed his opposition to war and violence, was an early source of peace education.[63] He advised the prince's tutor to make sure that his pupil learned to know the people of his kingdom—their traditions, customs, work, and problems. Unlike Niccolo di Bernardo Machiavelli (1469–1527), an Italian humanist, who urged the king to rule by fear and manipulation, Erasmus advised the prince to gain his people's love and respect by studying the arts of peace, especially diplomacy, to avoid war.

FOCUS The Renaissance humanist educators regarded themselves as well-educated models and critics. In your own educational experience, have you encountered teachers who acted as models and critics? Do you plan to be such a model and critic?

3-9b The Renaissance Significance for World Education

Renaissance humanists emphasized knowledge of Latin and Greek as necessities of the educated person. For centuries, this classical preference shaped Western secondary and higher education. In Europe and the United States, many colleges and universities required students to pass entry tests in Latin for admission until the late nineteenth century.

3-10 THE REFORMATION AND EDUCATION

Political, economic, and technological change in Europe set the context for the Protestant Reformation of the sixteenth and seventeenth centuries. Humanist criticism of the medieval Scholastics' scriptural interpretations raised questions about the Catholic Church's authority to enforce doctrinal conformity. The new economic wealth of the middle classes generated their efforts to gain a political voice. The invention of the printing press made it cheaper and easier to produce tracts and books. The emergence of national states shifted people's loyalty from the pope to their own kings.

John Calvin, Martin Luther, Philipp Melanchthon, Ulrich Zwingli, and other Protestant religious reformers sought to free themselves and their followers from papal

---

[61]For biographies of Erasmus, visit **www.newadvent.org/cathen/05510b.htm**; Maurice Wilkinson, *Erasmus of Rotterdam* (Charleston, SC: BiblioBazaar, 2008).

[62]For Erasmus and his texts, access **www.archive.org/details/erasmuse00caperich**; also, see **www.kjvonly.org/doug/kutilek_erasmus.htm**.

[63]Desiderius Erasmus, *The Education of Children* (Tredition Classics, 2012); Robert D. Sider and John B. Payne, eds., *Collected Works of Erasmus* (Toronto: University of Toronto Press, 1994).

OVERVIEW 3.3

SIGNIFICANT EVENTS IN THE HISTORY OF WESTERN EDUCATION TO 1650 CE

Period	Political and Social Events		Significant Educational Events	
Greek	1200 BCE	Trojan War	c. 1200 BCE	Homer's *Iliad* and *Odyssey*
	594 BCE	Athenian constitutional reforms	399 BCE	Trial of Socrates
	479–338 BCE	Golden Age of Greek (Athenian) culture	395 BCE	Plato's *Republic*
	445–431 BCE	Age of Pericles	392 BCE	Isocrates established rhetorical school in Athens
	431–404 BCE	Peloponnesian War between Athens and Sparta	387 BCE	Plato founds Academy
	336–323 BCE	Alexander the Great	330 BCE	Aristotle's *Politics*
Roman	753 BCE	Traditional date of Rome's founding	449 BCE	Latin primary schools, or *ludi*, appear
	510 BCE	Roman republic established	167 BCE	Greek grammar school opened in Rome
	272 BCE	Rome dominates Italian Peninsula		
	146 BCE	Greece becomes Roman province	96 CE	Quintilian's *Institutio Oratoria*
	49–44 BCE	Dictatorship of Julius Caesar		
	31 BCE	Roman empire begins		
	476 CE	Fall of Rome in the West		
Medieval	713 CE	Arab conquest of Spain	1079–1142 CE	Abelard, author of *Sic et Non*
	800 CE	Charlemagne crowned Holy Roman Emperor	1180 CE	University of Paris granted papal charter and recognition
	1096–1291 CE	Crusades to the Holy Land	1209 CE	University of Cambridge founded
	1182–1226 CE	St. Francis of Assisi	1225–1274 CE	Thomas Aquinas, author of *Summa Theologiae*
Renaissance	1295 CE	Explorations of Marco Polo	1428 CE	Da Feltre, classical humanist educator, established court school at Mantua
	1304–1374 CE	Petrarch, author of odes and sonnets		
	1313–1375 CE	Boccaccio, founder of Italian vernacular literature	1509 CE	Erasmus's *The Praise of Folly*
	1384 CE	Founding of Brethren of the Common Life		
	1393–1464 CE	Cosimo de'Medici encourages revival of art and learning in Florence		
	1423 CE	Invention of printing press		
Reformation	1455 CE	Gutenberg Bible printed	1524 CE	Luther's "Letter ... in Behalf of Christian Schools"
	1492 CE	Columbus arrives in America		
	1517 CE	Luther posts "Ninety-Five Theses" calling for church reform	1524 CE	Melanchthon, an associate of Luther, writes school codes in German states
	1509–1564 CE	John Calvin, Protestant reformer, founder of Calvinism	1630–1650 CE	John Knox organizes Calvinist schools in Scotland
	1509–1547 CE	King Henry VIII of England, founder of the Church of England		
	1540 CE	Jesuit order founded by Loyola		
	1545 CE	Council of Trent launches Roman Catholic Counter-Reformation		

authority and to redefine Christian doctrines and practices.[64] These religious reformers wanted to use education and schools to promote Protestantism. They asserted that every person had not only the right but also the religious obligation to read the Bible as the primary authority of truth. Their emphasis on reading the scriptures created a demand for more Bibles, which was met by the appearance of printed books.

The invention of the printing press in 1423 dramatically advanced literacy and schooling. Before the printing press, students painstakingly created their own copies of texts by recording dictation from teachers. By the mid-fifteenth century, European printers were experimenting with movable metal type. Johannes Gutenberg, a German jeweler, invented a durable metal alloy to form letters for the printing press. In 1455, Gutenberg's Bible was the first major book printed. Printing spread throughout Europe, multiplying the output and cutting the costs of books. It made information accessible to a growing population of readers.[65] It brought more textbooks into the schools and made the text part of the teacher's method of instruction. The printing press inaugurated an *information revolution*, whose consequences were similar to the advent of data storage, retrieval, and dissemination by personal computers. (See Overview 3.3 for the invention of the printing press and other significant events in the history of education.)

vernacular schools Primary institutions that provided instruction in students' common language, in contrast to schools that instructed in classical languages such as Greek or Latin.

Protestants established **vernacular schools** to instruct children in spoken languages such as German, Swedish, or English used in their religious services rather than the Catholic Church's Latin. Protestant primary schools offered a basic curriculum of reading, writing, arithmetic, and religion. While Catholic liturgies remained in Latin, Catholic schools, to compete with Protestants, also began to teach vernacular languages along with Latin.

Both Protestants and Catholics used schools to instill religious beliefs and practices approved by the particular denominations. Only members of the particular officially sanctioned church were hired as teachers. Religious authorities closely supervised teachers to make certain they were teaching approved doctrines. In fact, teacher supervision and licensing developed during the Reformation.

---

[64]Patrick Collinson, *The Reformation: A History* (New York: Modern Library, 2004); Diarmaid Mac-Culloch, *The Reformation* (New York: Penguin, 2005); John Calvin, *Institutes of the Christian Religion* (Peabody, MA: Hendrickson Publishers, 2008); and F. Bruce Gordon, *Calvin* (New Haven: Yale University Press, 2011).

[65]Lucien Febvre and Henri-Jean Martin, *The Coming of the Book: The Impact of Printing, 1450–1800* (Verso World History Series, 2010); and Elizabeth L. Eisenstein, *The Printing Revolution in Early Modern Europe* (Cambridge, UK: Cambridge University Press, 2005).

TIMELINE
THE RENAISSANCE

Georgios Kollidas/Shutterstock.com

| 1300 | 1340 | 1380 | 1420 |

1310 CE Dante's "Divine Comedy" published

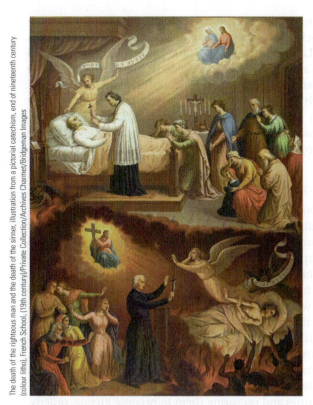

The death of the righteous man and the death of the sinner, illustration from a pictorial catechism, end of nineteenth century (colour litho), French School, (19th century)/Private Collection/Archives Charmet/Bridgeman Images

∧ **PHOTO 3.3** Illustration from a catechism shows the death of a religiously righteous man.

catechistic method of instruction Catechisms—religious textbooks—were organized into questions and answers that summarized the particular denomination's doctrines and practices.

Religious educators developed the **catechistic method** of instruction. Catechisms, religious textbooks, were organized into questions and answers that summarized the particular denomination's doctrines and practices (Photo 3.3). Students were expected to memorize the set answers and to recite them as the teacher read the particular questions. Although memorization had always been a feature of schooling, the catechistic method reinforced it. The belief was that if children memorized the catechism, they would internalize the doctrines of their church. The question-and-answer format gained such a powerful hold on teaching methods that it was also used to teach secular subjects such as history and geography.

For example, Calvin's *Catechism of the Church of Geneva* used the question and answer method:

Master: What is the chief end of human life?
Scholar: To know God by whom men were created.

In the nineteenth century, the same method appeared in Davenport's *History of the United States:*

Q. When did the battle of Lexington take place?
A. On the 19th of April, 1775; here was shed the first blood in the American Revolution.[66]

Religious and economic change worked to increase primary (elementary) school attendance and literacy rates. The Protestant emphasis on Bible reading caused more children, both girls and boys, to attend primary vernacular schools. The middle classes (the commercial and merchant sectors) sent their children to school to learn the practical skills of reading, writing, and arithmetic. For example, only 10 percent of men and 2 percent of women in England were literate in 1500. By 1600, literacy rates had increased to 28 percent for men and 9 percent for women; by 1700, nearly 40 percent of English men and about 32 percent of English women were literate. Literacy rates tended to be higher in northern than in southern and eastern Europe and in urban rather than rural areas.[67]

---

[66]John Calvin, *Tracts and Treatises on the Doctrine and Worship of the Church,* II, trans. Henry Beveride (Grand Rapids, MI: Wm. B. Eerdmans Publishing Co., 1958), p. 37; and Bishop Davenport, *History of the United States* (Philadelphia: William Marchall and Co., 1833), p. 31.
[67]Mary Jo Maynes, *Schooling in Western Europe: A Social History* (Albany: State University of New York Press, 1985).

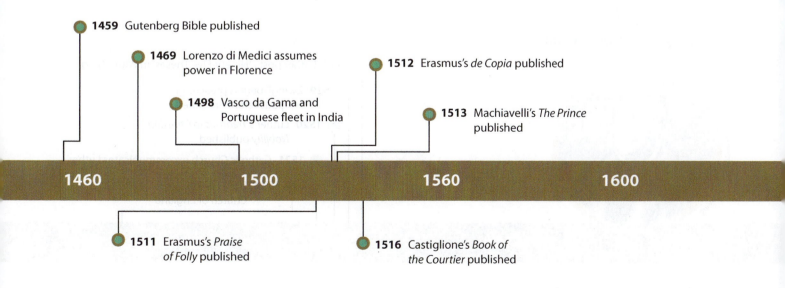

1459 Gutenberg Bible published

1469 Lorenzo di Medici assumes power in Florence

1498 Vasco da Gama and Portuguese fleet in India

1512 Erasmus's *de Copia* published

1513 Machiavelli's *The Prince* published

| 1460 | 1500 | 1560 | 1600 |

1511 Erasmus's *Praise of Folly* published

1516 Castiglione's *Book of the Courtier* published

Protestant educators continued to reserve the prestigious classical humanist preparatory and secondary schools for upper-class boys. Preparatory and secondary schools, such as the German *gymnasium*, the English Latin grammar school, and the French *lycée,* prepared upper-class boys in the classical Latin and Greek languages needed for university entry. The members of this male elite were prepared for leadership roles in the church and state.

Many strong personalities such as Calvin, Zwingli, Ignatius Loyola, and Henry VIII were leaders of the Protestant Reformation and the Roman Catholic Counter-Reformation. Martin Luther was a leading German Protestant reformer, whose influence extended throughout northern Europe.

3-10a Luther: Protestant Reformer

Martin Luther (1483–1546) stands out as one of the most important religious reformers in shaping Western history and education.[68] Luther, an Augustinian monk, posted his famous *Ninety-Five Theses* on the door of the castle church at Wittenberg in 1517 as a challenge to the authority of the pope and the Roman Catholic Church.

Luther saw the church, state, family, and school as interrelated agencies of education. Believing the family had a key role in forming the character of children, Luther encouraged family Bible reading and prayer. He wanted parents to provide their children with vocational training so they could support themselves as adults and become productive citizens.

Luther's "Letter to the Mayors and Aldermen of All the Cities of Germany in Behalf of Christian Schools" held public officials responsible for supporting and supervising schools. Government should support schools because they promoted civil order, economic growth, and religious values.[69] State officials should inspect schools to ensure teachers were educating children in correct religious doctrines and preparing them to become literate, orderly, and productive citizens. Higher education in the *gymnasien* (German secondary schools) and universities were to prepare well-educated ministers for the Lutheran Church.

Luther's views on women's education blended traditional gender roles with some more open ideas. Influenced by Saint Paul, he believed the husband, as the head of the

---

[68]Biographies of Luther are James A. Nestigen, *Martin Luther: A Life* (Minneapolis, MN: Augsburg, 2003); Fredrick Nohl, *Luther: Biography of a Reformer* (St. Louis, MO: Concordia Publishing House, 2003); Michael A. Mullett, *Martin Luther* (New York: Routledge, 2015); Stephen T. Nichols, *The Reformation: How a Monk and a Mallet Changed the World* (Wheaton, IL: Crossway Books, 2007); and Heiko A. Oberman, *Luther: Man Between God and the Devil* (New Haven: Yale University Press, 2006).

[69]For a biographical sketch, a commentary on Luther's educational ideas, and an excerpt from his "Letter to the Mayors and Aldermen of All the Cities of Germany in Behalf of Christian Schools," see Madonna M. Murphy, *The History and Philosophy of Education: Voices of Educational Pioneers* (Upper Saddle River, NJ: Pearson/Merrill/Prentice Hall, 2006), pp. 143–149.

TIMELINE
THE REFORMATION

Steven Wynn/iStockphoto.com

1517 Luther posts "Ninety-Five Theses" in Wittenberg

1519 Zwingli begins preaching religious reform in Geneva

1520 Luther's *Treatises to Christian Nobility* published

1521 Catholic Church excommunicates Luther

1534 Henry VIII declared head of Church of England

| 1500 | 1510 | 1520 | 1530 |

household, had authority over his wife. Domestic duties and child-rearing remained appropriate roles for women. However, Luther's emphasis that everyone should read the Bible in one's own language meant that girls, as well as boys, attended primary vernacular schools to learn to read.

To implement educational reforms, Luther relied heavily on the humanist educator, Philipp Melanchthon (1497–1560). In 1559, Melanchthon drafted the *School Code of Württemberg,* which became a model for other German states. The code specified that primary vernacular schools be established in every village to teach religion, reading, writing, arithmetic, and music. Classical secondary schools, *gymnasien,* were to provide Latin and Greek instruction for those select young men expected to attend universities.

3-10b The Reformation's Significance in World Education

The Protestant Reformation gave renewed emphasis to the role of religion in education. It also led to greater supervision of teachers to ensure that they were teaching approved religious doctrines. Religious conformity contributed to the catechetical, question and answer, method of teaching. Many schools were and are sponsored by churches, temples, synagogues, and mosques.

FOCUS The question-and-answer response to previously memorized lessons was used during the Reformation. Have you encountered this method in your own schooling? What are its strengths and weaknesses? Has religion influenced your views of education and its purposes?

3-11 THE ENLIGHTENMENT AND EDUCATION

In the eighteenth century, the naturalism and rationalism of the Enlightenment, in Europe and the Americas, generated new ideas about education, schools, and teaching. Enlightenment scientists and educators used the scientific method of empirical observation to discover how the natural world functioned. They observed children—especially their activities and play—to construct a natural method of instruction based on stages of human development. The Enlightenment worldview that children were naturally good and that teachers should base instruction on children's interests and needs influenced the educational reformers—Rousseau, Pestalozzi, and the progressive educators, discussed in Chapter 4, Pioneers of Teaching and Learning, and Chapter 6, Philosophical Roots of Education.

Enlightenment ideas took root in the United States, where they nourished an optimistic faith in political democracy and universal education. They influenced Franklin's emphasis on utilitarian and scientific education and Jefferson's arguments for separation of church and state and education in state-supported schools. Convinced of their ability to direct their own future, Americans saw education as the key to progress.

3-11a The Enlightenment's Significance in American Education

Leaders of the American Revolution, such as Benjamin Franklin and Thomas Jefferson, whose ideas are discussed in Chapter 5, Historical Development of American Education, were especially influenced by Enlightenment political philosophy. The Declaration of

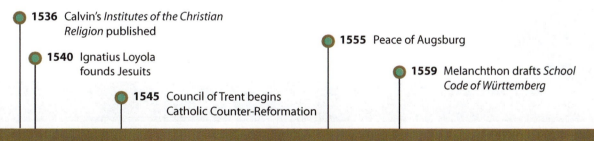

1536 Calvin's *Institutes of the Christian Religion* published

1540 Ignatius Loyola founds Jesuits

1545 Council of Trent begins Catholic Counter-Reformation

1555 Peace of Augsburg

1559 Melanchthon drafts *School Code of Württemberg*

| 1540 | 1550 | 1560 | 1570 |

Independence and the Constitution embodied such Enlightenment principles as the natural rights of life, liberty, and pursuit of happiness, and republican government free from absolutism. The discussion of the influence of the Enlightenment on education is continued in Chapter 4, Pioneers of Teaching and Learning, and Chapter 5, Historical Development of American Education.

SUMMING UP

1. The skills and tools of preliterate societies helped them survive in an often-hostile environment. To ensure a group's survival, adults passed on these skills to their children. Through the stories, songs, and myths, these societies transmitted their cultural beliefs and values to the young. The use of an oral tradition remains an important part of education as individuals and groups are encouraged to tell their stories.

2. Educators in ancient China, especially Confucius, sought to use education to promote social and political harmony. Confucius devised a hierarchical system of ethics in which every member of society had particular duties and responsibilities that they were expected to fulfill. Children knew exactly was what expected of them. Confucianism remains an important cultural and educational influence in contemporary China, Japan, Korea, and Singapore, as well as for many Asian Americans.

3. The ancient Egyptians developed hieroglyphics, a script that enabled them to record their knowledge of medicine, embalming, engineering, and their religious beliefs about the afterlife. The need for literate officials led to the development of scribal schools where teachers taught reading and writing.

4. The ancient Hebrews developed the religious concept of monotheism, a belief in one God as Creator of the world. This concept was shared by other religions such as Christianity and Islam. It became part of the Judeo-Christian tradition that has influenced Western, including American, culture.

5. Many Western and American ideas about education, especially the liberal arts and sciences, originated in ancient Greece and Rome. Socrates, Plato, Aristotle, and Isocrates developed concepts of the educated person, rational inquiry, freedom of thought, and the ideal of liberal education. The concept and methods of rhetorical education were devised by the Sophists, refined by Isocrates, and further developed by the Roman rhetorician Quintilian.

6. Scholastic educators in the Middle Ages sought to reconcile Christian doctrines and scriptures with Greek and Roman classical learning, especially Aristotle's philosophy. The idea of the university as an institution of higher education originated in the medieval universities of Paris, Bologna, Oxford, and Cambridge.

7. Islamic scholars made advances in medicine and mathematics that were transmitted to Western educators. They also

TIMELINE
THE ENLIGHTENMENT

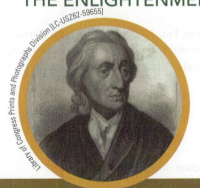

Library of Congress Prints and Photographs Division [LC-USZ62-59655]

1690	1700	1710	1720	1730

1690 Locke's *Two Treatises on Government* published

translated some works of Aristotle that were used by the Scholastics in the Middle Ages. To interpret the contemporary global situation and its tensions, teachers need to understand Islam's world significance.

8. Renaissance educators shifted the emphasis from theology to a more humanist-centered literature. They founded humanist schools that taught the Greek and Latin classics. Their educational imprint persisted until the end of the nineteenth century as the classical languages dominated secondary schools and college entry examinations.

9. Because Protestant reformers such as Luther and Calvin emphasized Bible reading, more students, both girls and boys, attended a growing number of primary schools conducted in vernacular languages. To ensure their conformity to denominational doctrines, teachers were supervised by church and state officials.

10. The Enlightenment's emphasis on nature and science contributed to the entry of science courses in the curriculum and to teaching methods based on children's stages of natural development.

SUGGESTED RESOURCES

INTERNET RESOURCES

For education in preliterate societies, access the PROJECT–History of Education–Education in Preliterate Societies website.

For an essay on children and youth in ancient China, access the Children and Youth in History website.

For the Chinese imperial examination system, access the Society for Anglo-Chinese Understanding (SACU) website.

For a discussion of "Greek Thought: Socrates, Plato, and Aristotle," access The History Guide website.

For a discussion of ancient Greek philosophy, access the Internet Encyclopedia of Philosophy website.

For a discussion of Islam, access the Foundation for Islamic Education website.

For a discussion and sources of Aquinas and Thomist philosophy, visit the Aquinas Online website.

For resources on Cicero, access The Cicero Homepage website.

For a list of extensive topics on ancient Jewish history, access the Jewish Virtual Library website.

For Confucius's life, philosophy, and educational ideas, go to the Stanford Encyclopedia of Philosophy website.

PUBLICATIONS

Altman, William H. F. *Plato the Teacher: The Crisis of the Republic*. Lanham, MD: Lexington Books, 2012. *Discusses Plato's educational ideas in terms of the Republic, politics, and community.*

Baines, John. *Visual and Written Culture in Ancient Egypt*. New York: Oxford University Press, 2007. *An examination of the visual and written aspects of Egyptian culture, with a discussion of writing and scribal culture.*

Barrow, Robin. *Plato and Education*. New York: Routledge, 2014. *Provides a comprehensive analysis of the implications of Plato's philosophy for education.*

Black, Robert. *Humanism and Education in Medieval and Renaissance Italy: Tradition and Innovation in Latin Schools from the Twelfth to the Fifteenth Century*. Cambridge, UK: Cambridge University Press, 2007. *Discusses the history of the Italian Renaissance in its intellectual, philosophical, and political context.*

Botticini, Maristella, and Eckstein, Zvi. *The Chosen Few: How Education Shaped Jewish History, 70-1492*. Princeton, NJ: Princeton University Press, 2012. *Examines the importance of literacy and education in the Jewish tradition.*

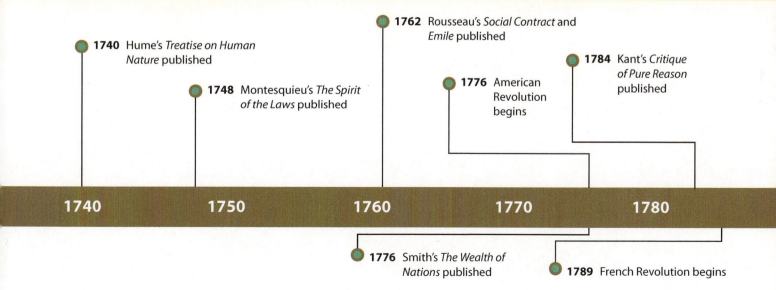

1740 Hume's *Treatise on Human Nature* published

1748 Montesquieu's *The Spirit of the Laws* published

1762 Rousseau's *Social Contract* and *Emile* published

1776 American Revolution begins

1784 Kant's *Critique of Pure Reason* published

1740 **1750** **1760** **1770** **1780**

1776 Smith's *The Wealth of Nations* published

1789 French Revolution begins

Cribiore, Rafaella. *Gymnastics of the Mind: Greek Education in Hellenistic and Roman Egypt.* Princeton, NJ: Princeton University Press, 2005. *Provides an analysis of the transference of Greek education to Egypt.*

De Bary, William Theodore. *Confucian Tradition and Global Education.* New York: Columbia University Press, 2007. *Considers the relevance of Confucianism in the contemporary world, especially to globalization.*

Fergus, Kerr. *Thomas Aquinas: A Very Short Introduction.* New York: Oxford University Press, 2009. *Provides a readable entry into the ideas of the medieval thinker.*

Gardner, Daniel K. *The Four Books: The Basic Teachings of the Later Confucian Tradition.* Indianapolis, IN: Hackett Publishing Co., 2007. *Provides an introduction to the basic Confucian texts.*

Gutek, Gerald. *Historical and Philosophical Foundations of Education: A Biographical Introduction.* Columbus, OH: Pearson, 2011. *Contains essays that provide biographies and discussions of the educational ideas of Confucius, Plato, Aristotle, Aquinas, Erasmus, Calvin, and others in their historical contexts.*

Li, Jin. *Cultural Foundations of Learning: East and West.* Cambridge, UK: Cambridge University Press, 2012. *Provides a comparison of the different approaches to education in Asian and Western cultures.*

MacCulloch, Diarmaid. *The Reformation.* New York: Penguin, 2005. *Examines the major actors and social and intellectual trends of the Reformation.*

Mcdougall, Iain, J. C. Yardley, and Mark Joyal. *Greek and Roman Education: A Source Book.* London: Routledge, 2008. *A comprehensive edition of the major sources of ancient Greek and Roman education.*

Nichols, Aidan. *Discovering Aquinas: An Introduction to His Life, Work and Influence.* Grand Rapids, MI: William B. Eerdmans Publishing, 2002. *Provides a biography and commentary on Thomas Aquinas and his theology and philosophy.*

Nichols, Stephen J. *The Reformation: How a Monk and a Mallet Changed the World.* Wheaton, IL: Crossway Books, 2007. *An engaging account of leading Protestant reformers such as Luther, Zwingli, and Calvin.*

Oldstone-Moore, Jennifer. *Confucianism.* Oxford and New York: Oxford University Press, 2002. *A highly readable account of Confucius and his ethical system.*

Pedersen, Olaf. *The First Universities: Studium Generale and the Origins of University Education in Europe:* Cambridge, UK: Cambridge University Press, 2009. *Provides a well-researched discussion of how the entry of the liberal arts through the general studies curriculum contributed to the founding of the medieval universities.*

Poulakos, Takis, and David DePew. *Isocrates and Civic Education.* Austin: University of Texas Press, 2009. *A well-done edition of Isocrates's ideas on education.*

Raaijmakers, Janneke. *The Making of the Monastic Community of Fulda, c. 744–c. 900.* New York: Cambridge University Press, 2012. *Offers carefully researched insights into monastic life in the Middle Ages based on the Carolingian era monastery at Fulda.*

Scott, Dominic. *Recollection and Experience: Plato's Theory of Learning and its Successors.* New York: Cambridge University Press, 2007. *An analysis of Plato's "Reminiscence" as a learning theory.*

Silverstein, Adam J. *Islamic History: A Very Short Introduction.* Oxford: Oxford University Press, 2010. *Provides a useful entry to the study of Islamic history and its sources.*

Teegarden, David A. *Death to Tyrants! Ancient Greek Democracy and the Struggle against Tyranny.* Princeton, NJ: Princeton University Press, 2014. *Analyzes how democrats in the Greek poleis devised and implemented antityrannical laws and strategies.*

Tolan, John, Gilles Veinstein, and Henry Laurens. *Europe and the Islamic World: A History.* Princeton, NJ: Princeton University Press, 2013. *Examines the interactions between Islamic and European cultures in historical perspective.*

PIONEERS OF TEACHING AND LEARNING

LEARNING OBJECTIVES

4-1 Describe Comenius's pansophism as a child-centered approach to make schools more humane and ecumenical.

4-2 Discuss Rousseau's proposal for natural education in *Emile* as a challenge to traditional views about knowledge, education, teachers, and children.

4-3 Determine how Pestalozzi's emphasis on educating the whole child reshaped teaching and learning in elementary schools.

4-4 Explain why teachers in the upper grades and high school were so attracted to Herbart's systematizing of instruction.

4-5 Describe Froebel's kindergarten as a liberating movement in early childhood education.

4-6 Comment on Spencer's Social Darwinism as a rationale for individual competition in schools and society.

4-7 Assess Dewey's use of the scientific method in problem solving as a method of instruction.

4-8 Assess Addams's socialized education as a forerunner of multicultural education.

4-9 Discuss how Montessori's training and background contributed to her design of the prepared learning environment.

4-10 Explain how Piaget's theory of stage-based human development changed elementary schools and teaching.

4-11 Appraise Freire's liberation pedagogy as a challenge to the social, political, economic, and educational status quo.

Christopher Futcher/iStockPhoto.com

This chapter was revised by Gerald L. Gutek.

THIS CHAPTER EXAMINES how leading educational pioneers developed new ideas about education. They designed innovative teaching and learning strategies that improved schools, curriculum, and methods of instruction.

Pioneers such as Johann Amos Comenius, Jean-Jacques Rousseau, and Johann Heinrich Pestalozzi challenged traditional concepts of child depravity and passive learning that had long dominated schooling. The **child depravity theory**, claiming that children are born with an inclination to evil, led to authoritarian teaching methods in which teachers used psychological and physical coercion to exorcise the child's presumed willfulness and laziness. In contrast, the educational pioneers asserted the **naturalistic theory** that children are naturally good and that teachers should base instruction on children's natural development, interests, and needs.

Educators such as Friedrich Froebel, Maria Montessori, Herbert Spencer, John Dewey, Jean Piaget, and Paulo Freire argued that (1) education should be aligned with the natural stages of human growth and development, and (2) children learn by interacting with the objects and situations in their everyday environments. Froebel's kindergarten and Montessori's prepared environment proposed bold new vistas for early childhood education. Both Dewey and Piaget emphasized children's explorations and interactions with their environments as the most intelligent and effective way to learn. Herbert Spencer proposed a utilitarian and scientific curriculum to prepare individuals to adapt successfully to their environments. Freire wanted education to raise the consciousness of marginalized people so they could liberate themselves from oppressive social, economic, political, and educational conditions. Johann Herbart devised a method to systematize and structure instruction.

You might think about these pioneers in education as educational mentors from the past who can illuminate your ideas about teaching and learning in the present. A mentor is a significant person whose life, ideas, and behavior serve as a model, or an exemplar, for another person. For example, in Chapter 3, The World Origins of American Education, we saw that Socrates was a mentor for Plato, who, in turn, was Aristotle's mentor. You can relate these pioneers to your own mentors, especially teachers, who shaped your ideas on education and, perhaps, your decision to become a teacher. Then, you can reflect on how the pioneers in this chapter contributed to your ideas about teaching and learning.

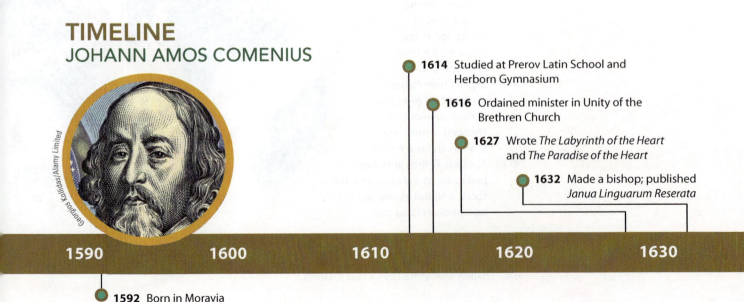

TIMELINE
JOHANN AMOS COMENIUS

Georgios Kollidas/Alamy Limited

1614 Studied at Prerov Latin School and Herborn Gymnasium

1616 Ordained minister in Unity of the Brethren Church

1627 Wrote *The Labyrinth of the Heart* and *The Paradise of the Heart*

1632 Made a bishop; published *Janua Linguarum Reserata*

| 1590 | 1600 | 1610 | 1620 | 1630 |

1592 Born in Moravia

4-1 COMENIUS: PANSOPHISM AS A NEW METHOD

child depravity theory A belief that children, because of their sinful nature, are inclined to be disorderly and lazy and need strict discipline to develop a personal sense of order and civility.

naturalistic theory The educational rationale that education and instruction should be based on the natural stages of human growth and development.

Jan Komensky (1592–1670), or Johann Comenius, was born in the Moravian town of Nivnitz, which is now in the Czech Republic.[1] He lived during Europe's post-Reformation religious wars between Catholics and Protestants—a time of intense sectarian violence. He was a bishop and educator of the Moravian Brethren, a small, often persecuted, Protestant church. Religious persecution forced Comenius to flee his homeland and live as a refugee in other countries. Working to end religious intolerance, he constructed a new educational philosophy, *pansophism,* to cultivate universal understanding. A pioneering peace educator, Comenius believed that universally shared knowledge would convince people to renounce their ethnic and religious hatreds and live harmoniously in a peaceful world order.[2]

Comenius was a transitional figure between the Renaissance humanist educators discussed in Chapter 3, The World Origins of American Education, and the naturalist reformers examined in this chapter (Photo 4.1). Comenius's sensory method of teaching, rather than passive memorization, inspired later educators such as Rousseau, Pestalozzi, Montessori, and Dewey. Because Latin was still an important language in education, he wrote *Gate of Tongues Unlocked,* which related teaching Latin to the students' own spoken vernacular language. Lessons began with short, simple phrases and gradually moved to longer, more complex sentences. The innovative Comenius wrote and illustrated the early picture book, *The Visible World in Pictures,* as a teaching aid.[3]

4-1a Principles of Teaching and Learning

Comenius rejected the child depravity doctrine that children were inherently bad and that teachers needed to use corporal punishment to discipline them. Instead, he wanted teachers to be caring persons who respected children's dignity and created engaging

[1] For biographies of Comenius, see Will S. Monroe, *Comenius: And the Beginnings of Educational Reform* (London: Forgotten Books, 2012) and M. W. Keatinge, *The Historical Life of John Amos Comenius* (Whitefish, MT: Kessinger Publishers, 2007).

[2] Johann Comenius, *The Labyrinth of the World and the Paradise of the Heart,* translated and introduced by Howard Louthan and Andrea Sterk (New York: Paulist Press, 1998), pp. 17–26. Also, access *The Labyrinth of the World and the Paradise of the Heart* at The Online Books Page at **http://onlinebooks.library.upenn.edu.** Reprints of Comenius's works are M. W. Keatinge, *The Great Didactic of John Amos Comenius* (Whitefish, MT: Kessinger Publishers, 2012); Comenius, *Orbis Pictus* (Whitefish, MT: Kessinger Publishers, 2007); Comenius, *School of Infancy,* Will S. Monroe ed. (London: FB&c Ltd. Forgotten Books, 2012); Comenius, *Why God Gives Children and In What Parents Ought to Educate Them* (Whitefish, MT: Kessinger Publishers, 2010).

[3] For a brief biography and excerpt from Comenius's *Great Didactic,* see Madonna M. Murphy, *The History and Philosophy of Education: Voices of Educational Pioneers* (Upper Saddle River, NJ: Pearson/Merrill/Prentice Hall, 2006), pp. 150–156.

1642 In England, in Sweden, and Prussia

1648 Publishes *Lux in Tenebris*

1655–1656 Lives in Amsterdam

1655 Publishes *Opera Didactica*

1658 Publishes *Orbis Pictus*

1670 Death in Amsterdam

1640   1650   1660   1670   1680

> **PHOTO 4.1** Illustrations of panels in Comenius's *Orbis Pictus*, which depict the work of the scientist, theologian, and educator.

Interfoto/Personalities/Alamy

and pleasant classrooms. An early advocate of learning readiness, Comenius warned against hurrying or pressuring children. He believed children learn most efficiently when they are developmentally ready to learn a particular skill or subject. Teachers should calibrate lessons to children's natural stages of development. He advised teachers to organize their lessons into easily assimilated small steps that made learning gradual, cumulative, and pleasant.

The following Comenian principles apply to the preservice preparation of teachers and to classroom practice: (1) use objects or pictures to illustrate concepts; (2) organize lessons around students' everyday experience; (3) be clear and direct in presenting material; (4) emphasize the general aspect rather than the details in a lesson; (5) extend children's horizons by emphasizing that we live in an environment shared with plants, animals, and other people; (6) present lessons in sequence, stressing one thing at a time; (7) do not leave a specific skill or subject until students thoroughly

TIMELINE
JEAN-JACQUES ROUSSEAU

Georgios Kollidas/Shutterstock.com

1728 Supported by patroness Madame de Warens

1743 Secretary at French embassy in Venice

1739 Tutor to sons of Jean Bonnot de Mably in Lyon

1710   **1720**   **1730**   **1740**

1712 Born in Geneva, Switzerland

1745 Begins relationship with Therese Levasseur

understand it.[4] Comenius's emphasis on children's readiness, using concrete objects, and proceeding gradually in instruction became an integral part of preservice teacher-education programs.

4-1b Education and Schooling

Comenius, a pioneer in multicultural and peace education, respected religious and cultural diversity but also believed all persons were members of a common human family. He believed that schooling, by cultivating universal knowledge and values, could promote international understanding and peace and create a nonviolent world.

An innovator, Comenius used the technological inventions of his time, such as the printing press, to diffuse his ideas. He also wrote textbooks that included illustrations.

4-1c Influence on Educational Practices Today

Comenius advised teachers against rushing or pressuring children to learn things they weren't ready for and to create pleasant and caring classroom climates.

He wanted teachers to:

- Respect universal human rights and children's dignity as persons.
- Recognize children's stages of development and learning readiness.
- Use objects and pictures to encourage children to use their senses in learning.

FOCUS Why did Comenius create a new model of the school? What features of contemporary schools would Comenius favor, and which would he try to reform? In your educational experience, were there teachers who used Comenius's principles? Do you plan to include Comenius's ideas in your teaching?

4-2 ROUSSEAU: EDUCATING THE NATURAL CHILD

Jean-Jacques Rousseau (1712–1778) was a Swiss-born French theorist who lived during the eighteenth-century Enlightenment, which influenced the American and French Revolutions.[5] He was among the Parisian intellectuals who questioned the authority of the established church and absolute monarchy. (For more on the Enlightenment, see Chapter 3, The World Origins of American Education.)

---

[4]Gerald L. Gutek, *Historical and Philosophical Foundations of Education: Selected Readings* (Columbus, OH: Merrill, 2001), pp. 50–57.

[5]For Rousseau's life and ideas, see Jean-Jacques Rousseau, *Confessions,* Patrick Coleman, ed., and Angela Scholar, trans (New York: Oxford University Press, 2000); Rousseau and Russell Gaulbourne, *Reveries of the Solitary Walker* (New York: Oxford University Press, 2011); David Gauthier, *Rousseau: The Sentiment of Existence* (Cambridge, UK: Cambridge University Press, 2006); Robert Walker, *Rousseau: The Age of the Enlightenment* (Princeton: Princeton University Press, 2012); Leo Damrosch, *Jean-Jacques Rousseau: Restless Genius* (New York: Houghton Mifflin, 2007).

1755 Publishes *Discourse on the Origin and Foundations of Inequality among Men*

1762 Publishes *The Social Contract* and *Emile*

| 1750 | 1760 | 1770 | 1780 |

1750 Writes essay "Has the Progress of the Arts and Sciences Contributed More to the Corruption or Purification of Morals?"

1778 Death

OVERVIEW 4.1

EDUCATIONAL PIONEERS

Pioneer	Historical Context	Purpose of Education	Curriculum
Comenius 1592–1670 (Czech)	Seventeenth-century religious war following Protestant Reformation	Relate instruction to children's natural growth and development; contribute to peace and social justice	Vernacular language, reading, writing, mathematics, religion, history, Latin; universal knowledge
Rousseau 1712–1778 (Swiss-French)	Eighteenth-century French Enlightenment	Create learning environments in which children's natural goodness can grow	Nature; the environment
Pestalozzi 1747–1827 (Swiss)	Early nineteenth century, post-Napoleonic period and early industrialism	Develop the human being's moral, mental, and physical powers harmoniously; use sense perception in forming clear ideas	Object lessons; form, number, sound (name)
Herbart 1776–1841 (German)	Mid-nineteenth-century developments in European philosophy and psychology	Develop multiple interests and moral character	Academic and humanistic studies, especially history and literature
Froebel 1782–1852 (German)	Nineteenth-century resurgence of philosophical idealism and nationalism	Develop the latent spiritual essence of the child in a prepared environment	Songs, stories, games, gifts, occupations
Spencer 1820–1903 (English)	Darwin's theory of evolution in 1859 and rise of nineteenth-century industrial corporations	Provide competitive situations in which the most able are rewarded	Practical, scientific, and applied subjects
Dewey 1859–1952 (American)	Early twentieth-century American progressive movement, growth of science, and rise of pragmatic philosophy	Contribute to the individual's personal, social, and intellectual growth	Making and doing; history and geography; science; problems
Addams 1860–1935 (American)	First half of twentieth century, period of massive immigration and urban change	Assimilate immigrants into American society while preserving their ethnic cultural heritages	Wide range of practical skills for life in urban centers, along with arts and sciences, and problem solving
Montessori 1870–1952 (Italian)	Late nineteenth- and early twentieth-century assertion of feminism; greater attention to early childhood education	Assist children's sensory, physical, and intellectual development in a prepared environment	Motor and sensory skills; preplanned materials
Piaget 1896–1980 (Swiss)	Twentieth-century developments in psychology by Freud, Hall, Jung, and others	Structure instruction on children's patterns of growth and stages of development	Concrete and formal operations
Freire 1921–1997 (Brazilian)	Late twentieth-century critique of neocolonialism and globalism	Raise consciousness about exploitative conditions	Literary circles and critical dialogues

Methods of Instruction	Role of the Teacher	Significance	Influence on Today's Schools
Based on readiness and stages of human growth; gradual, cumulative, orderly; use of objects	A permissive facilitator of learning; calibrates instruction to child's stages of development	Developed a more humane view of the child; educational method incorporating sensation	Schools organized according to children's stages of development
Reliance on sensation; experience with nature	Assists nature, rather than imposing social conventions on the child	Led a Romantic revolt against the doctrine of child depravity; a forerunner of child-centered progressivism	Permissive teaching based on child freedom
Reliance on sensation; object lessons; simple to complex; near to far; concrete to abstract	Acts as a caring facilitator of learning by creating a homelike school environment; skilled in using the special method	Devised an educational method that introduced object teaching and sensory learning in elementary schools	Schooling based on emotional security and object learning
Systematic organization of instruction: preparation, presentation, association, generalization, application	A well-prepared professional who follows the prescribed sequence in teaching	Devised an education method that stressed sequential organization of instruction and moral character development	Teacher preparation based on a prescribed method and entry of history and literature into curriculum as a moral core
Self-activity; play; imitation	Facilitates children's growth	Created the kindergarten, a special early childhood learning environment	Preschools designed to liberate the child's creativity
Reliance on sensation and the scientific method; activities	Organizes instruction in basic activities	A leading curriculum theorist who stressed scientific and applied knowledge	Schooling that stresses scientific knowledge and competitive values
Problem solving according to the scientific method	Creates a learning environment based on learners' shared experiences	Developed the pragmatic experimentalist philosophy of education	Schooling that emphasizes problem solving and activities in a context of community
Begin with learner's neighborhood, culture, and needs; lead to broader social realities and connections	Engages in a reciprocal or mutual learning experience with students	Developed a progressive theory of urban and multicultural education	Respect for multicultural pluralism in a shared American cultural context
Spontaneous learning; activities; practical, sensory, and formal skills; exercises for practical life	Acts as a director of learning by using didactic materials in a prepared environment	Developed a widely used method and philosophy of early childhood education	Early childhood schooling that is intellectually and developmentally stimulating
Individualized programs; exploration and experimentation with concrete materials	Organizes instruction according to stages of cognitive development	Formulated a theory of cognitive development	Schooling organized around cognitive developmental stages
Use of personal and group autobiographies	Stimulates awareness of real conditions of life	Formulated a theory and praxis of critical consciousness	Influenced critical theory and liberation pedagogy

Rousseau's *On the Origin of the Inequality of Mankind* and *The Social Contract* condemned social inequalities based on birth, wealth, and property.[6] In the original state of nature, Rousseau asserted, people were "noble savages," who were innocent, free, and uncorrupted by socioeconomic artificialities. Rousseau is often criticized for his personal inconsistency regarding children. Although he championed children's rights in his books, he abandoned his own children in orphanages instead of rearing and educating them himself.

Rousseau conveyed his educational philosophy in 1762 through his novel *Emile*, the story of a boy's education from infancy to adulthood.[7] Rousseau's highly controversial novel rejected the principle that education should socialize the child. Attacking the child-depravity doctrine and book-dominated education, he argued that children's instincts and needs are naturally good and should be satisfied rather than repressed by authoritarian schools and coercive teachers. He wanted to liberate people from society's imprisoning institutions, of which the school was one of the most coercive, in that it prepared people to accept the restrictions imposed by other institutions.

4-2a Principles of Teaching and Learning

Like Comenius, Rousseau emphasized the crucial importance of stages of human development. In *Emile*, he identified five developmental stages: infancy, childhood, boyhood, adolescence, and youth. Each stage is sequential, exhibiting its own conditions for readiness to learn and leading to the next stage.[8] To preserve the child's natural goodness, a tutor homeschools Emile on a country estate away from the conformity and role-playing of artificial and corrupt society and schools. Homeschooling is preferred to schools that miseducate children to follow social conventions rather than their own natural instincts.

In Rousseau's first stage, infancy (birth to age 5), his fictional character, Emile, constructs his initial impressions about reality; he learns directly by using his senses to examine the objects in his environment.

During childhood (from age 5 to 12), Emile constructs his own personal self-identity as he learns that his actions cause either painful or pleasurable consequences. Naturally curious, Emile continues to use his senses to learn more about the world. Calling the eyes, ears, hands, and feet the first teachers, Rousseau judged learning through sensation to be much more effective than teaching children words they do not understand. The tutor deliberately refrains from introducing books at this stage so Emile will not substitute reading for direct experience with nature.

During boyhood (from age 12 to 15), Emile learns natural science by observing how plants and animals grow. He learns geography by directly exploring his surroundings rather than from studying maps. Emile also learns a manual trade, carpentry, to connect mental and physical work.

When he reaches adolescence (from age 15 to 18), Emile is ready to learn about the broader world of society, politics, art, and commerce. Visits to museums, theaters, art galleries, and libraries cultivate his aesthetic tastes. During the last stage

---

[6]Jean-Jacques Rousseau, *Discourse on Political Economy and the Social Contract* (trans. Christopher Betts) (New York: Oxford University Press, 2009); Joshua Cohen, *Rousseau: A Free Community of Equals* (New York: Oxford University Press, 2010); Ethan Putterman, *Rousseau, Law, and the Sovereignty of the People* (Cambridge, UK: Cambridge University Press, 2010); Christie McDonald and Stanley Hoffman, *Rousseau and Freedom* (Cambridge, UK: Cambridge University Press, 2010).

[7]Jean-Jacques Rousseau, *Emile, or on Education* (includes Emile and Sophie; or the Solitaries). Christopher Kelly ed., Allan Bloom, trans. (Lebanon, NH: Dartmouth College Press, 2009); Jean-Jacques Rousseau, *Emile,* with an introduction by Gerald L. Gutek (New York: Barnes and Noble, 2005). For a critique of *Emile* by a contemporary of Rousseau, see H. S. Gerdil, *The Anti-Emile: Reflections on the Theory and Practice of Education against the Principles of Rousseau* (South Bend, IN: St. Augustine Press, 2011).

[8]Christopher Winch, "Rousseau on Learning: A Re-Evaluation," *Educational Theory* (Fall 1996), pp. 424–425. For a commentary on the role of parents and the state in education, see Laurence B. Reardon, *The State as Parent: Locke, Rousseau, and the Transformation of the Family* (Scranton, PA: University of Scranton Press, 2011).

of education (from age 18 to 20), Emile visits Paris and Europe's major cities to broaden himself intellectually and culturally. After he meets his future wife, Sophie, Emile tells his tutor as the book ends that he plans to educate his children just as he was educated, according to nature.

4-2b Education and Schooling

Rousseau was suspicious of schools, which he believed taught children to conform to society's artificial rules rather than live spontaneously according to nature. School-induced socialization forced children into the routines and the roles adults preferred instead of letting them follow their own natural instincts, interests, and needs.[9] By forcing children to memorize books, traditional teachers thwarted the child's own power to learn from direct experience. Emile, a child of nature, expresses rather than represses his natural instincts and impulses. If pleasure is enjoyed, Emile earned his reward. If his actions cause pain, Emile brought these consequences upon himself. Either way, he learned from the experience. Rousseau highlighted the following principles in his philosophy of education: (1) childhood is the natural foundation for future human growth and development; (2) children's natural interests and instincts will lead to a thorough exploration of the environment; (3) human beings go through necessary stages of development in their life cycles; and (4) adult coercion negatively impacts children's development.

4-2c Influence on Educational Practices Today

Although his critics disparage the story of Emile's education as an impractical story of a fictitious student and teacher relationship, Rousseau has influenced modern education. His argument that the curriculum should be based on children's interests and needs profoundly affected child-centered progressive educators. (See Chapter 6, Philosophical Roots of Education, for more on progressive education.) Rousseau's ideas also anticipated constructivism, in which children interpret their own reality rather than learn information from indirect sources. Despite his distrust of schools, Rousseau's insights—that teachers should follow children's interests and that children should learn from their direct interaction with the environment—have shaped preservice preparation and classroom practice.

FOCUS How did Rousseau's ideas about nature and society shape his philosophy of education? Why did he prefer home schooling to institutionalized learning? In your educational experience, were there teachers who used Rousseau's principles? Do you plan to incorporate Rousseau's ideas in your teaching?

4-3 PESTALOZZI: EDUCATING THE WHOLE CHILD'S MIND, BODY, AND EMOTIONS

The Swiss educator Johann Heinrich Pestalozzi (1747–1827) lived in the early stage of Western industrialization when factory-made products were beginning to replace handicrafts. More children were working as poorly paid laborers in mines and factories.[10] Concerned about the negative impact of this economic change on families and children, Pestalozzi sought to develop schools that, like loving families, would nurture children's holistic development. His ideas remain viable as globalization impacts families and children, especially in economically developing countries. An attentive reader

---

[9]Eugene Iheoma, "Rousseau's Views on Teaching," *Journal of Educational Thought* 31 (April 1997), pp. 69–81.

[10]For Pestalozzi's educational novel, see Johann Heinrich Pestalozzi, *Leonard and Gertrude* (Toronto: University of Toronto Libraries, 2011); for Pestalozzi's worldwide influence on education, see Daniel Tröhler, *Pestalozzi and the Educationalization of the World* (New York: Palgrave Macmillan, 2013); for a brief biography and excerpts from Pestalozzi's *Diary* and *Methods,* see Madonna M. Murphy, *The History and Philosophy of Education: Voices of Educational Pioneers* (Upper Saddle River, NJ: Pearson/Merrill/Prentice Hall, 2006), pp. 179–186.

of *Emile*, Pestalozzi agreed with Rousseau that humans are naturally good but were spoiled by a corrupt society, that traditional schools imposed dull routines of memorization and recitation, and that educational reform was needed to improve society.[11] Although Rousseau inspired him, Pestalozzi significantly revised Rousseau's method. While Rousseau rejected schools, Pestalozzi believed that schools, if properly organized, could become centers of effective learning. He reconstituted Rousseau's homeschool approach into simultaneous group instruction in schools.

In his schools at Burgdorf and Yverdon, Pestalozzi developed a preservice teacher-education program where he served as a mentor to the future teachers being trained in his method. Like Comenius, Pestalozzi emphasized the right of children to be taught by caring teachers in a safe environment.[12]

Philosophically, Pestalozzi, a realist like Aristotle, believed that the mind formed concepts by abstracting data conveyed to it by the senses. His method of object-centered instruction influenced Froebel and Montessori, discussed later in this chapter, as well as later progressive educators. (See Chapter 6, Philosophical Roots of Education, for more on realism and progressivism.)

4-3a Principles of Teaching and Learning

Pestalozzi organized his approach to teaching into "general" and "special" methods. The general method, which had to be in place before more specific instruction occurred, sought to create a caring and emotionally healthy homelike school environment. This required teachers who, emotionally secure themselves, could win students' trust and affection and nurture their self-esteem.

After the general method was in place, Pestalozzi implemented his special method, which stressed direct sensory learning. Guided by Rousseau's warnings against highly abstract lessons that were remote from children's everyday life, Pestalozzi began instruction with children's direct experiences in their environment. In this approach,

---

[11]Gerald L. Gutek, *Pestalozzi and Education* (Prospect Heights, IL: Waveland Press, 1999), pp. 21–51.
[12]Johann Heinrich Pestalozzi, *How Gertrude Teaches Her Children* (Ann Arbor, MI: University of Michigan Library, 2009).

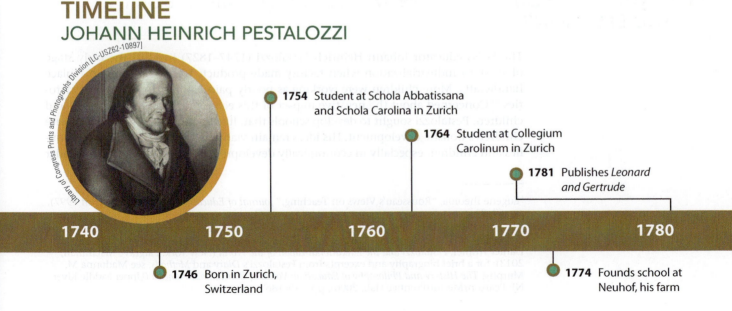

TIMELINE
JOHANN HEINRICH PESTALOZZI

Library of Congress Prints and Photographs Division [LC-USZ62-10897]

1754 Student at Schola Abbatissana and Schola Carolina in Zurich

1764 Student at Collegium Carolinum in Zurich

1781 Publishes *Leonard and Gertrude*

| 1740 | 1750 | 1760 | 1770 | 1780 |

1746 Born in Zurich, Switzerland

1774 Founds school at Neuhof, his farm

Library of Congress Prints and Photographs Division [LC-US262-41995]

> **PHOTO 4.2** Pestalozzi teaching students at his institute in Burgdorf, Switzerland; note the large wall charts used in teaching counting and arithmetic.

object lesson A method developed by Johann Heinrich Pestalozzi, who used concrete objects as the basis of form, number, and name lessons.

children studied the objects—plants, rocks, animals, and man-made items—they encountered in their daily experience in the environment.

Pestalozzi devised **object lessons** in which children learned the form, number, and names of objects. To learn an object's form, they traced, outlined, and sketched its shape. To learn numbers, they counted the objects. Then they learned the names given to objects. The students moved gradually from drawing exercises to writing and reading. The first writing exercises consisted of drawing lessons in which the children drew a series of rising and falling strokes and open and closed curves. Developing children's motor coordination and hand muscles, these drawing and tracing exercises prepared them for writing. From counting exercises, they moved to adding, subtracting, multiplying, and dividing objects (Photo 4.2).

Pestalozzi incorporated the following strategies in his preservice teacher-preparation program. Teachers should (1) begin with concrete objects before moving to more abstract concepts; (2) begin with the learner's immediate environment before moving to what is distant and remote; (3) begin with easy and simple exercises before moving to complex ones; and (4) always proceed gradually and cumulatively. Pestalozzi's method was incorporated into elementary schools and teacher-education programs in Europe and the United States.

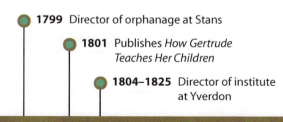

1799 Director of orphanage at Stans

1801 Publishes *How Gertrude Teaches Her Children*

1804–1825 Director of institute at Yverdon

1790	1800	1810	1820	1830

1800–1804 Director of institute at Burgdorf

1827 Death at Neuhof

4-3b Education and Schooling

Both Rousseau and Pestalozzi defined "knowing" as understanding nature, its patterns, and its laws. Pestalozzi stressed empirical, or sensory, learning, through which children learn about their environment by carefully observing natural phenomena. Like Comenius, Pestalozzi believed children should learn gradually, not be hurried, and should understand what they are studying before moving on to the next lesson.

Educating Children with Special Needs   Pestalozzi was dedicated to teaching children with special needs. He opened his schools to children who were poor and hungry victims of poverty and to those who had social, emotional, and psychological problems. If children came to school without breakfast, he fed them before he attempted to teach them. If they were frightened, he comforted them. For him, a teacher needed to be a caring person as well as an expert in teaching methods. Pestalozzi's principles are applicable to teaching children with special needs as well as children generally.

Influence on Educational Practices Today   Pestalozzi's object lessons were introduced into American elementary schools in the nineteenth century. His emphasis on object lessons anticipated process-based learning. His belief in holistic education stimulated educators to encourage both cognitive and affective learning. Pestalozzi's general method remains highly meaningful for American teachers of at-risk children.[13] His stress on emotional security as a necessary precondition for skill and subject learning anticipated the contemporary emphasis on safe and secure schools that are free of bullying and violence.

FOCUS How did Pestalozzi define the purposes of education? How did he use children's sensory experience with objects in his teaching method? In your educational experience, were there teachers who used Pestalozzi's principles? Do you plan on incorporating Pestalozzian principles in your teaching?

---

[13]Arthur Bruhlmeier, *Head, Heart, and Hand: Education in the Spirit of Pestalozzi* (Cambridge, UK: Open Book Publishers, 2010); Rebecca Wild, *Raising Curious, Creative, Confident Kids: The Pestalozzi Experiment in Child-Based Education* (Boston: Shambhala, 2000). For the introduction of Pestalozzianism in the United States, see Henry Barnard, ed., *Pestalozzi and Pestalozzianism: Life, Education Principles and Methods of John Henry Pestalozzi* (Ann Arbor: University of Michigan University Library/Michigan Historical Reprint Series, 2005).

TIMELINE
JOHANN FRIEDRICH HERBART

Nicku/Shutterstock.com

1776 Born in Oldenburg, Germany

1788 Attends classical gymnasium

| 1700 | 1720 | 1740 | 1760 | 1780 |

1794 Student at University of Jena

4-4 HERBART: SYSTEMATIZING TEACHING

Johann Friedrich Herbart (1776–1841), a German professor of philosophy and psychology, devised an educational method that systematized instruction and encouraged students' moral development. In particular, he used history and literature to construct networks of ideas in students' minds.[14]

4-4a Principles of Teaching and Learning

Herbart defined *interest* as a person's ability to focus on and retain an idea in consciousness. He reasoned that a large mass or network of ideas would generate a great number of interests. Ideas related to each other formed a network, or what he termed an "apperceptive mass," in the mind. Herbart advised teachers to introduce students to an increasing number of ideas and to draw relationships between them.

Concerned with students' character education, Herbart emphasized the humanities, especially history and literature as rich sources of moral values. By studying the lives of great men and women, students could discover how people made their defining moral decisions. Literature provided a framework for placing values into a humanistic perspective. Herbart was influential in bringing history and literature into the secondary-school curriculum at a time when it was dominated by the classical Greek and Latin languages.

4-4b Education and Schooling

Seeking to systematize teaching, Herbart structured instruction into a precise sequence of five steps:

1. Preparation, in which teachers encourage readiness in students to receive the new concept or material they are planning to introduce
2. Presentation, in which teachers clearly identify and present the new concept

---

[14]For a biography and excerpts from Herbart's *Outlines of Educational Doctrine*, see Madonna M. Murphy, *The History and Philosophy of Education: Voices of Educational Pioneers* (Upper Saddle River, NJ: Pearson/Merrill/Prentice Hall, 2006), pp. 194–201. Also, see Andrea R. English, *Discontinuity in Education: Dewey, Herbart, and Education as Transformation* (New York: Cambridge University Press, 2013).

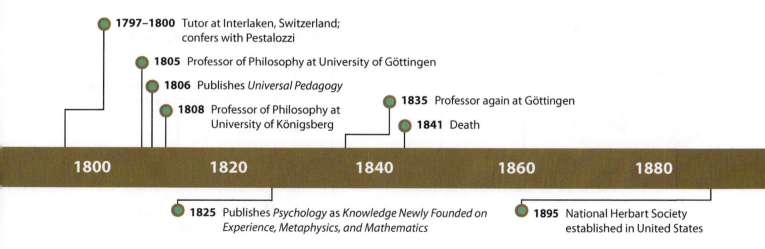

1797–1800 Tutor at Interlaken, Switzerland; confers with Pestalozzi

1805 Professor of Philosophy at University of Göttingen

1806 Publishes *Universal Pedagogy*

1835 Professor again at Göttingen

1808 Professor of Philosophy at University of Königsberg

1841 Death

1800   1820   1840   1860   1880

1825 Publishes *Psychology as Knowledge Newly Founded on Experience, Metaphysics, and Mathematics*

1895 National Herbart Society established in United States

3. Association, in which the new concept is compared and contrasted with ideas that students already know
4. Generalization, in which a principle is formed that combines the new and previous learning
5. Application, in which appropriate examinations and exercises assess whether students have mastered and learned the new principle[15]

4-4c Influence on Educational Practices Today

In the late nineteenth and early twentieth centuries, teacher-preparation programs featured Herbart's method of systematic and sequential instruction, which became especially popular in the United States and Japan. Despite its popularity, John Dewey and progressive educators criticized Herbart's method, claiming that it reduced students to passive receivers of information rather than active learners.

Herbart's method is especially relevant to the No Child Left Behind (NCLB) guidelines that time spent on instruction should be efficient and effective and that students should be tested to assess the degree to which they have mastered skills and subjects. The implications of Herbart's method for teachers today are to (1) clearly identify the skills and concepts they plan to introduce to students; (2) develop well-organized and clearly presented lessons; and (3) test students to verify their comprehension and application of the skills and subjects presented to them.

FOCUS What was Herbart's instructional design? Did his method improve instruction? In your educational experience, were there teachers who used Herbart's principles? Do you plan to incorporate Herbart's method in your teaching?

4-5 FROEBEL: THE KINDERGARTEN MOVEMENT

The German educator Friedrich Froebel (1782–1852) created the *kindergarten*—literally, "children's garden"—a school for early childhood education.[16] Philosophically an idealist, like Plato, Froebel believed an inherent spirituality was at the core of

---

[15]Herbart's original four-step method was restructured by the American Herbartian educators into the five steps generally used in the United States. For more information about the American Herbartians, access "Herbart and the Herbartians" at **www.archive.org**.

[16]Norman Brosterman, *Inventing Kindergarten* (New York: Harry N. Abrams, 1997), pp. 14–18, 22–29. For Froebel's life, see Friedrich Froebel, *Autobiography of Friedrich Froebel,* translated and annotated by Emilie Michaelis and H. Keatley Moore (Memphis, TN: General Books, 2010).

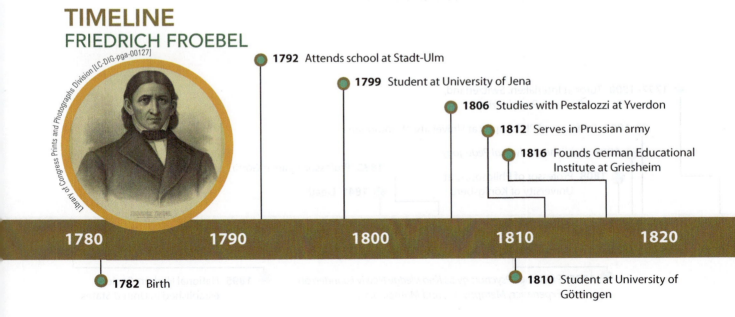

TIMELINE
FRIEDRICH FROEBEL

[LC-DIG-pga-00127]

Library of Congress Prints and Photographs Division

1792 Attends school at Stadt-Ulm

1799 Student at University of Jena

1806 Studies with Pestalozzi at Yverdon

1812 Serves in Prussian army

1816 Founds German Educational Institute at Griesheim

| 1780 | 1790 | 1800 | 1810 | 1820 |

1782 Birth

1810 Student at University of Göttingen

human nature. (For more on idealism, see Chapter 6, Philosophical Roots of Education.) He believed that every child possesses an innate interior spiritual essence, a power, striving to be externalized. Froebel designed his kindergarten as an educational environment in which children could actualize their inherent but latent spirituality through activity. A nationalist, he believed that the people of each country, including his native Germany, shared a common folk spirit that was manifested in the nation's stories, songs, and fables. Thus, storytelling and singing were important in the kindergarten.

Froebel's desire to become a teacher took him to Pestalozzi's institute at Yverdon, where from 1808 to 1810, he interned in the teacher-training program. Pestalozzi served as a mentor for Froebel. Just as Pestalozzi had revised Rousseau's ideas, Froebel restructured Pestalozzi's method. While he endorsed Pestalozzi's use of object teaching in an emotionally secure school atmosphere, Froebel believed that Pestalozzi's method needed a more philosophical foundation. Giving Pestalozzi's object lesson a more symbolic meaning, Froebel claimed that the concrete object would stimulate recall of a corresponding concept in the child's mind. Enthusiastically accepting Pestalozzi's vision of schools as emotionally secure places for children to learn, Froebel added that they should also be places where children grew spiritually. Like Comenius, Rousseau, and Pestalozzi, Froebel envisioned a new kind of teacher who would be sensitive to children's readiness and needs, not pedantic taskmasters who forced children to memorize words they did not understand.

4-5a Principles of Teaching and Learning

Froebel designed the kindergarten as a prepared environment in which children externalized their inner spirituality through activity. His first kindergarten, founded in 1837 at Blankenburg, was a permissive learning environment that featured games, play, songs, stories, and crafts.[17] The kindergarten's activities, now a standard part of early childhood education, stimulated children's imaginations and introduced them to their culture's folk heroes and heroines and values through songs and stories. Play, especially games, socialized children in group activities and developed their physical and motor skills.[18] The curriculum included what Froebel called *gifts*, or objects with fixed form, such as spheres, cubes, and cylinders, intended to bring to consciousness

---

[17]For a brief biography, time line, and excerpt from Froebel's *The Education of Man*, see Madonna M. Murphy, *The History and Philosophy of Education: Voices of Educational Pioneers* (Upper Saddle River, NJ: Pearson/Merrill/Prentice Hall, 2006), pp. 201–209. For an online text of Froebel's *Education of Man*, access **www.archive.org**.

[18]Evelyn Lawrence, ed., *Routledge Library Editions: Education Mini-Set K Philosophy of Education: Friedrich Froebel and English Education*, Vol. 18 (New York and London: Routledge, 2012). For Froebel's *Education of Man, Mother Songs*, and reminiscences, access the Froebel Web at **www.froebelweb.org**.

1837 Establishes kindergarten at Blankenburg

1852 Death

| 1830 | 1840 | 1850 | 1860 | 1870 |

FROM PRESERVICE TO PRACTICE

USING A STORY TO CONNECT THE PAST AND PRESENT

The chapter's author shares a children's book he had written, *My Grandfather Owns a Grocery Store,* with a kindergarten class.

My grandson, Luke, invited me to read my book, *My Grandfather Owns a Grocery Store,* to his kindergarten class. The book was a self-published family project—I wrote the text about my grandparents' neighborhood grocery store where I helped out as a child. My daughters, their husbands, and my grandchildren illustrated the book with drawings and sketches.

The kindergarten class sat in a circle in front of me; I was seated on a stool. I told the children about the book—how I wrote it from childhood memories of my grandparents, their neighborhood grocery store, and how I helped to stock the shelves and arrange the fruit. I would read a page or two, then show them the illustrations and ask them if they had any questions.

I read about how my grandparents opened their store early in the morning so that the women in the neighborhood could buy fresh bread and lunch meat to pack their husbands' and their children's lunches. I explained that when I was a child, many people did not have refrigerators and used iceboxes instead. The children did not know what an icebox was. So, I explained that it was a large wooden chest that contained a large block of ice. I told them that an iceman came on a truck and delivered big blocks of ice to use to keep the food cold

so it wouldn't spoil. I asked them what happens to ice—they said it melts. Then, I asked them if they had refrigerators. They all raised their hands. Some volunteered that they had two refrigerators.

Then I read on and told them how my grandfather showed me how to arrange the cans of beans and peas so that people could see the labels. I told them how I arranged the oranges and apples in pyramids. I asked them what a pyramid is. One child raised his hand and showed the class the shape of a pyramid. I said it was difficult to arrange a pyramid with apples and oranges because they are shaped like balls and will roll away. Then I explained how I made a pyramid.

After the class, my daughter, Laura—who is Luke's mother and an elementary teacher—and I discussed my visit to the kindergarten. She believed that the lesson was positive in that it made a connection with the children's own experiences—all the children had been in large grocery stores somewhat like the smaller neighborhood grocery stores of the past. As a historian of education, I also thought about how Friedrich Froebel would critique my teaching. I think he would approve of the use of a story to build a cultural connection to the children's heritage. I think he would have also approved of my use of the geometric shape, the pyramid, to illustrate how I arranged oranges and apples.

CASE QUESTIONS

1. What aspects of Froebel's kindergarten philosophy did the author use?

2. Would you use Froebel's method if you were teaching the class?

3. Have you had an educational experience like the one in the excerpt?

---

the underlying concept represented by the object. The kindergarten also featured what Froebel called *occupations,* materials children could shape and use in building and construction activities. For example, clay, sand, cardboard, and sticks could be shaped into castles, cities, and mountains.[19]

4-5b Education and Schooling

We often form our first impressions of schools and teachers in kindergarten and carry these ideas with us throughout our lives. Froebel believed the kindergarten teacher's personality to be of paramount importance. Did the teacher really

---

[19]Scott Bultman, *The Froebel Gifts: 1–6 The Solids; The Froebel Gifts: The Building Gifts 2–6* (Grand Rapids, MI: Froebel USA, 2014). For applying Froebel's kindergarten philosophy to contemporary education, see Helen Tovey, *Bringing the Froebel Approach to Your Early Years Practice* (New York and London: Routledge, 2011) and Tina Bruce, ed., *Early Childhood Practice: Froebel Today* (London: Sage Publications, 2012).

understand the child's nature and respect the dignity of the child's personality? Did the teacher personify the highest cultural values so that children had a model they could emulate? Preservice experiences should help teachers become sensitive to children's needs and give them the knowledge and skills to create caring and wholesome learning environments. Froebel encouraged kindergarten teachers to resist contemporary trends to introduce academic subjects into kindergartens as a premature pressure that comes from adults, often parents, rather than children's needs and readiness.[20]

4-5c Influence on Educational Practices Today

Kindergarten education grew into an international movement. German immigrants imported the kindergarten to the United States, where it became part of the American school system. Elizabeth Peabody, who founded an English-language kindergarten, worked to make the kindergarten part of the American school system.[21] Froebel's innovative ideas are now well integrated into American early childhood education.

FOCUS How did Froebel use idealist philosophy in his concept of childhood? Why did he emphasize children's play as contributing to learning? In your educational experience, were there teachers who used Froebel's principles? Do you plan to incorporate Froebel's ideas into teaching?

4-6 SPENCER: SOCIAL DARWINIST AND UTILITARIAN EDUCATOR

Herbert Spencer (1820–1903) was an English social theorist whose ideas were very popular and influential in the United States in the late nineteenth and early twentieth centuries. Spencer based his social and educational philosophy on his interpretation of Charles Darwin's theory of evolution.[22] According to Darwin, species evolved naturally and gradually over long periods of time. Members of certain species survived and reproduced themselves by successfully adapting to changes in the environment. As their offspring inherited these favorable adaptive characteristics, they too survived and continued the life of the species. Those unable to adapt—the unfit—perished.[23]

social Darwinism Spencer's ideology applied Darwin's biological principles of the "survival of the fittest" and competition to individuals in society.

Spencer, a key proponent of **social Darwinism**, applied Darwin's biological theory to society and believed that the fittest individuals of each generation would survive because of their skills, intelligence, and adaptability.[24] For Spencer, competition, a natural ethical force, motivated the best-equipped members of the human species to climb to the top of the socioeconomic ladder. Winning the competitive race over slower and duller individuals, the fittest would inherit the earth and populate it with their intelligent and productive children. The unfit—lazy, stupid, or weak individuals—would slowly disappear. Competition would improve the human race and result in gradual

---

[20]For a discussion of academic pressures on children, see Shama Olfman, *All Work and No Play: How Educational Reforms Are Harming Our Preschoolers* (Westport, CT: Praeger, 2003).

[21]Bertha von Marenholtz-Bulow, *How Kindergarten Came to America: Friedrich Froebel's Radical Vision of Early Childhood Education* (New York and London: The New Press, 2007).

[22]For a succinct and clearly written exposition on Darwin, see Mark Ridley, *How to Read Darwin* (New York: W. W. Norton, 2006).

[23]Charles Darwin, *The Autobiography of Charles Darwin, 1809–1883,* Nora Barlow, ed. (New York: W.W. Norton, 1993); David Quammen, *The Reluctant Mr. Darwin: An Intimate Portrait of Charles Darwin and the Making of His Theory of Evolution* (New York: W.W. Norton, 2007); Charles Darwin, *From So Simple a Beginning: Darwin's Four Great Books (Voyage of the Beagle, The Origin of Species, The Descent of Man, The Expression of Emotions in Man and Animals,* Edward O. Wilson, ed. (New York: W.W. Norton, 2005).

[24]Reprints of Spencer's works are Herbert Spencer, *Essays: Scientific, Political, and Speculative* (London: Routledge/Thoemmes Press, 1996); Spencer, *Essays on Education and Kindred Subjects Everymans Library* (New York: Dutton, 2012); Spencer, *Collected Writings* (London: Routledge/Thoemmes Press, 1996); Spencer, *The Principles of Psychology* (London: Routledge/Thoemmes Press, 1996).

but inevitable progress.[25] Many American educators applied Spencer's ideas of competition to students in their classrooms. Later, Dewey and the progressives fought to replace competition in schools with cooperation.

Spencer believed that schools should compete against each other so that strong academic schools prevailed against inferior ones. He opposed state-funded public schools, which he argued would create a monopoly for mediocrity by catering to the average rather than the gifted students in the school-age population. Private schools, in contrast, as they competed for the most able students, would become centers of educational innovation. Like contemporary proponents of vouchers, Spencer believed the best schools would attract the brightest students and the most capable teachers.

4-6a Principles of Teaching and Learning

utilitarian education The teaching of skills and subjects applicable to daily life, work, and society. Herbert Spencer argued that the subject of most use, or utility, was science.

Spencer defined nature differently than Rousseau and Pestalozzi. To Spencer, nature meant the law of the jungle and survival of the fittest.[26] He believed that people in an industrialized society needed a **utilitarian education** to learn useful scientific and technological skills and subjects. Spencer emphasized science and technology in the curriculum as the best way to prepare individuals to be efficient producers in a competitive industrial society.[27]

4-6b Education and Schooling

Spencer was highly critical of traditional schools because they resisted change and continued to transmit an obsolete curriculum of Latin and Greek languages, literature, and history. In contrast, he wanted teachers to be curriculum and instructional innovators who promoted science and technology in their classrooms. He wanted to modernize the curriculum so that it focused on the physical, biological, and social sciences as well

---

[25]Mark Francis, *Herbert Spencer and the Invention of Modern Life* (Ithaca, NY: Cornell University Press, 2007); Mark Francis and Michael W. Taylor, eds., *Herbert Spencer: Legacies* (London: Routledge, 2015).

[26]For a critique of Spencer, see Kieran Egan, *Getting It Wrong from the Beginning: Our Progressivist Inheritance from Herbert Spencer, John Dewey, and Jean Piaget* (New York: Yale University Press, 2002).

[27]Alberto Mingardi and John Meadowcraft, *Herbert Spencer (Major Conservative and Libertarian Thinker)* (New York: Bloomsbury Academic, 2013).

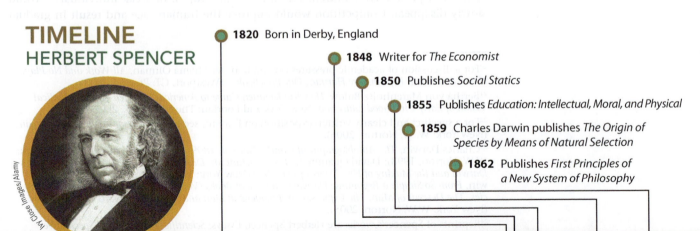

TIMELINE
HERBERT SPENCER

Ivy Close Images / Alamy

1820 Born in Derby, England

1848 Writer for *The Economist*

1850 Publishes *Social Statics*

1855 Publishes *Education: Intellectual, Moral, and Physical*

1859 Charles Darwin publishes *The Origin of Species by Means of Natural Selection*

1862 Publishes *First Principles of a New System of Philosophy*

1800   1820   1840   1860

as applied technology and engineering. Today, he would probably include computer literacy, genetics, and bioengineering in his list of useful subjects.

Developing a rationale used in modern curriculum making, Spencer ranked activities according to the degree that they promoted health, positive social relationships, and economic productivity. He gave science a high priority because individuals could apply it to all of their activities.[28] For example, sciences such as anatomy and physiology explain human growth, especially physical development. Scientific information about nutrition can be applied to a healthy diet. Spencer identified five types of activities to be used in constructing the curriculum: (1) self-preservation activities needed to perform all other activities; (2) occupational or professional activities that enable a person to earn a living; (3) child-rearing activities; (4) social and political participation activities; and (5) leisure and recreation activities.

4-6c Influence on Educational Practices Today

American educators were highly receptive to Spencer's ideas. In 1918, a National Education Association committee, in its landmark *Cardinal Principles of Secondary Education,* reiterated Spencer's list of basic life activities. Contemporary curriculum designers continue to use Spencer's rationale when they organize the curriculum on human needs and activities.

Although social Darwinism dominated American social science and education in the late nineteenth century, John Dewey's experimentalism and progressive reform, which is discussed in the next section, eclipsed it in the early twentieth century. Key social Darwinist ideas reemerged in the 1980s and still continue in the contemporary neoliberal conservative educational agenda, which favors providing vouchers to attend private schools, reducing government's regulatory powers, and an emphasis on teaching market-driven basic skills to increase economic productivity. The standardized testing required in the NCLB (in the Bush administration) and The Race to the Top (RTTT) program (in the Obama administration) uses competition between schools to identify achieving and failing schools and teachers.

Spencer would raise entry standards for students seeking admission to preservice teacher-education programs to make them more competitive. Only the brightest applicants were accepted. The programs would stress science and technology. Ending tenure, teaching would be competitive, with competent teachers replacing incompetent ones, and merit pay would be used in teacher compensation.

----

[28]Michael Taylor, *Philosophy of Herbert Spencer* (New York: Continuum, 2007).

FOCUS How did Spencer borrow ideas from Charles Darwin's theory of evolution? Do you think his emphasis on competition and applied knowledge, such as engineering and technology is appropriate today? In your educational experience, were there teachers who used Spencer's principles? Do you plan to include Spencer's ideas in your teaching?

1896 Publishes *Synthetic Philosophy*

1903 Death

4-7 DEWEY: LEARNING THROUGH EXPERIENCE

John Dewey (1859–1952) developed his pioneering experimentalist philosophy of education in the context of the social, political, scientific, and technological changes taking place in the United States in the twentieth century.[29] Dewey's pragmatic philosophy, which encouraged progressive reforms, incorporated elements of the theories of evolution and relativity. Dewey believed that cooperative group activity enhanced social intelligence, and he rejected Spencer's social Darwinist emphasis on individual competition.[30] (For a discussion of pragmatism, see Chapter 6, Philosophical Roots of Education.)

In 1896, Dewey established his Laboratory School at the University of Chicago. Dewey saw the school as an experimental setting in which educational ideas were tested in classroom practice. He called the school a "miniature society" and an "embryonic community," in which children learned collaboratively by working together to solve problems. Dewey organized the curriculum into constructive, experimental, and creative activities to:

- Develop children's sensory and physical coordination
- Provide opportunities for children to make and do things based on their interests
- Stimulate children to formulate, examine, and test their ideas by acting on them

In Dewey's experimentalist philosophy, using the scientific method to solve problems is the key to both thinking and learning. Problem-solving became the central method of learning at the Laboratory School.[31]

---

[29]For a biography of Dewey, see Jay Martin, *The Education of John Dewey: A Biography* (New York: Columbia University Press, 2002). Also, see Richard Pring, *John Dewey* (London: Bloomsbury Academic, 2014).

[30]For Dewey's relationship to pragmatism, see Louis Menard, *The Metaphysical Club: The Story of Ideas in America* (New York: Farrar, Straus and Giroux, 2001). For Dewey as an American pragmatist, access **www.dewey.pragmatism.org**.

[31]John Dewey, *The Child and the Curriculum* (Toronto: University of Toronto Libraries, 2011). A commentary is Laurel N. Tanner, *Dewey's Laboratory School: Lessons for Today* (New York: Teachers College Press, 1997).

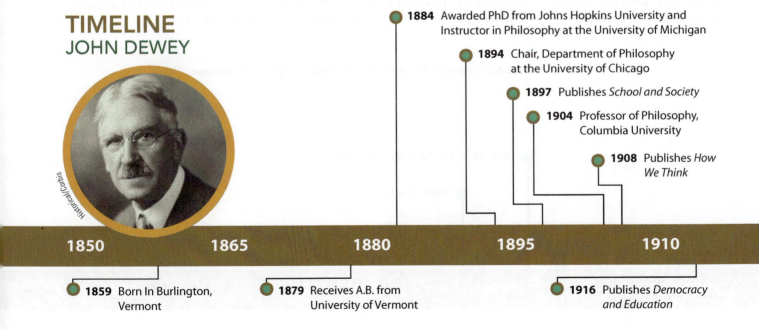

TIMELINE
JOHN DEWEY

Historical/Corbis

1884 Awarded PhD from Johns Hopkins University and Instructor in Philosophy at the University of Michigan

1894 Chair, Department of Philosophy at the University of Chicago

1897 Publishes *School and Society*

1904 Professor of Philosophy, Columbia University

1908 Publishes *How We Think*

| 1850 | 1865 | 1880 | 1895 | 1910 |

1859 Born In Burlington, Vermont

1879 Receives A.B. from University of Vermont

1916 Publishes *Democracy and Education*

4-7a Principles of Teaching and Learning

Dewey's *The Child and the Curriculum* emphasized his central experimentalist principles. Dewey believed that (1) children as socially active human beings are eager to explore their environment; (2) learners encounter personal and social problems as they interact with their environment; (3) these problems stimulate children to use their intelligence to solve the problem and expand their experience in an active, instrumental manner.[32]

scientific method A systematic approach to inquiry in which hypotheses are tested by replicable empirical verification.

Dewey believed the **scientific method** was the most effective process for solving problems. By using the scientific method, children learn how to think reflectively and to direct their experiences in ways that lead to personal and social growth. Dewey designed a method, "The Complete Act of Thought," which he believed facilitated using the scientific method to solve all kinds of life problems. Dewey's method involved a sequence of five steps:

1. Encountering a "problematic situation" that contains something new or different from past experience and that blocks ongoing activity
2. Locating and defining the specific new or different feature that is causing the problem
3. Reflecting on past experience and researching the problem to find information to use in solving it
4. Reflecting on the problem and constructing possible solutions to solve it
5. Testing the possible solution that is most likely to solve the problem to determine if it works[33]

For Dewey, genuine knowledge is not inert information that teachers transmit to students; it is an instrument to solve problems. We use our fund of human knowledge—past ideas, discoveries, and inventions—to frame hypothetical solutions to current problems and then test and reconstruct this knowledge in light of present needs. Because people and their environments constantly change, knowledge, too, is continually reconfigured or reconstructed. After a problem has been solved, its solution enters into past experience and can be used to solve future problems.

4-7b Education and Schooling

For Dewey, education is a social process in which the group's immature members, especially children, learn to share and participate in group life. Through education, children access their cultural heritage and learn to use it in problem solving. Seeing

---

[32]Gregory Pappas, *John Dewey's Ethics: Democracy as Experience* (Bloomington, IN: Indiana University Press, 2008). For Dewey's continuing relevance to contemporary global society, see Jim Garrison, Larry Hickman, and Daisaku Ikeda, *Living as Learning: John Dewey in the 21st Century* (Cambridge, MA: Ikeda Center, 2014).

[33]John Dewey, *Democracy and Education,* with an introduction by Gerald L. Gutek (New York: Barnes and Noble, 2005), pp. 164–65. (Originally published in 1916.)

1938 Publishes *Experience and Education*

1952 Death in New York City

| 1925 | 1940 | 1955 | 1970 | 1985 |

education's sole purpose as social growth, Dewey said, "(i) the educational process has no end beyond itself; it is its own end; and that (ii) the educational process is one of continual reorganizing, reconstructing, transforming."[34]

Dewey's curriculum consists of three levels of learning activities and processes. The first level, "making and doing," engages children in projects in which they explore their environment and act on their ideas. These activities develop sensory and motor skills and encourage socialization through collaborative group projects. The second level, "history and geography," broadens students' concepts of space and time through projects in those areas. The third level, "science," brings students into contact with various subjects such as biology, chemistry, and social studies that they can use as resources in problem solving. These three curricular levels move learning from simple impulses to careful observation of the environment, to planning actions, and finally to reflecting on and testing the consequences of action.

Dewey saw democratic education and schooling as open-ended processes in which students and teachers can test all ideas, beliefs, and values. Opposing the separation of people from each other because of ethnicity, race, gender, or economic class, Dewey believed that democratic communities encourage people to share their experiences to solve common problems.

4-7c Influence on Educational Practices Today

By applying pragmatism to education, Dewey worked to open schools to social reform and change. His ideas about socially expanding children's experience stimulated progressive education, which emphasized children's interests and needs. Today, educators who work for social change and reform are often following Dewey's pioneering educational concepts.[35]

Dewey's influence can be seen in "hands-on" or process-oriented teaching and learning. Dewey would construct the preservice education of teachers on the principles of (1) seeing education in broad social terms, and (2) developing competencies in using the scientific method to solve problems. Practicing teachers would use group activities, collaborative learning, and process-centered strategies in their classrooms.

[34]Ibid., p. 54.

[35]For analyses of Dewey's work in educational philosophy, see Matt Parmental, "The Structure of Dewey's Scientific Ethics," and Eric Bredo, "Understanding Dewey's Ethics," in *Philosophy of Education* (Urbana: Philosophy of Education Society/University of Illinois at Urbana-Champaign, 2000), pp. 143–154. Also, see Douglas J. Simpson, ed., and Sam F Stuck, Jr., ed., *Teachers, Leaders, and Schools: Essays by John Dewey* (Carbondale: Southern Illinois University Press, 2010).

FOCUS   How did Dewey think of the school as an educational laboratory? How did Dewey relate the learner's experience to problem-based learning? In your educational experience, were there teachers who used Dewey's problem-solving methods? Do you plan to include Dewey's experimentalism in your teaching?

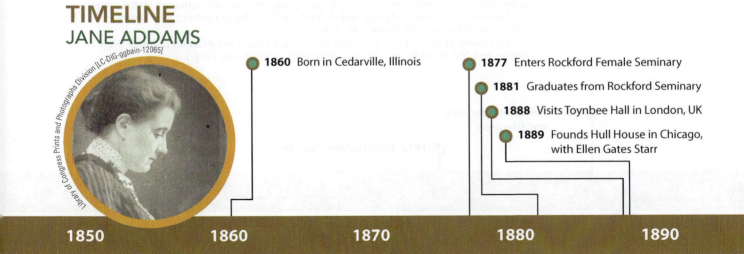

TIMELINE
JANE ADDAMS

Library of Congress Prints and Photographs Division (LC-DIG-ggbain-12065)

1860 Born in Cedarville, Illinois

1877 Enters Rockford Female Seminary

1881 Graduates from Rockford Seminary

1888 Visits Toynbee Hall in London, UK

1889 Founds Hull House in Chicago, with Ellen Gates Starr

| 1850 | 1860 | 1870 | 1880 | 1890 |

4-8 ADDAMS: SOCIALIZED EDUCATION

socialized education Jane Addams's educational philosophy in which the school curriculum includes units on multiculturalism, urbanization, industrialization, technology, and the peaceful resolution of international conflicts.

Jane Addams (1860–1935)—the founder of Hull House and a pioneering leader in social work, the peace movement, and women's rights—developed an educational philosophy called **socialized education**. She based her educational ideas on her efforts to improve the living and working conditions of immigrants in Chicago and to mobilize women to work for social and educational reforms. Addams was a pioneer of multicultural, international, peace, and women's education.

Rebelling against the Victorian era's gender restrictions on women, Addams rejected the traditional curriculum that limited women's educational choices and opportunities.[36] She wanted women to define their own lives, to choose their own careers, and to participate fully in politics, society, and education.[37]

In 1889, Jane Addams established Hull House on Chicago's Near West Side in a culturally diverse but impoverished neighborhood of immigrants from southern and eastern Europe. Addams and her coworkers, a cadre of young middle-class women, educated the immigrants and, in turn, were educated by them. Addams and the women at Hull House learned how the immigrants used their own initiative to survive in a new country. In turn, Hull House provided a settlement house where immigrants learned how to obtain jobs, pay rent, find health care, and educate their children.[38]

4-8a Principles of Teaching and Learning

Because of her work with immigrants in Chicago, Addams saw how urbanization, industrialization, and technology were changing society. She argued that education needed to take on new and broadened social purposes. Teachers needed to understand

---

[36]Victoria Bissell Brown, *The Education of Jane Addams* (Philadelphia: University of Pennsylvania Press, 2004), pp. 72–91.

[37]Jane Addams, *Peace and Bread in Time of War* (Urbana and Chicago: University of Illinois Press, 2002); and Jane Addams, Emily G. Balch, and Alice Hamilton, *Women at The Hague: The International Congress of Women and Its Results* (Urbana and Chicago: University of Illinois Press, 2003).

[38]Biographies of Addams are Allen F. Davis, *American Heroine: The Life and Legend of Jane Addams* (Chicago: Ivan R. Dee, 2000); James W. Linn, *Jane Addams: A Biography* (Urbana and Chicago: University of Illinois Press, 2000); Louise W. Knight, *Jane Addams: Spirit in Action* (New York: W. W. Norton, 2010). For Addams as a writer, see Katherine Joslin, *Jane Addams, a Writer's Life* (Urbana and Chicago: University of Illinois Press, 2004).

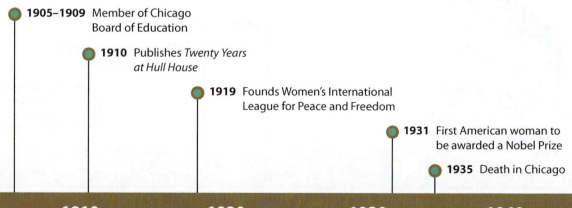

1905–1909 Member of Chicago Board of Education

1910 Publishes *Twenty Years at Hull House*

1919 Founds Women's International League for Peace and Freedom

1931 First American woman to be awarded a Nobel Prize

1935 Death in Chicago

| 1900 | 1910 | 1920 | 1930 | 1940 |

the economic, demographic, and technological trends that were reshaping American society from a rural to an urban society and prepare their students to deal with them in intelligent, socially responsible, and democratic ways.[39]

Believing that multicultural diversity would contribute to America's broad common culture, Addams sought to build connections between immigrants and the larger American society. Addams wanted public schools to feature a multicultural curriculum that included the history, customs, songs, crafts, and stories of ethnic and racial groups.[40]

4-8b Education and Schooling

Addams's socialized education was defined in very broad social, economic, and political terms. She believed schools, like settlement houses, should work to build a sense of community in a country undergoing a profound transition from a rural to an urban industrialized and technological society. She envisioned schools as multifunctional agencies that socialized as well as taught children academic skills and subjects. Teachers, like social workers, had many-faceted responsibilities for their students' social well-being. The curriculum should be reconstituted to provide broadened experiences that explored children's immediate environment and highlighted connections with a technological society.

Addams's enlarged concept of teaching with a social-justice mission has important implications for preservice teacher education. It means that prospective teachers need to examine issues of multiculturalism and social justice in relationship to education and schooling. For practicing teachers, it means that the classroom needs to be connected to the people in the community it serves.

---

[39]Jane Addams, *Democracy and Social Ethics* (Urbana and Chicago: University of Illinois Press, 2002, 1905), pp. 80–97. Also, see Sandra Opdycke, *Jane Addams and Her Vision for America* (New York: Prentice-Hall, 2011).

[40]Jane Addams, *The Spirit of Youth and the City Streets* (New York: Macmillan, 1909), pp. 98–103. Also, see Maurice Harringon, *The Social Philosophy of Jane Addams* (Urbana: University of Illinois Press, 2009).

TIMELINE
MARIA MONTESSORI

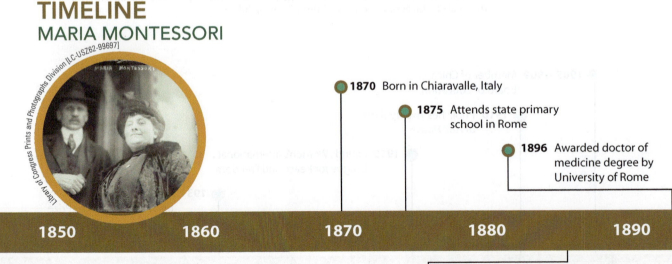

Library of Congress Prints and Photographs Division [LC-USZ62-99697]

1870 Born in Chiaravalle, Italy

1875 Attends state primary school in Rome

1896 Awarded doctor of medicine degree by University of Rome

| 1850 | 1860 | 1870 | 1880 | 1890 |

1886–1889 Studies engineering at a technical institute

4-8c Influence on Educational Practices Today

FOCUS How did Addams's experience in working with immigrants in an urban setting shape her philosophy of socialized education? Do Addams's ideas resonate well with contemporary multiculturalism and women's studies? In your educational experience, were there teachers who used Addams's principles? Do you plan to include elements of her socialized education in teaching?

Addams's belief that education must be free from inherited gender biases corresponds with the goals of contemporary women's education, especially equal rights for women and their freedom to define their lives and choose their careers.

Addams's argument that industrialism should be infused with broad social purposes applies to humanizing the effects of contemporary globalization. For her, technology should contribute to greater communication and sharing rather than generate consumer-oriented materialism and massive corporate profits. Her crusade for a world without war provides a needed message for peace education in a world wracked by violence and terrorism.

4-9 MONTESSORI: THE PREPARED ENVIRONMENT

The Italian educator Maria Montessori (1870–1952) devised an internationally popular method of early childhood education.[41] Like Pestalozzi and Froebel, Montessori recognized that children's early experiences have an important formative and continuing influence on their later lives.

As a pioneering women's educator, Montessori vigorously challenged those who, because of sexist stereotyping, argued that women should be excluded from higher and professional education. Defying the traditional barriers to women's education, Montessori, after an initial rejection, was admitted to the University of Rome and became the first woman in Italy to earn a degree of doctor of medicine.[42]

As a physician, Montessori worked with children categorized as mentally handicapped and psychologically impaired. Her methods with these children proved to be so effective that she concluded they were applicable to all children.

4-9a Principles of Teaching and Learning

In 1908, Maria Montessori established a children's school, the *Casa dei Bambini,* for impoverished children in the slums of Rome. In this school, Montessori designed a

---

[41]Biographies of Montessori are Rita Kramer, *Maria Montessori: A Biography* (Reading, MA: Perseus Books, 1988); and E. M. Standing, *Maria Montessori: Her Life and Work,* introduction by Lee Havis (New York: Plume/Penguin Books, 1998).

[42]For a brief biography and an excerpt from Montessori's *My System of Education,* see Madonna M. Murphy, *The History and Philosophy of Education: Voices of Educational Pioneers* (Upper Saddle River, NJ: Pearson/Merrill/Prentice Hall, 2006), pp. 368–375. For Montessori's educational theory, see Marion O'Donnell, *Maria Montessori* (*Continuum Library of Educational Thought*) (New York: Continuum, 2007), and Angeline S. Lillard, *Montessori: The Science behind the Genius* (New York: Oxford University Press, 2008).

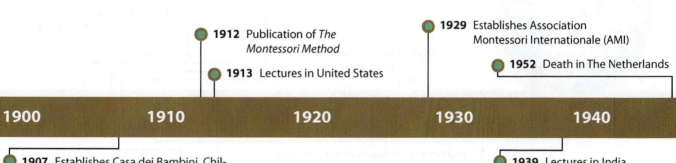

1912 Publication of *The Montessori Method*

1913 Lectures in United States

1929 Establishes Association Montessori Internationale (AMI)

1952 Death in The Netherlands

| 1900 | 1910 | 1920 | 1930 | 1940 |

1907 Establishes Casa dei Bambini, Children's House, in Rome

1939 Lectures in India

specially prepared environment that featured methods, materials, and activities based on her observations of children.[43] She had refined her theory by conducting extensive research on the work of Itard and Seguin, two early pioneers in special education. Contrary to the opinions of many conventional educators, Montessori believed that children possess an inner need to work at what interests them without the prodding of teachers and without being motivated by external rewards and punishments. Children, she found, are capable of sustained concentration and work. Enjoying structure and preferring work to play, they like to repeat actions until they master a given skill. In fact, children's capacity for spontaneous learning leads them to begin reading and writing on their own initiative.

4-9b Education and Schooling

Montessori's curriculum included three major types of activities and experiences: practical, sensory, and formal skills and studies. Children learned to perform such practical activities as setting the table, serving a meal, washing dishes, tying and buttoning clothing, and practicing basic manners and social etiquette. The practical life activities are designed so that children can do them independently of adults. Special exercises were used to develop sensory acuity and muscular and physical coordination. Children learned the alphabet by tracing movable sandpaper letters. They learned to write and then learned to read. They used colored rods of various sizes and cups to learn counting and measuring.

Montessori designed preplanned teaching (*didactic*) apparatus and materials to develop children's practical, sensory, and formal skills. Examples included lacing and buttoning frames, identifying packets by smell, and tracing movable letters. Because they direct rather than control learning in the prepared environment, Montessori educators are called "directresses" rather than "teachers." The directress prepares the

---

[43]Gerald Lee Gutek, ed., *The Montessori Method: The Origins of an Educational Innovation: Including an Abridged and Annotated Edition of Maria Montessori's* The Montessori Method (Lanham, MD: Rowman and Littlefield Publishers, 2004). For a digital copy of the *Montessori Method,* access **www.digital.library.upenn.edu**.

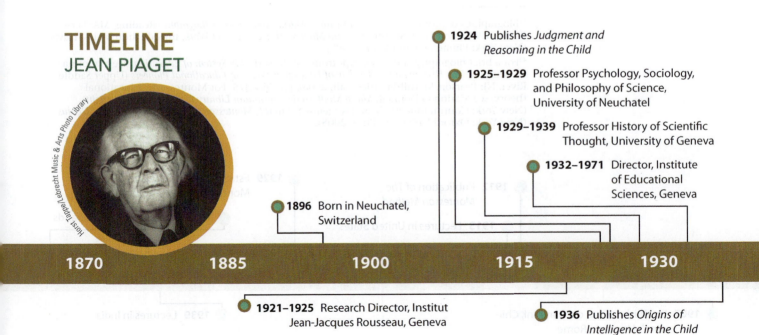

TIMELINE
JEAN PIAGET

Horst Tappe/Lebrecht Music & Arts Photo Library

1896 Born in Neuchatel, Switzerland

1921–1925 Research Director, Institut Jean-Jacques Rousseau, Geneva

1924 Publishes *Judgment and Reasoning in the Child*

1925–1929 Professor Psychology, Sociology, and Philosophy of Science, University of Neuchatel

1929–1939 Professor History of Scientific Thought, University of Geneva

1932–1971 Director, Institute of Educational Sciences, Geneva

1936 Publishes *Origins of Intelligence in the Child*

1870	1885	1900	1915	1930

> **PHOTO 4.3** Children in today's Montessori schools use specially designed didactic materials in an environment prepared to encourage learning.

Elizabeth Crews/The Image Works

FOCUS Why was the child's independence in performing practical life skills a priority for Montessori? Do you think the term "directress" is an appropriate designation for a teacher? In your educational experience, were there teachers who used the Montessori method? Do you plan to include elements of the Montessori method in your teaching?

school setting, stocking it with learning apparatus that children can easily access, but does not interfere with their choice of and working with the items they have selected. Neither does she correct the child's work because the apparatus itself is self-correcting. Children tend to persist with an activity until they have mastered it.

4-9c Influence on Educational Practices Today

Montessori made a pioneering contribution to education when she emphasized that early childhood education has a highly formative power over a person's adult development. Her significant educational contributions include her (1) concept of sensitive periods, or phases of development, when children are ready to work with materials that are especially useful in sensory, motor, and cognitive learning; (2) belief that children are capable of sustained self-directed work in learning a particular skill; and (3) emphasis on the school as part of the community and the need for parent participation and support (Photo 4.3). She anticipated the current movement to provide earlier enrichment opportunities for young children.[44]

[44]Gerald L. Gutek, "Maria Montessori: Contributions to Educational Psychology," in Barry J. Zimmerman and Dale H. Schunk, *Educational Psychology: A Century of Contributions* (Mahwah, NJ: Lawrence Erlbaum, 2003), pp. 171–186.

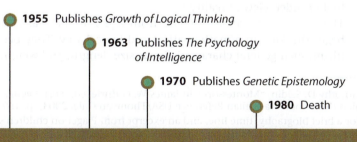

1955 Publishes *Growth of Logical Thinking*

1963 Publishes *The Psychology of Intelligence*

1970 Publishes *Genetic Epistemology*

1980 Death

| 1945 | 1960 | 1975 | 1990 | 2005 |

Montessori schools Early childhood institutions that follow Maria Montessori's philosophy and method of instruction with an emphasis on the development of children's sensory, motor, and intellectual skills by using didactic materials in a structured environment.

About six thousand of the world's twenty thousand **Montessori schools** worldwide are in the United States. Most of these are private schools, enrolling children between the ages of 2 and 6. Some public-school systems have established Montessori units, especially as magnet or charter schools.[45]

Although some universities have Montessori programs, most Montessori training programs are private, associated with either the American Montessori Association or the Montessori International Society. These organizations subscribe to Montessori's admonition that preservice training should closely follow the method she designed. Prospective directresses study the Montessori method and are trained in using the didactic materials in the prepared environment.

4-10 PIAGET: DEVELOPMENTAL GROWTH

The Swiss psychologist Jean Piaget (1896–1980) developed significant pioneering insights into children's cognitive, moral, and language development.[46] Like Montessori, Piaget used clinical observation to discover how children construct and act on their ideas.[47]

4-10a Principles of Teaching and Learning

Piaget discovered that children construct their concepts about reality by actively exploring their environment. According to Piaget, intelligence develops through a series of stages characterized by the child's set of mental structures and operations at a particular age. With each new stage, children develop new mental abilities that enable them to reconstruct the concepts they constructed at an earlier stage into a more complex cognitive map of the world.[48] Based on his stage-learning theory of development, Piaget identified four qualitatively distinct but interrelated periods of cognitive growth:

sensorimotor stage A stage of child development identified by Jean Piaget that occurs from birth to two years, when children construct their earliest concepts by environmental exploration.

1. The **sensorimotor stage**, from birth to 2 years, occurs when children learn by actively exploring their immediate environment. Children begin their earliest environmental explorations using their senses—their mouths, eyes, noses, and hands. Displaying a largely nonverbal intelligence, they learn to coordinate their senses and to construct simple concepts of space, time, and causality at the visual, auditory, tactile, and motor levels. These rudimentary concepts, however, are limited to children's immediate situations.[49]

preoperational stage A stage of human development identified by Jean Piaget that occurs from age 2 to 7 years, when children create categories, classify, add to, and reconstruct their conceptions of reality through systematic environmental explorations.

2. The **preoperational stage**, from age 2 to 7 years, occurs when intuition combines with speech to lead to operational thinking involving concepts of space, time, and cause-and-effect relationships that extend beyond the immediate situation. Children now reconstruct their concepts by grouping and naming objects. They use signs and symbols to represent their ideas and experiences as they reorganize the mental structures and networks constructed in the first stage into a more complex, higher-order, view of reality.[50]

concrete-operational period A stage of human development identified by Jean Piaget that occurs from ages 7 to 11 years, when children reorganize their concepts to perform increasingly complex mental operations.

3. The **concrete-operational period**, from age 7 to 11 years, occurs when children begin thinking in a mathematical and logical way. They become adept at recognizing such general characteristics as size, length, and weight, and in using them

---

[45]Timothy D. Seldin, "Montessori," in James W. Guthrie, ed., *Encyclopedia of Education,* 2nd ed., Vol. 5 (New York: Macmillan Reference USA/Thomson Gale, 2003), p. 1697.

[46]For a brief biography, time line, and an excerpt from Piaget on children's intellectual development, see Madonna M. Murphy, *The History and Philosophy of Education: Voices of Educational Pioneers* (Upper Saddle River, NJ: Pearson/Merrill/Prentice Hall, 2006), pp. 375–383.

[47]David Elkind, "Piaget, Jean (1896–1980)," in Guthrie, *Encyclopedia of Education,* 2nd ed., Vol. 5 (New York: Macmillan Reference USA/Thomson Gale, 2003), p. 1895.

[48]Ibid., p. 1897.

[49]Ibid.

[50]Ibid.

formal-operational period A stage of human development identified by Jean Piaget that occurs from age 11 through early adulthood, when individuals formulate abstract generalizations and learn how to perform complex problem-solving processes.

constructivism A learning theory in which learners actively create meaning by constructing and reconstructing their ideas about reality though their explorations of the environment.

FOCUS Were some of Piaget's ideas such as learning through the senses, exploring the environment, and using objects similar to the concepts developed by other pioneers such as Rousseau, Pestalozzi, Dewey, and Montessori? How did Piaget attempt to reduce the gap between how children learned informally outside of and formally within the school? In your educational experience, were there teachers who used Piaget's principles? Do you plan on incorporating Piaget's ideas into your teaching?

to perform more complex mental operations. As before, they reconstruct the concepts developed in earlier stages into more abstract and complex levels. Coinciding with the years of elementary school, children in the concrete-operational stage exercise their reasoning skills and deal with clock and calendar time, map and geographical space, and experimental cause and effect.[51]

4. At the **formal-operational period**, from age 11 through early adulthood, individuals construct logical propositions and interpret space, historical time, and multiple cause-and-effect relationships. They use such multivariate thinking to construct possible plans of action.[52] Now that adolescents understand cause-and-effect relationships, they can use the scientific method and can learn complex mathematical, linguistic, and mechanical processes.[53]

Piaget's stage-learning theory of development has many important applications to education. Because children are constantly reconstructing their view of reality as they grow and develop, their conceptions of reality often differ from the kinds of curriculum and instruction adults tend to impose on them.

Early-childhood and primary education should reflect on how children construct and learn to act on their own cognitive processes. As they move through the stages of development, children have their own readiness for new learning based on the cognitive level they have reached. This, in turn, determines their readiness for new and higher-order learning experiences.[54] Although a rich environment can stimulate readiness, learning cannot be forced on children until they are developmentally ready for it.

4-10b Education and Schooling

Piaget reconstructed the concept of the school to resemble the informal environment in which children learn on their own. Outside of school, children learn directly and informally from their explorations of their environment. The most effective classroom teaching replicates the informal learning children use in their everyday out-of-school lives.[55]

As they interact with their environment, children build knowledge of their world through a creative process known as **constructivism**.[56] As they discover gaps between their existing concepts and the new situations they encounter when exploring their environment, children reconceptualize their existing knowledge with their new information to construct more complete higher-order concepts.[57] To stimulate children's explorations, teachers can design their classrooms as learning centers stocked with materials that engage children's curiosity.[58] The following principles from Piaget can guide teachers' preservice preparation and classroom practice:

1. Encourage children to explore and experiment.
2. Individualize instruction so children can learn at their own level of readiness.
3. Design the classroom as a learning center stocked with materials that children can touch, manipulate, and use.

---

[51]Ibid.

[52]C. J. Brainerd, "Jean Piaget, Learning Research, and American Education," in Barry J. Zimmerman and Dale H. Schunk, ed., *Educational Psychology: A Century of Contributions* (Mahwah, NJ: Lawrence Erlbaum, 2003), p. 257; and Elkind, p. 1897.

[53]Jean Piaget, *The Origins of Intelligence in Children,* trans. Margaret Cook (New York: Norton, 1952), pp. 24–40; also see Ulrich Muller, Jeremy I. M. Carpendale, and Leslie Smith, eds., *The Cambridge Companion to Piaget* (Cambridge, UK: Cambridge University Press, 2009); and Richard Kohler, *Jean Piaget (Continuum Library of Educational Thought)* (New York: Continuum, 2008).

[54]Brainerd, p. 260.

[55]Ibid., p. 284.

[56]Susan Puss, *Parallel Paths to Constructionism: Jean Piaget and Lev Vygotsky* (Greenwich CT: Information Age Publishing, 2004).

[57]Brainerd, p. 271.

[58]Piaget, *Origins of Intelligence,* pp. 23–42.

4-10c Influence on Educational Practices Today

Piaget's cognitive psychology sought to connect children's cognitive development with curriculum and instruction in schools. His ideas stimulated a movement to remake classrooms into informal learning centers. Piaget's assertion that children construct rather than copy their versions of reality influenced contemporary constructivist instruction.[59]

4-11 FREIRE: LIBERATION PEDAGOGY

liberation pedagogy Paulo Freire's educational theory that encourages teachers and their students to develop a critical consciousness of the conditions that oppress them and to free themselves from this oppression.

Paulo Freire (1921–1997) constructed his philosophy of **liberation pedagogy** while conducting a literacy campaign among the impoverished illiterate peasants and urban poor in his native Brazil.[60] For Freire, literacy meant more than learning to read and write; it raised people's consciousness about the conditions of their lives, especially those that exploited and marginalized them.[61] Freire's *Pedagogy of the Oppressed* expressed his commitment to an education that empowered people to resist and overcome the forces that limited their freedom and pushed them to the edges of society.[62]

4-11a Principles of Teaching and Learning

Freire's philosophy emphasizes *conscientizaçao*, a Portuguese word, which means to be conscious and critically aware of the social, political, and economic conditions

---

[59]Elkind, p. 1894.

[60]For a brief biography and an excerpt from Freire's *Pedagogy of the Oppressed,* see Madonna M. Murphy, *The History and Philosophy of Education: Voices of Educational Pioneers* (Upper Saddle River, NJ: Pearson/Merrill/Prentice Hall, 2006), pp. 383–391. Also, access the Paulo Freire Institute, UCLA at **www.paulofreireinstitute.org**.

[61]Richard Shaull, preface to Paulo Freire, *Pedagogy of the Oppressed* (New York: Continuum, 1984), pp. 9–11. Also, see John Dale and Emory J. Hyslop-Margison, *Paulo Freire: Teaching for Freedom and Transformation: The Philosophical Influences on the Work of Paulo Freire* (London and New York: Springer, 2010); and Antonia Darder, *Freire and Education* (New York and London: Routledge, 2014).

[62]Among several editions is Paulo Freire, *Pedagogy of the Oppressed*, Myra Bergman Ramos, trans., and introduction by Donaldo Macedo (New York: Continuum, 2000). Also, see Freire, *Pedagogy of Hope: Reliving Pedagogy of the Oppressed* (New York: Continuum, 2004); and Freire, *Education for Critical Consciousness* (Continuum, 2005).

TIMELINE
PAULO FREIRE

Globo/Getty Images

1921 Born in Recife, Brazil

1946 Director Department of Education and Culture of Social Services in Pernambuco, Brazil

| 1910 | 1920 | 1930 | 1940 | 1950 |

TECHNOLOGY @ SCHOOL

PAULO FREIRE'S LIBERATION PEDAGOGY

You can research the Internet to broaden your perspectives on Paulo Freire's liberation pedagogy. For websites committed to Freire's pedagogy, go to the Paulo Freire Institute and the Freire Project. Relate the discussion of Freire's educational ideas on these sites to the commentary in this chapter.

and contradictions that affect a person's life. To raise their consciousness, students, in dialogue with their teachers, need to reflect on their own lives and write their personal and collective histories of their racial, ethnic, language, economic, and social groups. They must consciously examine the real, rather than the make-believe situations impacting their lives. They need to cut through the phoniness that may cloud their thinking and identify the people and conditions that deny them the freedom to define and express themselves.[63]

4-11b Education and Schooling

Freire asserted that the school's curriculum and instruction can either indoctrinate students to conform to an official version of knowledge, or it can challenge them to develop a critical consciousness that empowers them to engage in self-liberation. For example, an official version of history that celebrates the achievements of white Euro-American males and minimizes the contributions of women, African Americans, Latinos, and other minority groups creates a false consciousness. An education that defines a person's worth in terms of wealth and power and sees schooling as a ticket to success in an exploitative economic system cannot be truly humanizing.[64]

For Freire, teachers cannot be impartial or uncommitted on social, political, and economic issues.[65] Those who claim to be completely objective are really imposing social, economic, political, and educational structures erected and controlled by dominant classes. He urges teachers to develop a critical consciousness about the real power

[63]Paulo Freire, *Pedagogy of Freedom: Ethics, Democracy, and Civic Courage* (Lanham, MD: Rowman and Littlefield, 1998), p. 51.

[64]Stanley Aronowitz, introduction to Freire, *Pedagogy of Freedom*, p. 4.

[65]Paolo Freire, *Pedagogy of Freedom*, p. 22.

1964 Imprisoned by military regime in Brazil, then exiled to Chile

1967 Publishes *Pedagogy of the Oppressed*

1968 Visiting Professor at Harvard University

1969 Educational Advisor to World Council of Churches

1986 Awarded UNESCO Prize for Education for Peace

1988–1991 Secretary of Education for Sao Paulo

1997 Death

1960   1970   1980   1990   2000

1961 Organizes literacy campaign

1980 Returns to Brazil

TAKING ISSUE

Read the following brief introduction, as well as the Question and the pros and cons list that follows. Then, answer the question using *your* own words and position.

COMMITMENT TO SOCIAL JUSTICE IN EDUCATION?

You have just read about Paulo Freire who said that teachers cannot remain neutral on issues of social justice. Freire argued that teachers should be committed to empowering dispossessed and marginalized individuals and groups. Return to the earlier section on Herbert Spencer in this chapter. Spencer, a social Darwinist, argued that teachers who tried to promote social equality were making a serious mistake that attempted to interfere with the natural law of competition.

Question

Should teachers be committed to social justice education that seeks to empower marginalized groups? (Think about this question as you read the PRO and CON arguments listed here. What is *your* response to this issue?)

Arguments PRO	Arguments CON
1. If teachers do not take a stand on social issues, they are merely reinforcing the discriminatory status quo.	1. The teacher's function is to educate students in the skills and subjects needed to earn a living, not to indoctrinate them in a political ideology.
2. Education can be a positive agency of social change that promotes equality among individuals and groups.	2. Trying to change society is a utopian dream that interferes with economic progress.
3. Teachers need to raise students' consciousness about the agents and conditions that exploit them.	3. Teachers should encourage competition that brings out the best in people.
4. Teachers should join forces with progressive groups and organizations that are working for social justice.	4. Society is improved through individual efforts and hard work, not by "raising consciousness."

Question Reprise: What Is Your Stand?

Reflect again on the following question by explaining *your* stand about this issue. Should teachers be committed to social justice education that seeks to empower marginalized groups?

relationships in the schools and the conditions that affect their students. For example, teachers in schools in economically depressed ghettos need to know that their students' lives are being blighted by poverty, poor access to health care and recreational services, drug abuse, and gang violence. When they understand the true reality of their school situations, teachers can resist these oppressive conditions and work to empower their students.

For Freire, real learning takes place as teachers and students engage in open and ongoing dialogue. He attacks instruction, presented as transmitting information that creates false, rather than critical, consciousness in students' minds. An example is "teacher talk," which implies that teachers can transmit knowledge to students by telling them what is true: students memorize what the American teacher says and passively deposit it in their minds for later recall on tests. Freire calls the teacher-talking–student-listening method educational "banking," in which each bit of information is deposited to be cashed in the future, usually for an examination.[66]

For educators inspired by Freire, the standardized tests used in the contemporary standards movement, such as NCLB or RTTT, are examples of the banking model. The tests, constructed by bureaucratic experts, assess students' recall of officially

---

[66]Paolo Freire, *Pedagogy of the Oppressed*, pp. 57–59.

transmitted, approved information, rather than students' lived experience. Test results, which reflect statistics rather than people, become sorting devices that separate students into elite academic achievers destined for prestigious universities/positions in the corporate structure and others who will be pushed to the margins in society and the economy.

4-11c Influence on Educational Practices Today

FOCUS Why did Freire construct his theory of liberation pedagogy? Why is it called liberation pedagogy? Do you think the schools you attended and in which you are doing your clinical experience or teaching liberate or marginalize students and teachers? In your educational experience, were there teachers who used Freire's principles? Are there elements of Freire's liberation pedagogy that you plan to incorporate in your teaching?

Freire is esteemed as a genuine educational pioneer by contemporary critical theorists. (See Chapter 6, Philosophical Roots of Education, for more on critical theory.) Freire worked to transform teaching and learning from the limited concept of transmitting information to engaging in the project of completing one's identity and meaning in a world that needs to be made more equitable, humane, and just. According to Freire, preservice preparation should involve future teachers in dialogues in which they critically assess the social, economic, and political conditions that have an impact on schools and their students. In their classroom practice, teachers should help students work for social justice by creating a true consciousness which exposes the conditions that marginalize them and their communities.

SUMMING UP

1. Comenius's pansophism sought to reform schools from places where children were often physically and psychologically coerced by teachers into child-friendly and humane places where they learned to trust their peers and others.

2. Rousseau's *Emile*, which presented his ideas on education according to nature, challenged traditional concepts about schools and other institutions.

3. Pestalozzi's emphasis on educating the whole child, mentally, physically, and emotionally, challenged the traditional concept that teachers should transmit knowledge to students. His method of object teaching encouraged children to use their senses in interpreting their environment.

4. Herbart structured a sequence-based method of instruction that was widely used in the upper grades and in high schools.

5. Froebel created the kindergarten as a new early childhood school which featured children's growth through play, songs, stores, and activities using "gifts" and "occupations."

6. Spencer, who applied Darwin's theory of evolution society, saw schools as places where individuals competed to achieve. His curriculum design applied science to life.

7. Dewey, using his pragmatic experimentalist philosophy, designed the scientifically based method of problem solving, in which students learn from their experiences.

8. Based on her work with immigrants at Hull House, Addams constructed socialized education, a prototype of multicultural, peace, and women's education.

9. Montessori, a medical doctor, used her clinical observation of children to create a structured learning environment in which children were free to choose the apparatus on which they worked.

10. Piaget's theory of stage-based human development made instruction more informal so that the gap between learning inside and outside of schools was lessened.

11. Freire constructed liberation pedagogy as an educational weapon to free marginalized people from exploitation from dominant classes and groups.

SUGGESTED RESOURCES

INTERNET RESOURCES

For Comenius's methods on language instruction, access the Comenius Foundation website.

For an extensive collection of books and articles by and about Comenius, access The Online Books Library. To view Comenius's *Orbis Pictus*, access the HathiTrust Digital Library.

For Rousseau's *Emile,* access the Emile Project at the Institute for Learning Technologies.

For the lives and philosophies of Rousseau, Dewey, and Addams, access the Internet Encyclopedia of Philosophy website.

For biographies and a slide show on Pestalozzi, access the Pestalozzi World website.

For archives, links, and other resources about Froebel, access the International Froebel Society website.

For the philosophy, history, and projects related to Froebel, access the Froebel Foundation USA website.

For a biography of Dewey, access the Center for Dewey Studies page at the Southern Illinois University website.

For Jane Addams's life and philosophy, access the Stanford Encyclopedia of Philosophy website.

For a chronology and images of Jane Addams and her papers, access the Jane Addams Paper Project website.

For information on Maria Montessori, consult the International Montessori Index, Montessori Online, and the American Montessori Association websites.

For a biography and bibliography of Piaget, access the Jean Piaget Society website.

For a biography, resources, and videos about Freire, access the Freire Project website.

For an interpretation of Herbert Spencer's influence on economics, society, and education in late nineteenth-century America, access "The Richest Man in the World" at the WGBH American Experience website.

PUBLICATIONS

Brown, Victoria Bissell. *The Education of Jane Addams.* Philadelphia: University of Pennsylvania Press, 2004. *A biography of Jane Addams that explores the origin and sources of her concepts of social reform, education, women's rights, and world peace.*

Cochran, Molly, ed. *The Cambridge Companion to Dewey.* Cambridge, UK: Cambridge University Press, 2010. *Contains essays by scholars on Dewey's life, work, and philosophy.*

Damrosch, Leo. *Jean-Jacques Rousseau: Restless Genius.* Boston: Houghton Mifflin, 2005. *Damrosch's highly acclaimed biography provides a definitive account of the French philosopher's life and works.*

Darder, Antonia. *Freire and Education.* New York and London: Routledge, 2014. *Argues that Freire's educational ideas are especially relevant to today's teachers and their students.*

Dewey, John. *Democracy and Education,* introduction by Gerald L. Gutek. New York: Barnes and Noble, 2005. *An edition of Dewey's important book on philosophy of education, published originally in 1916, with an introductory essay that places the book in its historical and educational contexts.*

Dewey, John. *How We Think,* introduction by Gerald L. Gutek. New York: Barnes and Noble, 2005. *An edition of Dewey's important work on thinking as inquiry, published originally in 1910, with an introductory essay that places the book in its historical and educational contexts.*

Francis, Mark. *Herbert Spencer and the Invention of Modern Life.* Ithaca, NY: Cornell University Press, 2007. *Provides an interpretation of Spencer's relevance to contemporary society.*

Garrison, Jim; Larry Hickman, and Ikeda Daisaku. *Living as Learning: John Dewey in the 21st Century.* Cambridge, MA: Ikeda Center, 2014. *Examines Dewey's continuing relevance to contemporary global society.*

Freire, Paulo. *Pedagogy of the Oppressed.* Translated by Myra Bergman Ramos. New York: Continuum, 2000. *Freire establishes the educational and ideological rationale for his liberation pedagogy.*

Gutek, Gerald L. *Historical and Philosophical Foundations of Education: A Biographical Introduction.* Columbus, OH: Pearson, 2011. *Placing each educator in historical and cultural context, Gutek examines the educational ideas of Plato, Quintilian, Aquinas, Calvin, Rousseau, Pestalozzi, Froebel, Spencer, Montessori, Addams, Dewey, Du Bois, Gandhi, and Mao.*

Gutek, Gerald L. *The Montessori Method: The Origins of an Educational Innovation: Including an Abridged and Annotated Edition of Maria Montessori's* The Montessori Method. Lanham, MD: Rowman and Littlefield Publishers, 2004. *Provides an introductory biography of Maria Montessori and an analysis of her educational method.*

Johnston, James S. *Inquiry and Education: John Dewey and the Quest for Democracy.* Albany: State University of New York Press, 2006. *Examines Dewey's epistemology in relation to education.*

Knight, Louise W. *Citizen: Jane Addams and the Struggle for Democracy.* Chicago: University of Chicago Press, 2006. *Provides an engaging narrative of Jane Addams's intellectual journal to become an international social, educational, and political theorist and activist.*

Lilley, Irene M. *Friedrich Froebel: A Selection from His Writings.* New York and London: Cambridge University Press, 2010. *This reissuing of Lilley's book provides an excellent introduction and selections to Froebel's educational philosophy and method.*

Martin, Jay. *The Education of John Dewey.* New York: Columbia University Press, 2002. *A thorough discussion of John Dewey's life and education, with emphasis on how Dewey's emotional life influenced his philosophy.*

Monroe, Will S. *Comenius: And the Beginning of Educational Reform.* London: Forgotten Books, 2012. *A reissuing of Monroe's classic work on Comenius.*

Piaget, Jean. *The Child's Conception of the World: A 20th-Century Classic of Child Psychology.* Translated by Joan and Andrew Tomlinson. Lanham, MD: Rowman and Littlefield Publishers, 2007. *Piaget's analysis of how children develop their reasoning powers.*

Povell, Phyllis. *Montessori Comes to America: The Leadership of Maria Montessori and Nancy McCormick Rambusch.* New York: University Press of America, 2009. *Povell's insightful narrative provides the history of Montessori education in the United States and analyzes the leadership styles of Montessori and Rambush.*

Rossatto, Cesar Augusto. *Engaging Paulo Freire's Pedagogy of Possibility: From Blind to Transformative Optimism.* Lanham, MD: Rowman and Littlefield Publishers, 2005. *A teacher-educator provides a cross-cultural analysis of Freire's theory in light of contemporary trends and issues such as globalization.*

Rousseau, Jean-Jacques. *Emile*, introduction by Gerald L. Gutek. New York: Barnes and Noble, 2005. *An edition of Rousseau's classic work,* Emile, *published originally in 1762, with an introduction that identifies and examines the book's key concepts.*

Tovey, Helen. *Bringing the Froebel Approach to Your Early Years Practice.* New York and London: Routledge, 2011. *Tovey considers Froebel's principles and applies them to contemporary early childhood education.*

Tröhler, Daniel. *Pestalozzi and the Educationalization of the World.* New York: Palgrave Macmillan, 2013. *Examines how Pestalozzi's ideas and methods brought worldwide change to education, schooling, and teaching.*

Zimmerman, Barry J., and Dale H. Schunk, eds. *Educational Psychology: A Century of Contributions.* Mahwah, NJ: Lawrence Erlbaum, 2003. *This book, a project of the Educational Psychology division of the American Psychological Association, contains essays on Piaget and other leading educational psychologists of the twentieth century.*

CHAPTER 5

HISTORICAL DEVELOPMENT OF AMERICAN EDUCATION

LEARNING OBJECTIVES

5-1 Describe how European ideas about culture, education, and schools shaped education in North America during the colonial period and how these ideas are relevant for contemporary education.

5-2 Assess how the ideas of Benjamin Franklin, Thomas Jefferson, Benjamin Rush, and Noah Webster shaped American education in the early national period and their relevancy for contemporary education.

5-3 Clarify the ways in which the common school had an impact on the movement toward public education and teacher education.

5-4 Explain how the high school's rise as the major institution for secondary education completed the American educational ladder.

5-5 Indicate how political, religious, social, and economic developments shaped the American college and university.

5-6 Assess the policies public schools used to educate a racially, ethnically, and linguistically diverse population of students.

5-7 Summarize the history of the controversy over Common Core Standards.

CristinaMuraca/Shutterstock.com

___
This chapter was revised by Gerald L. Gutek.

STUDYING THE HISTORY of American education provides an opportunity for you to write your educational autobiography. This examination of the origin of your ideas about education also is useful to the construction of your own philosophy of education. You can trace the roots of your ideas and beliefs about education by looking into your grandparents' and parents' school experiences, as well as your own. As you discover your own educational origins, you can build a bridge between your experiences and the broader historical developments that shaped American education. To research your educational autobiography, you might (1) interview your grandparents, parents, and others about their school experiences; (2) identify and examine family artifacts, photographs, records, and other memorabilia that relate to attending and graduating from school; and (3) think deeply and reflectively about your own educational experiences, especially your teachers and their methods. Then you can record your findings and begin to write your own autobiography. You can use this chapter, which examines the history of elementary schools, high schools, and colleges and universities, as a framework on which to locate your own experiences. Your may find that the discussion of the public-school policy regarding the education of diverse racial, ethnic, and language groups relates to your own education or that of your ancestors.

This chapter on the history of American education analyzes how individuals and groups built schools and developed educational processes in the United States. It examines (1) the introduction of European educational ideas and institutions to North America during the colonial period; (2) the efforts to create a uniquely American educational system during the revolutionary and early national eras; (3) the establishment of public education during the common school movement; (4) the development of secondary education from the Latin grammar school, through the academy, to today's comprehensive high school; (5) the development of colleges and universities; (6) the immigration and the education of culturally diverse populations; and (7) the historical background of the contemporary standards controversy.

5-1 THE COLONIAL PERIOD

North America's colonization in the seventeenth and eighteenth centuries caused complex cultural encounters and often-violent conflicts between Europeans and the indigenous Native Americans. The Europeans, who carried contagious diseases such as measles and smallpox, infected the Native Americans who lacked immunity to these illnesses. Epidemics of these contagious illnesses ravaged the tribes living along the Atlantic coast. For example, a smallpox epidemic in 1618–1619 killed 90 percent of the Native Americans in the Massachusetts Bay Colony.[1]

Many Europeans who came to North America as explorers, conquerors, and colonists held an ethnocentric opinion that European culture and language—English, French, or Spanish—were superior to that of the Native Americans. They categorized the indigenous peoples they encountered as culturally inferior, lesser humans who needed to be saved, civilized, or eliminated.

The Native Americans and the European colonists had diametrically opposed perspectives on nature, the uses of the environment, and property that would lead to conflict. For the American Indians, the natural environment and its resources were not

---

[1]For European and Native Americans relationships, see Peter C. Mancell and James H. Merrell, *American Encounters: Natives and Newcomers from European Contact to Indian Removal, 1500–1850* (New York: Routledge, 2006); and Margaret Szasz, *Indian Education in the American Colonies, 1607–1783* (Lincoln: University of Nebraska Press, 2007).

privately owned properties; they were open to those who needed them for places to live and for shelter. For the Europeans, natural resources could be privately owned and developed, or exploited, for sustenance but also for wealth and profit.

The European colonists came from many ethnic and language backgrounds. The French established settlements in Canada and the Mississippi Valley; the Spanish in Mexico, Florida, and the Southwest; the Dutch in New Netherlands, now New York State; and the English in the original thirteen colonies that became the United States after the Revolutionary War. The English, who defeated the Dutch and the French, had the most pervasive impact on colonial American politics, society, and education.

The colonists at first re-created the socioeconomic-class–based **dual-track school system** that they had known in Europe. Boys and girls, especially in the New England colonies, attended primary schools where they learned reading, writing, arithmetic, and religion. Boys from the more privileged classes attended **Latin grammar schools**, which prepared them in the Latin and Greek languages and literatures needed for admission to colonial colleges. (For the origins of the dual-track school system, see Chapter 3, The World Origins of American Education.)

dual-track school system The traditional European pattern of separate primary schools for the masses and preparatory and secondary schools for males in the upper socioeconomic classes.

Latin grammar school A preparatory school of the colonial era that emphasized Latin and Greek languages and studies required for college admission.

5-1a New England Colonies

The New England colonies of Massachusetts, Connecticut, and New Hampshire were a crucible for the development of American educational ideas and institutions. Massachusetts enacted the first formal education laws in British North America. (See Overview 5.1 for significant events in American education.)

The English settlers in Massachusetts believed that a literate people who knew God's commandments as preached by their Puritan ministers could resist the devil's temptations. Following their Protestant injunction to read the Bible, the church-controlled schools emphasized reading, writing, arithmetic, and religion.

Following John Calvin's theology, Puritan schools were guided by interpenetrating economic and religious purposes. According to the Calvinist work ethic, good Puritans were to be responsible citizens and productive businessmen and farmers who attended church, read the Bible, and worked diligently. Puritan teachers stressed values of punctuality, honesty, obedience to authority, and hard work. American education continues to emphasize the relationship between education and economic productivity, asserting that individuals with more schooling earn more money than those with less schooling.

Child Depravity The concept of child depravity shaped the Puritan child-rearing and educational practices. Children were regarded as depraved, or at least, inclined to evil. Children's play was seen as idleness and children's talk as gibberish. Following the adage, "Spare the rod and spoil the child," Puritan teachers relied on firm discipline and corporal punishment to manage their classes. At home, children were to help with household and farm chores. Revisit Chapter 4, Pioneers of Teaching and Learning, to see how Comenius, Rousseau, Pestalozzi, and Froebel opposed the doctrine of child depravity.

"Old Deluder Satan" Believing that a literate people would be a Godly people, the Puritan settlers established schools soon after their arrival in Massachusetts. In 1642, the Massachusetts General Court, the colony's legislative body, enacted a law requiring parents and guardians to ensure that children in their care learned to read and understand the principles of religion and the commonwealth's laws. In 1647, the General Court enacted the "Old Deluder Satan" Act, a law intended to outwit Satan, whom the Puritans believed deceived ignorant people into sinning. The law required every town of fifty or more families to appoint a reading and writing teacher. Towns of one hundred or more families were to employ a Latin teacher to prepare young men to enter Harvard College.

town school The eighteenth- and early-nineteenth-century New England elementary school that educated children living in a designated area and was the common school's predecessor.

hornbook A single sheet of parchment containing the Lord's Prayer, letters of the alphabet, and vowels, which is covered by the translucent, flattened horn of a cow and fastened to a flat wooden board. It was used in colonial primary schools.

The Town School The New England colonists re-created the European dual-track system, establishing primary town schools for the majority of students and Latin grammar schools for upper-class boys. The New England **town school**, a locally controlled institution, educated both boys and girls from ages 6 to 13 or 14. Attendance could be irregular, depending on weather conditions and the need for children to work on family farms. The school's curriculum included reading, writing, arithmetic, catechism, and religious hymns. Children learned the alphabet, syllables, words, and sentences by memorizing the **hornbook**, a sheet of parchment covered by transparent material made by flattening cattle horns. The older children read the *New England Primer,* which included religious materials such as the Westminster Catechism, the Ten Commandments, the Lord's Prayer, and the Apostle's Creed.[2] Arithmetic was primarily counting, adding, and subtracting.

The New England town school, often a crude log structure, was dominated by the teacher's pulpit-like desk at the front of the single room. Seated on wooden benches, pupils memorized their assignments until called before the schoolmaster to recite. Most teachers were men, some of whom temporarily taught school while preparing for the ministry. Others took the job to repay debts owed for their voyage to North America. Very few elementary teachers were trained in educational methods, and they often relied on corporal punishment to maintain discipline.

The Latin Grammar School Upper-class boys attended Latin grammar schools, which prepared them for college entry. These boys generally had learned to read and write English from private tutors. Entering the Latin grammar school at age 8, the student would complete his studies at age 15 or 16. He studied such Latin authors as Cicero, Terence, Caesar, Livy, Vergil, and Horace. More advanced students studied such Greek authors as Isocrates, Hesiod, and Homer. Little attention was given to mathematics, science, or modern languages. Usually college graduates, the Latin masters who taught in these schools were better paid and accorded higher social status than elementary teachers. (For the importance of Latin in Western culture, see Chapter 3, The World Origins of American Education.)

Established in 1636, Harvard College was founded on the Puritan belief that future ministers and other leaders needed a thorough classical and theological education. The applicants were typically young men from the wealthier and more favored families. To be admitted to the College, the applicants had to demonstrate their competency in Latin and Greek. The four-year curriculum reflected the Puritan belief that ministers and other leaders needed a liberal arts education, with an emphasis on the classics. Harvard taught grammar, logic, rhetoric, mathematics, geometry, astronomy, ethics, philosophy, and natural science. Especially important for future ministers were Calvin's theology, Hebrew, Greek, and ancient history.

5-1b Middle Atlantic Colonies

Although the other colonial regions—the Middle Atlantic colonies and Southern colonies—shared a common English culture with New England, they exhibited significant differences in the provision and maintenance of schools. The settlers in the Middle Atlantic colonies—New York, New Jersey, Delaware, and Pennsylvania—were more culturally pluralistic than the homogenous Puritans of Massachusetts and Connecticut. The Dutch had settled New Netherlands, which later became New York; the Swedes had settled Delaware, and some Germans located in Pennsylvania. The Middle Atlantic colonies' ethnic, language, and religious diversity influenced education. While Puritan New England created uniform town schools, the different churches in the Middle Atlantic colonies established parochial schools to educate children in their own religious beliefs and practices.

---

[2]Melissa Freeman and Sandra Mathison, *Researching Children's Experiences* (New York: Guilford Publications, 2009), pp. 1–17. Also, see Jennifer E. Monaghan, *Learning to Read and Write in Colonial America* (Amherst: University of Massachusetts Press, 2007).

OVERVIEW 5.1

SIGNIFICANT EVENTS IN THE HISTORY OF AMERICAN EDUCATION

Major Political Events		Significant Educational Events	
1630	Massachusetts Bay Colony settled	1636	Harvard College, first English-speaking college in Western Hemisphere, founded
		1642	First education law enacted in Massachusetts
		1647	Massachusetts enacted Old Deluder Satan Act, requiring establishment of schools
		1751	Benjamin Franklin's Academy established in Philadelphia
1775–1783	American Revolution	1783	Noah Webster's *American Spelling Book* published
1788	US Constitution ratified	1785	Northwest Ordinance, first national education law, enacted
		1821	First public high school in the United States opened in Boston
			Emma Willard's Female Seminary, a school of higher education for women, established in Troy, New York
		1823	First private normal school in the United States opened in Concord, Vermont
1824	Bureau of Indian Affairs established	1825	Webster's *American Dictionary* completed
		1827	Massachusetts law requiring public high schools passed
1830	Indian Removal Act	1837	Horace Mann appointed secretary of Massachusetts Board of Education
1846–1848	Mexican-American War; US acquisition of southwestern territories	1839	First public normal school opened in Lexington, Massachusetts
1849	Gold rush to California	1855	First German-language kindergarten in the United States established
		1860	First English-language kindergarten in the United States established
1861–1865	Civil War	1862	Morrill Land Grant College Act passed, establishing in each state a college for agricultural and mechanical instruction
		1865	Freedmen's Bureau established
		1872	Kalamazoo decision upheld taxation for public high schools
1887	Dawes Act divides tribal lands	1881	Booker T. Washington established Tuskegee Institute
		1892	NEA established Committee of Ten
1898	Spanish-American War; US acquisition of Puerto Rico and the Philippines	1896	*Plessy v. Ferguson* decision upheld constitutionality of "separate but equal" doctrine
		1909	First junior high school established in Berkeley, California

Major Political Events		Significant Educational Events	
1914–1918	World War I	1917	Smith-Hughes Act passed, providing funds for vocational education, home economics, and agricultural subjects
		1918	*Cardinal Principles of Secondary Education* published
		1919	Progressive Education Association organized
1929	Beginning of the Great Depression	1930	New Deal programs provided federal funds for conservation projects and school construction
1939–1945	World War II	1944	GI Bill provided federal funds for continuing education of veterans
1950–1953	Korean War	1954	*Brown v. Board of Education of Topeka* ended *de jure*, or legally enforced, racial segregation of public schools
		1957	Soviet Union launched Sputnik, leading to a reevaluation of American education
		1958	National Defense Education Act passed, providing federal funds to improve science, math, and modern foreign-language instruction and guidance services
		1964	Civil Rights Act authorizes federal lawsuits for school desegregation
1965–1973	Vietnam War	1965	Elementary and Secondary Education Act passed, providing federal funds to public schools, especially for compensatory education
		1968	Bilingual Education Act enacted
		1972	Title IX Education Amendment passed, outlawing sex discrimination in schools receiving federal financial assistance
		1975	Education for All Handicapped Children (Public Law 94-142) passed
		1980	Department of Education established in federal government with cabinet status
		1983	Publication of *A Nation at Risk* stimulated national movement to reform education
1990	End of Cold War	1994	Goals 2000: The Educate America Act outlines national education goals
1991	Gulf War	1996	The nation's first educational technology plan: Getting Students Ready for the Twenty-First Century: Meeting the Technology Literacy Challenge
2001	Terrorist attacks on New York City and Washington, DC	2001	No Child Left Behind Act enacted
2003	Iraq War		
2009	Inauguration of first African American US president		
2009	Global economic recession	2010	21st Century Skills and Common Core Standards Movements

New York The Dutch originally settled in New Amsterdam, which was renamed "New York" after its conquest by the English. Members of the Reformed Church, the Dutch colonists established Dutch-language parochial schools to teach reading, writing, and religion. These Dutch parochial schools continued to operate after the colony came under England's domination.[3] When New York City grew into a thriving commercial port, private for-profit schools, called private-venture schools, offered navigation, surveying, bookkeeping, Spanish, French, and geography.

Pennsylvania As a proprietary colony founded by William Penn, Pennsylvania became a refuge for the Society of Friends, or Quakers, a religious denomination persecuted in England. As pacifist conscientious objectors, Quakers refused to support war efforts or serve in the military. Because of their tolerance, the Quakers welcomed members of other small churches, such as the German pietists, to Pennsylvania. Quaker schools were open to all children, including blacks and Native Americans. (Philadelphia had a small African American community, and some Native Americans remained in the colony.) While Quaker schools taught the standard reading, writing, arithmetic, and religion found in other colonial primary schools, they were unique in offering vocational training, crafts, and agriculture. Rejecting the doctrine of child depravity and corporal punishment, Quaker teachers used gentle persuasion to motivate their pupils.

Southern Colonies The Southern colonies—Maryland, Virginia, the Carolinas, and Georgia—presented still another economic and educational pattern. Except for flourishing tidewater cities such as Charleston and Williamsburg, the southern population was more dispersed than in New England or the Middle Atlantic colonies. This made it difficult for rural families to establish centrally located schools. The economically advantaged children of wealthy white plantation owners often studied with private tutors. Some families sent their children to private schools sponsored by the Church of England in towns such as Williamsburg or Charleston.

The slave system, which used the forced labor of captive Africans on plantations, profoundly shaped culture, economics, and politics in the South. Although slavery existed throughout the colonies, the largest population of enslaved Africans was in the Southern colonies. Africans were seized by force and brutally transported in slave ships to North America to work on southern plantations. The enslaved Africans were trained as agricultural field hands, craftspeople, or domestic servants, but they were generally forbidden to learn to read or write. Some notable exceptions learned to read secretly. Over time, the African heritage became the foundation of African American religion and culture.[4]

The slave system also affected economically disadvantaged whites. While wealthy plantation owners occupied the most productive land, the poorer farmers settled in less fertile backcountry or mountainous areas. The wealthy and politically powerful plantation elite focused on the education of their own children and provided few schools for the rest of the population.

5-1c Colonial Education: A Summary View

Despite regional religious and language differences, the New England, Middle Atlantic, and Southern colonies followed Western European, especially English educational patterns.[5] The schools operated by different churches in the Middle Atlantic colonies were forerunners of faith-based private schools. Gender affected educational opportunities

---

[3]For the Dutch in North America, see Evan Haefeli, *New Netherlands: The Dutch Origins of American Religious Liberty* (Philadelphia: University of Pennsylvania Press, 2012); and Russell Shorto, *The Island at the Center of the World: The Epic Story of Dutch Manhattan and the Forgotten Colony That Shaped America* (New York: Random House, 2004).

[4]James Walvin, *Crossings: Africa, the Americas, and the Atlantic Slave Trade* (London: Reaktion, 2013).

[5]Lawrence A. Cremin, *American Education: The Colonial Experience, 1607–1783* (New York: Harper and Row, 1970).

in all three regions. Both girls and boys attended primary schools, but Latin grammar schools and colleges were reserved for males. Women's education was limited to primary schools, where they learned the basics (reading and writing) to fulfill their familial and religious responsibilities. Many, especially men who controlled educational institutions, believed that women were intellectually incapable of higher studies.

FOCUS How were European educational ideas, institutions, and processes transported to North America during the colonial period? How were these ideas, institutions, and processes continued or changed over time? Have educational ideas from the colonial era shaped your educational experience? If so, consider including them in your educational autobiography.

The colonial school system reflected a European class orientation. Although primary schools provided basic education, they were not agencies of upward social mobility. The Latin grammar schools and colonial colleges educated only a small minority of males from the favored classes. During the nineteenth century, frontier egalitarianism, political democratization, and economic change would erode these European-based educational structures to create the American system of universal public education.

In the late colonial period, the 1760s and 1770s, the population of Britain's American colonies grew as their economies prospered. Businessmen in the commercial cities of New York, Boston, Philadelphia, and Charleston, as well as settlers on the frontier, especially the Scotch-Irish Presbyterians, began to resist increased taxation by the British government. Their resistance to taxation without their consent led to the American Revolution which began in 1776.

5-2 THE EARLY NATIONAL PERIOD

On October 19, 1781, the surrender of the British General Cornwallis to a combined American and French army at Yorktown brought the War for America's independence to an end. In the Treaty of Paris in 1783, Great Britain recognized the independence of its former colonies. Although the battles were over, the United States faced the momentous challenge of constructing a new nation out of thirteen victorious but cantankerous former colonies.

5-2a Articles of Confederation and the Constitution

During the early years of independence, the United States was a confederation of thirteen independent and sovereign states loosely tied together in *The Articles of Confederation and Perpetual Union* of 1781. The Confederation's government had jurisdiction over the Northwest Territory, an area of more than 260,000 square miles that included the present-day states of Ohio, Indiana, Illinois, Michigan, Wisconsin, and part of Minnesota. Marking the initial effort of the United States government in education, the Northwest Land Ordinance in 1785 reserved income from the sixteenth section in each township in the Territory for the support of education as "necessary to good government and the happiness of mankind." The Northwest Ordinance set the precedent for using federal **land grants** for education in the nineteenth century.

land grant A grant in which the income from a section of federal land is used to support education.

The US Constitution, which was ratified in 1788 and became the law of the land, did not specifically address education. The Tenth Amendment's "reserved powers" clause (which reserves to the states all powers not specifically delegated to the federal government or prohibited to the states by the Constitution) left responsibility for education with the individual states. The New England tradition of local school control also contributed to a state and local system rather than a national school system in the United States.

During the early national period, leaders such as Benjamin Franklin, Thomas Jefferson, Benjamin Rush, and Noah Webster developed proposals for schools in the new republic. Their proposals recommended that schools in the United States (1) prepare Americans for the duties of republican citizenship; (2) provide the utilitarian and scientific skills and subjects needed to develop the nation's vast expanses of frontier land and abundant natural resources; and (3) eliminate European attitudes in order to construct a uniquely American culture.[6]

---

[6]Jacqueline S. Reinier, *From Virtue to Character: American Childhood, 1775–1850* (New York: Twayne of Macmillan, 1996), p. xi.

5-2b Franklin: The Academy

academy A type of private or semipublic secondary school in the United States from 1830 to 1870 that was the high school's institutional predecessor. Today, some secondary schools, often private institutions, are called academies.

Benjamin Franklin (1706–1790), a leading statesman, scientist, and publicist, founded an **academy**, that is, a private secondary school, and described its curriculum in his "Proposals Relating to the Education of Youth in Pennsylvania."[7] Franklin's emphasis on useful knowledge and science differed notably from the traditional Latin grammar school. English grammar, composition, rhetoric, and public speaking replaced Latin and Greek as the principal language studies. Students could also elect a second language related to their future careers. For example, prospective clergy could choose Latin and Greek, and those planning on commercial careers could elect French, Spanish, or German. Mathematics was taught for its practical application to bookkeeping, surveying, and engineering rather than as an abstract subject. History and biography provided moral models for students to learn how famous people made their political and ethical decisions.

Prophetically, Franklin recognized how important science, invention, and technology would be in America's future. His curriculum featured the useful skills that schools had traditionally ignored, such as carpentry, shipbuilding, engraving, printing, and farming. By the mid-nineteenth century, the United States had many academies that resembled Franklin's plan.

---

[7]Walter Isaacson, *Benjamin Franklin: An American Life* (New York: Simon and Schuster, 2003), pp. 146–147. Other biographies of Franklin are: James Srodes, *Franklin: The Essential Founding Father* (Washington, DC: Regnery, 2002); Walter Isaacson, *Benjamin Franklin: An American Life* (New York: Simon and Schuster, 2003); and Edmund S. Morgan, *Benjamin Franklin* (New Haven, CT: Yale University Press, 2002). For Franklin on education and his idea of an English school, see Gerald L. Gutek, *An Historical Introduction to American Education* (Long Grove, IL: Waveland Press, 2013), pp. 42–46 and 65–70.

TIMELINE
BENJAMIN FRANKLIN

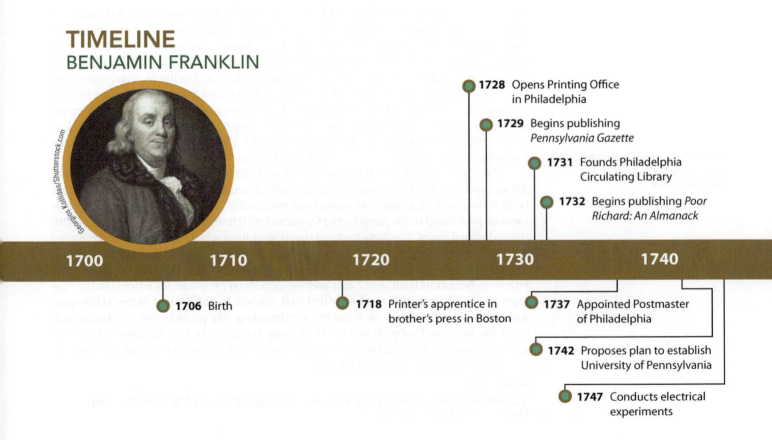

Georgios Kollidas/Shutterstock.com

- **1728** Opens Printing Office in Philadelphia
- **1729** Begins publishing *Pennsylvania Gazette*
- **1731** Founds Philadelphia Circulating Library
- **1732** Begins publishing *Poor Richard: An Almanack*

1700 — 1710 — 1720 — 1730 — 1740

- **1706** Birth
- **1718** Printer's apprentice in brother's press in Boston
- **1737** Appointed Postmaster of Philadelphia
- **1742** Proposes plan to establish University of Pennsylvania
- **1747** Conducts electrical experiments

5-2c Jefferson: Education for Citizenship

Thomas Jefferson (1743–1826), author of the Declaration of Independence and the third president of the United States, expressed his educational philosophy in his "Bill for the More General Diffusion of Knowledge," introduced in the Virginia legislature in 1779. Jefferson was also the principal founder of the University of Virginia.[8] Education's major purpose, Jefferson stated, was to promote a republican society of literate and well-informed citizens. Committed to separation of church and state, he believed that the state, not the churches, had the primary educational role. State-sponsored schools, not private ones, would be funded by public taxes.[9]

Jefferson's bill, though not passed, raised important issues for the new nation. For example, it promoted state-established public schools and sought to provide both equity and excellence in education. It would have subdivided Virginia's counties into districts. The bill stipulated that free children, both girls and boys, could attend an elementary school in each district, where they would study reading, writing, arithmetic, and history. The state would pay for the first three years of a student's attendance. Jefferson's proposal also would have established twenty grammar schools throughout the state to provide secondary education to boys. In these grammar schools, students would study Latin, Greek, English, geography, and higher mathematics.

Jefferson's bill anticipated the idea of academic merit scholarships. In each district school, the most academically able male student who could not afford to pay tuition

---

[8]For a discussion of Jefferson on education, see Gutek, *An Historical Introduction to American Education,* pp. 47–51. Also, see R. B. Bernstein, *Thomas Jefferson* (New York: Oxford University Press, 2003); and Maurizio Valsania, *Nature's Man: Thomas Jefferson's Philosophical Anthropology* (Charlottesville: University of Virginia Press, 2013).

[9]Julius P. Boyd, ed., *The Papers of Thomas Jefferson,* Vol. II (Princeton, NJ: Princeton University Press, 1950), pp. 526–533.

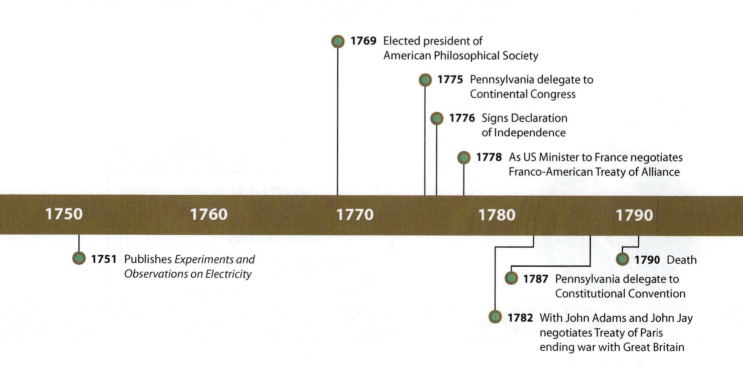

1769 Elected president of American Philosophical Society

1775 Pennsylvania delegate to Continental Congress

1776 Signs Declaration of Independence

1778 As US Minister to France negotiates Franco-American Treaty of Alliance

1750 1760 1770 1780 1790

1751 Publishes *Experiments and Observations on Electricity*

1790 Death

1787 Pennsylvania delegate to Constitutional Convention

1782 With John Adams and John Jay negotiates Treaty of Paris ending war with Great Britain

would receive a scholarship to continue his education at a grammar school. The ten scholarship students of highest academic achievement would receive additional state aid to attend the College of William and Mary.

Jefferson's plan represented an early compromise over issues of equity and excellence in American education. Although its provision of primary school for most children was a step toward equity, the concept of academic selectivity tilted toward the idea of secondary schools as "sorting machines" that identified and educated the most academically able students.

5-2d Benjamin Rush: Church-Related Schools

Benjamin Rush (1745–1813), a leading physician and medical educator of the early republic, did not subscribe to Jefferson's principle of separation of church and state. Seeing no conflicts among science, republican government, and religion, Rush wanted the Bible and Christian principles taught in schools and in colleges. Anticipating the contemporary theory of "intelligent design," Rush believed that science revealed God's perfect design in creating the natural order.[10] Unlike Jefferson, Rush did not believe that government support of church-related schools threatened freedom of religion and scientific inquiry.

Rush's plan for a comprehensive system of state schools and colleges combined private and public interests. Private citizens' groups, especially members of churches, would raise money for a school and then would receive a charter from the state to be eligible for public funds. Emphasizing the nation's Christian roots, Rush wanted schools to be denominationally affiliated and offer a faith-based education.

A determined advocate of women's education, Rush rejected the sexist bias that women were intellectually inferior to men and needed only a limited education. Arguing that women's intellectual powers were equal to men's, he proposed a system of academies and colleges for women.

---

[10]Hyman Kuritz, "Benjamin Rush: His Theory of Republican Education," *History of Education Quarterly* (Winter 1967), pp. 435–36. For a biography of Rush, see Alyn Brodsky, *Benjamin Rush: Patriot and Physician* (New York: St. Martin's Press, 2004).

TIMELINE
THOMAS JEFFERSON

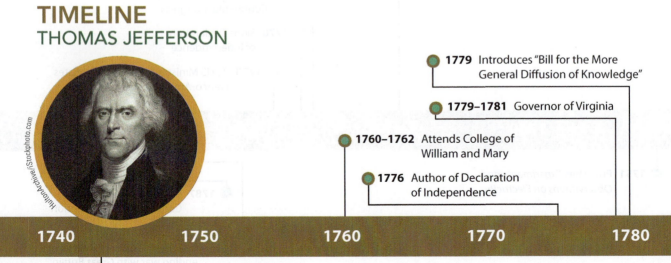

1779 Introduces "Bill for the More General Diffusion of Knowledge"

1779–1781 Governor of Virginia

1760–1762 Attends College of William and Mary

1776 Author of Declaration of Independence

| 1740 | 1750 | 1760 | 1770 | 1780 |

1743 Birth

Hulton Archive/iStockphoto.com

5-2e Webster: Schoolmaster of the Republic

Noah Webster (1758–1843), a prominent educator and lexicographer, was one of the early republic's leading cultural nationalists.[11] He wanted the United States to be culturally independent with its own "language as well as government." Believing that a common language and literature would build a sense of national identity, Webster worked to construct a distinctive American version of the English language with its own idiom, pronunciation, and style.

Believing that textbooks had a powerful influence on teaching and learning, Webster wrote spelling and reading books that emphasized American identity and achievements.[12] His *American Dictionary* was published in 1828 after years of intensive research.

Esteemed as the "schoolmaster of the republic," Noah Webster promoted a monocultural American identity with its own distinctive Americanized version of English as the national language. Until the mid-twentieth century, public schools "Americanized" immigrant children by imposing this monolithic cultural version on them. Today, multicultural and bilingual education programs recognize America's diversity by seeking to broaden the contours of American cultural identity.

FOCUS Why did Franklin, Jefferson, Rush, and Webster propose plans to use education and schooling to construct a distinctive American cultural identity? Did they succeed? How did political and social change in the early national period change the educational institutions and processes inherited from the colonial era? Have particular school subjects, ceremonies, or events shaped your cultural identity as an American?

5-3 THE MOVEMENT TOWARD PUBLIC SCHOOLING

In the early nineteenth century, when some children worked in the factories in the industrializing eastern states, philanthropic groups supported Sunday and monitorial schools to educate them in basic skills and religion. The Sunday school instructed children on Sunday when factories were closed. When public schools were established, the Sunday school model was used by Protestant churches to provide religious education to the children of their particular denomination. The American Sunday School Union was established to coordinate the activities and develop curricular materials for its member churches.

Of the various philanthropic educational efforts, the monitorial school was most popular. Monitorial education came to the United States from the United Kingdom, where Joseph Lancaster (1778–1838) had developed it to provide basic instruction in reading, spelling, and arithmetic to large numbers of children. In the **monitorial method**, a master teacher would train older and more advanced students as instructional aides (monitors) to teach reading, writing, and arithmetic to younger pupils. Because student monitors did most of the teaching, the costs were minimal. Lessons

monitorial method A method of instruction, also known as mutual instruction, developed by the English educators Andrew Bell and Joseph Lancaster, which was popular in the United States in the early nineteenth century.

---

[11]Joshua Kendall, *The Forgotten Founding Father: Noah Webster's Obsession and the Creation of an American Culture* (New York: G. P. Putnam's Sons, 2010), pp. 69–75.

[12]For Webster and his *Elementary Spelling Book,* see Gutek, *An Historical Introduction to American Education,* pp. 55–61.

1801–1809 US President

1825 Opening of University of Virginia

1826 Death

| 1790 | 1800 | 1810 | 1820 | 1830 |

were calibrated to groups of students who moved in unison from lesson to lesson; lessons were broken down into small parts, or units, with each phase of instruction assigned to particular monitors. Monitorial schools were popular in large eastern cities. For example, more than 600,000 children attended the New York Free School Society's monitorial schools.[13] In the 1840s, common schools replaced monitorial schools when their educational limitations become increasingly apparent.

5-3a The Common School

common school A publicly supported and locally controlled elementary school.

The **common school** movement of the first half of the nineteenth century is highly significant in American education because it created publicly controlled and funded elementary education. It was called a "common" school because it was open to children of all social and economic classes. Historically, however, enslaved African children in the South were excluded from common schools until the Civil War and the Thirteenth Amendment ended slavery, and more public schools were established during the Reconstruction period.

In the country's common schools, despite separation of church and state, the school day usually began with a Christian prayer, hymn, or reading from the Bible, which would be followed by the recitation of the pledge of allegiance to the flag and the reading of a short patriotic passage or the singing of a patriotic song. The teacher led the students through a basic standard curriculum of reading, writing, spelling, arithmetic, history, and geography. Often lessons in health, art (drawing), and music (singing) were included. Because the school contained students of a variety of ages, the teacher might arrange them into groups of a similar age. In this way, she could do some simultaneous group instruction. However, a considerable amount of time was spent on the individual recitation in which a student would stand before the teacher and recite a previously assigned lesson. In the early nineteenth century, it was not unusual for each student to bring the books their family owned with them to school. The teacher would make an assignment from the book, and the student would memorize and then recite it.

---

[13]William R. Johnson, "'Chanting Choristes': Simultaneous Recitation in Baltimore's Nineteenth-Century Primary Schools," *History of Education Quarterly* (Spring 1994), pp. 1–12.

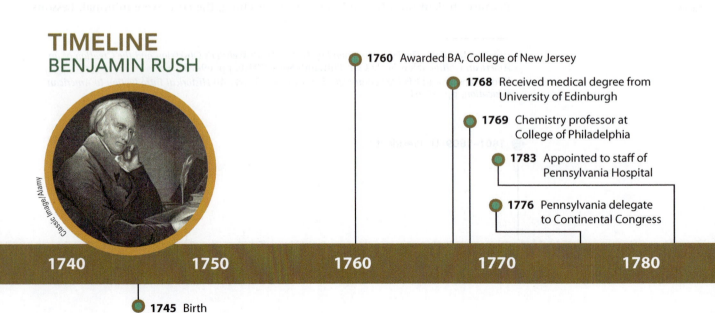

TIMELINE
BENJAMIN RUSH

Classic Image/Alamy

1760 Awarded BA, College of New Jersey

1768 Received medical degree from University of Edinburgh

1769 Chemistry professor at College of Philadelphia

1783 Appointed to staff of Pennsylvania Hospital

1776 Pennsylvania delegate to Continental Congress

1740   1750   1760   1770   1780

1745 Birth

Because of the historic tradition of local control and the Constitution's reserved powers clause in the Tenth Amendment, the states, rather than the federal government, were responsible for the establishment and support of public schools. The United States, unlike France and Japan, did not establish a national school system. The patterns by which common schools were established differed from state to state and even within a given state. Especially on the western frontier, where there were many small school districts, resources and support for schooling varied significantly from one district to another. Because of this history, public-education funding is still seriously uneven in the school districts and states.

The common-school movement gained momentum between 1820 and 1850. The New England states of Massachusetts and Connecticut, with a tradition of town and district schools, were the earliest to establish common schools. In 1826, Massachusetts required every town to elect a school committee responsible for all the schools in its area of jurisdiction. Ten years later, in 1836, Massachusetts established the first state board of education. Connecticut then followed its neighbor's example. Other northern states generally adopted New England's common school model. As the frontier moved westward, and new states were admitted to the Union, they, too, established common or public elementary-school systems. In the South, however, with some exceptions such as North Carolina, common schools were not generally established until the Reconstruction period, 1865–1876, after the Civil War.

State legislatures typically established common schools in the following sequence:

1. First, they allowed residents to organize local school districts with the approval of local voters.
2. Second, they deliberately encouraged, but did not mandate, establishing school districts, electing school boards, and levying taxes to fund schools.
3. Third, they made common schools compulsory by mandating the establishment of districts, election of boards, and collecting taxes to support schools.

The common school movement did not proceed easily, however. Opponents argued that education was a private, not a public concern. Some individuals, especially in the Midwestern rural areas, supported schools as strictly local institutions but did not want the state involved in their governance, control, and funding. Despite this opposition, common schools were established and laid the foundation of the American public-school system. Later in the nineteenth century, the American **educational ladder** was completed as high schools connected elementary schools to state colleges and universities. Horace Mann was one of the most prominent common school leaders.

educational ladder The system of public education in the United States that begins with kindergarten, proceeds through elementary school, continues through middle and high school, and leads to attendance at a community college, state college, or university.

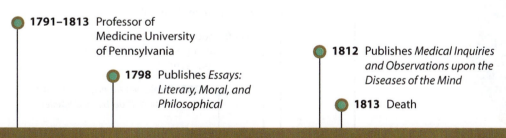

1791–1813 Professor of Medicine University of Pennsylvania

1798 Publishes *Essays: Literary, Moral, and Philosophical*

1812 Publishes *Medical Inquiries and Observations upon the Diseases of the Mind*

1813 Death

1790   1800   1810   1820   1830

5-3b Mann: The Struggle for Public Schools

When the Massachusetts legislature established a state board of education in 1837, it appointed Horace Mann (1796–1859), a prominent Whig political leader and a steadfast proponent of common schools, as its secretary.[14] His *Annual Reports* provided a rationale for public schools. As editor of the *Common School Journal*, Mann also sought to win national support for public schools.[15] (For Mann's appointment and other events in American education, see Overview 5.1.)

Mann used his political acumen to mobilize support and build a coalition for public education. He convinced taxpayers that it was in their self-interest to support public schools. Applying the Calvinist *stewardship theory* to his common-school campaign, Mann argued that wealthy people, as stewards of society, had a special responsibility to provide public education. He told businessmen that tax-supported public education was an investment in Massachusetts's economic growth. Common schools would train productive workers to be responsible citizens who obeyed the law and worked hard and diligently. Mann convinced workers and farmers that common schools would be the great social equalizer, providing their children with the skills and knowledge needed to climb the economic ladder.

Building on Jefferson's case for civic education, Mann argued that public education was necessary for a democratic society. Citizens needed to be literate to make intelligent and responsible decisions as voters, members of juries, elected public officials, and civil servants.

Whereas Jefferson sought to improve educational opportunity for academically talented young men, Mann wanted to provide greater equality of access to schools. Although common schools would minimize class differences, Mann, like a true Whig, believed the upper social classes should still control the economic and political system. Like Noah Webster, Mann supported an "Americanization" policy, arguing that a common-school system would provide the United States, as a nation of immigrants, with a unifying common culture.

---

[14]The definitive biography remains Jonathan Messerli, *Horace Mann: A Biography* (New York: Knopf, 1972). Reprints of books on Horace Mann are B. A. Hinsdale, *Horace Mann and the Common School Revival in the United States* (Whitefish, MT: Kessinger Publishing, 2007); Matthew Hale Smith, William B. Fowle, and Horace Mann, *The Bible, The Rod, and Religion in Common Schools* (Whitefish, MT: Kessinger Publishing, 2008); Joy Elmer Morgan, *Horace Mann: His Ideas and Ideals* (Whitefish, MT: Kessinger Publishing, 2008).

[15]For Mann and common schools and his Report No. 12, see Gutek, *An Historical Introduction to American Education*, pp. 86–89 and 108–114.

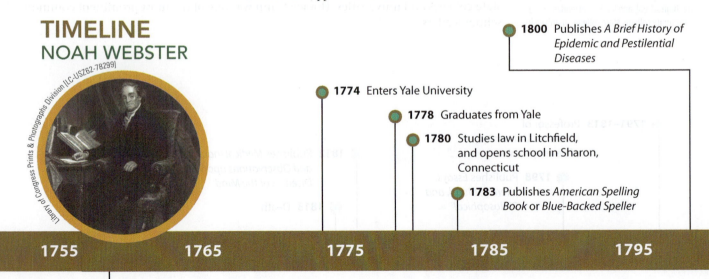

TIMELINE
NOAH WEBSTER

Library of Congress Prints & Photographs Division [LC-USZ62-78299]

1800 Publishes *A Brief History of Epidemic and Pestilential Diseases*

1774 Enters Yale University

1778 Graduates from Yale

1780 Studies law in Litchfield, and opens school in Sharon, Connecticut

1783 Publishes *American Spelling Book* or *Blue-Backed Speller*

1755   **1765**   **1775**   **1785**   **1795**

1758 Born

Mann constructed the general public-school philosophy in that public schools would be (1) organized as a statewide system, funded by local and state taxes; (2) governed by elected school boards who carried out state mandates; (3) staffed by professionally educated teachers; and (4) free of church control.

5-3c Normal Schools and Women's Education

In addition to providing publicly supported elementary education for the majority of American children, the common-school movement had two important complementary consequences: (1) it led to the establishing of **normal schools**, which provided early preservice teacher preparation; and (2) it opened elementary-school teaching as an important career path for women.

normal school A two-year teacher-education institution used to prepare elementary teachers in the nineteenth and early twentieth centuries.

Named after the French *école normale* on which they were modeled, normal schools were the dominant institution for preparing elementary-school teachers from the 1860s to 1920. While most normal schools were state institutions, others were part of public-school systems in large cities or were private or religious institutions. Normal-school enrollments increased from 29,100 in 1875 to 116,600 in 1899 and reached 119,000 students in 1915.

Although there were exceptions, most normal schools offered two-year teacher-education programs that were organized into three components: academic courses, pedagogical courses, and clinical experiences. Academic courses, often in the liberal arts and sciences, were related to the skills and subjects taught in elementary schools. For example, English language and literature courses related to teaching reading, writing, grammar, spelling, and literature; mathematics, algebra, and geometry related to arithmetic; American and European history and geography related to civics and social studies; and physics, chemistry, botany, and biology related to general science and nature studies. More directly related to teaching, pedagogical courses included the history, philosophy, and psychology of education; methods of instruction; and classroom management. Clinical experiences involved observation of experienced teachers in school classrooms and supervised practice teaching. In the twentieth century, many normal schools were reorganized as four-year teacher-education colleges.[16]

The establishment of common schools created a demand for professionally prepared teachers, and many women entered teaching careers in the expanding elementary-school system. The normal schools prepared women for these careers and also opened opportunities for higher education previously denied them. Although salaries were

---

[16]James W. Fraser, *Preparing America's Teachers: A History* (New York: Teachers College Press, 2007), pp. 27–40, 43–58. For the history of normal schools, see Christine A. Ogren, *The American State Normal School: "An Instrument of Great Good"* (New York: Palgrave Macmillan, 2005). For normal schools in Massachusetts, see Mary-Lou Breitborde and Kelly Kolodny, eds., *Remembering Massachusetts State Normal Schools: Pioneers in Teacher Education* (Westfield: Institute for Massachusetts Studies, 2014).

1806 Publishes *A Compendious Dictionary of the English Language*

1828 Publishes *An American Dictionary of the English Language*

1843 Death

| 1805 | 1815 | 1825 | 1835 | 1845 |

low and conditions demanding, teaching gave middle-class women an opportunity for careers outside the home. Until the Civil War, most rural schoolteachers were men. By 1900, however, 71 percent of rural teachers were women.

5-3d Catharine Beecher: Preparing Women as Teachers

In the nineteenth century, Elizabeth Cady Stanton, Emma Willard, and Susan B. Anthony led the movement for women's suffrage and educational equality. Prominent among these leaders was Catharine Beecher (1800–1878), a teacher educator, who connected the common school to women's education.[17] Beecher founded and operated the Hartford Female Seminary, in Hartford, Connecticut, from 1823 until 1831. She then created the Western Female Institute as a model for teacher-education institutions.

Teaching, Beecher reasoned, provided educated women with a socially useful career at a time when their access to higher education and the professions was severely limited. Importantly, it made women financially independent and gave them the opportunity to shape future generations morally.

Envisioning elementary-school teaching as a woman's profession, Beecher contributed to the feminization of elementary teaching. Women's colleges would open higher education to women and prepare them to staff the growing public-school system.[18] She argued that ninety thousand teachers were needed to bring civilization to America's untamed western frontier.[19] Beecher was part of a network of women educators such as Emma Willard, Zilpah Grant, and Mary Lyon who prepared women for teaching careers.

Beecher had clear ideas about preservice preparation and classroom practice. In their preservice preparation, students would study evangelical Christian morality, discuss the civilizing mission of women as teachers, and observe experienced teachers.[20] In practice, women teachers needed to use their "sensibility," their intuitive insights, about children to manage their classrooms, teach a common curriculum that encouraged literacy and civility, and serve as moral mentors.

---

[17]Kathryn Kish Sklar, *Catharine Beecher: A Study in American Domesticity* (New York: W. W. Norton & Co., 1976), p. xiv. Also, see Barbara A. White, *The Beecher Sisters* (New Haven, CT, and London: Yale University Press, 2003).

[18]Catharine Beecher, *An Essay on the Education of Female Teachers* (New York: Van Nostrand & Dwight, 1835), pp. 14–18.

[19]Ibid., p. 19.

[20]Ellen C. DuBois and Lynn Dumenil, *Through Women's Eyes: An American History with Documents* (Boston: Bedford/St. Martins, 2005), pp. 139–141.

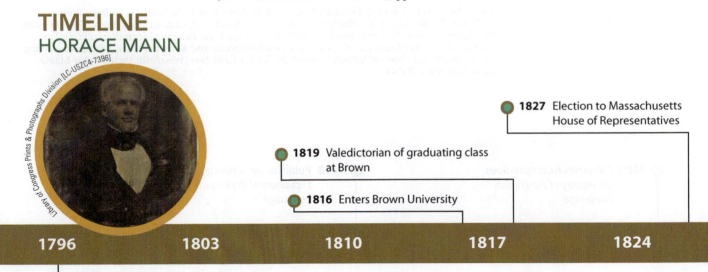

TIMELINE
HORACE MANN

Library of Congress Prints & Photographs Division [LC-USZC4-7396]

1827 Election to Massachusetts House of Representatives

1819 Valedictorian of graduating class at Brown

1816 Enters Brown University

1796   **1803**   **1810**   **1817**   **1824**

1796 Born in Franklin, Massachusetts

The Granger Collection, NYC

> **PHOTO 5.1** The small rural school also served as a cultural center for the community.

The One-Room School   In much of the country, especially in the rural areas of farms and small towns, the typical public school was a one-room building in which a single woman taught boys and girls, ranging in age from 6 or 7 to 16 or 17 (Photo 5.1). The local school district, with its single one-room school, could act as almost a direct democracy in which an elected school board set the tax rate and hired and supervised the teacher.[21] Or some board's members might be local tyrants, arbitrarily imposing their rules and regulations on teachers and students.

---

[21]A web presentation on the one-room school is "One Room Schools: Michigan's Educational Legacy," Clarke Historical Library, (Mount Pleasant: Central Michigan University).

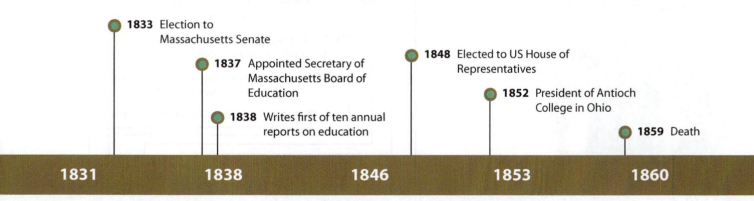

1833 Election to Massachusetts Senate

1837 Appointed Secretary of Massachusetts Board of Education

1838 Writes first of ten annual reports on education

1848 Elected to US House of Representatives

1852 President of Antioch College in Ohio

1859 Death

| **1831** | **1838** | **1846** | **1853** | **1860** |

On the Western frontier, the one-room log school was often the first community building constructed. By the 1870s, wood-frame schoolhouses, painted white or red, replaced the crude log structures. These improved buildings, heated by woodburning stoves, included slate blackboards and cloakrooms. The teacher's desk stood on a raised platform at the front of the room where there were portraits of George Washington, and in the northern states, Abraham Lincoln. Many classrooms had large double desks that seated two pupils. Later, these often were replaced with single desks, each with a desktop attached to the back of the chair in front of it. Thus, all the desks were immovable and arranged in straight rows, one behind the other.[22]

The pupils, ranging from age 6 to 17, studied a basic curriculum of reading, writing (penmanship), grammar, spelling, arithmetic, history, geography, music (singing), drawing, and hygiene (healthy living). Teachers typically used the drill and recitation method in which a student or a small group of students would come to the front of the room and recite a previously memorized passage from a textbook. Later in the nineteenth century, teachers who attended normal schools began to use Pestalozzi's object lessons and simultaneous group instruction. Some teachers (such as Helen Parkhurst, an innovative teacher educator) experimented with progressive methods in which some of the students worked individually on their lessons while she worked with others in small groups. Schools emphasized the values of punctuality, honesty, hard work, and patriotism. The rural one-room schoolteachers, expected to be disciplinarians as well as instructors, had "to be their own janitors, record keepers, and school administrators."[23] For more about one-room schools, see the Technology @ School box.

Teacher certification was simple but chaotic in that each board issued its own certificates to its teachers, which other districts often refused to recognize. Today's more uniform state certification and accreditation by the National Council for Accreditation of Teacher Education (NCATE) is a step toward greater professionalization for teachers. Many small districts were consolidated into larger ones in the early twentieth century, as described in Chapter 7, Governing and Administering Public Education.

---

[22]Wayne E. Fuller, *One-Room Schools of the Middle West: An Illustrated History* (Lawrence: University of Kansas Press, 1994), pp. 7–19, 18–27, 30–40.

[23]Ibid., p. 61.

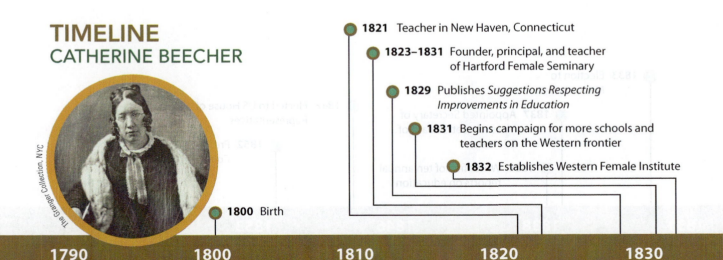

TIMELINE
CATHERINE BEECHER

The Granger Collection, NYC

1800 Birth

1821 Teacher in New Haven, Connecticut

1823–1831 Founder, principal, and teacher of Hartford Female Seminary

1829 Publishes *Suggestions Respecting Improvements in Education*

1831 Begins campaign for more schools and teachers on the Western frontier

1832 Establishes Western Female Institute

1790   **1800**   **1810**   **1820**   **1830**

TECHNOLOGY @ SCHOOL

You can research the one-room school to make a personal connection to the careers of America's pioneer teachers. Consult these websites for more on one-room schools:

- For one-room schoolhouse historical information, access the Northern Illinois University Blackwell Museum website.

- For information on one-room schools, McGuffey readers, and penmanship, access the Country School Association of America website.

- For an introduction to the Kansas One Room School House Project, access the Kansas Heritage website.

- For a state listing of sites, stories, photos, lessons, and a bibliography, access the One-Room Schoolhouse Center website.

These sites provide information about teachers, students, architecture, textbooks, and curriculum in one-room schools. You can continue your research at your local or school library to identify articles and books on this subject.

Contact local museums and history societies in your area to see if they have materials on one-room schools. You can also locate and interview individuals who attended one-room schools. Share your research with colleagues in the course.

FOCUS Did Horace Mann and Catharine Beecher achieve their goals in common schools and teacher education? How did the establishment of common schools relate to the growth and development of teacher education and to the entry of more women as teachers? Consider how public schools shaped your educational experience. Do some research to see if any members of your extended family attended one-room schools.

5-3e McGuffey Readers

The growth of public elementary schools, especially "graded" urban schools, and teacher-education programs generated a demand for series of textbooks on skills, especially graded reading and spelling books, and subjects such as mathematics, history, and geography. William Holmes McGuffey (1800–1873), clergyman, professor, and college president, wrote the widely used and highly popular McGuffey readers. McGuffey readers emphasized literacy, hard work, diligence, punctuality, patriotism, and civility. Stressing patriotism and heroism, reading selections included the orations of Patrick Henry, Daniel Webster, and George Washington. More than 120 million copies of McGuffey's readers were sold between 1836 and 1920.[24]

---

[24]James M. Lower, "William Holmes McGuffey: A Book or a Man? Or More?" *Vitae Scholasticae* (Fall 1984), pp. 311–320; Harvey C. Minnich, *William Holmes McGuffey and His Readers* (Whitefish, MT: Kessinger Publishing, 2008); for a reprint of a McGuffey reader, see Williams Holmes McGuffey, *McGuffey's Fifth Eclectic Reader* (Charleston, SC: Bibliolife, 2008).

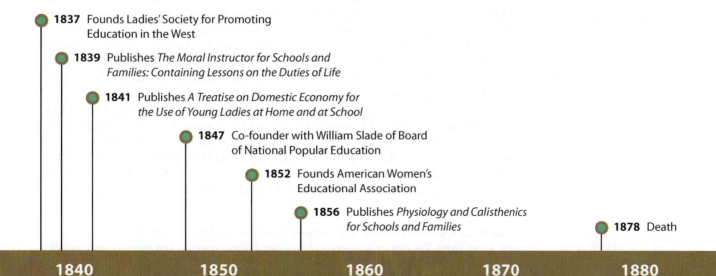

1837 Founds Ladies' Society for Promoting Education in the West

1839 Publishes *The Moral Instructor for Schools and Families: Containing Lessons on the Duties of Life*

1841 Publishes *A Treatise on Domestic Economy for the Use of Young Ladies at Home and at School*

1847 Co-founder with William Slade of Board of National Popular Education

1852 Founds American Women's Educational Association

1856 Publishes *Physiology and Calisthenics for Schools and Families*

1878 Death

1840   1850   1860   1870   1880

5-4 THE DEVELOPMENT OF AMERICAN SECONDARY SCHOOLS

With the establishment of public elementary schools, the first rung of the American educational ladder was now in place. The highest rung was filled by the state colleges. However, these upper and lower steps remained disconnected in the middle. The next section examines how the establishment of public high schools completed the ladder.

5-4a The Academy: Forerunner of the High School

Anticipated by Benjamin Franklin's plan, the academy replaced the colonial Latin grammar school as the major American secondary school in the first half of the nineteenth century. By 1855, more than 6,000 academies enrolled 263,000 students. Unlike the Latin grammar schools, which were exclusively attended by males preparing for college entry, academies were both single-sex and coeducational. They offered college-preparatory programs as well as a range of other programs.

Academy programs followed three patterns: (1) the traditional college-preparatory curriculum, which emphasized Latin and Greek; (2) the English-language curriculum, a general program for students who would end their formal education upon completing secondary school; and (3) the normal curriculum, which prepared elementary-school teachers. Some males also attended military academies such as the Citadel in South Carolina.

Some academies were founded to educate young women. For example, in 1821, Emma Willard, a leader in the women's rights movement, established New York's Troy Female Seminary. Along with domestic science (household management and family-related skills) and women's arts (sewing, weaving, and sketching), women's academies offered classical and modern languages, science, mathematics, art, music, and the teacher-preparation, or normal, curriculum. Although most academies were private, some were semipublic institutions partially funded by cities and states. Academies were popular secondary schools until the 1870s, when public high schools began to replace them. Today, private academies still provide secondary education for a small percentage of the school-age population.

5-4b The High School

high school A secondary school for students that typically includes grades 9 or 10 through 12.

Although a few **high schools**, such as the Boston English Classical School, were operating in the early nineteenth century, the high school became the country's dominant secondary school after 1860. In the 1870s, the courts ruled in a series of cases (especially the Kalamazoo, Michigan, case in 1874) that school districts could levy taxes to establish and support public high schools.[25] By 1890, public high schools enrolled more than twice as many students as private academies.[26]

In the late nineteenth and early twentieth centuries, the states passed compulsory attendance laws that established the age range that students had to attend school. While students could attend approved nonpublic schools, the states set minimum standards for all schools.

The progressives supported compulsory attendance legislation. They worked for the enactment of child labor laws, such as the Keating-Owen Child Labor Act of 1916, which restricted employment of children and adolescents so that they would attend school rather than enter the workforce. Compulsory attendance was sometimes opposed by immigrant parents, who feared it was a strategy to erode their children's ethnic heritage, and among farmers, who needed their children to work on the farm.[27]

[25]See *Stuart v. School District No. 1 of Village of Kalamazoo,* 30 Mich. 69 (1874).

[26]L. Dean Webb, *The History of American Education: A Great American Experiment* (Upper Saddle River, NJ: Pearson/Merrill/Prentice Hall, 2006), pp. 173–183.

[27]Michael McGeer, *A Fierce Discontent: The Rise and Fall of the Progressive Movement in America, 1870–1920* (New York: Free Press, 2003), pp. 190–111.

Urbanization and the High School   In the late nineteenth and early twentieth centuries, the convergence of several significant socioeconomic and educational trends created a favorable climate for the establishment of high schools. The United States was changing from an agricultural and rural society to an industrial and urban nation. For example, New York City's population quadrupled between 1860 and 1910. By 1930, more than 25 percent of all Americans lived in seven great urban areas: New York, Chicago, Philadelphia, Boston, Detroit, Los Angeles, and Cleveland. The high school was an educational response to an urban and industrial society's need for more specialized occupations, professions, and services.[28] This socioeconomic change was concurrent with important developments in adolescent psychology. G. Stanley Hall, for example, argued that adolescents, at a crucial stage in their development, were best educated in high schools.

Reshaping the High School Curriculum   Since its establishment, the purposes of high schools has been debated. Whereas liberal arts and science college professors saw them as college-preparatory institutions, vocational educators wanted high schools to prepare adolescents to enter the workforce. In some large cities, high schools, called "people's colleges," offered liberal arts and science courses as well as work-related programs.[29] In 1892, the National Education Association (NEA) established the **Committee of Ten**, chaired by Harvard University President Charles Eliot, to define the high school's mission and purposes. The committee made two important recommendations: (1) subjects should be taught uniformly for both college-preparatory students and those who completed their formal education upon graduation; and (2) an endorsement of the pattern of eight years of elementary and four years of secondary education.[30] It identified four curricula as appropriate for the high school: classical, Latin-scientific, modern language, and English. These recommendations reflected a general college-preparatory orientation because each curriculum included foreign languages, mathematics, science, English, and history.

By 1918, all states had enacted compulsory attendance laws, with thirty states mandating full-time attendance until age sixteen.[31] Increasing enrollments made high school students more representative of the general adolescent population and more culturally diverse than in the past when students came primarily from the upper- and upper-middle classes.

The NEA's **Commission on the Reorganization of Secondary Education** in the *Cardinal Principles of Secondary Education* (1918) responded to the socioeconomic changes in the high school student population. The Commission redefined the high school as a comprehensive institution serving the country's pluralistic social, cultural, and economic populations. It recommended the following: (1) establishing differentiated curricula to meet agricultural, commercial, industrial, and domestic as well as college-preparatory needs; and (2) maintaining the high school's integrative and comprehensive social character.[32] The Commission's recommendations paralleled Herbert Spencer's curriculum theory based on needs as discussed in Chapter 4, Pioneers of Teaching and Learning.

Committee of Ten A committee of the National Education Association chaired by Charles Eliot, which shaped the high school curriculum through its recommendations of a four-year program and a curriculum that included academic subjects for all students.

Commission on the Reorganization of Secondary Education A National Education Association commission that shaped the high school curriculum through its recommendations in *The Cardinal Principles of Secondary Education (1918).*

---

[28]William J. Reese, *The Origins of the American High School* (New Haven, CT: Yale University Press, 1995); David F. Labaree, *The Making of an American High School: The Credentials Market and the Central High School of Philadelphia, 1839–1939* (New Haven, CT: Yale University Press, 2009).

[29]Jurgen Herbst, *The Once and Future School: Three Hundred Years of American Secondary Education* (New York: Routledge, 1996), pp. 95–106.

[30]National Education Association, *Report of the Committee on Secondary School Studies* (Washington, DC: US Government Printing Office, 1893).

[31]L. Dean Webb, *The History of American Education: A Great American Experiment*, p. 176.

[32]Commission on the Reorganization of Secondary Education, Cardinal Principles of American Secondary Education, Bulletin no. 35 (Washington, DC: US Government Printing Office, 1918).

5-4c Secondary-School Organization

By the 1920s, four curricular patterns were used in high schools: (1) the college-preparatory program, which included English language and literature, foreign languages, mathematics, natural and physical sciences, and history and social studies; (2) the commercial or business program with courses in bookkeeping, shorthand, and typing; (3) the industrial, vocational, home economics, and agricultural programs; and (4) the general academic program for students planning to complete their formal education upon graduation.

Despite variations, the typical high school pattern followed a four-year sequence encompassing grades 9–12 and generally including ages 14 to 18. Variations included reorganized six-year schools, where students attended a combined junior-senior high school after completing a six-year elementary school; three-year junior high schools, comprising grades 7–9; and three-year senior high schools for grades 10–12.

junior high school A two- or three-year transitional school between elementary and high school, commonly for grades 7–9.

In the 1920s and 1930s, educators designed the **junior high school** as a transitional institution between elementary and high school that was oriented to early adolescents' developmental needs. Junior high schools were either two-year institutions that encompassed grades 7 and 8 or three-year institutions that also included ninth grade. The junior high school curriculum extended beyond that of elementary schools by including some vocational and commercial courses. By 1920, there were 883 junior high schools in the United States. By the 1940s, more than 50 percent of young adolescents were attending junior high schools.[33]

middle school A two- to four-year transitional school between elementary and high school, commonly for grades 6–8.

In the 1960s, **middle schools** became another type of transitional institution between elementary and high school.[34] They generally include grades 6–8 (ages 11–13) and facilitate a gradual transition from childhood to adolescence by emphasizing programs oriented to preadolescent development and needs. Often using new architectural designs, middle schools featured learning centers, language laboratories, and arts centers. Their numbers grew rapidly from 1,434 in 1971 to 9,750 in 2000.[35] Although most school districts today use the middle-school model, some retain the junior-high approach.[36]

5-4d The Development of Educational Technology

In the twentieth century, America's schools began to integrate educational technology into their classrooms. Using technology in classroom instruction is an important component of preservice teacher-education programs. Competency in educational technology is mandated by many state certification programs and is a standard in professional teacher accreditation.

In the late 1920s, radio and motion pictures were introduced in schools. The National Association of Educational Broadcasting was organized to implement radio instruction and the exchange of educational scripts. "Schools of the Air" on commercial frequencies brought cultural and music-appreciation programs into classrooms in the late 1930s and 1940s.

Alexander J. Stoddard initiated the National Program in the Use of Television in the Schools in 1957, and the Midwest Program on Airborne Television Instruction

---

[33]Douglas MacIver and Allen Ruby, "Middle Schools," in James W. Guthrie, ed., *Encyclopedia of Education,* 2nd ed., Vol. 5 (New York: Macmillan/Thomson Gale, 2003), p. 1630.

[34]For middle-school education, see Thomas Dickinson, ed., *Reinventing the Middle School* (New York: Routledge Farmer, 2001).

[35]MacIver and Ruby, "Middle Schools," p. 1630.

[36]For developments in middle-school education, see Anthony W. Jackson and Gayle A. Davis, *Turning Points 2000: Educating Adolescents in the 21st Century* (New York: Teachers College Press, 2000).

began telecasting lessons to schools in 1961.[37] Along with educational television, other instructional technologies such as programmed learning, computer-assisted instruction, and educational videos were being used in the schools by the early 1970s. Today many high schools have their own television studio and channel. Closed-circuit television frequently augments preservice teacher education, providing student teachers with an instant, videotaped critique of their teaching.

The 1990s saw large-scale development and implementation of computer-based educational technology. Electronic data retrieval, the Internet, and computer-assisted instruction brought significant change to instruction.[38] Tim Berners-Lee, with Robert Cilia, developed the prototype for the World Wide Web in 1990, creating an electronic means of quickly disseminating and accessing information. An important development occurred in 1993, when Marc Andreessen and Eric Bina developed Mosaic, a software program capable of electronically displaying graphics with accompanying texts.[39] States and local school districts rushed to increase the number of computers in classrooms, improve Internet access, and provide increased technical support for schools. The US Department of Education issued "Getting America's Students Ready for the Twenty-First Century: Meeting the Technology Literacy Challenge," in 1996, to provide greater access to information technology and develop technology and information literacy skills for teachers and students.[40] Today, teacher-education programs include preservice and in-service training in using educational technology in professional-development experiences.

5-5 THE AMERICAN COLLEGE AND UNIVERSITY

Colleges were established in North America as early as the colonial period of the seventeenth century, when Protestant denominations established church-affiliated institutions of higher learning. Believing that well-educated ministers were needed to establish Christianity in the New World, the Massachusetts General Court chartered Harvard College in 1636. By 1754, Yale, William and Mary, Princeton, and King's College (later Columbia University) had also been established as church-affiliated institutions of higher learning. Other colonial colleges were the University of Pennsylvania, Dartmouth, Brown, and Rutgers. The general colonial college curriculum included the following:

- First year: Latin, Greek, Hebrew, rhetoric, and logic
- Second year: Greek, Hebrew, logic, and natural philosophy
- Third year: natural philosophy, metaphysics, and ethics
- Fourth year: mathematics and a review of Greek, Latin, logic, and natural philosophy[41]

---

[37]Gutek, *An Historical Introduction to American Education,* pp. 224–226.

[38]Allan Collins and Richard Halverson, *Rethinking Education in the Age of Technology: The Digital Revolution and Schooling in America* (New York: Teachers College Press, 2009), pp. 66–90.

[39]Robert Cailliau and James Gilles, *How the Web Was Born: The Story of the World Wide Web* (New York: Oxford University Press, 2000). For networking among teachers, see Kira J. Baker-Doyle, *The Networked Teacher: How New Teachers Build Social Networks* (New York: Teachers College Press, 2011).

[40]See Office of Educational Technology, US Department of Education, at **www2.ed.gov /about/offices/list/os/technology/index.html**.

[41]John R. Thelin, *A History of American Higher Education* (Baltimore, MD: Johns Hopkins University Press, 2004), pp. 2–38; also, see Christopher J. Lucas, *American Higher Education: A History* (New York: St Martin's Press, 2006); and David J. Hoeveler, *Creating the American Mind: Intellect and Politics in the Colonial Colleges* (Lanham, MD: Rowman and Littlefield Publishers, 2007).

land-grant college A state college or university offering agricultural and mechanical curricula, funded originally by the Morrill Act of 1862. Today, many institutions originally established as land-grant colleges are large multipurpose state universities.

The University of Virginia, designed by Thomas Jefferson, was the model for the modern state university. Jefferson saw the University's purpose as encouraging the "illimitable freedom of the human mind . . . to follow truth wherever it may lead."[42] Since the University of Virginia opened in 1825, states have been establishing colleges and universities. Along with the state colleges and universities, churches continued to establish liberal arts colleges, especially in the new states that entered the Union. Thus, the pattern of both state and private institutions of higher learning was established in the United States.

In the 1850s, critics of traditional liberal arts colleges argued that the federal government should provide land grants to the states to establish more practical agricultural and engineering institutions. In response, the Morrill Act of 1862 granted each state 30,000 acres of public land for each senator and representative in Congress. The income from this land grant was to support state colleges for agricultural and mechanical (engineering) education.[43] **Land-grant colleges** and universities today are typically large institutions that include agriculture, teacher education, engineering, and other applied sciences and technologies as well as liberal arts and professional education. Still another important development in higher education came when Johns Hopkins University was founded in 1876 as a graduate research institution based on the German university seminar model.

The two-year community college is among the most available and popular higher-education institutions in the United States. Some two-year institutions originated as junior colleges in the late nineteenth and early twentieth centuries, when several university presidents recommended that the first two years of undergraduate education take place at another institution rather than at a four-year college. Others developed from the initiatives of high school administrators to provide courses in special subjects such as bookkeeping and vocational training for their recent graduates. After World War II, many junior colleges were reorganized into community colleges, and numerous new community colleges were established with broader functions of serving their communities' educational needs. States developed strategies that calibrated the two-year community colleges with their four-year colleges and universities as comprehensive systems of higher education. Community colleges tend to be highly responsive in providing training for technological change, especially those related to the communications and electronic data revolutions, as well as to the general educational needs of the people in their localities.

Congress passed the Servicemen's Readjustment Act (the GI Bill) in 1944, near the end of World War II, which marked a major change in the student population in American higher education. To help readjust society to peacetime and reintegrate returning military personnel into the economy, the GI Bill provided federal funds to subsidize veterans' tuition, fees, books, and living expenses. College and university enrollments expanded between 1944 and 1951, when 7.8 million veterans used the Bill's assistance to attend technical schools, colleges, and universities.[44] The result launched a continuing trend to open higher education to more diverse and previously underserved groups.

Since the 1960s, a massive growth of American higher-education institutions occurred as a fully articulated system of community colleges and four-year colleges and universities developed in the United States. However, higher education today faces the issue of the rising cost of attending college and student indebtedness.

---

[42]Noble E. Cunningham, Jr., *In Pursuit of Reason: The Life of Thomas Jefferson* (New York: Ballantine Books, 1987), pp. 344–345.

[43]Benjamin E. Andrews, *The Land Grant of 1862 and the Land-Grant College* (Washington, DC: US Government Printing Office, 1918).

[44]Gerald L. Gutek, *American Education 1945–2000: A History and Commentary* (Long Grove, IL: Waveland Press, 2000), pp. 9–14.

5-6 IMMIGRATION AND EDUCATION IN A CULTURALLY PLURALIST SOCIETY

The next section examines the origins of ethnic, racial, language, and cultural pluralism in American society and education. It presents a topical rather than a strictly chronological discussion of the United States as a nation of immigrants and examines the educational history of African-, Native-, Latino-, Asian-, and Arab Americans.

Historically, the United States has been, as it is today, a racially, ethnically, and culturally pluralist nation. With the exception of Native Americans, Americans trace their roots to other continents, especially to Europe, Africa, Asia, and South America.

5-6a European Immigration

Before the Civil War, European immigrants to the United States came mainly from northern Europe—England, Scotland, Ireland, Norway, Sweden, Denmark, and Germany. Most of these immigrants were Protestants—Anglicans, Presbyterians, Quakers, Baptists, Methodists, and Lutherans.

Irish and German Immigration   In the 1840s, more Irish and Germans immigrated to the United States because of economic and political pressures in their native countries. For example, the potato famine had devastated Ireland's economy. The Irish were predominately Roman Catholics, and the Germans were primarily Lutherans and Catholics. Until the arrival of the Catholic Irish and Germans, the population of the United States, though divided into a denominational array of churches, was generally Protestant. Despite separation of church and state, many public schools at that time began the school day with a reading from the King James Version of the Bible and emphasized a generalized Protestant value orientation. Led by their bishops, Catholics resisted what they believed was a Protestant orientation in public schooling and created their own system of parochial schools.

Changing Immigration Patterns   After the Civil War, immigration patterns shifted from northern to central, southern, and eastern Europe. The new immigrants were now Italians and Greeks; Slavic ethnic groups such as Poles, Russians, Czechs, Slovaks, Croats, Slovenes, and Serbs; Arabs from Syria and Lebanon; and Jews from eastern Europe, seeking to escape the pogroms in Russia. In the 1890s, 1,914,000 immigrants came from southern and eastern Europe. In the twentieth century's first decade, from 1900 to 1910, the number of European immigrants reached 6,224,000, swelling the total number of immigrants to 13,500,000. After 1910, the number of European immigrants declined.[45]

Immigration Policy Controversies   The twenty-first century debates over immigration policy are not new. Although it is a country of immigrants, periodic efforts have been made to restrict immigration to the United States. In 1924, Congress established a quota system designed to restrict immigration from southern and eastern Europe. The law set more generous quotas for immigrants from the United Kingdom, Ireland, and the countries of northern and western Europe than it did for those from southern and eastern Europe. The ideological rationale behind the quota system was that immigrants from the British Isles, Germany, and the Scandinavian countries could assimilate into American society more readily than immigrants from other countries.

---

[45]Oscar Handlin, "The Immigration Contribution," in Richard Leopold and Arthur Link, eds., *Problems in American History* (New York: Prentice-Hall, 1952), pp. 643–690; and *Population Abstract of the United States* (Washington, DC: Government Printing Office, 1980), p. 199.

Ethnicity The first generation of immigrants, especially in large northern cities such as New York, Chicago, and Cleveland, generally lived in homogenous communities with members of their own ethnic, language, and religious group. Except for some work situations, they generally spoke the language of their country of origin, attended church services in that language, and read the same foreign-language newspapers. They were members of the same ethnic, social, and athletic societies.

Through much of the twentieth century, public-school students attended schools in specifically designated attendance areas. When these attendance areas were coterminous with an ethnic community, the majority of a particular school's students were often from the same ethnic and language group. When the schools overlapped ethnic neighborhoods, their student populations were somewhat more ethnically and culturally diverse. Because immigrant adolescents in the late nineteenth and early twentieth centuries tended to drop out of high school to enter the labor force, secondary education had limited effects on their integration into the larger society.

The Assimilationist Ideology Ethnic groups sometimes ran into conflict with the dominant public-school ideology of Americanization, which stated that immigrant children should be assimilated as quickly as possible into American society. **Assimilation** meant that immigrant children should learn to speak and read the English language, learn the values of hard work and punctuality prescribed by the Protestant ethic, and obey the laws of the United States. The assimilationist ideology grew out of the common school philosophy that public schools should be agencies of constructing shared knowledge and values. When seen through the lenses of the assimilationist ideology, the ethnic neighborhoods were viewed as obstacles to bringing immigrants into American society. Public schools were identified as agencies that could teach immigrant children to become Americans. The prominent educator, Ellwood P. Cubberley, whose books were widely used in teacher-education programs, clearly articulated the assimilationist ideology. In describing the challenge to assimilate the new immigrants, Cubberley stated:

> Everywhere these people tend to settle in groups or settlements, and to set up here their national manners, customs, and observances. Our task is to break up these groups of people as a part of our American race, and to implant in their children, so far as it can be done, the Anglo-Saxon conception of righteousness, law and order, and popular government, and to awaken in them a reverence for our democratic institutions and for those things in our national life which we as a people hold to be of abiding worth.[46]

The strategy of assimilation that was applied to European immigrants was also used in the education of other racial and language groups such as African-, Latino-, Asian-, and Arab Americans.

5-6b African Americans

The Civil War, the Emancipation Proclamation, and the Thirteenth Amendment ended slavery in the United States. Emancipation brought with it the challenge of educating the freed men, women, and their children, especially in the South.

In 1865, Congress established the Freedmen's Bureau to provide economic and educational assistance to African Americans in the South during the Reconstruction period. Under the leadership of General O. O. Howard, the Bureau established schools that by 1869 had enrolled 114,000 African American students. Bureau schools followed a New England common-school curriculum of reading, writing, grammar, geography,

assimilation The strategy that immigrant children should be schooled into the dominant "American" culture by learning to speak and read the English language, the values of hard work and punctuality prescribed by the Protestant ethic, and respect for the laws of the United States.

---

[46]Ellwood P. Cubberley, *Changing Conceptions of Education* (Boston: Houghton-Mifflin, 1909), pp. 13–15.

FROM PRESERVICE TO PRACTICE

CONNECTING THE PAST AND THE PRESENT: CONSTRUCTING AN EDUCATIONAL AUTOBIOGRAPHY

Irene Stopek, a college sophomore, had enrolled in a course on the history of education that examined education from the earliest times to the present. Professor Grace Standish, the instructor, told the students during the first class meeting that they would be examining the most important ideas that had influenced our thinking about schools and teachers. She said that a study of such magnitude need not be overwhelming or remote; it could be very personal if the students began their journey into the history of education by reflecting on how they had developed their own ideas about schools and teaching. She advised them that they could construct their own educational autobiography as part of the course requirements. Several students, including Irene, who appeared to be overwhelmed by the challenge, asked how they might research and complete this assignment.

Reassuring them, Professor Standish told them her own story about how she decided to become a professor of education.

She told them about the importance her parents placed on education, about teachers who encouraged her, and how her experiences as a high school social studies teacher led her to pursue graduate study in education. She then described how a professor acted as her mentor and guided her through her graduate work and doctoral dissertation.

Irene now began to reflect on her decision to enter teacher education and how she envisioned herself as an elementary-school teacher. She searched her memories to discover how and why she formed that mental portrait of herself as a teacher. She remembered her mother telling the family story of how her own parents had emigrated from Czechoslovakia as refugees after World War II and how they struggled to learn English, find jobs, and send their own children to school. Irene planned to begin her research by asking her mother to narrate her own family's story—its history—about American education.

CASE QUESTIONS

1. What questions would you ask family members about their educational experiences?
2. Did your family's experience with education influence your decision to become a teacher?
3. How did your own educational experiences shape your ideas about schools and teachers?

---

arithmetic, and music, especially singing. Many schools functioned until 1872, when Bureau operations ended.[47]

Although the Freedmen's Bureau had prepared some African American teachers, many of its schools were staffed by northern white teachers, who carried their educational philosophies and teaching methods to the South. Though well intentioned, many of these teachers believed that African American students needed only a limited, basic education. Rather than encouraging educational self-determination, educators such as Samuel C. Armstrong, the mentor of Booker T. Washington, emphasized industrial training and social control that had the effect of keeping African Americans in a subordinate economic and social position.[48]

Washington: From Slavery to Freedom   Booker T. Washington (1856–1915) was the leading African American educational spokesperson after the Civil War. As illustrated in his autobiography, *Up from Slavery*, Washington was a transitional figure. Born a slave, he experienced the hectic years of Reconstruction and cautiously developed a compromise with the white power establishment.[49]

---

[47]Paul A. Cimbala and Hans L. Trefousee, *The Freedmen's Bureau: Reconstructing the American South after the Civil War* (Malabar, FL: Krieger Publishing Co., 2005).

[48]Robert Francis Engs, *Educating the Disenfranchised and Disinherited: Samuel Chapman Armstrong and Hampton Institute, 1839–1893* (Knoxville: University of Tennessee Press, 1999).

[49]Booker T. Washington, *Up from Slavery* (New York: Doubleday, 1938). For biographies of Washington, see Robert J. Norrell, *Up From History: The Life of Booker T. Washington* (Cambridge, MA: Harvard University Press, 2011); and Raymond W. Smock, *Booker T. Washington: Black Leadership in the Age of Jim Crow* (Chicago: Ivan R. Dee Publisher, 2009).

Bettmann/Corbis

∧ PHOTO 5.2 Students at the Tuskegee Institution in Alabama, where Booker T. Washington emphasized industrial education.

As a student at Hampton Institute, Washington endorsed industrial education, the educational philosophy of Armstrong, his mentor. Armstrong believed that African American youth should be trained as skilled domestic servants, farmers, and vocational workers in trades rather than educated for the professions (Photo 5.2). Washington subscribed to Armstrong's philosophy of moral and economic "uplift" through work.

In 1881, Washington was appointed principal of the educational institute that the Alabama legislature had established for African Americans at Tuskegee. Washington shaped the Tuskegee curriculum according to his belief that southern African Americans were a landless agricultural class. He wanted to create an economic base—primarily in farming but also in vocational trades—that would provide jobs. Even if they were low-level jobs, Washington believed they would build an economic foundation that African Americans could use to climb slowly upward. Thus, Tuskegee's curriculum emphasized basic academic, agricultural, and occupational skills; the values of hard work; and the dignity of labor. It encouraged students to become elementary-school teachers, farmers, and artisans, but discouraged entry to higher education and participation in law and politics. Entry into professional education and political action, Washington believed, were premature and would conflict with the South's dominant white power structure.

Washington, a dynamic and popular platform speaker, developed a symbiotic racial theory that blacks and whites were mutually dependent economically but could remain separate socially. In 1885, Washington voiced his philosophy to an approving white audience at the Cotton Exposition in Atlanta, Georgia, when he said, "In all things that are purely social, we can be as separate as the fingers, yet one as the hand in all things essential to mutual progress."[50]

Today, Washington is a controversial figure in history. Defenders say he made the best of a bad situation and that, although he compromised on racial issues, he preserved and slowly advanced African Americans' educational opportunities. Critics see Washington as the head of a large educational machine that he ruthlessly controlled

---

[50]Booker T. Washington, *Selected Speeches of Booker T. Washington* (New York: Doubleday, 1932); and Washington, *Character Building* (Radford, VA: Wilder Publications, 2008).

TIMELINE
BOOKER T. WASHINGTON

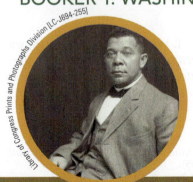

Library of Congress Prints and Photographs Division [LC-J694-255]

1872–1875 Attends Hampton Institute

1878 Attends Wayland Seminary

1881 Opens Tuskegee Institute

1855   **1865**   **1875**   **1885**

1856 Birth

to promote his own power rather than to improve the situation of African Americans. One of Washington's outspoken critics was W. E. B. Du Bois.[51]

Du Bois: Challenger to the System   A sociologist, historian, and civil rights activist, W. E. B. Du Bois (1868–1963) attacked the rigid system of racial segregation that had been established in the South in the late nineteenth and early twentieth centuries after Reconstruction ended in 1876.[52] Becoming an activist for civil rights, he challenged Washington's accommodationist philosophy.

Unlike Washington, whose roots were in southern agriculture, Du Bois's career spanned both sides of the Mason-Dixon Line. Born in Massachusetts, he attended Fisk University in Nashville, did graduate work in Germany, earned his doctorate at Harvard University, and directed the Atlanta University Studies of Black American Life.[53] His important book, *The Philadelphia Negro: A Social Study*, examined the social, economic, and educational problems of an urban African American community.[54] His *The Souls of Black Folk* told how African Americans had developed a dual consciousness—one side of which expressed their African roots and the other that presented the submissiveness demanded by many white Americans.[55]

In 1909, Du Bois helped organize the National Association for the Advancement of Colored People (NAACP). His editorials in *The Crisis,* the NAACP's major publication, argued that all American children and youth, including African Americans, should have genuine equality of educational opportunity. Du Bois and the NAACP were persistent adversaries of racially segregated schools, and his dedicated activism helped overturn racial segregation in public schools.

Unlike Booker T. Washington, Du Bois urged African Americans to organize and actively seek their civil rights. Believing that African Americans needed well-educated leaders, especially in the professions, Du Bois developed the concept of the "talented tenth," according to which at least 10 percent of the African American population should receive a higher education. Du Bois was adamant that a person's career should be determined by ability and choice, not by racial stereotyping. A prophetic leader, Du Bois set the stage for the significant changes in American race relations that came after the 1960s.

---

[51]For the controversy between Washington and Du Bois, see Jacqueline M. Moore, *Booker T. Washington, W. E. B. Du Bois, and the Struggle for Racial Uplift* (Wilmington, DE: Scholar Resources, 2003), pp. 61–87.

[52]For the definitive biography of Du Bois, see David Levering Lewis, *W. E. B. Du Bois: Biography of a Race, 1868–1919* (New York: Henry Holt, 1973); and Lewis, *W. E. B. Du Bois: The Fight for Equality and the American Century, 1919–1963* (New York: Henry Holt, 2000).

[53]For a highly useful edition of Du Bois's works, see Eugene F. Provenzo, Jr., ed., *Du Bois on Education* (Lanham, MD: Rowman & Littlefield, 2002).

[54]W. E. B. Du Bois, *The Philadelphia Negro: A Social Study* (Philadelphia: University of Pennsylvania Press, 1998).

[55]W. E. B. Du Bois, *The Souls of Black Folk* (New York: Simon and Schuster, 2005). For an analysis in relation to DuBois's philosophy, see Stephanie J. Shaw, *W. E. B. Du Bois and The Souls of Black Folk* (Chapel Hill: University of North Carolina Press, 2013).

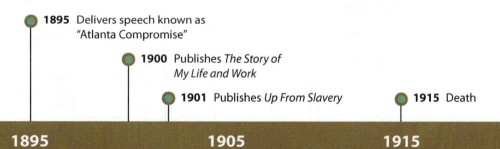

1895 Delivers speech known as "Atlanta Compromise"

1900 Publishes *The Story of My Life and Work*

1901 Publishes *Up From Slavery*

1915 Death

1895   1905   1915   1925

African American Demographic and Social Change   While Washington and Du Bois engaged in debates over social and educational policy, important changes were taking place in the African American population. No longer concentrated in the rural South, African Americans were moving to the large northern cities. World War I (1917–19) and World War II (1941–45) generated manpower needs in the war industries. An estimated 1.6 million African Americans migrated from the rural South to large northern cities to take jobs and improve their economic condition. The African American population in the North increased by an estimated 40 percent as large black communities developed in New York, Philadelphia, Boston, Chicago, Detroit, and Cleveland. Blacks joined labor unions, and a new spirit of activism was born. The African American situation was much more complex than it was in the post-Reconstruction era when Booker T. Washington constructed his philosophy of industrial education. An urban black community now existed along with the Southern rural and agricultural community. (Racial integration and social change is discussed in Chapter 11, Social Class, Race, and School Achievement, and elsewhere in this book.)

5-6c Native Americans

Education among pre-Columbian Native Americans was largely informal. Children learned skills, social roles, and cultural patterns from their group's oral tradition, from parents and elders, and from direct experience with tribal life. The role of tribal elders in helping children understand and use the possibilities and limitations of the place—the landscape's resources—in which the tribe lived was an especially valuable lesson. (See Chapter 3, The World Origins of American Education, for information about education in preliterate societies.)

Marked by suspicion and violence, encounters among Native Americans and European colonists affected both cultures. As colonists attempted to re-create European culture in North America, and Native Americans sought to preserve their culture, both groups changed. Europeans did not believe that they had anything to learn from Native people; rather, the Native people had much to learn from the Europeans, and if they failed to learn, then they were doomed for extinction.[56] European colonists' efforts to "civilize" North American indigenous peoples rested on the Europeans' belief

---

[56]Colin G. Calloway, *New Worlds for All: Indians, Europeans, and the Remaking of Early America* (Baltimore, MD: Johns Hopkins University Press, 1997), p. 42; also, see Milton Gaither, "The History of North American Education, 15,000 BCE to 1491," *History of Education Quarterly*, Vol. 54, No. 1 (August 2014), pp. 323–348, for the importance of landscape in American Indian education.

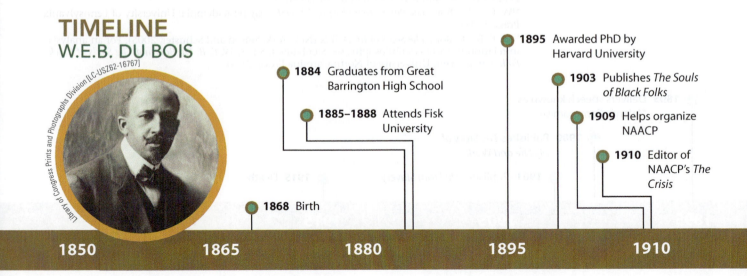

TIMELINE
W.E.B. DU BOIS

Library of Congress Prints and Photographs Division [LC-USZ62-16767]

1884 Graduates from Great Barrington High School

1885–1888 Attends Fisk University

1868 Birth

1895 Awarded PhD by Harvard University

1903 Publishes *The Souls of Black Folks*

1909 Helps organize NAACP

1910 Editor of NAACP's *The Crisis*

1850   1865   1880   1895   1910

in their own cultural superiority. In the Mississippi Valley, French missionaries, especially the Jesuits, sought to convert Native Americans to Catholicism and to educate French colonists' children in the language and culture of France.

In the Spanish-controlled Southwest, Jesuit and Franciscan priests sought to alleviate exploitation of Native Americans by Spanish landlords by establishing missions to protect, control, and convert the tribes to Catholicism. Mission schools taught religion, reading, writing, and craft skills.[57] The Moravians—religious followers of John Amos Comenius, in Pennsylvania, Ohio, and North Carolina—taught the Native American tribes and translated the Bible and religious tracts into Indian languages.

Among the early Native American educators, Sequoyah (1770–1831), a Cherokee, devised an alphabet in his native language that developed into Cherokee as a written language.

In the nineteenth century, the US government forcibly relocated the majority of Native Americans to reservations west of the Mississippi River in remote areas of the Great Plains and the Southwest. After 1870, the federal Bureau of Indian Affairs (BIA), encouraged by well-intentioned but misguided reformers, again attempted to "civilize" Native Americans by assimilating them into white society. These so-called reformers sought to eradicate tribal cultures and instill what they saw as white values through agricultural and industrial training.[58]

boarding schools Residential institutions where students live and attend school.

From 1890 to the 1930s, the BIA used **boarding schools** to implement the assimilationist educational policy. Boarding schools emphasized a basic curriculum of reading, writing, arithmetic, and vocational training. Ruled by military discipline, Native American youngsters in these schools were forbidden to speak their own native languages and were forced to use English.

Native American youngsters variously resisted, passively accepted, or accommodated to the boarding schools' regimens. Active resisters repeatedly ran away from the boarding schools.[59] Others passively accepted the boarding schools' programs as a way to learn a trade useful for earning a living.[60] Many students suffered a loss of cultural identity, feeling trapped in a never-never land between two different cultures.

After the boarding-school policy was discontinued in the 1930s, Native American education experienced significant changes. Many Native Americans left reservations to live in large cities where their children generally attended public schools. Children on tribal reservations attended BIA schools, public schools, or nonpublic schools.

Ending the assimilationist policies, the Indian Self-Determination and Education Assistance Act of 1975 encouraged Native Americans "to control their own education activities."[61]

---

[57]Christopher Vecsey, *On the Padres' Trail* (Notre Dame, IN: University of Notre Dame Press, 1996).

[58]David W. Adams, *Education for Extinction: American Indians and the Boarding School Experience, 1875–1928* (Lawrence: University Press of Kansas, 1995), pp. 12–24. Also, see Ruth Spack, *America's Second Tongue: American Indian Education and the Ownership of English, 1860–1900* (Lincoln: University of Nebraska Press, 2002), p. 75.

[59]Spack, *America's Second Tongue*, p. 131.

[60]David W. Adams, "From Bullets to Boarding Schools: The Educational Assault on Native American Identity, 1878–1928," in Philip Weeks, ed., *The American Indian Experience* (Arlington Heights, IL: Forum Press, 1988), pp. 218–239. For a history of a boarding school based on reflections of its students, see K. Tsianina Lomawaima, *They Called It Prairie Light: The Story of Chilocco Indian School* (Lincoln: University of Nebraska Press, 1994).

[61]For Native-American self-determination and education, see Julie L. Davis, *Survival Schools: The American Indian Movement and Community Education in the Twin Cities* (Minneapolis: University of Minnesota Press, 2013).

1935 Publishes *Black Reconstruction*   **1963** Death

1925   **1940**   **1955**   **1970**   **1985**

Although assimilation is no longer an official government policy, many Native Americans remain alienated from the educational system. Compared to the national population, a greater percentage of Native Americans are under age 20, but their participation in schooling is far lower than the national average. An extremely high dropout rate places Native American high school completion far below that of the US population at large.

5-6d Latino Americans

Latino Americans comprise the fastest-growing ethnic group in the United States. Latino, a collective term, identifies Spanish-speaking people whose ethnic groups originated in Mexico, Puerto Rico, Cuba, or other Central and South American countries. Although Latino Americans may speak Spanish as a common language and share many Spanish traditions, each group has its own distinctive culture.[62]

Mexican Americans are the largest Latino group in the United States.[63] The 1848 Treaty of Guadeloupe Hidalgo, which ended the Mexican War, forced Mexico to cede to the United States the vast territories that now comprise Arizona, California, Colorado, Nevada, New Mexico, and Utah. This territory, along with Texas, was home to a large Mexican population.[64] In these states, public schools followed the **Americanization** assimilationist policy then used throughout the United States. Mexican American children were taught in English, rather than their vernacular Spanish, and their Chicano cultural heritage was ignored. Consequently, schooling imposed a negative self-image, often portraying Mexican Americans as conquered people of an inferior culture.[65] Bilingual and multicultural education, replacing "Americanization," contributes to maintaining a Mexican American historical consciousness. (For more on bilingual and multicultural education, see Chapter 12, Providing Equal Educational Opportunity.)

The Mexican American population increased as migrant workers crossed the US-Mexican border to work in the United States. Because Mexicans provided cheap labor as ranch workers, railroad crews, and especially farm workers, employers encouraged their entry. Wages were low, housing was frequently squalid, and working conditions were harsh. Children of the migrant workers, even if not working in the fields with their parents, had few or no educational opportunities. Although many migrant workers returned to Mexico, others remained in the United States, either legally or illegally. Since World War II, many Mexican Americans have relocated from the Southwest to other states, often to the large Northeastern and Midwestern cities. Today, approximately 90 percent of Mexican Americans live in urban areas.

In the late 1960s, the *Chicano movimiento*, or movement, similar to the African American civil rights movement, pursued two goals: (1) organizing Mexican Americans to work for improved social, economic, and educational conditions; (2) preserving the Mexican American cultural heritage as a source of group identity.[66] Organized in 1929 to promote Latino civil rights, The League of United Latin American Citizens (LULAC) attracted middle-class professionals. Cesar Chavez organized the United Farm Workers

Americanization The dominant ideology in public schools imposed on immigrant and minority group children in the nineteenth and early twentieth centuries.

---

[62]Joseph A. Rodriguez and Vicki L. Ruiz, "At Loose Ends: Twentieth-Century Latinos in Current United States History Textbooks," *Journal of American History* 86 (March 2000), pp. 1689–1699.

[63]Victoria-Marie MacDonald, "Hispanic, Latino, Chicano, or 'Other'? Deconstructing the Relationship between Historians and Hispanic-American Educational History," *History of Education Quarterly* 41 (Fall 2001), pp. 368–369.

[64]Manuel G. Gonzales, *Mexicanos: A History of Mexicans in the United States* (Bloomington: Indiana University Press, 2009). Also, see Victor Zuniga and Ruben Hernandez-Leon, eds., *New Destinations: Mexican Immigration in the United States* (New York: Russell Sage Foundation, 2006).

[65]For the educational experience of Mexican American children, see Guadalupe San Miguel, Jr., *Chicano/a Struggles for Education: Activism in the Community* (College Station: Texas A&M University Press, 2013); and Patricia Gandora and Frances Contreras, *The Latino Education Crisis: The Consequences of Failed Social Policies* (Cambridge, MA: Harvard University Press, 2010).

[66]Richard Valencia, *Chicano Students and the Courts: The Mexican American Legal Struggle for Educational Equality* (New York: New York University Press, 2008).

to secure improved working conditions and higher wages for agricultural workers.[67] The Chicano movement encouraged Mexican American political activity, economic development, and educational participation. Despite increased Mexican American attendance in elementary and secondary education, higher-education enrollments fall below the national average.[68]

The history of Puerto Rican Americans, another large Latino group, begins with the Spanish-American War of 1898, when defeated Spain ceded Puerto Rico to the United States. Puerto Rico, a US possession, attained Commonwealth status in 1952.[69]

Believing that Puerto Rico needed American-style social and economic development, US officials overhauled the old Spanish school system. They made school attendance compulsory, established American-style public schools, and employed English-speaking teachers trained in US teaching methods. Although some classes continued to be taught in Spanish, English was made compulsory to promote "Americanization." Some teachers skillfully negotiated their teaching to include the concept of Puerto Rican identity within the larger context of an emerging American cultural presence.[70] Puerto Rican immigration to the US mainland has been continuous since the early twentieth century. Today more than two million Puerto Rican Americans live in large urban centers such as New York, Chicago, and Philadelphia. Historically, their high school dropout rates have been high and college attendance rates low. In recent years, however, Puerto Rican Americans have become more politically active, especially in New York and Chicago, and have improved their economic and educational position.

The Cuban American experience in the United States represents a different pattern from other Latino groups in that it originated as a community in political exile from its native land.[71] Several waves of emigration from Cuba combined to form the Cuban American community. The first exiles, from 1959 to 1973, fled Fidel Castro's repressive Communist regime. Many were upper- and middle-class Cubans who brought with them the political, economic, and educational background and organizations needed to create a distinctive Cuban American cultural community. The Mariel immigrants of the 1980s came from Cuba's disadvantaged underclass. The Cuban American community, mirroring some aspects of the Cuba they left, has created a unique but also a permeable culture.[72] In 2015, the Obama administration initiated the process of normalizing diplomatic relations with Cuba.

Cuban Americans have high rates of participation in higher education, with over 90 percent of the age group from 18 to 24 enrolled in colleges and universities. In the twenty-first century, Latino Americans are playing a larger role in American social, political, and economic life, as evidenced by the growing and influential Latino professional and business middle classes. The concept of "permeable cultures" is useful in interpreting Latino American cultures. The term *permeable* refers to the tendency to move back and forth from Latino to Anglo cultures. Latinos selectively create their own Hispanic American cultural patterns.[73]

---

[67]Frederick J. Dalton, *The Moral Vision of Cesar Chavez* (Maryknoll, NY: Orbis Books, 2003).

[68]Vicki L. Ruiz and John R. Chavez, eds., *Memories and Migrations: Mapping Boricua and Chicana Histories* (Urbana and Chicago: University of Illinois Press, 2008).

[69]For the history of Puerto Rico as a US possession, see Jose Trias Monge, *Puerto Rico: The Trials of the Oldest Colony in the World* (New Haven, CT: Yale University Press, 1997).

[70]Gervasio Luis Garcia, "I Am the Other: Puerto Rico in the Eyes of North Americans, 1898," *Journal of American History* 38 (June 2000), p. 41; and Solsiree del Moral, *Negotiating Empire: The Cultural Politics of Schools in Puerto Rico, 1898–1952* (Madison: University of Wisconsin Press, 2013), pp. 5–12.

[71]Alex Anton and Roger E. Hernandez, *Cubans in America: A Vibrant History of a People in Exile* (New York: Kensington Books, 2003).

[72]Maria Cristina Garcia, *Havana USA: Cuban Exiles and Cuban Americans in South Florida, 1959–1994* (Berkeley and Los Angeles: University of California Press, 1996), pp. 111–118. Also, see Alex Stepick, *This Land Is Our Land: Immigrants and Power in Miami* (Berkeley: University of California Press, 2003). For higher education participation, see Amy Chua and Jed Rubenfeld, *The Triple Package: What Really Determines Success* (New York: Penguin Press, 2014), p. 39.

[73]Rodriguez and Ruiz, "At Loose Ends," p. 1696.

Public schools, with the Bilingual Education Act (1968) and the Supreme Court decision in *Lau v. Nichols* (1974), replaced the assimilationist "Americanization" policies with bilingual and multicultural educational programs (see Chapter 12, Providing Equal Educational Opportunity). Recently, however, bilingual education has become politically controversial, with some states making English the official language. Led by California in 1998, several states have reduced or ended their bilingual education programs.[74]

5-6e Asian Americans

Asian immigrants arrived in the United States through the Pacific Coast cities of Seattle, Los Angeles, and San Francisco. The earliest Asian immigrants, from China and Japan, tended to settle in California, Oregon, and Washington.[75] More recent Asian immigrants include Filipinos, Indians, Thais, Koreans, Vietnamese, Laotians, and Cambodians.

Chinese Americans   From 1848 to 1882, 228,945 Chinese immigrated to the United States. They were often single, male contract laborers who worked in mining, farming, and railroad construction. Later, the immigrants who did not return to China were joined by their wives and family members. The Chinese settled in communities in larger West Coast cities such as Seattle, San Francisco, and Los Angeles where they established their own social, religious, cultural, fraternal, and educational societies.

As of 1880, 105,465 Chinese were living in the United States. In 1882, the US Congress enacted the Chinese Exclusion Act that prohibited further Chinese immigration and denied citizenship to Chinese already in the country. Chinese immigrants encountered serious racial discrimination. For example, California's Alien Land Law that prohibited aliens ineligible for citizenship from owning land was directed against Chinese immigrants. The San Francisco Board of Education required Chinese students to attend segregated schools. The Magnuson Act in 1943 repealed the Exclusion Act and permitted Chinese residing in the United States to become citizens. Currently, the Chinese American population stands at 3.8 million.[76]

In 1973, the US Supreme Court heard the *Lau v. Nichols* case, which had been appealed from lower district and appeals courts. Parents of non-English-speaking Chinese students had sued the San Francisco Unified School District. The plaintiffs charged that the District had failed to provide supplemental English language instruction to 1,800 students of Chinese ancestry who did not speak English. They alleged that the District's policy caused unequal educational opportunities in violation of the Fourteenth Amendment. Upholding the plaintiffs, the Supreme Court ruled that:

> Basic English skills are necessary to children to participate in the public-school educational program; children who do not understand English will find their classroom experiences wholly incomprehensible and in no way meaningful. . . . The failure of the San Francisco school system to provide English language instruction to approximately 1,800 students of Chinese ancestry who do not speak English, or to provide them with other adequate instructional procedures, denies them a meaningful opportunity to participate in the public educational program and thus violates . . . the Civil Rights Act of 1964. . . .[77]

---

[74]Guadalupe San Miguel, *Contested Policy: The Rise and Fall of Federal Bilingual Policy in the United States, 1960–2001* (Denton: University of North Texas Press, 2004).

[75]*Angel Island Immigrant Journeys: A Curriculum Guide for Grades 3–12* (San Francisco, CA: Angel Island Immigration Station Foundations, 2004). Also, see Xiaojian Zhao, *Remaking Chinese American Immigration, Family, and Community* (New Brunswick, NJ: Rutgers University Press, 2002).

[76]"Race Reporting for the Asian Population by Selected Categories," (Washington, DC: US Census Bureau, 2010). For an autobiographical perspective, see Jean Lau Chin, *Learning from My Mother's Voice: Family Legend and the Chinese American Experience* (New York: Teachers College Press, 2005).

[77]*Lau v. Nichols*, 414 US 563 (1974).

The enactment of the Bilingual Education Act (1968) and the Supreme Court decision in *Lau v. Nichols* (1974) dismantled the assimilationist ideology that had shaped public-school policies on the education of immigrant and non-English-speaking children. Public schools and teacher-education programs began to emphasize bilingual-bicultural and multicultural education. However, these programs remain controversial. Some states have reduced or eliminated bilingual education programs.[78]

Japanese Americans   Japanese immigration began in the 1860s when American labor contractors recruited Japanese men to work on sugar and pineapple plantations in Hawaii. Later, Japanese workers also immigrated to California. The largest Japanese immigrant communities were in Hawaii, Washington, Oregon, and California.[79] Japanese immigration continued until 1910, when it declined because of economic and political issues between Japan and the United States.[80] Of the 27,000,000 immigrants who came to the United States between 1881 and 1930, only 275,308 were Japanese.[81] The Japanese called the immigrants, *Issei,* and their children, *Nisei.*

In Los Angeles and Seattle, Japanese American communities developed as Japanese entrepreneurs operated hotels, restaurants, and grocery stores. Like the European and Chinese immigrants, Japanese Americans established Japanese-language newspapers, religious and benevolent societies, and recreational organizations. Seeking to maintain their language and culture, Japanese Americans established private Japanese-language schools that taught Japanese language, history, and geography.[82]

As with other immigrant children, state compulsory school-attendance laws required Japanese American children to attend school. The Issei, the first generation immigrants, were familiar with the schools that the Japanese government had established. Unlike some immigrants from southern and eastern Europe, Mexico, and China, who had limited experience with compulsory schooling, the Japanese were more familiar and receptive to it. Japanese American children encountered racial segregation and the assimilationist ideology in public schools. In 1906, the San Francisco Board of Education required Asian children to attend segregated schools. When the Japanese government protested, the Board rescinded its segregationist policy.

Japanese Americans faced strong anti-Japanese hostility after Japan attacked the US naval base at Pearl Harbor on Oahu in Hawaii on December 7, 1941. Suspicious that Japanese on the West Coast might commit acts of sabotage, the US Government interned 110,000 people of Japanese ancestry, many American citizens, in relocation camps. Located in remote areas in California, Arizona, Idaho, Wyoming, Colorado, and Arkansas, the internment camps, called relocation centers, lacked adequate housing and other basic services. Over time, the internees established social and recreational activities. Japanese American teachers organized schools for the children and adult-education classes.

The suspicions that led the US government to intern the Japanese Americans proved groundless. Not a single act of sabotage was committed by a Japanese American during World War II. Despite resentment over the government's repressive action, twenty thousand Japanese Americans (the majority from Hawaii but six thousand were recruits from the camps) served in the US armed forces during World War II.

---

[78]Guadalupe San Miguel, *Contested Policy: The Rise and Fall of Federal Bilingual Policy in the United States, 1960–2001.*

[79]Paul Spickard, *Japanese Americans: The Formation and Transformation of an Ethnic Group* (New Brunswick, NJ: Rutgers University Press, 2009), p. 11.

[80]David J. O'Brien and Stephen S. Fugita, *The Japanese American Experience* (Bloomington: Indiana University Press, 1991), pp. 4–17.

[81]Spickard, *Japanese Americans,* p. 22.

[82]Spickard, *Japanese Americans,* p. 79. For Japanese-language schools, see Agato Noriko, *Teaching Mikadoism: The Attack on Japanese Language Schools in Hawaii, California, and Washington* (Honolulu: University of Hawaii Press, 2006).

By 1945, most of the camps were closed. In the 1980s, the US government admitted that its wartime action had violated the internees' civil liberties, and compensated them. The Civil Liberties Act of 1988 provided a presidential letter of apology and monetary reparations for more than 82,000 persons of Japanese ancestry who had been interned without due process of law during World War II.[83]

Japanese Americans reconstituted their communities within the larger American society in the 1950s. Participation in postsecondary and professional education increased as nearly 90 percent of Japanese Americans were attending institutions of higher education.[84]

Other Asian Americans   After the 1960s, immigration increased among other Asian groups, especially Koreans and Indians. Following the collapse of the American-supported government in South Vietnam in the 1970s, Vietnamese, Cambodians, Laotians, and Hmong arrived with differing educational backgrounds. For example, among the South Vietnamese were former military officers, government officials, businesspersons, and professionals. The Hmong, by contrast, came from a rural culture without a written language. Along with the more recent Asian American immigrants, there is also an older, well-established Filipino American population.

5-6f Arab Americans

The designation "Arab," a cultural and linguistic rather than a racial term, refers to those who speak Arabic as their first language. The majority of Arab Americans are descendants of immigrants from Lebanon, Syria, Palestine, Iraq, Jordan, and Egypt and are Muslims. There is also a large Christian Arab American community.

The early Arab immigrants came to the United States from the Turkish Ottoman Empire in the late nineteenth century, especially between 1875 and 1915.[85] Many early immigrants from Lebanon and Syria were Orthodox or Catholic Christians who settled in ethnic neighborhoods in the northeastern states. Some became small business owners, merchants, and restaurateurs. Like other immigrant groups, they established fraternal organizations and recreational societies such as the Syrian Brotherhood Orthodox Society, often sponsored by a church or mosque.[86] One of the earliest Arabic newspapers, *Kawkab America* (trans. *The Star of America*), was founded in 1892.[87]

A more recent wave of Arab immigration, especially from Palestine, Egypt, and Jordan, which began after World War II, still continues.[88] More recent immigrants are predominately Islamic and generally have more formal education than earlier immigrants.

Arab Americans have much in common with other immigrant groups. Many older Arab Americans became assimilated by attending public schools, through membership in community and political organizations, and through business and work. While assimilating into the larger American society, many maintained their Arabic culture through language, customs, religion, music, literature, and storytelling.[89] Many

---

[83]Spickard, *Japanese Americans*, pp. 132–133. Also, see Minoru Kiyota and Ronald S. Green, *The Case of Japanese Americans during World War II: Suppression of Civil Liberty* (Lewiston, NY: E. Mellen Press, 2004); and Kenneth K. Takemoto, *Nisei Memories: My Parents' Talk about the War Years* (Seattle: University of Washington Press, 2006).

[84]Allan W. Austin, *From Concentration Camps to Campus: Japanese American Students and World War II* (Urbana: University of Illinois Press, 2004).

[85]Gregory Orfalea, *The Arab Americans: A History* (New York: Olive Branch Press, 2006).

[86]For the Arab American experience, see Amir B. Maruasti and Karen D. McKinney, *Middle Eastern Lives in America* (Lanham, MD: Rowman & Littlefield, 2004); and Randa A. Kayyali, *The Arab American* (Westport, CT: Greenwood Press, 2006).

[87]Elizabeth Boosahda, *Arab-American Faces and Voices: The Origins of an Immigrant Community* (Austin: University of Texas Press, 2003), pp. 84–86.

[88]For the Palestinian experience and the forming of Arab American identity, see Edward Said, *Out of Place* (New York: Knopf, 1999).

[89]Boosahda, *Arab-American Faces and Voices*, p. 9.

immigrants were bilingual and often established Arabic language, culture, and religion classes in churches or mosques.

The proportion of Arab Americans who attend college is higher than the national average, with many earning advanced degrees. Many Arab Americans are self-employed in family-owned businesses. About 60 percent of Arab Americans in the workforce are executives, professionals, and office and sales staff.

After the terrorist attacks on September 11, 2001, concerns arose that Arab Americans might be victims of stereotyping and discrimination. Isolated instances of discriminatory acts occurred, but the Arab American community took a proactive stance to educate the general population about its history and culture. Educators, too, have worked to include Arab Americans within multicultural education.

5-7 THE COMMON CORE: A HISTORICALLY REFERENCED ISSUE

Common Core State Standards Standards released by the National Governors Association Center for Best Practices (NGA Center) and the Council of Chief State School Officers (CCSSO) in 2010 to define and assess the knowledge and skills students should know by their graduation from high school.

FOCUS How did the United States become a culturally pluralistic society? Reflect on the roles of African-, Latino-, Asian-, and Arab Americans in American culture and their contributions. Reflect on the contributions and the problems of your own racial, ethnic, or language group as you write your educational autobiography. You may want to consult parents, family members, and others of your group about their educational experiences.

Today, a major controversy exists between proponents and opponents of a common core of skills and subjects for American elementary and secondary students. In 2010, the Council of Chief State School Officers (CCSSO) and the National Governors Association Center for Best Practices (NGA Center) approved **Common Core State Standards** in English language arts and mathematics for students from kindergarten through twelfth grade. The authors of the Standards asserted they were developed to ensure that American students were competent in skills and subjects related to literacy (such as reading) and mathematics (for example, algebra), ready for college, and prepared to compete in a global economy. Students' competencies in the English language and mathematics would be annually assessed by standardized testing.[90] The Common Core Standards, though they cut across state boundaries, relied on each state for adoption. When the standards were first announced, they received a positive response from forty-nine states. However, by 2014, the Common Core proposal was under attack, and several states had withdrawn from participation. To examine the issue, we first deal with standards in recent history.

In the 1970s, a "basic education" movement gained support across the country. Calling for the reassertion of rigorous academic standards, the movement's proponents contended that standards had declined because public schools had de-emphasized basic academic skills and subjects. They alleged that schools were using social promotion rather than academic competency to move students to higher grade levels.[91]

In the 1980s, President Reagan and his Secretary of Education, Terrel Bell, developed an agenda to raise educational standards that promoted (1) a basic skill and subject matter curriculum; (2) effective schools with high academic standards and expectations; and (3) education to improve American economic competition in the global economy. The academic standards movement moved ahead significantly when the National Commission on Excellence in Education issued its report, *A Nation at Risk,* which dramatically stated the following:

> Our Nation is at risk. Our once unchallenged preeminence in commerce, industry, science, and technological innovation is being overtaken by competitors throughout the world. . . .The educational foundations of our society are presently being eroded by a rising tide of mediocrity that threatens our very future as a Nation and a people.[92]

---

[90]Common Core State Standards Initiative site, **www.corestandards.org**; also, see Frederick M. Hess and Michael Q. McShane, eds. *Common Core Meets Education Reform: What It All Means for Politics, Policy, and the Future of Schooling* (New York: Teachers College Press, 2013).

[91]Diane Ravitch, "Why Basic Education," Conference on Basic Education, Council on Basic Education (Portland, OR, April 27, 1978).

[92]National Commission on Excellence in Education, *A Nation at Risk: The Imperative for Educational Reform* (Washington, DC: US Department of Education, 1983) p. 5.

TAKING ISSUE

Read the brief introduction below, as well as the question and the pros and cons list that follow. Then answer the question using *your* own words and position.

COMMON CORE STANDARDS

Question

Should the Common Core State Standards be adopted in your state? (Think about this question as you read the PRO and CON arguments listed here. What is *your* response to this issue?)

Arguments PRO

1. In the global economy, it is imperative that all American students, regardless of their state, be competent in English language and mathematics so they are well prepared for college and entry into the workforce.

2. The Standards will correct the inequity in which students in some states receive a higher quality of education than students in other states.

3. Standards will encourage states and schools within them to "Race to the Top" by improving curriculum and instruction.

4. Achieving or failing to meet standards informs parents and the public about the condition of American education.

Arguments CON

1. The Common Core State Standards initiative is a veiled attempt to impose a national curriculum on public schools that violates the historic tradition of state and local control of education.

2. The imposition of uniform standards will force teachers to teach for the standardized tests; this will limit their creativity and flexibility in meeting students' needs.

3. The assessments, through standardized testing, will be a source of profits for testing corporations that will drive the direction of public education.

4. Standards should be set at the local district level with the full participation of parents and teachers, not by bureaucrats and corporate executives.

Question Reprise: What Is Your Stand?

Reflect again on the following question by explaining *your* stand about this issue: Should your state adopt the Common Core State Standards?

"*Everything you need to know about Common Core,*" Diane Ravitch, *The Washington Post*", **www.washingtonpost.com** (December 1, 2014).

The report recommended a high school curriculum of "Five New Basics," which included four years of English; three years of mathematics, science, and social studies; and a half year of computer science.[93] However, the recommended reforms were left as they had been historically, to the states.

The standards movement gained more momentum when Congress enacted the No Child Left Behind Act (NCLB) in 2001, which President George Bush had strongly endorsed. NCLB put into federal law some of the earlier trends for setting higher academic standards, emphasizing basic skills, and school and teacher accountability. It emphasized, as did the later Common Core, the basic skills of reading and arithmetic as necessary foundations for later academic success and the need to assess students' competency in meeting standards in these subjects. Although it did not establish a national curriculum nor national testing, NCLB required the states to establish testing programs to assess annually all students' reading and mathematics competencies from grades 3 to 8. Throughout its history, NCLB has been controversial. Its proponents contend that the National Assessment of Educational Progress (NAEP) has shown improvements in reading and mathematics, and that schools and teachers are now being held accountable for the success or failure of instruction. Opponents allege that the NCLB's reliance on standardized testing forces teachers to spend too much time "teaching for the test," and not enough time on developing students' creativity and problem-solving skills.

[93]National Commission on Excellence in Education, *A Nation at Risk*, p. 24–27.

The next major phase in the Standards Movement was the development of the Common Core State Standards and the Obama Administration's Race to the Top (RTTT). Part of the Recovery Act of 2009, RTTT provided $4.35 billion to encourage states to adopt standards. Echoing earlier standards efforts, RTTT urged the adoption of standards to prepare students to succeed in college and the workplace and compete in the global economy. In effect, RTTT encouraged states to adopt the Common Core Standards.[94]

By 2014 the Common Core Standards were under attack from diverse opponents. Some conservatives believed the Standards were an attempt to create a national curriculum, which violated the historic tradition of state and local control of education. Others, like Diane Ravitch, a noted historian of education, opposed the Common Core Standards as serving the market interests of "testing corporations, charter chains, and technology companies. The Standards, she argues, were adopted "behind closed doors" without participation of educators and the public. While not opposed to the concept of standards, Ravitch argued that they should "not be rigid, inflexible, and prescriptive" and should permit teachers to adapt them to their students' needs.[95] See the Taking Issue Box on the previous page.

5-7a Connecting with the History of Education throughout This Book

This chapter relates the general historical context of American education to other chapters in this book. It provides the historical background for the following:

- Chapter 7, Governing and Administering Public Education, which discusses the federal government's educational role and the establishment of the US Department of Education.
- Chapter 12, Providing Equal Educational Opportunity, which discusses racial desegregation, compensatory education, bilingual education, education for children with disabilities, the Education for All Handicapped Children Act of 1975, and No Child Left Behind.
- Chapter 13, The Changing Purposes of American Education, which discusses major policy reports such as *High School* and a *Nation at Risk*.

---

[94]See **www.ed.gov**.

[95]"Everything you need to know about Common Core—Ravitch," *The Washington Post* (December 1, 2014) at **www.washingtonpost.com**.

SUMMING UP

1. The European colonists transported and established religious and socioeconomic class-based educational institutions in North America. Primary vernacular schools provided a basic curriculum of reading, writing, arithmetic, and religion. The Latin grammar school and the colonial college, reserved for upper-class boys and men, provided a classical curriculum to prepare them for leadership roles in church, state, and society.

2. In the early national period, Benjamin Franklin, Thomas Jefferson, and Benjamin Rush proposed plans for a uniquely American school system; Noah Webster's plan used an American version of the English language to create the country's national identity.

3. The common school, the nineteenth century prototype for the public elementary school, contributed to the development of teacher education, especially normal schools, and the entry of more women into teaching.

4. The public high school in the late nineteenth century completed the American educational ladder that connected public elementary schools to state colleges and universities. Important historical influences in shaping American

higher education were the Morrill Act, the German research concept, the GI Bill, and the rise of community colleges.

5. The United States is a racially, ethnically, and culturally diverse nation; the public policy toward this pluralism has ranged from Americanization in the nineteenth century to multiculturalism in the twentieth.

6. Since the mid-twentieth century, the infusion of technology, especially computers, has been transforming education and creating global economic and communications systems.

7. The controversy over Common Core Standards can been seen as a continuation of the basic education movement, *A Nation at Risk*, and the No Child Left Behind Act.

SUGGESTED RESOURCES

INTERNET RESOURCES

For primary sources, access "Benjamin Franklin's Autobiography," at the Early America website.

For a biography and chronology on Jefferson, access "Monticello's Online Resources" at the Monticello website.

For Rush's essay on education, access "Benjamin Rush on Public Schooling" at the School Choices website.

For a tour, history, research, and activities of the colonial period, access the Colonial Williamsburg website.

For Jefferson documents, access the Thomas Jefferson Digital Archive at the University of Virginia website.

For biographies of Mary Lyon, Jane Addams, Catharine Beecher, and other leaders in women's rights and education, access the resource center at the National Women's History Project website.

For a biography and resources on W. E. B. Du Bois, access the W.E.B. Du Bois website.

For images and discussion of the Chinese in California and the relocation of Japanese Americans during World War II, go to "Collections" at the Bancroft Library website.

For resources on one-room schools, access One-Room Schools at the Iowa Pathways web page.

For a "Day at School," access the Clarke Historical Library website.

For resources on African American, Native American, and immigration history, access the American Memories Collection at the Library of Congress website.

To read more about Indian Boarding Schools, access "Indian Boarding Schools in the Pacific Northwest," at the University Libraries, University of Washington website, and "American Indian Boarding Schools Haunt Many," at the NPR website

PUBLICATIONS

Austin, Allan W. *From Concentration Camps to Campus: Japanese American Students and World War II.* Urbana: University of Illinois Press, 2004. *Discusses how Japanese Americans overcame the trauma of internment during World War II.*

Chan, Sucheng, and Madeline Y. Hsu, eds. *Chinese Americans and the Politics of Race and Culture.* Philadelphia: Temple University Press, 2008. *An anthology of essays on Chinese American history, culture, and identity.*

Collins, Allan, and Richard Halverson. *Rethinking Education in the Age of Technology: The Digital Revolution and Schooling in America.* New York: Teachers College Press, 2009. *Discusses how technology is transforming American education.*

Connolly, Paula T. *Slavery in American Children's Literature, 1790–2010.* Iowa City: University of Iowa Press, 2013. *A commentary on the treatment of slavery in children's books that is especially useful for teachers in understanding how children form their ideas about the topic.*

Davis, Julie L. *The American Indian Movement and Community Education in the Twin Cities.* Minneapolis: University of Minnesota Press, 2013. *Focuses on education as an agency to improve the conditions of Native Americans.*

Del Moral, Solsiree. *Negotiating Empire: The Cultural Politics of Schools in Puerto Rico, 1898–1952.* Madison: University of Wisconsin Press, 2013. *Discusses how Puerto Rico's teachers mediated between American education and Puerto Rican identity.*

Fleegler, Robert L. *Ellis Island Nation: Immigration Policy and American Identity in the Twentieth Century.* Philadelphia: University of Pennsylvania Press, 2013. *Examines the changes in the US immigration policy from the 1882 Chinese Exclusion Act to the 1986 Immigration Reform and Control Act.*

Gandara, Patricia, and Frances Contreras. *The Latino Education Crisis: The Consequences of Failed Social Policies.* Cambridge, MA: Harvard University Press, 2010. *Provides a policy analysis on the impact of social and educational policies on Latino education.*

Gutek, Gerald L. *An Historical Introduction to American Education.* Long Grove, IL: Waveland Press, 2013. *Provides a topical approach to the historical development of educational institutions in the United States.*

Kloosterman, Valentina. *Latino Students in American Schools: Historical and Contemporary Views.* New York: Praeger, 2003. *Discusses the education of Latino students in a historical perspective.*

Kolodny, Kelly A. *Normalites: The First Professionally Prepared Teachers in the United States.* Charlotte, NC: Information Age Publishing, 2014. *Provides an insightful and engaging commentary on the education of teachers in normal schools.*

Lassone, Cynthia A., Robert J. Michael, and Jerusalem Rivera-Wilson. *Current Issues in Teacher Education: History, Perspectives, and Implications.* Springfield, IL: Charles C. Thomas, 2008. *Provides historical background on selected contemporary issues in teacher education.*

McMahon, Lucia. *Mere Equals: The Paradox of Educated Women in the Early American Republic.* Ithaca: Cornell University Press, 2012. *Explores early national women's education, examining tensions between the concept of intellectual equality and persistent traditional gender restrictions.*

Mitchell, Mary Niall. *Raising Freedom's Child: Black Children and Visions of the Future after Slavery.* New York: New York University Press, 2008. *Examines African American schooling in the general cultural context of emancipation from slavery.*

Moore, Jacqueline M. *Booker T. Washington, W. E. B. Du Bois, and the Struggle for Racial Uplift.* Wilmington, DE: Scholarly Resources, 2003. *Presents a well-balanced examination of the differences between Washington and Du Bois as well as alternatives to their positions.*

Ogren, Christine A. *The American State Normal School: "An Instrument of Great Good."* New York: Palgrave Macmillan, 2005. *Develops a historical appraisal of the importance of normal schools in the history of American teacher education.*

Patterson, James T. *Brown v. Board of Education: A Civil Rights Milestone and Its Troubled Legacy.* New York: Oxford University Press, 2001. *Examines the highly significant case that ended legally sanctioned racial segregation in the United States.*

Provenzo, Jr., Eugene F. *Du Bois on Education.* Lanham, MD: Rowman and Littlefield, 2002. *Provides a well-edited and comprehensive collection of Du Bois's major works on education and an extensive bibliography.*

Reyhner, Jon A., and Jeanne M. Oyawin Eder. *American Indian Education: A History.* Norman: University of Oklahoma Press, 2006. *Provides a comprehensive history of American Indian education, including discussions of missionary, government, and boarding schools.*

San Miguel Jr., Guadalupe. *Chicana/o Struggles for Education: Activism in the Community.* College Station: Texas A&M University Press, 2013. *Examines the changing educational patterns that have shaped the education of Mexican American children.*

Shaw, Stephanie J. *W.E.B. Du Bois and The Souls of Black Folk.* Chapel Hill: University of North Carolina Press, 2013. *Provides a thorough analysis of how Du Bois's philosophy shaped his book.*

Spack, Ruth. *America's Second Tongue: American Indian Education and the Ownership of English, 1860–1900.* Lincoln: University of Nebraska Press, 2002. *Examines English-language instruction in terms of federal policy and Indian schools.*

Urban, Wayne J., and Jennings L. Wagoner, Jr. *American Education: A History.* New York: Routledge, 2008. *Provides a comprehensive analysis of the major periods of American history of education in the broad context of national and international events.*

Valencia, Richard. *Chicano Students and the Courts: The Mexican American Legal Struggle for Educational Equality.* New York: New York University Press, 2008. *An in-depth treatment of issues on the legal rights of Chicano students such as school organization, financing, bilingual and bicultural education, and undocumented students.*

Watras, Joseph. *A History of American Education.* Boston: Allyn and Bacon, 2007. *This well-written and carefully organized history of American education examines the implications of the ideas of leading educators and reform movements for teachers and schools in a historical perspective.*

PHILOSOPHICAL ROOTS OF EDUCATION

LEARNING OBJECTIVES

6-1 Relate philosophy's special terminology of metaphysics, epistemology, axiology, and logic to education.

6-2 Appraise the relevance of idealism's goal of intellectual and spiritual growth in contemporary education and schools.

6-3 Explain realism's emphasis on classifying and categorizing subjects in the curriculum in relation to its view of reality.

6-4 Design lessons based on pragmatist epistemology that applies the scientific method to problem solving.

6-5 Generalize the existentialist belief that "existence precedes essence" to learning and social situations in high school.

6-6 Apply postmodernist deconstruction to a chapter in a textbook that you are using in a college course or to a textbook in a subject that you are teaching.

6-7 Construct curriculum models that reflect essentialist principles.

6-8 Select three books that meet the perennialist criteria of a "great book" for inclusion on the reading list of a high school class in American literature.

6-9 Design an elementary school field trip that is based on the child-centered progressive project method.

6-10 Appraise the critical theory argument that the official curriculum reinforces the domination of favored groups and marginalizes the contributions of disadvantaged ones.

Richard G. Bingham II / Alamy

This chapter was revised by Gerald L. Gutek.

TEACHERS MUST MEET such immediate daily demands as preparing lessons, assessing student performance, and creating and managing a fair and equitable classroom environment. Because of their urgency, these challenges often preoccupy teachers in their early professional careers from constructing what the National Council for Accreditation of Teacher Education (NCATE) standards call a "conceptual framework," an intellectual philosophy of education that gives meaning to teaching by connecting its daily demands with long-term professional commitment and direction.[1] A conceptual framework contributes to a sense of professional coherence that helps teachers place immediate short-term objectives into relationship with long-term goals.

We can define a philosophy as the most general way of thinking about the meaning of our lives in the world and reflecting deeply on what is true or false, good or evil, right or wrong, and beautiful or ugly.[2] This chapter provides you with a conceptual framework, a theoretical map, upon which you can locate your ideas about education and construct your own philosophy of education.

In Chapter 5, Historical Development of American Education, you were encouraged to write your own history of education and educational autobiography. You can now revisit and extend your historical and autobiographical reflections about the people and events that shaped your ideas about education, schooling, teaching, and learning as the background for constructing your own philosophy of education. Begin by asking yourself what you believe is true and valuable and how your educational experiences have shaped these beliefs. You can think about the relationship between knowledge and knowing and between teaching and learning. You can determine whether the philosophies and theories in this chapter are similar to or different from your own educational experiences. You can determine whether your encounters with these philosophies and theories confirm or cause you to revise your beliefs about what is true and valuable. Finally, you can make some judgments about how they influence what, why, and how you teach.

6-1 OVERVIEW AND SPECIAL TERMINOLOGY

This chapter examines five philosophies and four theories of education. Comprehensive **philosophies**, such as idealism and realism, present a general worldview that includes education. Educational **theories**, often derived from philosophies or arising from practice, focus more specifically on schools, curriculum, and teaching and learning (see Figure 6.1). The general philosophies examined in this chapter link to the more specific theories of education. For example, the philosophy of realism closely relates to the theories of perennialism and essentialism. Similarly, aspects of progressivism derive from pragmatism. To construct your own philosophy of education, you need to think like a philosopher and use philosophy's terminology.

Philosophies of education use the terms *metaphysics, epistemology, axiology,* and *logic*.[3] Figure 6.2 summarizes the relationship between these terms and education.

philosophies Systematic developed bodies of thought, each representing a generalized worldview about reality, logic, and values.

theories Sets of related ideas or beliefs, often based on research findings or generalizations from practice, that guide educational policies or procedures.

---

[1] **www.ncate.org/Standards/NCATEUnitStandards/UnitStandardsinEffect2008/tabid/476/Default.aspx**.

[2] For introductions to philosophy of education, see Nell Noddings, *Philosophy of Education* (Denver, CO: Westview, 2011); Steven M. Cahn, *Classic and Contemporary Readings in the Philosophy of Education* (New York: Oxford University Press, 2011); Harvey Siegal, ed., *The Oxford Handbook of Philosophy of Education* (New York: Oxford University Press, 2012); Gert J. J. Biesta, *The Beautiful Risk of Education* (Paradigm Publishers, 2014); Richard Bailey, *Philosophy of Education: An Introduction* (New York: Continuum, 2010); and David T. Hansen, *Ethical Visions of Education: Philosophy in Practice* (New York: Teachers College Press, 2007).

[3] For a discussion of philosophical terminology, see Gerald L. Gutek, *New Perspectives on Philosophy and Education* (Columbus, OH: Pearson, 2009), pp. 3–7.

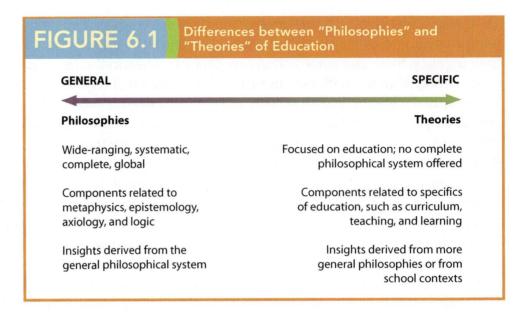

FIGURE 6.1 Differences between "Philosophies" and "Theories" of Education

GENERAL ← → SPECIFIC

Philosophies	Theories
Wide-ranging, systematic, complete, global	Focused on education; no complete philosophical system offered
Components related to metaphysics, epistemology, axiology, and logic	Components related to specifics of education, such as curriculum, teaching, and learning
Insights derived from the general philosophical system	Insights derived from more general philosophies or from school contexts

metaphysics The area of philosophy that examines issues of a speculative nature dealing with ultimate reality.

epistemology The area of philosophy that examines knowing and theories of knowledge.

Metaphysics considers questions about ultimate reality. What is ultimately real or not real? Is there a spiritual realm of existence separate from the material world? Idealists, for example, see reality primarily in nonmaterial intellectual, conceptual, or spiritual terms. Realists see it as an objective order that exists independently of humankind. The subjects taught in schools represent how curriculum designers, teachers, and textbook authors describe their beliefs about "reality" to students.

Epistemology, which deals with knowledge and knowing, influences methods of teaching and learning. It asks, "On what do we base our knowledge of the world and our understanding of truth? Does our knowledge derive from divine revelation, from ideas latent in our own minds, from empirical evidence, or from something else?" Teachers who believe that the universe exists as an orderly structure will emphasize the systematic and

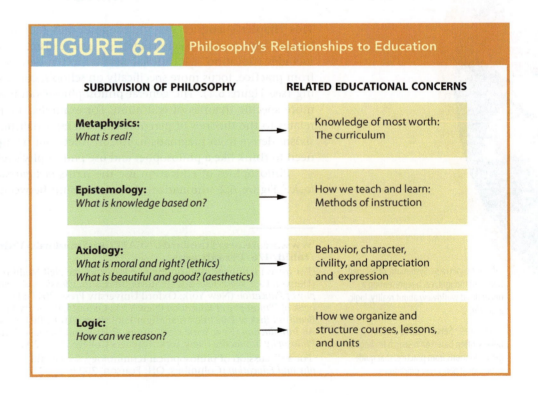

FIGURE 6.2 Philosophy's Relationships to Education

SUBDIVISION OF PHILOSOPHY	RELATED EDUCATIONAL CONCERNS
Metaphysics: *What is real?*	Knowledge of most worth: The curriculum
Epistemology: *What is knowledge based on?*	How we teach and learn: Methods of instruction
Axiology: *What is moral and right? (ethics) What is beautiful and good? (aesthetics)*	Behavior, character, civility, and appreciation and expression
Logic: *How can we reason?*	How we organize and structure courses, lessons, and units

sequential teaching of subjects to reproduce this order in students' minds. They will use subject matter to transmit this conception of reality to students. In contrast, teachers who believe the process of how we know is most important will involve students in problem solving to construct their own view of reality. There is an important difference between transmitting knowledge about an antecedent reality that exists prior to the students' experience and encouraging students to make or construct their own version of reality. Which of these approaches to reality will you emphasize in your philosophy of education?

Axiology, which prescribes and proscribes values—what we should or should not do—is subdivided into *ethics* and *aesthetics*. Teachers often refer to these prescriptions and proscriptions as appropriate or inappropriate behavior. **Ethics** examines moral values and prescribes the standards of ethical behavior; **aesthetics** addresses values in beauty and art. Teachers—like parents and society in general—convey their values to the young by rewarding and reinforcing behavior that corresponds to their conceptions of what is true, good, and beautiful, and what is right and wrong. Moreover, the classroom environment teachers create immerses students in a moral climate that reflects their ethical and aesthetic sensibilities. For example, sharing and respecting the rights of others are prescribed values. In contrast, cheating and bullying are proscribed as harmful, unethical behaviors.

Concerned with correct and valid thinking, logic examines the rules of inference used to order our propositions and arguments. **Deductive logic** moves from general principles and statements to particular instances and applications. For example, we begin with the premise that all deciduous trees seasonally drop their leaves, then state the sub-premise that the maple tree drops its leaves in the fall, and finally reach the conclusion that the maple is a deciduous tree. In terms of deductive inference, if the premises are true, then the conclusion must be true. **Inductive logic** moves from the particular instance to tentative generalizations that are subject to further verification and possible revision. It moves from limited data to a more general conclusion. For example, (a) the earth's temperature has been increasing over the past fifty years; (b) this global warming is due to the greenhouse effect caused by emissions from the burning of fossil fuels; (c) if we continue to generate emissions from fossil fuels, the earth's temperature will continue to rise. Curriculum and instruction are organized on conceptions of logic. Think about the differences in teaching a science course from the two examples used.[4] Does something in the subject itself logically dictate how lessons should be organized and presented to students (the deductive approach)? Or should teachers take their cues from students' interest, readiness, and experience in organizing instruction (an inductive approach)?

Using this terminology, we now examine the philosophies of idealism, realism, pragmatism, existentialism, and postmodernism. After studying each philosophy's key concepts, educational implications, and application to schools and classrooms, you can determine how they relate to your ideas about teaching and learning and decide if you will include them in your philosophy of education. (See Overview 6.1 for the philosophies discussed in this chapter.)

axiology The area of philosophy that examines value issues, especially in morality, ethics, and aesthetics.

ethics The subdivision of axiology that examines questions of right and wrong and good and bad.

aesthetics The subdivision of axiology that establishes criteria for judging that something, such as literature, music, and art, is either beautiful or not.

deductive logic The process of thinking by which consequences or applications are drawn out of general principles or assumptions; the process of thought in which conclusions follow from premises.

inductive logic The process of reasoning from particulars to generalities, from the parts to the whole, and from the individual to the general. It is the basis of the scientific method, emphasized by Dewey and the pragmatists.

FOCUS Reflect on the terms—*metaphysics, epistemology, axiology,* and *logic*—discussed in the chapter. In constructing your philosophy of education, what are your beliefs about reality, knowing, valuing, and thinking?

6-2 IDEALISM

idealism A philosophy which asserts that reality is spiritual, intellectual, and nonmaterial.

Idealism, one of the oldest Western philosophies, begins with Plato (428–347 BCE), who taught his philosophy in the ancient Greek city-state of Athens. Much later, in nineteenth-century Germany, Georg W. F. Hegel (1770–1831), a university professor, lectured to his students about a philosophy of history in which the major periods in human history represented the unfolding of the ideas in the mind of the Absolute,

---

[4]Samir Okasha, *Philosophy of Science: A Very Short Introduction* (Oxford, UK: Oxford University Press, 2002), pp. 18–24.

OVERVIEW 6.1

PHILOSOPHIES OF EDUCATION

Philosophy	Metaphysics	Epistemology	Axiology	Educational Implications	Proponents
Idealism	Reality is spiritual or mental and unchanging.	Knowing is the intuitive recall of ideas present in the mind.	Values are universal, absolute, and eternal.	A subject-matter curriculum that emphasizes the culture's great and enduring ideas.	Emerson Froebel Hegel Plato
Realism	Reality is objective and exists independently of us, but we can know it.	Knowing consists of conceptualization based on sensation and abstraction.	Values are absolute and eternal, based on universal natural laws.	A subject-matter curriculum that emphasizes the arts, humanities, and sciences.	Aquinas Aristotle Broudy Maritain Pestalozzi
Pragmatism (experimentalism)	Rejects metaphysics, asserting that hypotheses about reality are based on experience, the individual's interaction with a changing environment.	Knowing results from experiencing, testing ideas by acting on them, and using the scientific method.	Values are situational and culturally relative.	Instruction that uses the scientific method to solve problems.	Childs Dewey James Peirce
Existentialism	Discounts metaphysics, arguing that our beliefs about reality are subjective, with existence preceding essence.	Our knowing comes from making personal choices.	Values are to be freely chosen by the person.	Classroom dialogues to stimulate awareness that each person creates a self-concept through significant choices.	Kierkegaard Sartre Marcel Morris
Postmodernism	Rejects metaphysics as a historical construction used for socioeconomic domination.	Deconstructs texts (canons) to find their origin and use by dominant groups and classes.	Emphasizes the values of marginalized persons and groups.	Schools are sites of democratic criticism and social change to empower dominated groups.	Derrida Foucault

or God.[5] In the United States, Ralph Waldo Emerson (1803–1882) and Henry David Thoreau (1817–1862) developed an American version of idealism, called transcendentalism, that emphasized finding truth in nature. Friedrich Froebel (discussed in Chapter 4, Pioneers of Teaching and Learning) developed his kindergarten on idealist principles that emphasized the unfolding of children's spiritual nature. Asian religions such as Hinduism and Buddhism also rest on an idealist spiritual worldview.

6-2a Key Concepts

Metaphysics   Idealists believe that the spiritual, conceptual, nonmaterial world is ultimately real. They see the world as the creation of a great universal mind, the mind of the Absolute or God. For idealists, the person's spiritual essence, or soul, as the

---

[5] David Bostock, "Plato," in Ted Honderich, ed., *The Philosophers: Introducing Great Western Thinkers* (Oxford, UK: Oxford University Press, 1999), pp. 15–21; and J. M. Fritzman, *Hegel* (Cambridge, UK: Polity Books, 2014).

permanent element of human nature, gives individuals the power to think and feel. This intellectual or spiritual world of ideas is universal and eternal. Because it is perfect like its Creator, it does not need to change. Like the Universal Spirit itself, goodness, truth, and beauty are the same everywhere in the world throughout time.

Idealists, such as the American transcendentalists, use the concepts of macrocosm and microcosm to explain how they perceive reality. **Macrocosm** refers to the universal mind, the first cause, creator, or God. Regardless of what it is called, the macrocosmic mind is the whole of existence. It is the one, all-inclusive, and complete self of which all lesser selves are part. The universal, macrocosmic mind is continually thinking and valuing. The **microcosm**, the personal mind or spirit, is a lesser self but nevertheless spiritual and intellectual like the great being of which it is a part.

macrocosm The universal whole or entirety. In idealism, it is the most universal, complete, and abstract idea from which all subordinate ideas are derived.

microcosm A smaller part of the greater whole, the macrocosm, from which it is derived.

a priori **ideas** Ideas deduced from self-evident first principles that are conclusions based on reason alone. Associated with realism, Thomism, and perennialism, Dewey and the pragmatists argue that the epistemology of *a priori* ideas is not based on verifiable experience.

Epistemology Idealists believe the ideas that compose reality have always existed in the mind of the Absolute, or God. To know something means we have reached a conscious understanding of one or more of these ideas. Plato developed the epistemology of reminiscence, by which we remember *a priori* **ideas** that already are lodged deep in our minds but of which we are not yet conscious. The individual, through deep thought and introspection, searches his or her own mind and discovers in it the ideas that are copies of those in the macrocosmic mind. The teacher asks the probing questions that challenge students to become conscious of this interior but latent knowledge. The educational process of searching within for the truth is intended to stimulate students to arrive at a broad, general, and unifying perspective of the universe.[6] (See Chapter 3, The World Origins of American Education, for the Socratic method and Plato's theory of reminiscence.) Idealist teachers believe the Absolute or God has been revealed over time to those who have sought the truth. These truth-seekers have recorded their discoveries and revelations in bodies of knowledge, or "subjects," especially the liberal arts. Schools, as repositories of this universal and eternal truth, have organized teaching and learning into a hierarchical curriculum of academic subjects, in which some subjects are more important than others. At the top of the hierarchy are the most general disciplines, philosophy, and theology. These highly abstract subjects transcend the limitations of time, place, and circumstance and transfer to a wide range of situations and times. Mathematics is valuable, too, because it cultivates abstract thinking. History and literature, which portray how people make their important choices, rank high as sources of moral and cultural models. Somewhat lower in the curriculum, the natural and physical sciences address particular cause-and-effect relationships. Language is taught as a necessary means of communication and expression at all stages of human development and learning. In leading students through the learning process, the teacher's overarching purpose is to create a transdisciplinary integration of knowledge that relates these subjects to each other as a form of higher-order thinking.

Axiology Because they believe that truth, goodness, and beauty exist in a universal and eternal order, idealists prescribe values that are unchanging and applicable to all people everywhere. Thus, ethical behavior reflects the enduring knowledge and values of human culture. Philosophy, theology, history, literature, and art are rich sources for transmitting values because they provide the contents and the contexts through which students can encounter worthy models, especially in the classics—the great transgenerational works that have been enjoyed through the centuries.

Logic For idealists, logic, too, follows the whole-to-part relationship between the Absolute and individual minds. The part, a specific idea or principle, is derived from and agrees with the whole, which is more general. Idealist teachers would use deductive logic to organize lessons that begin with general principles or rules and use specific cases

---

[6]Gutek, *New Perspectives on Philosophy and Education*, pp. 28–29.

or examples to illustrate them. For example, an idealist teacher of literature might introduce the general concept of respect for others who are different from us by referring to Henry David Thoreau, who took his own path to civil disobedience at Walden Pond.

6-2b Educational Implications

If you were to ask an idealist teacher, "What is knowledge?" she or he would reply that knowledge is about the universal spiritual truths that underlie reality and about the ideas that reflect that truth. Because knowledge is about universal ideas, then education is the intellectual process of bringing these ideas to the learner's consciousness.

If you ask an idealist teacher, "What is the school?" she or he would answer that it is an intellectual institution where teachers and students pursue the questions Socrates and Plato asked: "What is truth? What is beauty? What is the good life?" To answer these questions, we need to think deeply and bring to consciousness the answers that are present in our minds. We need to read the great books and learn to appreciate the great works of art and music in which writers, artists, and composers have captured insights into this truth.

Who should attend school? The idealist would say everyone. Although students have varying intellectual abilities, all should have the opportunity to cultivate their minds as far as possible. While gifted students need the greatest intellectual challenges, all students have the right and opportunity to pursue the same intellectual curriculum.

How should we teach? The idealist would say that thinking and learning are the processes of bringing ideas to our conscious reflection. The **Socratic method**, in which the teacher stimulates the learner's awareness of ideas by asking leading questions, is a very engaging approach to learning.[7] Modeling is another part of idealist instruction. Teachers should be intellectual and ethical models that students can emulate.

Idealists want schools and teachers to maintain high intellectual standards of academic quality and resist the entry of anything that leads to mediocrity. In Plato's *Republic,* for example, intellectual standards were so high that only a gifted minority became philosopher-kings. Today's idealists would insist that individuals should have an education that will take them as far as their intellectual ability enables them to go.

Idealists would endorse standards that require teachers to have high intellectual expectations of students and require students to strive to achieve intellectual excellence. Standards, moreover, would not be geared to the statistical average but should raise expectations as high as possible. Standardization, however, can never be a substitute for individual intellectual and moral excellence.

6-2c Application to Schools and Classrooms

Rejecting the materialism, consumerism, and the momentary popularity of sensationalism in the contemporary mass media society, idealism wants schools to be stable places of teaching and learning. It wants teachers to be vital agents in guiding students to realize their fullest intellectual potential; it encourages teachers and their students to encounter and appreciate the finest and most enduring achievements of the culture. Teachers should introduce students to the classics—great and enduring works of art, literature, and music—so that they can experience and share in the time-tested cultural values these works convey.

In using technology or any innovation, idealists want educators to keep their attention focused on education's paramount purpose of searching for the truth in schools that are places of the mind. While they understand that Internet can make the

Socratic method The method of inquiry named for the ancient Greek philosopher, Socrates, who asked probing questions about truth, goodness, and beauty that caused his students to examine their beliefs and values.

---

[7]For Socrates, Plato, and Aristotle, see C. D. C. Reeve, "The Socratic Movement," in Randall Curren, ed., *A Companion to the Philosophy of Education* (Malden, MA: Blackwell Publishing, 2006), pp. 7–24. Also, see Paul Ricoeur, *Being, Essence and Substance in Plato and Aristotle* (Cambridge, UK: Polity Books, 2013).

great books and works of art accessible to more students, idealists insist that technology should be a means, an instrument, of education rather than an end. The content matters most, not the technical apparatus that conveys it.[8]

An idealist teacher has developed a lesson in her seventh-grade social studies class on the power of ideas as expressed by different persons at different times to respect human rights and social justice. She identifies three persons who students can imitate as models of ethical behavior: Henry David Thoreau, Mohandas Gandhi, and Martin Luther King, Jr. In the mid-nineteenth century, Thoreau, who refused to pay taxes to support the war against Mexico, was jailed in Massachusetts for his civil disobedience. Gandhi, who led a nonviolent movement against the repression of Indians in South Africa and India, like Thoreau, was imprisoned for his actions in the 1920s, 1930s, and 1940s. Martin Luther King, Jr., who like Gandhi led a nonviolent campaign for African American civil and voting rights in the American South in the 1960s also was jailed, like Thoreau, for his actions for social justice. In this unit, the teacher has provided three outcomes that reflect her commitment to idealism. One, the life and actions of Thoreau, Gandhi, and King show the power of ideas. Two, these ideas are universal in that they are shared by three men of difference races, living in different places. Three, these ideas are timeless in that the same basic idea is manifested at different times, the mid-nineteenth and the first half of the twentieth centuries and in the 1960s.

FOCUS What elements of idealism appeal to you as a teacher? Which appeal least? Why? Are there elements of idealism that you would like to incorporate into your philosophy of education?

6-3 REALISM

realism A philosophy which asserts that reality consists of an objective order of objects that, though they are external, can be known by humans through their senses and power of abstraction.

The Greek philosopher Aristotle (384–322 BCE), a student of Plato, developed **realism**, which asserts that reality exists outside of our minds or is objective, not latent or internal to our minds as Plato claimed. As described in Chapter 3, The World Origins of American Education, during the Middle Ages, Thomas Aquinas (1224–1274) constructed a synthesis of Aristotle's natural realism and Christian doctrine known as Thomism.[9] Bringing realism into the twenty-first century, scientific realists assert that the scientific method is the best way to get an accurate description of what the world is and how it works.[10] To explain and use our scientific findings, we have to construct theories. As scientific investigation provides more accurate and verified information about the world, we can revise and refine our theories so that they correspond more accurately to reality.

Realists assert that (1) there is a world of real existence, of objects, not made by human beings; (2) the human mind can know about the real world; and (3) such knowledge is the most reliable guide to individual and social action and behavior. Beginning with these principles, we can examine realism's educational implications.

6-3a Key Concepts

Metaphysics and Epistemology   Realists believe in a material world that is independent of and external to the knower's mind.[11] All objects are composed of matter. Matter, in turn, is organized as it takes on the form or structure of an object.

---

[8]For education, philosophy, and technology, see Christina E. Erneling, *Towards Discursive Education: Philosophy, Technology, and Modern Education* (New York: Cambridge University Press, 2010); and Marc de Vries, *Teaching about Technology: An Introduction to the Philosophy of Technology for Non-Philosophers* (Dordrecht, Netherlands: Springen, 2005).

[9]For biographies and the ideas of Aristotle and Aquinas, see David Charles, "Aristotle," in Honderich, *The Philosophers*, pp. 23–31; and Alexander Brodie, "St. Thomas Aquinas," in Honderich, *The Philosophers*, pp. 39–47. Also, see Jonathan Barnes, *Aristotle: A Very Short Introduction* (Oxford, UK: Oxford University Press, 2000), p. 30; and Vivian Boland, *St. Thomas Aquinas* (London and New York: Bloomsbury Academic, 2014).

[10]Okasha, *Philosophy of Science*, pp. 58–62.

[11]J. J. C. Smart, *Philosophy and Scientific Realism* (New York: Routledge, 2013).

> **PHOTO 6.1** Realist philosophy emphasizes sensory learning and organizing objects into categories such as chemistry, as these students are doing in a science class.

PhotoAlto/Alamy

Knowing (epistemology) involves two necessary and related stages: sensation and abstraction. First, the person perceives an object as his or her senses convey data about it to the person's mind, such as color, size, weight, smell, or sound. The mind sorts these data into qualities that are always found in the object from those that are sometimes present. By identifying the necessary qualities (those always present), the learner abstracts a concept of the object and recognizes it as belonging to a certain class. This classification affirms that the object shares certain qualities with other members of the same class but not with objects of a different class (Photo 6.1).

Like idealists, realists believe that a curriculum of organized, separate subjects provides the most accurate and efficient way for students to learn about reality. Organizing subject matter into categories, as scientists and scholars do, is an orderly method of classifying objects. For example, past human experiences can be organized into history. Botany studies plants systematically according to their classifications. Political organizations such as nations, governments, legislatures, and judicial systems can be grouped under political science. The realist acquires knowledge about reality through systematic inquiry into subjects like these.

Axiology   For realists, certain rules should govern intelligent rational behavior. Aristotle defined humans as rational animals. Therefore, people are most human when they act in a rational way, which means to make reasonable decisions based on knowledge. From their observations of natural and social realities, people can develop theories about how nature and society function. When their decisions are made on these theories, they are behaving rationally.

Logic   Realist teachers may use logic both deductively and inductively. For example, students in a botany class might examine roses that differ in color, scent, and size but conclude, through induction, that all are members of the same genus. However, when the class plants a rose garden on the school grounds as a project, the students can find information about roses in the library and on the Web and deduce the correct locations and amounts of fertilizer and water for each rose they plant.

6-3b Educational Implications

To find realism's educational implications, we again ask, "What is knowledge?" Realists would reply that knowledge is about the world in which we live. When we know something, our knowledge is always about an object. Our concepts are valid when they correspond to those objects as they really exist.[12] Scientific realists would add that our concepts, to be accurate, should be based on a scientific description and verification of this correspondence.

Formal education, the realists would say, is the study of knowledge organized and classified into subject-matter disciplines. History, languages, science, and mathematics are some of these organized bodies of knowledge. Knowledge of these subjects informs us about the world in which we live; this knowledge is our best guide in conducting our daily affairs.

For realists, society establishes schools as academic institutions to provide students with knowledge about the objective world in which they live. Because all persons have a rational potentiality, schooling should be available to all. Realists would oppose sorting students into separate academic and vocational tracks. All students should pursue the same academic curriculum, which will prepare them to make rational decisions, informed by knowledge.

6-3c Application to Schools and Classrooms

In realist classrooms, the teacher's primary responsibility is to bring students' ideas about the world into correspondence with reality by teaching skills (such as reading, writing, or computation) and subjects (such as history, mathematics, or science) that are based on authoritative and expert knowledge. Although they appreciate that their students are emotional as well as rational, realists focus on cognitive learning and subject-matter mastery. Realist teachers oppose the intrusion of nonacademic activities that interfere with the school's primary purpose as a center of disciplined academic inquiry.

In the preservice preparation of teachers, subject-matter knowledge and competency is given high priority. For example, the history teacher should be a historian with an academic major in history. In addition, realist teachers should have a general education in the liberal arts and sciences so that they understand and can demonstrate relationships between their special area of expertise and other subjects. Realist teachers use a wide repertoire of methods, such as lecture, discussion, demonstration, and experiment. Content mastery is most important, and methodology is a necessary but subordinate means to reach the goal of liberally educating students.

How might a realist high school physics teacher structure a unit on Isaac Newton's laws of motion? First, the teacher would help students place Newton in context within the history of science and discuss his scientific contributions. Second, the teacher might illustrate the laws of motion in a laboratory demonstration. Third, the students might discuss the demonstration and frame the scientific generalization it illustrates. Finally, students would be tested to assess their understanding of Newton's laws of motion.[13]

Realists welcome the use of standards, such as the Common Core State Standards, that establish academic achievement benchmarks. For students to progress through elementary and high school, and especially in college, they need to be competent in the indispensable skills of reading and mathematics. Standards in the basic skills as well as in English, higher mathematics, science, and history are needed across the curriculum. It is important that standards reflect what mathematicians, scientists, historians, and other academic specialists have identified as the concepts and processes that are necessary to understand an academic subject. Standardized tests provide reliable,

---

[12]Joshua Rasmussen, *Defending the Correspondence Theory of Truth* (Cambridge, UK: Cambridge University Press, 2014).

[13]Philip H. Phenix, *Philosophies of Education* (New York: Wiley, 1961), pp. 22–24.

objective, and comparable data about how well students are mastering academic subjects and about teachers' effectiveness in instructing students. However, standards set only the necessary foundation of what students should know. Students need to be challenged to achieve academic excellence in their subjects.

Realists tend to believe that if teachers know their academic subject they will devise ways of teaching it. They are open to a variety of methods of teaching such as lectures, discussions, research projects, and the use of technology as long as the teacher's aim remains focused on the subject. Educational technology that is calibrated to a subject can be used as an effective and dynamic enhancement to teaching a subject but never as a substitute for content.

FOCUS What elements of realism appeal to you as a teacher? Which appeal least? Why? Are there elements of realism that you would like to incorporate into your philosophy of education?

6-4 PRAGMATISM

pragmatism A philosophy that assesses the validity of ideas by acting on and testing them; the consequences of such action determines an idea's viability.

Pragmatism emphasizes the need to test the validity or workability of our ideas by acting on them. Among pragmatism's founders were Charles S. Peirce (1839–1914), William James (1842–1910), George Herbert Mead (1863–1931), and John Dewey (1859–1952). Peirce emphasized using the scientific method to validate ideas empirically; he substituted probability, or what is likely to happen, for certainty. Based on statistics, we can formulate an informed prediction—but not a certain—hypothesis of what is likely to happen. Emphasizing a pluralistic world, James applied pragmatic philosophy to psychology, religion, and education.[14] Mead emphasized that children develop and learn as they explore and interact with their environment. Advocating democracy as the fairest and most equitable kind of society, Dewey applied his version of pragmatism, called experimentalism, to education.[15] (For Dewey's biography and contributions to education, see Chapter 4, Pioneers of Teaching and Learning.)

Influenced by Charles Darwin's theory of evolution, Dewey applied the terms *organism* and *environment* to education. Dewey saw human beings as biological, social, and verbal organisms that use their life-sustaining impulses to promote their growth and development. Every organism, including human beings, lives in a habitat or environment. As people interact with their environments, they have experiences. From these experiences, they construct a usable network of experiential episodes that they can use to solve the problems they encounter in life. For Dewey, education's purpose is to promote the experiences that contribute to optimum human growth.

Whereas idealist and realists emphasize subject-matter disciplines, Dewey sees thinking and learning as problem solving. In his experimental epistemology, the learner, either as an individual or group member, uses the scientific method to test experience by solving personal and social problems. Problem solving, as a process method of general intelligence, can transfer and be applied to a wide range of problematic situations.[16]

6-4a Metaphysics and Epistemology

Unlike the idealist and realist philosophies based on a metaphysical foundation of universal and unchanging reality, pragmatism dismisses metaphysics as empirically unverifiable speculation. Pragmatists focus on epistemology, how we construct our

[14]James W. Garrison and Ronald Podeschi, *William James and Education* (New York: Teachers College Press, 2002).

[15]Reprints and recent editions of Dewey's books are John Dewey, *The School and Society & The Child and the Curriculum* (Mineola, NY: Dover Publications, 2001); *Democracy and Education* (New York: Cosimo Classics, 2005); *Schools of Tomorrow* (Mineola, NY: Dover Publications, 2006); *Art as Experience* (New York: Perigee Books, 2005); *Experience and Education: The 60th Anniversary Edition* (West Lafayette, IN: Kappa Delta Pi, 1998).

[16]For Dewey's discussion of thinking and problem solving, see John Dewey, *How We Think,* introduction by Gerald L. Gutek (New York: Barnes and Noble, 2005), originally published in 1910.

experience As defined by John Dewey, the interaction of a person with his or her environment.

knowledge in a constantly changing world rather than on alleged metaphysical certainties. For example, Peirce, who dismissed certainty as unattainable, replaced it with probability, which had practical applications in human affairs.

Experience, defined as the interaction of the person with the environment, is a key pragmatist concept. A person's interaction with his or her social, cultural, and natural environments constitutes the process of living, growing, and developing. This interaction may alter or change both the person and the environment. Knowing comes from a transaction—a process—between the learner and the environment.[17]

Dewey rejects the idealist and realist concepts that reality is *a priori* or antecedent to human involvement in the world. Rather, he is more concerned with how human beings interact with the environment and construct tentative and flexible conceptions about a changing reality. These tentative assumptions about reality are always subject to further testing and validation, which may lead to a revision, or reconstruction, of an existing assumption or to a new one. Ideas do not exist in their pure state as the idealists assert. Ideas are conceptual instruments that need to be used to determine if they work. Their validity needs to be tested by acting on them and determining what consequences they have for us. Although each interaction with the environment has generalizable aspects that carry over to the next problem, each episode will differ somewhat. It is this element of difference in the episode that causes a problem. When we have solved the problem that the different element has caused, we can add the solution to our network of experience and use it to solve the problems we encounter in the future. For example, attending college may have been a problematic situation for you in that it was a new or different experience. You may have defined the ways in which it was a new or different experience. You might have used your prior experiences in attending elementary and high school to give you ideas on dealing with and solving the new problem. After solving this new problem, you should be able to use your experience as a college student in dealing with the new element of graduate school. Dewey argued that we cannot keep on doing the same things over and over in schools just because they are traditional. We need to use the school as an educational laboratory to test what and how we teach to determine if it leads to the learner's understanding and growth. Does an educational program, curricular design, or teaching strategy achieve its anticipated goals and objectives, and in doing so, does it contribute to students' growth?[18]

Because we and the environment are constantly changing, pragmatists dismiss the idealist and realist curricula based on supposedly antecedent permanent realities or universal truths as empirically untenable. Rather, they assert that our decision making needs to be guided by our experience. Any claim to truth is really a tentative assertion that we can test and revise as we do more research. What we need, say the pragmatists, is a socially and scientifically intelligent method that gives us a process-oriented direction in a constantly changing world.

6-4b Axiology and Logic

Pragmatic axiology is highly situational and culturally relative. A constantly changing and pluralistic world means that values, too, are not universal and eternal as idealists and realists assert but are changing and relative to time, place, and circumstance. For pragmatists, whatever contributes to personal and social growth is valuable; what restricts or limits it is unworthy. Rather than blindly accepting inherited traditional and conventional values, we can clarify our values by testing and reconstructing them in our experience.

---

[17]For an analysis of Dewey's pragmatic perspective, see Christine L. McCarthy and Evelyn Sears, "Deweyan Pragmatism and the Quest for True Self," *Educational Theory* (Spring 2000), pp. 213–227.

[18]For interpretations of Dewey's philosophy to contemporary educational issues, see David T. Hansen, ed., *A Critical Engagement with Dewey's Democracy and Education* (Albany: State University of New York Press, 2006).

> PHOTO 6.2 The students in the pragmatist mode are engaged in interdisciplinary collaborative group interaction.

Birgit Koch/Fotosonline/Alamy Limited

Following the scientific method, experimentalist logic is inductive rather than deduced from first principles as in idealism and realism. Any claim to truth is a warranted assertion that is tentative and subject to further testing and revision.

6-4c Educational Implications

Rather than transmit subject matters of allegedly permanent truths, pragmatists are concerned with the process of constructing, using, and testing ideas. For pragmatists, education is an experimental process—a method of solving problems that challenges people as they interact with their world. For Dewey, the most intelligent and reflective way of solving problems is to use the scientific method.

Pragmatists favor interdisciplinary education rather than a departmentalized subject-matter curriculum (Photo 6.2). When you face a problem, pragmatists say, you find the information needed to solve it from many sources, not from a single academic subject. For example, to define the problem of global warming and suggest ways of solving it, we need to use information that comes from historical, political, sociological, scientific, and technological sources. A pragmatically educated person knows how to research and apply information from multiple sources to the problem. In contrast, idealists and realists strongly disagree because they believe students must first acquire a knowledge base by studying and mastering organized subjects before they can use applied interdisciplinary approaches.

Pragmatists such as Dewey see the school as a local community of learners and teachers intimately connected to the larger society. The school exercises three major functions: to simplify, purify, and balance the cultural heritage. To simplify, teachers select cultural, political, and economic elements in the society and reduce their complexity to units appropriate to learners' readiness, interest, and prior experience. To purify, they select valuable cultural elements such as collaboration and eliminate those such as bullying that limit human interaction and growth. To balance, the school helps learners integrate their experiences so that it is personally and socially meaningful.

In a pluralistic multicultural society, the pragmatic school provides experiences that encourage children of one culture to understand and appreciate members of other

FROM PRESERVICE TO PRACTICE

THE SCHOOL AS A SPECIAL ENVIRONMENT

In this scenario, students are meeting to discuss their preservice clinical observations. Professor Alcott encourages the students to relate their clinical observations to reflections on general concepts about education, schools, curriculum, and methods. Professor Alcott asks, "Now that you have observed classes in schools, what exactly is a school?" Martin Neswich, a student, replies, "Professor, we have all gone to school and have observed classes in schools. We all know what a school is." Professor Alcott replies, "Before we conclude that we know what a school is, I want you to listen to some guests I have invited to the class to answer that question as a panel." A panelist, a member of a veterans' organization, says, "Schools are not doing a good job in teaching American history, civic responsibility, and patriotism." Another panelist, a businessman, says, "Schools need to teach salable market skills needed in business. Some of the people I hire don't even know basic math skills." The third panelist says, "I am a mother of three elementary-age students but don't send my children to public schools because they do not provide the proper religious education and moral values." Professor Alcott thanks the panelists for their presentations. Then, he says, "We have heard from three members of the community who have very different ideas about what a school is and what it does. Before we end this unit, I want you to read what John Dewey, one of America's leading philosophers, said about schools. As teachers, we all need to go to the source." He passes out a short excerpt from John Dewey's, *Democracy and Education*, and says, "Let's read the selection and discuss the questions at the end of the reading next week."

...as soon as a community depends to any considerable extent upon what lies beyond its own territory and its own immediate generation, it must rely upon ... schools to insure adequate transmission of all its resources. ... Hence a special mode of social intercourse is instituted, the school, to care for such matters.

This mode of association has three functions. ... First, a complex civilization is too complex to be assimilated in toto. It has

to be broken up into portions ... and assimilated ... in a gradual and graded way. The relationships of our present social life are so numerous and so interwoven that a child placed in the most favorable position could not readily share in many of the most important of them. Not sharing in them, their meaning would not be communicated to him, would not become part of his own mental disposition. There would be no seeing the trees because of the forest. Business, politics, art, science, religion, would all at once clamor for attention; confusion would be the outcome. The first office of the ... school is to provide a simplified environment. It selects the features which are fairly fundamental and capable of being responded to by the young. ...

In the second place, it is the business of the school environment to eliminate, so far as possible, the unworthy features of the existing environment from influence upon mental habitudes. It establishes a purified medium of action. Selection aims not only at simplifying but at weeding out what is undesirable. Every society gets encumbered with what is trivial, with dead wood from the past, and with what is positively perverse. The school has the duty of omitting such things ... and ... doing what it can to counteract their influence in the ordinary social environment. ... As a society becomes more enlightened, that it is responsible not to transmit and conserve the whole of its existing achievements, but only such as make for a better future society. ...

In the third place, it is the office of the school ... to balance the various elements in the social environment, and to see ... that each individual gets an opportunity to escape from the limitations of the social group in which he was born, and to come into living contact with a broader environment. ... It is this situation which has ... forced the demand for an educational institution which shall provide something like a homogeneous and balanced environment for the young. ...

Source: John Dewey, *Democracy and Education* (New York: MacMillan Co., 1916), pp. 22–26. Abridged by the author.

CASE QUESTIONS

1. What does Dewey identify as three functions of the school?

2. How do Dewey's functions of the school differ from those of the panelists?

3. How do you define the role and functions of the school in your own personal philosophy of education?

cultures. Although cultural diversity enriches the entire society, pragmatists want all children to learn to use the scientific method. They believe that schools should build community consensus by emphasizing common problems and using shared processes to solve them. As genuinely integrated and democratic learning communities, schools should be open to all and encourage the widest possible sharing of resources among people of all cultures.

6-4d Application to Schools and Classrooms

Whereas idealist and realist teachers make teaching subject matter their primary responsibility, pragmatist teachers are more concerned with teaching students to solve problems using the scientific method as an interdisciplinary approach. Rather than transmitting subjects to students, pragmatist teachers facilitate student research and activities, suggesting resources useful in problem solving, including those found in the library as well as those online.[19]

Students in a pragmatist classroom share the collaborative experience of using the scientific method to solve a full range of personal, social, and intellectual problems. Teachers expect that students will learn to apply the problem-solving method to situations both in and out of school and thus connect the school to society. Social networking can create a larger, perhaps even a global, community with more opportunities to share ideas, insights, and experiences.

Pragmatist teachers want their classrooms to be collaborative learning communities where students share their interests and problems. Recognizing that every culture has something of value to share with other cultures, they stress multicultural communication between students of different cultures so that together they can create more inclusive democratic communities. Instead of transmitting the status quo, pragmatist teachers are risk takers who see education as an open-ended and uncertain process.

Pragmatists would raise serious questions about the standards movement, especially the Common Core State Standards, which emphasizes successful learning as mastering subjects and relies on standardized testing to assess students' competencies. The Core rationale burdens students with antecedent goals, and expectations are set by expert academicians and corporate testing agencies rather than those arising from the students' own experiences, issues, and problems. Further, standardized tests measure only how well students have memorized prescribed content, rather than genuine problem-solving skills. Teachers whose competency is judged by their students' performance on standardized tests are likely to focus instruction on passing tests rather than solving problems.

How might we apply pragmatism to classroom teaching? Let us say a college teacher-education class is examining the use of standardized tests to determine if standards of academic achievement are being achieved, as in the No Child Left Behind Act (NCLB) or the Common Core Standards. The class members do the following:

1. Establish the issue's context: Why is using standardized tests to measure achievement a controversial issue in education? Who supports and who opposes using standardized tests to set academic standards?
2. Define the problem's key terms: What is a standardized test, and how is it used?
3. Conduct interdisciplinary research to locate information about the issue from various sources such as professional educators, educational psychologists, government agencies, parents' organizations, state and federal legislators, and the Web.
4. Conjecture possible solutions, ranging from acceptance to rejection of the proposition.
5. Resolve the issue by reaching consensus and acting—for example, carry out an agreement to write a position paper and send it to newspapers, journals, and administrators in the department of education at your college or university.

FOCUS What elements of pragmatism appeal to you as a teacher? Which appeal least? Why? Are there elements of pragmatism that you would like to incorporate into your philosophy of education?

---

[19]For the philosophical implications of technology, see Larry A. Hickman, *Philosophical Tools for Technological Culture* (Bloomington: Indiana University Press, 2001).

6-5 EXISTENTIALISM

existentialism A philosophy that encourages individuals to define themselves by making significant personal choices.

Existentialism is more a process of philosophizing than a systematic philosophy (like idealism and realism). Representing feelings of desperation and hope, it calls for a personal examination of one's own life. An existentialist education encourages deep personal reflection on one's identity, commitments, and choices. It asks: Who am I? What am I doing here, and why am doing it? What difference does my presence make to myself and to the world?

The existentialist author Jean-Paul Sartre (1905–1980) stated that "Existence precedes Essence." Sartre, a playwright and philosopher, emphasized the role of human imagination as a way of knowing and feeling.[20] For Sartre, we are born into a world that we did not choose to be in and that we did not make. However, we possess the personal power, the will, to make choices and to create our own purposes for existence. We are thrust into choice-making situations. Some choices are trivial, but those that deal with the purpose and meaning of life lead to personal self-definition and meaning. We create our own definition as we make our own essence. We are what we choose to be. Human freedom is total, say the existentialists, as is our responsibility for choice.[21]

The existentialist belief that human beings are responsible for creating their own essences dramatically differs from idealist and realist beliefs that the person is already defined in a universal system. Whereas the idealist or realist sees the individual existing in a meaningful and explainable world, the existentialist believes the universe is indifferent to human wishes, desires, and plans. Existentialism focuses on the concept of *angst,* or dread. We know that our presence in the world is temporary and that our destiny is death and disappearance. With this knowledge about the human situation, each person can make meaningful choices about freedom or subordination, love and hate, peace and war, and justice or injustice. As we make these choices, we ask: "What difference does it make that I am here and that I have chosen to be who I am?"

According to the existentialists, we must cope with the constant threat that others—persons, institutions, and agencies—pose to our choice-making freedom. Each person's response to life reflects an answer to the question, "Do I choose to be a self-determined person, or am I content to let others define me?" But existentialism does see hope behind the desperation. Each person has the potential for being, loving, and creating. Each can choose to be a free, inner-directed, authentic person who realizes that every choice is an act of personal value creation.[22]

6-5a Educational Implications

Rejecting antecedent metaphysical descriptions that define the person at the moment of birth, existentialists assert that we create our own essence by making personal choices in our lives. Epistemologically, the individual chooses the knowledge that he or she wants to appropriate into his or her life. Existentialists consider axiology most important because human beings create their own values through their choices.

Recognizing that we live in a world of physical realities, existentialists accept that science provides useful information about the natural environment. However, the most meaningful aspects of our lives are personal, not scientific. Thus, existentialists

---

[20]Thomas Baldwin, "Jean-Paul Sartre," in Honderich, *The Philosophers,* pp. 245–252. Also, see Patrick Baert, *The Existential Moment: The Rise of Sartre as a Public Intellectual* (Cambridge, UK: Polity Books, 2015); and Katherine J. Morris, *Sartre* (Malden, MA: Blackwell Publishing, 2008).

[21]Gutek, *New Perspectives on Philosophy and Education,* pp. 113–125.

[22] Kevin Aho, *Existentialism: An Introduction* (Cambridge, UK: Polity Books, 2014). Also, access Scott Webster, "Existentialism: Providing an Ideal Framework for Educational Research in Times of Uncertainty" at **www.aare.edu.au**.

believe that our personal understanding about the human condition and the personal choices we make are crucial. Education's purpose is to awaken our consciousness about our freedom to choose and to create our own sense of self-awareness that contributes to our authenticity.

At school, existentialists say, teachers and students should engage in discussion about their own lives and choices. Because we are all in the same existential predicament, we all should have opportunities for meaningful, not routinized, schooling. Teachers and students should have the opportunity to ask questions, engage in dialogue, and consider alternatives in all areas of life.

An existentialist teacher would encourage students to philosophize, question, and participate in dialogues about the meaning of their hopes and fears; their desires; and living, loving, and dying. There are no correct or incorrect answers to these questions. They are personal and subjective, not measurable by standardized tests, nor reached by group consensus or by using the scientific method to solve problems. An existentialist curriculum consists of whatever leads to open-ended personal philosophizing. Particularly valuable are literature, biography, drama, and film that vividly portray individuals in the act of making choices in life, especially emotional and aesthetic ones. Students should read books, often autobiographies and novels, and discuss plays, movies, and television programs that vividly portray the human condition and the choice making it requires.

Students should be free to create their own authentic modes of self-expression.[23] They should be free to experiment creatively with music, art, poetry, drama, dance, film, and literature to dramatize their emotions, feelings, and insights.

Educational technology that portrays personal choice and freedom has a role in an existentialist education. For example, students can design multimedia productions to express themselves. However, technologies that generate conformity in thinking and subject a person to group-controlled expression, such as when social media is misused, should be viewed as another kind of oppression that limits freedom. The question is—does social media lead to greater freedom of expression or more conformity?

6-5b Applications to Schools and Classrooms

Teaching from an existentialist perspective is always difficult because curricula and standards are in place in schools before teachers and students walk through the doors on the first day of class. They are often imposed on teachers by external agencies. Further, existentialists warn that teachers cannot specify goals and objectives in advance because students should be free to choose their own educational purposes. They would oppose the standards movement, especially its emphasis on a common core curriculum for all students and standardized testing to measure academic success, as an impediment to personal choice and freedom. Rather than imposing external standards on students, the existentialist teacher seeks to stimulate an intense awareness in students of their ultimate responsibility for their own education and self-definition. To do this, the teacher encourages students to examine the institutions, forces, and conditions that limit freedom of choice. Further, existentialist teachers seek to create open classrooms to maximize freedom of choice. Within these open learning environments, instruction is self-directed rather than standardized.

6-5c An Existentialist School: Summerhill

Although Summerhill defies neat philosophical classification, the philosophy of its founder Alexander Sutherland Neill (1883–1973) illustrates some aspects of existentialism. A British educator, Neill founded Summerhill School, where he encouraged

---

[23]For narrative and education, see Mike Haylor, *Autoethnography, Self-Narrative, and Teacher Education* (Boston: Sense Publishers, 2011).

students to make their own choices about their own education. Liberated from a prescribed curriculum and academic requirements, students were free to choose what, when, and how they learned. Neill found his students actually wanted to learn and eagerly pursued their own educational agendas.[24]

Literature, drama, and film are especially powerful in existentialist teaching. An example of existentialist teaching might be a senior high school history class that is studying the Holocaust, the genocide of six million Jews in Europe during World War II by the Nazis. The class views Steven Spielberg's movie, *Schindler's List,* in which an industrialist, Oscar Schindler, who initially profited from the forced labor of Jewish concentration camp inmates, makes a conscious decision to save his workers from death in the Nazi gas chambers. The class then probes the moral situation of one man, Schindler, and the choice that he made in a senseless and cruel world.

FOCUS What elements of existentialism appeal to you as a teacher? Which appeal least? Why? Are there elements of existentialism that you would like to incorporate into your philosophy of education?

6-6 POSTMODERNISM

postmodernism A philosophy that is highly skeptical of the truth of meta-narratives, the canons that purport to be authoritative statements of universal or objective truth. Rather, postmodernists regard these canons as historical statements that rationalize one group's domination of another.

constructivism A theory of learning which argues that children learn most effectively and readily by constructing ideas based on direct explorations of the environment.

Postmodernism contends that the modern period of history has ended and that we now live in a postmodern era. It originated in the philosophies of the German philosophers Friedrich Nietzsche (1844–1900) and Martin Heidegger (1899–1976). Nietzsche dismissed metaphysical claims about universal truth, suggesting that they were contrived to replace worn-out myths and supernatural beliefs with newer but equally false assertions.[25] Formulating a philosophy called phenomenology, Heidegger asserted that human beings construct their own subjective truths about reality from their intuitions, perceptions, and reflections as they interact with phenomena. Postmodernism exerts a strong intellectual influence today, especially in the humanities and philosophy.[26]

Postmodernism has implications for **constructivism**, a psychology and method of education. Postmodernists and constructivists agree that we make, or construct, our beliefs about knowledge from our experiences of interacting with our environment. As a human construction, our knowledge is always tentative, conjectural, and subject to ongoing revision. Because our statements, or our texts, about knowledge are a construction of how we perceive reality rather than a correspondence with reality, they can be deconstructed, or taken apart. *Collaborative learning,* the sharing of experiences and ideas through language, makes our discourse about knowledge both a personal and a social construction.[27]

6-6a Key Concepts

The French philosophers Michel Foucault and Jacques Derrida were key figures in developing postmodernism. Like Nietzsche, Foucault totally rejected the premodern idealist and realist claims that there are universal and unchanging truths. However, Foucault's major attack was on the modern experts, especially scientists, social scientists, and educators, who claim that they are impartial, objective, and unbiased. He contends that what these experts pronounce to be objective truth is really a disguised rationale

---

[24]A. S. Neill, *Summerhill School: A New View of Childhood* (London: St. Martin's Griffin, 1995); Mark Vaughan, *Summerhill and A. S. Neill* (London: Open University Press, 2006). The website for Neill's Summerhill School is **www.summerhillschool.co.uk/pages/index.html**.

[25]For an incisive and insightful discussion of postmodernism, see Christopher Butler, *Postmodernism: A Very Short Introduction* (Oxford, UK: Oxford University Press, 2002). Also, see Dave Hill, Peter McLaren, Mike Cole, and Glen Ritowski, *Postmodernism in Educational Theory: Education and the Politics of Human Resistance* (London: Tufnell Press, 1999).

[26]David E. Cooper, *World Philosophies: An Historical Introduction* (Oxford, UK, and Cambridge, MA: Blackwell, 1996), p. 467.

[27]John A. Zahorik, *Constructivist Teaching* (Bloomington, IN: Phi Delta Kappa Educational Foundation, 1995), pp. 10–13. Also, see Marie Larouchelle and Nadine Bendarz, eds., *Constructivism and Education* (Cambridge, UK: Cambridge University Press, 2009).

for the elites who hold power and want to use it over others, especially the poor, minorities, and women.[28] In their analysis of education, postmodernists use the concepts of subordination (a powerful elite's control of disempowered groups and classes) and marginalization (the social, political, economic, and educational process of pushing powerless groups to the edges of society). An example of subordination occurs when politically powerful groups mandate certain educational requirements, such as a core curriculum and standardized testing of prescribed subjects, for other less powerful groups. For example, postmodernists would likely see the Common Core State Standards as a top-down imposition on schools and teachers by powerful elite groups. Marginalization takes place when schools teach an official history that focuses on the achievement of white males of the dominant group and either ignores or reduces the histories of women and minorities as a minor supplement to the story.

deconstruction Critical examination and dissection of texts or canons to determine the power relationships embedded in their creation and use. Often used by educators who follow postmodernist philosophy.

Claiming that knowledge as a human construction is expressed by language, Derrida developed **deconstruction** as a method to trace the origin and the meaning of texts or canons.[29] (A *canon* is a work, typically a book, prized as having authoritative knowledge.) A text is often a book, but it might also be a movie, a play, or another type of cultural representation. In education, a text is often a curriculum guide, a DVD, or a digital or print book, including a textbook, such as the one you are reading. The purpose of deconstruction is to show that texts, rather than reflecting metaphysical truths or objective knowledge, are biased historical and cultural constructions that involve political power relationships. For example, you can deconstruct this book or any textbook by answering such questions as the following: Who are the authors? Why did they write the book? What were their motives? Does the text endorse a particular ideology? Does that ideology support some people, groups, or classes over others?

Proponents of the Great Books curriculum, discussed later in this chapter, elevate certain books of Western culture to a high status, claiming that they provide highly valuable insights into life and society. However, some postmodernists criticize these texts for emphasizing Western culture while marginalizing Asian and African cultures. Postmodernists would say that texts such as Plato's *Republic* and Aristotle's *Nicomachean Ethics,* though exalted as having an enduring universal moral authority, are mere historical pieces that can be deconstructed to determine how they were and are used as rationales for the domination of one group over another.[30]

In deconstructing a canon or text, postmodernists ask the following questions: (1) What people, events, and situations at a particular time gave prominence to the canon? (2) Who gives a canon a privileged status in a culture or society, and who benefits from its acceptance as an authority? (3) Does the canon exclude underrepresented and marginalized individuals and groups? The answers to these questions point to those who hold actual social, economic, political, and educational power in a particular culture and society.

Postmodernists raise questions about who sets the standards for education and determines the skills and subjects found in the curriculum. For example, postmodernists would encourage the deconstruction of the Common Core State Standards by asking the following: Who set the standards and determined the curriculum? What skills and experiences do the standards include or exclude? Do the standards establish official knowledge and set power relationships among groups? (For an affirmation of these standards, see the section on essentialism later in this chapter.)

[28]For Foucault and education, see Gail McNicol Jardine, *Foucault & Education* (New York: Peter Lang, 2005); and Mark Olssen, *Michel Foucault: Materialism and Education* (Boulder, CO: Paradigm Publishers, 2006).

[29]Gert J. J. Biesta, *Derrida and Education* (New York: Routledge, 2011); and Peter P. Trifonas and Michael Peters, *Derrida, Deconstruction, and Education: Ethics of Pedagogy and Research* (Oxford, UK: Blackwell, 2004).

[30]David E. Cooper, "Postmodernism," in Randall Curren, ed., *A Companion to the Philosophy of Education* (Malden, MA: Blackwell Publishing, 2006), pp. 206–217.

6-6b Educational Implications

Like existentialists, postmodernist teachers want to raise their students' consciousness. While existentialists focus on consciousness about personal choice, postmodernists focus on consciousness about social inequalities by deconstructing traditional assumptions about knowledge, education, schooling, and instruction. They do not regard the school's curriculum as a repository of objective truths and scientific findings to be transmitted to students. It is an arena of conflicting viewpoints—some of which dominate and subordinate others.

Postmodernists see American public schools as battlegrounds, as contested sites in the struggle for social, political, or economic equality or domination. They contend that the official curriculum is full of rationales, constructed by powerful groups seeking to legitimize their own privileged socioeconomic status and to dominate, or socially control, other less-fortunate people. They dispute such official educational policy claims that public schools (1) fairly and equitably educate all children; (2) facilitate upward social and economic mobility; and (3) are necessary for maintaining a democratic society. In contrast, postmodernists argue that public schools, like other official institutions, help reproduce a society that is (1) patriarchal—it favors men over women; (2) Eurocentric—its so-called official knowledge is largely a construction of white people of European ancestry; and (3) capitalist—private property and the corporate mentality are glorified in the free-market ideology (particularly in the United States) that gives the false promise that individual initiative and competition will lead to social mobility. The experiences of other groups, such as people of color, the poor, and women, are given brief, marginal comments in the curriculum's official narratives.[31]

If we think of the school as a contested arena, we can see how postmodernists deconstruct the curriculum. Proponents of official knowledge want a standard cultural core curriculum in secondary and higher education that is based on the traditional canons of Western culture. Postmodernists challenge these canons as representing male-dominated, European-centered, Western, and capitalist culture. They argue that the contributions of underrepresented groups—Africans, Asians, Latinos, and Native Americans; women; the economically disadvantaged; and gays and lesbians—should be included in the curriculum, even at its core, if there is still a core. Postmodernists contend that a culturally diverse curriculum would reach all children, especially those marginalized in contemporary schools.

Postmodernists refer to instruction as a "representation" in which teachers use narratives, stories, images, music, and other cultural constructions to inform students about reality and values.[32] For example, a teacher in a social studies class who is presenting (making a representation) a unit on the history and controversy relating to immigration needs to be conscious that the sources she is using and the media coverage that her students hear are biased. Postmodernists urge teachers to become conscious of their powerful roles and to critically examine their representations to students. Rather than transmit only officially approved knowledge, teachers must critically represent a wider but more inclusive range of human experience.[33] Students are entitled to hear many voices and many stories, including their own autobiographies and biographies. While postmodernists and pragmatists agree that the curriculum should include discussion of controversial issues, postmodernists do not emphasize the scientific method as do pragmatists. The scientific method, for postmodernists, represents another meta-narrative (a narrative or exposition that is claimed to have global authority) used to

---

[31]Angeline Martel and Linda Peterat, "Margins of Exclusion, Margins of Transformation: The Place of Women in Education," in Rebecca A. Martusewicz and William M. Reynolds, *Inside/Out: Contemporary Critical Perspectives in Education* (New York: St. Martin's Press, 1994), p. 152.

[32]Elizabeth Ellsworth, "Representation, Self-Representation, and the Meanings of Difference: Questions for Educators," in Rebecca A. Martusewicz and William M. Reynolds, *Inside/Out: Contemporary Critical Perspectives in Education*, p. 100.

[33]Ibid., pp. 100–101

give an elite group power over others. In this instance, the scientific method as a meta-narrative has been elevated into what its advocates proclaim to be the sole method of arriving at verifiable claims to truth. Postmodernists would contend that the scientific method is only one of many ways to construct claims to truth and that dominant elites have expropriated it to justify their exploitation of people and resources.

6-6c Application to Schools and Classrooms

To empower their students, postmodernists argue that teachers must first empower themselves as professional educators. They need to deconstruct official statements about the school's purpose, curriculum, and organization, as well as the teacher's role and mission. Real empowerment means that teachers need to take responsibility for determining their own futures and for encouraging students to determine their own lives.

The process of empowering teachers and students begins in the schools and communities where they work and live. Postmodernists urge teachers to create their own site-based educational philosophy. Teachers, students, and community members must begin a local, site-based examination of such key control questions as (1) who actually controls their school, establishes the curriculum, and sets academic standards; (2) what motivates those who control the school; and (3) what rationale justifies the existing curriculum? This kind of deconstructive analysis will empower people and transform society by challenging special economic and political groups, exposing their powers and privileges.

Postmodernists would question the motives of the proponents of a core curriculum. They would deconstruct rationales for standards, asking critical questions about using standardized tests to measure student achievement, as in the NCLB Act and the Common Core State Standards. To find the real power relationships, they would ask who mandates the testing, develops the test, interprets the results, and determines how scores will be used.

Postmodernists apply the same critique to electronic representations that they do to other texts. Teachers and students need to look beyond the dynamic and rapid pace of the Internet and social media to determine who is writing the script and why they are doing so. Social media can be a means of linking oppressed groups, or it can be a more technological means of dominating them. The Internet, especially social media, can empower people by creating a means of quick communication for those interested in sharing ideas and common concerns with each other. Likewise, technology, if controlled by dominant groups, can indoctrinate people to accept the status quo that marginalizes and subordinates them, and it can be used to generate a rampant consumerism. A postmodernist teacher would examine the representations in software for student use, as well as to consider issues of power related to students' access to technology.

What would a postmodernist lesson be like? Students in a high school American history class might examine how Mexicans living in the territories that Mexico was forced to cede to the United States after the Mexican War were marginalized. They might deconstruct books, especially textbooks, which treat the topic, to find their authors' biases and positions. Next, they might discuss how Chicanos in the southwestern states were often relegated to subordinate social and economic status. The lesson might include a journal assignment in which students examine areas of their own lives where they feel either powerful or marginalized and suggest actions they believe would help make their voices heard in constructive ways.

In the following sections, we examine four educational theories: essentialism, perennialism, progressivism, and critical theory (see Overview 6.2). Whereas philosophies present highly generalized views of reality, knowledge, and values, theories explain more particular phenomena and processes. Educational theories examine the roles and functions of schools, curriculum, teaching, and learning. Some theories are

FOCUS What elements of postmodernism appeal to you as a teacher? Which appeal least? Why? Are there elements of postmodernism that you would like to incorporate into your philosophy of education?

OVERVIEW 6.2

THEORIES OF EDUCATION

Theory	Aim	Curriculum	Educational Implications	Proponents
Perennialism (rooted in realism)	To transmit universal and enduring truth and values	Fundamental skills, the liberal arts and sciences, the great books of Western civilization	Instruction that features transmission, discussion, and reflection on enduring truths and values	Hutchins Adler Maritain
Essentialism (rooted in idealism and realism)	To develop basic skills of literacy, numeracy, and subject-matter knowledge	Basic skills, essential subject matter—history, mathematics, language, science, computer literacy	To prepare competent and skilled individuals for the competitive global economy	Bagley Bestor Hirsch
Progressivism (rooted in pragmatism)	To educate individuals according to their interests and needs	Activities and projects	Instruction that features problem solving and collaborative learning; teacher acts as a facilitator	Dewey Kilpatrick Parker Johnson
Critical theory (rooted in neo-Marxism and postmodernism)	To raise consciousness about issues of marginalization and empowerment	Autobiographies of oppressed peoples	Focus on social conflicts, empowerment, and social justice	McLaren Giroux

derived from philosophies, and others are based on practice. We begin with the more traditional theories of essentialism and perennialism, which are rooted in idealism and realism and take a subject-matter approach to teaching and learning. Then we move to progressivism, influenced by pragmatism, and critical theory, influenced by existentialism and postmodernism, which relate education to social change.

6-7 ESSENTIALISM

essentialism An educational theory that emphasizes basic skills and subject-matter disciplines. Proponents favor a curriculum consisting of reading, writing, and arithmetic at the elementary level and five major disciplines (English, math, science, history, and foreign language) at the secondary level. Emphasis is on academic competition and excellence.

Essentialism establishes the school's primary or essential function as maintaining the achievements of human civilization by transmitting them to students as skills and subjects in a carefully organized and sequenced curriculum. William C. Bagley (1872–1946), a leading essentialist professor of education, believed that schools should provide all students with the skills and knowledge needed to function in a democratic society.[34] Failure to transmit these necessary skills and subjects puts civilization in peril. This essential knowledge includes the skills of literacy (reading and writing), computation (arithmetic), and the subjects of history, mathematics, science, languages, and literature. Because there is much to learn but only a limited time to learn it, the curriculum needs to emphasize essential knowledge, and teaching needs to be efficient. For effective learning, the curriculum needs to be sequential and cumulative. It is sequential when lower-order skills generate and lead to more complex higher-order ones. It

---

[34]J. Wesley Null, *A Disciplined Progressive Educator: The Life and Career of William Chandler Bagley* (New York: Peter Lang, 2003).

is cumulative when what is learned at a lower grade level leads to and is added to by knowledge in succeeding grades or levels.[35]

Bagley crafted a finely tuned program of teacher education that moved teachers forward from preservice to professional classroom practice. Teachers need a knowledge base in the liberal arts and sciences, mastery of the skills and subjects they teach, and a repertoire of professional education experiences and methods that enables them to transmit essential skills and subjects efficiently and effectively to students. The successful passage from preservice to practice means that teachers can competently organize skills and subjects into units appropriate to students' age and ability levels and competently teach them.

Arthur E. Bestor, Jr., a professor of history and a leader of the Council on Basic Education, reconceptualized essentialist principles into the theory of basic education. Bestor argued that schools should provide a sound education in the intellectual disciplines, which he defined as the fundamental ways of thinking found in history, science, mathematics, literature, language, and art. These intellectual disciplines were historically developed as people searched for cultural understanding, intellectual power, and useful knowledge.[36]

Essentialists charge that often popular and supposedly innovative methods that neglect systematic teacher-directed instruction in basic skills of reading, writing, computation, and the essential subjects have caused a serious decline in students' academic performance and civility. Social-promotion policies, which advance students to higher grades to keep them with their age cohort even if they have not mastered grade-appropriate skills and subjects, have further eroded academic standards. These policies caused a serious decline in student achievement scores on standardized tests such as the SAT and ACT. In addition, a morally permissive environment in the schools has weakened fundamental values of civility, social responsibility, and patriotism.

6-7a Contemporary Essentialist Trends

Since the 1980s, there has been a movement to reassert selected aspects of essentialism in the *Nation at Risk* report, the NCLB Act, and the Common Core State Standards initiative. (For the history of this movement, see Chapter 5, The Historical Development of American Education). *A Nation at Risk* recommended a core of subjects, called the "new basics," consisting of English, mathematics, science, social studies, and computer science that would have met the approval of Bagley, Bestor, and earlier essentialists.[37]

The Elementary and Secondary Education Act of 2001 (the NCLB) invoked the essentialist premise that schools should emphasize key basic skills, such as reading and mathematics, and that standardized tests should be used to objectively measure students' academic achievement.[38]

The Common Core State Standards, announced in 2010, reveal a modified essentialist orientation. The standards identify English (language arts) and mathematics as basic subjects whose mastery is needed for success in education and in life. E. D. Hirsch, the author of *Cultural Literacy: What Every American Needs to Know,* sees the Common Core Standards as addressing the need for nationally shared key ideas that can serve as a reference point for all Americans.[39] (See more discussion of the Common Core State Standards in Chapter 14, Curriculum and Instruction.)

---

[35]William C. Bagley, "An Essentialist Platform for the Advancement of American Education," *Educational Administration and Supervision* 24 (April 1938), pp. 241–256.

[36]Arthur E. Bestor, Jr., *Educational Wastelands: The Retreat from Learning in Our Public Schools* (Urbana: University of Illinois Press, 1953); and Bestor, *The Restoration of Learning: A Program for Redeeming the Unfulfilled Promise of American Education* (New York: Alfred A. Knopf, 1956).

[37]National Commission on Excellence in Education, *A Nation at Risk: The Imperative for Educational Reform* (Washington, DC: US Department of Education, 1983), pp. 5, 24.

[38]*No Child Left Behind* (Washington, DC: US Printing Office, 2001), pp. 1, 8–9.

[39]Common Core State Standards at **www.corestandards.org**, and the Core Subjects and 21st Century Themes at **www.p21.org**. Also, see Al Baker, "Culture Warrior, Gaining Ground: E. D. Hirsch Sees His Education Theories Taking Hold," NYTimes.com, December 1, 2014, **www.nytimes.com/2013/09/28/books/e-d-hirsch-sees-his-education-theories-taking-hold.html**.

TECHNOLOGY @ SCHOOL

SKILLS, SUBJECTS, AND STANDARDS

The Nation at Risk and NCLB emphasized that the curriculum needs to place emphasis on basic skills such as reading and mathematics and basic subjects such as the English language, mathematics, science, history, and computer science. It also emphasized that benchmarks need to be set to determine whether students are meeting these academic standards. A recent initiative emphasizing skills and subjects is the Common Core State Standard. Although some educators endorse skills, subjects, and standards as necessary to ensuring the academic quality of American education, others fear that the skill and subject emphasis may weaken process- and project-oriented learning and that standards may lead to a classroom standardization that limits creativity and problem solving. Explore this issue by accessing the following websites, and then make up your own mind.

Access the following sites for information about standards: US Department of Education website to survey state and national developments related to standards; Common Core State Standards and the Core Subjects and 21st Century Themes websites; Council for Basic Education website for its perspectives on the teaching of arts, English, geography, history, mathematics, and other subjects; The John Dewey Project on Progressive Education at the University of Vermont website; and the Rage and Hope: Critical Theory and Its Impact on Education website.

6-7b Educational Implications

Essentialists want schools and teachers to be committed to their primary academic mission and not be diverted into nonacademic areas. The schools' appropriate role is to teach students the basic skills and subjects that prepare them to function effectively and efficiently in a democratic society. Although social, economic, and political issues may be examined in relevant subjects such as history and social studies, this discussion should be objective and not politicized to promote a particular ideological agenda.

Essentialists favor a subject-matter curriculum that differentiates and organizes subjects according to their internal logical or chronological principles. The curriculum's skills and subjects should have a well-defined scope and a cumulative sequence that prepares students for future learning. Curriculum that ignores the past, rejects subject-matter boundaries, and claims to be interdisciplinary unnecessarily confuses students, blurs academic outcomes, and wastes valuable time and resources by failing to establish the necessary knowledge base.

Essentialists are suspicious of so-called innovative or process learning approaches, such as constructivism, in which students construct their own knowledge in a collaborative fashion, and of authentic assessment in which students evaluate their own progress. For essentialists, civilized people learn effectively and efficiently when they acquire the knowledge base that scientists, scholars, and other experts have developed and organized. We need not continually reinvent the wheel, wasting time and resources by rediscovering what is already known. We need to learn and use what we already know and move forward from that foundation into the future.

Although competent teachers always try to stimulate a student's interest, curriculum content should be based on the time-tested experience of the human race. Genuine freedom comes from staying with a task and mastering it. Bagley, for example, in emphasizing teacher-directed instruction, argues that children have the right to expect teachers, as trained professionals, to guide and direct their learning.[40] Similar to the scientific realists, essentialists argue that students need to learn about the objective real world rather than misguidedly following the constructivist view that they should create their own version of reality.

---

[40]J. Wesley Null, "Social Reconstruction with a Purpose: The Forgotten Tradition of William Bagley," in Karen Riley, ed., *Social Reconstruction: People, Politics, Perspectives* (Greenwich, CT: Information Age Publishing, 2006), pp. 27–44.

6-7c Application to Schools and Classrooms

For essentialists, the purpose of education is to transmit and maintain the necessary fundamentals of human culture. Schools have the specific mission of transmitting essential human skills and subjects to the young to preserve and pass them on to future generations.[41] As effective professional educators, teachers should (1) adhere to a carefully structured curriculum of basic skills and subjects; (2) inculcate traditional Western and American values of patriotism, hard work, effort, punctuality, respect for authority, and civility; (3) manage classrooms efficiently, effectively, and fairly as spaces of discipline and order; and (4) promote students on the basis of academic achievement, not social considerations.

Essentialist teachers would use deductive logic to organize instruction. They first teach basic concepts and factual information, and then they lead students to make generalizations based upon that knowledge. Consider a high school American history class studying the controversy between the two African American leaders, Booker T. Washington and W. E. B. Du Bois. First, the teacher assigns primary sources such as Washington's *Up from Slavery* and Du Bois's *The Souls of Black Folk.* (Washington and Du Bois are discussed in Chapter 5, Historical Development of American Education.) Then she leads a discussion in which the students, based on their reading and research, carefully identify Washington's and Du Bois's differences in background, education, and policy. After such teacher-guided research and discussion, the students develop generalizations about why Washington and Du Bois acted as they did and assess their influence in African American and US history.

FOCUS What elements of essentialism appeal to you as a teacher? Which appeal least? Why? Are there elements of essentialism you plan to incorporate into your philosophy of education?

6-8 PERENNIALISM

perennialism An educational theory that emphasizes rationality as the major purpose of education, asserting that the essential truths are recurring and universally true. Proponents generally favor a curriculum consisting of the language arts, literature, and mathematics at the elementary level, followed by the classics, especially the "great books," at the secondary and higher levels.

Perennialism shares many features with essentialism, such as using subject matter to transmit the cultural heritage across generations. It differs, however, in that perennialism is derived from the realist philosophy of Aristotle and Aquinas, while essentialism is based more on what has worked as a survival skill throughout history. (For more on Aristotle and Aquinas, see Chapter 3, The World Origins of American Education.) Perennialism asserts that education, like the truth it conveys, needs to be universal and authentic during every period of history and in every place and culture. Neither truth, nor education, is relative to time, place, or circumstances.

Education's primary purpose is to bring each new generation in contact with truth by exercising and cultivating the rationality each person possesses as a human being. Perennialist epistemology contends that due to their common human nature, people possess a potentiality to know and a desire to find the truth. This potentiality is activated when students come in contact with humankind's highest achievements, especially the great books and the classics in art, music, and literature. Truth exists in and is portrayed in the classic, or enduring, works of art, literature, philosophy, science, and history created by earlier generations and passed on to succeeding generations as a cultural inheritance.

Perennialism, derived heavily from realism, is also congenial to idealism. However, leading perennialists such as Jacques Maritain, Robert Hutchins, and Mortimer Adler based their educational theories on Aristotle's and Thomas Aquinas's realism. For them, the school's primary role is to develop students' rationality. They oppose turning schools into multipurpose agencies, especially economic ones that emphasize vocational training. Although perennialists understand the need for vocational skills and competencies, they believe that business and industry can provide up-to-date job

---

[41]Diane Ravitch, *Left Back: A Century of Failed School Reforms* (New York: Simon and Schuster, 2000), pp. 465–467.

training more efficiently than schools. Placing nonacademic demands on schools, such as social adjustment or vocational training, diverts time and resources from the school's primary purpose of developing students intellectually.

Because truth is universal and unchanging, the curriculum should consist of permanent, or perennial, studies that emphasize the recurrent themes of human life. It should contain subjects that cultivate rationality and the moral, aesthetic, and religious values that contribute to ethical behavior and civility. Like idealists, realists, and essentialists, perennialists favor a subject-matter curriculum that includes history, language, mathematics, logic, literature, the humanities, and science. Religious perennialists, such as Jacques Maritain, also include religion and theology in the curriculum.

Robert Hutchins, a former president of the University of Chicago, described the ideal education as "one that develops intellectual power" and is not "directed to immediate needs; it is not a specialized education, or a preprofessional education; it is not a utilitarian education. It is an education calculated to develop the mind."[42]

Hutchins recommended reading and discussing the great books of Western civilization to bring each generation into an intellectual dialogue with the great minds of the past. Among the great books are Homer's *Iliad* and *Odyssey,* Plato's *Dialogues,* Cicero's *Orations,* St. Augustine's *Confessions,* St. Thomas Aquinas's *Summa Theologica,* Dante's *Divine Comedy,* Machiavelli's *The Prince,* Erasmus's *The Praise of Folly,* More's *Utopia,* Calvin's *Institutes of the Christian Religion,* Locke's *An Essay Concerning Human Understanding,* Newton's *Mathematical Principles of Natural Philosophy,* Rousseau's *Social Contract,* Smith's *The Wealth of Nations,* Austen's *Pride and Prejudice,* Tocqueville's *Democracy in America,* Mill's *On Liberty,* Darwin's *Origin of the Species,* Marx's *Das Kapital,* Tolstoy's *War and Peace,* and Freud's *The Interpretation of Dreams.* These classic works, with their reoccurring themes, stimulate intellectual discussion and critical thinking. With the classics, Hutchins urged the study of grammar, rhetoric, logic, mathematics, and philosophy.

As noted earlier, postmodernists attack Hutchins's Great Books curriculum as giving Western European canons dominance over other cultures, such as those of Asia and Africa. Maritain, a French philosopher, based his perennialist "integral humanism" on Aristotle's natural realism and Thomas Aquinas's theistic realism.[43] Maritain wanted religion to be an integral part of the curriculum.[44] Rejecting cultural relativism and existentialism, Maritain asserted that education needed to be guided by the ultimate direction that religion provides. His religious emphasis fits the contemporary resurgence of faith-based values in American society. Like Hutchins, Maritain endorsed the great books as indispensable for understanding the development of civilization, culture, and science.[45]

For Maritain, elementary education should develop correct language usage, cultivate logical thinking, and introduce students to history and science. Secondary and undergraduate college education should focus on the liberal arts and sciences.

---

[42]Robert M. Hutchins, *A Conversation on Education* (Santa Barbara, CA: The Fund for the Republic, 1963), p. 1; and Robert M. Hutchins, *The Higher Learning in America* (New York: Transaction, 1995). For biographies of Hutchins, see Milton Mayer, *Robert Maynard Hutchins: A Memoir* (Berkeley: University of California Press, 1993); and Mary Ann Dzuback, *Robert Hutchins: Portrait of an Educator* (Chicago: University of Chicago Press, 1991). For a highly readable and engaging discussion of Hutchins, Mortimer Adler, and the Great Books curriculum, see Alex Beam, *A Great Idea at the Time: The Rise, Fall, and Curious Afterlife of the Great Books* (New York: Public Affairs, 2008).

[43]Douglas A. Ollivant, *Jacques Maritain and the Many Ways of Knowing* (Washington, DC: American Maritain Association, 2002).

[44]For a reappraisal of Maritain, see Gerald L. Gutek, "Jacques Maritain and John Dewey on Education: A Reconsideration," Madonna Murphy, "Maritain Explains the Moral Principles of Education to Dewey," and Wade A. Carpenter, "Jacques Maritain and Some Christian Suggestions for the Education of Teachers," in Wade A. Carpenter, guest ed., *Educational Horizons* 83 (Summer 2005), pp. 247–263, 282–301.

[45]Jacques Maritain, *Education at the Crossroads* (New Haven, CT: Yale University Press, 1960), pp. 70–73.

The Paideia Proposal Mortimer J. Adler's educational proposal that uses the Greek term *paideia*, the total educational formation, or upbringing of a child in the cultural heritage, to assert that all students should pursue the same curriculum consisting of intellectual skills and organized knowledge in language, literature, the arts, sciences, and social studies. It is a modern form of perennialism.

6-8a The Paideia Proposal

Mortimer J. Adler's *The Paideia Proposal: An Educational Manifesto* is a revival of perennialism.[46] *Paideia,* a Greek word, refers to a person's complete educational and cultural formation. Adler, who opposed streaming students into different curricular tracks, wants all students to have the same high quality of schooling. The *Paideia* curriculum includes language, literature, fine arts, mathematics, natural sciences, history, geography, and social studies. These studies are especially useful in helping students develop a repertoire of intellectual skills such as reading, writing, speaking, listening, calculating, observing, measuring, estimating, and problem solving. Together, these skills lead to higher-order critical thinking and reflection.[47]

6-8b Educational Implications

Perennialists assert that in a democratic society, all students have the equal right to the same high-quality intellectual education. To track some students into academic and others into vocational curricula denies them equality of educational opportunity.

ethical relativism Asserting that ideas and values are constructed by specific cultural groups during a particular historical period, they depend on the place, time, circumstances, and situations in which they arise. Ethical relativism denies the existence of universal and eternal truths and values. It is associated with pragmatism, progressivism, social reconstructionism, and critical theory.

Perennialists strongly oppose pragmatism's and postmodernism's **ethical relativism**, which contends that our "truths" are temporary statements based on how we cope with changing circumstances. Perennialists, such as Allan Bloom in *The Closing of the American Mind,* condemn ethical and cultural relativism for denying universal standards by which certain actions are consistently either morally right or wrong.[48]

6-8c Applications to Schools and Classrooms

For perennialists, the school's primary role is to develop students' reasoning powers by studying the great cultural works of Western civilization. To fulfill this academic mission, teachers in their preservice preparation need an education in the liberal arts and sciences and need to read and discuss the great books. As practicing professionals, teachers need a solid academic foundation to act as intellectual mentors and models for their students.

In primary grades, perennialist teachers would teach fundamental skills, such as reading, writing, computation, and research skills, and stimulate a desire for learning so students are prepared to begin their lifelong quest for truth. Perennialist secondary teachers would emphasize the enduring human concerns explored in the great works of history, literature, drama, art, and philosophy. Like idealists, perennialists emphasize the classics that speak to people across generations. Endorsing high academic standards, perennialists want those standards to be based on intellectual content, especially knowledge of the classics. They especially want standards to be based on a cultural core grounded in the Western cultural tradition.

Kindle and other electronic and digital versions of the great books and other classics are an effective way of transmitting them to a larger audience. Also, chat rooms and other social networking tools can enhance communication about the classics. Technology, including posts on social media, however, is not a substitute for reading the classics.

An illustration of the perennialist emphasis on recurring human concerns and values can be seen in a middle-school literature class that is reading and discussing Louisa

---

[46]Mortimer J. Adler, *The Paideia Proposal: An Educational Manifesto* (New York: Macmillan, 1982); see also Mortimer J. Adler, *Paideia Problems and Possibilities* (New York: Macmillan, 1983). For the Paideia philosophy, materials, and teaching practices, access the National Paideia Center at **www.paideia.org**. Also, see Tim Lacey, *The Dream of a Democratic Culture: Mortimer J. Adler and the Great Books Idea* (New York: Palgrave Macmillan, 2013).

[47]Adler, *Paideia Proposal*, pp. 22–23.

[48]Allan Bloom, *The Closing of the American Mind* (New York: Simon and Schuster, 1987).

May Alcott's *Little Women*. The students have discussed the main characters—Marmee, Jo, Beth, Meg, and Amy—and the issues of war, poverty, and illness that the March family faces. The class discussion reveals that the March family's sad and happy times reoccur perennially in family life today. That evening at dinner, the grandmother of Alice, a student in the class, asks, "What are you studying in school?" Alice replies, "We just finished reading *Little Women*." Alice's mother and grandmother say that they, too, read and enjoyed the book when they were girls. In the ensuing conversation, Alice, her mother, and her grandmother share their impressions of the book. In such ways, perennial themes can become memories that speak across time to generations.

FOCUS   What aspects of perennialism appeal to you as a teacher? Which appeal least? Why? Are there elements of perennialism you would like to incorporate into your philosophy?

6-9 PROGRESSIVISM

progressivism   An antitraditionalist theory in American education associated with child-centered learning through activities, problem solving, and projects. The Progressive Education Association promoted progressivism as an educational movement.

Progressivism originated as a general reform movement in American society and politics in the late nineteenth and early twentieth centuries. Although they agreed in opposing traditional education and wanting to reform schools, progressives did not always agree on how and what to change in curriculum and instruction. Whereas child-centered progressives wanted to liberate children from authoritarian schools, social reconstructionists wanted to use schools to reform society.[49] Administrative progressives, who were school superintendents and principals, wanted to make schools more efficient and cost effective by building larger schools that could house more class sections and offer a more diverse curriculum.

In their revolt against traditional schools, progressive educators oppose essentialism and perennialism. Educators such as Marietta Johnson, William H. Kilpatrick, and G. Stanley Hall rebelled against rote memorization and authoritarian classroom management for children and adolescents.

Marietta Johnson (1864–1938), founder of the Organic School in Fairhope, Alabama, epitomized child-centered progressive education. Believing that prolonging childhood is especially needed in a technological society, Johnson wanted childhood lengthened rather than shortened. Children, she said, should follow their own internal timetables rather than adults' scheduling.[50] Possessing their own stages of readiness, children should not be pushed by teachers or parents to do things for which they are not developmentally ready.

Anticipating contemporary constructivist learning, Johnson believed children learn most successfully and satisfyingly by actively exploring their environments and constructing their own conception of reality based on their direct experiences. Johnson's activity-based curriculum accentuated physical exercise, nature study, music, crafts, field geography, storytelling, dramatizations, and games. Creative activities such as dancing, drawing, singing, and weaving took center stage, while reading and writing were delayed until the child was 9 or 10 years old.[51]

Johnson designed a teacher-education program that went from preservice to practice. During preservice, caring and effective teachers needed to develop (1) a sincere affection for and sympathetic interest in children; (2) a knowledge base in child and adolescent development and psychology and in the skills and subjects they taught; and (3) a commitment to social justice. As in-service practitioners, teachers should create safe, developmentally friendly, and engaging classrooms in which children, following their own interests, learn at their own pace.

---

[49]For social reconstructionism, see Karen L. Riley, ed., *Social Reconstructionism: People, Politics, Perspectives* (Greenwich, CT: Information Age Publishing, 2006).

[50]Marietta Johnson, *Thirty Years with an Idea* (Tuscaloosa: University of Alabama Press, 1974), pp. 20–21.

[51]Johnson, *Thirty Years with an Idea*, pp. 52–55, 62–63, 86–95.

William Heard Kilpatrick (1871–1965), a professor of education at Columbia University's Teachers College, made progressivism an integral part of teacher preparation. In restructuring Dewey's problem solving into the project method, Kilpatrick used three guiding principles: (1) genuine education involves problem solving; (2) learning is enriched as students collaboratively research and share information to formulate and test their hypotheses; and (3) teachers can guide students' learning without dominating it. Using these principles, Kilpatrick designed four types of projects: (1) implementing a creative idea or plan; (2) enjoying an aesthetic experience; (3) solving an intellectual problem; and (4) learning a new skill or area of knowledge.[52]

Kilpatrick believed that teachers who used the project method could transform their classrooms into collaborative, democratic, learning communities. As they worked collaboratively, students motivated by their own interests would be engaged in wholehearted, purposeful activity in which they designed and completed a project. Unlike the prestructured objectives of the essentialist and perennialist curricula, the project method was open ended in that its outcomes were not specified in advance but came out of the project.[53] (Visit the Project-Based Learning Space website for the background, theory, and application of the project method.)

6-9a Key Concepts

The Progressive Education Association opposed (1) authoritarian teachers, (2) exclusively book-based instruction, (3) passive memorization of factual information, (4) the isolation of schools from society, and (5) using physical or psychological coercion to manage classrooms. These progressive educators positively affirmed that (1) the child should be free to develop naturally; (2) interest, motivated by direct experience, is the best stimulus for learning; (3) the teacher should facilitate learning; (4) there needs to be close cooperation among the school, home, and community; and (5) the progressive school should be a laboratory to test educational ideas and practices.

Opposing the conventional subject-matter curriculum, progressives experimented with alternative curricula, using activities, experiences, problem solving, and projects. Child-centered progressive teachers sought to free children from conventional restraints and repression. More socially oriented progressives, called social reconstructionists, sought to make schools the centers of larger social reforms.[54] Led by George Counts and Harold Rugg, the social reconstructionists believed that teachers and schools need to investigate and deliberately work to solve social, political, and economic problems. In many ways, **social reconstructionism** anticipated critical theory, discussed in the next section of the chapter.[55]

social reconstructionism The theory developed by a group of progressive educators who believe schools should deliberately work for social reform and change.

6-9b Educational Implications

For progressives, knowledge is an instrument that does or creates something. Although it can come from many sources—books, experiences, experts, the library, the laboratory, and the Internet—knowledge becomes meaningful when used

---

[52]William H. Kilpatrick, "The Project Method: The Use of the Purposeful Act in the Educative Process," *Teachers College Record,* Vol. XIX, No. 4 (September 1918).

[53]John A. Beineke, *And There Were Giants in the Land: The Life of William Heard Kilpatrick* (New York: Peter Lang, 1998), pp. 106–107.

[54]The definitive history of progressive education remains Lawrence A. Cremin, *The Transformation of the School* (New York: Random House, 1961).

[55]William B. Stanley, "Education for Social Reconstruction in Critical Context," in Karen Riley, ed., *Social Reconstructionism: People, Politics, Perspectives,* pp. 89–110.

instrumentally as a tool to accomplish a purpose. Agreeable to using technology in instruction, progressives want it to be an open means to accessing information in a larger community setting. For example, social media can be used to share ideas and information with individuals around the world. When students work together collaboratively, especially on projects, the results are open ended in that they lead to more experiences and are socially charged in that they bring individuals into social interaction.

For progressives, children's readiness and interests, rather than predetermined subjects, should shape curriculum and instruction. They resist the imposition of standards from outside the school by government agencies and special interest groups as a new form of authoritarian control that can block open-ended, problem-based inquiry. Instructionally flexible, progressive teachers use a repertoire of learning activities such as problem solving, field trips, creative artistic expression, and projects. Constructivism, like progressivism, emphasizes socially interactive and process-oriented hands-on learning in which students work collaboratively to expand and revise their knowledge base.[56]

In professional education, progressives warn against separating preservice from practice, which are phases in the same flow, or continuum, of a teacher's experience. Preservice experiences, such as clinical observation, should be directly connected to classroom practice and not regarded as preparatory to it. In turn, practice should be considered as a continuing process of in-service professional development, in which teachers construct innovative and effective teaching strategies. The teacher should guide students to new activities, new projects, and new problems, thus enlarging and broadening their social and cultural relationships.

6-9c Applications to Schools and Classrooms

The West Tennessee Holocaust Project, designed by teachers and students at the Whitwell Middle School in Whitwell, Tennessee, offers an excellent illustration of the project method.[57] The project's purpose was to teach respect for different cultures and to understand the consequences of intolerance.[58] Linda Hooper, the school's principal, saw the project as providing an opportunity "to give our children a broader view of the world...that would crack the shell of their white cocoon."[59]

In preparing for the project, students read Anne Frank's *Diary of a Young Girl* and Elie Wiesel's *Night,* studied aspects of Judaism, and viewed the motion picture *Schindler's List.* Overwhelmed by the immensity of the Holocaust's toll of six million Jews killed in Nazi extermination camps, the students experienced difficulty in understanding why and how this genocide had occurred.

The students learned that some courageous Norwegians, expressing solidarity with their Jewish fellow citizens, pinned ordinary paper clips to their lapels as a silent protest against the Nazi occupation. One student reacted, saying, "Let's collect six million paper clips and turn them into a sculpture to remember the victims." The students decided to do so as a memorial to the six million Jewish victims of the Holocaust.

---

[56]For translating constructivist epistemology into classroom practice, see Peter W. Airasian and Mary E. Walsh, "Constructivist Cautions," *Phi Delta Kappan* (February 1997), pp. 444–449. Also, see David J. Martin and Kimberly S. Loomis, *Building Teachers: Constructivist Approach to Introducing Education* (Stamford, CT: Cengage Learning, 2007).

[57]Dita Smith, *Washington Post* (April 7, 2002), p. C01, at **www.truthorfiction.com/rumors /s/studentmemorial.htm.**

[58]**www.whitwellmiddleschool.org/?PageName=bc&n=69256.**

[59]Smith, *Washington Post.*

AP Image/Mark Gilliland

∧ **PHOTO 6.3** The Whitwell Tennessee Holocaust Memorial and Paper Clip Project is an example of a progressive, collaborative learning strategy with community involvement.

FOCUS What aspects of progressivism appeal to you as a teacher? Which appeal least? Why? Are there elements of progressivism you would like to incorporate into your philosophy?

The students collected paper clips from their family and friends, set up a web page about the project, and asked for donations of clips. Although they collected 100,000 clips in the project's first year, the goal of collecting 6 million paper clips seemed insurmountable. When Lena Gitter, a 94-year-old Holocaust survivor, learned about the project, she contacted two German journalists, Peter Schroeder and Dagmar Schroeder-Hildebrand, who were doing research at the US Holocaust Memorial Museum in Washington, DC. Intrigued that American children in a small Southern town were engaged in a unique project to honor the victims of the Holocaust, the journalists wrote articles about the project that appeared in Germany and Austria.

After that, the school was deluged with paper clips. The Schroeders visited the Whitwell school and community. Their visit was a culturally enriching experience for the students, who met persons from another country for the first time. It was especially significant because the Schroeders were from Germany, the country whose Nazi leaders had perpetrated the Holocaust. The Schroeders wrote a book about *The Paper Clip Project* that was published in Germany.[60]

During the project, students developed an array of skills. They recorded correspondence and contributions in a ledger, wrote letters to acknowledge contributions, and responded to e-mails sent to their website.

Although none of Whitwell's students had ever met a Jew when the project began, several Jewish Holocaust survivors visited and spoke to the students and residents of the town. In 2005, Whitwell eighth graders visited the Holocaust Museum in Washington, DC.

The students decided to house their paper clip collection in a German railroad car, like those that transported Jews to the extermination camps. With the help of the Schroeders, an actual German railway car was brought to Whitwell. With the help of the entire community, the students created a permanent museum, in which the paper clips, stored in the car, are a memorial to the Holocaust victims (Photo 6.3).

The Whitwell Holocaust project illustrates the open-endedness of the project method. The project's activities permeated the school and the community, bringing residents and students together in a collaborative effort. It would get the attention of the president and vice president of the United States, become the subject of a book, and become an international cause. When they began the project, the Whitwell students and teachers had no idea how many lives they would touch. A student, summing up the project, said, "Now, when I see someone, I think before I speak, I think before I act, and I think before I judge."[61]

6-10 CRITICAL THEORY

critical theory (critical pedagogy) A theory of education which contends that some public-school systems limit educational opportunities for students marginalized due to race, class, and gender biases. Proponents argue that teachers should be "transformative intellectuals" who work to change the system. Also known as "critical discourse."

Critical theory, an influential contemporary theory of education, urges a rigorous critique of schools and society to uncover exploitative power relationships and bring about equity, fairness, and social justice.[62] Many of its assumptions are derived from

---

[60]Peter W Schroeder and Dagmar Schroeder-Hildebrand, *Six Million Paper Clips: The Making of a Children's Holocaust Memorial* (Minneapolis, MN: Kar-Ben Publishing Co., 2004). Also, see the DVD, Eliott Berlin and Joe Fab, Directors, *Paper Clips.*

[61]Smith, *Washington Post.*

[62]Douglas Kellner, "Critical Theory," in Randall Curren, ed., *A Companion to the Philosophy of Education* (Malden, MA: Blackwell Publishing, 2006), pp. 161–175.

postmodernist and existentialist philosophies, neo-Marxism, feminist and multicultural theories, and Paulo Freire's liberation pedagogy. (Freire is discussed in Chapter 4, Pioneers of Teaching and Learning.) Henry Giroux and Peter McLaren are leading critical theorist philosophers.[63]

6-10a Key Concepts

Some of the ideas of Karl Marx, a nineteenth-century philosopher, have influenced critical theory. Arguing that all institutions rest on an economic base, Marx saw human history as a class struggle for social and economic power.[64] Critical theorists often use such Marxist concepts as class conflict and alienation to analyze social and educational institutions. Alienation refers to feelings of powerlessness experienced by people who have been marginalized and pushed to society's edges.

According to critical theorists, critical consciousness requires recognition that an individual's social status, including educational and economic expectations and opportunities, is largely determined by race, ethnicity, gender, and class. The dominant socioeconomic class that controls social, political, economic, and educational institutions uses its power to maintain, or reproduce, its favored position and to subordinate socially and economically disadvantaged classes.[65] In the United States, historically subordinate groups are the urban and rural poor, African and Native Americans, Latinos, women, and gays and lesbians.[66] Through a critical education, however, subordinated classes and groups can become conscious of their exploitation, resist domination, overturn the patterns of oppression, and empower themselves.

6-10b Educational Implications

Critical theorists want to raise consciousness about questions dealing with knowledge, education, the school, and teaching and learning. For them, knowledge is about issues of social, political, economic, and educational power and control. In particular, critical theorists want to raise the consciousness of people who have been forced into marginal and subordinate positions in society due to poverty, race, ethnicity, language, class, or gender.[67]

Critical theorists contend that economically, politically, and socially dominant classes control and use schools to reproduce and maintain their privileged social and economic position. To maintain their commanding status, children of the dominant classes attend prestigious schools and universities that prepare them for high-level careers in business, industry, and government. Children of subordinate groups and classes are indoctrinated to accept the conditions that disempower them as the best of all possible worlds. Schools in economically disadvantaged

[63]Henry Giroux, *On Critical Pedagogy* (London: Continuum International Publishing Group/Bloomsbury Academic, 2011); *Neoliberalism's War on Higher Education* (Chicago: Haymarket Books, 2014); *Border Crossings: Cultural Workers and the Politics of Education* (New York: Routledge, 2005).

[64]Peter E. Jones, *Marxism and Education: Renewing the Dialogue, Pedagogy, and Culture* (New York: Palgrave Macmillan, 2011).

[65]Martin Carnoy, "Education, State, and Culture in American Society," in Henry A. Giroux and Peter L. McLaren, eds., *Critical Pedagogy, the State, and Cultural Struggle* (Albany: State University of New York Press, 1998), pp. 6–7.

[66]Angeline Martel and Linda Peterat, "Margins of Exclusion, Margins of Transformation: The Place of Women in Education," in Rebecca A. Martusewicz and William Reynolds, eds., *Inside/Out: Contemporary Critical Perspectives in Education* (New York: St. Martin's Press, 1994), pp. 151–154.

[67]Henry A. Giroux and Peter L. McLaren, "Schooling, Cultural Politics, and the Struggle for Democracy," in Giroux and McLaren, *Critical Pedagogy, the State, and Cultural Struggle*, pp. xi–xii.

urban and rural areas, for example, serve mainly the poor, African Americans, and Latinos. Typically underfinanced, these schools are often deteriorating physically and lack needed resources.

Inner-city schools, as well as many other schools, are ensnared in large, hierarchical educational bureaucracies. With orders coming down from the top, teachers have little or no decision-making power about how schools will run. Within the school, teachers tend to be isolated from each other in self-contained classrooms. Further, parents and others in the local community are kept at a distance, with little school involvement. The curriculum, too, is determined by higher-level administrators, with little room for local initiatives that relate to the life experiences of students or community members.

"hidden" curriculum What students learn, other than academic content, from the school milieu or environment.

Critical theorists identify two curricular spheres: the formal official curriculum and the **"hidden" curriculum**. Mandated by state and local districts, the officially approved curriculum requires teachers to teach certain specific skills and subjects to students. The dominant classes use the official curriculum to transmit their particular beliefs and values as the legitimate version of knowledge for all students. Transmission, instead of critical thinking and analysis, reproduces in students the officially sanctioned and mandated version of knowledge. For example, the official version of history portrays America's past as a largely white, male-dominated, Euro-American series of triumphs in conquering the wilderness of the frontier, industrializing the nation, and making the United States the greatest country on earth. Women, African- and Native Americans, and Latinos are marginalized or treated as afterthoughts to the official narrative. NCLB and the Common Core State Standards, a new version of the old official curriculum, impose outside requirement demands on teachers and students that Giroux says standardizes knowledge and assessment and "is very deadly" for critical and creative thinking.[68]

The "hidden curriculum" is a key element in school-based social control in that it imposes approved dominant group behaviors and attitudes on students through the school climate. "Hidden" because it is not stated in published state mandates or local school policies, it permeates the public-school milieu. For example, sexist attitudes that males have a greater aptitude than females in mathematics and science maintain and reproduce gender-specific patterns of entry into education and careers in those fields. The student cliques and groups that are either "in or out" in popularity often mirror the socioeconomic status found in the surrounding community.

Although the privileged classes have historically dominated schools, critical theorists do not see their domination as inevitable.[69] They believe that teachers, as critically minded activists, can transform schools into democratic public spheres in which they raise the consciousness of the exploited and empower the dispossessed.

The multicultural society in the United States provides many more versions of the American experience than the officially approved story. Members of each racial, ethnic, and language group can tell their own stories rather than having the stories told for them. After exploring their own identities, students can develop ways to recognize stereotyping and misrepresentation and to resist indoctrination both in and out of school. They can learn how to take control of their own lives and shape their own futures.[70]

---

[68]Al Baker, "Culture Warrior, Gaining Ground: E. D. Hirsch Sees His Education Theories Taking Hold," NYTimes.com, December 1, 2014, **www.nytimes.com/2013/09/28/books/e-d-hirsch-sees-his-education-theories-taking-hold.html**

[69]Patricia H. Hinchey, *Becoming a Critical Educator: Defining a Classroom Identity, Designing a Critical Pedagogy* (New York: Peter Lang, 2004).

[70]"Rage and Hope: Critical Theory and Its Impact on Education" at **www.perfectfit.org/CT/index2.html.**

6-10c Application to Schools and Classrooms

Critical theorists want teachers—in both their preservice preparation and classroom practice—to focus on issues of power and control in school and society. They urge teachers to (1) find out who their real friends are in the struggle for control of schools; (2) learn who their students are by helping them explore their own self-identities; (3) collaborate with local people to improve their school and community; (4) join with like-minded teachers in teacher-controlled professional organizations to empower themselves; and (5) participate in critical dialogues about political, social, economic, and educational issues that confront American society.

Critical theorists find that teachers' power in determining their own professional lives is severely limited. State boards, not teachers' professional organizations, largely determine entry requirements into the profession. Where standardized tests are used to determine schools' effectiveness and teachers' competency, teachers are judged by criteria mandated by state legislators and prepared by so-called experts external to their own schools and classrooms.

Michael Apple, a neo-Marxist curriculum theorist, warns that too much discussion about using educational technology in the classroom is rhetorical rather than motivated by a desire for genuine change. Unless educational technology is used to uncover the root issues of discrimination and poverty, he believes it is likely to bring an externally derived, "impersonal, prepackaged style" to education rather than one based on the schools' real internal conditions.[71]

Critical theorists want students to construct their own meaningful knowledge and values in their local contexts, that is, the immediate situations and communities in which they live and in the schools they attend. Teachers should begin consciousness-raising with the students by examining the conditions in their neighborhood communities. Students can share their life stories to create a collaborative group autobiography that recounts experiences at home, in school, and in the community. They can further connect this group autobiography to the larger histories of their respective economic classes and racial, ethnic, and language groups. For example, *The Freedom Writers Diary* is a compelling narrative of how Erin Gruwell, an English teacher at Woodrow Wilson High School in Long Beach, California, used autobiographical writing as a teaching method. Gruwell's students, categorized as at-risk students, wrote their autobiographies in diaries. They wrote about the conditions that they were experiencing in their own situations—violence, gang warfare, drug abuse, and poverty.[72]

Teachers using a critical-theory approach might, like the example in Freedom Writers, design a unit in which middle-school social studies students explore their racial and ethnic heritages. Students begin by sharing their impressions of their heritage by telling stories about their families, their customs, and their celebrations. Then, parents and grandparents are invited in as guest speakers to share their cultural experiences with the students. Students then create a multicultural display that includes family photographs, artifacts, and other items that illustrate the lives and cultures of the people who live in the local community.

Throughout the chapter, you have been encouraged to reflect on how the philosophies and theories can be used in constructing your own philosophy of education. Now, it is time to bring your thoughts together in a summative experience—in

FOCUS What elements of critical theory appeal to you as a teacher? Which appeal least? Why? Are there elements of critical theory that you would like to incorporate into your philosophy of education?

---

[71]Michael W. Apple, *Official Knowledge: Democratic Education in a Conservative Age* (New York and London: Routledge, 2000), pp. 132–133.

[72] The Freedom Writers, with Erin Gruwell, *The Freedom Writers Diary: How a Teacher and 150 Teens Used Writing to Change Themselves and the World Around Them* (New York: Doubleday/Random House, 1999). Also, see the Freedom Writers Foundation at **www.freedomwritersfoundation.org**.

TAKING ISSUE

Read the brief introduction below, as well as the Question and the pros and cons list that follows, and then answer the question using *your* own words and position.

TEACHER OBJECTIVITY OR COMMITMENT ON SOCIAL, POLITICAL, AND ECONOMIC ISSUES

There have been longstanding debates over the issue of whether teachers should teach matters dealing with society, politics, and the economy as objectively as possible or if they should teach in a way that is committed to deliberate social reform. In particular, the essentialists, progressives, and critical theorists take very different positions on teacher objectivity or commitment to social reform in their classrooms.

Question

Should teachers be objective when they teach about social, political, or economic issues in their classrooms? (Think about this question as you read the PRO and CON arguments listed here. What is *your* response to this issue?)

Arguments PRO

1. Teachers should not use their classrooms to indoctrinate students to accept a particular ideology of social, political, and economic change.

2. Teachers should be objective and present the various opinions on issues as fairly as possible.

3. Teachers should provide students with objective information on social, political, and economic issues, but student action on these issues should take place when they are adults not when they are children or teenagers.

Arguments CON

1. Teaching, like education, represents commitment to certain values; teachers need to endorse democratic and egalitarian values that are committed to social justice.

2. Objectivity or neutrality is not possible for teachers. When teachers claim to be objective, they are really supporting the status quo.

3. If teachers really want to have a voice in curriculum and instruction, they need to be actively—not passively—engaged in the political and economic decision-making process.

Question Reprise: What Is Your Stand?

Reflect again on the following question by explaining *your* stand on this issue: Should teachers be objective when they teach about social, political, or economic issues in their classrooms?

---

which you sum up your ideas on your philosophy of education and state your views on knowledge, education, schooling, and teaching and learning. In summing up your philosophical project, you can reconsider such questions as the following:

- Do you believe that knowledge is based on universal and eternal truths, or is it relative to different times and places?
- What is the purpose of education? Is it to transmit the culture, to provide economic and social skills, to develop critical-thinking skills, or to criticize and reform society?
- What are schools for? Are they to teach skills and subjects, encourage personal self-definition, develop human intelligence, or create patriotic and economically productive citizens?
- What should curriculum contain? Should it include basic skills and subjects, experiences and projects, the great books and the classics, inquiry processes, and/or critical dialogues?
- What should the relationship be between teachers and students? Should it be based on teaching academic skills and subjects, students' interests, problems, or changing the society?

SUMMING UP

1. Philosophy's special terminology has the following relationship to education: metaphysics relates to curriculum; epistemology to methods of instruction; ethics to character formation and social justice; aesthetics to the fine arts; and logic to organizing the school's program.

2. Idealism, which is grounded in the intellectual and spiritual nature of reality, sees education's primary purpose as students' intellectual and moral development.

3. Realism's metaphysical view that humans live a knowable world of objects emphasizes a curriculum in which subjects are based on particular categorizations and classifications of these objects.

4. Pragmatism, which sees reality in a constant state of change and flux, emphasizes that the best probability for directing this change is by using the scientific method to solve problems.

5. Existentialists, who assert that individuals have the responsibility for defining themselves, encourage teachers and students to choose experiences in schools that resist conformity and lead to personal authenticity.

6. Postmodernism proposes that we learn to search under the surface of texts and other sources that claim to represent objective official knowledge by deconstructing them.

7. Educational theories, which arise from practice or are derived from a philosophy or ideology, represent a generalized design that can be transferred and applied to schools.

8. Emphasizing an academic curriculum of basic skills and subjects such as English, mathematics, science, and history, essentialism has had a continuous influence on American education that has surfaced in the basic education movement, *A Nation at Risk,* the NCLB Act, and the Common Core State Standards.

9. Perennialism emphasizes the school's primary role in transmitting the achievements of Western civilization to students through the classics, the great books, and the fine arts.

10. Progressivism has two related branches: the child-centered, which stressed instruction arising from children's interests and needs, and the social reconstructionist, which urges teachers and schools to create a new social order.

11. Critical theorists emphasize constructing a site-based philosophy that is grounded on the lives of students in their schools and communities as a means of empowering marginalized groups.

SUGGESTED RESOURCES

INTERNET RESOURCES

For the relationship of existentialism to education, access Scott Webster, "Existentialism: Providing an ideal framework for educational research in times of uncertainty" at the Australian Association for Research in Education website.

For the Paideia philosophy, teaching strategies, and materials, access the National Paideia Center website.

For Movietone News footage on John Dewey and audio excerpts on George Counts and Boyd Bode, access the Education Museum at the University of South Carolina website.

For recent research, projects, and programs on John Dewey and progressive education, consult the John Dewey Project on Progressive Education at the University of Vermont website.

For resources on John Dewey's life and philosophy, consult the Center for Dewey Studies on the Southern Illinois University website.

For information and materials about basic education, consult the Council for Basic Education website.

PUBLICATIONS

Barrow, Robin, and Ronald G. Woods. *An Introduction to Philosophy of Education.* New York: Routledge, 2006. *Provides a useful commentary about philosophy of education as a field.*

Beam, Alex, *A Great Idea at the Time: The Rise, Fall, and Curious Afterlife of the Great Books.* New York: Public Affairs, 2008. *A highly readable and engaging discussion of Hutchins, Adler, and the Great Books curriculum.*

Butler, Christopher. *Postmodernism: A Very Short Introduction.* Oxford, UK: Oxford University Press, 2002. *A succinct and clearly written analysis of the major features of postmodernism.*

Cahn, Steven M. *Classic and Contemporary Readings in the Philosophy of Education.* New York: Oxford University Press, 2011. *Provides primary source selections from such classic theorists as Plato and Aristotle and contemporary theories such as feminism and multiculturalism.*

Curren, Randall, ed. *A Companion to the Philosophy of Education.* Malden, MA: Blackwell Publishing, 2006. *Contains interpretive essays and bibliographies on historical and contemporary movements in philosophy of education.*

Cutrofello, Andrew, and Paul Livingston. *The Problems of Contemporary Philosophy: A Critical Guide for the Unaffiliated.* Cambridge, UK: Polity Book, 2015. *Provides an engaging commentary on issues in contemporary philosophy.*

Erneling, Christina E. *Towards Discursive Education: Philosophy, Technology, and Modern Education.* New York: Cambridge University Press, 2010. *Considers the relationships of education, philosophy, psychology, and technology.*

Giroux, Henry, *On Critical Pedagogy.* London: Continuum International Publishing Group/Bloomsbury Academic, 2011. *A leading critical theorist discusses education and cultural politics.*

Grinberg, Jaime G. A., Lewis Tyson, and Megan Laverty. *Playing with Ideas: Modern and Contemporary Philosophies of Education.* Dubuque, IA: Kendall Hunt Publishing, 2007. *An engaging and lively discussion of significant contemporary educational philosophies.*

Gutek, Gerald. *Philosophical, Ideological, and Theoretical Perspectives on Education.* Columbus, OH: Pearson, 2014. *A discussion and commentary on how philosophies, ideologies, and theories impact education, schools, curriculum, and instruction.*

Gutek, Gerald L. *Philosophical and Ideological Voices in Education.* Boston: Allyn and Bacon, 2004. *Provides discussions of the major philosophies, ideologies, and theories of education with representative primary source selections.*

Hansen, David T. *Ethical Visions of Education: Philosophy and Practice.* New York: Teachers College Press, 2007. *Discusses how leading philosophers and theorists of education sought to integrate their ideas into classroom practice.*

Hansen, David T., ed. *John Dewey and Our Educational Prospect: A Critical Engagement with Dewey's Democracy and Education.* Albany: State University of New York Press, 2006. *Provides an analysis of Dewey's highly influential book,* Democracy and Education.

Hinchey, Patricia H. *Becoming a Critical Educator: Defining a Classroom Identity, Designing a Critical Pedagogy.* New York: Peter Lang, 2004. *Applies critical theory to schools and classrooms.*

Lacey, Tim. *The Dream of a Democratic Culture: Mortimer J. Adler and the Great Books Idea.* New York: Palgrave Macmillan, 2013. *A historical perspective on Mortimer Adler and the great books as a perennial issue in American education.*

Noddings, Nel. *Education and Democracy in the 21ˢᵗ Century.* New York: Teachers College Press, 2013. *Provides an eminent philosopher's commentary on policy issues, curriculum, citizenship, and schools in a democratic society.*

Noddings, Nel. *Philosophy of Education.* Boulder, CO: Westview Press, 2011. *Provides an excellent overview of philosophy of education in relation to teaching, learning, schools, and policy with attention to contemporary issues such as standards and tests.*

Riley, Karen, ed. *Social Reconstruction: People, Politics, Perspectives.* Greenwich, CT: Information Age Publishing, 2006. *Contains analyses of social reconstructionism in historical and educational perspectives.*

Siegel, Harvey, ed. *The Oxford Handbook of Philosophy of Education.* New York: Oxford University Press, 2012. *Provides essays and commentaries on philosophy of education from leading authorities in the field.*

Watras, Joseph. *Philosophical Conflicts in American Education, 1893–2000.* Boston: Allyn and Bacon, 2004. *Analyzes major movements in curriculum and instruction from philosophical and historical perspectives.*

Watts, Leonard J., ed. *Leaders in Philosophy of Education: Intellectual Self-Portraits.* Boston: Sense Publishers, 2008. *Discusses the work of leading philosophers of education in examining intellectual and practical virtues, women's education, creativity, multiculturalism, and globalization.*

CHAPTER 7

GOVERNING AND ADMINISTERING PUBLIC EDUCATION

LEARNING OBJECTIVES

7-1 Describe the role of the local school board and how it works with the district superintendent, the central office, school principals, and the broader community to maintain effective schools.

7-2 Define the role of the intermediate unit in relation to the local school district and the state department of education.

7-3 Identify the various roles and responsibilities of the governor, state legislature, state board of education, state department of education, and chief state school officer in determining school policy.

7-4 Explain how the role of the federal government in education has changed over the years.

7-5 Discuss how nonpublic schools compare to the public-school systems in the United States.

Steven Georges/ZUMA Press/Newscom

This chapter was revised by Dr. David E. Vocke, Towson University.

EDUCATION IN THE UNITED STATES is organized on four governmental levels: local, intermediate (in some states), state, and federal. Understanding the formal organization of schools and how they are governed can help you make wise choices and realistic decisions about schools and take appropriate political action. In this chapter, we examine the various governmental levels and how they affect education.

The United States does not have a centralized, national education system like those in Great Britain, France, or Japan. We have fifty different state educational systems and many differences among local school systems even within the same state.

The US Constitution makes no mention of public education, but the Tenth Amendment to the Constitution reserves to the states all powers not specifically delegated to the federal government or prohibited to the states by the Constitution. This amendment is the basis for allocating to the states primary legal responsibility for public education. However, the states have delegated varying degrees of responsibility for day-to-day school system operations to local districts. So we begin our discussion of how schools are governed and administered at the local level.

7-1 LOCAL RESPONSIBILITIES AND ACTIVITIES

Every public school in the United States is part of a local school district. The district is created by the state. The state legislature, subject to the restrictions of the state constitution, can modify a local district's jurisdiction, change its boundaries and powers, or even eliminate it altogether. In most states, the local district encompasses a relatively small geographical area and operates schools for children within specific communities. However, because a school district operates on behalf of the state, local policies must be consistent with policies set forth in the state school code.

7-1a Characteristics of Local School Boards

local school board A body of citizens, either appointed or elected, who set policy regarding schools in a local school district.

Despite the fact that the state limits their prerogatives, **local school boards** have been delegated and assume significant decision-making responsibility. Many school boards have the power to raise money through local tax initiatives. They exercise power over personnel and school property. Most states leave student policy largely to local school boards, but others, by law, impose specific requirements or limitations.

Methods of selecting board members are prescribed by state law. The two standard methods are election and appointment. Election is thought to make for greater accountability to the public, but some people argue that appointment leads to greater competence and less politics. Election, by far the most common practice, accounts for more than 94 percent of school board members nationwide.[1] A few states specify a standard number of board members, others specify a permissible range, and a few have no requirements. Most school boards have five to eight members.

School board members typically do not come from the education profession; they are representative of the larger community they serve. In most cases, they are not paid or are paid very little for their service; 75 percent of board members in small districts receive no pay. They serve as volunteers performing a valuable community service.

Many educators are concerned about whether school boards adequately reflect the diversity of the communities they serve. A nationwide survey from the National

---

[1]Frederick M. Hess and Olivia Meeks, *School Boards Circa 2010: Governance in the Accountability Era* (Alexandria, VA: National School Boards Association, 2010).

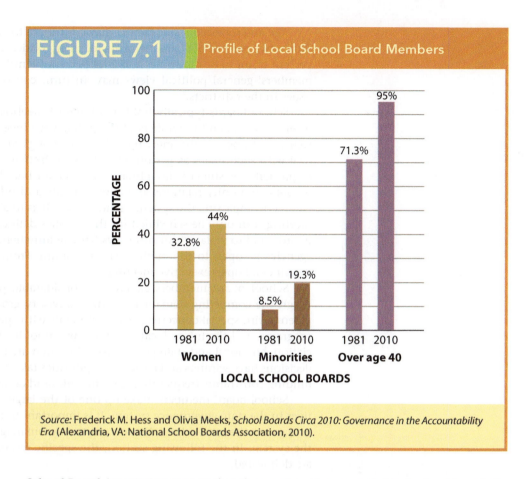

FIGURE 7.1   Profile of Local School Board Members

Source: Frederick M. Hess and Olivia Meeks, *School Boards Circa 2010: Governance in the Accountability Era* (Alexandria, VA: National School Boards Association, 2010).

School Board Association reports that the number of women on local school boards in 2010 stood at 44 percent, up from 33 percent in 1981 (see Figure 7.1). Minority representation increased over the same period, from 8.5 percent to 19.3 percent, but continues to lag behind the rising proportion of minority students in US public schools (48 percent in 2011).[2] Large school systems (those enrolling fifteen thousand or more students) tend to have more racially heterogeneous boards. The survey indicated that minority members constituted approximately 28 percent of the school board membership in these systems; women made up 51.7 percent.[3]

The majority of school board members (60 percent) are between 40 and 59 years of age, and 34 percent are over the age of 60. Board members tend to be more educated than the general population (74 percent have had four or more years of college) and wealthier (48.6 percent earn more than $100,000 annually). They are likely to be educators, professionals, or businesspeople (59 percent). Thirty-eight percent have children currently enrolled in school. School districts are aware that whether or not board members have children in the district's schools can affect the board members' policy-making agendas, although different districts react to this knowledge differently. Some school districts require board members to have school-age children; other districts permit children of board members to attend school *outside* the district.

[2]Ibid., p. 38; Frederick M. Hess, *School Boards at the Dawn of the 21st Century: Conditions and Challenges of District Governance* (Alexandria, VA: National School Boards Association, 2002); and Grace Kena, Susan Aud, Frank Johnson, Xiaolei Wang, Jijun Zhang, Amy Rathbun, Sydney Wilkinson-Flicker, and Paul Kristapovich, "Racial/Ethnic Enrollment in Public Schools," *The Condition of Education 2014 (NCES 2014-083)*, (Washington, DC: US Department of Education, National Center for Education Statistics, 2014), at **http://nces.ed.gov/programs/coe /indicator_cge.asp**.

[3]Frederick M. Hess and Olivia Meeks, *School Boards Circa 2010: Governance in the Accountability Era; and "Frequently Asked Questions," National School Boards Association* at **www.nsba.org /about-us/frequently-asked-questions** (January 19, 2015).

Age and socioeconomic factors may contribute to board members' political views. Thirty-two percent of board members see their political affiliation as conservative, 47.3 percent claim to be moderate, and 20.4 percent identified themselves as liberal. Board members' general political views may, in turn, contribute to their votes on school issues in their districts.[4]

School boards typically hold two types of meetings: regular and closed. Regular meetings are open to members of the public with meeting times and agendas posted well in advance of the meeting. Closed meetings are not open to the public and deal with such issues as personnel actions, collective bargaining matters, acquisition of property, or student disciplinary cases. Open board meetings obviously enhance school-community relations and allow parents and other citizens to understand the issues encompassing the system's schools as well as to air their concerns. Closed board meetings can only be scheduled for those issues delineated in the state's school code in order not to violate "sunshine laws," the requirement that meetings of government agencies be open to the public.[5] The upcoming From Preservice to Practice feature describes an open executive meeting.

School board members experience considerable pressure as they listen to and weigh the competing demands of citizen advisory groups, the business community, parents with special concerns (such as students with special needs, gifted and talented programs, and the future location of a new school in the district), the teachers' association, and local and state politicians, who often are key in funding decisions. Some decisions have winners and losers; high priorities take precedence over lower ones, and funding constraints frequently mean difficult (and occasionally unpopular) decisions.

School board members make up one of the largest groups of elected representatives in the state governance system. It is important to remember that the board's role is to *govern* the local school district, not to micromanage the day-to-day operations of the system. In the following section, the specific responsibilities of the school board are delineated.[6]

7-1b School Board Responsibilities

School administration and management is big business, and school board members must understand good business practices. Overall, US school boards have fiscal responsibility for $604 billion each year and employ more than 6.2 million teachers, administrators, and support staff (such as guidance counselors, librarians, and instructional aides).[7] They constitute the largest nationwide employer. Many school board members (41 percent) will spend more than twenty-five hours per month on school board business.[8] Board members must be fair and mindful of the law when dealing with students, teachers, administrators, parents, and other community residents.

[4]Frederick M. Hess and Olivia Meeks, *School Boards Circa 2010: Governance in the Accountability Era.*

[5] "Types of School Board Meetings," Oswego Community Unit School District No. 308 (December 9, 2013) at **www.sd308.org/oswego**; and Kirk D. Strang, "Protection from Open Meetings Violations," *School Administrator* (June 2014), p. 9.

[6]John Cassel and Tim Holt, "The Servant Leader," *American School Board Journal* (October 2008), pp. 34–35.

[7]Patrick Keaton, "Number of Full-Time-Equivalent (FTE) Staff for Public Schools, by Staff Category and State or Jurisdiction: School Year 2010–11," *Public Elementary and Secondary School Student Enrollment and Staff Counts from the Common Core of Data: School Year 2010–11 (NCES 2012-327)*, (Washington, DC: National Center for Education Statistics, 2012), at **http://nces.ed.gov/pubs2012/2012327.pdf**; and Stephen Q. Cornman, "Table 8: Total Expenditures for Public Elementary and Secondary Education and Other Related Programs, by Type of Expenditure and State or Jurisdiction: Fiscal Year 2011," *Revenues and Expenditures for Public Elementary and Secondary Education: School Year 2010–11 (Fiscal Year 2011) (NCES 2013-342)*, (Washington, DC: National Center for Education Statistics, 2013) at **www2.census .gov/govs/school/12f33pub.pdf** (January 16, 2015).

[8]Frederick M. Hess and Olivia Meeks, *School Boards Circa 2010: Governance in the Accountability Era.*

FROM PRESERVICE TO PRACTICE

A PARTNERSHIP IN DECISION MAKING?

As everyone assembled for the school board's regular meeting, Dr. Clore, superintendent of schools, nodded to the president of the school board that he was ready for the meeting to commence.

This would be a difficult meeting. They would be considering all administrative contracts, but special concerns had arisen about the contract of Tom Day, the principal of Westside Elementary–Middle School. Many parents and teachers were upset that the school had performed so poorly on the state assessments for a second straight year, even with the greater flexibility for meeting standards that had been announced by the state department of education. These groups had generated a small mountain of documentation to support their point of view and had pushed their request for his termination through all of the school district's required steps up to tonight's announcement of the decision. Dr. Clore, too, had recommended that the board not renew Mr. Day's contract. He had worked with him but had seen no improvement. In his mind, Principal Day was not an instructional leader. Day had poor communication with faculty, staff, and parents and seemed to lead from behind the principal's desk rather than through proactive interaction with others.

Other parents and former students, however, continued to support Principal Day and had been lobbying both publicly and privately with individual board members for his retention.

Dr. Clore looked around. On one side of the room sat the parents and teachers who supported Mr. Day, ready to raise their objections if—more like "when," thought Dr. Clore—the board announced Day's departure. On the other side sat those who had worked to remove him. It looked like a no-win situation. Tonight, Dr. Clore thought, we are all at a crossroad.

Dr. Clore wished, again, that the state's sunshine laws, designed to encourage openness in governmental decision making, permitted a little more privacy about personnel matters. Although much of the deliberation had already been conducted behind closed doors in executive session, the announcement of contracts had to be made in an open meeting.

Well, he thought to himself, at least it will all finally be over with fairly quickly. The policy of this board was to allow a maximum of five minutes of citizen input on any agenda item. Each group with a similar view would have to select a representative to speak. Dr. Clore was certain that the pro and con groups of parents were prepared to have a representative speak before the board, although he was less sure about the teachers. That meant at least ten minutes of unpleasantness.

He hoped nothing got out of hand. The school board president was relatively new to his position, and personnel considerations could become emotional. Dr. Clore knew that if the procedures were not followed exactly, a lawsuit could follow.

CASE QUESTIONS

1. Ideally, school boards and superintendents work in partnership. How would you define the roles of the superintendent and school board in this situation?

2. What legal issues could arise if the mandated procedures were not followed at this meeting?

3. What role, if any, might teachers have in such personnel decisions?

4. In a larger district, how might central office staff other than the superintendent be involved in an issue such as this?

5. What might be a better way for the school board to handle this potentially explosive situation?

The powers and responsibilities of school boards may be classified as follows:

1. *Policy.* School boards set the general rules about what is done in the schools, who does it, and how. The current practice of school-based management has allocated greater involvement of teachers, school-based administrators, and parent groups in day-to-day school operation and direction.

2. *Staffing.* Technically, the board is responsible for hiring all school district employees. In practice, however, school boards usually confine themselves to recruiting and selecting the school superintendent (the district's chief executive officer) and high-ranking members of the central office staff. Decisions on hiring and retaining principals, teachers, and school-based staff are usually delegated to the district's administrators.

3. *Employee relations.* School board members are responsible for all aspects of employee relations, including collective bargaining with teacher unions. Large school districts rely on consultants or attorneys to negotiate with teachers, but small school districts may use the superintendent or a school board committee.

4. *Fiscal matters.* The board oversees the budget and must keep the school district solvent and get the most out of every tax dollar. The school district usually has a larger budget than any other aspect of local government. This is an especially critical responsibility in harsh economic times.

5. *Students.* The board addresses questions of student rights and responsibilities, requirements for promotion and graduation, extracurricular activities, and attendance.

6. *Curriculum and assessment.* The school board develops curriculum—especially development related to federal and state law and guidelines—and approves textbook selections. Boards today are especially focused on enhancing the academic achievement of students in their district's schools.

7. *Community relations.* The school board must respond not only to parents but also to other members of the community.

8. *Intergovernmental requirements.* Federal and state agencies establish a variety of requirements for local schools, and the local school board is responsible for seeing that these mandates are addressed.[9]

Board members are expected to govern the school system without encroaching on the superintendent's authority. Members, in theory, have no authority except during a board meeting and while acting as a collective group or board.[10] They also must be politically prudent. Eventually, someone will ask for a favor, and members must be able to resist this pressure.

7-1c The School Superintendent and Central Office Staff

superintendent of schools The chief executive officer of the local school district who implements policies adopted by the school board.

One of the board's most important responsibilities is to appoint a competent **superintendent of schools**.[11] The superintendent is the chief executive officer (CEO) of the school system, whereas the board is the legislative policy-making body. Sometimes, the superintendent literally is a CEO. Although the vast majority of superintendents are professional educators, a number of school districts in recent years, most notably Seattle, New York, Pittsburgh, Providence, and Los Angeles, have hired leaders from the private sector or the military as superintendents.[12]

As with school boards, concerns have emerged that superintendents fail to reflect the diversity of the districts they serve. Currently, 76 percent of school superintendents are men, 24 percent are women—up from 6.6 percent in 1992—and only 6 percent are members of minority groups.[13]

The school board, which consists of laypeople rather than experts in school affairs, is responsible for seeing that schools are properly run by the professional education personnel. The board of education often delegates many of its own legal powers to the superintendent and staff, especially in larger districts, although the superintendent's policies are subject to board approval.

[9]Arnold F. Shober and Michael T. Hartney, *Does School Board Leadership Matter?* (Washington, DC: Thomas B. Fordham Institute, 2014); Education Commission of the States, "Governance: School Boards," at **http://ecs.org/html/issue.asp?issueid=68&subissueID=327** (January 19, 2015); and National School Boards Association, "What School Boards Do," at **www.nsba.org /about-us/what-school-boards-do** (January 19, 2015).

[10]Robert L. Zorn, "Educating New Board Members," *American School Board Journal* (August 2008), pp. 26–27; and Jason Cabico and Erica E. Harrison, "Getting on Board," *Kennedy School Review* (2009), pp. 19–24.

[11]Edgar B. Hatrick, "Searching for Excellence in a Superintendent," *School Administrator* (2010), p. 41.

[12]Ericka Mellon, "Army Strong, Superintendent Savvy," *District Administration* (May 2011), pp. 71–77; Fenwick English and Zan Crowder, "Assessing Eli Broad's Assault on Public School System Leadership," *Democracy & Education* (2012), pp. 1–4, at **http://democracyeducationjournal .org/cgi/viewcontent.cgi?article=1078&context=home** (April 25, 2015); and Vanessa Romo, "A Superintendent Shortage Is Shaking Up America's Schools," *TakePart* (May 10, 2013) at **www.takepart.com/article/2013/05/10/superintendent-shortage-shake-up-schools**.

[13]Angela Pascopella, "State of the Superintendency," *District Administration* (February 2008), pp. 32–36; Theodore J. Kowalski, Robert S. McCord, George J. Petersen, I. Phillip Young, and Noelle M. Ellerson, *The American School Superintendent: 2010 Decennial Study* (Lanham, MD: Rowman & Littlefield Education, 2010); and Daniel A. Domenech, "AASA's Status Check on the Superintendency," *School Administrator* (December 2010), p. 47.

A major function of the school superintendent is to gather and present data so that school board members can make intelligent policy decisions. The superintendent advises the school board and keeps members abreast of problems; generally, the school board refuses to enact legislation or make policy without the school superintendent's recommendation. However, in cases of continual disagreement or major policy conflict between the school board and the superintendent, the latter is usually replaced. The average tenure of superintendents is about 7 years. In large urban districts, the average is lower, at 3.2 years.[14] The reasons most superintendents give for losing their jobs are communication breakdowns and micromanagement by the board (interference in school administration), especially when they are forced to make unpopular decisions brought on by budget restrictions.[15] What would Dr. Clore's feelings be about school board interference and micromanagement?

Besides advising the board of education, the superintendent is responsible for many other functions, including the following:

● *Management of professional and nonteaching personnel* (for example, custodians and cafeteria workers)
● *Leadership in curriculum, instruction, and assessment* (ensuring decisions about curriculum and instruction are based on data derived from district assessments and that such decisions are impacting student performance)
● *Administrative management* (including district organization, budgeting, long-range planning, and complying with directives from state and federal agencies)

In addition, the superintendent oversees day-to-day operation of the district schools and serves as the major spokesperson for the schools.[16]

Superintendents often experience strong pressure from various segments of the community, such as concerned parents or organized community groups with their own agendas (sometimes overt, sometimes covert). Much of the superintendent's effectiveness depends on his or her ability to deal with such pressure groups. Only a confident school leader can balance the demands and expectations of parents and community groups with the ultimate goal of improving learning for all students in the district. Experts agree that the key to success as a superintendent is communication—with school board members, citizen groups, teachers, parents, unions, and elected officials. Failure to build citizen, legislative, and political support quickly leads to discord between the superintendent and the various stakeholders.[17]

central office staff A cadre of supervisors and specialists who work closely with the superintendent to carry out school board policy.

A **central office staff** assists the superintendent (see Figure 7.2). Large districts of twenty-five thousand or more students, which represent slightly more than 2 percent of all school districts in the United States, may have many levels in the staff hierarchy: a deputy superintendent, associate superintendents, assistant superintendents, directors, department heads, and coordinators and supervisors—each with their own support staffs, resulting in several hundred employees in the central office.[18] Small school districts usually have a less bureaucratic central office and far fewer administrative personnel.

Critics charge that the many-layered bureaucracies of large school districts are inefficient and a waste of taxpayers' money. Actually, the responsibilities of central offices are diverse and complex, including interacting with federal and state education

---

[14]J. H. Snider, "The Superintendent as Scapegoat," *Education Week* (January 11, 2006), pp. 40–41; and "Urban School Superintendents Tenure Slips, Says New Report," *News . . . News . . . Council of the Great City Schools* (November 6, 2014).

[15]Donald R. McAdams, "Getting Your Board Out of Micromanagement," *School Administrator* (November 2008), p. 6; and Vanessa Romo, "A Superintendent Shortage Is Shaking Up America's Schools."

[16]Doug Eadie, "Prescription for Success," *American School Board Journal* (August 2008), pp. 46–47; and Lee Mitgang, "Flipping the Script," *School Administrator* (December 2010), pp. 15–18.

[17]Edgar B. Hatrick, "Searching for Excellence in a Superintendent," *School Administrator* (October 2010), p. 41; and Art Stellar, "Welcome to the Jungle," *School Administrator* (November 2011), pp. 28–33.

[18]Kathleen Vail, "The Changing Face of Education," *Education Vital Signs* (2003) at **www.nsba .org**; and *Digest of Education Statistics* (2012) at **http://nces.ed.gov/programs/digest/d12 /tables/dt12_099.asp,** Table 99 (January 16, 2015).

FIGURE 7.2   Typical Medium-Sized School District (5,000–25,000 Students)

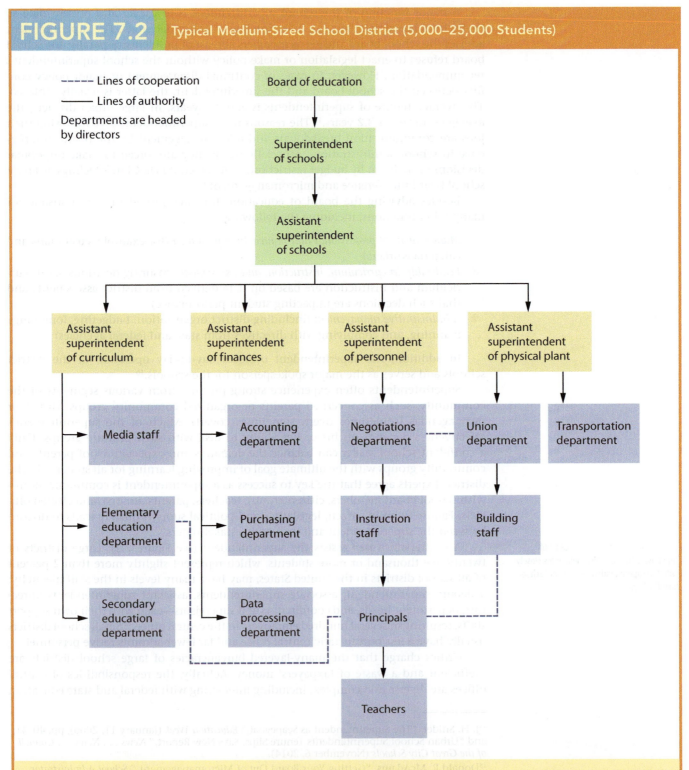

This figure shows the organizational chart of a medium-sized school district with 5,000 to 25,000 students, representative of almost 12 percent of school districts nationwide. Small school districts, with 1,000 to 5,000 students—about 38 percent of all districts nationally—have much simpler organizational structures. The organizational hierarchy of larger school districts is cumbersome; a chart of a district with 100,000 or more students would extend off the page. *Source:* Digest of Educational Statistics, 2010, Table 91, at **http://nces.ed.gov/programs/digest/d10/tables/dt10_091.asp?referrer=list**

agencies, processing payroll and contracts, monitoring human resources, and overseeing construction, transportation, and purchasing. Recent efforts in several major school districts are transforming central offices to partner more with school-based personnel, especially school principals, to help improve instruction in every classroom.[19]

7-1d The Principal and the School

principal The chief administrative officer of the school who is responsible for school operation.

Most schools have a single administrative officer, a **principal**, who is responsible for school operations. Interestingly, 64 percent of primary school and 30 percent of high school principals are women. In small schools, the principal may teach part-time as well; large schools may have one or more assistant or vice principals to share the administrative responsibilities. The administrative hierarchy may also include department chairpersons, discipline officers (for instance, a dean of students), and guidance counselors. Each of these individuals works closely with the school principal and under his or her direction. Furthermore, most principals work with a community-based school improvement group, often a Parent-Teacher Association (PTA) or a professional learning community.[20]

Traditionally, the most important aspect of the principal's job is the role of manager: dealing with day-to-day school operations, meetings, paperwork, phone calls, and community relations. Today, however, there is increasing pressure to demonstrate improved student performance on mandated assessments. Principals must focus on the cycle of curriculum development, instruction, assessment, and data analysis. The successful principal has to be adept at collaborating with various stakeholders to make data-driven decisions that raise student achievement.[21]

In the past, secondary-school principals were often considered primarily as general managers, whereas elementary-school principals viewed themselves as leaders in curriculum and instruction.[22] This was likely because larger secondary schools create more managerial work for the principal. Today, however, because of the emphasis on raising academic achievement for all students, principals are taking a more active role as an instructional leader focused on improving teaching and learning (Photo 7.1). Additionally, they are spending more of their time in formal observations of teachers due to the new requirements from the state and federal levels.

As a teacher, how will you interact with your principal? In large secondary schools, a teacher's interaction with the principal might be minimal, consisting of primarily formal observations; faculty meetings; cafeteria, hall, or bus duty; and conversations in the main office. In contrast, many elementary-school teachers have frequent, almost daily, contact with the principal, and these encounters can cover a wide range of school- and student-related issues.

Customarily, authority concerning school policies flows from the top down, from the school board through the superintendent and central office staff to the principal.

[19]Christina Samuels, "District Central Offices Take on New Roles," *Education Week* (July 18, 2012), p. 13; and University of Washington Center for Educational Leadership and Meredith I. Honig, *The Central Office Transformation Toolkit*, (Seattle: University of Washington Center for Educational Leadership, November 2013).

[20]Laura A. Cooper, "The Principal as Instructional Leader," *Principal* (January 1989), pp. 13–16; Allan C. Ornstein, "Leaders and Losers," *Executive Educator* (August 1993), pp. 28–30; and Amy Bitterman, Rebecca Goldring, and Lucinda Gray, "Table 2: Average and Median Age of School Principals, and Percentage Distribution of Principals, by Age Category, Sex, School Type, and Selected School Characteristics: 2011–12," *Characteristics of Public and Private Elementary and Secondary School Principals in the United States: Results from the 2011–12 Schools and Staffing Survey (NCES 2013-313)*, (Washington, DC: National Center for Education Statistics, 2013) at **http://nces.ed.gov/pubsearch/pubsinfo.asp?pubid=2013313** (January 16, 2015).

[21]Douglas B. Reeves, "Looking Deeper into the Data," *Educational Leadership* (December 2008), pp. 89–90; and Center for the Future of Teaching and Learning, and International SRI, "School Leadership: A Key to Teaching Quality. A Policy Brief on the Role of Principals in Strengthening Instruction," *Center for the Future of Teaching and Learning* (January 1, 2011).

[22]Lynn K. Bradshaw, "The Changing Role of Principals in School Partnerships," *NASSP Bulletin* (May 2000) pp. 86–96; and Lesi A. Maxwell, "Principals Hard-Pressed for Time to Be Instructional Leaders," *Education Week* (March 26, 2014), pp. 1, 24; and David DeMatthews, "Getting Teacher Evaluation Right: What Principals Need to Know," *The Educational Forum* (January 2015).

> PHOTO 7.1 Principals have multiple responsibilities, but it is probably most important that they view themselves as leaders in curriculum, instruction, and assessment.

In some districts, however, as explained in Chapter 2, The Teaching Profession, *Professional Learning Communities* (PLCs) have provided principals and teachers increased responsibility for such matters as developing and aligning curriculum with instructional practices and assessments, participating in peer observations, and allocating time for professional development. Collaboration with teachers and other school staff to create school policies that improve student learning calls for a more participatory governance style by school principals.[23]

7-1e Parent and Community Involvement

Many collaborative school programs go beyond principals and teachers by giving important roles to parents and other community members, as well. In doing so, they build on a movement for increased parent and community involvement evident since the 1970s.

Many educators have promoted parent involvement for the most basic of reasons: research indicates that it pays off in higher student test scores on standardized tests, lower absenteeism, improved behavior at home and school, and higher motivation to study.[24] Across the nation, polls indicate that the public overwhelmingly supports the idea of parent involvement and believes that parents play a major role in children's education. As a result of this support, parent involvement was a key component of NCLB and is a major focus of the Obama administration's New Family and Community Engagement Framework.[25]

Nevertheless, teachers perceive that parents are reluctant to take full advantage of existing opportunities to involve themselves with their children's schooling. In a Department of Education survey of parents, 42 percent of parents claimed that they

[23]NASSP, *Changing Role of the Middle Level and High School Leader: Learning from the Past – Preparing for the Future* (Reston, VA: National Association of Secondary School Principals, 2007); and The Wallace Foundation, *The School Principal as Leader: Guiding Schools to Better Teaching and Learning* (New York: The Wallace Foundation, January 2013).

[24]Asnat Dor and T. Brooke Rucker-Naidu, "Teachers Attitudes toward Parents' Involvement in School: Comparing Teachers in the USA and Israel," *Issues in Educational Research* (September 2012), pp. 246–262.

[25]Jennifer DePlanty, Russell Coulter-Kern, and Kim A. Duchane, "Perceptions of Parent Involvement in Academic Achievement," *Journal of Educational Research* (July 2007), pp. 361–368; and *Family and Community Engagement* (Washington, DC, April 2014) at **www.ed.gov/family-and -community-engagement**.

volunteered at school, while 76 percent reported that they attended a parent-teacher conference.[26] Some parents, according to research, avoid school involvement because of feelings of inadequacy, negative experiences in schools as students, and negative perceptions of administrator and teacher attitudes.[27] However, in a survey of parents with children enrolled in urban schools, 83 percent of respondents indicated they felt respected by school personnel.[28]

The pressure for school reform has produced formal arrangements that give parents and other community members a voice in local educational decisions. For purposes of discussion, we can divide community involvement into three broad categories: community participation, community control, and community schools.

community participation Citizen advisory committees at either the local school or school board level.

Community Participation The usual form of **community participation** involves advisory committees at either the neighborhood school or central board level. These committees are commonly appointed by school officials and offer the school board help and advice. Citizen advisory councils provide advice and assistance in many areas: (1) identification of goals, priorities, and needs; (2) feedback on developing district policy; (3) support for financing schools; (4) recruitment of volunteers; and (5) assistance to students in school and in "homework hotline" programs. Nearly every state has a parent involvement law.[29]

community control An elected community council or board that shares decision-making power with the local school board.

Community Control In a system of **community control,** an elected community council or board does more than offer advice—it shares decision-making power with the central school board.

Since the 1990s, Chicago Public Schools have practiced a form of community control, known as *local school councils* (LSCs), as part of local educational reform designed to improve academic achievement. Members of LSCs, which include the principal, six parents, two community members, two teachers, and one nonteaching staff representative, are elected to two-year terms. The councils are responsible for approving how funds and resources are allocated, developing and monitoring school improvement plans, and monitoring and evaluating the school's principal. The LSC system recently marked its twenty-fifth anniversary and is still noted as an example for parent and community control of schools.[30]

charter school A public school governed by a community group granted a special contract (charter) by the state or the local school board. Charter schools often form to offer educational alternatives unavailable in regular public schools.

A more recent development in community involvement in education is the establishment of **charter schools** (discussed in more detail in Chapter 16, School Effectiveness and Reform in the United States). In this arrangement, the local school board or state board of education grants a community group or private organization a *charter* (a contract listing specific rights, privileges, and expectations), which permits the group to establish and operate a public school. Specific arrangements about finance, school operation, physical location, student enrollment, teacher work conditions, and

---

[26]Larry Ferlasso, "Involvement or Engagement?" *Educational Leadership* (May 2011), pp. 10–14: and *Data Bank – Parental Involvement in Schools* (Bethesda, MD: Child Trends, September 2013).

[27]Lauri Goldkind and G. Lawrence Farmer, "The Enduring Influence of School Size and School Climate on Parents' Engagement in the School Community," *School Community Journal* (Spring/Summer 2013); and Kantahyanee W. Murray, Nadine Finigan, Vanya Jones, Nikeea Copeland-Linder, Denise L. Haynie, and Tina L. Cheng, "Barriers and Facilitators to School-Based Parent Involvement for Parents of Urban Public Middle School Students," *SAGE Open* (November 2014) at **http://sgo.sagepub.com/content/4/4/2158244014558030**.

[28]Brian Perkins, *What We Think: Parental Perceptions of Urban School Climate* (Alexandria, VA: National School Boards Association, 2008); and Ann Bradley, "Poll: Urban Parents Find Schools Safe," *Education Week* (May 7, 2008), p. 4.

[29]Gavin Shatkin and Alec Ian Gershberg, "Empowering Parents and Building Communities," *Urban Education* (November 2007), pp. 582–615; Kavitha Mediratta, Seema Shah, Sara McAlister, Norm Fruchter, Christina Mokhtar, and Dana Lockwood, *Organized Communities, Stronger Schools* (New York: Annenberg Institute for School Reform at Brown University, March 2008); and "Parent/Family," *ECS – Education Commission of the States* at **www.ecs.org/html/issue.asp?issueid=85** (January 21, 2015).

[30]Denisa R. Superville, "Power of Parents Tested by Changes in Chicago Schools," *Education Week* (October 8, 2014), pp. 1, 15; and Chicago Public Schools, *Local School Councils* at **www.cps.edu/Pages/Localschoolcouncils.aspx** (January 21, 2015).

TAKING ISSUE

Read the brief introduction below, as well as the Question and the pros and cons list that follows. Then, answer the question using *your* own words and position.

CHARTER SCHOOLS AS PUBLIC-SCHOOL REFORM

As the pressure for school choice increases, so has the public's desire for greater participation in its schools. The Obama administration and Secretary of Education Duncan have provided funds for charter schools as an avenue for school choice and a way to spur reform.

Question

Should local boards of education continue to support charter schools as a better way to educate students? (Think about this question as you read the PRO and CON arguments listed here. What is *your* response to this issue?)

Arguments PRO	Arguments CON
1. Charter schools provide an alternative vision of schooling that is not realized in the traditional public-school system.	1. Accountability goals frequently are not clearly spelled out by sponsors in charter schools, leading to misunderstanding and confusion as to their mission.
2. Charter schools have increased autonomy from state and local school district regulations.	2. State and federal regulations still apply to charter schools and tend to restrain their independence.
3. Special populations of students may be better served by charter schools.	3. Charter schools often receive inadequate funding for start-up and operating expenses, especially if they serve special populations that require high expenditures.
4. Students, teachers, and parents participate by choice and are committed to making charter schools work; true collaboration is possible. Teachers are given freedom to craft the curriculum in creative ways, as long as standards are met.	4. Charter schools have difficulty finding staff, and there is high teacher attrition.
5. Charter schools are generally smaller and more manageable in size.	5. Charter schools tend to "skim" the more talented students for admission, thus ignoring more challenging students.
6. Parental involvement and overall communication are increased in charter schools. There is a sense of community among stakeholders.	6. Insufficient planning time for charter school boards, principals, and staff makes for management and communication problems later on.

Question Reprise: What Is Your Stand?

Reflect again on the following question by explaining *your* stand about this issue: Should local boards of education continue supporting charter schools?

accountability are negotiated. Charter school administrators agree to meet prescribed accountability standards; if they fail to do so, the charter is revoked, and the school is closed.[31] See the Taking Issue box for a discussion of the pros and cons of charter schools.

Community Schools   Since the early 1980s, the school has come to be seen as only one of several educational agencies within the community. Under this concept—called **community schools**—the school serves as a partner, or coordinating agency, in providing educational, health, social, family support, recreational, and cultural activities to the community. Such concentrated efforts are designed to not only increase student achievement but to also provide a safe and supportive environment where the whole

community schools When the school is seen as only one of the educational agencies within the community, and the school serves as a partner, or coordinating agency, in providing educational, health, social, family support, recreational, and cultural activities to the community.

[31]National School Boards Association, "Frequently Asked Questions – What are Charter Schools?" at **www.nsba.org/about-us/frequently-asked-questions** (January 21, 2015).

child can develop. In Tulsa, Oklahoma, for example, research suggests that students in the Tulsa Area Community School Initiative (TACSI) that implemented the community schools characteristics outperformed noncommunity schools in math by 32 points and reading by 19 points. TACSI schools also exhibited greater student trust of teachers, school identification among students, and parent trust in school than comparison schools.[32] Programs such as these are especially helpful for low-income families.

As part of the community schools plan, schools share their personnel and facilities with other community agencies or even businesses. In return, schools may expect to share facilities, equipment, and personnel with other community agencies, local businesses, and area universities. This type of sharing is especially important in a period of retrenchment and school budget pressures.

7-1f Size of Schools and School Districts

Educators have long debated the question of size: How many students should be enrolled in a single district? How large should a school be? Five decades ago, James Conant argued that the most effective high schools were the ones large enough to offer comprehensive and diversified facilities. More recently, however, other educators have contended that small schools are more effective.[33]

In 1987, after reviewing several studies, two researchers concluded that high schools should have no more than 250 students. Larger enrollments, according to this analysis, result in a preoccupation with control and order, and the anonymity of a large school makes it harder to establish a sense of community among students, teachers, and parents.[34] More than twenty-five years later, school systems are applying these lessons to high schools. For example, a recent study of more than 100 small high schools in New York City, known as small schools of choice (SSCs), which are limited to 100 students per grade, found that the SSCs improved graduation rates of educationally and economically disadvantaged students without increasing school operating costs.[35]

Countering the small school research, past studies indicated that learning is most effective in high schools of 600 to 900 students; learning declines as school size shrinks, and students in very small schools learn less than students in moderate-size schools. Teachers in schools with populations larger than the 600 to 900 range were more likely to report that apathy, tardiness, and drug use were serious problems than were teachers in relatively smaller schools.[36]

The debate about school size parallels similar disputes about the optimum size of school districts. Larger school districts, according to their proponents, offer a broader tax base and reduce the educational cost per student; consequently, these districts can

[32]Curt M. Adams, *The Community School Effect Evidence from an Evaluation of the Tulsa Area Community School Initiative* (Tulsa, OK: The Oklahoma Center for Educational Policy, 2010); Coalition for Community Schools, *What is a Community School?* at **www.communityschools .org/aboutschools/what_is_a_community_school.aspx** (January 21, 2015); and Virginia Myers, "Community Schools," *American Teacher* (May 2012), pp. 12–15.

[33]James B. Conant, *The American High School Today* (New York: McGraw-Hill, 1959); and Kenneth Leithwood and Doris Jantzi, "A Review of Empirical Evidence about School Size Effects: A Policy Perspective," *Review of Educational Research* (January 1, 2009), pp. 464–490.

[34]Thomas B. Gregory and Gerald R. Smith, *High Schools as Communities: The Small School Reconsidered* (Bloomington, IN: Phi Delta Kappa, 1987); and Hanna Skandera and Richard Sousa, "Why Bigger Isn't Better," *Hoover Digest* (Summer 2001).

[35]Howard Bloom and Rebecca Unterman, "Can Small High Schools of Choice Improve Educational Prospects for Disadvantaged Students?" *Journal of Policy Analysis & Management* (Spring 2014), pp. 290–319.

[36]David C. Berliner, "By the Numbers: Ideal High School Size Found to Be 600 to 900," *Education Week* (April 24, 1996), p. 10; Board on Children, Youth and Families, *Engaging Schools: Fostering High School Students' Motivation to Learn* (Washington, DC: The National Academies Press, 2003); and Brian V. Carolan, "An Examination of the Relationship among High School Size, Social Capital, and Adolescents' Mathematics Achievement," *Journal of Research on Adolescence* (September 2012), pp. 583–595.

better afford high-quality personnel, a wider range of educational programs and special services, and efficient transportation systems. Most studies of this subject over the past sixty years have placed the most effective school district size as between ten thousand and fifty thousand students.[37]

Today, however, small is often considered better in school districts as well as in individual schools; the perception is there is too much waste in large systems. Proponents of smaller districts contend they are more cost effective and efficient. The small size is more inviting to parental involvement, and management of the system is more transparent to the citizens of the community than in larger districts.[38]

Arguments and counterarguments aside, the trend in American education has been toward larger school districts. By the 2008–2009 school year, 22.63 percent of all public-school students were in the 100 largest districts—.6 percent of all public-school districts, each serving 47,000 or more students. In most cases, the larger school systems are located in or near cities, the largest being the New York City system with approximately 1,041,000 students in more than 1,500 schools, followed by the Los Angeles Unified School District with 662,000 students.[39]

consolidation The combining of small or rural school districts into larger ones.

Consolidation   School districts increase enrollment through population growth and through consolidation, when several smaller school districts combine into one or two larger ones. As Figure 7.3 illustrates, consolidation dramatically reduced the overall number of districts from more than 130,000 in 1930 to 13,567 in 2012, with the bulk of the decline taking place in the thirty years between 1930 and 1960.[40]

School districts consolidate for a variety of reasons; chief among them are the following:

- *Size*. Larger school districts permit broader, more rigorous curriculum offerings and more specialized teachers.
- *Services*. Larger districts justify hiring counselors, assistant principals, and team leaders not normally found in smaller districts.
- *Economics*. There is an efficiency of scale where purchasing decisions (for example, books, paper, and art supplies) should yield significant cost savings when ordering in bulk. Consolidation also permits older buildings to be retired at considerable cost savings. Redundant high-salaried central-office positions may also be cut when school districts combine.[41]

Though thousands of districts were consolidated in the earlier part of the previous century as the United States transitioned away from a rural economy, state legislatures

---

[37]Donna Driscoll, Dennis Halcoussis, and Shirley Svorny, "School District Size and Student Performance," *Economics of Education Review* (April 2003), pp. 193–201; and John T. Jones, Eugenia F. Toma, and Ron W. Zimmer, "School Attendance and District and School Size," *Economics of Education Review* (April 2008), pp. 140–148.

[38]Craig Howley and Robert Bickel, "The Influence of Scale," *American School Board Journal* (March 2002), pp. 28–30; S. L. Bowen, "Is Bigger That Much Better? School District Size, High School Completion, and Post-Secondary Enrollment Rates in Maine," *Maine View*, (2007), pp. 1–5; and Joshua Bendor, Jason Bordoff, and Jason Furman, *An Education Strategy to Promote Opportunity, Prosperity, and Growth* (Washington, DC: The Brookings Institution, 2007), p. 14.

[39]Jennifer Sable, Chris Plotts, and Lindsey Mitchell, *Characteristics of the 100 Largest Public Elementary and Secondary School Districts in the United States: 2008–2009* (Washington, DC: US Department of Education, National Center for Education Statistics, 2011) at **http://nces .ed.gov/pubs2011/2011301.pdf** (January 19, 2015); and "2013 AS&U 100: Largest School Districts by Enrollment," *American School & University* at **http://asumag.com/research /2013-asu-100-largest-school-districts-enrollment#node-34011** (January 19, 2015).

[40]Nora Gordon, *The Causes of Political Integration: An Application to School Districts* (Cambridge, MA: National Bureau of Economic Research, 2006); and *Digest of Education Statistics, 2013*, Table 214.30 (January 2014) at **http://nces.ed.gov/programs/digest/d13/tables /dt13_214.30.asp** (May 28, 2015).

[41]Glenn Cook, "The Challenges of Consolidation," *American School Board Journal* (October 2008), p. 10; and William D. Duncombe and John M. Yinger, "School District Consolidation: The Benefits and Costs," *School Administrator* (May 2010), pp. 10–17.

FIGURE 7.3   Declining Number of Public-School Districts, 1930–2012

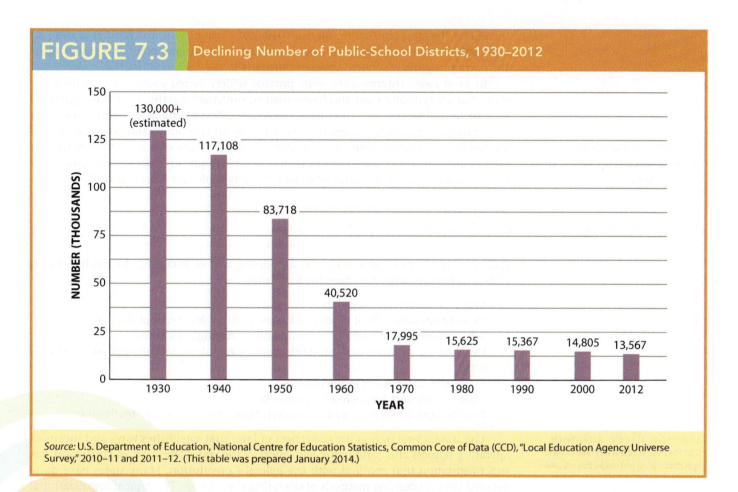

Source: U.S. Department of Education, National Centre for Education Statistics, Common Core of Data (CCD), "Local Education Agency Universe Survey," 2010–11 and 2011–12. (This table was prepared January 2014.)

FOCUS As you follow various news media in your area, what educational issues are discussed at the local school district level? How do these issues impact board members, the superintendent, school principals, and the community in the local district in which you have your internships?

today continue the push for consolidation as enrollment numbers in rural districts continue to decline. States such as Arizona, Arkansas, Indiana, Kansas, Maine, Nebraska, New York, and Vermont are enacting merger plans that encourage district consolidation. Maine, for example, enacted legislation in 2007 that mandated the state's 290 school districts consolidate into 80 districts.[42] Consolidating districts usually means closing schools, and this has proved to be a serious and emotional matter, especially in small and rural districts where the local school is likely the focal point of community identity. A less drastic method of consolidation is for neighboring districts to share programs and personnel.[43]

7-2 INTERMEDIATE UNITS

intermediate unit or regional educational service agency (RESA) An educational unit or agency in the middle position between the state department of education and the local school district; usually created by the state to provide supplementary services and support staff to local school districts.

The term **intermediate unit** or **regional educational service agency (RESA)** refers to an office or agency in a middle position between the state department of education and local school districts. This agency provides coordination and supplementary services to local districts, and it links local and state educational authorities. The intermediate unit is usually a legal and political extension of the state department of education

---

[42]Craig Howley, Jerry Johnson, and Jennifer Petrie, *Consolidation of Schools and Districts: What the Research Says and What It Means* (Boulder, CO: National Education Policy Center, 2011) at **http://nepc.colorado.edu/publication/consolidation-schools-districts** (January 22, 2015); and Scott Lafee, "The Emotions of Consolidation," *School Administrator* (June 2014), pp. 14–19.

[43]Charles S. Dedrick, "Leadership Squeeze of Proposed Mergers," *School Administrator* (June 2014), pp. 20–27.

created by the state legislature. By the 2010–2011 school year, thirty-three states had some form of intermediate unit. Approximately 1,550 intermediate or regional agencies currently provide services to school districts in the United States.[44]

In most cases, intermediate units provide widely varied assistance to school districts that are typically rural and have small administrative staffs. They have provided support in finding teachers in critical needs areas, developing assessments, operating online delivery systems, serving the needs of special-education students, and providing services for English language learning students.[45] Many educators believe that an intermediate unit covering several districts can economically provide assistance that many small or financially strapped school districts could not afford on their own.

FOCUS Does your state have intermediate units or RESAs? If so, how do they assist local schools?

7-3 STATE RESPONSIBILITIES AND ACTIVITIES

Each state has legal responsibility for supporting and maintaining the public schools within its borders. The state does the following:

- Enacts school-related legislation.
- Determines state school taxes and financial aid to local school districts.
- Sets minimum standards for training and recruiting personnel.
- Develops state curriculum standards (some states also establish approved textbook lists).
- Establishes assessment requirements.
- Makes provisions for accrediting schools.
- Provides special services such as student transportation or free textbooks.

state school code A collection of state laws that establish ways and means of operating schools and conducting education.

The **state school code** is the collection of laws that establishes ways and means of operating schools and conducting education in the state. The state, of course, cannot enact legislation that conflicts with the federal Constitution. Many states have quite detailed laws concerning methods of operating the schools. The typical organizational hierarchy, from state to local levels, is shown in Figure 7.4.

7-3a The Governor and State Legislature

Although a governor's powers vary widely, authority on educational matters is spelled out in law. Usually a governor is charged with making educational budget recommendations to the legislature. In many states, the governor has legal access to any accumulated balances in the state treasury, and these monies can be used for school purposes. The governor can generally appoint or remove school personnel at the state level and, in some states, even remove local superintendents. But these powers often carry restrictions, such as approval by the legislature. In most states, the governor can appoint members of the state board of education and, in several states, the chief state school officer.[46] Governors can veto educational measures or threaten to veto to discourage the legislature from enacting opposed educational laws.

In most states, the legislature is primarily responsible for establishing and maintaining the public schools and has broad powers to enact laws pertaining to education. These powers are limited by restrictions in the form of federal and state constitutions and court decisions. The legislature usually decides major financial matters, including the nature and level of state taxes for schools and the taxing powers of local school districts. It may also determine basic parameters of teaching and instruction, including

---

[44]*Digest of Education Statistics, 2012,* Table 100 at **http://nces.ed.gov/programs/digest/d12/tables/dt12_100.asp** (January 19, 2015).

[45]AESA Governmental Relations Committee, *Improving American Education through Educational Service Agencies* (Arlington, VA: The Association of Educational Service Agencies, 2010).

[46]NASBE, *State Education Governance Models: 2014* (Arlington, VA: National Association of State Boards of Education, 2014).

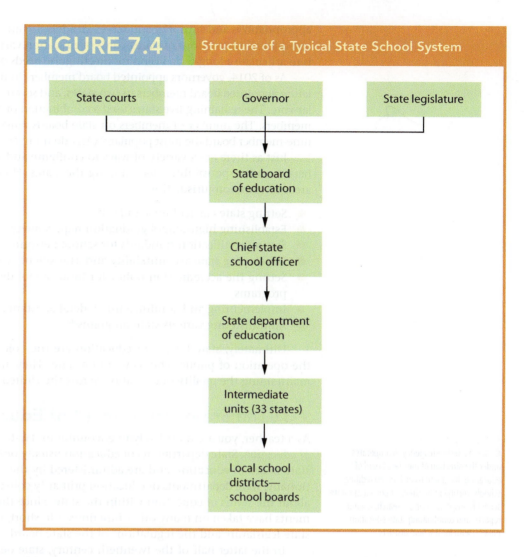

FIGURE 7.4   Structure of a Typical State School System

State courts → Governor → State legislature

State board of education

Chief state school officer

State department of education

Intermediate units (33 states)

Local school districts— school boards

(1) what may or may not be taught, (2) how many years of compulsory education will be required, and (3) the length of the school day and school year. In addition, the legislature may establish testing and assessment procedures, authorize school programs, and set standards for building construction. Where the legislature does not enact these policies, they are usually the responsibility of the state board of education, which we describe in the next section.

As a teacher, you will need to comply with various state laws. State legislatures have had to comply with the accountability mandates under the federal ESEA. As a result, state statutes have been enacted that increase academic standards, mandate assessments, and establish systems for reporting student data.[47] Not since the wave of school reform that followed the passage of the ESEA of 1965 have state legislatures played such a prominent role in educational policy.

7-3b The State Board of Education

state board of education An influential state education agency that advises the state legislature and establishes policies for implementing legislative acts related to education.

The **state board of education** is usually the most influential and important state education agency. With the exception of New Mexico, Wisconsin, and Minnesota, all states have some sort of state board of education, which depends on the state legislature for

[47]"Policies for Jurisdiction of the Education Committee," National Conference of State Legislatures (2014) at **www.ncsl.org/ncsl-in-dc/task-forces/policies-education.aspx** (January 22, 2015).

appropriations and authority and serves an advisory function for the legislature. The precise duties and functions of state boards of education vary, but their overarching purpose is to articulate a long-term vision for meeting the needs of the state's education system.[48]

As of 2014, governors appointed board members in thirty-three states, the state legislature appointed board members in two states, and seven states elected members by popular vote. The remaining five states used a combination of appointed members and elected members. The number of members on state boards ranges from six to seventeen, with a nine-member board the most popular.[49] (An odd number of members eliminates tie votes.)

Just as there are a variety of ways to configure and select state school board members, board responsibilities vary among the states. However, state boards share some areas of common jurisdiction:

- Setting state curriculum standards
- Establishing high school graduation requirements
- Setting certification standards for school personnel
- Developing state accountability and assessment systems
- Setting the accreditation policy for local school districts and teacher-preparation programs
- Implementing and administering federal assistance programs
- Administering various state programs[50]

Ultimately, state boards of education are the voice of the citizens in overseeing the operation of public schools within a state. They are an important component in maintaining the quality of education across the United States.

7-3c The State Department of Education

state department of education An agency that operates under the direction of the state board of education. Its functions include accrediting schools, certifying teachers, apportioning state school funds, conducting research, issuing reports, and coordinating state education policies with local school districts.

As a teacher, you are most likely to encounter in day-to-day work the **state department of education**. State departments of education usually operate under the direction of the state board of education and are administered by the chief state school officer. Traditionally, state departments of education primarily collected and disseminated statistics about the status of education within the state. Since the 1950s, however, state departments have taken on many other functions.[51] In short, they implement the laws of the state legislature and the regulations of the state board.

In the latter half of the twentieth century, state departments of education had to grapple with controversial issues such as desegregation, compensatory education, appropriate education for all students, student rights, school finance reform, and minimum competency testing. During the past decade, state departments, in addition to their traditional duties, have been required to develop accountability systems, implement statewide assessments, and develop data systems needed to support districts and schools.[52]

7-3d The Chief State School Officer

chief state school officer The chief executive of the state board of education; sometimes called the state superintendent or commissioner of education.

The **chief state school officer** (sometimes known as the state superintendent or commissioner of education) heads the state department of education and is also the chief

---

[48]NASBE, "State Boards of Education," at **www.nasbe.org/about-us/state-boards-of -education/** (January 22, 2015).

[49]NASBE "State Education Governance," *National Association of State Boards of Education* (July 2014), at **www.nasbe.org/about-us/state-boards-of-education/** (January 22, 2015).

[50]NASBE, "State Boards of Education," at **www.nasbe.org/about-us/state-boards-of -education/** (January 22, 2015).

[51]Fred C. Lunenburg and Allan C. Ornstein, *Educational Administration: Concepts and Practices,* 6th ed. (Belmont, CA: Wadsworth, 2011).

[52]Thomas J. Sergiovanni, Paul Kelleher, Martha McCarthy, and Frances Fowler, *Educational Governance and Administration,* 6th ed. (Boston: Allyn and Bacon, 2008); and Betheny Gross, Ashley Johim, Paul Hill, Larry Miller, Marguerite Roza, Kelly Hupfield, and Suzan Simburg, *The SEA of the Future: Building the Productivity Infrastructure* (Denver, CO: CRPE, 2014).

executive of the state board of education (if the state has one). He or she is most often a professional educator.

The office is filled in one of three ways: in 2014, fifteen states filled the position through appointment by the governor, twenty-three states through appointment by the state board of education, and twelve states by popular election. Additionally, as of 2015, two chief state school officers were African American; however, 44 percent of chief officers were women—an increase of 10 percent from four years earlier.[53] The greater number of women in the position represents a departure from the good-old-boy network that once dominated the upper echelons of educational administration.

The duties of chief state school officers and relationships between that position and state boards and state departments vary widely. Generally, an elected chief officer enjoys more independence than one who is appointed. It is interesting that in a thirty-three month period beginning in March of 2012, twenty-nine states replaced their state superintendent at least once. The high turnover has been attributed to the trend of state superintendents being held responsible for statewide student achievement results and to the political nature of the position; new governors generally prefer to have like-minded appointees in the position.[54]

FOCUS Talk to teachers and administrators in your local schools. In what ways do they see the state superintendent, state board of education, and state department of education affecting day-to-day school operations? Do they see this impact as positive or negative?

7-4 THE FEDERAL ROLE IN EDUCATION

We'll consider the federal government's role in four parts: (1) the federal agencies that promote educational policies and programs; (2) the trend that has shifted many educational decisions between the federal government and the state governments; (3) federal financing of education; and (4) the Supreme Court's decisions concerning education. In this chapter, we focus on the first two parts. Federal spending is examined in Chapter 8, Financing Public Education, and court decisions are discussed in Chapter 9, Legal Aspects of Education.

7-4a Federal Educational Agencies

During most of the nation's first 150 years, between 1787 and 1937, Congress enacted only a handful of significant educational laws. Since passage of the ESEA of 1965, however, hundreds of significant education laws have been passed by Congress.[55] Traditionally, the major organizations of teachers and administrators, such as the American Federation of Teachers, the National Education Association, and the National School Boards Association, have preferred that the federal government offer financial aid and special services but refrain from interfering in educational policy. Many educators now believe that the federal government has intruded on local and state responsibilities and added numerous unfunded mandates on state and local agencies struggling to improve the schools.[56]

The US Department of Education   Although many different federal agencies now encompass educational programs or activities, the **US Department of Education** is the primary federal educational agency. When the Department of Education was founded in 1867, as the Office of Education, its commissioner had a staff of three clerks and a

US Department of Education
A cabinet-level department in the executive branch of the federal government that is in charge of federal educational policy and the promotion of educational programs.

[53]NASBE, *State Education Governance Models: 2014* (Arlington, VA: National Association of State Boards of Education, 2014); and "Meet the Chiefs," *Council of Chief State School Officers* at **www.ccsso.org/who_we_are/meet_the_chiefs.html** (January 22, 2015).

[54]Andrew Ujifusa, "What's the Turnover for State Education Chiefs in Recent Years?" *Education Week's Blogs* (November 14, 2014) at **http://blogs.edweek.org/edweek/state_edwatch /2014/11/whats_the_turnover_for_state_education_chiefs_in_recent_years.html**.

[55]Don Wolfensberger, "Congress and Education Policy: ESEA at 40—The Evolving Federal Role in Education," *Woodrow Wilson International Center for Scholars* (March 2005) at **www.wilsoncenter.org/sites/default/files/education-intro.pdf** (January 22, 2015).

[56]Motoko Rich, "Holding States and Schools Accountable," *The New York Times* (February 10, 2013), p. A25.

total of $15,000 to spend. From those humble beginnings, the agency has grown to about 4,400 employees, and in 2012, its annual expenditures exceeded $99 billion. The department has the smallest staff of all the cabinet agencies, yet it has the third-largest discretionary budget.[57]

Over time, the Office of Education assumed the responsibilities of (1) administering grant funds and contracting with state departments of education, school districts, and colleges and universities; (2) engaging in educational innovation and research; and (3) providing leadership, consultative, and clearinghouse services related to education.

In 1979, after much congressional debate and controversy, the Office of Education was elevated to the Department of Education, with full cabinet-level status. A secretary of education was named, and the department officially opened in 1980.

The secretary of education has widespread visibility and influence. Besides advising the president, managing educational policies, and promoting programs to carry out those policies, the secretary can exert persuasion and pressure in political and educational circles. Over the years, secretaries of education—including William Bennett, Lauro Cavazos, Lamar Alexander, Richard Riley, Roderick Paige, Margaret Spelling, and Arne Duncan—have used the limelight to push their own brands of reform.[58] Current Secretary of Education Duncan has been extremely visible as he makes the case to reauthorize the ESEA.[59] The Technology @ School feature discusses Internet sources of information on the various levels of school governance.

7-4b Returning Responsibility to the Federal Government

In 2001, Congress approved President George W. Bush's educational reform initiative, the No Child Left Behind Act (NCLB), which increased the federal government's influence on education policy at the state and local levels. NCLB sought to improve low-performing schools and to hold states and local school districts accountable for all students meeting high standards as measured by annual performance tests in reading and mathematics. Local school districts that failed to improve student performance, especially in Title I schools, were required to offer parents the opportunity to choose other public schools or make available free tutoring programs.[60] Accountability pressure had superintendents, principals, and teachers scrambling to show increased test scores in reading and math to demonstrate that individual schools were making adequate yearly progress (AYP). Despite NCLB's far-reaching implications and somewhat increased funding levels, critics faulted NCLB as an "unfunded mandate" and for usurping the authority of state and local educational agencies.[61]

The Obama administration's education policy has continued under the framework of the NCLB Act, but it has implemented a number of important adjustments to the law,

[57]NCES, *Digest of Education Statistics*, 2012, "US Department of Education Outlays—Table 423," at **http://nces.ed.gov/programs/digest/d12/tables/dt12_423.asp** (January 2015); "About ED – Overview and Mission Statement," US Department of Education at **www2.ed.gov /about/landing.jhtml** (January 2015); and "About ED – The Federal Role in Education," US Department of Education at **www.ed.gov/about/overview/fed/role.html** (January 2015).

[58]Kenneth A. Dodge, Martha Putallaz, and David Malone, "Coming of Age: The Department of Education," *Phi Delta Kappan* (May 2002), pp. 674–676; and D. T. Stallings, *A Brief History of the United States Department of Education 1979–2002* (Durham, NC: Center for Child and Family Policy—Duke University, 2002) at **https://childandfamilypolicy.duke.edu/pdfs /pubpres/BriefHistoryofUS_DOE.pdf**.

[59]US Department of Education, "*US Education Secretary Arne Duncan Calls for Strong Education Law That Protects All Students, Ensures High-Quality Preschool, Supports Bold State and Local Innovation,*" (January 12, 2015) at **www.ed.gov/news/press-releases/us-education-secretary-arne -duncan-calls-strong-education-law-protects-all-stude**.

[60]*Helping Families by Supporting and Expanding School Choice*, US Department of Education (July 2008) at **www2.ed.gov/nclb/choice/schools/choicefacts.html** (January 23, 2015).

[61]Kimberly Scriven Berry and Carolyn D. Herrington, "States and Their Struggles with NCLB: Does the Obama Blueprint Get It Right?" *Peabody Journal of Education* (2011), pp. 272–290.

TECHNOLOGY @ SCHOOL

SCHOOL GOVERNANCE INFORMATION AVAILABLE ON THE INTERNET

As a prospective teacher, you can learn more about the different levels of school governance through research on the Internet. Below you will find the websites for the professional organizations of various school leaders that we have described in the chapter. Although the initial focus during your education career will be on classroom teaching and not administrative duties, these sites can be a valuable resource in your development as a professional educator.

Each of the sites provides up-to-date information about current issues that impact their respective constituencies. For example, the American Association of School Administrators (AASA), at its *Policy and Advocacy* page, provides access to its "Legislative Action Center," which describes the organization's position on various pieces of federal legislation, especially the reauthorization of ESEA. Each of the sites listed has a similar link; the National School Boards Association (NSBA) link is *Advocacy*, and the Education Commission of the States (ECS) has an *Education Issues A-Z* link. Examine these links at the various sites to discover which issues are on the radar for school leaders. What positions do the organizations take on the various issues (that is, accountability, charter schools, performance pay, Common Core State Standards, and so on)? How might these issues impact you as a classroom teacher?

In addition to the links to various reports and updated news, many sites are using different media to keep their membership informed. The National Association of Secondary School Principals (NASSP) has a page, the *School Leader's Review—Podcasts,* that allows you to subscribe to regularly posted discussions of important education topics. The Council of Chief State School Officers (CCSSO) site contains a link to the *Common Core Curriculum Implementation Video Series* that explains the standards in a series of video vignettes. Monitoring these sites will ensure that you are current with the education policy debates taking place around the country.

- National School Boards Association
- National Association of State Boards of Education
- Council of Chief State School Officers
- Education Commission of the States
- American Association of School Administrators
- National Association of Elementary School Principals
- National Association of Secondary School Principals
- US Department of Education Public Education Network (PEN)
- Center for Public Education

FOCUS What policies, programs, and recent changes in your local schools have been influenced by the president's education proposals? Are teachers in your local districts supportive of these efforts?

most notably flexibility to states regarding specific assessment proficiency requirements of NCLB in exchange for rigorous state-developed plans designed to close achievement gaps, increase equity, improve the quality of instruction, and increase outcomes for all students. For a majority of states, this has meant the adoption of the Common Core State Standards as the framework for "state-developed plans." As Secretary of Education Duncan urges reauthorization of the ESEA, it is evident that for the foreseeable future, the federal government will be influencing education policy that impacts local schools. While advocating for flexibility for schools and districts to design data-based improvement plans to increase achievement, the government assures its critics that it will not give districts a "pass" to avoid accountability.[62] Because schools function today in an era of accountability, new teachers will face rigorous expectations almost immediately, regardless of the level at which they teach. The key here is faculty cooperation and sharing, which is necessary for increased student academic achievement.

7-5 NONPUBLIC SCHOOLS

Although this chapter has focused on public education, nonpublic schools are not exempt from governmental influences. In particular, many state education laws apply to private and parochial schools as well as to public institutions—laws pertaining to

---

[62]*Elementary and Secondary Education Act*, US Department of Education at **www.ed.gov/esea** (January 23, 2015); and Maggie Severns, "The Plot to Overhaul No Child Left Behind," *Politico* (January 2, 2015).

health standards, building codes, child welfare, student codes, and so forth. In addition, legislative bodies in many states have passed laws to help private schools and to provide public-funded aid in such areas as student transportation, health services, dual enrollment or shared-time plans, school-lunch services, book and supply purchases, student testing services, student tuition, and student loans.

As indicated in Chapter 1, Motivation, Preparation, and Conditions for the Entering Teacher, nonpublic schools in 2011 accounted for slightly less than 10 percent of total enrollments in US elementary and secondary schools, or a total of 5.2 million students. Catholic schools still enroll the most private-school students, although their numbers have declined from 85 percent of all private-school students in 1969 to 39 percent in 2011. Nonsectarian, independent schools increased their share of students from 8 percent of private-school enrollments in 1969 to 22 percent in 2011. Conservative Christian school enrollments now account for 13.8 percent of nonpublic-school enrollment, down from a peak of approximately 16 percent in 2005–2006.[63]

Private schools typically operate differently from public schools. They have a principal or headmaster but generally lack the cadre of support people mentioned earlier in this chapter. They usually derive their authority from a board of directors or school committee, which, unlike a public-school board, addresses the operation of one particular private school.

Many commentators see public and private sectors as competing for students and for funds. Other educators, however, prefer to envision cooperation between public and private schools in an effort to meet the needs of students. In fact, certain distinctions between public and private schools are becoming blurred. For example, programs of *school choice* may include public charter schools; magnet and alternative schools; private independent and religious schools; virtual schools; and homeschooling. In some cases, there is a blending of the public and private by allowing students to apply public funds to a private education.[64] (Privatization is also discussed in Chapter 16, School Effectiveness and Reform in the United States, and school choice is covered in Chapter 8, Financing Public Education.)

FOCUS How many nonpublic schools are there in your area? What affiliations do they have with the various religious denominations? Examine the governance structure of at least one school.

SUMMING UP

1. The governance of education is organized on four governmental levels: local, intermediate (in some states), state, and federal.

2. Schools are organized into school districts; approximately 13,600 public-school districts currently operate in the United States.

3. At the local level, the school board, the school superintendent, the central office staff, and school principals all take part in governing and administering the schools.

4. Educators have attempted to increase parent and community involvement in the schools. Forms of public

involvement include community participation, community control, community schools, and charter schools.

5. Educators have long debated the optimum size for schools and school districts. Many believe that increases in size do not necessarily mean increases in efficiency or effectiveness and might result in the opposite.

6. Small and rural school districts continue to undergo significant consolidation, a movement that began in the 1930s.

7. More than half of the states have one or more intermediate units that support local school districts and assist districts in meeting their needs.

---

[63]Allan C. Ornstein, "The Growing Popularity of Private Schools," *Clearing House* (January 1990), pp. 210–213; and NCES, "Enrollment and Percentage Distribution of Students Enrolled in Private Elementary and Secondary Schools, by School Orientation and Grade Level," *Digest of Education Statistics 2013* at **http://nces.ed.gov/programs/digest/d13/tables/dt13_205.20.asp** (January 23, 2015).

[64]Bruno V. Manno, "The New Marketplace of School Choice," *Education Week* (December 1, 2010), pp. 24–25; and Tamara Wilder Linkow, "Disconnected Reform: The Proliferation of School Choice Options in US School Districts," *Journal of School Choice* (October 2011), pp. 414–443.

8. In most states, the legislature is primarily responsible for establishing and maintaining public schools and has broad powers to enact laws pertaining to school education.
9. All states except New Mexico, Wisconsin, and Minnesota have state boards of education. The state boards oversee state departments of education headed by the chief state school officer.
10. Overall, the federal role in education has dramatically expanded since the 1950s. Federal policy in the twenty-first century has given increasing influence over education to the federal government.
11. Nonpublic schools account for approximately 10 percent of total enrollments in US elementary and secondary schools, with Catholic schools comprising almost 39 percent of these enrollments, and nonreligious, independent schools 22 percent.

SUGGESTED RESOURCES

INTERNET RESOURCES

Visit the US Department of Education's home page to evaluate the pages for the major stakeholders addressed in this chapter: students, parents, teachers, and administrators. Take the time to fully explore the other various pages for information about fellowships, lesson plans, ideas for organizing instruction, blogs, online workshops and webinars, and answers to FAQs.

You may also find Secretary Duncan's Facebook page or Twitter feed useful. Follow him around the country as he promotes the administration's education reform efforts. This resource will ensure that you are up to date on the issues being promoted by the Obama administration.

PUBLICATIONS

Auerbach, Susan, ed., *School Leadership for Authentic Family and Community Partnerships: Research Perspectives for Transforming Practice.* New York: Routledge, 2012. *Provides information for school leaders to pursue meaningful partnerships with families and community groups, so they can build relationships, dialogue, and power-share to develop socially just, democratic schools.*

Kahlenberg, Richard D., and Halley Potter. *A Smarter Charter: Finding What Works for Charter Schools and Public Education.* New York: Teachers College Press, 2014. *Takes a comprehensive look at the topic of charter schools from their origins to current research on various facets of the topic.*

Maeroff, Gene I. *School Boards in America: A Flawed Exercise in Democracy.* New York: Palgrave Macmillan, 2010. *Gives an inside view of local school boards and how they work.*

Nash, Ron, and Kathleen Hwang. *Collaborative School Leadership: Practical Strategies for Principals.* Lanham, MD: Rowman & Littlefield Publishers, 2013. *Emphasizes ways that principals can develop a school environment where all stakeholders pursue school improvement.*

Ravitch, Diane. *The Death and Life of the Great American School System: How Testing and Choice Are Undermining Education.* New York: Basic Books, 2010. *Examines issues such as school choice, evaluating the quality of teaching, and charter schools. Ravitch advocates for strong educational values and the revival of strong neighborhood public schools.*

Reed, Douglas S. *Building the Federal Schoolhouse: Localism and the American Education State.* New York: Oxford University Press, 2014. *Examines fifty years of federal education policy and expanding influence of the federal government on local schools.*

Sergiovanni, Thomas J. *The Principalship: A Reflective Practice Perspective,* 6th ed. Boston: Pearson, 2009. *A comprehensive examination of the role of the principal in the complex schools of today.*

Walser, Nancy. *The Essential School Board Book: Better Governance in the Age of Accountability.* Boston: Harvard Education Press, 2009. *Discusses strategies that school boards can incorporate to increase student achievement.*

Warren, Mark R., and Karen L. Mapp. *A Match on Dry Grass: Community Organizing as a Catalyst for School Reform.* Oxford: Oxford University Press, 2011. *Based on a national study, the book presents case studies of organizing efforts by parents.*

CHAPTER **8**

FINANCING PUBLIC EDUCATION

LEARNING OBJECTIVES

8-1 Analyze property taxes as a school revenue source and the problems created by relying on this form of taxation for local school support.

8-2 Examine how states generate revenue to fund education, and describe how those funds are distributed to local school districts.

8-3 Describe the federal government's responsibilities in financing PreK–12 public schooling.

8-4 Identify major issues that have impacted the efforts to reform school finance, and describe how the recent economic climate affects school finances.

Littleny/Shutterstock.com

This chapter was revised by Dr. David Vocke, Towson University.

EDUCATION IN THE UNITED STATES is big business. By 2012, public-education (K–12) revenue was more than $594 billion annually, and elementary and secondary education represented approximately 4.1 percent of the nation's annual gross domestic product.[1] The three major sources of revenue for public schools are local, state, and federal governments, and education consumes a significant portion of the budget for each of these entities. Although the percentages of funds provided by these three sources have changed, the total amount of money available for schools concerns most local school districts. During shifts in economic conditions, the business of schooling is forced to respond to the ups and downs of the changes. In a survey of local school board members, almost 92 percent of respondents identified "budget/funding" as an extremely or very urgent issue for their district.[2] This chapter explores the mechanics of education funding and the overall changes in school financing in recent years. Today's educators must deal with budget fluctuations, equity and adequacy in school financing, accountability, and various plans to restructure the system of financial support.

8-1 TAX SOURCES OF SCHOOL REVENUES

Public-school funding relies primarily on revenues generated from taxes, especially local property taxes and state sales and income taxes (Photo 8.1). Policy makers realize that some taxes are considered fairer than others. Most people today accept the following criteria for evaluating taxes:

1. *A tax should not cause unintended economic distortions.* It should not change consumer-spending patterns or cause the relocation of business, industry, or people.
2. *A tax should be equitable.* It should be based on the taxpayer's ability to pay. Those with greater incomes or with greater property worth should pay more taxes. Taxes of this sort are called **progressive taxes**. Inequitable taxes and those that require lower-income groups to pay a higher proportion of their income than higher-income groups are called **regressive taxes**.
3. *A tax should be easily collected.* Administration by the responsible agency and ability to comply with the requirements by the taxpayer should be simple.[3]
4. *The tax should respond to changing economic conditions,* rising during inflation and decreasing in a recession.[4] Responsive taxes are *elastic;* those not responsive are *inelastic.*

progressive taxes Taxes based on the taxpayer's ability to pay, for example, income taxes.

regressive taxes Taxes that require lower-income groups to pay relatively more of their income than higher-income groups.

As we review the various taxes collected to support public schools, note the impact they have on the spectrum of America's taxpayers.

8-1a Local Financing for Public Schools

Although states are responsible for education, traditionally much of this responsibility has fallen to local school districts. Overview 8.1 summarizes governmental income sources and spending patterns for education at local, state, and federal levels.

[1]National Center for Education Statistics, "Table 106.10—Expenditures of Education Institutions Related to Gross Domestic Product, By Level of Institution," *Digest of Education Statistics 2013* at **http://nces.ed.gov/programs/digest/d13/tables/dt13_106.10.asp**.
[2]Frederick M. Hess and Olivia Meeks, *School Boards Circa 2010: Governance in the Accountability Era* (Alexandria, VA: National School Boards Association, 2010).
[3]Allan R. Odden and Lawrence O. Picus, *School Finance: A Policy Perspective*, 4th ed. (Boston: McGraw-Hill, 2008).
[4]James W. Guthrie, Mathew G. Springer, R. Anthony Rolle, and Eric A. Houck, *Modern Education Finance and Policy* (Boston: Pearson/Allyn and Bacon, 2007).

Marjorie Kamys Cotera/Bob Daemmrich Photography/Alamy

> **PHOTO 8.1** Taxes are major sources of both local and state school funding. Property taxes, personal income taxes, and sales taxes provide much school funding. Historically, some citizens in many parts of the country have resisted tax increases.

As indicated earlier, local contributions to school financing have decreased over the past several decades but still amount to more than 44 percent of total school expenditures.

property tax The main source of revenues for local school districts, based on the value of real property (land and improvements on land).

8-1b Property Tax

Property tax is the main source of tax revenue for local school districts, accounting for 74.2 percent of local tax revenue received. Connecticut, New Hampshire,

---

OVERVIEW 8.1

OTHER INCOME SOURCES BY LEVEL AND SPENDING PATTERN

Level	Income Sources	Spending Patterns
Local	• Property tax • Exclusive product rights • Special taxes and user fees	Funding goes to local schools in the district. Districts vary widely in their ability to fund their schools, and state aid does not always equalize the discrepancies.
State	• Personal income tax • Sales tax • Excise taxes • Corporate income tax • Lotteries	States vary in ability to finance education. Local districts are funded using combinations of four plans: flat grant, foundation, power-equalizing, or weighted student. Many states are striving to provide an adequate education for all students.
Federal	• US Treasury	Funding is distributed primarily to states for designated purposes, such as assisting students in low-income schools, developing new assessments, and providing special education.

New Jersey, and Rhode Island are most reliant on property taxes to generate local revenue.[5]

Property taxes are determined by first arriving at the *market value* of a property—the probable selling price for the property. In most states, the market value is converted to an *assessed value* using a predetermined index or ratio, such as one-fourth or one-third; for example, a property with a market value of $200,000 might have an assessed value of only $50,000. The assessed value is generally less than the market value. Finally, the local tax rate, often expressed in mills, is applied to the assessed value. A **mill** represents one-thousandth of a dollar; thus, a tax rate of 25 mills amounts to $25 for each $1,000 of assessed value (or $25 × 50 = $1,250 tax). Levying of property taxes is often dependent upon approval of the local voters; passage of such tax levies can be difficult during tough economic times.

Property tax is not considered to be an equitable tax and is difficult and costly to administer. Differing assessment practices and lack of uniform valuation may lead people owning equivalent properties to pay different taxes. Also, the property tax may fail to distribute the tax burden according to ability to pay. A retired couple may have a home whose market value has increased substantially over the years, along with their taxes, but because they live on a relatively low fixed income, they cannot afford the increasing taxes. In this respect, the property tax is regressive.[6]

In addition, the property tax is not immediately responsive to changing economic conditions. Some states reassess properties every one to two years, but others reassess only every three to four years. Thus a property's assessed value and actual tax are often based on outdated market conditions.

8-1c Other Sources of Local Funding

In addition to the property tax, local school districts can gather revenues through special income taxes and other taxes or fees. Some municipalities, especially small villages and towns, depend on such sources as traffic fines and building permits to help raise revenues for the local coffers.

User fees are a type of special assessment charged for select services and materials in public schools. User fees can be levied on bus service, textbooks, laptops, extracurricular activities, and after-school centers. School districts are more often charging students to participate in sports, which is a form of a user fee. User fees tend to be utilized more frequently when school districts face budget shortfalls. Because they are not based on ability to pay, user fees are considered a regressive tax.[7]

A growing number of school boards have signed lucrative contracts with corporations for **exclusive product rights** and exclusive naming rights. Exclusive rights contracts allow districts or their schools to receive payments for the right to be a sole provider of a service or product. For example, schools will sign an exclusive product contract with a soft drink company to allow only that particular brand to be sold on school property in exchange for a set fee. School districts have also developed fund-raising campaigns

mill A unit of the local tax rate representing one-thousandth of a dollar.

user fees Special fees charged specifically to those who use a facility or service (for example, recreational facilities, bus service, or after-school centers).

exclusive product rights Special privileges whereby commercial enterprises pay a fee for the exclusive right to market their product (for example, Pepsi) in the school district.

---

[5]"Revenues for Public Elementary and Secondary Schools, by Source of Funds and State or Jurisdiction: 2010–11," *Digest of Education Statistics 2013* at **http://nces.ed.gov/programs /digest/d13/tables/dt13_235.20.asp?current=yes**; and Jeffrey L. Barnett, Cindy L. Sheckells, Scott Peterson, and Elizabeth M. Tydings, 2012 Census of Governments: Finance: *State and Local Government Finance Summary Report* (Washington, DC: US Census Bureau, December 17, 2014); and "Local Property Taxes as a Percentage of Local Tax Revenue: Selected Years 1977–2012," *Tax Policy Center* (January 12, 2015) at **www.taxpolicycenter.org/taxfacts /displayafact.cfm?Docid=518**.

[6]"Property Taxes," *The Institute on Taxation & Economic Policy (ITEP)* at **www.itep.org/tax _topics/property_taxes.php** (January 30, 2015).

[7]Fred C. Lunenburg, "The Practice of Charging User Fees in Public Schools," *Schooling* (January 2010); Stephanie Simon, "Public Schools Charge Kids for Basics, Frills," *Wall Street Journal— Eastern Edition* (May 25, 2011), pp. A1–A14; and Scott Laffee, "The Affordability Question," *School Administrator* (February 2012), pp. 27–34.

with corporate sponsors, generating everything from cash donations to new stadiums, scoreboards, and equipment purchases in exchange for advertising the donor's services. Nevertheless, these contracts are negotiated on a district-by-district basis, with some districts benefiting handsomely while others struggle to fund their school district budgets. A recent study found that approximately 70 percent of high schools and half of the nation's middle schools have exclusive drink contracts.[8] The Taking Issue box debates school-based commercial activities.

8-1d Local Resources and Disparities

tax base Basis upon which taxes to support public schools are assessed at state and local levels—for example, property tax, sales tax, or income tax.

Despite state and federal aid, some school districts have greater difficulty supporting education than others do. A school district located in a wealthy area or an area with a broad **tax base** (for example, expensive residential neighborhoods, shopping malls, businesses, and industry) generates more revenue than a poor school district. As a result, in most states, the wealthiest school districts often spend two to three times more per student than the poorest school districts do. As we discuss later in this chapter, state courts and legislatures have attempted to reduce these disparities through reforms in the system of educational finance. In most states, however, substantial disparities in funding persist, and the recession that began in 2007 exacerbated the problem as most states had to reduce revenue and resources provided to the public schools.[9]

municipal overburden Severe financial crunch caused by population density and a high proportion of disadvantaged and low-income groups.

Although financial problems affect many rural and suburban districts, the greatest financial troubles are usually found in large cities. Cities are plagued by what is commonly called **municipal overburden**, a severe financial crunch caused by high population density, a high proportion of low-income citizens, and aging infrastructure. The additional spending needed for social services and infrastructure upkeep prevents large cities from generating enough tax revenue to meet all of the demands on the city's budget.

Another problem is that city schools have a greater proportion of special-needs students—namely, English language learners, students in poverty, and students with disabilities. This growing number of students often requires programs and related services that are consuming a larger portion of education funding nationally.[10]

FOCUS Are budget constraints impacting local schools in your area? Is the school infrastructure in local school districts in need of updating?

Despite their dire need for more revenues, cities often cannot realistically raise property taxes. Ironically, tax increases contribute to the decline of urban schools because they cause businesses and middle-income residents to depart for the suburbs, which tend to have a lower tax burden. Thus, the city's tax base is undermined. Declining services due to lack of revenues also cause residents to leave—a no-win situation.

8-2   STATE FINANCING OF PUBLIC SCHOOLS

Although the states have delegated many educational powers and responsibilities to local school districts, each state remains legally responsible for educating its children and youth, and the states' portion of education funding has increased steadily; elementary and secondary education now account for the largest category in the percentage

---

[8]"905.00 Commercial Activities," Quaker Valley School District (January 22, 2013) at **www .qvsd.org/pageprint.cfm?p=5896&keywords=Search** (January 31, 2015); and Sarah Sparks, "Commercialism in US Elementary and Secondary School Nutrition Environments," *Education Week* (January 22, 2014), p. 5.

[9]Bruce Baker, David Sciarra, and Danielle Fairrie, *Is School Funding Fair? A National Report Card*, 3rd ed. (Newark, NJ: Education Law Center, 2013); and Bruce D. Baker, *America's Most Financially Disadvantaged School Districts and How They Got That Way* (Washington, DC: Center for American Progress, July 2014) at **https://cdn.americanprogress.org/wp-content/uploads/2014/07 /BakerSchoolDistricts.pdf**.

[10]"In Fairness to Cities," *Scientific American* (September 2011), p. 14; "Individuals with Disabilities Education Act – Cost Impact on Local School Districts," *Federal Education Budget Project* (Washington, DC: New America Foundation, April 25, 2014); and *Good News about Urban Public Schools* (Washington, DC: The Council of the Great City Schools, October 2014).

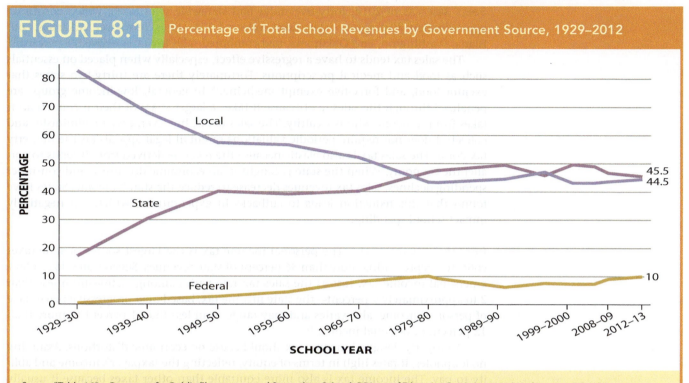

FIGURE 8.1 Percentage of Total School Revenues by Government Source, 1929–2012

Source: "Table 162 – Revenues for Public Elementary and Secondary Schools," *Digest of Education Statistics, 2007* (Washington, DC: US Department of Education, National Center for Education Statistics, 2008) at **http://nces.ed.gov/programs/digest/d07/tables/dt07_162.asp**; "Table 1 – Revenues and Percentage Distribution of Revenues for Public Elementary and Secondary Education," *Revenues and Expenditures for Public Elementary and Secondary Education, School Year 2008–2009* (Washington, DC: US Department of Education, National Center for Education Statistics, June 2011) at **http://nces.ed.gov/pubs2011/expenditures/tables/table_01.asp**; and "Percentage Distribution of Public Elementary-Secondary School System Revenue by Source and State," *American FactFinder* (May 22, 2014) at **http://factfinder.census.gov/faces/tableservices/jsf/pages /productview.xhtml?pid=SSF_2012_SSF005.US01&prodType=tabl**.

of state spending at 25 percent.[11] In this section, we look at the principal types of state taxes used to finance education, variations in school funding from state to state, methods by which state aid is apportioned among local districts, and the role of state courts in promoting school finance reform.

8-2a State Revenue Sources

sales tax A tax based on purchase of taxable goods (generally not food or services).

personal income tax A tax based on a percentage of personal income.

Sales taxes and **personal income taxes** are the two major state revenue sources. Because states currently pay approximately 45 percent of the cost of public elementary and secondary education (see Figure 8.1), these two taxes are important elements in the overall support of public schools.[12] As Figure 8.1 shows, revenues from federal sources have increased from less than half a percent in 1929–1930 to 10 percent currently. State contributions also rose from less than 17 percent in 1929–1930 to just more than 45 percent by 2013. As state and federal contributions have risen, local revenues have fallen in proportion, from more than 82 percent to 44.5 percent.[13]

[11]*Policy Basics: Where Do Our State Tax Dollars Go?* (Washington, DC: The Center on Budget and Policy Priorities: March 27, 2014) at **www.cbpp.org/files/policybasics-statetaxdollars.pdf**.

[12]**Mark** Dixon, *Public Education Finance: 2012* (Washington, DC: US Census Bureau, May 2014) at **www2.census.gov/govs/school/12f33pub.pdf**.

[13]US Census Bureau, "Percentage Distribution of Public Elementary-Secondary School System Revenue by Source and State," *American FactFinder* (May 22, 2014) at **http://factfinder .census.gov/faces/tableservices/jsf/pages/productview.xhtml?pid=SSF_2012 _SSF005.US01&prodType=table**.

Sales Tax As of 2014, forty-five states had statewide sales taxes, which constitute approximately 30 percent of state taxes collected. Five states, Tennessee, Arkansas, Louisiana, Washington, and Oklahoma, had combined sales tax rates above 8.5 percent.[14]

The sales tax tends to have a regressive effect, especially when placed on essentials such as food and medical prescriptions. Fortunately there are thirty-two states that exempt food, and forty-five exempt medicine.[15] In general, low-income groups are penalized through the sales tax because it takes a larger share of their income than it takes from someone who is wealthy. The sales tax is, however, easy to administer and collect; it does not require periodic valuations or entail legal appeals (as the property tax does). The sales tax is also elastic because the revenue derived from it tends to parallel the economy. When the state is caught in an economic downturn and consumer spending declines, sales tax revenues decrease to reduce the state's income. States have found that this reduction leads to cutbacks in expenditures, which can negatively impact school spending.[16]

Personal Income Tax The personal income tax is the largest source of state taxes collected, representing more than 36 percent of state revenues. Seven states do not levy a personal income tax. Just as the sales tax rate varies among states—from less than 2 to approximately 9 percent—the state income tax, based on a progressive percentage of personal income, also varies and may range from less than 1 percent to more than 12 percent of personal income.[17]

A properly designed income tax should cause no economic distortions. Assuming no loopholes, it rates high in terms of equity, reflecting the taxpayer's income and ability to pay. The income tax is also more equitable than other taxes because it usually considers special circumstances of the taxpayer, such as dependents, illness, disability, and the like. In a number of states, state income taxes have become more progressive because of the Earned Income Tax Credit, and several states have eliminated taxes on poor families altogether.[18]

The personal income tax is easy to collect, usually through payroll deductions. It is also highly elastic, allowing state government to vary rates according to the economy. However, its elasticity makes it vulnerable to recession, which drives income revenue down.

Other State Taxes Other state taxes contribute limited amounts to education but provide revenue for the state budget. These include (1) excise taxes on motor fuel, liquor, and tobacco products; (2) estate and gift taxes; (3) severance taxes (on the output of minerals and oils); and (4) corporate income taxes.

Another trend that emerged in the past fifty years has been to establish state lotteries and other gaming enterprises, such as casinos, to support education. Although

---

[14]"2013 State Tax Collection by Source," *Federation of Tax Administrators* at **www.taxadmin .org/fta/rate/13taxdis.html** (January 30, 2015); and "State and Local Sales Tax Rates in 2014," *Tax Foundation* (March 18, 2014) at **http://taxfoundation.org/article/state-and -local-sales-tax-rates-2014**.

[15]"State Sales Tax Rates and Food & Drug Exemptions," *Federation of Tax Administrators – January 2015* at **www.taxadmin.org/fta/rate/sales.pdf** (January 2015).

[16]Institute on Taxation and Economic Policy, "Tax Fairness Fundamentals," *Fair State and Local Taxes* (Washington, DC: ITEP, 2011) at **www.itep.org/pdf/guide1.pdf** (January 30, 2015).

[17]"2013 State Tax Collection by Source (2013)," *Federation of Tax Administrators* at **www.taxadmin .org/fta/rate/13taxdis.html** (January 30, 2015); Rick Olin and Sandy Swain, *Individual Income Tax Provisions in the States* (Madison, WI: Wisconsin Legislative Fiscal Bureau, January 2013); "State and Local Sales Tax Rates in 2014," *Tax Foundation* (March 18, 2014) at **http:// taxfoundation.org/article/state-and-local-sales-tax-rates-2014**; and "State Individual Income Taxes," *Federation of Tax Administrators* (December 2014).

[18]Carl Davis, Kelly Davis, Matthew Gardner, Harley Heimovitz, Sebastian Johnson, Robert S. McIntyre, Richard Phillips, Alla Sapozhnikova, and Meg Wiehe, *Who Pays? A Distribution Analysis of the Tax Systems in All 50 States*, 5th ed. (Washington, DC: Institute on Taxation and Economic Policy, January 2015).

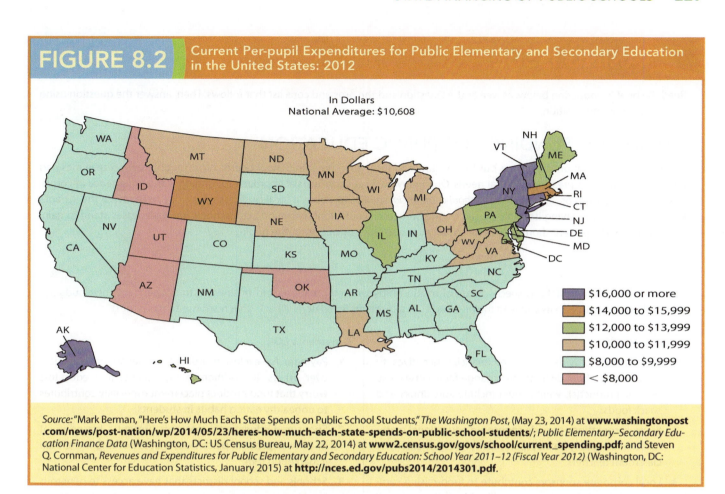

FIGURE 8.2 Current Per-pupil Expenditures for Public Elementary and Secondary Education in the United States: 2012

In Dollars
National Average: $10,608

$16,000 or more
$14,000 to $15,999
$12,000 to $13,999
$10,000 to $11,999
$8,000 to $9,999
< $8,000

Source: "Mark Berman, "Here's How Much Each State Spends on Public School Students," *The Washington Post*, (May 23, 2014) at **www.washingtonpost.com/news/post-nation/wp/2014/05/23/heres-how-much-each-state-spends-on-public-school-students/**; *Public Elementary–Secondary Education Finance Data* (Washington, DC: US Census Bureau, May 22, 2014) at **www2.census.gov/govs/school/current_spending.pdf**; and Steven Q. Cornman, *Revenues and Expenditures for Public Elementary and Secondary Education: School Year 2011–12 (Fiscal Year 2012)* (Washington, DC: National Center for Education Statistics, January 2015) at **http://nces.ed.gov/pubs2014/2014301.pdf**.

this was a major purpose of the early lotteries, funds have been diverted to the general fund of state budgets to meet other social priorities such as health care, social welfare agencies, and road construction. As a result, in most of the forty-four states where lotteries currently exist and the thirty states that offer other forms of legalized gambling, a majority dedicates a portion of lottery revenues for education, but the lottery actually contributes less than 5 percent of those states' total revenue allocated to education. Lotteries are regressive because more low-income individuals play the lottery than do high-income individuals, and they spend larger percentages of their annual income on it.[19]

8-2b States' Ability to Finance Education

Some students are more fortunate than others, simply by geographic accident. State residence has a lot to do with the type and quality of education a child receives. In 2012, eight states spent more than $15,000 per year to educate the average student. In contrast, thirteen states spent less than $9,000 per student. Utah and Idaho spent approximately $6,500 per student (see Figure 8.2).[20]

---

[19]Matt Villano, "All In: Gambling Options Proliferate Across USA," *USA Today* (January 26, 2013); Liz Malm and Ellen Kant, *The Sources of State and Local Tax Revenues* (Washington, DC: Tax Foundation, January 28, 2013); Bryce Covert, "Why State Lotteries Never Live Up to Their Promises," *ThinkProgress* (February 25, 2014) at **http://thinkprogress.org/economy/2014/02/25/3326421/state-lottery-education/**; and "Lottery Results," *USA.gov* (January 29, 2015) at **www.usa.gov/Topics/Lottery-Results.shtml**.

[20]Steven Q. Cornman, *Revenues and Expenditures for Public Elementary and Secondary Education: School Year 2011–12 (Fiscal Year 2012)* (Washington, DC: National Center for Education Statistics, January 2015) at **http://nces.ed.gov/pubs2014/2014301.pdf**.

TAKING ISSUE

Read the brief introduction below, as well as the Question and the pros and cons list that follows. Then, answer the question using *your* own words and position.

EXPANDING FUNDING FOR PUBLIC EDUCATION

Funding public education is a serious burden for state and local governments. School boards have sought new tax revenues and creative ways to meet pressing financial needs. One innovative yet controversial approach to funding is the emergence of corporate–school relationships, also known as *school commercialism*. For example, a local business might pay to renovate the school's gym in exchange for having its name placed on the basketball court floor. Although both schools and businesses stand to gain, these relationships present thorny issues for school administrators, as well as for the public.

Question

Should school boards establish special financial relationships with corporations and businesses to supplement their budgets? (Think about this question as you read the PRO and CON arguments listed here. What is *your* response to this issue?)

Arguments PRO	Arguments CON
1. Corporations provide significant financial incentives to schools and school districts in exchange for exclusive use of their product(s), which could include soft drinks and snack foods.	1. Payment for exclusive product use favors one business over others. In addition, many parents and educators worry that food product placement especially contributes to unhealthy eating habits in students.
2. Some corporations provide sponsored educational materials that can easily be incorporated into the curriculum by classroom teachers.	2. Sponsored educational materials present a biased point of view or product placement that is nothing more than a marketing tool.
3. Local corporate sponsors contribute to fund-raising campaigns for needed upgrades to build stadiums, install scoreboards, or renovate auditoriums.	3. Schools and school districts that have access to generous local sponsors receive favored treatment, while others struggle to fund their school district budgets. Schools in low-income areas may have trouble recruiting benefactors.
4. Providing exclusive naming rights for school facilities in exchange for contributions is a way to recognize the philanthropic efforts of the corporate entity.	4. Businesses engaged in exclusive naming rights are granted a captive audience of young consumers for a relatively small investment.
5. Partnerships between schools and the business community provide an integrated effort to improve the educational program in local schools in a time of funding shortfalls.	5. Children are exposed to advertising in all realms of life. School should provide an environment free of marketing messages and implicit endorsements of particular brands.

Question Reprise: What Is Your Stand?

Reflect on the following question by explaining *your* stand about this issue: Should school boards establish special financial relationships with corporations and businesses to supplement their budgets?

Do these figures mean that some states set their education priorities higher than other states do? No, they reflect what states can afford, which has much to do with the personal incomes and property values of their inhabitants. We must consider what the states spend on all other services and functions, such as medical care, transportation, and human services.

Since the beginning of the recession in 2007, the downturn in the national economy has had a negative impact on state budgets and their ability to fund vital services such as K–12 schooling. As a result, at least thirty-five states have provided less funding per student to local school districts in the 2013–2014 school year, and per-pupil funding has been cut by more than 10 percent from prerecession levels in fourteen states. Oklahoma and Alabama have reduced funding by more than 20 percent from pre-2008 levels.[21]

Educational Support and Aging Baby Boomers   Another factor that diminishes states' abilities to finance public education is an aging population. The average age of the US population is projected to continue growing as it has since 1900, largely due to the baby boom generation reaching retirement age. The proportion of people older than 65 was 4.1 percent in 1900. In 2000, it was 12.4 percent and will likely be greater than 20 percent by 2030.[22] Older people who no longer have children in school are generally more resistant to increased taxes for schools. Yet government per capita costs for the elderly are more than double those for children, which is due largely to spending on Social Security and Medicare benefits provided to retirees.[23]

The increase in average age is a nationwide trend; however, some parts of the country are graying faster than others. According to the 2010 census, fourteen of the twenty-one "oldest" states are in the Northeast and Midwest, where the graying population is more likely to be reluctant to provide financial and political support for schools.[24] In contrast, areas with a higher concentration of youth can offset the growing influence of older age groups.

8-2c State Aid to Local School Districts

States use four basic methods to finance public education. Some states have financial strategies that combine methods.[25]

1. *Flat grant model.* This is the oldest and most unequal method of financing schools. State aid to local school districts is based on a fixed amount multiplied by the number of students in attendance. This fails to consider students with special needs (English Language Learners cost more to educate than do native English speakers), special programs (vocational and special education), or the wealth of school districts.

   The remaining three methods each pursue greater equality of educational opportunity by allocating more funds to school districts in greatest need of assistance.

2. *Foundation plan.* This most common approach—thirty-six states use a variation of this plan—guarantees a minimum annual expenditure per student to all school districts in the state. However, reformers usually consider the minimum level too low, and wealthy school districts easily exceed it. School districts with a high percentage of children from low-income families suffer with this plan.

3. *Power-equalizing plan.* Each school district retains the right to establish its own expenditure levels, but the state pays a percentage of local school expenditures

[21]Michael Leachman and Chris Mai, "Most States Funding Schools Less Than Before the Recession," *The Center on Budget and Policy Priorities* (May 20, 2014) at **www.cbpp.org/cms/index .cfm?fa=view&id=4011**.

[22]Administration on Aging, *Projected Future Growth of the Older Population* (Washington, DC: Administration for Community Living, n.d.) at **www.aoa.acl.gov/Aging_Statistics /future_growth/future_growth.aspx#age** (February 1, 2015).

[23]Jeffrey S. Passel, "Demography of Immigrant Youth: Past, Present, and Future," *Future of Children* (Spring 2011), pp. 19–41; and Jennifer M. Ortman, Victoria A. Velkoff, and Howard Hogan, *An Aging Nation: The Older Population in the United States, Current Population Reports, P25-1140* (Washington, DC: US Census Bureau, 2014).

[24]Linda A. Jacobsen, Mary Kent, Marlene Lee, and Mark Mather, "America's Aging Population," *Population Bulletin 66*, no. 1 (2011); and "Resident Population by Age and State: 2010," *The 2012 Statistical Abstract* (Washington, DC: The US Census Bureau, 2011) at **www.census.gov /compendia/statab/cats/population.html**.

[25]Amy M. Hightower, Hajime Mitani, and Christopher B. Swanson, *State Policies That Pay: A Survey of School Finance Policies and Outcomes* (Bethesda, MD: Editorial Projects in Education, Inc., 2010); and Michael Griffith, "Understanding State School Funding," *The Progress of Education Reform* (Denver, CO: The Education Commission of the States, June 2012) at **www.ecs.org /clearinghouse/01/02/86/10286.pdf**.

based on district wealth and taxation effort. Wealthier school districts receive fewer matching state dollars, and poorer districts receive more.

4. *Weighted student plan.* Students are weighted in proportion to their special characteristics (for example, special needs, low-income) or special programs (for example, vocational or English for Speakers of Other Languages [ESOL]) to determine the cost of instruction per student. For example, a state might provide $4,000 for each regular student, one and a half times that amount ($6,000) for vocational students, and two times that amount ($8,000) for students with special needs. This plan is often used in conjunction with the foundation plan and at least thirty-seven states employ this approach.[26]

8-2d The Courts and School Finance Reform

Efforts to equalize educational opportunities among school districts within a state have been spurred by a series of court decisions that have fundamentally changed the financing of public education in most states. The 1971 landmark decision in *Serrano v. Priest* radically altered the way California allocated education funds. California, like nearly all the states, depended primarily on local property taxes to support the schools, and plaintiffs argued that this system of financing resulted in unconstitutional disparities in expenditures between wealthy and poor school districts. The California Supreme Court agreed and declared the state's funding formula unconstitutional.

After the *Serrano* decision, the US Supreme Court ruled in 1973 in *San Antonio v. Rodriguez* that expenditure disparities based on differences in local property taxes between school districts in a state were not unconstitutional under the US Constitution but might be unconstitutional under state constitutions. The *Rodriguez* decision placed the issue of inequities in school finance in the hands of the state courts and legislatures, where many believed it belonged.[27]

Since *Rodriguez*, certain state courts have ruled that school financing arrangements are unconstitutional if they result in large disparities in per-pupil expenditures based on wealth differences among school districts. For example, in *Rose v. Council for Better Education* (1989), the Kentucky Supreme Court declared the entire state educational system, including the method of funding schools with property taxes, unconstitutional. This decision prompted the legislature to hike average education spending some 30 percent and to undertake an extensive plan of educational reform (described in Chapter 16, School Effectiveness and Reform in the United States).[28] In all, forty-five of the fifty states have encountered lawsuits challenging state methods of funding public schools.[29] The From Preservice to Practice box shows how teachers might be affected by the distribution of money to local school districts in their states.

Recent state court decisions have focused on both adequacy, providing adequate resources to help students meet the call for higher student achievement, and equity, the belief that students in low-income school districts have the right to the same

---

[26]"Funding, Formulas, and Fairness," *Education Law Center* (February 2013) at **www.elc-pa.org/wp-content/uploads/2013/02/ELC_schoolfundingreport.2013.pdf**.

[27]Camille Walsh, "Erasing Race, Dismissing Class: San Antonio Independent School District v. Rodriguez," *Berkeley La Raza Law Journal* (March 2011), pp. 133–171.

[28]David J. Hoff, "The Bottom Line," *Education Week* (January 6, 2005), pp. 28–36; and Anne Rebecca Newman, "Transforming a Moral Right into a Legal Right: The Case of School Finance Litigation and the Right to Education," *Philosophy of Education Society* (2006), pp. 82–90.

[29]Allan R. Odden and Lawrence O. Picus, *School Finance: A Policy Perspective,* 4th ed. (Boston: McGraw Hill, 2008), pp. 42–43; and "School Funding Litigation Overview," *Access Quality Education* (March 2013) at **http://schoolfunding.info/legal-developments/**.

FROM PRESERVICE TO PRACTICE

FUNDING WOES

"Can you believe the budget cuts that were proposed at last night's school board meeting?" Karen asked. "I thought the state's economy was improving, but our district is facing cuts to extracurricular activities and technology upgrades, Stuart. We should be getting more state money per pupil than the wealthy districts. I thought that's what the legislature approved a few years back with the new funding formula!"

"You're right, Karen, it's not fair. But that's the way it is. We both chose to work here," Stuart replied. "Although the state unemployment picture is improving, overall tax revenues are still down. Since wages have been down, folks have not been willing to spend as much, so income and sales tax revenues are still not meeting projections to cover the state's expenditures. The state budget is facing a $600 million deficit, so state aid to schools is going to be down. The board is in a real bind."

Karen sighed. "I just wish that education received the priority it needs to serve all students fairly. I know that the money comes from local, state, and federal sources, but it seems that the state is unable to keep up with needs of the local districts. It seems the state it saying it has done all it can."

"I think you are on target with that assessment. Of course the school board could seek a new tax levy to increase local funding, but there seems to be little chance that voters in our community would be willing to approve an increase in property taxes. I have to admit I can understand their resistance to vote for the levy," Stuart noted. "Increasing those taxes would also affect renters like me, too. My landlord told me that if a school levy was approved, he would pass along the costs by raising my rent."

"Even if local taxes were increased, I think our school district still would have less than area suburban schools," Karen responded. "If the situation gets worse, what will the board's next move be? I'm guessing they'll increase class sizes in the upper grades and begin laying off high school teachers."

"I'll bet you're right, Karen," Stuart agreed. "Wealthy districts have figured out ways to generate local money in addition to property taxes. Several of them have established foundations through booster clubs. The businesses that are located in the community contribute heavily each year and get a tax write-off."

"Too bad we don't have a few more generous businesses!" Karen said, laughing. Then, turning serious, she asked, "Do you think I have to worry about my job, as a beginning teacher?"

"Probably not this year because it looks like the primary grade teachers are safe. But you never know; most of a school's budget is in personnel costs. That's you and me. In the meantime, I guess the best thing we can do is just keep focusing on the students."

CASE QUESTIONS

1. Why is it important for beginning teachers like Karen and Stuart to have a basic understanding of school finance?

2. How does the current economic situation relate to school financing in your state?

3. How does school-district wealth relate to school financing in your state?

4. What percentages of your local school district's money are derived from local sources? From state sources? From federal sources? If you don't know, estimate the amounts. Then check to see how close your estimates are.

educational opportunity as students from high-income districts.[30] In short, states need to close the gap between the best- and worst-financed local school districts.

Some states may also need to factor private schools into their distribution plans. In June 2002, the US Supreme Court, in a five-to-four vote, ruled in favor of the Cleveland voucher program, which was funded by the state of Ohio. This program provides state money in the form of educational vouchers that may be used by the parents of low-income students to attend religious or nonsectarian private schools. Subsequent state legislation established the EdChoice Scholarship Program, which extended the tuition vouchers, now labeled as scholarships, to Ohio's public-school students who attend the state's lowest-rated public schools. In the 2013–2014 school year, 18,080 students received Ohio vouchers worth $4,250 for students in grades K–8 and $5,000 for high

---

[30]"Systems for Determining Adequacy," *The Education Commission of the States* (2011) at **www .ecs.org/html/issue.asp?issueid=48&subissueID=35** (February 9, 2015); and Michael J. Hoffman, "State School Finance System Variance Impacts on Student Achievement: Inadequacies in School Funding," *JEP: Ejournal of Education Policy* (Fall 2013), pp. 1–8.

FOCUS What are the benefits and drawbacks to the forms of taxation states use to fund schools? Explain your reasoning.

school students.[31] Forty states, by 2013, had either passed or had pending bills for funding vouchers, tax credits, or other benefits for private education.[32]

Yet, some critics of school finance reform have argued that money alone makes little difference in the quality of education.[33] They contend that educational improvement demands commitment and responsibility on the part of students, teachers, and parents. Moreover, unless we address a variety of social and cognitive factors, especially family structure, reform efforts may be useless. With all of these issues unresolved, school finance reform will be hotly debated for years to come.

8-3 FEDERAL EDUCATION FUNDING

Until the middle of the twentieth century, the federal government gave states (or local schools) little financial assistance in educating American students (see Chapter 5, Historical Development of American Education). This attitude aligned with a constitutional argument that the federal government should have little to do with education, which was a state responsibility. After the Soviet Union launched the *Sputnik* satellite in 1957, national policy became more closely linked to education, and federal funding dramatically increased and focused on specific, targeted areas; increased federal monies were allocated for improvement of science, mathematics, and foreign language instruction and for teacher education.

From the mid-1960s through the 1970s, the full force of the federal government came into play to enforce US Supreme Court decisions on school desegregation. The impetus came from the equal protection clause of the Fourteenth Amendment and the Civil Rights Act of 1964, which provided that all programs supported by federal funds must be administered and operated without discrimination or all federal funds would be withheld.

In addition to these desegregation efforts, the educational needs of minority groups and women received considerable attention and funding from the mid-1960s to the late 1970s. Diverse groups such as non-English-speaking students, Native Americans, students in low-income schools, and those with special needs were targeted for special programs.

8-3a Trends in Federal Aid to Education

In the 1980s, the Reagan administration brought its new conservatism to the federal level, and the trend of increasing federal contributions to public schooling ended. Federal education spending declined over the course of the decade (compare Table 8.1 on the following page with Figure 8.1 on p. 227).

During this time, school-funding methods also changed. **Categorical grants** (funds targeted for specific groups and designated purposes) gave way to **block grants** (funds for a general purpose without precise categories). This move was part of the "new federalism" that shifted responsibility for many federal social and educational programs from the national government to state governments based on the theory that states, which were closer to the programs, would know best how to spend the funds.

The 1990s saw another shift in the trend of federal involvement in funding K–12 schooling. The federal *Goals 2000* program, supported by both the George H.W. Bush and Clinton administrations, reversed the reduction in federal dollars put in place

categorical grants Funds designated for specific groups and purposes; the standard method of federal education funding before the 1980s and again more recently.

block grants General-purpose funding from the federal government, allowing each state considerable freedom to choose specific programs on which to spend the funds.

---

[31]"Ohio Legislature Expands School Voucher Program," *Church & State* (September 2005), pp. 3, 21; Alexandra Usher and Nancy Kober, *Keeping Informed about School Vouchers: A Review of Major Developments and Research* (Washington, DC: Center on Education Policy, July 2011); and "EdChoice Scholarship Program," *School Choice Ohio* (2015) at **www.ecs.org/html/Document.asp?chouseid=9459**.

[32]Peter Schrag, "Vouchers: They're Baaaaaack!" *The Nation* (June 20, 2011), pp. 25–26.

[33]Gerald W. Bracey, "Schools-Are-Awful Bloc Still Busy in 2008," *Phi Delta Kappan* (October 2008), pp. 103–114; and Bruce Baker, *Does Money Matter in Education* (Washington, DC: The Albert Shanker Institute, 2012).

TABLE 8.1	Federal Funds for Elementary and Secondary Education, 1970–2012	
Year	**Amount (billions)**	**Federal Government Share of Funding (percentage)**
1970	$3.2	8.0
1972	4.4	8.9
1974	4.9	8.5
1976	6.3	8.9
1978	7.7	9.4
1980	9.5	9.8
1982	8.2	7.4
1984	8.6	6.8
1986	9.9	6.7
1988	10.7	6.3
1990	12.7	6.1
1994	18.3	7.1
1996	22.1	6.8
2000	27.0	7.3
2002	33.1	7.9
2005	44.8	9.2
2009	56.7	9.6
2012	59.5	10

Note: As a result of the Education Consolidation and Improvement Act in 1981, many programs and funds were shifted among various federal departments; the base of comparison has not been exactly the same since then.
Source: "Revenues for Public Elementary and Secondary Schools, by Source of Funds: Selected Years, 1919–20 through 2004–05," *Digest of Education Statistics: 2007* at **http://nces.ed.gov/programs /digest/d07/tables/dt07_162.asp**; Mark Dixon, *Public Education Finance: 2012* (Washington, DC: US Census Bureau, May 2014) at **www2.census.gov/govs/school/12f33pub.pdf**; and "Percentage Distribution of Public Elementary-Secondary School System Revenue by Source and State," *American FactFinder* (May 22, 2014) at **http://factfinder.census.gov/faces/tableservices/jsf/pages/productview .xhtml?pid=SSF_2012_SSF005.US01&prodType=table.**

during the Reagan presidency appropriated to support education programs. Gone, too, was the emphasis on block grants as categorical programs began to remerge. A major target for federal dollars that were awarded to the states was the development and implementation of state curriculum standards.[34]

The trend toward more categorical funding gained momentum as we entered the new millennium. The No Child Left Behind (NCLB) Act of 2001 focused federal funding on standards, testing, accountability measures, and teacher quality. States were required to refine curriculum standards, develop assessments of the standards in reading and math for grades 3 through 8 and once in high school, and establish an accountability plan. Additionally, school systems had to ensure that all teachers were highly qualified.[35]

---

[34]Gail L. Sundeman, "The Federal Role in Education: From the Reagan to the Obama Administration," *VUE* (Summer 2009) at **http://vue.annenberginstitute.org/sites/default/files /issuePDF/VUE24.pdf** (February 9, 2015).

[35]Pamela Karwasinski and Katharine Shek, "A Guide to the No Child Left Behind Act," *The Center for Public Education* (March 15, 2006) at **http://www.education.com/reference /article/Ref_guide_No_Child_Left/** (February 9, 2015); and Editorial Projects in Education Research Center, "Issues A-Z: No Child Left Behind," *Education Week* (September 19, 2011) at **www.edweek.org/ew/issues/no-child-left-behind/**.

With the passage of NCLB, the federal government became more involved with the state and local education agencies by taking an active role in implementing education policy. The law not only required that assessments be developed and administered, it also required that benchmarks for adequate yearly progress (AYP) be established to ensure that all students are proficient in meeting standards as measured by the assessments. Additionally, the achievement results were categorized by student ethnicity, family income, home language, and disability, and schools could only meet AYP when each of the student groups met AYP.[36]

Critics labeled NCLB an unfunded mandate because federal funding lagged behind states' ability to cover the costs of developing and administering achievement tests, identifying criteria to determine highly qualified teachers, and other provisions of the act. This lack of funding was frustrating to school officials at both state and local levels, especially as schools' budgets constricted during the economic downturn.[37]

The transition from the Bush administration to the Obama administration saw a shift in focus on a number of issues related to NCLB. The new administration believed that parts of the act were flawed and reforms were needed as work began on the reauthorization of the Elementary and Secondary Education Act (ESEA), which was to take place in 2007. Interestingly, due to Congressional inaction, the ESEA is still awaiting reauthorization in 2015. In the intervening years, the Obama White House pushed forward a number of initiatives and programs designed to reform federal education policy. During the global recession, the administration secured passage of the American Recovery and Reinvestment Act (ARRA) of 2009, which awarded $77 billion to strengthen elementary and secondary education and helped save jobs in school districts across the nation. Another initiative, Race to the Top (RTTT), a $4.35 billion competitive education grant, was designed to encourage states to make improvements in teacher effectiveness, improve achievement in low-performing schools, develop more rigorous standards and better assessments, and enhance data systems. The administration also granted greater flexibility in providing relief from certain provisions of NCLB in exchange for adopting college- and career-ready standards and new principal and teacher evaluations. Nineteen states received funding under the grant and thirty-four states modified state laws or policies to facilitate changes to address the federal emphasis. Additionally, forty-eight states worked together to develop the college- and career-ready standards now known as the Common Core State Standards.[38]

FOCUS Do you believe that the federal government contributes sufficient support to public education in the United States? Explain your position.

8-4 SCHOOL FINANCE TRENDS

Financial crises in education often make the headlines. For example, the recent national recession triggered large state-revenue shortfalls. Coupled with rising costs and enrollments, the loss of state revenue placed many local school districts in a bleak fiscal situation. Although such crises may have come and gone in the past with changes in the economy and in federal, state, and local budgets, we are still faced with several long-lasting concerns about school finance. As we examine historical trends, keep in mind that educators today are being asked to show proof that they are spending public money wisely. To find out more about current school funding, see the Technology @ School box.

---

[36]*The No Child Left Behind Act of 2001* at **www2.ed.gov/policy/elsec/leg/esea02/index .html** (February 8, 2015); and Mary Branham Dusenberry, "NCLB: Not as Easy as ABC," *State News* (May 2007), pp. 19–23.

[37]Alyson Klein, "Focus Turns to Congress after High Court's Denial of Challenge to NCLB Law," *Education Week* (June 16, 2010), p. 24.

[38]"Race to the Top," *White House* (n.d.) at **www.whitehouse.gov/issues/education/k-12/race -to-the-top**; "Reforming No Child Left Behind," *White House* (n.d.) at **www.whitehouse.gov /issues/education/k-12/reforming-no-child-left-behind**; and "K–12 Education," *White House* (n.d.) at **www.whitehouse.gov/issues/education/k-12**.

TECHNOLOGY @ SCHOOL

FINDING SCHOOL FINANCING INFORMATION ON THE INTERNET

As a teacher, you should remain informed about issues and trends in school financing. As discussed in this chapter, financing decisions at every level of government can affect your school community.

One way to stay informed about school finance issues is to monitor the website of the Education Commission of the States. This site provides access to a number of relevant resources. From the home page, click on "Education Issues A-Z," and then click on "Finance," and you will find a wealth of information about *funding formulas, litigation* related to *adequacy* of funding, and the status of *state budgets*. Also available are research reports, additional articles on school finance issues, and access to other websites.

The Education Law Center website, which focuses on Pennsylvania school issues, has a "Fighting for Fair School Funding" section. It provides updated information on state court cases and current research reports on the status of school funding issues. Because school equity is such a topical issue, this site provides clear information on this complex topic.

One additional site that provides helpful information on school funding issues is the Center on Budget and Policy Priorities. It is easiest to find education-related articles through the "Press Release" header or by utilizing the search box. It consistently provides updates on the news about school budgets across the country.

8-4a Taxpayer Resistance

Beginning in the late 1970s, a tax revolt swept the country, putting a damper on the movement for school finance reform. In California, a 1978 taxpayer initiative called Proposition 13 set a maximum tax of 1 percent on the fair market value of a property and limited increases in assessed valuation to 2 percent a year. By 2013, forty-seven states had imposed some type of property tax limitations or caps.[39] Additionally, as a result of this **taxpayer resistance**, thirty states operate under spending limits that are intended to restrain the growth of state budgets.[40]

taxpayer resistance When taxpayers show reluctance to continue paying increased taxes to support public schools.

The late twentieth-century educational reform movement emphasized the need to improve the quality of education. Taxpayers are typically willing to support increased education spending for that purpose; however, they want to know what they are getting for the dollars they spend. This concern led to increased educator accountability for the use of public funds.

8-4b The Accountability Movement

accountability Holding teachers, administrators, and/or school board members responsible for student performance or for wise use of educational funds.

Although definitions of **accountability** vary, the term generally refers to the notion that teachers, administrators, school board members, and even students themselves must be held responsible for the results of their efforts. Teachers must meet some standard of competency, and administrators must demonstrate that their efforts are improving student academic achievement.

The accountability movement stems from various factors. Parents realize that schooling is important for success, and research suggests that the quality of a teacher has important consequences for student achievement. As the cost of education has increased, parents and policy makers demand to know what they are paying for.

---

[39]"Capping Property Taxes: A Primer," *ITEP – Institute on Taxation and Economic Policy* (September 2011) at **http://itepnet.org/pdf/pb26caps.pdf**; and Dylan Scott, "Property Tax Revenue Limits Squeeze School Budgets," *Governing the States and Localities* (February 6, 2013) at **www.governing.com/blogs/view/gov-revenue-limits-put-squeeze-on-wisconsin-schools.html**.

[40]Bert Waisanen, "State Tax and Expenditure Limits – 2010," *NCLS* (n.d.) at **www.ncsl.org/research/fiscal-policy/state-tax-and-expenditure-limits-2010.aspx#studies**.

Taxpayers, who want to keep the lid on school spending, want to hold schools and educators responsible for students' academic achievement.[41]

In 2001, the newly passed NCLB brought the issue of accountability to the forefront of federal education policy. The act required statewide assessment programs in reading and mathematics for all children in grades 3 through 8. The purpose was to hold schools accountable for the performance of all students, especially underserved populations, on the assessments. If a school failed to meet AYP toward performance targets for a set number of years, sanctions were placed on the school. The focus of this accountability effort was referred to as a "test and punish" approach that had drastic implications for school funding at both the state and local district level.[42]

The Obama administration has implemented a number of adjustments to the accountability measures in its efforts to reauthorize the ESEA. The administration has been granting states waivers from certain accountability requirements related to student achievement. While there has been some easing of pressure in this area, the trade-off is that states receiving federal funds are being required to implement teacher and principal evaluations systems that incorporate measures of student growth. Teachers will be held accountable by measuring the value that a given teacher adds to the achievement of his or her students.[43]

8-4c Tax Credits, Educational Vouchers, and School Choice

tuition tax credits Tax reductions offered to parents or guardians of children to offset part of their school tuition payments.

Tuition tax credits allow parents to claim a state tax reduction for approved education expenses they pay to send their child to nonpublic school. The tax-credit movement reflects the public's desire for increased choice in schools as well as the continuing quest of nonpublic schools for support. Since the 1950s, Minnesota has employed tax deductions for educational expenses; at least seven other states also use a type of tax credit for such expenses.[44] An expanding version of the tuition tax credit is the scholarship tax credit program where corporations and individuals can donate a portion of the state taxes that are owed to private nonprofit school tuition organizations that award scholarships to K–12 students. The scholarship can be used for private schools or public schools outside of the student's home district. Fourteen states currently have scholarship tax credit programs.[45]

educational voucher A flat grant or payment representing a child's estimated school cost or portion of the cost. Under a typical voucher plan, the parent or child may choose any school, public or private, and the school is paid for accepting the child.

Use of **educational vouchers** is another growing trend in school finance reform. Under a voucher system, the state or local school district gives parents of school-age children a tax-subsidized voucher or flat grant, representing a portion of their children's educational cost. Children then use this voucher to attend a school of the family's choosing.[46] Thirteen states and the District of Columbia had voucher programs in

[41]Peter Hart and Robert M. Teeter, *Equity and Adequacy: Americans Speak on Public School Funding* (Princeton, NJ: Educational Testing Service, 2004) at **www.ets.org/americans_speak/funding**; and *Teachers Matter: Understanding Teachers' Impact on Student Achievement* (Santa Monica, CA: Rand, 2012) at **www.rand.org/education/projects/measuring-teacher-effectiveness/teachers-matter.html**.

[42]Todd Ziebarth and Bryan Hassel, *ECS Issue Brief—School Restructuring via the No Child Left Behind Act: Potential State Roles* (Denver, CO: Education Commission of the States, November 2005) at **www.ecs.org/html/Document.asp?chouseid=6578**; and Allie Bidwell, "Coalition Wants New School Accountability," *US News and World Report* (October 28, 2014).

[43]Bidwell, "Coalition Wants New School Accountability"; and Marc S. Tucker, *Fixing Our National Accountability System* (Washington, DC: The National Center on Education and the Economy, 2014).

[44]Lawrence Hardy, "The Voucher Revival," *American School Board Journal* (November 11, 2011), pp. 14–18; and Josh Cunningham, *Comprehensive School Choice Policy: A Guide for Legislators* (Denver, CO: National Conference of State Legislatures, September 2013).

[45]"School Choice: Scholarship Tax Credits," *NCLS.org* (2015) at **www.ncsl.org/research/education/school-choice-scholarship-tax-credits.aspx**.

[46]Bruce D. Baker, Preston Green, and Craig E. Richards, *Financing Education Systems* (New York: Merrill Prentice Hall, 2008), pp. 318–321.

2013, and pro-voucher legislators in forty states had introduced bills to use state tax dollars to send students to nonpublic schools.[47]

Debates over tax credits and voucher programs have been vigorous and emotional. The NEA, the AFT, and other educational organizations contend that vouchers or tax credits offer no real choice to most students, split the public along socioeconomic lines, and reduce financial support for the public schools.[48] Opponents have also argued that such programs do not raise student achievement for all, provide unconstitutional support for church-related schools, undermine the public-school system by supporting and encouraging the movement of students to nonpublic schools, and produce a large drain on public-school budgets or state treasuries. Critics also contend that tax dollars are ultimately going to private entities with little accountability and uncertain outcomes.[49]

Proponents of tuition tax credits and vouchers generally link the issue with the concept of **school choice**, which is discussed in detail in Chapter 16, School Effectiveness and Reform in the United States. By widening a parent's choices for schooling, supporters contend we can increase competition among schools and raise the overall level of educational quality. The idea is to depend on education to follow the laws of the marketplace: If students and parents can choose schools, the effective schools will stay in operation, and the less desirable ones will either go out of business or improve.

In addition, supporters of tuition tax credits and voucher programs argue that such credits are not unconstitutional and do not seriously reduce federal revenues or hamper public-school tax levy efforts. They also argue that these programs provide wider opportunity for students to attend schools outside the inner city; thus, tax credits or vouchers do not contribute to, and might even reduce, racial and socioeconomic isolation. Many supporters also believe that tax credits or vouchers, besides providing parents with a choice in selecting schools, stimulate public-school improvement, particularly when families have choices within the public-school district.[50]

The call for school choice is most obvious with the growth of *charter schools*, discussed in Chapter 7, Governing and Administering Public Education. Minnesota was first to adopt a charter school law in 1991; by the 2012–2013 school year, there were 5,997 charter schools across forty-two states and the District of Columbia, which accounted for more than 6 percent of all US public schools. Most charter school organizers contend that they receive less public funding than noncharters. Many school boards counter that they are frugal in allocating operating funds for charter schools, fearing a financial drain on already tight budgets for existing public schools.[51]

school choice A system that allows students or their parents to choose the schools they attend.

---

[47]"School Vouchers: The Wrong Choice for Public Education," *Anti-Defamation League* (2011) at **www.adl.org/assets/pdf/civil-rights/religiousfreedom/religfreeres/School -Vouchers-docx.pdf**; and "School Vouchers: Legal and Constitutional Issues" (webinar) (Denver, CO: National Conference of State Legislatures, June 20, 2013) at **www.ncsl.org /documents/educ/voucher-webinar.pdf**.

[48]NEA, "Issues and Action – Vouchers" at **www.nea.org/home/16378.htm** (February 4, 2015); and AFT, "AFT Statement on Louisiana Supreme Court Decision on Vouchers" (May 7, 2013) at **www.aft.org/press-release/aft-statement-louisiana-supreme-court-decision -vouchers** (February 4, 2015).

[49]Lyndsey Layton, "GOP Measure Would Promote School 'Choice' with Federal Funding," *Washington Post* (January 27, 2014); and NSBA, "Issue Brief – Private School *Voucher*" (January 17, 2015) at **www.nsba.org/sites/default/files/012015_Vouchers_Issue_Brief.pdf** (February 4, 2015).

[50]Greg Anrig, "An Idea Whose Time Has Gone," *Washington Monthly* (April 2008), pp. 29–33; "Vouchers," *Education Week* (August 11, 2011) at **www.edweek.org/ew/issues/vouchers** (February 5, 2015); Jeff Bryant, "The New Push for School Vouchers at State, Federal Levels," *Washington Post*, (February 12, 2014); and "Commonly Asked Questions about School Choice and Vouchers," *Rethinking Schools Online* (2015) at **www.rethinkingschools.org/special _reports/voucher_report/vouchersorig/vq&a.shtml**.

[51]Katrina E. Bulkley, "Charter Schools: Taking a Closer Look," *Kappa Delta Pi Record* (March 1, 2011), pp. 110–115; and "Charter Schools: Overview," *NCSL.org* (2014) at **www.ncsl.org /research/education/charter-schools-overview.aspx** (February 4, 2015).

8-4d School Budgets during Difficult Economic Times

The economic downturn that began with the Great Recession in 2008 forced school officials to face funding challenges that had been unprecedented for several generations. Most local school boards grappled with reduced funding from both the state and local levels. The reliance on property taxes at the local level made it difficult to project when the decline in those revenues would turn around because home property values remained low for several years. State revenues, which rely on sales and personal income taxes, have remained flat in spite of a recovering economy.[52]

The lingering fiscal stress on school districts requires that they find additional funding streams or cut spending; there is much greater likelihood the latter will be the only option for most local boards of education, and national data shows that spending for instruction decreased by 3.3 percent and total support services decreased by 2.5 percent from 2011 to 2012. Raising existing tax rates or implementing new taxes does not seem to be an option in the current political climate. The option left to school districts is to reduce spending. Terms such as "efficient spending," "downsizing," and "enhanced productivity" are being used to advise school boards concerning how to balance their school district budgets.[53]

States and local school systems continue to take action to reduce spending despite some recent improvements in overall state revenues. The most current analysis of school finance data reveals the impact of the nation's economic circumstance on school funding:

- Per-pupil expenditures were less in thirty-five states in 2014 than they were before the recession in 2008.
- At least fifteen states provided less per-pupil funding to local school districts in 2014 than 2013. Most states did see a modest increase in tax revenues during this same time period.
- In states where funding was increased, the increase did not make up for cuts in previous years. New Mexico, for example, increased school funding by $72 per pupil from 2013 to 2014, but it had cut spending by $946 per pupil the previous five years. Thirty-eight percent of impacted districts reduced extracurricular programs and activities.
- As of August 2013, a total of 324,000 jobs had been eliminated by local school districts since 2008. During this time period, school enrollment increased by approximately three quarters of a million students.
- In at least fourteen states, per-pupil expenditures are 10 percent or more below 2008 levels. Oklahoma and Alabama have cut per-pupil funding by more than 20 percent over the same time frame.[54]

While state revenues have risen in the recent past, they have still not reached levels established prior to the recession. With state legislatures reluctant to raise new revenue streams—taxes—it seems schools will continue to be asked to do more with less.

[52]"Cutting to the Bone: At a Glance," *The Center for Public Education* (October 7, 2010) at **www .centerforpubliceducation.org/Main-Menu/Public-education/Cutting-to-the-bone -At-a-glance** (February 11, 2015); and Center on Education Policy, *Summary of Two Reports by the Center on Education Policy* (Washington, DC: Center on Education Policy February, 2012).

[53]Michael J. Petrilli and Margerite Roza, *Stretching the School Dollar: A Brief for State Policy Makers* (Washington, DC: Thomas B. Fordham Institute, January 2011); and Allie Bidwell, "How States are Spending Money in Education," *US News & World Report* (January 29, 2015).

[54]James W. Guthrie and Elizabeth A. Ettema, "Public Schools and Money," *Education Next*, (Fall 2012), pp. 19–23; Michael Leachman and Chris Mai, "Most States Funding Schools Less Than Before the Recession," *The Center on Budget and Policy Priorities* (May 20, 2014) at **www.cbpp .org/cms/index.cfm?fa=view&id=4011**; and Emma Brown, "Nation's Per-Pupil Funding Fell for Second Consecutive Year in 2012," *The Washington Post* (January 29, 2015).

Rachel Epstein/The Image Works

> PHOTO 8.2 School boards are being pressed to eliminate unnecessary spending, and school budgets must stand up to close scrutiny. Many districts are trying to "do more with less," in spite of demands for smaller schools, teacher shortages, and deteriorating old school buildings.

school infrastructure The basic physical facilities of the school plant (plumbing, sewer, heat, electric, roof, windows, and so on).

8-4e School Infrastructure and Environmental Problems

The nation's **school infrastructure** is in critical disrepair. By *infrastructure*, we mean the basic physical facilities of the school plant (plumbing, sewer, heat, electric, roof, carpentry, and so on). Building experts estimate that schools in the United States are deteriorating faster than they can be repaired and faster than most other public facilities. Plumbing, windows, electrical wiring, and heating systems in many schools are dangerously out of date; roofing is below code; and exterior brickwork, stone, and wood are in serious disrepair. Over the past twenty-five years, school districts have had to defer maintenance of school facilities due to a lack of funds for upkeep and repair (Photo 8.2). Estimates of the costs of this deferred maintenance is estimated to range from $270 billion to more than $542 billion.[55] When maintenance and repair work is delayed, students are subjected to potentially dangerous conditions: unsafe drinking water, poor air quality from mold, outdated security systems, reduced curricular offerings as specialized spaces such as gyms are closed, and danger from structural problems.[56]

Even as school boards struggle to meet the needs of an aging infrastructure, demographers are projecting continued growth of the school-age population. From 2015 to 2021, the Pre-K through 12th grade population is expected to grow by more than 2 million students. In 2012, $10 billion was spent on new buildings and modernization of existing ones to prepare for these new students. This is half of the funding level for the year prior to the recession. Repairs aside, concern continues to grow about where the money will come from to build the additional classrooms we continue to need.[57]

---

[55] 21st Century School Fund, *Through Your Lens: Student and Teacher Views of School Facilities across America* (2010) at **www.eric.ed.gov/PDFS/ED509518.pdf** (February 8, 2015); "2013 Report Card for America's Infrastructure: Schools," *ASCE – America' Society of Civil Engineers* (2013) at **www.infrastructurereportcard.org/schools/**; and "The State of Our Schools 2013," *The Center for Green Schools* (January 14, 2013) at **http://centerforgreenschools.org/Libraries /State_of_our_Schools/2013_State_of_Our_Schools_Report_FINAL.sflb.ashx**.

[56] "PK–12 Public School Facility Infrastructure Fact Sheet," *The 21st Century School Fund and Building Educational Success Together (BEST)* (February 2011) at **www.21csf.org/csf-home/Documents /FactSheetPK12PublicSchoolFacilityInfrastructure.pdf**.

[57] "Actual and Projected Numbers for Enrollment in Grades PK–12, PK–8, and 9–12 in Elementary and Secondary Schools, by Control of School: Fall 1996 through Fall 2021," *Projections of Education Statistics to 2021* (January 2013) at **http://nces.ed.gov/programs/projections /projections2021/tables/table_01.asp**.

SUMMING UP

1. Schools are financially supported by state and local governments and—to a lesser extent—by the federal government. Overall, since the early twentieth century, state support has increased dramatically, and local support has declined; the percentage of federal support grew until the early 1980s, then declined, but has since recovered to earlier levels.
2. Although property tax is the main local source of school revenue, it is considered a regressive tax.
3. There is wide variation in the financial ability among states and within states (at the local district level) to support education. Poorer school districts tend to receive more money from the state than do wealthier school districts, but the amount rarely makes up for the total difference in expenditures per pupil.
4. School finance reform, initiated by the state courts and carried forward by state legislatures, has attempted to reduce or eliminate funding disparities between poorer and wealthier districts. The basic goal is to provide for adequate educational opportunities and give poorer districts the means to improve their performance.
5. Since the *Sputnik era*, federal funding of education has become increasingly linked to national policy. As policy emphasis has changed, so has the level of funding.
6. Controversies over accountability, tuition tax credits, educational vouchers, charter schools, and school choice reflect increasing public concern with the educational system.
7. Taxpayer resistance, especially to increases in property taxes, results in strong pressure to be more accountable with school revenue.
8. Deteriorating school infrastructure poses significant financial liabilities for many school districts.

SUGGESTED RESOURCES

INTERNET RESOURCES

The Center on Budget and Policy Priorities conducts research and analysis on budget and tax policies. Its focus is broader than just education issues, but its reports are accessible to the general public and are informative regarding issues of the day. By entering "education" as a keyword in the search box, numerous reports related to education financing are provided. Charts, graphs, and tables are generally incorporated into the reports to illustrate economic issues discussed in the articles. This site is an excellent resource for keeping current with education finance issues. It also provides videos, podcasts, blogs, and slideshows to present its reports.

PUBLICATIONS

Chaikind, Stephen. *Education Finance in the New Millennium.* Hoboken NJ: Taylor and Francis, 2013. *Gives a comprehensive, contemporary view of school finance and focuses on the myriad topics that impact school district expenditures.*

Feinberg, Walter, and Christopher Lubienski, eds. *School Choice Policies and Outcomes: Empirical and Philosophical Perspectives.* Albany, NY: SUNY Press, 2008. *Provides an examination of varying voices in the choice debate and suggests choice, directed by the appropriate goals, might advance education.*

Hanushek, Eric A., and Alfred A. Lindseth. *Schoolhouses, Courthouses, and Statehouses: Solving the Funding-Achievement Puzzle in America's Public Schools.* Princeton, NJ: Princeton University Press, 2009. *Suggests that court rulings requiring states to spend more on funding education in the name of equity has not reduced the achievement gap. Proposes a performance-based system that offers incentives to raise achievement.*

Johnston, J. Howard, and Ronald Williamson. *Leading Schools in an Era of Declining Resources.* New York: Routledge, 2014. *Offers practical advice to school administrators which help tackle a variety of critical issues that surface during difficult financial times.*

Ladd, Helen F., and Margaret E. Goertz, eds. *Handbook of Research in Education Finance and Policy,* 2nd ed. New York: Routledge, 2015. *A comprehensive review of the field of education finance; includes a historical evolution of the field.*

Molnar, Alex. *School Commercialism: From Democratic Ideal to Market Commodity.* New York: Routledge, 2013. *Offers an examination of how marketing impacts school policy and practice and raises questions about the influence of commercialism in public schools.*

Odden, Allen R., and Lawrence O. Picus. *School Finance: A Policy Perspective,* 4th ed. New York: McGraw-Hill, 2008. *Examines school productivity formulas, fiscal policy, and fiscal federalism.*

Roza, Marguerite. *Educational Economics: Where Do School Funds Go?* Washington, DC: Urban Institute Press, 2010. *Considers the sources of school finance—federal block funding, foundation grants, earmarks, set-asides, and union mandates—and how they can easily be diverted from where they are most needed.*

Shelly, Bryan. *Money, Mandates, and Local Control in American Public Education.* Ann Arbor: University of Michigan Press, 2011. *Examines school finance, including an analysis of unfunded and underfunded mandates and regulations that the author suggests are the true cause of the loss of community control over public education.*

Stewart, Thomas, and Patrick J. Wolf. *The School Choice Journey: School Vouchers and the Empowerment of Urban Families.* New York: Palgrave Macmillan, 2014. *Sheds light on parental school choice in Washington, DC, within the broader context of urban poverty and education reform in the United States.*

Goodluz/Shutterstock.com

CHAPTER 9

LEGAL ASPECTS OF EDUCATION

LEARNING OBJECTIVES

9-1 Identify the fundamental elements and concepts in the legal system.
9-2 Describe the legal rights and responsibilities of teachers.
9-3 Discuss the legal rights of students and the limitations on student behavior.
9-4 Describe the basic religious activities that can and cannot be conducted in public schools and the ways in which the government can and cannot assist nonpublic schools.

_____
This chapter was revised by Daniel U. Levine.

DURING THE PAST SIX DECADES, the courts have increasingly been asked to resolve issues relating to public education in the United States. This rise in educational litigation reflects the fact that education has assumed a greater importance in our society than it had a few decades ago. The growth in litigation has been paralleled, and to some extent spurred on, by an enormous increase in state and federal legislation affecting education. As litigation and legislation regarding the schools continue to increase, teachers and administrators are increasingly responsible for learning about the ins and outs of school law.

This chapter presents a general overview of the US court system and examines the legal topics and court decisions that have most affected today's schools and teachers. The major topics we will consider are (1) the rights and responsibilities of both teachers and students and (2) religion and the schools.[1]

9-1 THE COURT SYSTEM

plaintiffs Persons who sue.

litigants Parties in a lawsuit.

Cases involving education-related issues can be heard either in federal or state courts, depending on the allegations of the **plaintiffs** (the persons who sue). Federal courts decide cases that involve federal laws and regulations or constitutional issues. State courts adjudicate cases that involve state laws, state constitutional provisions, school board policies, or other nonfederal problems. Most cases pertaining to elementary and secondary education are filed in state courts. However, to keep from overburdening court calendars, both federal and state courts usually require that prospective **litigants** (the parties in a lawsuit) exhaust all administrative avenues available for resolution before involving the court system.

9-1a State Courts

State court organization has no national uniformity. The details of each state's judicial system are found in its constitution. At the lowest level, most states have a court of original jurisdiction (often called a municipal or superior court) where cases are tried. The facts are established, evidence is presented, witnesses testify and are cross-examined, and appropriate legal principles are applied in rendering a verdict.

The losing side may appeal the decision to the next higher level, usually an intermediate appellate court. This court reviews the trial record from the lower court and additional written materials submitted by both sides. The appellate court is designed to ensure that appropriate laws were properly applied, that they fit with the facts presented, and that no deprivation of constitutional rights occurred.

If one side remains unsatisfied, another appeal may be made to the state's highest court, often called its supreme court. A state supreme court decision is final unless a question involving the US Constitution has been raised. The side that wishes to appeal may then petition the US Supreme Court to consider the case.

9-1b Federal Courts

Federal courts are organized into a three-tiered system: district courts, circuit courts of appeals, and the Supreme Court. The jurisdiction and powers of these courts are set forth in the Constitution and are subject to congressional restrictions. The lowest level, the district court, holds trials. For appeals at the next federal level, the nation is divided into twelve regions called circuits. Each circuit court handles appeals only from district

---

[1]Other chapters of this book also discuss selected legal issues in education. For court decisions regarding school finance, see Chapter 8, Financing Public Education. Desegregation law and legislation regarding special education are considered in Chapter 12, Providing Equal Educational Opportunity.

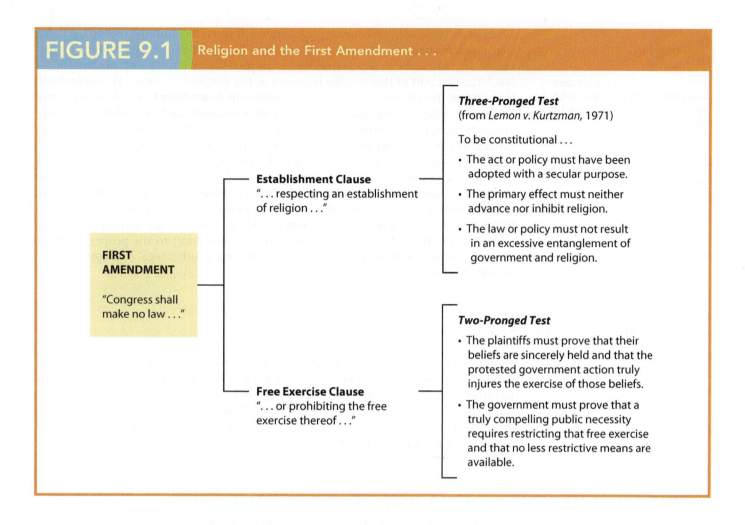

FIGURE 9.1 Religion and the First Amendment . . .

FIRST AMENDMENT

"Congress shall make no law . . ."

Establishment Clause
". . . respecting an establishment of religion . . ."

Free Exercise Clause
". . . or prohibiting the free exercise thereof . . ."

Three-Pronged Test
(from *Lemon v. Kurtzman,* 1971)

To be constitutional . . .

- The act or policy must have been adopted with a secular purpose.
- The primary effect must neither advance nor inhibit religion.
- The law or policy must not result in an excessive entanglement of government and religion.

Two-Pronged Test
- The plaintiffs must prove that their beliefs are sincerely held and that the protested government action truly injures the exercise of those beliefs.
- The government must prove that a truly compelling public necessity requires restricting that free exercise and that no less restrictive means are available.

courts within its particular geographic area. Unsuccessful litigants may request that the US Supreme Court review their case. If four of the nine justices agree, the Supreme Court will take the case; if not, the appellate court ruling stands.[2]

Decisions of a court below the US Supreme Court have force only in the geographic area served by that particular court. For this reason, it is possible to find conflicting rulings in different circuits. Judges often look to previous case law for guidance in rendering decisions, and they might find precedents for a variety of legally defensible positions on a single issue.

The First and the Fourteenth Amendments Although education is considered a state responsibility, it has produced an abundance of federal litigation, particularly in connection with the First and Fourteenth Amendments to the US Constitution. The First Amendment concerns freedom of religion, speech, press, and assembly, and the right "to petition the government for redress of grievances." Many First Amendment cases have dealt with the role of religion in public education and with the extent of protection guaranteed to freedom of expression by students and teachers. Two First Amendment clauses are frequently cited in lawsuits: the **establishment clause**, which prohibits the establishment of a government-sanctioned religion, and the **free exercise clause**, which protects rights of free speech and expression. To interpret these clauses, the courts generally use the criteria, or "tests," shown in Figure 9.1.

establishment clause A constitutional provision that prohibits the establishment of a government-sanctioned religion.

free exercise clause A constitutional provision that protects rights of free speech and expression.

[2]Some case citations in this chapter include the term *cert. denied.* This means that the losing parties petitioned the US Supreme Court for review, but their request was denied.

due process clause A formalized legal procedure with specific and detailed rules and principles designed to protect the rights of individuals.

equal protection clause A Fourteenth Amendment statement that government shall not deny any person the equal protection of the law.

Court cases involving the Fourteenth Amendment often focus on the section declaring that no state shall "deprive any person of life, liberty, or property, without due process of law; nor deny to any person within its jurisdiction the equal protection of the law." The first part of this passage is known as the **due process clause**. The second part is known as the **equal protection clause**. Fourteenth Amendment cases have addressed the issue of school desegregation as well as the suspension and expulsion of students. Litigants citing the Fourteenth Amendment must show that a "liberty" or a "property" interest is a major element in the case. A liberty interest is involved if "a person's good name, reputation, honor, or integrity is at stake." A property interest might arise from legal guarantees granted to tenured employees; for instance, teachers beyond the probationary period have a property interest in continued employment. Similarly, students have a property interest in their education. If either a liberty or a property interest is claimed, a school district must provide due process (guaranteeing a fair and impartial hearing and the opportunity to present evidence) to the people involved. The rest of this chapter will explore the use of these and other legal concepts in actual school settings.

9-2 TEACHERS' RIGHTS AND RESPONSIBILITIES

As pointed out in Chapter 2, The Teaching Profession, teachers historically were vulnerable to dismissal by local boards of education for virtually any reason and without recourse. Collective negotiation statutes, tenure laws, mandatory due-process procedures, and other legal measures have been established to curb such abuses and to guarantee teachers certain rights. Along with rights come responsibilities, and many of these, too, have been written into law.

9-2a Testing and Investigation of Applicants for Certification or Employment

Almost everywhere in the United States, individuals who want to teach in grades K–12 must possess teaching certificates, which are usually granted by the state. In recent years, many states have passed legislation requiring thorough background checks of prospective teachers, and some extend this requirement to currently employed teachers seeking recertification. For example, New York and Texas now require that all candidates for certification be fingerprinted as part of a check for criminal histories. Several school districts have initiated drug testing of teacher applicants. In addition, some states electronically share background information about candidates for government positions. Prospective teachers should be careful about what they post online because many districts are examining sites such as Twitter, Instagram, and Facebook for information about job applicants.[3]

These trends have been fueled by two complementary developments. One consideration is that technology has made it more feasible to use fingerprints and other information sources in checking with local, state, and federal law enforcement agencies. The other is that the public has become increasingly concerned about dangers posed by child molesters and potential school employees with other criminal records.

As described in Chapter 1, Motivation, Preparation, and Conditions for the Entering Teacher, in addition to background checks, states require that prospective teachers pass one or more competency tests for certification. In some cases, current teachers

---

[3]"Texas Now Requiring Fingerprints from School Employees," *American School Board Journal* (March 2008), p. 10; and Jonathan Shorman, "Legislation Requires Fingerprints Every Five Years for School Workers," *The Topeka Capital-Journal*, March 18, 2015, available at **www.cjonline .com**.

also must pass competency tests for continued employment. States where minority candidate passing rates are considerably lower than those for nonminorities have faced several lawsuits charging that specific tests discriminate against minority applicants. To answer such a lawsuit, employers must be able to specify the characteristics a test measures, establish that these characteristics are necessary in carrying out the job, and demonstrate that the test correlates with the work behavior in question.

Most lawsuits charging that teacher tests are discriminatory have either failed or been withdrawn because the available data did not demonstrate a clear pattern of discrimination nor an intent to discriminate. On the other hand, several challenges have succeeded, and worries about possible legal challenges, particularly from minority candidates, have occasionally led states to keep passing scores low. For example, concerns regarding a legal challenge alleging discrimination in part led the Massachusetts State Board of Education to substantially reduce the minimum score required to pass a proposed certification test in that state.[4]

9-2b Employment Contracts and Tenure

In choosing which teachers to hire, local school boards must comply with laws that prohibit discrimination with respect to age, sex, race, religion, or national origin. Upon appointment, the teacher receives a written contract to sign. The contract may specify that the teacher must adhere to school board policies and regulations. If the school district has negotiated with a teacher organization, the provisions of that agreement apply as well.

Contracts are binding on both parties. When one side fails to perform as agreed—called a **breach of contract**—the contract is broken. In such instances, the party that breached the contract may be sued for damages. Some states permit a teacher's certificate to be revoked if the teacher breaches the contract. If a school district breaks a contract, teachers may be awarded payments for damages or be reinstated to their former positions.

Every state also has some type of tenure law. **Tenure** protects teachers from dismissal without cause. Each state defines "cause"; the usual reasons include incompetency, immorality, insubordination, and unprofessional conduct. In addition, as explained in the next section, the school district must follow due process if it wants to dismiss a tenured teacher. From its inception, the notion of tenure has been controversial. Arguments for and against tenure are presented in this chapter's Taking Issue box.

Once granted tenure, rather than sign an annual contract, many teachers are employed under a **continuing contract**. The term means that their reemployment for the next year is guaranteed unless school officials give notice by a specific date that the contract will not be renewed.

Most states have a probationary period before teachers achieve tenure. Moreover, many tenured teachers who change districts lose their tenure and must serve another period of probation. The probationary period often consists of three years of consecutive, satisfactory service, but some states have been considering whether to establish shorter periods, at the end of which new teachers can be quickly removed from their positions, or longer periods before teachers can attain tenure.

Probationary contracts in some states allow the teacher to be discharged at the end of the contract term for any reason and without explanation—no due process is required, unless the teacher can demonstrate that his or her dismissal involves a constitutionally guaranteed liberty or property interest. (See the next section for information on the meaning of due process.) In other states, probationary teachers have

breach of contract What occurs when one side fails to perform as agreed in a contract.

tenure Permanence of position granted to educators after a probationary period, which prevents their dismissal except for legally specified causes and through formalized due-process procedures.

continuing contract An employment contract that is automatically renewed from year to year without need for the teacher's signature.

---

[4]Mark Walsh, "Appeals Court Upholds N.Y.C. Liability Over Teacher Test," *Education Week* (February 5, 2014).

TAKING ISSUE

TENURE FOR TEACHERS

At one time, many teaching positions in large cities were controlled by political patronage. In some cities, principalships were available for a price at the ward committeeman's office, and teaching jobs were won or lost on the basis of precinct work. In general, teachers were afraid to contradict an administrator or an influential parent. Tenure was introduced partly to stop these abuses and to give teachers independence in and out of the classroom. However, some educators now contend that the tenure system has outlived its usefulness.

Question

Should the tenure system for teachers continue? (Think about this question as you read the PRO and CON arguments listed here. What is *your* response to this issue?)

Arguments PRO

1. Teaching is, by its nature, controversial. A good teacher cannot help but offend someone at some level. Teachers can do their jobs properly only with the academic freedom that tenure helps to protect.

2. A tenure system does not protect incompetence. Procedures exist for removing a teacher who is clearly ineffective. The responsibility for teacher incompetence lies with lax state licensing procedures and with administrators who are too reluctant to dismiss teachers during probationary periods.

3. Teachers must cope with pressure from a bewildering array of sources, including parents, other community members, administrators, and legislators. A complaint from any one of these parties might lead to a teacher's dismissal. For this reason, teachers need—and deserve—the special protection offered by tenure.

4. Tenure was originally a response to serious political and administrative abuses, especially in large cities. The same forces that caused these problems still exist, and they will create similar abuses if the protection of tenure is ever removed.

Arguments CON

1. Some teachers use their positions to advance personal, social, or political views under the guise of controversial discussion. Other teachers are simply lazy or incompetent. Often these marginal teachers—not the good teachers—benefit from tenure protection.

2. The procedures for removing a tenured teacher are often so complex and arouse so much resentment among other teachers that administrators are discouraged from trying. Furthermore, even with upgraded screening methods, many ineffective teachers will continue to slip through. The only solution is to give school officials, like private employers, the right to fire an unproductive employee.

3. The many sources of pressure actually enhance a teacher's security. Active parents and community members often use their influence to protect good teachers. The layers of school administration offer avenues of appeal if a teacher's position is threatened. Thus, even without a tenure system, competent teachers will be secure in their jobs.

4. Teachers now have powerful professional organizations that shield them from undue political and administrative interference. With these organizations looking after teachers' rights, the tenure system has become an anachronism.

Question Reprise: What Is Your Stand?

Reflect again on the following question by explaining *your* stand on this issue: Should the tenure system for teachers continue?

general due-process rights, but the process may be streamlined to expedite dismissal of candidates rated as incompetent.[5]

Tenure May Be Eroding   As the quality and effectiveness of elementary and secondary schools have become of increasing public concern, questioning of tenure policies and arrangements has grown substantially. Some state governments and school

[5]Mark F. Bernstein, "Delaying Teacher Tenure for Education's Good," *School Administrator* (May 2006), available at **www.aasa.org**; and Neelesh Moorthy, "Elimination of Teacher Tenure Faces State Legal Battle," *The Chronicle* (February 4, 2015), available at **www.dukechronicle.com**.

TABLE 9.1	Due-Process Rules for Dismissing a Tenured Teacher

1. The teacher must be given a timely, detailed, written notice of the charges.

2. The teacher must be accorded a hearing and sufficient time to prepare.

3. The teacher has a right to be represented by legal counsel.

4. The teacher may present written and oral evidence, including witnesses.

5. The teacher may cross-examine witnesses and challenge evidence.

6. The hearing is to be conducted before an impartial body. The US Supreme Court has ruled (in *Hortonville District v. Hortonville Education Association*) that, under the US Constitution, a school board may be that impartial body unless bias can be proven.

7. The teacher is entitled to a written transcript of the proceedings.

8. The teacher has the right to appeal an adverse ruling to a higher legal authority, usually the state court system.

Source: See *Hortonville District v. Hortonville Education Association,* 426 US 482 (1976); Richard S. Vacca, "Teacher Evaluation and the Courts," *CEPI Education Law Newsletter* (December 2003), available at **www.cepi.vcu.edu/publications/newsletters**; Richard S. Vacca, "Public School Teachers," *CEPI Education Law Newsletter* (October 2006), available at **www.cepi.vcu.edu/publications/newsletters**; and Stephen Sawchuk, "Due Process Laws Vary for Teachers by State," *Education Week*, September 24, 2014.

districts have moved to increase the pre-tenure probationary period, usually from two years to three, and some administrators have increased their scrutiny and data collection regarding possibly incompetent teachers to solidify their position in due-process hearings.

Questioning of tenure accelerated nationally in 2014 and 2015 after a judge ruled in ***Vergara v. California*** that tenure unconstitutionally deprives students at low-achieving schools of equal educational opportunity. Many educators and researchers disputed the underlying theories, which presuppose that tests generally used to assess achievement can distinguish between effective/competent and ineffective/incompetent teachers. In addition, eliminating tenure and moving to fire supposedly unfit teachers would make an appreciable dent in the low-achievement status of low-income students. Whether the Vergara ruling will be upheld in a long appeals process and whether it will have much influence on school district policies and practices are open issues to be determined in the future.[6]

Vergara v. California A state-court ruling that tenure unconstitutionally deprives students at low-achieving schools of equal educational opportunity.

9-2c Due Process in Dismissal of Teachers

Due process refers to the use of legal rules and principles established to protect the rights of the accused. These principles are especially important to a teacher being dismissed from a job. The core element of due process is fairness. Although requirements vary from state to state, the rules shown in Table 9.1 are generally recognized in teacher dismissal cases.

due process A formalized legal procedure with specific and detailed rules and principles designed to protect the rights of individuals.

Firing a teacher for incompetence requires documentation of efforts to help that person improve. Obtaining this documentation can be burdensome for everyone involved, and few tenured teachers are dismissed using formal legal procedures. Instead, administrators sometimes use less formal procedures for excluding incompetent

---

[6]Carl Cohn, "What's Wrong With the Vergara Ruling," *Ed Source* (October 5, 2014), available at **www.edsource.org**; Liz Dwyer, "Can America Really Fire Its Way to Better Teachers?" *Take Part* (June 11, 2014), available at **www.takepart.com**; and Nick Gillepsie, "Teacher Tenure on Trial in NYC," *Reason* (March 16, 2015), available at **www.reason.com**.

teachers from their school districts. These procedures include counseling incompetent teachers out of the profession and suggesting and financing early retirement.[7]

9-2d Negotiation and Strikes

Teachers have the right to form and belong to unions and other professional organizations. Since the 1960s, such teacher groups have lobbied for state legislation to permit school boards to negotiate agreements with them. This effort has been successful in most states; however, a few continue to prohibit negotiations between teachers and school boards. Although the laws enacted vary widely, they usually allow the two sides to bargain collectively or at least to "meet and confer." Some states specify the procedure that must be followed if the two sides fail to agree (for example, fact-finding in Kansas; binding arbitration in Maryland).

Because education is considered a vital public service, the law generally prohibits employee strikes. (A few states allow teachers to withhold services under specific conditions written into state law.) However, teachers sometimes do strike despite legal prohibitions. In such instances, school officials can seek court injunctions ordering teachers to return to their classrooms. Defiance of a court order can result in penalties. Florida and Minnesota, for example, prohibit striking teachers from receiving salary increases for one year after a strike; New York law allows striking teachers to be penalized two days' pay for each day on strike; and Michigan permits dismissal of striking teachers.

9-2e Protection against Assault

In recent decades, physical assault on teachers and administrators has become an important problem at some schools, particularly secondary schools in big cities. In such cases, courts generally have convicted defendants who violated either educational statutes or state criminal codes. Some analysts have concluded that educators can help protect themselves and their fellow employees by vigorously pressing criminal charges and initiating civil suits for assault and battery. In addition, many school districts have developed policies that stress punishment of students, parents, or others who assault teachers and that also assist teachers in pursuing legal responses. On the other hand, due to various legal complications, it is often difficult to prosecute or otherwise punish special-education students who assault teachers.[8]

9-2f Protection against Unreasonable Search and Surveillance

Teachers have Fourth Amendment privacy rights that protect them against unreasonable open-ended search of their property, such as a locked desk in their classroom or a car in the school parking lot. School officials, police, or others must have some kind of evidence that provides a reasonable basis to support their search.

In several instances, administrators have installed video and/or audio in classrooms to provide surveillance of actions that allegedly might be dangerous to students. In one case in which audio recording devices were placed in special-education

---

[7]Edwin M. Bridges, *Managing the Incompetent Teacher*, 2nd ed. (Eugene, OR: ERIC Clearinghouse on Educational Management, 1990). See also Zach Miner, "Ratting Out Bad Teachers," *District Administration* (May 2008), p. 12, available at **www.districtadministration.com**; and Richard S. Vacca, "Teacher Employment Contracts," *CEPI Education Law Newsletter* (February 2015), available at **www.cepi.vcu.edu/publications/newsletters**.

[8]Kevin Bushweller, "The Return of Laura Marks," *Teacher Magazine* (November/December 2001), pp. 22–29; Perry A. Zirkel, "Assaults on School Personnel," *Principal* (September/October 2002); Michael D. Simpson, "When Educators Are Assaulted," *NEA Today* (February 2011), available at **www.nea.org**; and "Report Shows Assaults on Students and Teachers Are a Continuing Problem," June 27, 2014, posting by the Wisconsin Education Association Council, available at **www.weac.org**.

classrooms, a federal court ruled that this did not violate teachers' rights because a classroom is a public-use area subject to constant scrutiny. However, a state court subsequently found the district in violation of that state's eavesdropping laws.

9-2g Freedom of Expression

Courts have tended to uphold teachers' rights to express themselves in public or in school (see Overview 9.1). However, in determining whether the expression is protected under the First Amendment, the court considers the effects on school operation, teacher performance, teacher–superior relationships, and coworkers, as well as the appropriateness of the time, place, and manner of the teacher's remarks.

An example is the case of Marvin Pickering, a tenured high school teacher who published a letter to the editor of the local newspaper criticizing the board and superintendent about bond proposals and expenditures. The letter resulted in his termination. In *Pickering v. Board of Education,* the US Supreme Court held that publishing the letter did not impede the "proper performance of his daily duties in the classroom or... [interfere] with the regular operation of schools generally." For this reason, Pickering's dismissal was found to be improper. Similarly, the court system awarded $1 million to a Portland, Oregon, teacher whose district fired her for speaking out against what she viewed as insufficient opportunities provided for her special-education students. These precedents have made school officials uncertain about how to respond when teachers use social media such as Twitter to make critical or crude comments about their schools or students.[9]

On the other hand, two teachers in Alaska were dismissed for writing a letter that was highly critical of their superintendent and contained many false allegations. Reaction to the letter was immediate and prolonged. The Alaska Supreme Court held that the teachers' effectiveness had been impaired by their remarks and that their ability to work closely with colleagues had been diminished.[10]

A comparison of these cases shows that the decision rested not just on the behavior itself but also on its results. The courts have developed a three-step analysis for assessing teachers' rights to freedom of expression: (1) Did the teacher's expression of opinion involve a public matter of political, social, or other concern to the community? (2) If yes, courts still must weigh First Amendment rights against the employer's responsibility to promote a productive and harmonious climate for the delivery of education. The latter consideration led the courts to reject teachers' rights to wear political buttons if that might affect their communicating the curriculum. Finally, (3) the teacher is entitled to judicial relief only if his or her expression of opinion can be shown to be a motivating factor in dismissal or other punitive action. The Supreme Court largely reaffirmed this line of reasoning in the *Garcetti v. Ceballos* decision in 2006.[11]

[9]*Pickering v. Board of Education,* 391 US 563 (1968). See also Richard S. Vacca, "Teacher First Amendment Speech 2006," *CEPI Education Law Newsletter* (January 2006), available at **www .cepi.vcu.edu/publications/newsletters**; Frank D. LoMonte, "Tweet Police," January 3, 2014, posting by Slate, available at **www.slate.com**; and Doug Oakley, "Teachers and Social Media: Trekking on Treacherous Terrain," *eSchool News* (September 22, 2014), available at **www.eschoolnews.com**.

[10]*Watts v. Seward School Board,* 454 P. 2d 732 (Alaska 1969), cert. denied, 397 US 921 (1970). See also Edwin C. Darden, "When Speech Isn't Free," *American School Board Journal* (December 2007), pp. 42–43; and Anshu Agarwal and Bart Miller, "When Is Public Employee Speech Protected by the First Amendment," July 29, 2014, posting by Colorado LegiSource, available at **http:// legisource.net**.

[11]Benjamin Dowling-Sendor, "Is Speaking Out Cause for Dismissal?" *American School Board Journal* (March 1990), pp. 8, 46; Richard. S. Vacca, "*Garcetta v. Ceballos,*" *CEPI Education Law Newsletter* (October 2007), available at **www.cepi.vcu.edu/publications/newsletters**; and Paul M. Secunda, "US Supreme Court Review: Lane V. Franks," July 10, 2014, posting by the Marquette University Law School, available at **www.law.marquette.edu**.

OVERVIEW 9.1

SELECTED US SUPREME COURT DECISIONS AFFECTING TEACHERS' RIGHTS AND RESPONSIBILITIES

Case	Summary of Decision
Pickering v. Board of Education (1968)	Teachers may speak their opinions as long as the school's regular operation is not disrupted.
Board of Regents of State Colleges v. Roth (1972)	After the probationary period, teachers have a property interest in continued employment.
Cleveland Board of Education v. LeFleur (1974)	Boards of education may establish leave policies for pregnant teachers, but these policies may not contain arbitrary leave and return dates.
Hortonville District v. Hortonville Education Association (1976)	In a due-process hearing a school board may be the impartial body conducting the hearing.
Washington v. Davis (1976)	Underrepresentation of a group in the workforce does not, in itself, prove unconstitutional employment discrimination, but the employer in this situation must prove that hiring has not been discriminatory.
School Board of Nassau County v. Arline (1987)	Dismissing a teacher because of a physical impairment or contagious disease is unconstitutional.
Lehnert v. Ferris Faculty Association (1991)	Employees who are not union members cannot be required to pay dues used for political purposes unrelated to collective bargaining agreements.

Pickering and similar decisions would not be applicable to teachers in schools not publicly funded. The civil rights of private- and parochial-school teachers—tenure, freedom of expression, due process, and the like—depend primarily on the terms of their individual contracts with the school.

Verbal and Emotional Abuse of Students Teachers' rights to freedom of expression do not extend, of course, to verbal or emotional abuse of students. Teachers can be sued and/or suspended or dismissed for engaging in such behavior. For example, a teacher who also served as a basketball and football coach was accused of using terms (while coaching) such as "tontos" in dealing with Native American students and "jungle bunnies" in referring to African American students. Although allowed to continue teaching science and physical education, he was suspended from coaching for unprofessional conduct. Another teacher's name was placed on a statewide child abuse registry after a student's mother alleged that the teacher had ridiculed her son's weight and pinched his cheeks. Other teachers have had their employment terminated or interrupted for directing obscene curses at students they perceived as troublesome or for persistently using sarcasm and ridicule to pressure or embarrass students. Teachers also can be sued personally under civil liability or criminal statutes by parents who believe their children have been injured by verbal or emotional abuse or even by allegedly vulgar materials assigned by the teacher.[12]

---

[12]Perry A. Zirkel and Ivan B. Gluckman, "Verbal Abuse of Students," *Principal* (May 1991), pp. 51–52; Mark Walsh, "'Slave Ship' Case Settled," *Education Week* (July 8, 1998); Edwin C. Darden, "The Words That Wound," *American School Board Journal* (March 2008), pp. 42–43; and "Ed Law Briefly: Teacher Who Verbally Insults Young Student Can Be Listed on a Statewide Child Abuse Registry," *Real Clear Education* (September 16, 2014), available at **www.realcleareducation.com**.

9-2h Academic Freedom

academic freedom A protection permitting teachers to teach subject matter and choose instructional materials relevant to the course without restriction from administrators or other persons outside the classroom.

Academic freedom refers to the teacher's freedom to choose subject matter and instructional materials relevant to the course without interference from administrators or outsiders. Recent years have witnessed hundreds of incidents in which parents or others have tried to remove or restrict use of public-school materials, including allegedly immoral or unwholesome works such as *Little Red Riding Hood,* the Harry Potter series, *Snow White, Huckleberry Finn,* and the *Goosebumps* series. There have been many thousands of attempts to ban materials from US schools and libraries. Several courts have ruled that materials can be eliminated on the basis of vulgarity but not to censor ideas. In general, teachers should have a written rationale for the materials they select, explaining how they fit into the curriculum, and they should give students a choice of alternate materials if the students or their parents object to the materials selected.[13]

Appeals courts have upheld a high school teacher's right to assign a magazine article containing "a vulgar term for an incestuous son"; another teacher's use of a film in which citizens of a small town randomly killed one person each year; school library inclusion of books involving witchcraft and the occult; and elementary-school teachers' use of a literary anthology in which students were instructed to pretend they were witches and write poetic chants.[14]

On the other hand, decisions of school officials to restrict teachers' academic freedom have sometimes been upheld. For example, a West Virginia art teacher was suspended for (unwittingly) distributing sexually explicit cartoons, an Ohio English teacher was prohibited from assigning the books *One Flew over the Cuckoo's Nest* and *Manchild in the Promised Land* to juvenile students unless their parents consented, a North Carolina teacher was disciplined after her students performed a play containing adult language in a state drama competition, and an Ohio teacher was dismissed for inappropriate religious activities that included branding crosses electrically onto students' arms.

In general, courts have considered the following issues: (1) students' age and grade level, (2) the relevancy of the questioned material to the curriculum, (3) the duration of the material's use, (4) the general acceptance of a disputed teaching method within the profession, (5) the prior existence of board policy governing selection of materials and teaching techniques, (6) whether the materials are required or optional, and (7) whether actions against the teacher involved retaliation for free expression.[15]

9-2i Teacher Exemplars, Personal Behavior, Internet Use, and Dress Codes

Decades ago, teachers' behaviors were closely scrutinized because communities believed they should be role models and exemplars—that is, examples to their students of high moral standards and impeccable character, conservative dress and grooming,

[13]*Board of Education v. Pico,* 102 S. Ct. 2799 (1982); Jack L. Nelson, "The Need for Courage in American Schools," *Social Education* (November/December 2010), pp. 298–303; and "Banned and Challenged Classics," 2015 posting by the American Library Association, available at **www.ala.org**.

[14]*Keefe v. Geanakos,* 418 F. 2d 359 (1st Cir. 1969); *Pratt v. Independent School District No. 831,* 670 F. 2d 771 (8th Cir. 1982); and *Brown v. Joint Unified School District,* 42-15772 (9th Cir. 1994). See also Todd A. DeMitchell and John J. Carney, "Harry Potter and the Public School," *Phi Delta Kappan* (October 2005), pp. 159–165; and Leah Barkoukis, "Victory for Academic Freedom," March 24, 2014, posting by Town Hall, available at **www.townhall.com**.

[15]*DeVito v. Board of Education,* 317 S.E. 2d 159 (W. Va. 1984). See also Benjamin Dowling-Sendor, "Who Has the Right to Choose?" *American School Board Journal* (March 2002); Michael D. Simpson, "Defending Academic Freedom," *Social Education* (November/December 2010), pp. 310–315; "Supreme Court Rejects Appeal From Teacher Fired for Promoting Creationism," *Huff Post* (October 6, 2014); and Dave Bangert, "Evolution, Science Back in Bill's Cross Hairs," *Lafayette Journal & Courier* (January 21, 2015), available at **www.jconline.com**.

and polished manners. Although these standards have relaxed, in some places, teachers may still be dismissed under immorality statutes for a drunk-driving incident, homosexuality, or for living unmarried with a member of the opposite sex. Seemingly less weighty behaviors have also sometimes become grounds for dismissal, such as engaging in a water fight in which a student suffered mild skin irritations or joking about testes and menstrual periods when these topics were not part of the curriculum being taught by a science teacher. Teachers have been dismissed for actions such as participating in a "Slut Walk" intended to empower sexually assaulted women, and for modeling swimsuits.[16]

Recent years have seen occasional movement toward reemphasizing teachers' responsibilities as moral exemplars in and out of school. Many parents have demanded that schools reinforce traditional values among students, and many schools have introduced character education programs. School district policies generally still require that teachers serve as positive role models. Based in part on such requirements, Indiana courts upheld the dismissal of a teacher who drank beer in the presence of students at a local restaurant and then drove them home. A number of teachers have been reprimanded, suspended, or even fired for posting sexually oriented material on the Internet. In the past few years, some teachers have been dismissed for Internet postings such as one that indicated an intention to play "Crazy Bitch Bingo" at a local restaurant, and another for including an image of a male stripper at a bachelorette party. Numerous such dismissals have been reversed in court or voided by district officials or legal settlements.

According to attorneys for the National School Boards Association, misbehavior outside the school that reduces teachers' capacity to serve as positive role models can justify reprimands or dismissals as long as rights to free speech and free association (with friends or acquaintances of one's choice) are not violated. Some courts have followed this line of reasoning in allowing school districts to carry out drug testing of teachers and other staff. However, teachers are much less likely than professionals in general to be found or accused of using illegal drugs, and teacher groups have tended to view drug testing as an invasion of privacy. At least one federal court has ruled that such testing unconstitutionally violates teachers' rights to be free of unreasonable searches.[17]

Moral standards are also subject to changing social mores. In the past few years, for example, some states and numerous jurisdictions have passed laws prohibiting discrimination against gay or lesbian individuals. Several courts have cited such laws in rejecting job termination and other actions that may have been directed against gay or lesbian teachers. However, in some locations, schools still are moving to terminate gay or lesbian teachers.[18]

---

[16]*Everett Area School District v. Ault*, 548 A. 2d 1341 (Pa. Cmwlth. 1988); *Baldrige v. Board of Trustees*, No. 97–230 (Washington 1997); Richard S. Vacca, "Public Trust and the Role of Classroom Teachers," *CEPI Education Law Newsletter* (March 2005), available at **www.cepi.vcu.edu/publications/newsletters**; Edwin C. Darden, "Conduct Unbecoming," *American School Board Journal* (October 2007); and Suzanne E. Eckes, "Strippers, Beer, and Bachelorette Parties," *Principal Leadership* (September 2013), available at **www.nassp.org**.

[17]"Ed Law Briefly: Mississippi High Court Affirms School District's Right to Fire a Teacher Who Refused Drug Test," September 10, 2014, posting by Real Clear Education, available at **www.realcleareducation.com**; and Grace Chen, "Drug Testing Teachers," 2015 posting by Public School Review, available at **www.publicschoolreview.com/blog/drug-testing-teachers-testing-positive-or-negative**.

[18]Michael D. Simpson, "Big Legal Victories for Gay Students and Teachers," *NEA Today* (January 2003); Craig Sailor, "Tacoma District Apologizing for Firing Gay Teacher," *Washington Times* (July 10, 2014), available at **www.washingtontimes.com**; and Amanda Terkel, "Gay Teacher Fired after Posting Marriage Announcement on Facebook," January 14, 2015, posting by *Huff Post*, available at **www.huffingtonpost.com**.

Courts also have decided cases in which teachers' dress and grooming conflicted with school district policies or traditions. One California court ruled that women teaching at "back-to-basics" schools in Pomona could not be required to wear dresses if they preferred to wear outfits with pants. Another California court ruled that Paul Finot's wearing of a beard was a symbolic expression protected by the First Amendment as well as a liberty protected under the Fourteenth Amendment. On the other hand, when Max Miller's contract was not renewed because of his beard and long sideburns, the circuit court upheld the dismissal. "As public servants in a special position of trust," the judges stated, "teachers may properly be subjected to many restrictions in their professional lives which would be invalid if generally applied." In any case, proper attire and grooming are important considerations in the profession of teaching whether or not they are legally required.[19]

9-2j Tort Liability and Negligence

torts Civil wrongs.

Torts are civil wrongs. Under tort law, individuals who have suffered through the improper conduct of others may sue for damages. For example, educators may be found guilty of negligence when students are injured during classes, on the playground, or elsewhere if the injury resulted from failure to take appropriate preventive action. Of course, a case won't be filed every time a child is accidentally injured, but when injury results from negligent or intentional action, legal remedies can be pursued.

Generations ago, nearly every school district was immune from tort liability. This immunity had its origins in English common law, under which the king, as sovereign, could not be sued. Since 1960, most states have eliminated or modified this view of governmental immunity. In states that permit suits, the parties sued may include the school district as well as specific school administrators, teachers, and other staff. For example, school districts can be held liable for their employees' negligent or malicious actions (such as sexual abuse, neglect of hazing or bullying among students, or failure to report students' suicidal intentions) if school officials have provided little or no supervision or ignored persistent complaints. District officials may be guilty of negligence if a student is being harassed, and they knew about the situation but did nothing. These responsibilities even extend to malicious or neglectful action or inaction by volunteers who donate time to work with a school.[20]

Teachers are required by law to protect their students from injury or harm (Photo 9.1). In nearly all states, the traditional standard of care is what a reasonable and prudent person would do under similar circumstances. In one case, a kindergarten teacher was charged with negligence when a child fell from a playground structure while the teacher was attending to other children. The court ruled that the teacher was not required to have all children in sight at all times. Her presence in the immediate area was sufficient to establish that the teacher was fulfilling her duty. The New York State Supreme Court reached a similar conclusion in overturning a jury award to an injured high school athlete, on grounds that school officials had exercised "reasonable care" in operating their school's football program. In other cases, however, school districts or their

---

[19]*Miller v. School District No. 167 of Cook County, Illinois,* 495 F. 2d 65 (7th Cir. 1974); *Finot v. Pasadena City Board of Education,* 58 Cal. Rptr. 520 (1976); June Million, "Dress Codes for Teachers?" *Education Digest* (January 2004), pp. 59–61; Edward Graham, "Do Teachers Need Dress Codes to Know What to Wear at School?" *NEA Today* (June 2, 2014), available at **www.neatoday.org**; and "May a Teacher Wear Clothing Not Approved by a Teacher Dress Code?" 2014 posting by the First Amendment Center, available at **www.firstamendmentschools.org**.

[20]Richard S. Vacca, "Tort Liability and School Staff," *CEPI Education Law Newsletter* (January 2008), available at **www.cepi.vcu.edu/publications/newsletters**; "Ed Law Briefly: School Officials Had No Actual Knowledge of Harassment," November 12, 2014, posting by Real Clear Education, available at **www.realcleareducation.com**; and Matt M. Carver, "Sizing Up Volunteer Fitness," *School Administrator* (February 2015).

∧ PHOTO 9.1 Teachers must try to foresee potentially dangerous situations and prevent injuries to their students.

Catherine Ledner/Getty Images

employees have been found partially or wholly responsible for students' injuries that a reasonable person should have been able to foresee. Teachers and administrators must be particularly vigilant to ensure that precautions are taken to ensure the safety of students with disabilities, such as sometimes assigning an aide to watch an autistic child with a history of wandering away.[21]

An important principle is whether the injury could have been foreseen and thus prevented. An overweight student expressed concern to her physical education teacher about a class requirement to perform a back somersault. The teacher insisted the somersault be done, and the student's neck snapped in the attempt. The court said the teacher showed utter indifference to the student's safety, and the jury awarded $77,000 in damages. Similarly, a high school student in an introductory chemistry class blew away his hand while completing an assignment to make gunpowder. The court ruled that the injury was foreseeable, and the teacher was negligent. Typically, courts will take into account the age and maturity of students, the degree of difficulty and inherent danger of activities, the proper use of protective devices, and related considerations in determining whether adults were negligent in not foreseeing the likelihood of injuries.[22]

School districts require parents to sign consent forms when students are involved in activities such as field trips or athletic competitions. The form generally has two purposes: (1) to inform parents of their children's whereabouts and (2) to release school personnel from liability in case of injury. However, because parents cannot waive a child's right to sue for damages if an injury occurs, these forms actually serve only the first purpose. Obtaining a parental waiver does *not* release teachers from their legal obligations to protect the safety and welfare of students.

Recent decades have brought what some observers describe as an explosion in litigation related to liability and negligence. In addition, rather than accepting the exercise of reasonable precautions as a defense against negligence, recent judicial decisions have frequently emphasized "strict liability." In this situation, teachers cannot be too careful, for negligence might occur in numerous school settings. Physical education instructors, counselors, sponsors of extracurricular activities, and shop and laboratory teachers must take special care. Prudent safeguards include a clear set of written rules, verbal warnings to students, regular inspection of equipment, adherence to state laws and district policies regarding hazardous activities, thoughtful planning, and diligent supervision.[23]

---

[21]*Clark v. Furch*, 567 S.W. 2d 457 (Mo. App. 1978); Benjamin Dowling-Sendor, "Friday Night Tragedy," *American School Board Journal* (September 2004); "School Liability and Negligent Supervision of Children with Disabilities," January 16, 2014, posting by Education Expert, available at **www.education-expert.com**; and Paris Achen, "Lawsuit Filed on Behalf of Injured Teen Gymnast," *The Columbian* (February 10, 2015), available at **www.columbian.com**.

[22]*Landers v. School District No. 203, O'Fallon*, 383 N.E. 2d 645 (Ill. App. Ct. 1978). See also Edwin C. Darden, "A Slippery Slope," *American School Board Journal* (April 2007); Richard S. Vacca, "Student Safety," *CEPI Education Law Newsletter* (February 2011), available at **www.cepi.vcu.edu/publications/newsletters**; and "*Doe v New York Dept of Educ.*," May 7, 2014, posting by Justia US Law, available at **www.law.justia.com**.

[23]Mark S. Kapocius, "Sound Advice," *American School Board Journal* (March 2006); Richard S. Vacca, "The Duty of Care and Deliberate Indifference," *CEPI Education Law Newsletter* (May 2014), available at **www.cepi.vcu.edu/publications/newsletters**; and "Proving Negligence or Breach of Statutory Duty," 2015 posting by Lexis Nexis, available at **www.lexisnexis.com**.

TABLE 9.2	Selected Physical and Behavioral Indicators of Physical Abuse and Neglect, Sexual Abuse, and Emotional Abuse

Physical Indicators   **Behavioral Indicators**

Physical Abuse—nonaccidental injury to a child that may involve beatings, burns, strangulation, or human bites

Physical Indicators	Behavioral Indicators
• Unexplained bruises, swollen areas	• Self-destructive
• Welts, bite marks, bald spots	• Withdrawn and/or aggressive extremes
• Unexplained burns, fractures, abrasions	• Complaints of soreness or discomfort
• Evidence of inappropriate treatment of injuries	• Bizarre explanation of injuries

Physical Neglect—failure to provide a child with basic necessities

Physical Indicators	Behavioral Indicators
• Unattended medical need, lice, poor hygiene	• Regularly displays fatigue, listlessness
• Consistent lack of supervision	• Steals food, begs from classmates
• Consistent hunger, inadequate nutrition	• Frequently absent or tardy
• Consistent inappropriate clothing	• Reports no caretaker at home

Sexual Abuse—sexual exploitation, including rape, incest, fondling, and pornography

Physical Indicators	Behavioral Indicators
• Torn, stained, or bloody underclothing	• Withdrawal, chronic depression
• Pain, swelling, or itching in genital area	• Hysteria, lack of emotional control
• Venereal disease knowledge	• Inappropriate sex play, premature sex
• Frequent urinary or yeast infections	• Excessive seductiveness

Emotional Abuse—a pattern of behavior that attacks a child's emotional development such as name calling, put-downs, and so on

Physical Indicators	Behavioral Indicators
• Speech disorders	• Habit disorders (sucking, rocking, biting)
• Delayed physical development	• Emotional disturbance
• Substance abuse	• Neurotic traits (sleep disorders, play inhibition)
• Ulcer, asthma, severe allergy	• Antisocial, destructive, delinquent

Note: United Mothers (see "Source" below) emphasizes the following advice: "Symptoms, or indications of abuse, vary greatly from child to child…. Possibly only one or a few, or none of these symptoms…will be readily apparent in a child who IS being abused. Absence of any or all…does NOT mean that a child is NOT being abused. If you suspect there is a problem, do NOT try to diagnose or determine the extent of the problem on your own; please contact a professional immediately."

Source: Adapted from guidelines published by Safeguarding Our Children—United Mothers. Reprinted with permission. Also see material at **www.childabuse.com**; Felicia F. Romeo, "The Educator's Role in Reporting the Emotional Abuse of Children," *Journal of Instructional Psychology* (September 2000); Tracy W. Smith and Glenn W. Lambie, "Teachers' Responsibilities When Adolescent Abuse and Neglect Are Suspected," *Middle School Journal* (January 2005), pp. 33–40; "Mandatory Reporting of Child Abuse and Neglect State Statute Overview," December 9, 2011, posting by the National Conference of State Legislatures, available at **www.ncsl.org**; "Mandatory Reporters of Child Abuse and Neglect," 2014 posting by the Child Welfare Information Gateway, available at **www.childwelfare.gov**; and Richard S. Vacca, "Reporting Suspected Child Abuse," *CEPI Education Law Newsletter* (November 2014), available at **www.cepi.vcu.edu/publications/newsletters**.

9-2k Reporting Child Abuse

Because a high percentage of abuse is directed at school-age children, schools play an important role in protecting them. In most states, laws require educators to report suspected cases of child abuse to authorities or designated social service agencies. As a result, increasing numbers of school districts have written policies describing how teachers should proceed when they suspect abuse. Warning signs that may indicate a child is being abused are shown in Table 9.2.

9-2l Copyright Laws

A *copyright* gives authors and artists control over the reproduction and distribution of works they create; consequently, permission for reproduction usually must be obtained from the owner. Beginning in the 1970s, widespread use of copy machines bred serious

TABLE 9.3	Guidelines on Copying Materials for Educational Use

- Copying prose is limited to excerpts of no more than 1,000 words.

- Copies from an anthology or encyclopedia cannot exceed one story or entry, or 2,500 words.

- A poem may be copied if it is less than 250 words, and an excerpt of no more than 250 words may be copied from a longer poem.

- Distribution of copies from the same author more than once a semester or copying from the same work or anthology more than three times during the semester is prohibited.

- Teachers may make one copy per student for class distribution; if charges are made, they may not exceed actual copying costs.

- It is illegal to create anthologies or compilations by using photocopies as a substitute for purchasing the same or similar materials.

- Consumable materials, such as workbooks, may not be copied.

- Under the fair use doctrine, single copies of printed materials may be made for personal study, lesson planning, research, criticism, comment, and news reporting.

- Most magazine and newspaper articles may be copied freely. However, items in weekly newspapers and magazines designed for classroom use by students may not be copied without permission.

- Individual teachers must decide independently to copy material; they may not be directed to do so by higher authorities.

- There are three categories of material for which copies may be freely made: writings published before 1978 that have never been copyrighted, published works for which copyrights are more than seventy-five years old, and US government publications.

- It is safer to link to a source than to provide a full download if you are not sure you have fair use.

fair use A principle allowing use of copyrighted material without permission of the author, under specific, limited conditions.

and regular violations of copyright laws. To address this problem, in 1976, Congress amended the original 1909 copyright laws to include photocopying and the educational use of copyrighted materials. In addition, a committee of librarians, publishers, authors, and educators developed "fair use" guidelines. **Fair use** is a legal principle that allows use of copyrighted materials without permission from the author under specific, limited conditions. Table 9.3 summarizes fair use restrictions on copying for classroom use or other educational purposes.[24]

Authors usually copyright plays and musical productions, and schools must obtain permission from the author or the author's agent before presenting such works. Often a royalty fee is charged to secure permission, the amount of which may depend on whether or not admission is charged.

Recordings   Recordings, such as videos and DVDs, also fall within the fair-use guidelines of the copyright laws. These guidelines specify that educational institutions may not keep the recordings they make of copyrighted television programs for more than forty-five days without a license. During the first ten days, an individual teacher may use the recorded program once and may show it once again after that period when "instructional reinforcement is necessary." After forty-five days, the

---

[24]Linda Starr, "Copyrights and Copying Wrongs," 2010 paper posted at the Education World Internet site, available at **www.educationworld.com/a_curr/curr280a.shtml**; Louis Menand, "Crooner in Rights Spat," *New Yorker* (October 20, 2014); Meris Stansbury, "3 Must-Knows about Teachers and Copyright," *eSchool News* (May 28, 2014), available at **www .eschoolnews.com**; and US copyright legislation and practices at **www.copyright.gov**.

recording must be erased. Video recording may occur only when a faculty member requests it in advance; thus, it may not be done on a regular basis in anticipation of faculty requests.

Computer Software   Computer software is subject to the same fair use restrictions as other copyrighted materials. For example, teachers may not copy a protected computer program and distribute it for use on school computers. Downloading computer files from another source may require permission and/or fees. For example, after it was found that a Los Angeles school allegedly possessed pirated copies of hundreds of software programs, district officials agreed to pay $300,000 to rectify this infringement and to develop a multimillion-dollar plan to pay for violations at other schools.

Copyright issues involving the Internet have become an important concern for teachers, students, and administrators. Copyright holders have taken action to prohibit unauthorized use of text or images, to correct or restrict posting of incomplete or erroneous materials, or otherwise to reduce or eliminate potentially illegal publication of their materials on the Internet and other platforms. Business and commercial groups led by the entertainment and software industries worked with federal legislators to develop the No Electronic Theft Act of 1997; the Digital Millennium Act of 1998; the Technology, Education, and Copyright Harmonization Act of 2002; and the Enforcement of Intellectual Property Rights Act of 2008; all of these provide hefty penalties for possessing or distributing illegal electronic copies. These laws include provisions that allow copyright owners to prevent downloading of their material without permission and/or to require recipients to pay a fee. They also protect the copyrights of teachers whose material is posted online.[25]

FOCUS What areas of caution did the preceding material suggest to you as a teacher? What topics might require further study to make sure you do not violate the law but can also defend your rights as a teacher?

9-3 STUDENTS' RIGHTS AND RESPONSIBILITIES

in loco parentis The idea that schools should act "in place of the parent."

During the 1960s, students increasingly began to challenge the authority of school officials to control student behavior. Before these challenges, students' rights were considered limited by their status as minors and by the concept of *in loco parentis*, according to which school authorities assumed the powers of the child's parents during the hours the child was under the school's supervision. Use of this concept has declined, however, and the courts have become more active in identifying and upholding students' constitutional rights. Student responsibilities have been increasingly recognized as well—that is, understanding that students' educational rights are tied in with responsibilities on the part of both students and educators to ensure effective operation of the school.

The following sections and Overview 9.2 summarize some of the most important court decisions involving students' rights and responsibilities. These apply primarily to public schools. As with teachers, students in nonpublic schools may not enjoy all the constitutional guarantees discussed in this chapter. Unless a substantial relationship between the school and the government can be demonstrated, private-school activity is not considered action by the state and therefore does not trigger state constitutional obligations. However, the movement toward voucher plans

---

[25]Linda Howe-Stiger and Brian C. Donohue, "Technology Is Changing What's Fair Use in Teaching—Again," *Education Policy Analysis Archives*, 2002 posting available at **http://epaa .asu.edu**; Edwin C. Darden, "Copyright Rules for Schools," *American School Board Journal* (April 2011), available at **www.asbj.com**; and Kyle Wiens, "The End of Ownership," *Wired* (January 17, 2014), available at **www.wired.com**.

OVERVIEW 9.2

SELECTED US SUPREME COURT DECISIONS AFFECTING STUDENTS' RIGHTS AND RESPONSIBILITIES

Case	Summary of Decision
Tinker v. Des Moines Independent Community School District (1969)	Students are free to express their views except when conduct disrupts classwork, causes disorder, or invades the rights of others.
Goss v. Lopez (1975)	Suspension from school requires some form of due process for students.
Ingraham v. Wright (1977)	Corporal punishment is not cruel or unusual punishment and is permitted where allowed by state law.
New Jersey v. T.L.O. (1985)	To be constitutional, searches of students and students' property must meet a two-pronged test.
Bethel School District No. 403 v. Fraser (1986)	Schools need not permit offensive or disruptive speech.
Hazelwood School District v. Kuhlmeier (1988)	A school newspaper is not a public forum and can be regulated by school officials.
Honig v. Doe (1988)	Disabled students who are disruptive must be retained in their current placement until official hearings are completed.
Gebser v. Lago Vista Independent School District (1998)	School districts are not legally at fault when a teacher sexually harasses a student unless the school acted with "deliberate indifference" in failing to stop it.

(see Chapter 8 Financing Public Education) and other school choice arrangements (discussed in Chapter 16, School Effectiveness and Reform in the United States) that provide public funds for students who are attending nonpublic schools has begun to blur this distinction.

9-3a Freedom of Expression

In 1965, John Tinker, age 15, his sister Mary Beth, age 13, and their friend, Dennis Eckhardt, age 16, were part of a small group planning to wear black armbands to school as a silent, symbolic protest against the war in Vietnam. Hearing of this plan and fearing problems, administrators responded by adopting a policy prohibiting the wearing of armbands; the penalty was suspension until the armbands were removed. The Tinkers and Eckhardt wore the armbands as planned, refused to remove them, and were suspended. Their parents filed suit. In finding for the plaintiffs, the US Supreme Court outlined the scope of student rights, so that this case, *Tinker v. Des Moines Independent Community School District,* became the standard for examining students' freedom of speech guarantees.[26]

To justify prohibition of a particular expression of opinion, the Court ruled, school officials must be able to show that their actions were caused by "something more than a mere desire to avoid the discomfort and unpleasantness that always accompany an unpopular viewpoint." Student conduct that "materially disrupts classwork or involves substantial disorder or invasion of the rights of others" could be

---

[26]*Tinker v. Des Moines Independent Community School District,* 393 US 503 (1969). See also Benjamin Dowling-Sendor, "The Boundaries of Law," *American School Board Journal* (March 2005); Robert M. O'Neil, "Legal Issues in the Protection of Student Freedoms," *Social Education* (November/December 2010), pp. 322–325; Scott L. Sternberg, "Outside the Schoolhouse Gate," *Communications Lawyer* (September 2014), available at **www.americanbar.org**; and "Obscenity Case Files," 2015 posting by the Comic Book Legal Defense Fund, available at **www .cbldf.org**.

prohibited. In the absence of such good reasons for restraint, the students' constitutional guarantees of free speech would apply. But as the preceding statements suggest, free expression in public schools has limits. In *Bethel School District No. 403 v. Fraser,* the US Supreme Court confirmed that students may be punished for offensive or disruptive speech. In 2007, the Court added that administrators may prohibit a student from proclaiming statements such as "Bong Hits for Jesus" because they viewed this as promoting illegal drugs.[27]

Student publications may also raise problems. For example, in one case, school policy required the principal to review each proposed issue of *The Spectrum,* the school newspaper written by journalism students at Hazelwood East High School in St. Louis County, Missouri. The principal objected to two articles scheduled to appear in one issue. The principal claimed the articles were deleted not because of the subject matter but because he considered them poorly written, and there was insufficient time to rewrite them before the publication deadline.

Three student journalists sued, contending their freedom of speech had been violated. This case, *Hazelwood School District v. Kuhlmeier,* reached the US Supreme Court, which upheld the principal's action. The justices found that *The Spectrum* was not a public forum; rather, it was a supervised learning experience for journalism students. As long as educators' actions were related to "legitimate pedagogical concerns," they could regulate the newspaper's contents in any reasonable manner. The ruling further stated that a school could disassociate itself not only from speech that directly interfered with school activities but also from speech that was "ungrammatical, poorly written, inadequately researched, biased, prejudiced, vulgar or profane, or unsuitable for immature audiences." This decision was a clear restriction on student rights as previously understood.[28]

Controversies concerning publications written or distributed by students have prompted many school boards to develop regulations that can withstand judicial scrutiny. Generally, these rules specify a time, place, and manner of distribution; a method of advertising the rules to students; a prompt review process; and speedy appeal procedures. Students may not distribute literature that is by legal definition obscene or libelous, or that is likely to cause the substantial disruption specified in *Tinker.* School boards also have considerable leeway in determining whether nondisruptive material will be published in school newspapers and yearbooks. This chapter's case study involves a teacher concerned about her responsibilities as the school newspaper adviser.

9-3b Cyberbullying and Other Electronic Misdeeds

The Internet and the use of electronic devices have generated legal issues that educators will be contending with for a long time to come. Among the actions generating issues for educators are *cyberbullying, disparagement of school or staff, gaining access to prohibited materials,* and *sexting.* In the case of all four types of activity, students' negative actions more often than not take place outside the school, although they

cyberbullying Actions that involve the use of electronic means to torment, threaten, harass, humiliate, embarrass, or otherwise target another person.

sexting The act of using a smartphone or comparable electronic device to transmit sexually explicit images of oneself to individuals known to or in contact with the sender.

[27]*Bethel School District No. 403 v. Fraser,* 106 S. Ct. 3159 (1986). See also Josh Dunn and Martha Derthick, "Doubtful Jurisprudence," *Education Next* (Winter 2008), available at **www.educationnext.org**; Richard S. Vacca, "Student Expression and Assaultive Speech," *CEPI Education Law Newsletter* (March 2011), available at **www.cepi.vcu.edu/publications/newsletters**; and "Bethel V. Fraser and Morse V. Frederick," 2015 posting by Shmoop, available at **www.shmoop.com**.

[28]*Hazelwood School District v. Kuhlmeier,* 86-836 S. Ct. (1998). See also Richard S. Vacca, "Student Speech and Expression 2004," *CEPI Education Law Newsletter* (February 2004), available at **www.cepi.vcu.edu/publications/newsletters**; Perry A. Zirkel, "Bong Hits?" *Phi Delta Kappan* (October 2007), pp. 158–159; and "Hazelwood v. Kuhlmeier," 2014 posting by Shmoop, available at **www.shmoop.com**.

FROM PRESERVICE TO PRACTICE

ADVISING A STUDENT NEWSPAPER

Sara Rodriguez couldn't believe that she had been assigned to be the faculty adviser for the student newspaper. After all, she was just a beginning teacher. Sara had written for her high school and university student newspapers, but she had never been in charge of such a project. Now Sara found herself supervising and directing teenage students, some who were just three years her junior.

Sara, twenty-one, had recently graduated with an English major and journalism minor. She would be teaching English II and English III, and the student newspaper would be an extracurricular activity.

Bob Cartwright, the student editor, was a member of the senior class who was frequently outspoken about his beliefs and views. Just one month into the school year, all students attended a required assembly for an antidrug program. The next day, Bob came to her and said that he was going to write an editorial emphasizing student rights. He was tired of being forced to attend presentations when he had more important things to do with his time.

The next day Sara found this editorial written by Bob on her desk.

Student Rights Ignored!

Drug-free schools! Just say no!

Slogans without meaning were once again presented to an audience that was more knowledgeable about drugs than

any of the presenters. Every year we have to submit to this inane practice. What a colossal waste of time and energy! If the presenters were knowledgeable, they would already know that some drugs are being grown right on this very campus.

This editor just says NO to more assemblies about drug-free schools. Students are encouraged to walk out should another of these so-called educational opportunities present itself as a requirement. Let's stand up for our right to have a voice in determining what we must suffer. Write letters to this paper. Write to the principal and to the superintendent. Let them know what you think about this assembly and demand to have students involved in the planning process for all assemblies in the future.

Sara decided she must respond quickly, yet she did not want to cause a problem where there was none. She wondered if this editorial would cause trouble and thought she had better seek assistance from the principal. Her English classes were going well, but she wondered if problems serving as student newspaper adviser and dealing with this situation and other similar situations might jeopardize her chances for tenure or a continuing contract.

CASE QUESTIONS

1. What responsibilities and authority does Sara have as faculty adviser for the student newspaper?
2. What should Sara have determined before accepting such a position?
3. Should the student editor's action affect her evaluation?
4. What rights and responsibilities does the student newspaper editor have?

sometimes happen in the classroom or make use of school equipment or resources. Regarding all these types of activities, there is tension between students' rights to free speech and expression, and educators' duty to protect and enhance the welfare of students and staff.

Cyberbullying Cyberbullying involves the use of electronic means to torment, threaten, harass, humiliate, embarrass, or otherwise target another person. The consequences of cyberbullying have been of growing concern as individuals, particularly young people, seem to be frequently using their electronic devices to transmit materials that can be perceived as harmful or damaging to others' status, health, or reputation. In several incidents that were highly publicized in the mass media, children and youth who perceived themselves as targets or who were victims of such materials suffered damaging mental- and physical health effects; some even killed themselves. School officials generally have been reluctant to punish the originators or transmitters of cyberbullying materials, partly because doing so might be viewed as exposing their institutions to legal liability for violating students' free speech.[29]

In a few cases, however, schools have taken action against alleged cyberbullies, and then have been taken to court for doing so. In a California case, for example, an eighth-grade girl reported that a classmate had posted a YouTube video calling her a "brat" and a "slut." The classmate was suspended for two days, after which her family sued the district for violation of free-expression rights. The presiding federal judge said that to allow a school to suspend a student "simply because another student takes offense to their speech, without any evidence that such speech caused a sub-stantial disruption of the school's activities, runs afoul of the law," and ruled against the district. Fortunately, such restrictions do not prevent schools from implementing comprehensive policies to help students understand and avoid the negative conse-quences of cyberbullying, and many districts are introducing such policies.[30]

Changing definitions of bullying and cyberbullying may be raising issues and problems for educators more frequently than in the past. Several analysts believe a tendency is emerging to define even small acts of hostility and social exclusion as examples of bullying. For example, some children have been accused of bullying for not inviting others to their birthday parties or for indicating dislike of particular class-mates. Continuation or magnification of such a trend may make life more difficult for teachers and administrators.

Disparagement of School or Staff   Some students have been punished for send-ing e-mail or other material that school officials considered disparaging of the school or staff, to the extent that the material was potentially disruptive or destructive. Such punishment may be legal even if the computers involved are off school property. How-ever, electronic materials that might fit in these categories have the same legal standing as printed documents, which may require finding a delicate balance between legally protected individual rights on the one hand and prohibitions on harming individuals and institutions on the other. Incidents that have gone to court include the following:

- An Ohio school district had to pay $30,000 to a high school student after it lost a court case in which he challenged his suspension for posting material that ridi-culed his band teacher.
- A Florida school district had to pay monetary damages to a student it had sus-pended for posting negative material about a teacher on Facebook.
- The Third Circuit Court of Appeals ruled that two students who created Myspace profiles ridiculing their principals were protected by the First Amendment in the absence of disruptive effects within the schools.
- A US district court judge ruled against a Vermont district that had banned a critic from school property because district officials alleged that staff members were afraid of him.

On the other hand, some courts have upheld school officials who punished stu-dents for distributing derogatory cell-phone videos of teachers, and some judges have

---

[29]Richard S. Vacca, "Student Expression and Electronic Communication," *CEPI Education Law Newsletter* (April 2007), available at **www.cepi.vcu.edu/publications/newsletters**; Amy Williams, "What Bullying Looks Like in the Digital Age and How to Prevent It," *Edutopia* (October 23, 2014), available at **www.edutopia.org**; and Lauren C. Williams, "Why Illinois Schools Are Requiring Students to Hand Over Their Facebook Passwords," January 22, 2015, posting by Think Progress, available at **www.thinkprogress.org**.

[30]Kenneth S. Trump, "Managing Bullying in Politically Charged Climates," *District Administration* (January 2011), available at **www.districtadministration.com**; Nancy Willard, "What Are You Doing to Prevent Bullying?" *District Administration* (September 2014), available at **www.districtadministration.com**; "Bullying Prevention," 2015 posting by the Children's Safety Network, available at **www.childrenssafetynetwork.org**; and information available from the Cyberbullying Research Center at **www.cyberbullying.us**.

allowed administrators to ban the use of cell phones in classrooms, provided evidence was presented concerning the negative effects on discipline or morale.[31]

Children's Internet Protection Act (CIPA) An act providing that schools and libraries receive discounts on electronic equipment and media and are required to install a "technology protection measure" preventing minors from using computers to access "visual depictions that are obscene, child pornography, or harmful to minors."

Gaining Access to Prohibited Materials   Since the **Children's Internet Protection Act (CIPA)** went into effect in 2001, schools and libraries receiving discounts on electronic equipment and media have been required to install "a technology protection measure" that prevents minors from using computers with Internet capabilities to access "visual depictions that are obscene, child pornography, or harmful to minors." After CIPA was challenged in court, the US Supreme Court ruled that the law is a constitutional condition imposed on institutions in exchange for government funding. But the Court also said institutions must adopt a policy for unblocking the Internet for adults, without requiring the user to offer reasons for disabling the filter. However, CIPA requirements sometimes have been interpreted by school officials and the public as virtually prohibiting all access to YouTube and other sites that offer some prohibited material. Thus classroom use of YouTube and similar sites frequently has been viewed as unacceptable. The US Department of Education provides the following guidance to help teachers handle YouTube and other sites while complying with CIPA:[32]

● Accessing YouTube does not necessarily violate CIPA.
● Websites blocked for students are not always denied to teachers for use in school.
● "Brute force technologies" that shut down wide swaths of the Web, such as all of YouTube, are not required.

Sexting Brouhahas   Sexting frequently is defined as the act of using a smartphone or comparable electronic device to transmit sexually explicit images of oneself to individuals known to or in contact with the sender. A growing number of jurisdictions have been passing laws against sexting, generally raising child pornography charges if the sender or recipient is not yet an adult. Depending on the jurisdiction, sexters or transmitters of the images can be charged with either misdemeanors or felonies and can receive significant fines or jail sentences.

In some jurisdictions, sext messages have been circulated very widely and indiscriminately among young people, and sometimes have served to embarrass and/or intimidate subjects of the images and/or others who circulated them. In these situations, police and other government officials have been torn between assertive punishment to inhibit sexting and reluctance to prosecute sexting participants as child pornographers and thereby punish them with a label to follow them the remainder of their lives.

Because sext messages can be sent easily to numerous classmates and acquaintances and sometimes can create conflicts as well as damage reputations and social relationships, educators have become increasingly concerned with this type of behavior among their students. Some districts have introduced courses or other learning activities to inform students of the negatives and dangers involved in sexting. In general, school officials concerned with sexting should follow legal principles and guidelines described elsewhere in this chapter with respect to search (for example, of cell phones), discipline, and harassment.[33]

This chapter's Technology @ School feature offers more information on legal issues involved with student computer use.

---

[31]Michael D. Simpson, "No More Classroom Paparazzi," *NEA Today* (October 2008); and Daniel Marcus-Toll, "*Tinker* Gone Viral," *Fordham Law Review* (May 2014), available at **www.fordhamlawreview.org**.

[32]Tina Barseghian, "Straight from the DOE," *Mind/Shift* (April 26, 2011); and "Children's Internet Protection Act," 2014 posting by the Federal Communications Commission, available at **www.fcc.gov**.

[33]Zara Kessler, "First Sex and Then Sexting and Now Sext Education," *Standard Examiner* (October 23, 2014), available at **www.standard.net**; and Hanna Rosin, "Why Kids Text," *Atlantic* (November 2014), available at **www.theatlanic.com**.

TECHNOLOGY @ SCHOOL

LEGAL ISSUES INVOLVING TECHNOLOGY IN SCHOOLS

The widespread and still growing emphasis on using technology in education increases the likelihood that you, as a teacher, will face legal issues involving the use of computers and other electronic media. Some of these issues are spelled out in the "Navigate the Legal Maze" paper by Rita Oates (available on the Scholastic website). Among the technology-related issues dealt with are teachers' acceptable use of material (taking copyright laws into account), surveillance and privacy concerns when using cameras or other recorders, students' misappropriation of text or images from websites, and educators' obligations to filter digital material accessible to students. Oates points out that teachers do not have privacy protections when using district computers, and teachers can check with their district's legal counsel if there are serious questions about their responsibilities regarding the lawful use of technology.

9-3c Dress Codes and Regulations

Many courts have had to determine whether dress codes and regulations constitute an unconstitutional restriction on students' rights to free expression. In some instances, as in a Louisiana case dealing with requirements that football team members shave their mustaches, judges have ruled that the Constitution allows school boards to impose dress and grooming codes to advance their educational goals. Similarly, a US district court upheld a ban on boys' earrings as part of a policy prohibiting display of gang emblems.

In other cases, however, judges have ruled that prohibitions against boys' long hair were arbitrary and unreasonable. Several courts have stopped school districts from banning rosary beads that allegedly indicate gang membership, concluding that there are better ways to limit gangs than such a restriction on student expression. A federal court ruled that a school district could not prevent students from wearing bracelets stating "I heart Boobies" because the bracelets might be expressing support for breast-cancer awareness. Much depends on the arguments and evidence regarding the educational purposes served by such restrictions, the likelihood that violations will be disruptive, and the extent to which dress codes and restrictions are intended to accomplish a valid constitutional goal.[34]

In general, school officials must demonstrate a rational basis for prohibiting language or symbols they think may contribute to school problems. Applying this test, several courts also have ruled that public schools can require students to wear a designated uniform if school officials present evidence indicating that uniforms could help make schools safer or more productive. In several cases, dress codes have been upheld under this standard, but in some cases, dress codes have been challenged successfully on the grounds that they were arbitrary or capricious.[35]

Allegations of Sexism Involving Dress Codes   Controversies over dress codes also have erupted over perceptions that they unfairly lead to punishment of girls for

---

[34]Benjamin Dowling-Sendor, "A Matter of Disruption, Not Dress," *American School Board Journal* (August 1998); Kelly R. Taylor, "What Not to Wear," *Principal Leadership* (February 2009); David L. Hudson Jr., "Students Should Be Free to Wear Rosary Beads," 2011 posting by the First Amendment Center, available at **www.firstamendmentcenter.org**; James R. Marsh, "Court Reverses Boobies Bracelet Ban," 2011 posting by Childlaw Blog, available at **www.childlaw .us**; and Joanna Grossman, "Hair Makes the Man," *Verdict* (March 18, 2014), available at **www .verdict.justia.com**.

[35]Perry A. Zirkel, "A Uniform Policy," *Phi Delta Kappan* (March 1998), pp. 550–551; Benjamin Dowling-Sendor, "What Not to Wear," *American School Board Journal* (August 2005); and Richard S. Vacca, "Mandatory School Uniforms and the First Amendment," *CEPI Education Law Newsletter* (September 2014), available at **www.cepi.vcu.edu/publications /newsletters**.

infractions not applicable to boys. Some schools specify inflexibly how a girl must dress, excluding any departure from a school uniform, exposure of skin below the neck and arms, or use of items such as leggings or yoga pants. In many cases, such restrictions are defended on the grounds that departures would distract boys from their academic responsibilities. However, some girls perceive these codes to be sexist restrictions that attempt to use so-called "slut shaming" to embarrass and punish them. In some cases, the restrictions appear to be imposed more to carry out school officials' definition of "good taste" than to further a legally defensible purpose involving orderly behavior or safety in the school.[36]

9-3d Suspension and Expulsion

The issue of expulsion is illustrated in the case of nine students who received ten-day suspensions from their Columbus, Ohio, secondary schools for various alleged acts of misconduct. The suspensions were imposed without hearings but in accordance with state law; the school board had no written procedure covering suspensions. The students filed suit, claiming deprivation of their constitutional rights. In defense, school officials argued that without a constitutional right to education at public expense, the due process clause of the Fourteenth Amendment did not apply.

When this case, *Goss v. Lopez,* reached the Supreme Court in 1975, a majority of the Court disagreed with the school officials, reasoning that students had a legal right to public education. In other words, students had a property interest in their education that could not be taken away "without adherence to the minimum procedures" required by the due-process clause. Further, the justices said that students facing suspension "must be given some kind of notice and afforded some kind of hearing," including "an opportunity to explain [their] version of the facts." Also, "as a general rule, notice and hearing should precede removal of the student from school." Applying these principles to suspensions of up to ten days, the Court added that longer suspensions or expulsions might require more elaborate due-process procedures.[37]

In response to such court decisions, most school districts have developed policies governing suspensions and expulsions. These policies usually distinguish between short- and long-term suspensions. Short-term suspension rights typically include oral or written notice describing the misconduct, the evidence on which the accusation is based, a statement of the planned punishment, and an opportunity for the student to explain his or her version or refute the stated facts before an impartial person. Expulsions require full procedural due process similar to that necessary for teacher terminations.[38]

Controversy in Suspending Students with Disabilities   Recent court decisions have limited school officials' authority to suspend or expel disabled students who are disruptive or violent. In the case of *Honig v. Doe,* the Supreme Court ruled that

---

[36]"Students Protest 'Slut-Shaming' High School Dress Codes with Mass Walkouts," *The Guardian* (September 24, 2014), available at **www.theguardian.com**; and Giana Ciapponi, "School Dress Codes: Slut-Shaming or Empowering?" June 2, 2014, posting by Ravishly, available at **www.ravishly.com**.

[37]*Goss v. Lopez,* 419 US 565 (1975). See also Perry A. Zirkel, "Supporting Suspenders," *Phi Delta Kappan* (November 1994), pp. 256–257; Richard S. Vacca, "Student Procedural Due Process," *CEPI Education Law Newsletter* (February 2006), available at **www.cepi.vcu.edu/publications /newsletters**; and Mark Walsh, "School Discipline Upheld Over 'Stab' Tweets, Knife Possession," *Education Week* (February 12, 2014).

[38]Perry A. Zirkel and Ivan B. Gluckman, "Due Process for Student Suspensions," *NASSP Bulletin* (March 1990), pp. 95–98; Richard S. Vacca, "Student Discipline 2010," *CEPI Education Law Newsletter* (March 2010), available at **ww.cepi.vcu.edu/publications/newsletters**; and Krista Gesaman, "Student Media Guide to Due Process Claims," March 23, 2015, posting by the Student Press Law Center, available at **www.splc.org**.

such students must be retained in their current placement pending the completion of lengthy official hearings. The Individuals with Disabilities Education Act (IDEA) of 1990 specified additional rights that make it difficult to suspend or expel students with disabilities, including those who may be severely disruptive or prone to violence. As a result, educators are seeking new ways to guarantee the rights of students while dealing with disruptive pupils who are classified as disabled. Congress has passed legislation aimed at making it less cumbersome for administrators to suspend disabled students who violate school discipline rules, but educators report that practical issues are still murky. In addition, research indicates that low-income, disabled black students are suspended more frequently than low-income disabled white students, thus raising the possibility of legal challenges involving civil rights guarantees.[39]

Restraining and Secluding Disabled Students   About three-quarters of students physically restrained in school and about 60 percent of those placed in seclusion or some other form of involuntary confinement are students with disabilities. Many of these students are emotionally disturbed children and youth who sometimes pose serious dangers to themselves and others. Although restraining or secluding disabled students frequently is wholly or partly intended to keep schools safe in the face of difficulties described previously regarding suspension, sometimes the main motive is punishment that can cause serious injury. In any case, schools that rely heavily on restraint and seclusion may be violating IDEA guarantees of "free appropriate education," and if their disabled students are mostly minority students, they may be violating civil rights laws. Thus, it is not surprising that many schools seek to implement alternative approaches to student control.[40]

9-3e Protection from Violence

Educators have a duty to protect students against violent actions that occur at school or at school-sponsored events, which frequently extends to off-campus events such as graduations, proms, and parties. Depending on the circumstances, the courts or other government agencies may find school districts or their employees legally liable for failing in this duty. For example, a Louisiana court held a school district partly responsible for the gunshot wound suffered by a student after a school security guard warned the student of trouble but refused to escort him to his car. Virginia Tech University was fined $55,000 by the US Department of Education for its slow response in moving to protect students under gunfire from a mentally ill attacker. By contrast, an Illinois appellate court held Chicago high school officials not liable for the shooting of a student because they did not know that the weapon had been brought into school. In general, if the chance of harm to students is highly foreseeable, the educator's "duty to care" becomes a "duty to protect." Of course, regardless of questions involving legal culpability, educators should do everything possible to protect their students from violence.[41]

---

[39]Mitchell L. Yell, "*Honig v. Doe,*" *Exceptional Children* (September 1989), pp. 60–69; Richard S. Vacca, "Student Procedural Due Process 2006," *CEPI Education Law Newsletter* (February 2006), available at **www.cepi.vcu.edu/publications/newsletters**; and Judith Saltzman, "Disciplinary Protections for Children with Disabilities," 2014 posting by Milestones Autism Resources, available at **www.milestones.org**.

[40]Michelle Diament, "Harsh Discipline More Common For Students With Disabilities," March 21, 2014, posting by Disability Scoop, available at **www.disabilityscoop.com**; and Angela Pascopella, "District Changes Restraint and Seclusion Policy," *District Administration* (September 2014), available at **www.districtadministration.com**.

[41]Perry A. Zirkel, "Safe Promises?" *Phi Delta Kappan* (April 2000), pp. 635–636; Richard S. Vacca, "The Duty to Protect Students from Harm," *CEPI Education Law Newsletter* (November 2002), available at **www.cepi.vcu.edu/publications/newsletter**; and Kelly Schwartz, "Avoiding Sorrow in *Morrow,*" *Boston College Law Review*, Supp. 127 (2014), available at **www.bclawreview.org**.

Zero Tolerance and Its Positive and Negative Effects on Schools   Although school laws and policies dealing with school safety are primarily the responsibility of state and local governments (including public-school districts), growing national concern with violence in and around schools helped stimulate passage of the federal Gun-Free Schools Act of 1994. This legislation prohibits districts from receiving federal grants to improve performance among disadvantaged students unless their respective state governments have legislated "zero tolerance" of guns and other potentially dangerous weapons. By 1995, all fifty states had introduced such legislation, which in general provides for automatic suspension of students who possess objects that school officials decide are dangerous. Most districts have policies specifying how the legislation will be implemented and any additional grounds, such as possession of illegal substances, for automatic suspension.[42]

Zero-tolerance laws and policies may have made schools safer than before, but they have also had negative effects. Evidence indicates that they have contributed to repeat offenses and thereafter student dropouts. A study by the Harvard University Civil Rights Project found that zero-tolerance practices frequently had spun out of control in dishing out harsh punishments for minor infractions. For example, certain items leading to student suspensions or involvement of the police have generated a great deal of public ridicule of school districts, including a broken BB gun a 10 year-old found outside his school, a kitchen knife in a lunch box, a belt buckle with a sharp edge, the finger of a kindergarten student who used it as a play gun during recess, and a strong rubber band that could make a powerful slingshot. Some researchers believe that many disadvantaged students have been derailed from schooling into incarceration by minor infractions of zero-tolerance policies. Consequently, numerous organizations such as the American Bar Association are arguing for rejection of zero tolerance. To avoid negative outcomes and improve school climate through actions involving safety in schools, analysts urge educators to do the following:[43]

● Make sure students have opportunities to talk with and connect with caring adults.
● Provide flexibility and consider alternatives to expulsion.
● Clearly define what constitutes a weapon, a misbehavior, or a drug.
● Comply with due-process laws.
● Tailor policies to local needs, and review them annually.
● Implement a positive discipline policy.

Strict Discipline Issues in Urban Schools   Zero tolerance and related strict-discipline policies appear to be raising important issues involving the functioning of many urban schools. This is particularly the case with certain charter schools that appear to have had impressive results attracting low-income minority students and then improving their motivation and academic performance. Some of these schools have introduced exceedingly rigorous requirements regarding classroom and school behavior. In many cases, parents and students have sought out these schools because they believe that very strict discipline and highly structured expectations will help protect against negative forces outside the school and will teach students to overcome difficult obstacles.

However, even when strict discipline may have helped accomplish important educational goals, some negative consequences have been apparent. Some students have been disgruntled and decided to withdraw or drop out; others have become disruptive influences within the schools. A few have challenged teachers or administrators,

---

[42]"Violence Prevention," 2014 posting by the Institute of Education Sciences, available at **www.nces.ed.gov**.

[43]Judith A. Browne, *Derailed: The Schoolhouse to the Jail Track* (Washington, DC: Advancement Project, 2003); Stephanie F. Ward, "Schools Start to Rethink Zero Tolerance Policies," *ABA Journal* (August 1, 2014), available at **www.abajournal.com**; Matt Zalaznick, "Closing the School-to-Prison Pipeline," *District Administration* (October 2014), available at **www.districtadministration.com**; and Mary E. Flannery, "The School-to-Prison Pipeline," *NEA Today* (January 5, 2015), available at **www.neatoday.org**.

and some of their parents have raised legal objections to school actions. Educators are responding by reviewing their policies and attempting to maintain strong discipline while also taking into account the students' individual situations and circumstances.[44]

Discipline Often Shifting to the Police   Given the apparently increasing incidence of fatal shootings and other homicides in and near schools, as well as the exploding media attention they frequently ignite, educators and other government officials have moved toward stationing police officers and other full-time security personnel to protect students and staff at school. Thus, funds have been made available to support a growing police presence in US schools.

Although increase in police personnel at many schools probably has led to overall improvements in safety, several problems and issues also have been produced. For one thing, police interventions often result in legal charges being filed against students, sometimes contributing to students' entry or continuation in a so-called "pipeline" from school to prison. In addition, vigorous policing can encourage some students to believe they are in a coercive environment, and relatively innocent actions discouraged by zero-tolerance policies can result in arrest and even legal confinement. For example, one seventh-grader was arrested and charged with disturbing the peace after a minor hallway altercation, a teenager was charged with theft after sharing food from a classmate's meal, and some in-school fights have resulted in assault-and-battery charges. In response, some school districts are trying to reduce police intervention in minor infractions by students, and the US Department of Justice has advised school-based police to "not become involved in routine school disciplinary matters."[45]

9-3f Search and Seizure

A legal search usually requires a lawfully issued search warrant. But rising drug use in schools and accompanying acts of violence have led some school officials (particularly in big-city high schools) to install metal detectors or x-ray machines to search for weapons. Some schools have banned cell phones, which are sometimes used in drug sales; required students to breathe into alcohol-analysis machines; searched students' backpacks and book bags; and systematically examined lockers. Court challenges of such practices have usually centered on the Fourth Amendment, which states, "The right of the people to be secure in their persons, houses, papers, and effects, against unreasonable searches and seizures, shall not be violated, and no warrants shall issue, but upon probable cause, supported by oath or affirmation, and particularly describing the place to be searched, and the person or things to be seized."

Legal terms express suspicion in differing degrees. The "probable" cause mentioned in the Fourth Amendment means that searchers believe it is more probable than not that evidence of illegal activity will be found. This is the degree of suspicion required for police searches. In contrast, where school searches have been upheld, courts have said "reasonable" cause was sufficient for school officials to act. Searches usually are conducted because administrators have reason to suspect that illegal or dangerous items are on the premises.

These principles were considered in a case involving a teacher who discovered two girls in a school restroom smoking cigarettes. This was a violation of school rules, and the students were taken to the vice principal's office and questioned. One of the girls admitted smoking, but T.L.O., age 14, denied all charges. The vice principal opened T.L.O.'s purse and found a pack of cigarettes. While reaching for the cigarettes he noticed some rolling papers and decided to empty the purse. The search revealed marijuana, a pipe, some empty plastic bags, a large number of dollar bills, and a list entitled, "People

---

[44]Sarah Carr, "How Strict Is Too Strict?" *Atlantic* (November 2014), available at **www .theatlantic.com**

[45]Gary Fields and John R. Emshwiller, "For More Teens, Arrests by Police Replace School Discipline," *Wall Street Journal* (October 20, 2014), available at **www.wsj.com**.

who owe me money." T.L.O.'s mother was called, and the evidence was turned over to the police. T.L.O. confessed to the police that she had been selling marijuana at school.

After she was sentenced to one year's probation by the juvenile court, T.L.O. appealed, claiming the vice principal's search of her purse was illegal under the Fourth Amendment. In finding for school authorities in *New Jersey v. T.L.O.*, the US Supreme Court set up a two-pronged standard to be met for constitutionally sanctioned searches. Courts consider (1) whether the search is justified at its inception, and (2) whether the search, when actually conducted, is "reasonably related in scope to the circumstances which justified the interference in the first place." Using these criteria, the Court found the search of T.L.O.'s purse justified because of the teacher's report of smoking in the restroom. This information gave the vice principal reason to believe that the purse contained cigarettes. T.L.O. denied smoking, which made a search of her purse necessary to determine her veracity. When the vice principal saw the cigarettes and came across the rolling papers, he had reasonable suspicion to search her purse more thoroughly.[46]

Courts have also ruled that the suspicions of school officials sometimes were not sufficiently reasonable to justify the searches that followed. Using trained dogs to sniff student lockers and cars for evidence of drugs has been accepted because it occurred when the lockers and cars were unattended and in public view. The use of such dogs with students, however, can raise problems. In Highland, Indiana, 2,780 junior-high students and senior-high students waited for hours in their seats while six officials using trained dogs searched for drugs. A school official, police officer, dog handler, and German shepherd entered the classroom where Diane Doe, age 13, was a student. The dog went up and down the aisles sniffing students, reached Diane, sniffed her body, and repeatedly pushed its nose on and between her legs. The officer interpreted this behavior as an alert signaling the presence of drugs. Diane emptied her pockets as requested, but no drugs were found. Finally, Diane was taken to the nurse's office and strip-searched. No drugs were found. Before school, Diane had played with her own dog, and this smell remaining on her body had alerted the police dog.

The Does filed suit. Both the district court and the appeals court concluded that although the initial procedures were appropriate, the strip search of Diane was unconstitutional. The court of appeals said, "It does not require a constitutional scholar to conclude that a nude search of a thirteen-year-old child is an invasion of constitutional rights of some magnitude. More than that: It is a violation of any known principle of human decency." In a similar ruling in 2009, the Supreme Court ruled that a strip search of a girl accused of providing ibuprofen to a friend was unconstitutional because "directing a 13-year-old girl to remove her clothes, partially revealing her breasts and pelvic area, for allegedly possessing ibuprofen, was excessively intrusive."[47]

In sum, when searches are conducted without a specific warrant, the following guidelines seem appropriate:[48]

- Searches must be particularized. Reasonable suspicion should exist that *each student* being searched possesses specific contraband or evidence of a particular crime.
- Lockers are considered school property and may be searched if reasonable cause exists.

---

[46]*New Jersey v. T.L.O.*, 105 S. Ct. 733 (1985). See also Perry A. Zirkel, "Outstripping Students Again," *Phi Delta Kappan* (March 2008), pp. 538–541; and Mark Walsh, "Judge Rejects Administrators' Search of Student's Cellphone," *Education Week* (September 12, 2014).

[47]*Doe v. Renfrow*, 635 F. 2d 582 (7th Cir. 1980), cert. denied, 101 US 3015 (1981). See also Perry A. Zirkel, "Searching Students," *Principal Leadership* (September 2005), pp. 64–68; David L. Stader et al., "Drugs, Strip Searches, and Educator Liability," *Clearing House* (March 2010), pp. 109–113; and Frank LoMonte, "Supreme Court Cellphone-Search Ruling Sends a Cautionary Message to Schools," June 25, 2014, posting by the Student Press Law Center, available at **www.splc.org**.

[48]Kate Ehlenberger, "The Right to Search Students," *Educational Leadership* (December 2001/ January 2002), pp. 31–36; Edwin C. Darden, "Trouble on the Line," *American School Board Journal* (January 2007); and Richard S. Vacca, "Search and Seizure 2014," *CEPI Education Law Newsletter* (April 2014), available at **www.cepi.vcu.edu/publications/newsletters**.

- Dogs may be used to sniff lockers and cars. Generalized canine sniffing of students is permitted only when the dogs do not touch them.
- Strip searches usually are unconstitutional and should not be conducted unless available evidence clearly indicates that a significant threat to student safety is present.
- School officials may perform a pat-down search for weapons if they have a reasonable suspicion that students are bringing dangerous weapons to school.
- School officials may conduct searches on field trips, but the usual standards for searches still apply.
- School officials' judgments are protected by government immunity if the search is not knowingly illegal.

Video Surveillance and Search   Because videos can help with searches to identify those who have threatened or might threaten the safety of students and staff, school officials increasingly have been installing cameras and other means of surveillance. On the other hand, extensive video surveillance can violate Fourth Amendment protections against unreasonable search and seizure. Thus, the constitutionality of video surveillance hinges on its continuing reasonableness in a given situation. Few cases examining this issue have reached the courts, but in one instance, the Sixth Circuit Court of Appeals has ruled that it was not permissible to have ongoing scrutiny of athletic locker rooms.[49]

Drug Testing as a Form of Search   Some school board members and other policy makers have urged administrators to introduce random testing of student athletes' urine to detect marijuana, steroids, and other illegal substances. Historically, such testing was viewed as a potentially unconstitutional search. In 1995, however, the US Supreme Court ruled that this type of drug search is not necessarily unconstitutional even without specific reason to suspect a particular individual. A majority of the justices concluded that school officials have reasonable grounds to be especially concerned with drug use among athletes, who presumably set an example for other students. Since then, the Supreme Court has also permitted drug testing of students engaged in other activities. Students in violation of disciplinary policies involving the possession, sale, or use of prohibited substances on school property or at school-sponsored or school-sanctioned activities can be subject to appropriate disciplinary sanctions.[50]

9-3g Classroom Discipline and Corporal Punishment

Classroom discipline was the issue in a case involving a sixth grader who was placed in a time-out area of the classroom whenever his behavior became disruptive. The student had a history of behavioral problems, and the teacher had tried other methods of discipline without success. While in time out, the boy was allowed to use the restroom, eat in the cafeteria, and attend other classes. His parents sued, charging that the teacher's actions (1) deprived their son of his property interest in receiving a public education; (2) meted out punishment disproportionate to his offense, in violation of his due-process rights; and (3) inflicted emotional distress.

---

[49]Richard S. Vacca, "Student Search and Seizure," *CEPI Education Law Newsletter* (March 2008), available at **www.cepi.vcu.edu/publications/newsletters**; Amy M. Steketee, "The Legal Implications of Video Surveillance Cameras," *District Administration* (February 2012), available at **www.districtadministration.com**; and Andy Sevilla, "Elementary Student, Bus Driver Shot with BB Gun," *Hays Free Press* (October 22, 2014).

[50]Richard S. Vacca, "Search and Seizure," *CEPI Education Law Newsletter* (April 2010), available at **www.cepi.vcu.edu/publications/newsletters**; and "Frequently Asked Questions about Drug Testing in Schools," September 2014 posting by the National Institute on Drug Abuse, available at **www.drugabuse.gov**.

The district court said that school officials possess broad authority to prescribe and enforce standards of conduct in the schools, but this authority is limited by the Fourteenth Amendment. In this case, the student remained in school and thus was not deprived of a public education. "Time out" was declared to be a minimal interference with the student's property rights. The court noted that the purpose of a time out is to modify the behavior of disruptive students and to preserve the right to an education for other students in the classroom. All of the student's charges were dismissed.[51]

Use of Corporal Punishment   A particularly controversial method of classroom discipline is corporal punishment, which has a long history in American education dating back to the colonial period. Corporal punishment remains legal in nineteen states. It is unacceptable to many educators, although it enjoys considerable support within some segments of the community and is administered more frequently than educators like to admit. Surveys indicate that hundreds of thousands of children are spanked or paddled each school year, and thousands sustain injuries that require medical attention. But if the punishment results in even a small bruise, the punisher may be investigated for or charged with child abuse.[52]

Certain state legislatures have prohibited all corporal punishment in public schools. In states where the law is silent on this issue, local boards have wide latitude and may ban physical punishment if they choose. However, where a state statute explicitly permits corporal punishment, local boards may regulate but not prohibit its use. In this context, many school boards have developed detailed policies restricting the use of corporal punishment. Violations of policy can lead to dismissal, and legal charges are possible for excessive force, punishment based on personal malice toward the student, or unreasonable use of punishment.

Florida is an example of a state that allows corporal punishment. In 1977, the US Supreme Court, in *Ingraham v. Wright,* ruled on the constitutionality of this law from two federal perspectives: (1) whether use of corporal punishment was a violation of the Eighth Amendment barring cruel and unusual punishment, and (2) whether prior notice and some form of due process were required before administering punishment.

In this case, James Ingraham and Roosevelt Andrews were junior-high students in Dade County, Florida. Because Ingraham had been slow to respond to the teacher's instructions, he received twenty paddle swats administered in the principal's office. As a consequence, he needed medical treatment and missed a few days of school. Andrews was also paddled, but less severely. Finding that the intent of the Eighth Amendment was to protect those convicted of crimes, the justices said it did not apply to corporal punishment of schoolchildren. As to due process, the Court said, "We conclude that the Due Process clause does not require notice and a hearing prior to the imposition of corporal punishment in the public schools, as that practice is authorized and limited by common law."[53]

---

[51]*Dickens v. Johnson County Board of Education,* 661 F. Supp. 155 (E.D. Tenn. 1987). See also Darcie A. Mulay, "Keeping All Students Safe," *Stetson Law Review* (March 24, 2014), available at **www.stetson.edu/law/lawreview/media/42-1mulay.pdf**; and "What Is Responsive Classroom Time-Out?" July 28, 2014, posting by Responsive Classroom, available at **www.responsiveclassroom.org**.

[52]Perry A. Zirkel and David W. Van Cleaf, "Is Corporal Punishment Child Abuse?" *Principal* (January 1996), pp. 60–61; Martha M. McCarthy, "Corporal Punishment in Public Schools," *Educational Horizons* (Summer 2005), pp. 235–240; and Arit John, "Kansas Bill Would Legalize Spanking That Leaves Bruises to Deal with 'Defiant Children'," *The Wire* (February 19, 2014).

[53]*Ingraham v. Wright, 430* US (1977). See also Perry A. Zirkel, "You Bruise, You Lose," *Phi Delta Kappan* (January 1990), pp. 410–411; Benjamin Dowling-Sendor, "A Shock to the Conscience," *American School Board Journal* (April 2001); Rose Everleth, "Nineteen States Allow Teachers to Spank Children," *Smithsonian* (February 19, 2014), available at **www.smithsonianmag.com**; and Carla Vestal, "The Low-Down on the Beat-Down," January 13, 2015, posting by Civil Rights Clinic Blog, available at **http://cslcivilrights.com**.

Despite this ruling, the Court also commented on the severity of the paddlings. In such instances, the justices stated, school authorities might be held liable for damages to the child. Moreover, if malice is shown, the officials might be subject to prosecution under criminal statutes. In a later action, the Court also indicated a role for the due-process clause discussed earlier in this chapter. By declining to hear *Miera v. Garcia,* the Court let stand lower-court rulings that "grossly excessive" corporal punishment may constitute a violation of students' due-process rights. Thus teachers can be prosecuted in the courts for using excessive force and violating students' rights.[54]

Indeed, lower courts have ruled against teachers or administrators who have used cattle prods to discipline students, slammed students' heads against the walls, or spanked students so hard they needed medical attention, and the Supreme Court will probably continue to uphold such rulings. Overall, recent judicial decisions, together with the ever-present possibility of a lawsuit, have made educators cautious in using corporal punishment.

9-3h Sexual Harassment or Molestation of Students

The Supreme Court's decision in *Ingraham v. Wright* regarding physical punishment and a later decision in *Franklin v. Gwinnett* strengthened prohibitions against sexual harassment and sexual molestation. Definitions of these terms vary, but for interactions between students and teachers, the terms generally include not only sexual contact that calls into question the teacher's role as exemplar but also unwelcome sexual advances or requests for favors, particularly when the recipient might believe that refusal will affect his or her academic standing. Recent years have seen a dramatic increase in court cases involving school employees accused of sexually harassing students. Although the courts have been vague on what constitutes illegal sexual harassment of students, it is clear that both staff members and the districts that employ them can be severely punished if found guilty in court.[55]

School officials' legal responsibilities regarding teachers' sexual harassment of students were somewhat clarified in a 1998 Supreme Court decision (*Gebser v. Lago Vista Independent School District*) that involved a ninth grader who was seduced by a science teacher but never informed administrators about this sexual relationship. Her parents sued for damages from the school district using the argument that Title IX of the Education Amendments of 1972 requires schools to proactively take action to identify and eliminate sexual harassment. The Supreme Court ruled that school officials are not legally liable unless they know of the harassment and then proceed with "deliberate indifference." Some analysts were unhappy because they believed this decision allowed officials to avoid identifying and combating harassment, but others believed it reinforced administrators' resolve to implement policies that demonstrate their concern about harassment.[56]

Despite the relief from liability that *Gebser* provides for school officials, individual staff members must be wary of any action a student or parent might interpret as

[54]*Miera v. Garcia,* 56 USLW 3390 (1987); Edwin C. Darden, "Legal Problems with Corporal Punishment," *School Administrator* (January 2009); Rachel Chason, "As More Schools Ban Paddling, Others Defend It," *USA* Today (July 18, 2014), available at **www.usatoday.com**; and "School Corporal Punishment," January 27, 2015, posting by Inquisitr, available at **www .inquisitr.com**.

[55]Martha M. McCarthy, "The Law Governing Sexual Harassment in Public Schools," *Phi Delta Kappa Research Bulletin* (May 1998), pp. 15–18; and Ada Meloy, "What Title IX Has to Do with Sexual Assault," September 9, 2014, posting by the American Council on Education, available at **www.acenet.edu**.

[56]*Gebser v. Lago Vista Independent School District,* 98-1866 S. Ct. (1998). See also *Revised Sexual Harassment Guidance* (Washington, DC: US Department of Education Office of Civil Rights, 2001), available at **www.ed.gov**; Allison Fetter-Harrott, "Staff-to-Student Sexual Harassment," *District Administration* (March 2010), available at **www.districtadministration.com**; and "Sexual Harassment," 2015 posting by MRSC, available at **www.mrsc.org**.

sexual harassment or assault. Given the numerous allegations brought against teachers in recent years, many teacher organizations have been advising their members to avoid touching students unnecessarily. They also recommend that teachers make sure that doors are open and/or that other persons are present when they meet with a student. Legal advisers recognize the necessity for or benefits of touching or even hugging a student, as when a kindergarten teacher helps students put on coats, comforts a distressed pupil, grabs the aggressor in a fight between students, but many advise teachers to avoid physical contact as much as possible, particularly with older students.

Sexual abuse or harassment of one student by another is also a serious problem. As in the case of students allegedly harassed by teachers, the law regarding harassment by other students is poorly defined and murky. Name calling and teasing with sexual overtones have been interpreted as illegal harassment that educators have a legal obligation to suppress, but, in certain situations, school staff have been absolved of legal responsibility. Some school districts' antiharassment policies have prohibited so-called unwelcome statements about gays and lesbians, but a federal appeals court prevented punishment of students who made such statements when it ruled they were exercising First Amendment rights to religious expression. On the other hand, several districts have paid settlements to gay or lesbian students who were harassed by peers. The following guidelines have been suggested for educators who think sexual harassment may be occurring:[57]

1. Don't ignore the situation or let it pass unchallenged.
2. Don't overreact; find out exactly what happened.
3. Don't embarrass or humiliate any party to an incident.
4. Initiate steps to support the alleged victim.
5. Apply consequences in accordance with school behavior codes.
6. Don't assume that the incident is an isolated occurrence.
7. Provide comprehensive awareness programs for students, teachers, parents, and administrators.
8. School psychologists, counselors, and social workers should be available on request to the victim and his or her parents.

9-3i Student Records and Privacy Rights

Until 1974, students or their parents could not view most student records kept by schools. However, prospective employers, government agencies, and credit bureaus could do so. As might be guessed, abuses occurred. In 1974, Congress passed the **Family Educational Rights and Privacy Act** (also called either FERPA or the **Buckley Amendment**) to curb possible abuses in institutions receiving federal funds.

The Buckley Amendment requires public-school districts to develop policies allowing parents access to their children's official school records. The act prohibits disclosure of these records to most third parties without prior parental consent. Districts must have procedures to amend records if parents challenge the accuracy or completeness of the information they contain. Hearing and appeal mechanisms regarding disputed information must also be available. Parents retain rights of access to their child's school records until the child reaches age 18 or is enrolled in a postsecondary institution.

Family Educational Rights and Privacy Act (Buckley Amendment) A law passed in 1974 to curb possible abuses at institutions receiving federal funds.

[57]Perry A. Zirkel, "Student-to-Student Sexual Harassment," *Phi Delta Kappan* (April 1995), pp. 448–450; Richard S. Vacca, " Student-Peer Sexual Harassment 2009," *CEPI Education Law Newsletter* (February 2009), available at **www.cepi.vcu.edu/publications/newsletters**; and John Stephens, "Physical and Sexual Abuse," *District Administration* (August 2014), available at **www.districtadministration.com**.

However, the Buckley Amendment allows several exceptions. Private notes and memoranda of teachers and administrators (including grade books) are exempt from view. In addition, records kept separate from official files and maintained for law-enforcement purposes (for example, information about criminal behavior) cannot be disclosed, and nothing may be revealed that would jeopardize the privacy rights of other pupils. On the other hand, many schools have become more open to making information available about students who may threaten security on campus.[58]

Although social media are not explicitly addressed in the Buckley Amendment, educators must be careful not to reveal information about students, grades, enrollment, schedules, and related matters on Facebook, Twitter, or other social platforms.

Student-privacy policies also are affected by the Protection of Pupil Rights Amendment to the federal General Education Provisions Act of 1978. This Amendment specified that instructional materials used in connection with "any research or experimentation program or project" must be "available for inspection" by participating students' parents and guardians. In addition, no student can be required to participate in testing, psychological examination, or treatments whose "primary purpose is to reveal information" concerning political affiliations, sexual behaviors or attitudes, psychological or mental problems, income, and other personal matters. It has been difficult to define terms such as "instructional materials" and "research program," and many parents have used the Protection of Pupil Rights Act to object to school activities that probe students' feelings or beliefs. Consequently, teachers and other staff must consider carefully whether collecting information on students' background or beliefs serves a legitimate goal.[59]

9-3j Need for Balance between Rights and Responsibilities

During the past several decades, as courts have upheld the constitutional rights of students and placed restrictions on school officials, many educators and parents have decided that the legal process is out of balance. They believe the courts place too much emphasis on student rights and too little on the need for school discipline. The result, said former AFT president Albert Shanker, "is schools where little or no learning goes on because teachers have to assume the role of warden."[60]

However, some scholars believe that since the mid-1980s, the Supreme Court has moved to redress the balance. In this view, the Court's decisions in *T.L.O.* (1985), *Bethel v. Fraser* (1986), and *Hazelwood v. Kuhlmeier* (1988) place fewer burdens on school officials than the 1969 *Tinker* decision. Rather than demonstrating that certain rules are necessary, school officials now need to show only that the rules are reasonable. This

[58]Richard S. Vacca, "Student Records 2004," *CEPI Education Law Newsletter* (May 2004), available at **www.cepi.vcu.edu/publications/newsletters**; Meris Stansbury, "Feds Take Huge Steps to Protect Student Privacy," *eSchool News* (April 7, 2011), available at **www.eschoolnews.com**; and "Department Releases New Guidance on Protecting Student Privacy While Using Online Educational Services," US Department of Education (February 25, 2014), available at **www .ed.gov**.

[59]Benjamin Dowling-Sendor, "A Matter of Privacy," *American School Board Journal* (November 2004); Perry A. Zirkel, "Parental Discretion Advised?" *Phi Delta Kappan* (March 2006), pp. 557–558; Perry D. Drake, "Is Your Use of Social Media FERPA Compliant?" *Educause* (February 24, 2014), available at **www.educause.edu**; and Richard Yeakley, "Court Rejects Mother's Religious Home-School Arguments," *Belief Net News* (March 18, 2011), available at **www .beliefnet.com**.

[60]Albert Shanker, "Discipline in Our Schools," *New York Times* (May 19, 1991, p. E7). See also Benjamin Dowling-Sendor, "Balancing Safety with Free Expression," *American School Board Journal* (December 2001); and Frank LoMonte, "Tennessee Judge Strikes Careful Balance in Student's Twitter Suspension Case," January 6, 2014, posting by the Student Press Law Center, available at **www.splc.org**.

emphasis on reasonableness indicates that the Court "is placing considerable confidence in school officials," trusting those officials to maintain a proper balance between student rights and the school's needs.[61]

9-4 RELIGION AND THE SCHOOLS

The framers of our Constitution were acutely aware of religious persecution and sought to prevent the United States from experiencing the serious and often bloody conflicts that had occurred in Europe. As noted at the beginning of this chapter, the First Amendment, adopted in 1791, prohibits the establishment of a nationally sanctioned religion (the establishment clause) and government interference with individuals' rights to hold and freely practice their religious beliefs (the free exercise clause). Judge Alphonso Taft succinctly stated the position of government toward religion more than one hundred years ago: "The government is neutral, and while protecting all, it prefers none, and it disparages none."[62]

9-4a Prayer, Bible Reading, and Religious Blessings and Displays

Before 1962, students in New Hyde Park were required to recite daily this nondenominational prayer composed by the New York State Board of Regents: "Almighty God, we acknowledge our dependence upon thee, and we beg thy blessings upon us, our parents, our teachers, and our Country." Although exemption was possible upon written parental request, the US Supreme Court in *Engle v. Vitale* (1962) ruled the state-written prayer unconstitutional. According to the Court, "Neither the fact that the prayer may be denominationally neutral nor the fact that its observance on the part of students is voluntary can serve to free it from the limitations of the Establishment Clause."[63]

The decision created a storm of protest that has barely subsided to this day. A year later, the Court again prohibited religious exercises in public schools. This time, the issue involved oral reading of Bible verses and recitation of the Lord's Prayer. These were clearly religious ceremonies and "intended by the State to be so," even when student participation was voluntary. In 2000, the Court excluded student-led prayer at a football game because the game and therefore the prayer were officially sponsored by the school. On the other hand, the courts have ruled that students can lead or participate in prayers at commencement ceremonies, as long as decisions to do so are

---

[61]Lowell C. Rose, "Reasonableness—The Court's New Standard for Cases Involving Student Rights," *Phi Delta Kappan* (April 1988), pp. 589–592. See also Richard S. Vacca, "The Roberts Court," *CEPI Education Law Newsletter* (December 2008), available at **www.cepi.vcu.edu /publications/newsletters**; and Thomas A. Jacobs, "Will the Supreme Court Consider Cyberbullying?" May 7, 2014, posting by Legal Solutions Blog, available at **http://blog .legalsolutions.thomsonreuters.com/government/will-supreme-court-consider -cyberbullying**.

[62]Quoted by Justice Tom Clark in *School District of Abington Township v. Schempp*, 374 US 203 (1963). See also Richard S. Vacca, "Free Exercise of Religion in Public Schools," *CEPI Education Law Newsletter* (November 2006), available at **www.cepi.vcu.edu/publications /newsletters**; Thomas C. Berg, "The Story of the School Prayer Decisions," 2011 posting by the Social Science Research Network, available at **www.ssrn.com**; and Justin Murphy, "Schempp Still Stands Against Forced School Prayer," *USA Today* (April 7, 2014), available at **www.usatoday.com**.

[63]*Engle v. Vitale*, 370 US 421 (1962). See also "Guidelines on Constitutionally Protected Prayer," 2003 paper available at **www.ed.gov**; Perry A. Zirkel, "Friday Night Rites," *Phi Delta Kappan* (October 2008), pp. 146–147; and "Time to Pray at School!" 2014 posting by Adam Laats, available at **http://iloveyoubutyouregoingtohell.org/?s=time+to+pray+at+school**.

made by students without the involvement of clergy and are not sponsored by school officials.[64]

The Supreme Court also has ruled against invocations and benedictions in which a clergyman opens or closes a public-school ceremony by invoking blessings from a deity. In a 1992 decision, the Court concluded that such blessings violate the standards established in *Lemon v. Kurtzman* (see Figure 9.1 on page 245), which prohibits the government from advancing religion. However, Justice Anthony Kennedy's majority opinion noted that state actions implicating religion are not necessarily unconstitutional because some citizens might object to them, and that the decision was not meant to require a "relentless and pervasive attempt to exclude religion from every aspect of public life."

One effect of the decision was to postpone full constitutional review of several important questions, such as whether schools can implement "moment of silence" policies that allow voluntary silent prayer in classrooms, whether a school choir can perform clearly Christian songs at a graduation ceremony, and whether private groups can distribute free Bibles on school premises.

Displaying religious symbols (such as a cross or a menorah) in public schools in a manner that promotes a particular religion is clearly unconstitutional. However, the Supreme Court has ruled that religiously oriented artifacts such as a Nativity scene can be displayed in public settings if the overall atmosphere is largely secular. The interpretation of this ruling is controversial. In one nonschool case, the Court banned a Nativity scene in front of the Allegheny County (Pennsylvania) Courthouse because it had not been "junked up" (in the words of a county official) with Santa Claus figures or other secular symbols. After that decision, a federal judge required the removal of a crucifixion painting from the Schuylerville (New York) School District, on the grounds that the painting lacked any "meaningful" secular features. In 2002, an Ohio school district was prohibited from posting the Ten Commandments in front of four high schools. Since then, the Supreme Court ruled that government institutions may display the Ten Commandments as part of a historical exhibit, but not as a lone display of religious messages.[65]

9-4b Access to Public Schools for Religious Groups

Bridget Mergens, an Omaha high school senior, organized a group of about twenty-five students who requested permission to meet on campus before school every week or so to read and discuss the Bible. Although similar Bible clubs were allowed to meet at other schools, administrators refused the request, partly to avoid setting a precedent for clubs of Satanists, Ku Klux Klanists, or other groups the school would find undesirable. Bridget's mother brought suit, and, in 1990, the US Supreme Court found in her favor. Public high schools, the Court ruled, must allow students' religious, philosophical, and political groups to meet on campus on the same basis as other extracurricular

---

[64]*School District of Abington Township v. Schempp and Murray v. Curlett*, 374 US 203 (1963). See also Benjamin Dowling-Sendor, "A Defeat for Pregame Prayer," *American School Board Journal* (August 2000); Richard S. Vacca, "Graduation Prayer Revisited," *CEPI Education Law Newsletter* (May 2008), available at **www.cepi.vcu.edu/publications/newsletters**; and Alison DeNisco, "New Laws Make More Room for Prayer in Schools," *District Administration* (June 2014), available at **www.districtadministration.com**.

[65]Rob Boston, "The Klan, a Cross, and the Constitution," *Church and State* (March 1995), pp. 7–9; Benjamin Dowling-Sendor, "The Ten Commandments Ruling," *American School Board Journal* (October 2005); Charles C. Haynes, "County Can Uphold Religious Freedom by Taking Commandments Down," 2011 posting by the First Amendment Center, available at **www .firstamendmentcenter.org**; and Jonathan S. Tobin, "Freedom for Religion, Not From It," *Commentary* (May 5, 2014), available at **www.commentarymagazine.com/2014/05/05 /freedom-for-religion-not-from-it-greece-v-galloway-church-state-separation**.

groups. Permitting such meetings, the Court stated, does not mean that the school endorses or supports them. Many analysts and some courts have emphasized this point in supporting equal access for gay, lesbian, bisexual, and transgendered students. Courts have ruled that this equal access applies to not only before and after school but also to noninstructional time during the school day.[66]

Implications of the *Mergens* case have aroused great uncertainty. Schools apparently must choose between allowing practically any student group to meet or dropping all extracurricular activities. Similar considerations apply concerning the distribution of flyers about religious activities. A third option would be to permit meetings only by groups whose activities relate directly to the curriculum, but difficult problems arise in defining such activities. Recent Supreme Court cases have failed to fully clarify the issue, but it is clear that religious and other groups and activities must receive equivalent access and must satisfy criteria such as the following:[67]

- The activity must be student initiated.
- The school may not sponsor the activity, but its employees may attend meetings, and it may pay incidental costs such as heating.
- Outsiders may not direct the group or regularly attend meetings.
- The group cannot be disruptive.
- Each group must have equal access to meeting spaces, school periodicals, bulletin boards, and other facilities and resources.

9-4c The Pledge of Allegiance in Limbo

The separation of church and state also applies to statements of allegiance to the state. In one case, several Jehovah's Witnesses went to court over a West Virginia requirement that their children recite the pledge of allegiance at school each morning. The parents based their objection on religious doctrine. The US Supreme Court supported school officials' actions in expelling students who would not recite the pledge and salute the flag. However, three years later, after Witnesses in several locations had been accosted in the streets and forced to salute the flag, the Court reversed itself and concluded that students could be excused from reciting the pledge (Photo 9.2). The court ruled that the children could be exempted because the requirement to pledge conflicted with their religious beliefs. Subsequent decisions have provided further support for this conclusion.[68]

In 2002, a federal court of appeals ruled the Pledge of Allegiance unconstitutional because it includes the words "under God." This decision predictably sparked nationwide controversy; however, final disposition of the issue has yet to be determined by the Supreme Court and other courts.[69]

---

[66]*Board of Education of the Westside Community Schools v. Mergens,* 88 S. Ct. 1597 (1990). See also "Transgender and Gender Non-Conforming Students," April 2014 posting by the National Center for Transgender Equality, available at **www.transequality.org/sites/default/files /docs/kyr/KnowYourRightsSchools_April2014.pdf**.

[67]Benjamin Dowling-Sendor, "Opening Your Schools," *American School Board Journal* (May 1999); "A Question of Equity," *American School Board Journal* (February 2003); Colby M. May, "Religion's Legal Place in the Schoolhouse," *School Administrator* (October 2006), available at **www .aasa.org**; and "Overview of the Federal Equal Access Act," 2014 posting by Religious Tolerance, available at **www.religioustolerance.org/equ_acce.htm**.

[68]*West Virginia State Board of Education v. Barnette,* 319 US 624 (1943); *Lipp v. Morris,* 579 F. 2d 834 (3rd Cir. 1978); Perry A. Zirkel and Ivan B. Gluckman, "Pledge of Allegiance," *NASSP Bulletin* (September 1990), pp. 115–117; Garrett Epps, "Beware," *American Prospect* (October 2011), available at **www.prospect.org**; and "Pledge of Allegiance Fast Facts," November 11, 2014, posting by CNN, available at **www.cnn.com**.

[69]Margaret M. McCarthy, " Controversy Continues over the *Pledge of Allegiance*," *Educational Horizons* (Winter 2005), pp. 92–97; Grace Y. Kao and Jerome E. Coplulsky, "The Pledge of Allegiance and the Meanings and Limits of Civil Religion," *Journal of the American Academy of Religion* (March 2007), pp. 121–149; Kathleen Hopkins, "Lawsuit Challenges 'Under God' in Pledge of Allegiance," *USA Today* (November 19, 2014), available at **www.usatoday.com**; and "The Pledge of Allegiance Cases," undated posting by The Becket Fund, available at **www.becketfund.org**.

Elyse Lewin/Photographer's Choice/Getty Images

> **PHOTO 9.2** Federal judges have concluded that students who refuse to stand and recite the pledge of allegiance cannot be compelled to do so if participation violates their religious or other personal beliefs.

9-4d Religious Objections Regarding Curriculum

In Tennessee in the mid-1980s, fundamentalist Christian parents brought suit against the Hawkins County School District, charging that exposure of their children to the Holt, Rinehart and Winston basal reading series was offensive to their religious beliefs. The parents believed that "after reading the entire Holt series, a child might adopt the views of a feminist, a humanist, a pacifist, an anti-Christian, a vegetarian, or an advocate of a one-world government." The district court held for the parents, reasoning that the state could satisfy its compelling interest in the literacy of Tennessee schoolchildren through less restrictive means than compulsory use of the Holt series. However, an appellate court reversed this decision, stating that no evidence had been produced to show that students were required to affirm their belief or disbelief in any idea mentioned in the Holt books. The textbook series, the court said, "merely requires recognition that in a pluralistic society we must 'live and let live.'"[70]

In somewhat similar cases, district judges upheld a group of parents in Alabama who contended that school textbooks and activities advanced the religion of secular humanism,[71] as well as a New York group whose members contended that Bedford Public Schools were promoting pagan religions when students recited a liturgy to the Earth or sold worry dolls. The first decision was reversed by a federal appeals court, which held that the textbooks did not endorse secular humanism or any other religion, but rather attempted to instill such values as independent thought and tolerance of diverse views. The appeals court noted that if the First Amendment prohibited mere "inconsistency with the beliefs of a particular religion, there would be very little that could be taught in the public schools." The second case also was resolved in favor of the schools.

---

[70]*Mozert v. Hawkins County Board of Education*, 86-6144 (E.D. Tenn. 1986); *Mozert v. Hawkins County Board of Education*, 87-5024 (6th Cir. 1987); Vivian E. Hamilton, "Immature Citizens and the State," *BYU Law Review* No. 4 (2010), available at **www.lawreview.byu.edu**; and John Light, "Sherman Alexei's Young Adult Novel Pulled from Curriculum in Idaho Schools," *Moyers & Company* (April 8, 2014), available at **www.billmoyers.com**.

[71]The secular humanism philosophy de-emphasizes religious doctrines and instead emphasizes the human capacity for self-realization through reason.

Similar conclusions have been reached by courts hearing complaints about New Age classroom materials in California and several other states.[72]

In 1987, the US Supreme Court considered *Edwards v. Aguillard,* a case that challenged Louisiana's Balanced Treatment for Creation-Science and Evolution-Science Act. Creation science, or creationism, is the belief that life has developed through divine intervention or creation rather than initially through biological evolution. The Louisiana act required that creation science be taught wherever evolution was taught and that appropriate curriculum guides and materials be developed. The Supreme Court ruled this law unconstitutional. By requiring "either the banishment of the theory of evolution...or the presentation of a religious viewpoint that rejects evolution in its entirety," the Court reasoned, the Louisiana act advanced a religious doctrine and violated the establishment clause of the First Amendment.[73]

Intelligent Design   Controversy sometimes associated with the creationist point of view escalated in the twenty-first century as the **intelligent design** concept was introduced in a growing number of schools. This point of view argues that life is too complex to be formed through natural selection as portrayed by Darwin; therefore, it must be directed by a so-called intelligent designer. Many advocates of intelligent design avoid explicit references to divine creation, instead emphasizing what they view as flaws (including lack of valid evidence) in the theories developed by Darwinists.[74]

Actions initiated by advocates of intelligent design included a Cobb County (Ga.) school board requirement that biology texts have stickers stating that "This textbook contains material on evolution. Evolution is a theory, not a fact....This material should be approached with an open mind, studied carefully, and critically considered," and a similar curriculum-statement in which the Dover (Pennsylvania) school board suggested that students learn about intelligent design. These and several comparable actions have been challenged in federal courts, where judges have concluded that intelligent design involves support for particular religions and is not a scientific theory that can be required or inserted in the science curriculum. However, some analysts have noted that intelligent design still might be studied appropriately in social studies or elsewhere in the curriculum.[75]

intelligent design The argument that life is too complex to be formed through natural selection as portrayed by Darwin; therefore, it must be directed by an "intelligent designer."

9-4e Teaching about Religion

Guarantees of separation between church and state do not prohibit public schools from teaching *about* religion or about controversial topics involving religion. Some states and school districts have been strengthening approaches for developing an understanding of religious traditions and values while neither promoting nor detracting from any particular religious or nonreligious ideology. In addition, many scholars have been preparing materials for such constitutionally acceptable instruction.[76]

---

[72]*Smith v. Board of School Commissioners of Mobile County,* 87-7216, 11th Cir. (1987); and Doktor Zoom, "Academic Freedom to Teach Bible as Science Upheld in Lucky Louisiana," April 24, 2014, posting by Wonkette, available at **www.wonkette.com/547520/academic -freedom-to-teach-bible-as-science-upheld-in-lucky-louisiana**.

[73]*Edwards v. Aguillard,* 197 S. Ct. 2573 (1987); and Simon Brown, "The Evolution of Creationism," March 2014 posting by Citizens United, available at **www.au.org**.

[74]Elizabeth Culotta, "Is ID on the Way Out?" *Science* (February 10, 2006, p. 570); and "Darwin Shmarwin," *Economist* (February 19th, 2014), available at **www.economist.com**.

[75]Joseph Dunn and Martha Derthick, "A Setback in Dover," *Education Next,* No. 2 (2006), available at **www.educationnext.org**; and "What Has Been the Outcome of Court Cases Testing Creationism and Intelligent Design?" June 20, 2014, posting by David H. Bailey, available at **www.sciencemeetsreligion.org/evolution/court-cases.php**.

[76]For example, see Susan Black, "Teaching about Religion," *American School Board Journal* (June 2003); C. M. Bailey, 'Teaching the Bible in Public Schools," 2011 posting by Blog Critics, available at **www.blogcritics.org**; and Lisa Webster, "Taking (Public School) Teachers to Church, and the Mosque, and the Temple...," August 4, 2014, posting by Religion Dispatches, available at **www.religiondispatches.org**.

OVERVIEW 9.3

GUIDELINES ON RELIGION IN THE SCHOOLS, FROM THE US DEPARTMENT OF EDUCATION

Student prayer and religious discussion: The US Constitution does not prohibit purely private religious speech by students. Students therefore have the same right to engage in individual or group prayer and religious discussion during the school day as they do to engage in other comparable activity.

Generally, students may pray in a nondisruptive manner when not engaged in school activities or instruction and subject to the rules that normally pertain in the applicable setting.

Graduation prayer: Under current Supreme Court decisions, school officials may not mandate or organize prayer at graduation nor organize religious baccalaureate ceremonies.

Official neutrality: Teachers and school administrators...are prohibited by the Constitution from soliciting or encouraging religious activity and...from discouraging activity because of its religious content.

Teaching about religion: Public schools may not provide religious instruction, but they may teach about religion..., the history of religion, comparative religion, the Bible (or other scripture) as literature, and religion's role in the history of the United States and other countries are all permissible public-school subjects.

Although public schools may teach about religious holidays...and may celebrate the secular aspects of holidays, schools may not observe holidays as religious events or promote such observance by students.

Student assignments: Students may express their beliefs about religion in the form of homework, artwork, and other written and oral assignments....Such home and classroom work should be judged by ordinary academic standards.

Religious literature: Students have a right to distribute religious literature to their schoolmates on the same terms as they are permitted to distribute other literature that is unrelated to school curriculum or activities.

Religious exemptions: Schools enjoy substantial discretion to excuse individual students from lessons that are objectionable to the student or the student's parents on religious or other conscientious grounds.

Released time: Schools have the discretion to dismiss students to off-premises religious instruction, provided that schools do not encourage or discourage participation....Schools may not allow religious instruction by outsiders on school premises during the school day.

Teaching values: Though schools must be neutral with respect to religion, they may play an active role with respect to teaching civic values and virtue.

Student garb: Students may display religious messages on items of clothing to the same extent that they are permitted to display other comparable messages.

The Equal Access Act: Student religious groups have the same right of access to school facilities as is enjoyed by other comparable student groups.

Source: Richard W. Riley, "Secretary's Statement on Religious Expression" (statement released by the US Department of Education, Washington, DC, 1998).

According to guidelines issued in 1995 and reissued in 1998 by the US Department of Education, schools can teach subjects such as "the history of religion, comparative religion, the Bible (or other scripture) as literature, and the role of religion in the history of the United States and other countries." These federal guidelines, which also touched on many other controversies concerning religion and schools, are summarized in Overview 9.3. However, courts may not necessarily support what the executive branch deems correct.[77]

---

[77]Charles C. Haynes, "Religion in the Public Schools," *School Administrator* (January 1999), available at **www.aasa.org**; Jill Heinrich, "The Devil Is in the Details," *Educational Review* (February 2015); and information at **www.teachingaboutreligion.org**.

9-4f Government Guidelines Regarding Prayer and Religion in Schools

In 2003, the Department of Education issued more detailed guidelines involving prayer and related activities in public schools. Guidelines and commentary included the following:[78]

- Students may organize prayer groups and religious clubs before school to the same extent that students are permitted to organize other noncurricular student-activity groups....
- Teachers may...take part in religious activities where the overall context makes clear that they are not participating in their official capacities. Before school or during lunch, for example, teachers may meet with other teachers for prayer or Bible study to the same extent that they may engage in other conversation or nonreligious activities.....
- If a school has a "moment of silence" or other quiet periods during the school day, students are free to pray silently, or not to pray.... Teachers and other school employees may neither encourage nor discourage students from praying during such time periods....
- Students may express their beliefs about religion in homework, artwork, and other written and oral assignments, free from discrimination based on the religious content of their submissions. Such home and classroom work should be judged by ordinary academic standards of substance and relevance and against other legitimate pedagogical concerns.

9-4g Government Regulation and Support of Nonpublic Schools: A Legal Muddle

In 1925, *Pierce v. Society of Sisters* established that a state's compulsory school-attendance laws could be satisfied through enrollment in a private or parochial school. Attention then turned to the question of how much control a state could exercise over the education offered in nonpublic schools. A 1926 case, *Farrington v. Tokushige*, gave nonpublic schools "reasonable choice and discretion in respect of teachers, curriculum, and textbooks." Within that framework, however, states have passed various kinds of legislation to regulate nonpublic schools. Some states have few regulations; others require the employment of certified teachers, specify the number of days or hours the school must be in session, or insist that schools meet state accreditation standards. Many of these regulations may also apply to homeschooling; thus several current controversies involve the possible application of state standards (such as permitting participation in public-school athletics) to homeschooled students. Charter schools that are nonpublic also may or may not be required to provide special education, depending on the state where it is located.[79]

---

[78]Rod Paige, "Guidance on Constitutionally Protected Prayer in Public Elementary and Secondary Schools," 2003 paper posted at the US Department of Education Internet site, available at **www.ed.gov**. See also Edwin C. Darden, "Pause and Ponder," *American School Board Journal* (May 2008), pp. 48–49; and Mark A. Chancey, "How Should We Teach the Bible in Public Schools?" January 7, 2014, posting by Religion & Politics, available at **www .religionandpolitics.org**.

[79]*Pierce v. Society of Sisters*, 268 US 510 (1925); and *Farrington v. Tokushige*, 273 US 284 (1926). See also Julia Zhou, "State Regulation of Private Schools," June 24, 2014, posting by Private School Review, available at **www.privateschoolreview.com/articles/9**; and Paul T. O'Neill and Lauren M. Rhim, "Equity at Scale," January 2015 posting by the National Alliance for Public Charter Schools, available at **www.publiccharters.org**.

On the other side of the coin, states have offered many types of support for non-public schools, including transportation, books, and health services. In the 1947 case *Everson v. Board of Education of Erving Township,* the Supreme Court considered a provision in the New Jersey Constitution that allowed state aid for transportation of private and parochial students. The Court held that where state constitutions permitted such assistance, they did not violate the US Constitution. Since the Everson decision, the distinction between permissible and impermissible state aid to nonpublic schools has usually been based on the **child benefit theory**: aid that directly benefits the child is permissible, whereas aid that primarily benefits the nonpublic institution is not.[80]

child benefit theory A theory that government aid directly benefits the child rather than a nonpublic institution he or she attends.

In *Wolman v. Walter* (1977), *Agostini v. Felton* (1997), *Mitchell v. Helms* (2000), and *Zelman v. Simmons-Harris* (2002), the Supreme Court went further. Addressing state support for nonpublic schools permitted by the Ohio and New York constitutions, the Court decided specific questions by applying the three-pronged *Lemon v. Kurtzman* test illustrated in Figure 9.1. The Court's decisions were as follows:[81]

- Providing for the purchase or loan of secular textbooks, standardized tests, and computers is constitutional.
- Providing speech, hearing, and psychological diagnostic services at the nonpublic-school site is constitutional.
- Providing for the purchase and loan of other instructional materials and equipment, such as projectors, science kits, maps and globes, charts, media players, and so on, was ruled unconstitutional because this involves excessive government entanglement with religion.
- Providing funds for field trips is unconstitutional because "where the teacher works within and for a sectarian institution, an unacceptable risk of fostering religion is an inevitable byproduct."
- Providing Title 1 remedial services from public-school staff located at neutral facilities does not constitute excessive entanglement of church and state.
- Providing students with vouchers used to pay for tuition at nonpublic schools is constitutional if no financial incentives skew the program toward religious schools and such vouchers do not violate the state constitution.

The material outlined above shows why many legal scholars believe that constitutional law regarding government aid to nonpublic schools is something of a muddle. Why should the government purchase of textbooks, tests, and computers for nonpublic schools be constitutional but not the purchase of maps, globes, charts, and record players? Why can government-supported psychological services be provided at nonpublic schools, whereas remedial services must be provided at a neutral site? How can vouchers to attend nonpublic schools be legal in some states but not others? Questions as convoluted as these help explain why Court attempts at clarification have been only partly successful.

Policies and legislation regarding public funding of vouchers for students who attend nonpublic schools also reflect complex situations that involve another kind of muddle. In this case, the laws and practices are set by state governments that vary greatly in their decisions regarding important issues. For example, in Arizona, nonpublic schools are not required to administer state tests to voucher recipients; in Florida

---

[80]Barbara Miner, "A Brief History of Milwaukee's Voucher Program," *Rethinking Schools* (Spring 2006), available at **www.rethinkingschools.org**; and Jason Bedrick, "School Tax Credits Are Good for Parents, Taxpayers," *New Hampshire Business Review* (October 8, 2014), available at **www.cato.org**.

[81]Clint Bolick, "Voting Down Vouchers," *Education Next* (Spring 2008), available at **www.educationnext.org**; Greg Mild, "Bill Would Apply Reading Guarantee to Private School Students," April 6, 2014, posting by Plunderbund, available at **www.plunderbund.com**; and "The Lemon Test," 2015 posting by Shmoop, available at **www.shmoop.com**.

FOCUS Do you think controversies involving church and state will affect you directly as a teacher? Which aspects are most relevant in your subject field? What difficulties or challenges relating to religion might arise in the schools in your community?

and Georgia, they also are not required to give the exams, but parents can ask that their children with vouchers take the test, and schools must then cooperate. In Maine, if at least 60 percent of a school's attendance is publicly funded, the school must administer state tests. The thirteen states and Washington, DC, in which students receiving state-funded vouchers can use them at nonpublic schools also vary substantially regarding which students are eligible, whether or how receiving schools participate in special education, limits on amounts received by the schools, the dollar value of the vouchers, and several related considerations. These differences lead to somewhat muddled discussions of controversial and emotional issues such as whether the public schools are being negatively over-burdened with special-education students, and whether public funds are being used to attract motivated pupils out of the public schools.[82]

SUMMING UP

1. Education-related court cases have significantly increased in the past few decades. Such cases can be heard in both federal and state courts, depending on the issues involved. Only decisions of the US Supreme Court apply nationally.

2. Tenure protects teachers from dismissal, except on such specified grounds as incompetence, immorality, insubordination, and unprofessional conduct. Teachers accused of such conduct are entitled to due-process protections.

3. Teachers have the right to form and belong to unions and other professional organizations, but most states prohibit teachers from striking.

4. Teachers' rights regarding freedom of expression and academic freedom depend on a balance between individual and governmental interests. Teachers have rights guaranteed to individuals under the Constitution, but school boards have obligations to ensure the "proper" and "regular" operation of the schools, taking into account the rights of parents, teachers, and students.

5. Restraints on teachers' behavior outside school and on their dress and grooming are not as stringent as they once were in the United States, but teachers still are expected to serve as role models and to behave in an exemplary manner.

6. Schools must uphold definite safety standards to avoid legal suits charging negligence when students are injured. In addition, teachers must obey copyright laws.

7. The courts have clarified and expanded such students' rights as freedom of expression, due process in the case of suspension or expulsion, prohibition against bodily searches in the absence of specific grounds, limitations on corporal punishment, and privacy of records.

8. With regard to cyberbullying, the use of digital media to disparage the school or the staff, gaining access to prohibited materials, or circulating intimate images of oneself or classmates, students' negative actions more often than not take place outside the school, although they sometimes happen in the classroom or make use of school equipment or resources. Regarding all these types of activities, there is tension between students' rights to free speech and expression, and educators' duty to protect and enhance the welfare of students and staff.

9. Organized and mandated prayer and Bible reading are not allowed in public schools. School curricula do not automatically constitute unconstitutional discrimination against religion when they ignore religious points of view or explanations.

10. The legal basis for government support for nonpublic schools is mixed. For example, the government may provide textbooks, tests, and psychological services for students at nonpublic schools, but providing funds for field trips, projectors, science kits, or maps is thought to entangle church and state.

---

[82]"School Vouchers: State-by-State Comparison," January 2014 posting by the National Conference of State Legislatures, available at **www.ncsl.org**; and Emily Le Coz, "Special-Needs Vouchers Could Face Legal Fight," *The Clarion-Ledger* (March 12, 2015), available at **www.clarionledger.com**.

SUGGESTED RESOURCES

INTERNET RESOURCES

The American Civil Liberties Union gives considerable attention to education-related cases.

A wealth of law-related material involving school safety and student discipline is available at the Keep Schools Safe website.

As indicated by its frequent citation in this chapter's footnotes, the Education Law Newsletter provides detailed information about legal issues involving teachers, students, classrooms, and schools. The newsletter is available at the Commonwealth Educational Policy Institute at Virginia Commonwealth University website.

PUBLICATIONS

Alexander, Kern, and David M. Alexander. *American Public School Law,* 8th ed. Belmont, CA: Wadsworth, 2012. *This venerable text has been providing solid and reliable information and analysis regarding school law for decades.*

Schimmel, David, et al., *Teachers and the Law,* 9th ed. Boston: Pearson, 2014. *This nontechnical, question-and-answer book format considers a wide and comprehensive range of topics.*

Yudof, Mark G., et al. *Educational Policy and the Law,* 5th ed. Boston: Cengage, 2011. *Provides extensive background material, analysis, and discussion on a comprehensive set of school law topics.*

CHAPTER **10**

InTASC INTASC
STANDARDS
ADDRESSED IN
THIS CHAPTER

1 Learner Development
2 Learning Differences
3 Learning Environments
7 Planning for Instruction
8 Instructional Strategies

CULTURE, SOCIALIZATION, AND EDUCATION

LEARNING OBJECTIVES

10-1 Summarize how families, peer groups, school cultures, and electronic media contribute to the socialization of children and youth.

10-2 Discuss how sex roles and sex differences influence learning and achievement.

10-3 Describe how schools have been affected by adolescent and youth culture.

Monkey Business Images/Shutterstock.com

This chapter was revised by Daniel U. Levine.

WE ARE ALL AWARE THAT the world is changing rapidly. Communications and the economy are becoming globalized, career success requires increasingly advanced skills, immigration has accelerated in the United States and many other countries, and family patterns today differ greatly from those just thirty years ago. Each such change has a major impact on education from elementary school through the university level.

Nevertheless, certain underlying imperatives and influences regarding how we rear children and youth necessarily remain important. Student development still is strongly influenced by families, neighborhoods, and friends, as well as by wider cultural and social forces such as the mass media, just as it was thirty, sixty, or ninety years ago.

On the other hand, the specific ways in which such forces exert their influence on children and youth change over time. For example, you, as a teacher, may have increasing difficulty capturing students' attention in a digitized world that offers myriad competing stimuli. To respond adequately, you must understand what is happening in the family, the mass media, and the peer group, and how cultural and social trends are influencing the behaviors and ideas that students bring to the classroom.

culture Patterns of acquired behavior and attitudes transmitted among the members of society.

socialization The process of preparing persons for a social environment.

A society ensures its unity and survival by means of culture. The term **culture** has been broadly defined to encompass all the continually changing patterns of acquired behavior and attitudes transmitted among the members of a society. Culture is a way of thinking and behaving; it is a group's traditions, memories, and written records; its shared rules and ideas; and its accumulated beliefs, habits, and values. No individual, group, or entire society can be understood without reference to culture. Habits of dress, diet, and daily routine—the countless small details of ordinary life that seem to require little reflection—all constitute cultural patterns and identities. **Socialization**, which prepares children to function first as young people and then as adults, transmits culture and thereby allows society to function satisfactorily.

In a diverse society such as our own, schools are responsible for helping young people learn to participate in a national culture, but they also must be sensitive to cultural differences and make sure that students from minority groups have equal opportunities to succeed in education. We discuss the challenges posed by this imperative in the multicultural education sections of Chapter 12, Providing Equal Educational Opportunity.

10-1 AGENTS OF SOCIALIZATION

Various social institutions help to transmit culture to children and youth. For many societies, the most important institutions historically have been the church, peer group, school, and, of course, family. Some of these institutions, such as the church, have become less influential in Western societies, while others, such as the mass media, have emerged as a socializing force. In this section, we discuss several issues concerning the influence of family patterns on young people and their education. We then go on to consider the peer group's socializing role and educational implications, school culture, and the influences of television and other mass media. Overview 10.1 summarizes the socializing contributions of each of these institutions.

10-1a The Family

Although its organization varies, the family is a major early socializing agent in every society. As such, it is the first medium for transmitting culture to children. Because the family is the whole world to young children, its members teach a child what matters in life, often without realizing the enormous influence they wield. The behaviors adults encourage and discourage and the ways in which they provide discipline also affect a child's orientation toward the world.

OVERVIEW 10.1

EFFECTS OF MAJOR SOCIALIZING INSTITUTIONS

Institution	Trends and Characteristics	Socializing Effects
Family	• Poverty • Single-parent families • Increase in working mothers • Cohabitation • Latchkey children • Pressures on children • Overindulged children • Homelessness	Some trends, such as expanding options for before- and after-school activities, hold positive potential, but most put children at risk for difficulty in school.
Peers	• Popularity, athletics, attractiveness more important than academics • Extracurricular activities • Bullying • Active learner role carries risks	Cooperative activities can reduce bullying and foster peer relationships that promote academics. Extracurricular activities tend to promote academic achievement.
School culture	• Hidden curriculum diverse with frequently important impacts • Classroom cultures stress • Accommodations, bargaining, compromise • Teacher overload leading to rationing attention	School often teaches students to reduce their enthusiasm and to prefer passive learning.
Television and digital media	• Unclear relationship of television to achievement • Television may socialize aggression, undesirable attitudes • Internet promising for active learning • Electronic social networking becoming more important but might pose problems for students	Television and other media can contribute to academic achievement, but their content and use must be carefully planned, or they can become agents of negative socialization and mislearning.

Many children do well in school because their family environments have provided them with good preparation for succeeding in the traditional classroom. Others do poorly, in part because they have been poorly prepared. Recent changes in the nature of the family have important implications for children's educational development and success in school. This section discusses several of the most important changes and conditions affecting families, including increases in poverty, single-parent families, and cohabitation. We'll also discuss how families may create educational difficulties by pressuring or overindulging children. Finally, we'll examine the severe problems some children face in their home situations, including abuse and homelessness.

10-1b Poverty, Marriage, and Parenting Problems

Poverty is a major problem for many children. More than 20 percent of American children live in poverty. Poor children often face educational difficulties. We'll discuss the relationship between social class and educational achievement in more detail in Chapter 11, Social Class, Race, and School Achievement.

Many observers connect the substantial poverty rates among children and youth with the high and growing incidence of single-parent families, particularly when the mother has low status and a high school degree or less. Less than 10 percent of births to college-educated mothers occur out of wedlock, compared with more than 60 percent among mothers with less education. The percent of births to unmarried women with less education has risen steadily from less than 10 percent in 1970. Of all non-Hispanic white children, about one-quarter are living in single-parent households, compared with less than 10 percent in 1960. The figures for African American children and youth are even more startling: nearly 60 percent are living in single-parent households.[1]

Much research has concentrated on the specific effects of growing up in a single-parent family. Recent studies indicate that, on average, the children of always-married parents have better cognitive, emotional, and educational outcomes than those of never-married or discontinuously married parents, in part because the former have more income but even more because the two-parent families can provide their children with more attention and support. Some analysts perceive the resulting gains for children as indicating not only that more should done to advance stable marriages but also to help unmarried parents develop more skill in parenting.[2]

Dealing with Students from Single-Parent Families   To help you, as a teacher, respond to the trend toward single-parent families, analysts have recommended steps such as the following:[3]

- Do not assume that all or even most children from single-parent families have unusual problems.
- Send copies of communications to the noncustodial parent.
- Include representation of single-parent families in the curriculum; add library materials that show varied lifestyles and help children cope with divorce.
- Cooperate with other agencies in improving child-care arrangements before and after school.
- Conduct workshops to help teachers avoid any negative expectations they may have developed for children from single-parent families.
- Assign school counselors to help students succeed in academic and social tasks.
- Serve as advocates in providing appropriate help for individual students.
- Schedule meetings and events at times convenient for single parents.
- Form school-sponsored support groups for single parents and their children.
- Assist parents in learning how to supervise their children successfully.
- Cooperate with available specialized personnel, such as social workers, who may advise on handling difficult students from single-parent families.

Cohabitation Increase and Effects   In recent years, an increasing number and percentage of children have been growing up in cohabiting households in which their parent or parents have a sexual relationship but are not legally married. The incidence of cohabiting households has increased more than ten times since 1970. By 2012,

[1]Steven L. Nock, "Marriage as a Public Issue," *The Future of Children* (Fall 2005), available at **www.futureofchildren.org**; Isabel V. Sawhill and Joanna Venator, "Families Adrift," October 13, 2014, posting by Brookings, available at **www.brookings.edu**; and Sara McLanahan and Christopher Jencks, "Was Moynihan Right?" *Education Next* (Spring 2015), available at **www.educationnext.org.**

[2]David Blankenhorn, *The Future of Marriage* (New York: Encounter, 2009); "Family Structure and Children's Education," 2014 posting by The Heritage Foundation, available at **www.familyfacts.org**; Kimberly Howard and Richard V. Reeves, "The Marriage Effect," September 4, 2014, posting by Brookings, available at **www.brookings.edu**; and James N. Quane, William J. Wilson, and Jackelyn Hwang, "Black Men and the Struggle for Work," *Education Next* (Spring 2015), available at **www.educationnext.org**.

[3]Adele M. Brodkin and Melba Coleman, "Teachers Can't Do It Alone," *Instructor* (May–June 1995), pp. 25–26; and Valerie Strauss, "Teacher to Parents," *Washington Post*, November 14, 2014, available at **www.washingtonpost.com**.

about 25 percent of children were born to cohabiting couples—more than were born to single mothers living alone. Relatively little research has examined the effects on children, but analysts have begun to provide support for the following conclusions:[4]

- On many social and educational indicators, children in cohabiting households score poorly compared with children from intact, married families.
- Children in cohabiting households are more likely to suffer from child abuse than children in married or single-parent families.
- Cohabitation is occurring at a younger age than years ago. Because younger cohabiters are more likely to separate later than older ones, children they may have are more likely than others to end up in single-parent families.

latchkey children Children unsupervised after school.

Latchkey Children and Community Learning Centers   The situation of latchkey children who return to unsupervised homes after school is particularly problematic because many of these children spend much of their time watching television or roaming the streets. National data indicate that millions of latchkey children return to empty homes or go to community locations such as malls or street corners. Partly for this reason, many school officials as well as civic and political leaders have taken action to expand opportunities for children and youth to participate in extended-day programs at school or in recreational and learning activities at community centers after school. After-school programs thus have become an important aspect of services for young people in many locations, and you are likely to find that many of the students you teach will attend before- or after-school programs. However, an overemphasis on academics in after-school or other out-of-school programs can make for "hurried children," described in the next section.[5]

Hurried and/or Overparented Children   Awareness of the growing importance of education in contemporary society has stimulated many parents to push their children to excel in learning beginning in infancy. The desire to raise so-called "superbabies" appears particularly prevalent among middle-class parents, for whom the ABCs of childhood frequently center on "Anxiety, Betterment, [and] Competition." According to some analysts, these children are "overparented." To meet the demands of such parents, many preschool and primary classrooms might focus so systematically on formal instruction that they harm children in a misplaced effort to mass-produce little Einsteins. Some developmental psychologists characterize such parental pressure as a type of "miseducation" that creates hurried children and deprives young people of childhood.[6]

hurried children Children highly pressured to excel at an early age.

Overindulged Children   Whereas many children might be pressured to meet parental demands for high achievement, others are overindulged by parents who provide them with too many material goods or protect them from challenges that would foster

---

[4]W. Bradford Wilcox, "When Marriage Disappears," 2010 report prepared for The National Marriage Project and the Institute for American Values, available at **www.stateofourunions .org**. See also Richard Fry and D'Vera Cohn, "Living Together," 2011 report prepared for the Pew Foundation, available at **www.pewresearch.org**; Charles Murray, *Coming Apart* (New York: Crown Forum, 2012); Lauren Fox, "The Science of Cohabitation," *Atlantic* (March 20, 2014), available at **www.theatlantic.com**; and Rachel Sheffield, "What's the Real Story on Marriage and Family Trends?" January 19, 2015, posting by The Daily Signal, available at **www.dailysignal.com**.

[5]Brian Libby, "Fourteen Million Kids, Unsupervised," *Edutopia* (January 16, 2007), available at **www.edutopia.org**; Sara Neufeld, "To Close the Achievement Gap, Extra Hours in School Have to Be Better Hours," *Hechinger Report* (December 4, 2014), available at **www .hechingerreport.org**; and Peggy Olson, "Latchkey Kids," undated posting available at **www.study.com**.

[6]Amanda Morin, "The Benefits of Under-Scheduling Your Child," *Education.Com* (August 25, 2008), available at **www.education.com**; Bruce Feiler, "Overscheduled Children," *New York Times* (October 13, 2013); and M. Lin, "10 Signs Your Kid Is Too Busy," *Huffington Post* (October 24, 2014), available at **www.huffpost.com**.

emotional growth. (Of course, some children may be simultaneously overly pressured and overindulged.) Many observers believe that overindulgence is a growing tendency, particularly among young, middle-class parents trying to provide their children with an abundance of advantages. Some psychologists argue that overindulgence is an epidemic afflicting as many as 20 percent of the children in the United States. These "cornucopia kids" may find it hard to endure frustration, and thus may present special problems for their teachers and classmates.[7]

Child Abuse and Neglect   Children from any social class may suffer abuse or neglect by their parents or other household members. As we note in Chapter 9, Legal Aspects of Education, as a teacher, you will have a major responsibility to report any evidence that a student has been maltreated. Our society has become more aware of the extent and consequences of child abuse and neglect, and the number of children confirmed as victims of abuse and neglect has reached nearly one million a year. More than half of these cases involve neglect of such needs as food, clothing, or medical treatment; about one-seventh involve sexual mistreatment; and approximately one-fourth involve beatings or other physical violence. Many child-welfare agencies have been overburdened by the extent of the problem. Although they work to keep families together when safe for children, such agencies often must remove children from their homes and place them in foster care.[8]

Research on child abuse indicates that its victims tend to experience serious problems in emotional, intellectual, and social development. As adults, they have relatively high rates of alcohol and drug abuse, criminal behavior, learning disorders, and psychiatric disturbance. However, this research is difficult to interpret because a relatively large proportion of abuse victims are low-income children. The links between poverty and developmental problems and delinquent or criminal behavior make it harder to separate out the influence of abuse. The relationship is by no means simple; in fact, many abused children manage to avoid serious emotional and behavioral problems.[9]

In any case, educators must recognize that abused or seriously neglected students might not only have a difficult time learning but might also behave in ways that interfere with other students' learning. For this reason, organizations such as the Children's Television Workshop and the National Education Association have developed materials to help teachers deal with abused children, and they are working with other agencies to alleviate abuse and neglect.

Homelessness   Several studies indicate that homeless children disproportionately suffer from child abuse and physical ill health. As we would expect, they also are frequently low in school attendance and achievement. The federal government has done relatively little to provide for homeless adults and children, and many local governments have been unwilling or unable to provide much assistance. However, many schools are striving to provide appropriate help. Some districts and schools, for instance, hire additional counselors, sponsor after-school programs, employ a full-time

---

[7]Bruce A. Baldwin, *Beyond the Cornucopia Kids* (New York: Direction Dynamics, 1988); and Robert Locke, "7 Things You Must Know about Spoiling Children," January 9, 2014, posting by How to Learn, available at **www.howtolearn.com**.

[8]"Children, Families, and Foster Care," *The Future of Children* (Winter 2004), available at **www .futureofchildren.org**; Richard S. Vacca, "Parent Rights and Child Abuse Issues," *CEPI Education Law Newsletter* (October 2008), available at **www.cepi.vcu.edu/publications /newsletters**; Richard S. Vacca. "Reporting Child Abuse," *CEPI Education Law Newsletter* (November 2014), available at **www.cepi.vcu.edu/publications/newsletters**; and Kathleen D. Viezel and Andrew S. Davis, "Child Maltreatment and the School Psychologist," *Psychology in the Schools* (January 2015). See also material at **www.childhelp.org** and **www .childabuse.com**.

[9]Douglas LaBier, "Childhood Psychological Abuse Has Long-Lasting Impact," *Huffington Post* (December 15, 2014), available at **www.huffpost.com**; and Assaf Oshri et al., "Child Maltreatment Types and Risk Behaviors," *Personality & Individual Differences* (January 2015).

person to coordinate services with shelters for homeless families, or try to avoid transferring homeless children from one school to another.[10]

Problems related to homeless children were greatly magnified when the economic decline began in 2008. In Minneapolis, for example, nearly one in ten students were thought to be homeless at some point in 2009. School districts are required by federal law to help homeless children stay in one school continuously, but following this policy can greatly expand costs for transportation and other necessities such as supplies and counseling. The National Center on Family Homelessness reported that more than 2.5 million children were homeless nationally in 2013, and it urged communities to do more to overcome the multiple difficulties caused by this undesirable situation.

nuclear family Mother and father living with their children.

Assessment of Trends Related to the Family Historically, according to many analysts, our system of universal education drew support from the development of the **nuclear family** (two parents living with their children), which grew to prominence in Western societies during the past two centuries. The nuclear family has been described as highly child centered, devoting many of its resources to preparing children for success in school and later in life. With the decline of the nuclear family since World War II, the tasks confronting educators appear to have grown more difficult.[11]

David Popenoe, examining family trends in highly industrialized countries such as Sweden and the United States, concluded that these trends are creating the *postnuclear* family, which emphasizes individualism (individual self-fulfillment, pleasure, self-expression, and spontaneity), as contrasted with the nuclear family's child-centered familism. Adults, Popenoe further concluded, "no longer need children in their lives, at least not in economic terms. The problem is that children . . . still need adults . . . who are motivated to provide them with . . . an abundance of time, patience, and love."[12]

In the context of these family changes and the problems they create, social agencies established to help children and youth sometimes become too overloaded to provide services effectively. For example, one Maryland social worker, when asked why a 6-year-old had not been removed from a known crack house run by his mother, responded that he had "twenty similar cases on his desk, and that he didn't have time to go through the time-consuming process of taking a child from a parent" unless there was an immediate emergency. Overload of social-service agencies seems to have widely increased in recent years due to economic recession and resulting cuts in state and local budgets.[13]

According to the National Commission on Children, although most American children remain "healthy, happy, and secure," many are now "in jeopardy." Even those children free from extreme misfortune may confront difficult conditions. "They . . . attend troubled schools and frequent dangerous streets. The adults in their lives are often equally hurried and distracted . . . The combined effects are that too many children enter adulthood without the skills or motivation to contribute to society."[14] The From Preservice to Practice box describes the efforts of two teachers to motivate children with difficult home lives.

---

[10]John H. Holloway, "Addressing the Needs of Homeless Students," *Educational Leadership* (December 2002/January 2003); Jon Quella, "More Homeless Children Now Than Any Point in US History," November 17, 2014, posting by Common Dreams, available at **www.commondreams.org**; Peter M. Miller, "Families' Experiences in Different Homeless and Highly Mobile Environments," *Education and Urban Society* (January 2015); and information available at **www.homelesschildrenamerica.org**.

[11]Edward Shorter, *The Making of the Modern Family* (New York: Basic Books, 1975). See also Isabel V. Sawhill, *Generation Unbound* (Washington, DC: Brookings Institution Press, 2014); and material posted by the National Marriage Project, available at **www.stateofourunions.org**.

[12]David Popenoe, *Disturbing the Nest* (New York: Aldine de Gruyter, 1988), pp. 329–330; David Popenoe, *Families without Fathers* (New York: Transaction, 2009); and Paul Raeburn, *Do Fathers Matter?* (New York: Farrar, Straus and Giroux, 2014).

[13]William Zinsmeister, "Growing Up Scared," *Atlantic Monthly* (June 1990), p. 67; and Claire Galifaro, "Social Worker Turnover Leads to High Caseloads," *The Courier-Journal* (February 10, 2015), available at **www.courier-journal.com**.

[14]National Commission on Children, *Beyond Rhetoric* (Washington, DC: US Government Printing Office, 1991), pp. xvii–xviii. See also "Every Day in America," January 2014 posting by the Children's Defense Fund, available at **www.childrensdefense.org**.

FROM PRESERVICE TO PRACTICE

TUNING IN

Mark and Claudia have students in their classes who are dealing with difficult home lives and other issues. The two teachers are discussing ways to motivate these children and support their learning.

Mark: Claudia, what else can I be doing to motivate these kids? I have tried everything we were taught in our methods class. What do you do to attract and hold your students' attention?

Claudia: Early in the year, I try and find out what their favorite TV programs are. Then I use the programs' dilemmas and our discussions of the characters to introduce major units. It seems to work, but you have to do your homework on the students first. You might give that a try, Mark.

Mark: How do I even begin to figure out their favorite TV programs? What do you do, have them fill out a survey form on the first day of class?

Claudia: No, I just talk to them as they come in and ask if they saw this or that program last night. They tell me what programs they watched, and in a week, I have a pretty good list of programs that most of the kids watch. Just talk to them and ask them. They'll tell you.

Mark: I wonder how much TV they actually watch. I hardly have time to turn my TV on, but if I'm going to use this approach, I guess I'd better start making it part of my own homework assignment. What else do you think would help, Claudia?

Claudia: By now, you should know which students are your potential troublemakers. Find out what they like. And ask their guidance counselor what he or she can share about the student. Many of our students come from troubled families, families in poverty, and homeless families. As the economy worsens, we're seeing more qualifiers for free and reduced-price breakfast and lunches. That's just one small indicator that we are dealing with many students who lack the advantages we had when we were growing up.

Mark: Some of my students want to sleep most of the time. Do you think drugs have much to do with their inattention in class?

Claudia: Maybe in a few cases, but there's no single answer. I'm betting some of your students have bad home situations and possibly poor nutrition, and others are overscheduled with sports and jobs, besides school. They get less sleep than they need for many reasons. Plus, I've read recent research that suggests the brain chemistry of adolescents changes their sleep schedules. Teachers deal with all of this. Also, I don't want to make you feel bad, but when *all* of my students seem sleepy, the first thing I check is whether I could be boring them.

Mark: Okay, I'll make sure it isn't me! But I'll talk to the counselor about some of these kids, and the athletic director, too. She and the other coaches have a pretty good handle on students who go out for sports. Maybe some of my underachievers or troublemakers are playing volleyball or football this fall. Maybe between us, we can benefit everyone—the students, the coaches, and the teacher.

CASE QUESTIONS

1. Do you think teachers should use television programs to help promote attention to concepts they teach? Explain your answer.

2. Why is it important that teachers understand the backgrounds of students in their classrooms?

3. What other steps do you think Mark should take to help his effectiveness as a teacher?

10-1c The Peer Group

Whereas family relationships may constitute a child's first experience of group life, peer-group interactions soon begin to make their powerful socializing effects felt. From playgroup to teenage clique, the peer group affords young people many significant learning experiences—how to interact with others, how to be accepted by others, and how to achieve status in a circle of friends. Peers are equals in a way that parents and their children or teachers and their students are not. A parent or a teacher sometimes can force young children to obey rules they neither understand nor like, but peers do not have formal authority to do this; thus children can learn the true meaning of exchange, cooperation, and equity more easily in the peer setting.

Peer groups increase in importance as the child grows, and they reach maximum influence in adolescence, by which time they sometimes dictate much of a young person's behavior both in and out of school. Some researchers believe that peer groups

Richard G. Bingham II/Alamy Limited

> **PHOTO 10.1** Teachers should help students develop positive peer relationships conducive to learning.

are more important now than in earlier periods—particularly when children have little close contact with their parents and few strong linkages with the larger society.

peer culture Behaviors and attitudes of similar-age children or youth in an institution or society.

Peer Culture and the School   Educators are particularly concerned with the characteristics of student culture within the school. **Peer culture** frequently works against academic goals at school. For example, a landmark 1961 study by James Coleman found that high school students gained the esteem of their peers by a combination of friendliness and popularity, athletic prowess, an attractive appearance and personality, or possession of valued skills and objects (cars, clothes, music collections). Scholastic success was not among the favored characteristics; in general, the peer culture hindered rather than reinforced the school's academic goals.[15]

More than two decades later, John Goodlad and his colleagues asked more than seventeen thousand students, "What is the one best thing about this school?" The most frequent response by far was "my friends." Respondents also were asked to identify the types of students they considered most popular. Only 10 percent of respondents in junior and senior high schools selected "smart students"; instead, 70 percent of students selected either "good-looking students" or "athletes." Pondering these data, Goodlad concluded that "physical appearance, peer relationships, and games and sports" are more than mere concerns students carry into the school; these phenomena "appear to prevail" there. Noting that Coleman and others reported similar findings in earlier decades, he further wondered "why we have taken so little practical account of them in schools."[16]

To foster peer relationships that support rather than impede learning, some educators recommend conducting activities that encourage students to learn cooperatively. In addition, teachers should promote children's interaction with peers, teach interpersonal and small-group skills, assign children responsibility for the welfare of their peers, and encourage older children to interact with younger children (Photo 10.1).

---

[15]James S. Coleman, *The Adolescent Society* (New York: Free Press, 1961). See also "The Adolescent Society," *Education Next*, no. 1 (2006), available at **www.educationnext.org**; and William A. Corsaro, *The Sociology of Childhood* (Thousand Oaks, CA: Sage, 2014).

[16]John I. Goodlad, *A Place Called School* (New York: McGraw-Hill, 1984), p. 75. See also Amanda Ripley, *The Smartest Kids in the World* (New York: Simon & Schuster, 2013).

Such steps may help counteract peer pressure for antisocial behavior. However, each of these approaches requires considerable planning and dedication in implementation.[17]

Participation in Extracurricular Activities   Polls continually show that students consider their cooperation and interaction with peers in extracurricular activities a highlight of their school experience. Many educators believe this participation is a positive force in the lives of students, but the effect has been difficult to measure. The difficulty lies in determining whether participation in extracurricular activities is a cause or an effect of other aspects of students' development. It is known, for example, that students who participate in many extracurricular activities generally have higher grades than those who do not participate, other things being equal. It may also be true, however, that students with higher grades are more likely to participate than are those with lower grades.

Despite these difficulties, research suggests that participation—especially in athletics, service, leadership activities, and music—fosters emotional and physical health as well as students' aspirations to higher educational and occupational attainment (for example, more years of school completed later). The research also suggests that positive effects are more likely in small schools than in large schools.[18]

These conclusions have great significance for educators. Participation outside the academic curriculum probably is more *manipulable* (alterable by the school) than most other factors related to educational outcomes. For example, home environments may cause problems, but educators can rarely change a student's home environment. Nevertheless, teachers and administrators can promote student participation in extracurricular activities, and this may be one of the most effective ways to improve students' performance.

Research on Bullying and Its Prevention   In recent years, research has begun to address the problems caused by bullies—youngsters who severely harass their peers either inside or outside the school. Most schools have implemented policies to reduce bullying, particularly with respect to sexual orientation and to bullying involving the use of computers, cell phones, and other new media (cyberbullying). Factors frequently cited as causing some children to behave as bullies include neglect and abuse in their homes, the influence of television, and a lack of social skills that leads to a cycle of aggressive behavior. The majority of bullies are male, but the incidence of bullying by girls has been rising. Educators are concerned about not only the harm bullies do to others but also the tendency of bullies to exhibit criminal behavior as adults. Approaches you might apply to modify bullying behaviors include behavioral contracts, instruction in peaceful conflict resolution, classroom activities designed to reduce teasing, and enlisting parental involvement in supervising behavior.[19]

Adolescent Culture as a Determinant of Later Success, or Not   Some scientists studying adolescent culture in the schools have reported that it frequently has negative consequences for the futures of students who feel or are perceived as different from

[17]Robert E. Slavin, "Making Cooperative Learning Powerful," *Educational Leadership* (October 2014).

[18]Alyce Holland and Thomas Andre, "Participation in Extracurricular Activities in Secondary Schools," *Review of Educational Research* (Winter 1987), pp. 437–466; and "Adolescents Benefit from Structured Extracurricular Activities," 2014 posting by Educational Research Newsletter, available at **www.ernweb.com**.

[19]Matthew S. Robinson, "Scared Not to Be Straight," *Edutopia* (February 2008), available at **www.edutopia.org**; Kenneth S. Trump, "Managing Bullying in Politically Charged Climates," *District Administration* (January 2011), available at **www.districtadministration.com**; Amy Williams, "What Bullying Looks Like in the Digital Age and How to Prevent It," *Edutopia* (October 23, 2014), available at **www.edutopia.org**; and Elizabeth Whittaker and Robin M. Kowalski, "Cyberbullying via Social Media," *Journal of School Violence* (January–March 2015). Also see material at **www.bullyonline.org**, **www.stopbullyingnow.com**, and **www.cyberbullying.us**.

most other students. For example, Robert Crosnoe has found that feelings of not fitting in among students who were bullied because they were obese or gay sometimes led not only to depression, drug use, or other dysfunctions, but also to increased risk of not obtaining postsecondary educations. Related research indicates that lack of popularity in adolescence is associated with the subsequent emergence of career and adjustment problems in young adulthood.[20]

On the other hand, some analysts point out that many students who are excluded or are otherwise treated as outsiders in their high schools experience much success in college and later life. For example, Alexandra Robbins has studied the culture in a large high school and found that many "geeks," "nerds," and other outsiders are not popular, and they are frequently ridiculed and even bullied. But later in life, her "quirk theory" speculates, many are successful, in part because they are viewed as refreshingly different and interesting. Thus, there is considerable uncertainty about possible effects of high school culture on subsequent careers, and much variation in how it may affect particular students.

10-1d School Culture

Education in school, compared with learning experiences in family or peer-group contexts, occurs in relatively formal ways. Group membership is not voluntary but determined by age, aptitudes, and, frequently, gender. Students are tested and evaluated; they are told when to sit, when to stand, how to walk through hallways, and so on. The rituals of school assemblies, athletic events, and graduation ceremonies—as well as the school insignia, songs, and cheers—all convey the school culture and socialize students. Less-ritualized activities and teacher behaviors also acculturate students to the school.

Student Roles and the Hidden Curriculum   Gita Kedar-Voivodas has examined teacher expectations for student roles—that is, desired student behaviors and characteristics—in the elementary classroom. She identified three main types of expected student roles: the pupil role, the receptive learner role, and the active learner role.

The *pupil role* is one in which teachers expect students to be "patient, docile, passive, orderly, conforming, obedient and acquiescent to rules and regulations, respectful to authority, easily controllable, and socially adept." The *receptive learner role* requires students to be "motivated, task-oriented, . . . good achievers, and as such, receptive to the institutional demands of the academic curriculum." In the *active learner role,* according to Kedar-Voivodas, students go "beyond the established academic curriculum both in terms of the content to be mastered and in the processes" of learning. Traits of the active learner include "curiosity, active probing and exploring, challenging authority, an independent and questioning mind, and insistence on explanations." Kedar-Voivodas noted that many educational philosophers, among them John Dewey and Maria Montessori, have stressed the value of active learning.[21]

Kedar-Voivodas also found, however, that students exemplifying the active learner role sometimes are rejected by teachers. That is, many teachers respond negatively to active, independent, and assertive children. The difference can be large, Kedar-Voivodas said, between the school's academic curriculum, which demands successful mastery of cognitive material, and its "hidden" curriculum, which demands "institutional conformity."[22]

---

[20]Robert Crosnoe, "The Burden of the Bullied," 2011 paper posted by The University of Texas, available at **www.utexas.edu/features**; Adele Melander-Dayton, "Why It's Good to Be a High School Loser," *Salon* (May 1, 2011), available at **www.salon.com**; and Lexine A. Stapinski et al., "Peer Victimization during Adolescence," *Anxiety, Stress and Coping* (January 2015).

[21]Gita Kedar-Voivodas, "The Impact of Elementary Children's School Roles and Sex Roles on Teacher Attitudes," *Review of Educational Research* (Fall 1983), p. 417. See also Regina D. Langhout and Cecily A. Mitchell, "Engaging Contexts," *Journal of Community & Applied Social Psychology* (November/December 2008), pp. 593–614.

[22]Ibid., p. 418. See also Michael Apple, *Education and Power,* 2nd ed. (New York: Routledge, 1995); and Ali Nouri and Seyed M. Sajjadi, "Emancipatory Pedagogy in Practice," *International Journal of Critical Pedagogy*, v.5, no. 2, 2014, available at **www.libjournal.uncg.edu**.

hidden curriculum What students learn, other than academic content, from the school milieu or environment.

The **hidden curriculum**—a term used by many critics of contemporary schools—is what students learn, other than academic content, from what they do or are expected to do in school. In addition to teaching children to passively conform in the classroom, the hidden curriculum may be preparing economically disadvantaged students to be docile workers later in life. It can communicate negative racial and sexual stereotypes through material included in (or omitted from) textbooks. It can lead children to believe that bullying is acceptable or that copying others' work is expected and excusable. Excessive emphasis on competition for grades may create a hidden curriculum which teaches students that beating the system is more important than anything else.[23]

Classroom Culture   In his study of classroom processes in elementary schools, Philip Jackson found relatively few different types of classroom activity. The terms *seatwork, group discussion, teacher demonstration,* and *question-and-answer period* described most of what happened in the classroom. Further, these activities were performed according to well-defined rules such as "no loud talking during seatwork" and "raise your hand if you have a question." The teacher served as a "combination traffic cop, judge, supply sergeant, and timekeeper." In this cultural system, the classroom often becomes a place where events happen "not because students want them to, but because it is time for them to occur."[24]

The rules of order that characterize most elementary-school classrooms, Jackson concluded, focus on preventing disturbances. Thus, the prevailing socialization pattern in the culture of the school and classroom places its greatest emphasis on what Kedar-Voivodas called the obedient pupil role. Other studies have reached essentially the same conclusion. For example, "A Study of Schooling" conducted by John Goodlad and his colleagues described the following widespread patterns:[25]

1. The classroom is generally organized as a group that the teacher treats as a whole. This pattern seems to arise from the need to maintain orderly relationships among twenty to thirty people in a small space.
2. "Enthusiasm and joy and anger are kept under control." As a result, the general emotional tone is flat or neutral.
3. Most student work involves "listening to teachers, writing answers to questions, and taking tests and quizzes." Textbooks and workbooks generally constitute the media of instruction.
4. These patterns become increasingly rigid and predominant as students proceed through the grades.
5. Instruction seldom goes beyond "mere possession of information." Relatively little effort is made to arouse curiosity or to emphasize thinking.

In summary, Goodlad wrote, students "rarely planned or initiated anything, read or wrote anything of some length, or created their own products. And they scarcely ever speculated on meanings."[26]

---

[23]Mary Breuing, "Problematizing Critical Pedagogy," *The International Journal of Critical Pedagogy*, v.3, no. 3 (2011); and "Hidden Curriculum," December 2, 2014, posting by the Great Schools Partnership, available at **www.edglossary.org**.

[24]Philip W. Jackson, *Life in Classrooms* (New York: Holt, 1968), pp. 8–9, 13. See also Philip W. Jackson, *The Practice of Teaching* (New York: Teachers College Press, 1986); and Carolina Blatt-Gross, "Why Do We Make Students Sit Still in Class?" December 10, 2014, posting by CNN Living, available at **www.cnn.com**.

[25]Goodlad, *A Place Called School*, pp. 123–124, 236, 246. See also Donald J. Willower and William L. Boyd, *Willard Waller on Education and Schools* (Berkeley, CA: McCutchan, 1989); and Antonia Lewandowski, "Seen and Heard," *Teacher Magazine* (March 2006).

[26]John I. Goodlad, "A Study of Schooling," *Phi Delta Kappan* (March 1983), p. 468. See also Edgar H. Schuster, "The Persistence of the 'Grammar of Schooling,'" *Education Week* (April 30, 2003); and Paul E. Barton and Richard J. Coley, "The Mission of the High School," *ETS Policy Information Perspective* (July 2011), available at **www.ets.org**.

As we discuss elsewhere in this book, such systematic emphasis on passive learning by rote is in opposition to most contemporary ideas of what education should accomplish. Much has changed since Goodlad and his colleagues collected their data, but many classrooms still exemplify passive, rote learning. In particular, passive learning is more likely to be emphasized in schools with low-achieving, working-class students than in schools with high-achieving, middle-class students. To study this topic, Jean Anyon examined five elementary schools that differed markedly in social class. In the two predominantly working-class schools, Anyon found that instruction emphasized mostly mechanical skills such as punctuation and capitalization. In contrast, instruction in the schools she categorized as predominantly middle-class or "affluent professional" emphasized working independently and developing analytical and conceptual skills. Similar patterns have been reported by other researchers.[27]

Why do classrooms so often function in this way? This is an important question, and many analysts have addressed it. Reasons they have offered include the following:

1. *Institutional requirements to maintain order.* As Jackson points out, a multitude of routines seek to govern interactions between twenty or thirty students and a teacher. Researchers use terms such as *institutional realities* and *organizational dynamics* to describe the forces that translate a need for order into an emphasis on passive learning.[28]

2. *Student preferences for passive learning.* We should not underestimate the degree to which many students resist active learning. As Walter Doyle writes, students may "restrict the amount of output they give to a teacher to minimize the risk of exposing a mistake." By holding back, students can also persuade other students or the teacher to help them. As one older student said, "Yeah, I hardly do nothing. All you gotta do is act dumb, and Mr. Y will tell you the right answer. You just gotta wait, you know, and he'll tell you."[29]

3. *Accommodations, bargains, and compromises between students and teachers.* In a context that combines institutional requirements for order with student preference for passive learning, the teacher and students may reach an *accommodation* or *bargain* by which they *compromise* on a set of minimal standards. For example, Martin Haberman has observed what he calls "the Deal" in many urban classrooms: students are nondisruptive as long as the teacher ignores the fact that they are not diligent in their classwork. The widespread existence of such "ABCs" has been documented in major studies. Michael Sedlak and his colleagues called such an arrangement "a complex, tacit conspiracy to avoid rigorous, demanding academic inquiry."[30]

---

[27]Jean Anyon, "Social Class and the Hidden Curriculum of Work," *Journal of Education* (Winter 1980), pp. 67–92; Jean Anyon, *Ghetto Schooling* (New York: Teachers College Press, 1997); and Catherine Cornbleth, "School Curriculum-Hidden Curriculum," 2014 posting by State University, available at **http://education.stateuniversity.com**.

[28]Goodlad, "A Study of Schooling," pp. 469–470; Max Angus, *The Rules of School Reform* (London: Falmer, 1998); Daniel U. Levine and Rayna F. Levine, "Considerations in Introducing Instructional Interventions," in Barbara Presseisen, ed., *Teaching for Intelligence*, 2nd ed. (Thousand Oaks, CA: Corwin, 2007); and Nancy J. Ratcliff et al., "The Elephant in the Classroom," *Education* (Winter 2010), pp. 306–314.

[29]Walter Doyle, "Academic Work," *Review of Educational Research* (Summer 1983), pp. 184–185. See also David Ferrero, "Tales from the Inside," *Education Next* (No. 2, 2006), available at **www.educationnext.org**; and Roxy Harris, "Urban Classroom Culture," *Education Review* (Winter 2011–2012).

[30]Michael W. Sedlak et al., *Selling Students Short* (New York: Teachers College Press, 1986), p. 13; Martin Haberman, "The Ideology of Nonwork in Urban Schools," *Phi Delta Kappan* (March 1997), pp. 499–503; Jeffrey Mirel, "The Traditional High School," *Education Next* (No. 1, 2006), available at **www.educationnext.org**; and Harry Wong and Rosemary Wong, "Making Deals Is Ineffective," *Teachers Net Gazette* (December 2014/January 2015), available at **www.teachers.net**.

4. *Teachers' allocation of attention.* Many teachers feel compelled to give most of their time and attention to a few students. In some cases, these will be the slowest students—whomever the teacher believes most need help. In many other cases, however, attention goes primarily to the brightest students, who teachers frequently believe will benefit the most from extra attention. This attitude is particularly prevalent when teachers have so many "slow" students that helping them all seems impossible.

Helen Gouldner and her colleagues found these dynamics in an inner-city, all-black elementary school with a large proportion of students from low-income home environments that failed to prepare them to function well in the classroom. The few well-prepared students (generally from relatively high-status families) were the "pets"—those whom teachers helped throughout their school careers. The largest group of students (the "nobodies") received relatively little teacher attention and generally was neither disruptive nor particularly successful. The remaining students, a small group of "troublemakers," were unable or unwilling to conform to the routine demands of the classroom. These patterns were well in line with the school's "sorting and selecting" function because the teachers, most of whom were African American, could feel they were promoting success for at least some black students in a difficult learning environment.[31]

5. *Society's requirement that students learn to conform.* Underlying schools' emphasis on passive learning is the reality that young people must learn to function in social institutions outside the school. Because most people in contemporary society must cope with large economic, political, and social institutions, children must be socialized to follow appropriate routines and regulations. Philip Jackson summarizes this part of a school's socialization mission as follows: "It is expected that children will adapt to the teacher's authority by becoming 'good workers' and 'model students.' The transition from classroom to factory or office is made easily by those who have developed 'good work habits' in their early years." This goal of schooling is part of the hidden curriculum mentioned earlier.[32]

6. *Teacher overload.* It is difficult for teachers to provide active, meaningful learning experiences when they must cope with the demands of large classes and class loads, a variety of duties and tasks outside their classrooms, pressures to cover a wide range of material and skills, and other such responsibilities.[33] As we document elsewhere in this book, recognition is growing of the heavy burdens on teachers, and many reformers are working to reduce teacher overload.

We could offer many additional reasons why classroom instructional patterns have been relatively unaffected by contemporary learning theory, but most of them in some way involve institutional constraints that favor passive, rote learning.[34] Overcoming such constraints requires significant innovations in school organization and pedagogy, as we will see in Chapter 16, School Effectiveness and Reform in the United States.

---

[31]Helen Gouldner, *Teachers' Pets, Troublemakers, and Nobodies* (Westport, CT: Greenwood, 1978), pp. 133–134. This self-fulfilling prophecy and the way it operated at the school studied by Gouldner and her colleagues are described at greater length in Ray C. Rist, *The Urban School* (Cambridge, MA: MIT Press, 1973). See also Cris Tovani, "I Got Grouped," *Educational Leadership* (March 2010), available at **www.ascd.org**; and Shao-I Chiu, Jiezhi Lee, and Tzanglang Liang, "Does the Teachers' Pet Phenomenon Inevitably Cause Classroom Conflict?" *School Psychology International* (February 2013**)**.

[32]Jackson, *Life in Classrooms*, p. 32. See also Allen Mendler and Brian Mendler, "What Tough Kids Need from Us," *Reclaiming Children and Youth* (Spring 2010), pp. 27–31.

[33]Linda M. McNeil, *Contradictions of School Reform* (New York: Routledge, 2000); and Linda M. McNeil, "Teaching Boldly in Timid Schools," in M. C. Fehr and D. E. Fehr, eds., *Teach Boldly!* (New York: Peter Lang, 2010).

[34]Other frequently cited reasons include the tendency for teachers to teach the way they were taught, the high costs involved in introducing new approaches, and the lack of adequate preservice and in-service training.

Our focus in this section on negative aspects of school culture merits a reminder regarding the many positive aspects of elementary and secondary schools in the United States. Most schools provide an orderly learning environment, and most students learn to read and compute at a level required to function in our society. Relationships among teachers, students, and parents are generally positive. Most students receive a high school diploma, and many proceed to various postsecondary educations. We describe in greater detail many successful aspects of the US education system in Chapter 5, Historical Development of American Education; Chapter 11, Social Class, Race, and School Achievement; Chapter 15, International Education; Chapter 16, School Effectiveness and Reform in the United States; and elsewhere in this book.

Establishing a Productive Classroom Culture   As we pointed out in the preceding sections, traditional classroom practices and arrangements created classroom and school cultures that in a variety of ways hampered active learning of challenging material and concepts. Many educators have advised teachers to overcome these limiting conditions by establishing more productive cultural patterns that advance student engagement and learning. The vast quantity of reforms that have been disseminated for this purpose are too numerous and diverse to describe or even summarize here. But it is potentially rewarding to consider a few recent suggestions such as the following:[35]

- If students do not know how to be active learners, explicitly teach them how to fulfill this function.
- Devise lessons and assignments that produce high student engagement.
- Develop activities to enhance peer cooperation.
- Regularly emphasize the importance of kind and respectful behavior among students.
- Make sure that instruction is challenging and students feel comfortable asking questions.

10-1e Television and Digital Media

Some social scientists refer to television as the "first curriculum" because it appears to affect the way children develop learning skills and orient themselves toward acquiring knowledge and understanding. Because using television and other media may require little in the way of effort and skills, educators face a formidable challenge in maintaining students' interest and motivation in schoolwork. The average eighth grader spends more than three times as much time viewing television, surfing the Internet, and playing video games as doing homework and reading outside school. In addition, a large proportion of children and youth believe their peers' values are significantly influenced by what they see in the media. For more on the influence of television, see the Taking Issue box.

Although research shows a relationship between school achievement and television viewing, the nature of this relationship is not entirely clear. Some studies suggest that viewing television may reduce students' reading activities, but this conclusion is not well documented, and international studies show that students in some countries that rank high on television viewing among children also have relatively high

---

[35]Deborah L. Smith and Brian J. Smith, "Urban Educators' Voices," *Urban Review* (October 2, 2008); David Greene, *Doing the Right Thing* (Neche, ND: Friesen, 2013); "Using Positive Student Engagement to Increase Student Achievement," April 30, 2014, posting by Education.com, available at **www.education.com**; and Charlene Blohm, "Students Using Productive Struggle Experience Deeper Learning," *District Administration* (January 15, 2015), available at **www.districtadministration.com**.

TAKING ISSUE

Read the brief introduction below, as well as the Question and the pros and cons list that follows. Then, answer the question using *your* own words and position.

THE INFLUENCE OF TELEVISION

Television is a fixture in almost every home; its influence is so pervasive that it has been called another parent. Because most children spend more time watching television than attending school, debate continues over television's effect on student learning and behavior.

Question

Does television's influence on students generally benefit the teacher? (Think about this question as you read the PRO and CON arguments listed here. What is *your* response to this issue?)

Arguments PRO

1. Television enriches students' background knowledge so that they can understand much instruction more readily. Teachers who take advantage of what students already have learned from television can accelerate subject matter presentation.

2. In addition to providing useful information, television awakens interest in a wide range of topics. Teachers can draw on the interests that television arouses and involve students more deeply in many parts of the curriculum.

3. Television assists teachers by making learning palatable at an early age. Programs such as *Sesame Street* have increased student achievement in the early years by showing children that learning can be fun.

4. Television provides a catharsis for feelings of hostility and anger. Children who watch television dramas can work out potentially violent impulses that might otherwise be directed at classmates, parents, or teachers.

5. Television can provide a good socializing experience. Research has shown that programs such as *Sesame Street* can increase cooperative behavior among children. Furthermore, many children's shows offer their viewers a welcome relief from the world of adults.

Arguments CON

1. Most often, the information that students gain from television is a superficial collection of facts, not useful background knowledge. Moreover, television may delude students into thinking that these scattered facts represent genuine understanding.

2. Television viewing creates mental habits that teachers must try to counteract. Although television may provoke a fleeting interest in a topic, it accustoms students to learning through passive impressions rather than thoughtful analysis. In addition, extensive television viewing by children is associated with a reduced attention span.

3. Early exposure to "fun" learning often raises false expectations about school. The teacher cannot be as entertaining as Big Bird. The need to compete with such television shows makes the teacher's job more difficult.

4. Research on modeling indicates that many children, confronted with a situation parallel to one they have seen on television, respond with the same behavior used by the television characters. In other words, violent television programs often encourage violent behavior.

5. For every *Sesame Street*, dozens of television programs tend to alienate children from the values of the school and the wider society. For example, some programs reinforce negative peer attitudes toward social institutions; some present simplistic or distorted notions of right and wrong; and many encourage dangerous fantasies.

Question Reprise: What Is Your Stand?

Reflect again on the following question by explaining *your* stand about this issue: Does television's influence on students generally benefit the teacher?

achievement scores. It is difficult to separate cases in which television causes reduced attention to reading from those in which low-performing students turn to television for escape. Nevertheless, many educators are concerned that use of television and other media may lower achievement for many students, particularly because surveys indicate that millions of children watch television and use other media late into the night and then yawn their way through school the next day.[36]

Apart from their possibly negative effects on school achievement, television and other media—such as movies, video games, and the music industry—deeply influence the socialization of children and youth. The media both stimulate and reflect fundamental changes in attitudes and behaviors that prevail in our society, from recreation and career choices to sexual relationships, consumerism, and drug use. Unfortunately, no conclusive data determine just how much the media affect children and youth or whether overall developments and effects are positive or negative (depending, of course, on what one values as positive or negative). For example, twenty-four-hour-a-day rock-music programming on cable television has been viewed both as a means to keep young people off the streets and as the beginning of the end of Western civilization.[37]

Many adults are particularly worried that television, video games, and other media may encourage aggressive or violent behavior. The average child now witnesses thousands of simulated murders and tens of thousands of other violent acts by the time he or she completes elementary school. The effects depend in part on situational factors, for example, the child's degree of frustration or anger, potential consequences such as pain or punishment, previous receptivity to violence, and opportunity to perform an act of violence. Overall, however, according to a committee of behavioral scientists, "television violence is as strongly correlated with aggressive behavior as any other behavioral variable that has been measured." The American Academy of Pediatrics and the American Psychological Association also have concluded that repeated exposure to violence on television and in other media promotes violent behavior.[38]

Social scientists also are becoming particularly concerned about media effects on the socialization of girls. Recent research indicates that the depiction of sex in the media is implicated in producing teen pregnancies. In addition, a task force of the American Psychological Association has examined research on the influence of television, music videos, music lyrics, magazines, movies, video games, and the Internet, as well as advertising and merchandising, and concluded that effects include damage to girls' self-image and healthy development. The Association deplored the "sexualization" of children and youth, which it defined as "occurring when a person's value comes only from her/his sexual appeal or behavior, to the exclusion of other characteristics, and when a person is sexually objectified, e.g., made into a *thing* for another's sexual use."[39]

It also is true, however, that television and digital media can be an important force for positive socialization. For example, research shows that the children's television program *Sesame Street* has helped both middle-class and working-class youth academically, and children can become more cooperative and nurturing after viewing programs emphasizing these behaviors. Research also indicates that computer software programs such as *Cyberchase* can help elementary students improve in mathematics.

---

[36]*Survey of Sixth Grade School Achievement and Television Viewing Habits* (Sacramento: California State Department of Education, 1982); "Children and Electronic Media," *The Future of Children* (Spring 2008), available at **www.futureofchildren.org**; and "Selected Research on Screen Time and Children," 2014 posting by the Campaign for a Commercial-Free Childhood, available at **www.screenfree.org**.

[37]Mark Bauerlein, *The Dumbest Generation* (New York: Tarcher, 2008); Mark Bauerlein, "The Anti-Intellectual Environment of American Teens," *Education Next* (Spring 2009), available at **www.educationnext.org**; Mark Bauerlein, "Why the Millennials Are Doing So Poorly," June 8, 2014, posting at Minding the Campus, available at **www.mindingthecampus.com**; and Ronald Bailey, "Kill Pixels, Not People," *Reason* (February 2015).

[38]US Department of Health and Human Services, *Television and Human Behavior: Ten Years of Scientific Progress and Implications for the Eighties*, Vol. 1, Summary Report (Washington, DC: US Government Printing Office, 1982), pp. 6, 38–39; Christopher J. Ferguson, "Video Games and Youth Violence," *Journal of Youth and Adolescence* (April 2011), pp. 377–391; and "Kids & the Media," 2014 posting by the American Psychological Association, available at **www.apa.org**.

[39]Eileen L. Zurbriggen et al., "Report of the APA Task Force on the Sexualization of Girls," 2007 paper prepared for the American Psychological Association, executive summary available at **www.apa.org**; and Barrie Gunter, *Media and the Sexualization of Childhood* (London: Routledge, 2014).

Some analysts believe that video games, computer games, and other digital media are helping children and youth develop many kinds of problem-solving and motor skills. However, research on this possibility is limited and difficult to interpret.[40]

Recognizing both the good and the damaging effects media can have on children and youth, many people are working for improvements. The Parent-Teacher Association has made television reform—particularly reduction in sex, commercialism, and violence during prime time—one of its major national goals, and organizations such as the National Citizens Committee for Broadcasting have lobbied for change.

Progress has been slow, however. A typical afternoon of "kidvid" still can be a mind-numbing march of cartoon superheroes, and many programs insistently instruct children to demand another trip to the nearest toy store. In 1990, the federal government introduced a requirement that television stations broadcast at least three hours per week of educational and informational programs for children, but much of this programming has few viewers, and programs emphasizing sex and/or violence continue mostly unabated.

Possibly Negative Effects of Social Media and the Internet   Many analysts have expressed concern about the possibly negative effects that social media and the Internet may be having on children and youth. The most obvious danger that observers—particularly parents—frequently discern is the possibility that young people may encounter disreputable persons and even criminals among their social contacts. In some cases, these contacts can result in threats, harassment, and stalking. In addition, as we pointed out in the previous chapter, numerous teenagers have become involved in sending, receiving, and/or transmitting images and messages that can cause difficulties in their relationships and even get them arrested on charges involving pornography. Among the other potentially negative outcomes for children and youth that perhaps are being widely produced by social media and the Internet are the following:[41]

- Loss of ability or failure to develop ability to sustain focused attention
- Difficulty in pursuing coherent courses of action when experiencing multiple, frequent distractions and/or attempting to multitask with a variety of devices and media streams
- Reduction in the capacity to weigh evidence and arguments in a considered manner
- Increase in self-perceptions of unattractiveness due to viewing glamorized images in general and pornography in particular
- Distortion of children's sense of reality due to viewing too many digitized images

However, many observers of young peoples' use of social media and the Internet also point out that these technologies provide enormous opportunities for improving the lives of children and adults, as well as the functioning of social, political, and economic institutions. Some of the suggestions they have made regarding actions that should be emphasized in the schools include the following:[42]

- Teach about the safe and appropriate use of social media and the Internet, rather than excluding sources and leaving students to fend for themselves.

---

[40]Catherine de Lange, "Children Benefit from the Right Sort of Screen Time," *New Scientist* (March 2014), available at **www.newscientist.com**; Elena Malykhina, "Fact or Fiction? Video Games Are the Future of Education," *Scientific American* (September 12, 2014).

[41]Kathy Cook, "Social Media Tips for Teachers," *District Administration* (April 2014), available at **www.distictadministration.com**; Andrew M. Seaman, "Online Life for Teens May Lead to Real Problems," *Reuters* (November 17, 2014), available at **www.reuters.com**; and Stuart Wolpert, "In Our Digital World, Are Young People Losing the Ability to Read Emotions?" August 21, 2014, posting by UCLA Newsroom, available at **www.newsroom.ucla.edu**.

[42]Adam D. Thierer, "Understanding Our Digital Kids," *City Journal* (October 10, 2008), available at **www.city-journal.com**; and Antero Garcia et al., *Teaching in the Connected Learning Classroom* (Digital Media + Learning Research Hub: 2014), available at **www.dmlhub.net**.

TECHNOLOGY @ SCHOOL

HELPING STUDENTS DEVELOP MEDIA LITERACY

Media literacy involves skill in learning from and critically evaluating different forms of electronic and print media. Helping students develop media literacy will be an important part of your job as a teacher. Most of your students will not only spend time watching television but also playing computer games and video games and using the Internet for many purposes. One way to avoid negative outcomes, such as potential school achievement problems, unfavorable socialization, and unquestioning acceptance of media values, is to encourage active listening, viewing, and surfing.

You can teach about many aspects of media literacy. For example, you might help your students understand basic issues regarding the functioning and effects of mass media. Renee Hobbs offers suggestions in the article "Teaching Media Literacy: YO! Are You Hip to This?" (and in other articles) on the University of Rhode Island's Media Education Lab website. The Center for Media Literacy's Media-Lit Kit, which is available on its website, provides advice for implementing media literacy instruction that addresses a wide range of curriculum standards.

FOCUS To what extent did your high school teachers emphasize active learning? Do you recall any obvious obstacles to active learning that emphasized higher-order goals?

- Draw not just on popular sites, such as Facebook and Twitter, but also specialized social-networking sites such as GlobalSchoolNet.
- Make sure students are learning and writing acceptable English rather than truncated versions used in text messaging.
- Change instruction from a teacher-focused model to one based on students' skills.
- Emphasize skills, such as group projects carried out on the Web, that will be beneficial in future employment.
- Encourage students to pursue sources that emphasize art, history, or science rather than violence or sex.
- Help students balance relationships and contacts they have on the computer and smartphone with real-life activities, such as sports and clubs.
- Develop digital literacy, visual literacy, and other aspects of media competence.
- Create links between academic pursuits, students' digital interests, and peer culture.

See the Technology @ School box for more on "media literacy."

10-2 GENDER ROLES AND SEX DIFFERENCES AND OUTCOMES

gender roles Socially expected behavior patterns for girls and boys, and men and women.

Not only does society demand conformity to its fundamental values and norms, but it also assigns specific roles to each of its members, expecting them to conform to certain established behavioral patterns. Socialization is particularly forceful regarding **gender roles**—ideas about the ways boys and girls and men and women are "supposed" to act. Gender roles vary from culture to culture, but within a given culture, they are rather well defined, and children are socialized in them through an elaborate schedule of selective reinforcement. For example, a preschool boy may be ridiculed for playing with dolls, and young girls may be steered away from activities considered too physically rough. By age 3, as Robert Havighurst has remarked, there is already a "noticeable difference in behavior between boys and girls." Even at such an early age, boys are more "active," and girls are more "dependent" and "nurturant." As documented by David Rosenberg and JeongMee Yoon, girls' pinkishness and boys' blueishness now is becoming even more pronounced internationally.[43]

---

[43]Robert J. Havighurst, "Sex Role Development," *Journal of Research and Development in Education* (Winter 1983), p. 61. See also Timothy J. Lensmire, "Learning Gender," *Educational Researcher* (June–July 1995), pp. 31–32; David Rosenberg, "In Kids' Rooms, Pink Is for Girls, Blue Is for Boys," *Slate* (April 9, 2013), available at **www.slate.com**; and Enrico Gnaulati, "Why Girls Tend to Get Better Grades Than Boys Do," *Atlantic* (September 18, 2014), available at **www.theatlantic.com**.

When children go to school, they discover that it is dominated by traditional norms of politeness, cleanliness, and obedience. Teachers generally suppress fighting and aggressive behavior. This can be a problem for boys because, as research indicates, on the average, they are more aggressive than girls almost from the time they are born, probably because of hormone differences. Some scholars believe that teachers' tendency to reward passive behavior and discourage aggressiveness helps account for boys' relatively high rates of alienation and violation of school rules. Boys receive many more reprimands from teachers than do girls, and by the time students enter the secondary grades, boys greatly outnumber girls in remedial classes and in classes for those with emotional disturbances.[44]

By way of contrast, the problems that girls encounter in the educational system generally reflect their socialization for dependence rather than assertiveness. Historically, most girls were not encouraged to prepare for high-status fields such as law or medicine or high-paying technical occupations. Instead, they were expected to prepare for roles as wives and homemakers. The few occupations women were encouraged to consider, such as elementary school teacher, social worker, and nurse, tended to have relatively low pay and low status. This type of socialization did not motivate girls to acquire skills useful for later economic success. Furthermore, verbal skills of the kind in which girls tend to excel failed to prepare them for success in mathematics and science. As a result, many girls were excluded from educational opportunities.[45]

Although socialization in the elementary school frequently intends to make boys obedient and cooperative, in high school, the emphasis placed on athletics means that boys have often received more opportunities than girls to learn leadership and competitive skills that can be useful in later life. Girls, expected to be cooperative and even docile, traditionally have had relatively little encouragement to learn such skills, and those who did were perceived as violating proper norms for female behavior in American society.

Raphaela Best found that school peer groups also help communicate traditional expectations for boys and girls. Best reported that boys' peer groups stress "canons" such as "always be first" and "don't hang out with a loser," whereas girls' peer groups place relatively more emphasis on having fun rather than winning and on cooperation rather than competition. Best also reported that as the students she studied grew older, they made some progress in overcoming stereotypes that limited the aspirations of girls and restricted the emotional growth of boys. Similarly, Barrie Thorne studied elementary-school students and concluded that gender roles are socially constructed at an early age. She also concluded that teachers should try to counteract gender stereotypes by facilitating cooperative behaviors and enhancing opportunities to participate in diverse activities.[46]

---

[43]Robert J. Havighurst, "Sex Role Development," *Journal of Research and Development in Education* (Winter 1983), p. 61. See also Timothy J. Lensmire, "Learning Gender," *Educational Researcher* (June–July 1995), pp. 31–32; David Rosenberg, "In Kids' Rooms, Pink Is for Girls, Blue Is for Boys," *Slate* (April 9, 2013), available at **www.slate.com**; and Enrico Gnaulati, "Why Girls Tend to Get Better Grades Than Boys Do," *Atlantic* (September 18, 2014), available at **www.theatlantic.com**.

[44]Christina H. Sommers, *The War against Boys* (New York: Simon and Schuster, 2000); Gerry Garibaldi, "How the Schools Shortchange Boys," *City Journal* (Summer 2006), available at **www.city-journal.org**; Janet Mulvey, "The Feminization of Schools," *Education Digest* (April 2010), pp. 35–38; and Ryan D'Agostino, "The Drugging of the American Boy," *Esquire*, March 27, 2014, available at **www.esquire.com**.

[45]Susan L. Gabriel and Isaiah Smithson, eds., *Gender in the Classroom* (Urbana: University of Illinois Press, 1990); Richard Whitmire and Susan M. Bailey, "Gender Gap," *Education Next* (Spring 2010), available at **www.educationnext.org**; and Cordelia Fine, "Why Are Toys So Gendered?" *Slate* (April 5, 2014), available at **www.slate.com**.

[46]Raphaela Best, *We've All Got Scars: What Boys and Girls Learn in Elementary School* (Bloomington: Indiana University Press, 1983); Barrie Thorne, *Gender Play* (New Brunswick, NJ: Rutgers University Press, 1993). See also Eva Anggard, "Barbie Princesses and Dinosaur Dragons," *Gender and Education* (December 2005), pp. 539–553; and Laura D. Hanish and Richard A. Fabes, "Peer Socialization of Gender in Young Boys and Girls," August 2014 posting by the Encyclopedia of Early Childhood Development, available at **www.child-encyclopedia.com**.

10-2a Sex Differences in Achievement and Ability

Recent studies in the United States indicate that sex differences in academic achievement are relatively small to nonexistent. For example, data on the reading performance of 9-, 13-, and 17-year-olds indicate that girls score only a little higher than boys. Conversely, among 17-year-olds, boys score slightly higher than girls in higher-order mathematics achievement, but this difference is smaller than it was in 1970; 9- and 13-year-olds show little meaningful difference in mathematics scores for girls and boys. Research also indicates that female gains in mathematics probably are partly due to greater participation in math courses during the past few decades.[47]

Although sex differences in achievement are narrowing or disappearing, much controversy remains about possible differences in innate ability. These arguments often focus on whether a larger proportion of boys than girls have unusually strong innate ability for higher-order mathematics or abstract thinking in general. Research on this topic indicates more variability in ability among boys than among girls: boys are more likely to be either markedly high or markedly low in ability. However, some recent research indicates that girls and women are constituting a growing percentage of the highest-ability students.[48]

Those who believe that ability differences between the sexes are present at birth point to differences in brain function between boys and girls. For most people, the left hemisphere of the brain specializes in verbal tasks, whereas the right hemisphere specializes in nonverbal ones, including spatial functions important in mathematics. In this respect, brain research suggests some differences associated with sex hormones that begin to function at birth or even earlier. Among right-handed people (the majority), women handle spatial functions more with the *left* hemisphere than do men. Women also use the *right* hemisphere more in verbal functions. Numerous other differences have also been reported.[49]

Other observers, however, argue that differences in experience and expectations account for most or all of the learning and achievement differences between boys and girls. Particular attention has been paid to "math anxiety" among women—the possibility that the relatively poor performance of certain women in math (and therefore in science and other fields dependent on math) stems from socialization practices that make them anxious and fearful about mathematical analysis. A related line of argument is that women fear success in traditionally male activities and occupations because succeeding would violate sex stereotypes, thereby inviting ridicule. Still other analysts believe that girls tend to divert their attention more toward social relationships as they enter adolescence. But the situation is complex, and few large-scale generalizations can be made.[50]

---

[47]Yupin Bae et al., *Trends in Educational Equity of Girls and Women* (Washington, DC: National Center for Education Statistics, 2000), available at **www.nces.ed.gov**; and "Think Again: Men and Women Share Cognitive Skills," August 2014 posting by the American Psychological Association, available at **www.apa.org**.

[48]Elizabeth Fennema et al., "New Perspectives on Gender Differences in Mathematics," *Educational Researcher* (June–July, 1998), pp. 19–21; Doreen Kimura, *Sex and Cognition* (Cambridge, MA: MIT Press, 2000); Heather MacDonald, "Math *Is* Harder for Girls," *City Journal* (July 28, 2008), available at **www.city-journal.com**; Hanna Rosin, "The Genius Gap," *New York* (June 4, 2010), available at **www.nymag.com**; "Boys' Impulsiveness May Result in Better Math Ability" (July 27, 2012) posting by Science Daily, available at **www.sciencedaily.com**; and Vlatcheslav Wlasoff, "Mars vs. Venus—Differences in Male and Female Brains," January 13, 2015, posting by Brain Blogger, available at **www.brainblogger.com**.

[49]Richard M. Restak, "The Other Difference between Boys and Girls," *Educational Leadership* (December 1979), pp. 232–235; Louann Brizendine, *The Female Brain* (New York: Morgan Road Books, 2006); Louann Brizendine, *The Male Brain* (New York: Three Rivers Press, 2011); and Cordelia Fine, "His Brain, Her Brain?" *Science* (November 21, 2014).

[50]Lynn Friedman, "The Space Factor in Mathematics," *Review of Educational Research* (Spring 1995), pp. 22–50; Sarah D. Sparks, "Researchers Probe Causes of Math Anxiety," *Education Week* (May 18, 2011); and Carol Dweck and Rachel Simmons, "Why Do Women Fail?" July 30, 2014, posting by CNN, available at **www.cnn.com**.

10-2b Educational and Occupational Attainment of Women

Throughout most of US history, women completed fewer years of schooling than did men. In 1979, however, women for the first time outnumbered men among college freshmen. Since 1992, more than half of all bachelor's and master's degrees have been awarded to women. Women now constitute nearly 60 percent of college and university enrollment.[51]

Related gains have also been registered in the occupational status of women. For example, in 1950, only 15 percent of accountants were women, compared to over 50 percent by 2011; the comparable percentages for female lawyers were 4 percent in 1950 and 34 percent in 2014. In the twenty-first century, more women than men have earned doctorate degrees. Thus both our schools and the wider society are seeing the effects of efforts to eliminate sexism from school curricula, by encouraging girls to attend college and prepare for the professions, providing support for girls and women to enter scientific fields and computing, and other actions to equalize opportunity.[52]

Nevertheless, much remains to be achieved. Despite recent gains, many women still are concentrated in low-paying, low-status occupations. Although the percentage of female scientists and engineers with doctoral degrees has more than doubled since 1973, women still constitute less than one-quarter of the total. Researchers' suggestions for further improving educational opportunities and equity for girls and women include the following:[53]

- Increase teacher training dealing with gender issues.
- Introduce "gender-fair" curricula that accommodate learning-style differences.
- Introduce special programs to encourage girls to participate in math, computing, and science programs (Photo 10.2).
- Work to counteract the decline in self-esteem that many girls experience as they become concerned with their appearance.
- Expose girls to the different areas within science and math and opportunities for specializing in them.

10-2c The Increasing Plight of Working-Class and Low-Skilled, Middle-Class Men

We noted previously that traditional socialization practices in the classroom have created problems for many boys and that women have been gaining in education and employment, particularly when compared with men. Associated with but beyond these patterns, there is widespread concern regarding the status and future of working-class men and of low-skilled, middle-class men—those who have not acquired technical skills in higher education and were in the middle class mainly because of relatively high income. As a group, men in these categories have faced difficult circumstances as our economy has moved away from manufacturing and construction. Such circumstances have been apparent in data on the following trends and patterns:[54]

---

[51]Stephanie Coontz, "The M.R.S. and the P.H.D.," *New York Times* (February 11, 2012); and Mark H. Lopez and Ana Gonzalez-Barrera, "Women's College Enrollment Gains Leave Men Behind," March 6, 2014, posting by the Pew Research Center, available at **www.pewresearch.org**.

[52]"A Current Glance at Women in the Law," July 2014 posting by the American Bar Association, available at **www.americanbar.org**.

[53]Jill King, "Empowering Girls to Take Their Rightful Place in STEM," *HPC Wire* (November 5, 2014), available at **www.hpcwire.com**; and Phoebe Parke, "How Do We Get Girls into STEM?" October 27, 2014, posting by CNN, available at **www.cnn.com**.

[54]Hanna Rosin, "The End of Men," *Atlantic* (July/August 2010), available at **www.theatlantic .com**; Don Peck, "Can the Middle Class Be Saved?" *Atlantic* (September 2011), available at **www.theatlantic.com**; Adam Serwer, "The Bell Swerve," *American Prospect* (May 2011), available at **www.prospect.org**; Isabel V. Sawhill, "The Economics of Marriage and Family Breakdown," July 5, 2014, posting by Brookings, available at **www.brookings.edu**; Joanna Venator and Isabel V. Sawhill, "Where Have All the Good Men Gone?" October 8, 2014, posting by Brookings, available at **www.brookings.edu**; and Eric Westervelt, "Lessons in Manhood," *Education Digest* (January 2015).

Rhoda Sidney/The Image Works

> **PHOTO 10.2** Although sex differences in achievement are narrowing, much controversy remains about possible sources of sex differences and ways to address them.

- Many men are seeking work in a dwindling number of manual-labor jobs outside the service sector.
- After adjusting for inflation, the wages of men have fallen significantly since 1973.
- Among men who did not attend college, unemployment increased from 5–10 percent in the 1960s to 20–25 percent in 2000, before recession pushed it even higher.
- As marriage rates for the working class have fallen rapidly, many more less-educated men have become absent fathers who have child-support payments deducted from their already low wages.

Some of the educational reforms and innovations described in this book and elsewhere may produce improvements in students' opportunities, including those of working-class males. A few, such as high school career academies, can be particularly helpful for working-class and poverty-level students. But widespread national efforts to address the plight of working-class and low-skilled, middle-class segments of the population necessarily will involve complicated programs involving on-the-job training, family support, accelerated job creation, and related efforts. No programs along these lines are likely to be inexpensive or easy to implement.

FOCUS What might you do as a teacher to encourage girls, or boys, for that matter, to overcome overly passive tendencies?

10-3 ADOLESCENT AND YOUTH PROBLEMS

In many traditional, nonindustrialized cultures, the young are initiated into adult life after puberty. This initiation sometimes takes place through special rituals designed to prove the young person's worthiness to assume adult roles. In such societies, one is either a child or an adult; only a brief gap—if any gap at all—separates the two.

In modern technological societies, the young are forced to postpone their adulthood for a period of time called adolescence or youth. A major reason is that modern society no longer has an economic need for young people in this age group. One unfortunate result is that youth have become more and more isolated from the rest of society. In recent decades, this isolation has intensified many youth-centered problems, such as drug use, drinking, suicide, early pregnancy, and delinquency. At the same time, the isolation of youth hampers efforts of schools and other social institutions to prepare young people for adulthood.[55]

[55]James E. Cote, *Arrested Adulthood* (New York: New York University Press, 2000); Renee P. Denison, "Rites of Passage," February 11, 2014, posting by the Society for Research on Adolescence, available at **www.s-r-a.org**; and "School Performance in Context," January 2015 posting by the Horace Mann League and the National Superintendents Roundtable, available at **www.hmleague.org**.

10-3a Drugs and Drinking

Many high school students are regular users of alcohol and/or marijuana, and small percentages use cocaine, crack, methamphetamines, and other drugs. Research indicates that many teenagers have driven an automobile while intoxicated, and that an alarming number of teenagers frequently drink alone when they are bored or upset. The National Center on Addiction and Substance Abuse surveyed high school students and found that nearly half reported use of cigarettes, alcohol, marijuana, cocaine, or other addictive substances within the previous thirty days.[56]

Educators worry that young people's use of alcohol, marijuana, and other relatively mild drugs may reinforce or stimulate alienation from social institutions or otherwise impede the transition to adulthood. This is not to say that drug use invariably leads to problems such as low academic performance, rebelliousness, and criminal activity; it is just as likely that the problems arise first and lead to the drug use. Many young people are using drugs and alcohol to escape from difficulties they encounter in preparing for adult life. But whatever the sequence of causation, usage rates among US youth remain higher than other industrialized nations. Young people themselves believe that drugs and alcohol are a negative influence in their lives. National surveys consistently show that many high school students cite either drugs or alcohol as the "single worst influence" in their lives.[57]

10-3b Suicide

Educators have become increasingly concerned about suicide among young people. The suicide rate among children and youth has about quadrupled since 1950, and some surveys suggest that as many as one in ten school-age youth may attempt suicide. Reasons for this increase appear to include a decline in religious values that inhibit suicide, influence of the mass media, bullying by peers—particularly of gay and lesbian students—perceived pressures to excel in school, uncertain effects of commonly prescribed medications, failed relationships with peers, and pressures or despondency associated with divorce or other family problems.[58]

Teachers and other school personnel need to be alert to the suicide problem. Warning signs include the following: withdrawal from friends, family, and regular activities; violent or rebellious behavior; running away; alcohol or drug abuse; unusual neglect of personal appearance; radical change in personality; persistent boredom; difficulty in concentrating; decline in schoolwork quality; and emotional or physical symptoms such as headaches and stomachaches. Teachers also should keep in mind a US District Court ruling that found school officials partly responsible for a student's suicide when they failed to provide reasonable care and help for a young man who had displayed suicidal symptoms.[59]

10-3c Teenage Pregnancy

Among teenagers as a whole, the number and rate of births have fallen substantially during the past half-century, partly because of the availability of contraceptives and abortion and the success of abstinence campaigns in some communities. On the other

---

[56]"Use of Alcohol, Cigarettes, and a Number of Illicit Drugs Declines among US Teens," *Michigan News*, December 16, 2014.

[57]Diane Ravitch, "Sex, Drugs—and More Sex and Drugs," *Education Next*, no. 1 (2006), available at **www.educationnext.org**; Abigail S. Moore, "This Is your Brain on Drugs," *New York Times* (October 29, 2014); and Edmund Silins et al., "Young Adult Sequelae of Adolescent Cannabis Use," *Lancet* (September 2014), available at **www.thelancet.com**.

[58]Janice S. Crouse, "Sad Truths about Teen Suicide," *American Thinker* (January 9, 2014).

[59]Burr Snider, "Loss Prevention," *Edutopia* (October 2006), available at **www.edutopia.org**; Carolyn M. Rutledge, Don Rimer, and Micah Scott, "Vulnerable Goth Teens," *Journal of School Health* (September 2008), pp. 459–464; and Madeline Kennedy, "School-Wide Prevention Program Lowers Teen Suicide Risk," *Reuters* (January 23, 2015), available at **www.reuters.com**. See also "Teen Suicide Theme Page" and links provided at **www.cln.org/themes/suicide .html**.

hand, the percentage of births to teenage mothers that occur out of wedlock has sky-rocketed from 15 percent in 1960 to almost 90 percent in recent years. Researchers have linked this trend to various social problems. For example, families headed by young mothers are much more likely than other families to live below the poverty line, and teenage mothers are much less likely to receive prenatal care than are older mothers. Not surprisingly, then, children of teenage mothers tend to have poor health and to perform poorly in school. Moreover, society spends billions of dollars each year to support the children of teenage mothers.[60]

Teenage births constitute a substantially higher percentage of births in the United States than in most other industrialized nations. According to social scientists who have analyzed fertility data, high incidence of out-of-wedlock births among teenagers results from such interrelated factors as social acceptance of teenage sexuality, earlier and more frequent sexual intercourse, a decrease in early marriages, glamorization in some media, lack of potential marriage partners, a decline in community and parental influence over the young, and the assumption by social agencies of responsibility for helping younger mothers.[61]

Many schools have responded by establishing school-based clinics for pregnant teenagers and new mothers and by expanding courses that focus on sex education, health, personal development, and family life. Although early data on these activities were generally negative, recent studies indicate that they can be effective in preventing or at least alleviating problems associated with teenage pregnancy. Positive results also have been reported for a variety of approaches implemented as part of the federally sponsored National Campaign to Prevent Teen Pregnancy. In addition, organizations such as Girls, Inc. have conducted projects that provide girls with a combination of assertiveness training, health services, communications skills, personal counseling, and information about sexuality. Recent data show that these efforts appear to have helped in substantially reducing the incidence of teenage pregnancies.[62]

10-3d Delinquency and Violence

Juvenile delinquency has been an important issue for decades. Problems connected with violence and delinquency are particularly acute among young African American males, whose rate of death from homicide has more than doubled since 1965. Even among young white males, however, homicide rates are more than twice as high as in any other industrialized country.

Research on delinquency and violence among youth supports several generalizations:[63]

- Significant delinquency rates appear among youth of all social classes. However, violent delinquency is much more frequent among working-class youth than among middle-class youth.

[60]Kay S. Hymowitz, "It's Morning After in America," *City Journal* (Spring 2004), available at **www.city-journal.org**; and Dennis Thompson, "US Birth Rate Continues Decline, CDC Reports," *US News and World Report* (January 15, 2015).

[61]Kingsley Davis, "A Theory of Teenage Pregnancy in the United States," in Catherine S. Chilman, ed., *Adolescent Pregnancy and Childbearing* (Washington, DC: US Government Printing Office, 1980); R. Y. Langham, "What Are the Causes of Teenage Pregnancy?" August 16, 2013, posting by Live Strong, available at **www.livestrong.com**; and Stephen J. McCall et al., "Evaluating the Social Determinants of Teenage Pregnancy," *Journal of Epidemiology and Community Health* (January 2015).

[62]Brendan L. Smith, "Expanding School-Based Care," September 2013 posting by the American Psychological Association, available at **www.apa.org**; and Elizabeth Dickson, "School-Based Health Centers," 2014 posting by the Robert Wood Johnson Foundation, available at **www.rwjf.org**.

[63]Kay S. Hymowitz, "The Children's Hour," *City Journal* (Winter 2009), available at **www.city-journal.com**; and Abigail A. Fagan, Emily M. Wright, and Gillian M. Pinchevsky, "Exposure to Violence, Substance Use, and Neighborhood Context," *Social Science Research* (January 2015).

- Although a large proportion of crimes are committed by people under age 25, most delinquents settle down to a productive adult life.
- An increase in gangs has helped generate greater violence among youth.
- Family characteristics related to delinquency include lack of effective parental supervision and lack of a father.
- Delinquency is related to learning disabilities and low school achievement.
- One of the strongest predictors of delinquency is peer influence, but this influence interacts with the family, the neighborhood, and other factors.
- Violent youth crime has increased substantially in suburban and rural areas.

10-3e Effects on Schools

As we have seen, young people do not simply leave larger cultural patterns behind when they enter the schoolhouse door. Like the other topics discussed in this chapter, the characteristics of youth culture have enormous consequences for the US educational system. The most direct problems are drugs and alcohol in the schools, and violence, theft, and disorder on school grounds. Indicators of antisocial behavior in and around the schools have been a continuing topic of debate during the past thirty years.[64]

Although violence and vandalism are most common at low-income schools in big cities, they are serious problems at many schools outside the inner city, especially when the schools are afflicted by teenage and young-adult gangs, by crime connected with substance abuse and drug sales, and by trespassers who infiltrate school buildings. More than two hundred students have been killed in or around schools during the past fifteen years, some of them in the highly publicized shootings at Columbine, Sandy Hook, and other schools. In recent years, elaborate security plans have been put in place, zero-tolerance policies (described in Chapter 9, Legal Aspects of Education) have been introduced, and schools have implemented multiple programs to reduce bullying and intergroup hostilities.

In response to youth problems in general, schools now employ many more counselors, social workers, and other social service personnel than they did in earlier decades. Urban high schools, for example, use the services of such specialized personnel as guidance and career counselors, psychologists, security workers, nurses, truant officers, and home–school coordinators. Many of these specialists help conduct programs that target alcohol and drug abuse, teenage sex, school dropout, and suicide.

In addition, many schools are cooperating with other institutions in operating school-based clinics and/or in providing coordinated services that help students and families receive assistance with mental and physical health problems, preparation for employment, and other preoccupations that detract from students' performance in school. Thousands of schools also are implementing programs to improve school-wide discipline, teach students conflict-resolution skills, develop peer-mediation mechanisms, and control gang activities. Related chapters of this book provide additional information on efforts to improve school climates and environments.

FOCUS How do you think your teaching will be affected by problems of adolescence such as violence, drug use, and pregnancy? What kind of help might you need in dealing with such problems?

---

[64]James N. Loque, "Violent Death in American Schools in the 21st Century," *Journal of School Health* (January 2008), pp. 58–61; Michael Ficked, "What We Should Fear at School," *School Planning and Management* (July 2014); and Tina Rosenberg, "For Better Crime Prevention, a Dose of Science," *New York Times* (January 6, 2015).

SUMMING UP

1. Changes in family composition may be detrimentally influencing children's behavior and performance in school. Although the situation is complicated, an increase in single-parent families headed by females with little education appears to be having a negative effect. In recent years, cohabitation has become much more frequent and seems to be frequently producing children who perform poorly in school.

2. Peer culture becomes more important as children proceed through school, but it has an important influence on education at all levels of schooling. Educators should be aware of the potentially positive effects of participation in extracurricular activities.

3. The school culture (that is, regularities in school practice) appears to stress passive, rote learning in many elementary and secondary schools, particularly in working-class schools and mixed-class schools with relatively large numbers of low-achieving students. This happens in part because schools, as institutions, must maintain orderly environments; because many students prefer passive learning; because teachers generally have difficulty attending to the learning needs of all students; and because society requires that students learn to function within institutions.

4. Television probably increases aggressiveness and violent behavior among certain children and youth, and it may tend to detract from achievement, particularly in reading. Analysts have also been studying the social and cultural effects of digital technologies. Recommendations are being made to teach Internet skills and promote media literacy.

5. Girls traditionally have not been encouraged to seek education that prepares them for full participation in the larger society, and both girls and boys have experienced gender-role pressures in school. Even so, educational and occupational opportunities for women have been improving rapidly. Although gender differences in school achievement have been declining, certain differences in ability may persist in verbal skills (favoring females) and advanced mathematics (favoring males). Working-class males are facing increasingly difficult economic and social conditions as manufacturing and construction declines in importance for citizens with relatively low education levels.

6. Youth has become a separate stage of life marked by immersion in various subcultures. Teenage drug use and drinking, suicide, pregnancy, delinquency, and violence raise serious concerns about the development of adolescents and youths both inside and outside the school.

DISCUSSION QUESTIONS

1. How do adolescents' socialization experiences differ in urban and rural communities? Are such differences declining over time? If so, why?

2. How does "schooling" differ from "education"? As a prospective teacher, what implications do you see in this line of analysis?

3. In your experience, which types of students are most popular? Do you believe that popularity patterns have changed much in recent decades? If so, why?

4. What might the schools do to alleviate problems of drug use, violence, and teenage pregnancy? What should they do? Do you believe the "might" and "should" are different? Why or why not?

SUGGESTED RESOURCES

INTERNET RESOURCES

The Spring 2008 issue of *The Future of Children* is devoted to "Children and Electronic Media."

The theme of the February 2011 issue of *Educational Leadership* is "Teaching Screenagers."

Possibilities for improving media literacy among children and youth are explored in the Temple University Media Education Lab and the Center for Media Education. Their sites review projects underway at media labs where developers are devising interactive learning experiences that can foster students' skills in constructing meaning, solving problems, and generally learning to learn. Such projects have great potential for shaping children's growth in a positive direction.

PUBLICATIONS

Cillessen, Antonius H., David Schwartz, and Lara Mayeux, eds. *Popularity in the Peer System.* New York: Guilford, 2011. *Research-based contributions regarding many aspects of youth culture and its consequences.*

Gruenert, Steve, and Todd Whitaker. *School Culture Rewired.* Washington, DC: Association for Supervision and Curriculum Development, 2015. *Emphasizes methods for assessing school culture and how to improve it.*

Hansen, David T., Mary E. Driscoll, and Rene V. Arcilla, eds. *A Life in Classrooms.* New York: Teachers College Press, 2007. *A collection of essays on Philip Jackson's work, including his classic studies of school culture.*

Lareau, Annette, *Unequal Childhoods,* 2nd ed. Berkeley: University of California Press, 2011. *An ethnographic study of family cultures and parenting practices in low-income, working-class, and middle-class families.*

Sedlak, Michael W., Christopher W. Wheeler, Diana C. Pullin, and Philip Cusick. *Selling Students Short.* New York: Teachers College Press, 1986. *Evaluates classroom "bargains" that result in low-level learning and analyzes the weaknesses of bureaucratic school reform that takes little account of these classroom realities.*

SOCIAL CLASS, RACE, AND SCHOOL ACHIEVEMENT

LEARNING OBJECTIVES

11-1 Describe the relationship between social class and success in the educational system.

11-2 Discuss whether—after accounting for social class—race and ethnicity are associated with school achievement.

11-3 Identify the major reasons for low achievement among students with low socioeconomic status.

11-4 Defend arguments for and against the conclusion that the educational system has accomplished its goals to equalize opportunity.

ZUMA Press, Inc./Alamy

This chapter was revised by Daniel U. Levine.

WE BEGIN THIS CHAPTER by briefly explaining social class and examining relationships among students' social class, racial and ethnic background, and performance in the educational system. Then we discuss why students with low social status, particularly disadvantaged minority students, typically rank low in educational achievement and attainment. We conclude the chapter by examining the implications of these relationships in the context of our nation's historic commitment to equal educational opportunity.

This chapter, like Chapter 10, Culture, Socialization, and Education, offers no easy answers; nevertheless, we hope it will provide you with a deeper understanding. We will show how inadequate achievement patterns have become most prevalent among students with socioeconomic disadvantages, especially if those students also belong to minority groups that have experienced widespread discrimination. Other chapters will look at efforts to change the prevailing patterns and improve the performance of disadvantaged students. First, however, we must focus on the multiple root causes of the problem and their implications for teaching and learning.

11-1 SOCIAL CLASS AND SUCCESS IN SCHOOL

American society is generally understood to consist of three broad classes: working, middle, and upper. A well-known and strong relationship exists between social class and educational achievement. Traditionally, working-class students have performed less well than middle- and upper-class students. As you read the analysis in this section, you should ask yourself why it has been so difficult to improve the achievement of working-class students and what can be done to improve their achievement in the future.

11-1a Categories of Social Class

In the 1940s, W. Lloyd Warner and his colleagues used four main variables—occupation, education, income, and housing value—to classify Americans and their families into five groups: upper class, upper middle class, lower middle class, upper lower class, and lower lower class. Individuals high in occupational prestige, amount of education, income, and housing value ranked in the higher classes. Such people are also said to be high in **socioeconomic status (SES)**; that is, others see them as upper-class persons, and they are influential and powerful in their communities. Conversely, people low in socioeconomic status are considered low in prestige and power.[1]

Today, the term *working* class is more widely used than lower class, but social scientists still identify three to six levels of SES, ranging from upper class at the top to lower working class at the bottom. The **upper class** is usually defined as including wealthy persons with substantial property and investments. The **middle class** includes professionals, managers, and small-business owners (upper middle) as well as technical workers, technicians, sales personnel, and clerical workers (lower middle). The **working class** is generally divided into upper working class (including skilled crafts workers) and lower working class (unskilled manual workers). Skilled workers may be either middle class or working class, depending on their education, income, and other considerations such as the community in which they live.[2]

socioeconomic status (SES) Relative ranking of individuals according to economic, social, and occupational prestige and power; usually measured in terms of occupation, education, and income and generally viewed in terms of social-class categories ranging from working class to upper class.

upper class Wealthy persons with substantial property and investments.

middle class Professionals and small-business owners, as well as technicians and sales and clerical workers.

working class Skilled crafts workers and unskilled manual workers.

---

[1]W. Lloyd Warner, Marcia Meeker, and Kenneth Eells, *Social Class in America* (Chicago: Science Research Associates, 1949). See also Sarah Lubienski and Corinna C. Crane, "Beyond Free Lunch," *Education Policy Analysis Archives* (Vol. 18, 2010), available at **http://epaa.asu.edu/ojs**; "What Is Socioeconomic Status (SES)?" 2011 posting by Peter Levine, available at **www.peterlevine.ws**; and Tori DeAngelis, "Class Differences," *Monitor on Psychology* (February 2015), available at **www.apa.org**.

[2]Diana T. Sanchez and Julia A. Garcia, "Social Class in America," *RSF Review* (May 7, 2012); Tina L. Cheng and Elizabeth Goodman, "Race, Ethnicity, and Socioeconomic Status in Research on Child Health," *Pediatrics* (January 2015); and "American Class System and Structure," undated posting by Education Portal, available at **www.education-portal.com**. A bibliography is available at **www.pbs.org/peoplelikeus,** where you can also participate in an interactive game to characterize your home furniture preferences in social-class terms.

underclass Section of the lower working class subject to intergenerational transmission of poverty.

In recent years, observers have identified an **underclass** group within the working class. The underclass has been growing; the population of US neighborhoods with at least 40 percent of their inhabitants in poverty has increased by about a third since 2000. The underclass generally resembles the lower working class, but many of its members are the third or fourth generation to live in poverty and depend on public assistance to sustain a relatively meager existence. Usually concentrated in the inner slums of cities or in deteriorated areas of rural poverty, many members of the underclass frequently have little hope of improving their economic and social situations. Recent data indicate that many immigrant children and youth will be entering or are in danger of becoming part of an underclass. In particular, there is growing concern about the achievement of children whose parents or grandparents came to the United States from Mexico or elsewhere in the Americas. The percentage of Hispanic children in the United States is expected to about double in the next forty years, making it imperative that their relatively low achievement be raised and their high level of school dropout be lowered.[3]

Also, some analysts have identified an "overclass" that they believe is prospering in a competitive international economy at the same time that much of our population is stagnating economically. Alternatively, some analysts have identified a "creative class" or "cognotariat" consisting of highly educated urban dwellers whose work involves an emphasis on creativity. More frequently, observers may discuss an "establishment class" defined largely in terms of inherited wealth and status. As do observers studying underclass development, these analysts generally emphasize the importance of education in determining one's social status and income.[4]

11-1b Research on Social Class and School Success

One of the first systematic studies investigating the relationship between social class and achievement in school was Robert and Helen Lynd's study of "Middletown" (a small Midwestern city) in the 1920s. The Lynds concluded that parents, regardless of social class, recognize the importance of education for their children; however, many working-class children come to school unequipped to acquire the verbal skills and behavioral traits required for success in the classroom. The Lynds' observations of social class and the schools were repeated by W. Lloyd Warner and his associates in a series of studies of towns and small cities in New England, the Deep South, and the Midwest. Thousands of studies have since documented the close relationship between social class and education in the United States and throughout the world. Furthermore, research also confirms that transmission of status often is multigenerational. That is, higher-status parents generally transmit educational and related advantages to their children, who in turn frequently transmit advantages to their own children. From this point of view, the education of a child begins generations before he or she is born.[5]

For example, we have a clear picture of this relationship from the **National Assessment of Educational Progress (NAEP)** and other agencies that collect achievement information from nationally representative samples of students. As shown in

National Assessment of Educational Progress (NAEP) A periodic assessment of educational achievement under the jurisdiction of the Educational Testing Service, using nationally representative samples of elementary and secondary students.

[3]Christopher Jencks and Paul E. Peterson, eds., *The Urban Underclass* (Washington, DC: The Brookings Institution, 1991); Dalton Conley, "The Geography of Poverty," *Boston Review* (March/April 2007), available at **www.bostonreview.net**; Elizabeth Kneebone, Cary Nadeau, and Alan Berube, "The Re-Emergence of Concentrated Poverty," 2011 posting by the Brookings Institution, available at **www.brookings.edu**; Matt Miller, "Why Aren't the Poor Storming the Barricades?" *Economist* (January 21, 2014), available at **www.economist.com**; and "Impoverished We Stand," January 26, 2015, posting by Black Business Now, available at **www.blackbusinessnow.com/impoverished-we-stand-americas-growing-underclass**.

[4]David Brooks, *Bobos in Paradise* (New York: Simon and Schuster, 2000); Christopher Newfield, "The Structure and Silence of the Cognotariat," *Globalization, Societies and Education* (June 2010), pp. 175–189; and "Kicking against the Establishment," December 14, 2014, posting by Global Research, available at **www.globalresearch.ca**.

[5]Robert S. Lynd and Helen M. Lynd, *Middletown: A Study in American Culture* (New York: Harcourt, Brace and World, 1929); and Richard Adams, "Father's Educational Level Strongest Factor in Child's Success at School—Study," *The Guardian* (September 23, 2014), available at **www.theguardian.com**.

TABLE 11.1	Average Scores of Eighth Graders, by Parental Education and by Type of Community		
		Mathematics	**Reading**
Parental Education			
Not graduated high school		267	251
Graduated high school		270	255
Some education after high school		285	270
Graduated college		296	278
Type of Community			
Central city		273	257
Urban fringe/large town		283	266
Rural/small town		279	263

Note: Scores are from testing by the National Assessment of Educational Progress, which defines community type as follows: "Central city" includes central cities in metropolitan areas. "Urban fringe/large town" generally includes other locations in metropolitan areas. A "large town" is a place with at least 25,000 people outside metropolitan areas. Scores are from 2011 for Community Type and 2013 for Parental Education.

Source: The Condition of Education 2014 (Washington, DC: US Department of Education, 2014); and extractions from National Center for Education Statistics data sets at **www.nces.ed.gov /nationsreportcard/naepdata**.

Table 11.1, mathematics and reading proficiency scores of groups of students vary directly with their social class. Students with well-educated parents (one primary measure of social class) score much higher than students whose parents have less education. This holds to such an extent that 9-year-olds whose parents had at least some college had average scores not far below those for 13-year-olds whose parents had not completed high school. Income is another component of social class that is correlated with school performance. Recent data shows that whereas about half of eighth graders at low-poverty schools (with 25 percent or fewer students eligible for free or reduced-price lunch) scored at the Proficient level or above on the NAEP reading test, only about ten of the eighth graders at high-poverty schools (with 75 percent of their students eligible) attained those levels.

School achievement also correlates with the type of community, which reflects the social class of people who reside there. As shown in Table 11.1, the average mathematics and reading scores of students in "urban fringe/large town" areas (with a relatively high proportion of residents in professional or managerial occupations) are higher than those of students in "central city" areas, which have a high proportion of residents who receive public assistance or are unemployed.[6]

Further evidence of the relationship between social class and school achievement can be found in studies of impoverished neighborhoods in large cities. For example, Levine and his colleagues examined sixth-grade achievement patterns at more than a thousand predominantly low-income schools (which they called *concentrated poverty schools*) in seven big cities and reported that all but a few had average reading scores below the national average for more than two years. They also pointed out that at least one-fourth of the students at these schools cannot read well enough when they enter high school to be considered functionally literate.

---

[6]Sean F. Reardon, "The Widening Income Achievement Gap," *Educational Leadership* (May 2013), available at **www.ascd.org**; and Sean F. Reardon and Ann Owens, "60 Years After Brown," *Annual Review of Sociology* (Vol. 40, 2014).

This pattern can be found at concentrated poverty schools in big cities throughout the United States.[7]

Many educators also are concerned about the achievement of rural students, especially those who live in low-income regions and pockets of rural poverty. Although rural students generally achieve near the national average, research indicates that poverty and inequality can hamper their progress, and that two-thirds of rural educators believe the academic performance of their low-income students is in either "great need" or "fairly strong need" of improvement.[8]

We also should emphasize, however, that methods exist for improving the achievement of students with low SES. In particular, the "effective schools" movement that came to prominence in the 1980s showed that appropriate school-wide efforts to enhance instruction can produce sizable gains in the performance of disadvantaged students, even in concentrated poverty schools in big cities and rural schools in poor areas. It is easier today than only ten or fifteen years ago to find schools that have improved achievement among their low-income students. We describe the effective schools movement and other efforts to improve performance among disadvantaged students in other chapters, particularly Chapter 16, School Effectiveness and Reform in the United States.

Social Class, College Participation, and National Problems   Social class is associated with many educational outcomes in addition to achievement in reading, math, and other subjects. On average, working-class students not only have lower achievement scores but also are less likely than middle-class students to complete high school or to enroll in and complete college. Only about 25 percent of high school graduates from the lowest two socioeconomic quartiles (the lowest 50 percent of students measured in terms of family income) enter college and attain a postsecondary degree, compared with more than 80 percent of high school graduates in the highest quartile. (Each "quartile" contains one-quarter of the population.) Researchers find that social class relates to college attendance and graduation even when they compare students with similar achievement levels. For example, one study showed that low-status high school seniors were nearly 50 percent less likely to enter a postsecondary institution than were high-status seniors with similar reading achievement scores. Limitations in public financial aid, among other reasons, have caused this discrepancy to grow in recent years.[9]

FOCUS Have you visited schools where many students were from a social class that was different from most students in schools you attended? What differences did you observe? How do you think these differences would affect achievement?

11-2 RACE, ETHNICITY, AND SCHOOL SUCCESS

race Groups of people with common ancestry and physical characteristics.

ethnicity A shared cultural background based on identification and membership with an ethnic group.

ethnic group A group of people with a distinctive history, culture, and language.

Patterns of social class and educational achievement in the United States are further complicated by the additional factors of race and ethnicity. **Race** identifies groups of people with common ancestry and physical characteristics. **Ethnicity** identifies people who have a shared culture. Members of an **ethnic group** usually have common ancestry and share language, religion, and other cultural traits. Because no pure races exist, some scholars avoid referring to race and instead discuss group characteristics under the heading of ethnicity.

[7]Daniel U. Levine and Rayna F. Levine, *Society and Education,* 9th ed. (Needham Heights, MA: Allyn and Bacon, 1996). See also Susan Popkin, "The Costs of Concentrated Poverty," 2011 posting by Metrotrends blog, available at **www.metrotrends.org**; and Richard D. Kahlenberg, "An Opening for Montgomery's Schools to Lead the Way on Opportunity for All," *Washington Post* (April 25, 2014), available at **www.washington.com**.

[8]Alan J. DeYoung and Barbara K. Lawrence, "On Hoosiers, Yankees, and Mountaineers," *Phi Delta Kappan* (October 1995), pp. 104–112; and Alison DeNisco, "Rural Schools Hit Hard by Budget Cuts," *District Administration* (January 2015), available at **www.districtadministration.com**.

[9]Paul L. Barton and Richard J. Coley, *Windows on Achievement and Inequality* (Princeton, NJ: ETS Policy and Research Center, 2008), available at **www.ets.org**; Russell W. Rumberger, "Education and the Reproduction of Economic Inequality in the United States," *Economics of Education Review* (April 2010), pp. 246–254; Marni Bromberg and Christina Theokas, "Falling Out of the Lead," April 2014 posting by The Education Trust, available at **www.edtrust.org**; and Tim Goral, "Confronting a Low-Income Crisis in U.S. Schools," *District Administration* (April 2015), available at **www.districtadministration.com**.

As we saw in Chapter 5, Historical Development of American Education, the US population is a mix of many races and ethnicities. Some racial and ethnic minority groups in this country have experienced social and economic oppression as a *group* despite the accomplishments of many individuals. For example, African Americans have a lower average SES than that of non-Hispanic whites, even though many individual African Americans may be of higher SES than many whites. Other major ethnic minority groups, such as Mexican Americans and Puerto Ricans, are also disproportionately low in SES. (These two groups, combined with Cuban Americans and citizens with Central and South American ancestry, constitute most of the Hispanic/Latino population, which is growing rapidly and now outnumbers the African American population. This chapter uses the term *Hispanic* in reporting data from government publications employing this terminology and generally uses *Latino* elsewhere.) An ongoing concern for educators is the fact that these racial and ethnic minority groups are correspondingly low in academic achievement, high school and college graduation rates, and other measures of educational attainment.

We can see the close association among social class, race or ethnicity, and school performance in Figure 11.1, which presents average math and reading scores attained by nationally representative samples of eighth graders. African American students

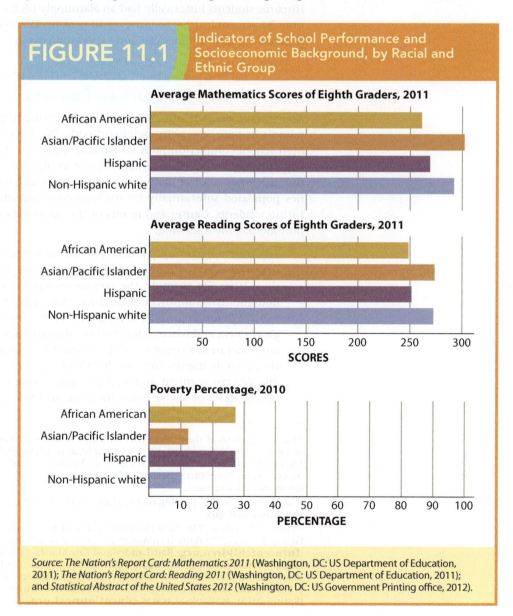

FIGURE 11.1 Indicators of School Performance and Socioeconomic Background, by Racial and Ethnic Group

Average Mathematics Scores of Eighth Graders, 2011

Average Reading Scores of Eighth Graders, 2011

SCORES

Poverty Percentage, 2010

PERCENTAGE

Source: The Nation's Report Card: Mathematics 2011 (Washington, DC: US Department of Education, 2011); *The Nation's Report Card: Reading 2011* (Washington, DC: US Department of Education, 2011); and *Statistical Abstract of the United States 2012* (Washington, DC: US Government Printing office, 2012).

have the lowest SES scores (as reflected by higher percentages in poverty). They also have the lowest math and reading scores. In contrast, non-Hispanic whites are highest in SES, second highest in math, and just below the highest in reading. In general, school achievement scores parallel SES scores; the higher the SES score, the higher the achievement scores.[10]

Data collected by the NAEP indicate that the gap between African American and Latino students on the one hand and white students on the other is narrowing somewhat. African American and Latino students have registered gains in reading, math, and other subjects. Some observers attribute these improvements partly to the federal Title I and No Child Left Behind (NCLB) programs and/or to increases in desegregation. (See Chapter 12, Providing Equal Educational Opportunity, for discussions of Title I, NCLB, and desegregation.) The gap is by no means closed, however. African American and Latino students still score far below non-Hispanic whites in reading and other subjects, and African American and Latino 17-year-olds still have approximately the same average reading scores as white 13-year-olds.

High school dropout rates have been decreasing for some years, and are now less than 10 percent for African American, Asian/Pacific Islander, and non-Hispanic white students. Hispanic students historically had an alarmingly high dropout rate, but it has decreased from 33 percent in 1990 to just over 10 percent. However, dropout rates are disturbingly high among African American and Latino students in some big-city poverty areas.[11]

11-2a The Special Problem of Minority Status Plus Urban Poverty

As we have pointed out, educational achievement generally is distressingly low at schools in poor inner-city neighborhoods. We have also pointed out that although high school completion rates for African American students have been rising nationally, the dropout problem remains severe in big cities. These problems reflect the fact that the inner cores of many large US urban areas have become segregated communities populated substantially by working-class and underclass African American and Latino residents. Causes and results of this socioeconomic and racial/ethnic stratification include the following:

1. *The African American population of the United States has become more economically polarized.* The overall SES and income of this population have increased substantially since 1950. For example, the average income (in real dollars) of African American households has almost doubled since 1965. However, many other African Americans still live in urban poverty, in neighborhoods where most families are headed by single women, and where rates of crime, delinquency, drug abuse, teenage pregnancy, and other indicators of social disorganization remain extremely high. Similarly for Hispanics, in many communities, there is a substantial split that divides a growing middle-class segment and a large segment residing in big-city poverty neighborhoods. Rates of social disorganization in these latter neighborhoods are high.[12]

---

[10]Further analysis of these and other data also indicates considerable variation within broad racial and ethnic classifications. For example, among Hispanics, Cuban Americans have much higher SES and achievement scores than do Mexican American and Puerto Rican students. Among Asian American subgroups, Hmong and Vietnamese students tend to be relatively low in status and achievement.

[11]"Fast Facts," annual posting by the National Center for Education Statistics, available at **www.nces.ed.gov**.

[12]William J. Wilson, *The Truly Disadvantaged* (Chicago: University of Chicago Press, 1987); George J. Borjas, "Making It in America," *The Future of Children* (Fall 2006), available at **www.futureofchildren.org**; Bart Landry and Kris Marsh, "The Evolution of the New Black Middle Class," *Annual Review of Sociology* (August 2011); Patrick Sharkey, "Spatial Segmentation and the Black Middle Class," *American Journal of Sociology* (January 2014); and James N. Quane, William J. Wilson, and Jackelyn Hwang, "Black Men and the Struggle for Work," *Education Next* (Spring 2015), available at **www.educationnext.org**.

The From Preservice to Practice feature in this chapter shows challenges that teachers face in these neighborhoods.

2. *Social institutions such as the family, the school, and the law-enforcement system often appear to have collapsed in the inner city.* Parents find it difficult to control their children, and law-enforcement agencies in some cities are unable to cope with high rates of juvenile delinquency and adult crime.[13]

3. *The concentration of low-income minority populations in big-city poverty areas has increased their isolation from the larger society.* In contrast to the urban slums and ghettos of fifty or a hundred years ago, today's concentrated poverty areas are larger geographically, and, in many cases, their residents are more homogeneous in (low) SES. Unskilled and semiskilled jobs are more difficult to obtain, and many jobs have been moved overseas or to the suburbs where they are practically inaccessible to central-city residents. Andrew Hacker observed that the contemporary "mode of segregation, combining poverty and race, is relatively new. To reside amid so many people leading desultory lives makes it all the harder to break away."[14]

4. *The problems experienced by young black males have escalated enormously.* Some knowledgeable observers believe that the plight of young males in inner-city poverty areas is at the root of a series of other serious problems: high rates of out-of-wedlock births, the persistence of welfare dependency, and violent crime and delinquency. The growth in female-headed families in urban poverty areas relates directly to the high rates at which young African American men drop out of the labor force, are incarcerated in prisons or placed on parole, or otherwise are excluded or exclude themselves from mainstream institutions. The result is a great reduction in the pool of men available to participate in stable families and accumulate resources for upward mobility.[15]

11-2b Comparing the Influence of Social Class and Ethnicity

The close interrelationship among social class, race and ethnicity, and school achievement leads researchers to frequently ask whether race and ethnicity are associated with performance in the educational system even after one takes into account the low SES of African Americans and other disadvantaged minority groups. In general, the answer has been that social class accounts for much of the variation in educational achievement by race and ethnicity. That is, if you know the social class of a group of students, you can predict with a good deal of accuracy whether their achievement, ability scores, and college attendance rates are high or low. Information about their racial or ethnic group generally does relatively little to improve such a prediction. This also means that working-class white students as a group are low in achievement and college attainment, whereas middle-class minority students, as a group, rank relatively high on these variables.

Disadvantaged minorities in the United States remain disproportionately working class and underclass, and their children remain much less successful in the educational system than are the children of the middle class. Moreover, because education is an

[13]William J. Wilson, "Being Poor, Black, and American," *American Educator* (Spring 2011), available at **www.aft.org**; Jamelle Bouie, "Down and Out," *Slate* (April 3, 2014), available at **www .slate.com**; and Jill Leovy, *Ghettoside* (New York: Spiegel and Grau, 2015).

[14]Andrew Hacker, *Two Nations* (New York: Ballantine, 1995); Karl Alexander, "The Roots of Poverty Are Many and Deep," October 29, 2014, posting by the Brookings Institution, available at **www.brookings.edu**; and Patrick Sharkey, "Where You Live Matters," 2015 posting by Spotlight on Poverty and Opportunity, available at **www.spotlightonpoverty.org**.

[15]Douglas S. Massey and Robert J. Sampson, *The Moynihan Report Revisited* (Thousand Oaks, CA: Sage, 2009); Ron Haskins, "Poverty and Opportunity," January 28, 2014, posting by the Brookings Institution, available at **www.brookings.edu**; and Sara McLanahan and Christopher Jencks, "Was Moynihan Right?" *Education Next* (Spring 2015), available at **www .educationnext.org**.

FROM PRESERVICE TO PRACTICE

HOPING FOR SUCCESS

David Rusciatti looked over his first class in eighth-grade English. He had agreed to teach in this inner-city school because that's where he began his own schooling, but the neighborhood was a different place now from just a few years ago when he had lived here.

David knew that this would be a challenging first year. In fact, a couple of the more experienced teachers had told him that they wouldn't like to be in his shoes. His schedule was full, with five classes of eighth-grade English. This first class seemed to have a mix of students of differing ethnicities and vastly different backgrounds. According to the guidance counselor, most of the students were low achievers. He knew that at least four of the boys and two of the girls had already attended eighth grade last year.

David heard quite a bit of giggling and chatting. As he took roll call, he noted back and hand slapping as each student raised his or her hand to indicate they were present. He remembered what his supervising professor had told him last year, "Remember, David, the first day and the first week are all-important. You must set the pace and lay down the rules then, or you are finished for the year."

David had prepared the first day's class with his professor's advice about setting the tone in mind. Following the premise that he must involve the students in their own active learning, he had developed a series of questions and activities. Before he could implement his plan of action, however, the assistant principal came in and took him aside. He whispered, "Don't rile Thomas Davis, over there. I've been told that he has a small pistol concealed under his shirt. I've called the campus police, and they'll nab him as soon as class is dismissed. He's upset about something to do with his girlfriend. If you have trouble before then, you can call me at the office using that phone on the wall. Think you'll be okay?"

"I'll be okay. I have the day well planned." As the assistant principal left, David wondered if he actually would be okay. All went well until he asked the students to write a short paragraph telling about their best experiences of the summer. Several students began commenting to each other, joking and laughing. David was unsure how much of this he should allow, so he smiled and encouraged those who were writing to continue. At the same time, he began to walk around the class to talk to each student not writing.

He scanned the class, noting the different levels of involvement. He would have to learn more about how to teach a group of students with such varying backgrounds and learn more about each individual, too. Maybe that should come first.

CASE QUESTIONS

1. Should first-year teachers be assigned difficult classes such as this one? Justify your answer.
2. What obstacles must David hurdle to be considered an effective teacher?
3. How would you prepare for and handle a class such as this?
4. What instructional policies might David want to introduce?

---

important channel for gaining access to the job market, minority students with low SES have relatively fewer opportunities for economic success later in their lives. From this point of view, the schools' ineffectiveness in educating students from working-class homes helps to perpetuate the current class system, and the burden of poverty and low achievement falls disproportionately on the nation's racial and ethnic minority groups.

For educators, the challenge is to improve the performance of all low-status students, from whatever ethnic group. The US population as a whole has become more divided, with a growing high-income segment, a growing low-income segment, and a shrinking middle segment. Many commentators share the alarm of former Secretary of Labor Robert Reich: "If we lose our middle class and become a two-tiered society, we not only risk the nation's future prosperity but also its social coherence and stability. As the economy grows, people who work the machines and clean the offices and provide the basic goods and services are supposed to share in the gains, but that hasn't been happening."[16]

FOCUS If the middle-income segment of the population is shrinking, and the low-income segment is growing, chances are good that, as a teacher, you will have low-income students in your classes. What are you doing to prepare yourself to teach children from all social classes effectively?

---

[16]Quoted in Keith Bradsher, "Productivity Is All, But It Doesn't Pay Well," *New York Times* (June 25, 1995), p. 4E. See also Emmanuel Saez and Gabriel Zucman, "Wealth Inequality in the United States Since 1913," National Bureau of Economic Research, Working Paper 2065 (October 2014), available at **www.nber.org**; and Estelle Sommeiller and Mark Price, "The Increasingly Unequal States of America," January 26, 2015, posting by the Economic Policy Institute, available at **www.epi.org**.

OVERVIEW 11.1

OBSTACLES TO ACHIEVEMENT FOR WORKING-CLASS STUDENTS BY AREA OF INFLUENCE

Area of Influence	Potential Obstacles to Achievement for Working-Class Students
Home	Disadvantages in home environment of some working-class students, especially in the first few years of life, may leave children unprepared to learn in school. Specifically: • *Knowledge and understandings.* Lack of exposure to the cultural and technological world may limit understandings needed in school. • *Cognitive and verbal skills.* Restricted language does not help prepare children for school. • *Values and attitudes.* Focus on control does not encourage higher-order thinking or independent problem-solving skills needed in school.
Heredity versus Environment	Working-class children average lower scores on intelligence tests, which may be related to environment, heredity, or both. The debate over why scores are low includes at least three views: • *Hereditarian.* Differences in intellectual capacity are inborn, affected little by environment. • *Environmentalist.* Family, school, and cultural environments are major factors in determining IQ test performance. • *Synthesis.* Both environment and heredity contribute to IQ and school performance. Teachers and parents should provide the best possible environment for each child to make the most of their inherited abilities.
Classroom	Obstacles in the classroom that can contribute to low achievement by working-class students include the following: • Inappropriate curriculum and instruction • Lack of previous success in school • Ineffective fixation on low-level learning • Difficult teaching conditions in working-class schools • Teacher perceptions of student inadequacies • Ineffective homogeneous grouping • Delivery-of-service problems • Overly large classes • Lack of teacher preparation and experience • Negative peer pressure • Differences between teacher and student backgrounds • Incompatibility between classroom expectations and students' behavioral patterns/learning styles • Accumulating effects of information-poor homes and neighborhoods

11-3 REASONS FOR LOW ACHIEVEMENT AMONG LOW-STATUS STUDENTS

Over the past forty years, much research has been aimed at understanding and overcoming the academic deficiencies of low-achieving students in general and low-achieving students from working-class or poor families in particular. Although the explanations are not necessarily mutually exclusive, we will group them under the following major factors (summarized in Overview 11.1): home environment, heredity versus environment, and obstacles in the classroom.

11-3a Home Environment

Chapter 10, Culture, Socialization, and Education, points out that children's families are the most important agent in their early socialization and education. We also noted that characteristics of the home environment closely reflect the family's social class. Thus, social-class differences in home environments associate with educational performance and student attainment. Many working-class students grow up in homes that fail to prepare them well for school. Even though their parents may stress the importance of education, these students tend to function poorly in the typical classroom.

Children's home environments cultivate three key sets of characteristics important to their school achievement: (1) knowledge and understandings, (2) cognitive and verbal skills, and (3) values and attitudes. Regarding *knowledge and understandings,* middle-class children are more likely than working-class children to acquire a wide knowledge of the world outside the home through access to books and cultural institutions (for example, museums), parental teaching, and exploration of diverse environments (Photo 11.1). Knowledge and understandings acquired through exposure to the wider world are helpful to children when they enter school. Working-class students today may experience even greater disadvantages than in earlier eras because they tend to have less access to computers at home than do middle-class students.[17]

Students' *cognitive and verbal skills* also reflect social-class differences in family language environments. Basil Bernstein has found that both middle- and working-class children develop adequate skills with respect to "ordinary" or "restricted" language, but middle-class children are superior in the use of "formal" or "elaborated" language. Ordinary, restricted language is grammatically simple, relying on gestures and further explanations to clarify meaning. Elaborated, formal language is grammatically complex and provides greater potential for organizing experience within an abstract meaning system. Many scholars believe that facility in using elaborated language helps middle-class children excel in cognitive development.[18]

Regarding *values and attitudes,* socialization practices in many working-class homes ill-prepare children to function independently in the school and classroom. Many children from lower socioeconomic backgrounds are at a disadvantage because their socialization appears to emphasize obedience and conformity, whereas middle-class families tend to stress independent learning and self-directed thinking. In particular, research indicates that many low-income students are reluctant to ask questions during their lessons because their parents have taught them that this is disrespectful. After an intensive study of seven hundred families in Nottingham, England, John and Elizabeth Newson summarized some of these socialization patterns as follows:

> Parents at the upper end of the social scale are more inclined on principle to use democratically based, highly verbal means of control, and this kind of discipline is likely to produce personalities who can both identify successfully

∧ PHOTO 11.1 Middle-class children are more likely than working-class children to attain a wide knowledge of the world through access to books and parental teaching.

Monkey Business Images/Shutterstock.com

---

[17]"Education and Socioeconomic Status," 2014 posting by the American Psychological Association, available at **www.apa.org**; and Nicole M. Stephens, Hazel R. Markus, and L. Taylor Phillips, "Social Class Culture Cycles," *Annual Review of Psychology* (January 2014).

[18]Basil Bernstein, *The Structuring of Pedagogic Discourse* (New York: Routledge, 1990); Jeanne S. Chall and Vicki A. Jacobs, "Poor Children's Fourth-Grade Slump," *American Educator* (Spring 2003), available at **www.aft.org**; and V. Heller, "Discursive Practices in Family Dinner Talk and Classroom Discourse," *Learning, Culture and Social Interaction* (June 2014).

with the system and use it for their own ends later on. At the bottom end of the scale . . . [many] parents choose on principle to use a highly authoritarian, mainly non-verbal means of control, in which words are used more to threaten and bamboozle the child into obedience than to make him understand the rationale behind social behavior. . . . Thus the child born into the lowest social bracket has everything stacked against him including his parents' principles of child upbringing.[19]

Differences in child-rearing practices reflect the fact that many working-class environments are relatively dangerous for children, and parents use methods that do not help at school but do prepare their children to function in this hostile environment. Other differences arise from parents' own limits in education, resources, and knowledge of what practices help children develop intellectually.

The importance of the home and family environment for general intellectual development has also been documented in studies by J. McVicker Hunt, Martin Deutsch, and other researchers. These studies generally indicate that environmental stimulation in working-class homes is less conducive to intellectual development, on the average, than it is in middle-class homes. Deutsch outlined factors, such as lack of productive visual and tactile stimulation, that limit learning readiness in many disadvantaged children. Deutsch and others developed indexes of environmental disadvantage that correlate even more closely with IQ scores and school success than do social-class indicators.[20]

The environmental disadvantage theory holds that early developmental years are more important than later years. As pointed out by Benjamin Bloom and others, the most rapid development of many human characteristics, including cognitive skills, occurs during the preschool years. Furthermore, the child's intellectual development is affected even during the prenatal stages by the mother's general health, her diet, her alcohol intake and drug usage, and stress and other emotional factors. Although we can counteract learning deficits that arise from disadvantaged early environments, it is, as this implies, more difficult to produce changes for older children; we need a more powerful environment to bring about these changes. It further implies that, as a society, we should use more of our resources to address early environmental problems and disadvantages.[21]

11-3b Stressful, Difficult Environments

Concern is growing regarding the negative outcomes that impoverished and stressful environments can produce as scientists learn more about how the brain develops and what this knowledge might mean for educators. In general, neurologists and other

---

[19]John Newson and Elizabeth Newson, *Seven Years Old in the Home Environment* (London: Allen and Unwin, 1976), p. 406. See also Felix Montes, "Study Shows That Model Learning Community Bears Fruit for Young Children," *IDRA Newsletter* (September 2006), available at **www.idra.org**; and Rebecca Klein, "Working-Class Kids Ask Fewer Questions in Class, and Here's Why," *Huffington Post* (September 10, 2014), available at **www.huffingtonpost.com.**

[20]Martin Deutsch, "The Role of Social Class in Language Development and Cognition," in A. H. Passow, M. I. Goldbery, and A. J. Tannenbaum, eds., *Education of the Disadvantaged* (New York: Holt, 1967), pp. 214–224; James Heckman, "The Economics of Inequality," *American Educator* (Spring 2011), available at **www.aft.org**; James Heckman and Stefano Mosso, "The Economics of Human Development and Social Mobility," *National Bureau of Economic Research* **Working Paper** (February 2014), available at **www.nber.org**; and Margaret Talbot, "The Talking Cure," *New Yorker* (January 12, 2015).

[21]Benjamin S. Bloom, *Stability and Change in Human Characteristics* (New York: Wiley, 1964); Benjamin S. Bloom, *Human Characteristics and School Learning* (New York: McGraw-Hill, 1976); Paula Braverman et al., "Early Childhood Experiences Shape Health and Well-Being Throughout Life," August 2014 posting by the Robert Wood Johnson Foundation, available at **www.rwjf .org**; William Huntsberry, "Pre-K Pays Off by Lowering Special Ed Placements," February 4, 2015, posting by NPRED, available at **www.npr.org**; and Greg Duncan et al., "The Long Reach of Early Childhood Poverty," undated paper prepared for the Harvard Center on the Developing Child, available at **www.developingchild.harvard.edu.**

investigators have reinforced Bloom's conclusions about the importance of a positive environment in the first two or three years of life, when the brain is growing rapidly and establishing billions of neural connections.[22]

In addition, scientists also have been discovering how growing up in disorganized or dangerous circumstances sometimes generates stress and related reactions that negatively affect the development of a young person's brain and personality. Some of these dynamics have been described in Paul Tough's *How Children Succeed* and related works by social scientists, neurologists, and other analysts. Several of these analysts have concluded that experiences involving neighborhood or home disturbances, family violence, inability to satisfy basic needs, and other difficult challenges can result in behaviors and attitudes such as poor self-control and self-regulation, problems in maintaining attention and persevering with distant goals, and other temperamental traits that can hamper progress in school and later life. (Several analysts have summarized some of the resulting traits as involving "character" issues that do much to determine a person's later successes and failures. We would rather refer to "temperament problems" because we think referring to character implies inherent deficiencies that might be overcome by constantly imploring persons to shape up.) Educators working with many students who manifest resulting behaviors and attitudes such as short attention spans, "acting out" in the classroom, or difficulty in pursuing intellectual tasks are trying to devise and implement approaches that help students become successful inside and outside the school.[23]

11-3c Social-Class Advantages and Disadvantages Are Not Universal

Socialization differentials such as those we have discussed in this section reflect *average* differences across social-class groups. They describe family and neighborhood patterns that are present in many locations, but they are not descriptions of universal problems that confront all low-income children and youth. As a teacher, you must remember that no universal patterns distinguish all middle-class families and students from all working-class families. Many children from working-class families do well in school, and many middle-class children do not. Many families with low SES do provide a home environment conducive to achievement, and the great majority of low-income parents try to offer their children a positive environment to support growth and learning. It also appears that the child-raising methods of working-class families probably are becoming more like those of middle-class families. Nevertheless, children from low-income, working-class homes are still disproportionately likely to grow up in an environment that inadequately prepares them to succeed in contemporary schools. In subsequent chapters we describe expanded programs for young children, as well as in-school reforms, that have been initiated to counteract and overcome the negative outcomes experienced by many low-income children and youth.

11-3d The Heredity versus Environment Debate

The past century has seen heated controversy about whether intelligence, which relates strongly to school achievement, is determined primarily by heredity or by environment.

---

[22]Ian Leslie, *Curious* (New York: Basic Books, 2014).

[23]"Back to School," September 14, 2012, posting by This American Life, available at **www .thisamericanlife.org/radio-archives/episode/474/transcript**; Paul Tough, *How Children Succeed* (Boston: Houghton Mifflin, 2013); Monica Potts, "Stress, Poverty, and the Childhood Reading Gap," *American Prospect* (February 12, 2014), available at **www.prospect .org**; and Derek Thompson, "The Curse of Segregation," *Atlantic* (May 5, 2015), available at **www.theatlantic.com**.

hereditarian view of intelligence The belief that intelligence is mostly determined by heredity.

Hereditarian View When IQ tests were undergoing rapid development early in the twentieth century, many psychologists believed that intelligence was determined primarily by heredity. Those who took this **hereditarian view of intelligence** thought that IQ tests and similar instruments measured innate differences, present from birth, in people's capacity. When economically disadvantaged groups and some minority groups, such as African Americans, scored considerably below other groups, the hereditarians believed that the groups with the lower scores were innately inferior in intellectual capacity.

The hereditarian view underwent a major revival in the 1970s and 1980s, based particularly on the writings of Arthur Jensen, Richard Herrnstein, and a group of researchers conducting the Minnesota Study of Twins. Summarizing previous research as well as their own studies, these researchers identified heredity as the major factor in determining intelligence—accounting for up to 80 percent of the variation in IQ scores.[24]

Jensen published a highly controversial study in the *Harvard Educational Review* in 1969. Pointing out that African Americans averaged about 15 points below whites on IQ tests, Jensen attributed this gap to a genetic difference between the two races in learning abilities and patterns. Critics have countered Jensen's arguments by contending that a host of environmental factors that affect IQ, including malnutrition and prenatal care, are difficult to measure and impossible to separate from hereditary factors. IQ tests are biased, they said, and do not necessarily even measure intelligence.[25]

After his 1969 article, Jensen continued to cite data that he believed linked intelligence primarily to heredity. His critics continue to respond with evidence that environmental factors, schooling in particular, have a major influence on IQ.[26]

environmentalist view of intelligence The belief that intelligence is mostly determined by environment.

Environmentalist View By the middle of the twentieth century, numerous studies had contradicted the hereditarian view, and most social scientists took the position that environment is as important as or even more important than heredity in determining intelligence. Social scientists who stress the **environmentalist view of intelligence** generally emphasize the need for continual compensatory programs beginning in infancy. Many also criticize the use of IQ tests on the grounds that these tests are culturally biased. Many attribute the differences in IQ scores between blacks and whites, for example, to differences in social class and family environment and to systematic racial discrimination.

Sandra Scarr and Richard Weinberg studied differences between African American children growing up in their biological families and those growing up in adopted families. They concluded that the effects of environment outweigh the effects of heredity. Thomas Sowell, after examining IQ scores collected for various ethnic groups between 1920 and 1970, found that the scores of certain groups, including Italian Americans and Polish Americans, have substantially improved. Other studies indicate that the test scores of African Americans and Puerto Ricans have risen more rapidly than scores in the general population in response to improvements in teaching and living conditions.[27]

---

[24]Arthur R. Jensen, "How Much Can We Boost IQ and Scholastic Achievement?" *Harvard Educational Review* (Winter 1969), pp. 1–123; Richard J. Herrnstein and Charles Murray, *The Bell Curve* (New York: Free Press, 1994); and Tanya Lewis, "Twins Separated at Birth Reveal Staggering Influence of Genetics," August 11, 2014, posting by Live Science, available at **www.livescience.com**.

[25]Jensen, "How Much Can We Boost IQ and Scholastic Achievement," pp. 273–356; H. Nyborg, ed., *The Scientific Study of Human Intelligence* (New York: Pergamon, 2003); Carl Zimmer, "The Nature of Intelligence," *Scientific American* (October 2008), pp. 68–75; and Ewen Callaway, "'Smart Genes' Prove Elusive," *Nature*, September 8, 2014, available at **www.nature.com**.

[26]Arthur R. Jensen, *The g Factor* (Westport, CT: Praeger, 1998); Arthur R. Jensen, "Race Differences, G, and the 'Default Hypothesis,'" *Psychology* (January 1, 2000); Stephen Ceci and Wendy M. Williams, "Darwin 200," *Nature* (February 12, 2009), available at **www.nature.com**; and Peter Wilby, "Psychologist on a Mission to Give Every Child a Learning Chip," *The Guardian* (February 18, 2014), available at **www.theguardian.com**.

[27]Sandra Scarr and Richard A. Weinberg, "I.Q. Test Performance of Black Children Adopted by White Families," *American Psychologist* (July 1976), pp. 726–739. See also Richard E. Nisbett et al., "Intelligence," *American Psychologist* (January 2012); and Scott B. Kaufman, "The Heritability of Intelligence," *Scientific American* (October 17, 2013), available at **www.scientificamerican.com**.

James Flynn, who collected similar data on other countries, found that massive gains in IQ scores in fourteen nations occurred during the twentieth century. These improvements, according to Flynn's analysis, largely stemmed not from genetic improvement but from environmental changes that led to gains in the kinds of skills assessed by IQ tests. Research also indicates that IQ has been increasing even in previously high-scoring populations, suggesting that there may be multiple causes such as early-childhood education, challenging media environments, and increasingly complex work assignments. Torsten Husen and his colleagues have concluded, after reviewing large amounts of data, that improvements in economic and social conditions, and particularly in the availability of schooling, can produce substantial gains in average IQ from one generation to the next. In general, educators committed to improving the performance of low-achieving students find these studies encouraging.[28]

synthesizers' view of intelligence The belief that intelligence is determined by interaction of environment and heredity.

Synthesizers' View   Certain social scientists have taken a middle, or synthesizing, position in this controversy. The **synthesizers' view of intelligence** holds that both heredity and environment contribute to differences in measured intelligence. For example, Christopher Jencks, after reviewing a large amount of data, concluded that heredity is responsible for 45 percent of the IQ variance, environment accounts for 35 percent, and interaction between the two ("interaction" meaning that particular abilities thrive or wither in specific environments) accounts for 20 percent. Robert Nichols reviewed all these and other data and concluded that the true value for heredity may be anywhere between .40 and .80, but that the exact value has little importance for policy.

In general, Nichols and other synthesizers maintain that heredity determines the fixed limits of a range; within those limits, the interaction between environment and heredity yields each individual's actual intelligence. This view has been supported by recent studies indicating that in impoverished families, much of the IQ variation correlates with quality of environment, whereas in wealthier families (which presumably provide an adequate environment), heredity exerts a greater influence on children's intelligence. In this view, even if interactions between heredity and environment limit our ability to specify exactly how much of a child's intelligence reflects environmental factors, teachers (and parents) should provide each child with a productive environment in which to realize her or his maximum potential.[29]

11-3e Obstacles in the Classroom

We have noted that the home and family environment of many working-class students lacks the kind of educational stimulation needed to prepare students for success in the classroom. However, certain school and classroom dynamics also foster low achievement. The following list highlights some of the most important obstacles to achievement that working-class students face.

1. *Inappropriate curriculum and instruction.* Curriculum materials and instructional approaches in the primary grades frequently assume that students are familiar with vocabulary and concepts to which working-class students have had little

---

[28]Marguerite Holloway, "Flynn's Effect," *Scientific American* (January 1999); Bryan Roche, "Ignore IQ Tests," *Discover* (August 27, 2014), available at **www.discovermagazine.com**; and William Kremer, "Are Humans Getting Cleverer?" March 1, 2015, posting by the BBC, available at **www .bbc.com**.

[29]Robert C. Nichols, "Policy Implications of the IQ Controversy," in Lee S. Shulman, ed., *Review of Research in Education* (Itasca, IL: Peacock, 1978); David L. Kirp, "Nature, Nurture, and Destiny," *American Prospect* (November 2007), available at **www.prospect.org**; and Diane Ravitch, "Learning More about How Environment Affects Intelligence," January 25, 2014, posting available at **http://dianeravitch.net/2014/01/25/learning-more-about-how -environment-affects-intelligence/**.

or no exposure. After grade 3, much of the curriculum requires advanced skills that many working-class students have not yet acquired; hence, they fall further behind in other subject areas.[30]

2. *Lack of previous success in school.* Lack of academic success in the early grades not only detracts from learning more difficult material later but also damages a student's perception that he or she is a capable learner who has a chance to succeed in school and in later life. Once students believe that they are inadequate learners and lack control over their future, they are less likely to work vigorously at overcoming learning deficiencies.[31]

3. *Ineffective fixation on low-level learning.* When a student, or group of students, functions far below grade level, teachers tend to concentrate on remediating basic skills in reading, math, and other subjects. This reaction is appropriate for some low achievers who need intensive help in acquiring initial skills, but it is damaging for those who could benefit from more challenging learning experiences and assignments. Although helping low-achieving students master higher-order learning skills presents a difficult challenge to teachers, certain instructional strategies make it possible to move successfully in this direction.[32]

4. *Difficulty of teaching conditions in working-class schools.* As students fall further behind academically and as both teachers and students experience frustration and discouragement, behavior problems increase in the classroom. Teachers have more difficulty providing a productive learning environment. Some give up trying to teach low achievers or leave the school to seek less-frustrating employment elsewhere.[33]

5. *Teacher perceptions of student inadequacy.* Teachers in working-class schools may see low achievement in their classrooms and conclude that many of their students cannot learn. This view easily becomes a self-fulfilling prophecy because teachers who question their students' learning potential are less likely to work hard to improve academic performance, particularly when improvement requires an intense effort that consumes almost all of a teacher's energy.[34]

6. *Ineffective homogeneous grouping.* Educators faced with large groups of low achievers frequently address the problem by setting them apart in separate classes or subgroups where instruction can proceed at a slower pace without detracting from the performance of high achievers. Unfortunately, both teachers and students tend to view concentrations of low achievers as "slow" groups for whom learning expectations are low or nonexistent.

---

[30]Lisa Delpit, "Lessons from Teachers," *Journal of Teacher Education* (May/June 2006), pp. 220–231; Barbara McClanahan, "Help! I Have Kids Who Can't Read in My World History Class!" *Preventing School Failure* (Winter 2009), pp. 105–112; Eric Jensen, "How Poverty Affects Classroom Engagement," *Educational Leadership* (May 2013), available at **www.ascd.org**; and Natalie Wexler, "High Test Scores at Many Charter Schools May Actually Be 'False Positives'," January 20, 2015, posting by Greater Great Washington, available at **www.greatergreaterwashington.org**.

[31]Jim Wright, "Learning Interventions for Struggling Students," *Education Digest* (January 2006), pp. 35–39; and Linda Shaw, "High Poverty, High Test Scores," *Seattle Times* (April 27, 2014), available at **www.seattletimes.com**.

[32]Christine S. Beck, "No More Lost Ground," *Educational Leadership* (April 2011), available at **www.ascd.org**; and "How We Know Kids in Poverty Can Meet the Common Core Standards," January 30, 2014, posting by ASCD Whole Child Bloggers, available at **www.wholechildeducation.org**.

[33]Richard D. Kahlenberg and Bernard Wasow, "What Makes Schools Work?" *Boston Review* (October–November 2003), available at **www.bostonreview.net**; Paul Tough, *Whatever It Takes* (Boston: Houghton Mifflin, 2008); Sarah D. Sparks, "Study Gauges 'Risk Load' for High Poverty Schools," *Education Week*, November 6, 2014; and Nicole Mirra and John Rogers, "The Negative Impact of Community Stressors on Learning Time," *Voices in Urban Education* (No. 40, 2015), available at **http://vue.annenberginstitute.org**.

[34]Charles M. Payne, *Getting What We Ask For* (Westport, CT: Greenwood, 1984); Lisa Delpit, *Other People's Children* (New York: New Press, 1995), pp. 173–174; Charles M. Payne, *So Much Reform, So Little Change* (Cambridge, MA: Harvard Education Press, 2008); Jessica Sinn, "The Cost of Lower Expectations," *emPower* (September 18, 2013), available at **www.empowermagazine.com**; and John Buntin, "Changing a Culture Inside and Outside of School," *Governing* (January 2015), available at **www.governing.com**.

homogeneous grouping
Involves the sorting of students into groups or subgroups based on their ability and/or previous achievement, following the assumption or belief that this makes it easier to provide effective instruction.

Ray Rist studied this type of arrangement, called **homogeneous grouping**, at a working-class school in St. Louis. A kindergarten class was divided into groups, the "fast learners" and the "slow learners." The fast group received "the most teaching time, rewards, and attention from the teacher." The slow group was "taught infrequently, subjected to more control, and received little if any support from the teacher." Naturally, by the end of the year, differences had emerged in how well prepared these children were for first grade, and the first-grade teacher grouped the students on the basis of their perceived readiness.[35]

Situations like the one Rist described might benefit from keeping the students in heterogeneous classes (that is, groups with a diversity of previous achievement) but giving them individualized instruction so that each can progress at his or her own rate. However, individualization is extremely difficult to implement and often requires such system-wide change in school practices that it becomes almost an economic impossibility. Thus, teachers in schools with mostly low-income students, confronted with heterogeneous classes, generally have failed to work effectively with their numerous low achievers.

One solution is to group low achievers homogeneously for blocks of instruction in reading, mathematics, or other subjects but make sure that the groups are small and temporary and are taught by highly skilled teachers who work well with such students. This alternative aligns with research indicating that restrictive settings (that is, separate arrangements for low achievers) may have either positive or negative outcomes, depending on what educators do to make instruction effective. An approach of this kind frequently is called "flexible grouping." We further discuss the issue of homogeneous versus heterogeneous grouping in Chapter 16, School Effectiveness and Reform in the United States, and in this chapter's Taking Issue box.[36]

7. *Service-delivery problems.* The problems we have described suggest the great difficulty in delivering educational services effectively in classes or schools with a high percentage of low achievers. For example, a teacher in a working-class school who has ten or twelve low-achieving students in a class of twenty-five has a many times more difficult task of providing effective instruction than does a teacher who has only four or five low achievers in a middle-class school. Not only may teachers in the former situation need to spend virtually all of their time overcoming low achievers' learning problems, but the negative dynamics that result from students' frustration and misbehavior make the task much more demanding. These problems are particularly acute for new teachers, who lack the experience to deal with them expeditiously. Administrators, counselors, and other specialized personnel in working-class schools experience the same predicament: the burden of addressing learning and behavior problems may leave little time for improving services for all students. The serious problems endemic in such **overloaded schools** make it difficult for educators to function effectively.[37]

overloaded schools Schools with a high incidence of serious problems that make it difficult for educators to function effectively.

8. *Overly large classes.* As suggested previously, classes too large for teachers to provide sufficient help to overcome learning problems often lead to ineffective

---

[35]Ray C. Rist, *The Urban School: A Factory for Failure* (Cambridge, MA: MIT Press, 1973), p. 91. See also Ray C. Rist, "Student Social Class and Teacher Expectations," *Harvard Education Review* (Fall 2000), pp. 257–266; Tom Loveless, "Ability Grouping, Tracking, and How Schools Work," *Education Next* (April 8, 2013), available at **www.educationnext.org**; and Ben Johnson, "Student Learning Groups," *Edutopia* (January 29, 2014), available at **www.edutopia.org**.

[36]Michael Scriven, "Problems and Prospects for Individualization," in Harriet Talmage, ed., *Systems of Individualized Education* (Berkeley, CA: McCutchan, 1975), pp. 199–210; Gaea Leinhardt and Allan Pallay, "Restrictive Educational Settings: Exile or Haven?" *Review of Educational Research* (December 1982), pp. 557–558; Laura Robb, "But They All Read at Different Levels," *Instructor* (January/February 2008), pp. 47–51; Michael Petrilli, "All Together Now?" *Education Next* (Winter 2011), available at **www.educationnext.org**; and "A Teacher's Guide to Differentiating Instruction," April 30, 2014, posting by Education.com, available at **www.education.com**.

[37]David F. Feldon, "Cognitive Load and Classroom Teaching," *Educational Psychologist* (Summer 2007), pp. 123–137; Christian Bruhwiler and Peter Blatchford, "Effects of Class Size and Adaptive Teaching Competency on Classroom Processes and Academic Outcome," *Learning and Instruction* (February 2011), pp. 95–108; and Katrina Schwartz, "Low-Income Schools See Big Benefits in Teaching Mindfulness," January 17, 2014, post by Mind/Shift, available at **ww2.kqed.org /mindshift/2014/01/17/low-income-schools-see-big-benefits-in-teaching-mindfulness/**.

TAKING ISSUE

Read the brief introduction below, as well as the Question and the pros and cons list that follows. Then, answer the question using *your* own words and position.

HOMOGENEOUS GROUPING

Many schools and classrooms group students by ability in specific subjects, separating the slower learners from the faster ones or the more advanced from the less advanced. Advocates of homogeneous grouping argue that it is both fair and effective, but critics have charged that it harms students, particularly low achievers.

Question
Is placing students in homogeneous groups by ability a generally effective approach for classroom instruction?

Arguments PRO

1. In a large, heterogeneous class with students at many different levels, the teacher cannot give the slowest learners the special attention they need. In fact, teachers may begin to see students who struggle to master the lesson as problems and see quicker students as favorites. Therefore, it makes sense to separate students into ability groups for specific subjects.

2. It is unfair to high-achieving students who are capable of learning quickly to slow the pace of instruction to suit average students. The high achievers may become bored and discouraged unless they are separated into groups that can proceed at a faster rate.

3. Homogeneous grouping encourages the growth of an esprit de corps among group members. With cooperation and friendly competition, students at similar levels can spur each other forward.

4. Many teachers are more effective with certain kinds of students than with others. Homogeneous grouping allows teachers to spend more time with groups they enjoy teaching and are best suited to teach.

5. Homogeneous grouping indicates to parents that the school recognizes differences in learning styles. The school is seen as making a commitment to each child's individual needs.

Arguments CON

1. Research has shown that ability grouping tends to stereotype slower learners and hamper their progress. The instruction offered to such groups is often inferior. Because little is expected of them, they are seldom challenged, and thus they fall further behind the more advanced students. In general, slower learners will do better in heterogeneous classes.

2. Although high-achieving students may be hindered somewhat in a heterogeneous setting, they will remain motivated as long as they sense that the teacher appreciates their talents. Moreover, it is important for them to learn that students of all academic levels have something of value to contribute.

3. A group spirit may develop among high achievers who feel a special honor in being placed together, but low achievers will feel stigmatized, often leading to negative group attitudes. They may become increasingly alienated from school and society.

4. Only a few extraordinary teachers have the necessary skill, patience, and enthusiasm to work effectively with an entire group of low achievers. Other teachers assigned to such groups may become frustrated and demoralized.

5. Parents of low achievers are rarely pleased at seeing their children separated from others. A heterogeneous setting is the best indication that the school cares about all of its students.

Question Reprise: What Is Your Stand?
Reflect again on the following question by explaining *your* stand about this issue: Is placing students in homogeneous groups by ability a generally effective approach for classroom instruction?

instruction for low-achieving students (Photo 11.2). Teachers of large classes find it particularly hard to help low achievers master complex skills such as critical thinking, reading comprehension, mathematics problem solving, and other higher-order skills.[38]

---

[38]Barbara A. Nye, "Do the Disadvantaged Benefit More from Small Classes?" *American Journal of Education* (November 2000), pp. 1–25; "Why Class Size Matters Today," April 2014 posting by the National Council of Teachers of English, available at **www.ncte.org**; and Linda Darling-Hammond, "Want to Close the Achievement Gap?" *American Educator* (Winter 2014/2015), available at **www.aft.org**.

Jon Naso/Star Ledger/Corbis News/Corbis

> **PHOTO 11.2** Conditions such as overcrowded classes, inexperienced teachers, or mismatches between the expectation of schools and teachers and the backgrounds and learning styles of students can contribute to lower achievement.

The effects of class size were assessed in a major study of students in Tennessee. The researchers found that students in small classes scored substantially higher in reading and math in kindergarten and first grade than did students in average-sized classes. They also maintained their advantage in later grades. Effects were particularly impressive at schools that enrolled large proportions of students from low-income minority backgrounds. Several subsequent smaller studies have arrived at similar conclusions.[39]

9. *Teacher preparation and experience.* Studies of high-poverty schools in big cities have shown that teachers at schools with concentrations of low-SES students tend to have less preparation and experience in teaching their subjects than teachers at schools with mostly middle-class students. For this reason, many analysts believe that upgrading teacher training and preparation and hiring teachers with appropriate experience should be priority goals in efforts to improve the achievement of low-income and working-class students.[40]

10. *Negative peer pressure.* Several researchers have reported that academically oriented students in predominantly working-class schools are often ridiculed and rejected for accepting school norms. John Ogbu and Signithia Fordham, among others, have described negative peer influences as being particularly strong among working-class African American students. At some inner-city schools where significant numbers of students react in this way, high achievers who work hard are often labeled "brainiacs" and accused of "acting white." Commenting on these phenomena, an African American professor concluded that the "notion that someone with a hunger for knowledge would be regarded as a 'traitor to his race' . . .

[39]Jeremy D. Finn and Charles M. Achilles, "Answers and Questions about Class Size," *American Educational Research Journal* (Fall 1990), pp. 557–577. See also and David Zyngier, "Class Size and Academic Results, with a Focus on Children from Culturally, Linguistically and Economically Disenfranchised Communities," 2014 posting by Academia.edu, available at **www.academia.edu/6838463**.

[40]Linda Darling-Hammond, "Teacher Quality and Student Achievement," *Education Policy Analysis Archives* (January 2000), available at **http://epaa.asu.edu/ojs**; Richard J. Murnane and Jennifer L. Steele, "What Is the Problem?" *The Future of Children* (Spring 2007), available at **www.futureofchildren.org**; and Aly Seidel, "The Teacher Dropout Crisis," July 18, 2014, posting by NPR, available at **www.npr.org**.

would seem like some kind of sinister white plot. In a society where blacks had to endure jailings, shootings, and lynchings to get an education, it seems utterly unbelievable that some black youngsters now regard . . . academic failure as a sign of pride."[41]

Some researchers have reported that such attitudes appear to be much less prevalent or nonexistent among middle-class black students or those who attend desegregated schools. In addition, research by Lois Weis and her colleagues suggests that antischool peer pressures among working-class students lessen as they realize that education is important for future success. Although working-class adolescents historically tended to view academic learning as irrelevant to their future employment, the high school boys in her study perceived schooling as offering "utilitarian opportunities" for acquiring skilled jobs and thus were willing to "put in their time" in school and even go to college.[42]

11. *Differences in teacher and student backgrounds.* Teachers from middle-class backgrounds might have difficulty understanding and motivating disadvantaged pupils. Particularly in the case of white teachers working with disadvantaged minority students, differences in dialect, language, or cultural background may make it difficult for the teachers to communicate effectively with their students. Such mismatches may also hamper the work of middle-class minority teachers in low-income schools. In any case, many teachers are reluctant to accept assignment or to remain in high-poverty schools, to the extent that many such schools are left with numerous inexperienced teachers who have not learned to work well with low-income students and to teach them effectively.[43]

12. *Incompatibility between classroom expectations and students' behavioral patterns and learning styles.* Teachers may also be unprepared for diversity in their students' learning styles and behavior. Numerous analysts have concluded that the behavioral patterns and learning styles of many working-class students and some groups of minority students differ from those of middle-class or nonminority students. When teachers gear their classroom expectations to the learning styles and behavior of high-achieving, middle-class students, such style differences can lead to school failure.

For example, some researchers suggest that the following patterns of behaviors exist, and they recommended the following ways for teachers to adapt their instruction to help students who display these styles:[44]

● Many African American students tend to behave energetically in class (a pattern researchers refer to as having high "activation" levels). These students do not perform well if teachers require them to sit in one place for extended periods of time

[41]Signithia Fordham, "Racelessness as a Factor in Black Students' School Success," *Harvard Educational Review* (February 1988), pp. 54–84; Roland G. Fryer, "'Acting White,'" *Education Next* (No. 2, 2006), available at **www.educationnext.org**; and John McWhorter, "'Acting White' Remains a Barrier for Black Education," *Reason*, October 8, 2014, available at **www.reason.com**.

[42]Maxine Seller and Lois Weis, *Beyond Black and White* (Albany: State University of New York Press, 1997). See also Lois Weis, *Class Reunion* (New York: Routledge, 2004); Lois Weis, ed., *The Way Class Works* (New York: Routledge, 2007); and Nicola Ingram, "Within School and Beyond the Gate," *Sociology* (No. 2, 2011), pp. 287–302.

[43]Uvaney Maylor, "'They Do Not Relate to Black People like Us,'" *Journal of Education Policy* (January 2009), pp. 1–21; Julie Landsman, "Overcoming the Challenges of Poverty," *Educational Leadership* (Summer 2014), available at **www.ascd.org**; and Anna Egalite and Brian Kisidia, "The Benefits of Minority Teachers in the Classroom," March 6, 2015, posting by Real Clear Education, available at **www.realcleareducation.com**.

[44]LaVonne Neal et al., "The Effects of African American Movement Styles," *Journal of Special Education* (Spring 2003), pp. 49–58; Augusta Mann, Touching the Spirit," 2011 posting by Successful Urban Teachers, available at **www.successfulteachers.com**; and Terrance F. Ross, "How Black Students Tend to Learn Science," *Atlantic* (December 4, 2014), available at **www .theatlantic.com**.

or prohibit impulsive responses. If, as a teacher, you have highly active students, you should plan learning activities that allow students some physical movement.

● Some low-income African American students tend to become confused when teachers fail to act forcefully and authoritatively. Researchers therefore suggest that, as a teacher, you maintain authority and avoid treating students as "buddies."

● African American and Latino students may tend to be "field dependent"—that is, they learn poorly when instruction begins with abstract, decontextualized concepts. You can help field-dependent students by presenting concrete material before moving to abstract analysis. Providing opportunities for students to learn in pairs or cooperative groups may also help.

We should emphasize that research has not conclusively established the existence of such distinctive behavioral patterns or learning styles among working-class or minority students. Learning differences between low-income African American, Latino, or other minority students and nonminority students may stem mostly from SES rather than from race or ethnicity. Nevertheless, numerous studies do support the conclusion that you can help improve performance among your low-achieving students if you adjust for the various behavioral and learning styles of *all* your students. We'll discuss such alternative teaching practices in the multicultural education section in Chapter 12, Providing Equal Educational Opportunity.[45]

13. *Accumulating effects of information-poor homes and neighborhoods.* Disadvantages associated with growing up in an impoverished environment (for more information on home influences, see the "Home Environment" section earlier in this chapter) not only accumulate just in infancy and early childhood but also cascade further as children proceed through school. Research indicates that students in poverty neighborhoods and schools have relatively limited access to high-quality print and digital materials, and thus during summer vacations and other time away from school, they fall further and further behind middle-class students in achievement.[46]

Our analysis so far makes it clear that many students are economically disadvantaged and also experience educational disadvantages in schools and classrooms. Research indicates that disadvantaged students can increase their success in the educational system with outstanding teachers and appropriate instructional strategies.[47] However, the discouraging facts of achievement and social class have raised questions about whether or not schools do indeed make a difference: Do they generally help in significant ways in counteracting the disadvantages students experience? The rest of this chapter confronts this issue. Related chapters, particularly Chapter 16, School Effectiveness and Reform in the United States, will discuss ways to bolster student achievement by improving the organization and delivery of instruction.

FOCUS Which reasons for low achievement among many low-income students seem most important to you? Can you identify other possible explanations not listed in this chapter? (Hint: Many low-income parents move around a lot.)

[45]Madge G. Willis, "Learning Styles of African American Children," *Journal of Black Psychology* (Fall 1989), pp. 47–65; A. Wade Boykin and Pedro Noguera, *Creating the Opportunity to Learn* (Washington, DC: ASCD, 2011); and Janice E. Hale, "Thirty-Year Retrospective on the Learning Styles of African American Children," *Education and Urban Society* (June 2014).

[46]Donna Celano and Susan B. Neuman, "When Schools Close, the Knowledge Gap Grows," *Phi Delta Kappan* (December 2008), pp. 256–262; and Bridget Ansel, "The Case Against Summer Vacation," *Politico* (July 14, 2014).

[47]Daniel U. Levine and Beau Fly Jones, "Mastery Learning," in Richard Gorton, Gail Schneider, and James Fischer, eds., *Encyclopedia of School Administration and Supervision* (Phoenix, AZ: Oryx, 1988); Stanley Pogrow, "Teacher Feature," *Teachers Net Gazette* (January 2002), available at **www.teachers.net/gazette/JAN02**; "Pathways to Change," September 2013 posting by the California Teachers Association, available at **www.cta.org**; and Donald Aguillard, "Superintendent Shares Tale of School District Turn-Around," *District Administration* (October 2014), available at **www.districtadministration.com**.

11-4 DO SCHOOLS EQUALIZE OPPORTUNITY?

The research discussed in the preceding sections indicates that disproportionate numbers of students from low-income backgrounds enter school poorly prepared to succeed in traditional classrooms and in later years rank relatively low in school achievement and other indicators of success. If we define equal opportunity in terms of overcoming disadvantages associated with family background so that students on the average perform equally well regardless of SES, one must conclude that the educational system has failed to equalize opportunity.

Equal educational opportunity has received considerable attention since the 1966 publication of a massive national study conducted by James Coleman and his colleagues. Titled *Equality of Educational Opportunity*, this federally supported study collected data on approximately six hundred thousand students at more than four thousand schools. Its congressional sponsors expected it to show that low achievement among low-socioeconomic students stemmed from low expenditures on their education, thus justifying increased school funding.

As expected, Coleman and his colleagues reported that achievement related strongly to students' socioeconomic background and that schools with high proportions of working-class and underclass students generally received less funding than did middle-class schools. However, they also found that expenditures for reduced class size, laboratories, libraries, and other aspects of school operation were fundamentally unrelated to achievement after one took into account (1) a student's personal socioeconomic background and (2) the social-class status of other students in the school. Many readers incorrectly interpreted the data to mean that schools cannot improve the performance of economically disadvantaged students. In reality, the results supported two conclusions: (1) simply spending more on education for disadvantaged students was unlikely to substantially improve their achievement, and (2) moving students from mostly working-class schools to middle-class schools *could* improve achievement.[48]

In the next decade, two influential books by Christopher Jencks and his colleagues bolstered this analysis. After examining a great deal of data, Jencks and his colleagues reached the following conclusions:[49]

1. School achievement depends substantially on students' family characteristics.
2. Family background accounts for nearly half the variation in occupational status and up to 35 percent of the variation in earnings.
3. The schools accomplish relatively little in terms of reducing the achievement gap between students with higher and lower SES.

Studies from many other countries support similar conclusions. For example, scholars at the World Bank, after reviewing several decades of international research, reported that family background has an "early and apparently lasting influence" on achievement. Likewise, a review of studies in Great Britain concluded that schools

---

[48]James S. Coleman et al., *Equality of Educational Opportunity* (Washington, DC: U.S. Government Printing Office, 1966); Frederick Mosteller and Daniel P. Moynihan, eds., *On Equality of Educational Opportunity* (New York: Random House, 1972); and James S. Coleman, *Equality and Achievement in Education* (Boulder, CO: Westview, 1990). See also Adam Gamoran and Daniel A. Long, "Coleman Report, Forty Years On," 2007 paper prepared for the Wisconsin Center for Education Research, available at **www.wcer.wisc.edu**; and Richard D. Kahlenberg, "The New Segregation," *Washington Monthly* (November/December 2014), available at **www.washingtonmonthly.com**.

[49]Christopher Jencks et al., *Inequality* (New York: Basic Books, 1972); and Christopher Jencks et al., *Who Gets Ahead?* (New York: Basic Books, 1979). See also Daniel P. McMurrer and Isabel V. Sawhill, *Getting Ahead* (Washington, DC: Urban Institute, 1998); Eduardo Porter, "Income Equality," *New York Times* (March 25, 2014); Dimitra Hartas, "Parenting for Social Mobility?" *Journal of Education Policy* (January 2015); and "Christopher Jencks Interview," undated Internet posting by the Public Broadcasting System, available at **www.pbs.org/fmc/interviews/jencks.htm**.

there have served as "mechanisms for the transmission of privileges from one generation of middle-class citizens to the next."[50]

This does not mean, however, that all or even most students from low-income families will be unsuccessful as adults or that the schools should be viewed as mostly unsuccessful in helping provide opportunities for students with diverse socioeconomic backgrounds. Research supports the following general conclusions:

1. *Although students with low SES tend to perform poorly in school and later have restricted employment opportunities, a substantial proportion of working-class children and some from families living in poverty do eventually attain middle-class status.* For example, although nearly two-thirds of men in the US labor force grew up in working-class families or on a farm, more than 50 percent are in middle- or high-status jobs; nearly 40 percent are in upper-middle-class jobs even though less than 25 percent were raised in upper-middle-class families. Socioeconomic mobility of this kind has been present throughout US history. However, it may have diminished somewhat in recent years.[51]

2. *The educational system has helped many people surpass their parents' status.* The educational system's role in promoting socioeconomic mobility has grown more central as middle- and high-status jobs have become more complex and dependent on specialized educational skills and credentials, and technological and economic changes have eliminated many unskilled jobs.[52]

3. *As education increasingly determines SES and mobility, college attendance and graduation constitute a kind of dividing line between those likely to attain high SES and those not.* One hundred years ago, enrollment in high school probably was the best educational indicator of SES. As of fifty or sixty years ago, high school graduation was the clearest dividing line. Today, postsecondary education is almost a prerequisite for middle- or high-status jobs.

4. *Despite the success of many working-class students, opportunities—educational, social, and economic—are too few to overcome the disadvantages of the underclass.* Children who attend low-achieving poverty schools remain disproportionately likely to stay low in SES.

11-4a Traditional versus Revisionist Interpretations

Growing recognition of the strong relationship between social class and school achievement has led to a fundamental disagreement between two groups of observers of US education. According to the **traditional view of schools**, the educational system succeeds in providing economically disadvantaged students with meaningful opportunities for social and economic advancement. The **revisionist view of schools**, in contrast, holds that the schools fail to provide most disadvantaged students with a meaningful chance to succeed in society. You may hear **critical theory** or **critical pedagogy**

---

traditional view of schools The belief that the educational system provides students, including economically disadvantaged ones, with meaningful opportunities. Also, the historically based perception that schools should teach basic skills such as reading, writing, spelling, arithmetic, and academic subjects.

revisionist view of schools The belief that elite groups have channeled disadvantaged students into second-rate schools and inferior jobs.

critical theory (critical pedagogy) A theory of education which contends that some public-school systems limit educational opportunities for students marginalized due to race, class, and gender biases. Proponents argue that teachers should be "transformative intellectuals" who work to change the system. Also known as "critical discourse."

---

[50]Marlaine E. Lockheed, Bruce Fuller, and Ronald Nyirongo, *Family Background and School Achievement* (Washington, DC: World Bank, 1988), p. 23; Yossi Shavit and Hans-Peter Blossfeld, eds., *Persistent Inequality* (Boulder, CO: Westview, 1993); and Bhashkar Mazumder, "Inequality in Skills and the Great Gatsby Curve," 2015 posting by the Federal Reserve Bank of Chicago, available at **www.chicagofed.org**.

[51]Michael Hout, "More Universalism, Less Structural Mobility," *American Journal of Sociology* (May 1988), pp. 1358–1400; Emily Beller and Michael Hout, "Intergenerational Social Mobility," *The Future of Children* (Fall 2006), available at **www.futureofchildren.org**; Isabel V. Sawhill, "Opportunity in America," *The Future of Children* (Fall 2006), available at **www.futureofchildren .org**; Michael Hout, "Intergenerational Class Mobility and the Convergence Thesis," *British Journal of Sociology* (January 2010), pp. 221–224; and Miles Corak, "Social Mobility, Fixed Forever?" May 22, 2014, posting available at **www.milescorak.com**.

[52]Hout, "More Universalism"; Miles Corak, "Income Inequality, Equality of Opportunity, and Intergenerational Mobility," *Journal of Economic Perspectives* (Summer 2013), available at **www .milescorak.com**; and "America's New Aristocracy," *Economist* (January 24, 2015), available at **www.economist.com**.

used as synonyms for the revisionist view as well. The following sections explore the ramifications of these two arguments.[53]

11-4b The Traditional View

Proponents of the traditional view acknowledge the relationships among social class, educational achievement, and economic success, but they emphasize existing opportunities and data indicating that many working-class youth do experience social mobility through schools and other institutions. Most traditionalists believe that our educational and economic institutions balance a requirement for excellence with provision of opportunity. From this perspective, each individual who works hard, no matter how disadvantaged, has the opportunity to succeed in elementary and secondary schools and to go to college.

Traditionalists point out that the US educational system gives the individual more chances to attend college than do the educational systems of many other countries (see Chapter 15, International Education). Students in this country do not, as in some nations, face an examination at age 11 or 12 that shunts them into an almost inescapable educational track. Even if American students do poorly in high school, they can go to a community college and then transfer to a university. Furthermore, admission standards at many four-year colleges permit enrollment of all but the lowest-achieving high school graduates.

Traditionalists admit that schools serve as a screening device to sort different individuals into different jobs, but they do not believe that this screening is systematically based on race, ethnicity, or income. Instead, they believe, better-educated people obtain better jobs primarily because schools have made them more productive. Additional years of schooling are an indication of this greater productivity. The employer needs criteria to guide hiring choices, and in a democratic society that values mobility and opportunity, quality of education counts, not the applicant's family connections, race, ethnic origin, or social class.

11-4c The Revisionist View and Critical Pedagogy

Revisionists contend that elite groups control the schools and thus channel disadvantaged students into second-rate secondary schools and programs, third-rate community colleges, and fourth-rate jobs. Many critical pedagogists also believe that the educational system has been set up specifically to produce disciplined workers at the bottom of the class structure. This is accomplished in part by emphasizing discipline in working-class schools, just as the working-class family and the factory labor system emphasize discipline.[54]

Much analysis in critical pedagogy has been referred to as **resistance theory**, which attempts to explain why some students with low SES refuse to conform to school expectations or to comply with their teachers' demands. The students' resistance, in this view, arises partly because school norms and expectations contradict the traditional definitions of masculinity and femininity these students hold. In addition, an "oppositional peer life" stimulates students to resist what they perceive as the irrelevant middle-class values of their teachers. Some research indicates that oppositional behaviors are particularly prevalent among male students. As described in Chapter 6,

resistance theory The view that working-class students resist the school in part because a hegemonic traditional curriculum marginalizes their everyday knowledge.

---

[53]Revisionists are sometimes referred to as neo-Marxists if they believe that the capitalist system must be abolished or fundamentally changed for schools to provide truly equal opportunity for all students.

[54]Major writings of the revisionist scholars and critical pedagogists include the following: Martin Carnoy, ed., *Schooling in a Corporate Society* (New York: McKay, 1975); Samuel Bowles and Herbert Gintis, *Schooling in Capitalist America* (New York: Basic Books, 1976); Michael W. Apple, *Ideology and Curriculum* (New York: Routledge, 1994); Henry A. Giroux, "America's Education Deficit and the War on Youth," 2014 posting by Monthly Review Press, available at **www.monthlyreview .org**; and materials available at **www.henryagiroux.com**.

Philosophical Roots of Education, resistance theorists have further concluded that the traditional curriculum marginalizes the everyday knowledge of such students, thereby reinforcing anti-intellectual tendencies in working-class cultures.[55]

Critical theorists have been devoting considerable attention to ways educators can improve the situation. Using a variety of related terms such as *critical discourse, critical engagement,* and *critical literacy,* they have emphasized the goal of teachers becoming "transformative intellectuals" who work to broaden schools' role in developing a democratic society. For example, Pauline Lipman believes that teachers should promote not just the "personal efficacy" but also the "social efficacy" of working-class and minority students, and they should help them prepare to become leaders in their local communities. She also believes that teachers should pursue this type of goal as part of a larger effort to reform public schools. Some analysts believe that computers and other technologies can help low-income students overcome many of their disadvantages.[56] As the Technology @ School box discusses, however, students from some groups lack sufficient access to these technologies.

11-4d An Intermediate Viewpoint

This chapter provides data indicating that working-class students as a group underperform middle-class students. After examining reasons offered to account for this difference, we summarized several decades of research concluding that elementary and secondary schools frequently fail to overcome the disadvantages that working-class students bring to school. Although recent studies have pointed to a number of more successful schools, the overall pattern offers support for some of the revisionists' conclusions.

On the other hand, not all working-class students and minority students fail in the schools, and not all middle-class students succeed. An accurate portrayal of the relationships between social class and achievement lies somewhere between the revisionist and the traditional views. Schools do not totally perpetuate the existing social-class structure into the next generation; neither do they provide sufficient opportunity to break the general pattern in which a great many working-class students perform at a predictably low level. Levine and Levine, reviewing the research on each side of the debate, have offered an intermediate view that stresses the following:[57]

- Research on status mobility in the United States indicates that people at the bottom level mostly tend to freeze into their parents' status. Despite considerable intergenerational movement up the socioeconomic ladder and some movement down, large proportions of Americans with the lowest social-class backgrounds do not progress beyond the status of their parents.
- Social and demographic trends have concentrated many children in low-income urban and rural communities in schools extremely low on achievement measures. A disproportionately high percentage of students in these schools are from racial or ethnic minority groups.

---

[55]Robert W. Connell et al., *Making the Difference* (Boston: George Allen and Unwin, 1982); Kathleen K. Abowitz, "A Pragmatist Revisioning of Resistance Theory," *American Educational Research Journal* (Winter 2000), pp. 877–907; and Tim Walker, "How Engaging Student Resistance Works Better Than Punishment," *NEA Today* (March 3, 2015), available at **www.neatoday.org**.

[56]Henry A. Giroux, *Teachers as Intellectuals* (Granby, MA: Bergin and Garvey, 1988); Pauline Lipman, *Race, Class, and Power in School Restructuring* (Albany: State University of New York Press, 1998); and Elizabeth Bishop, "Critical Literacy," *Journal of Curriculum Theorizing*, vol. 30, no. 1 (2014).

[57]Levine and Levine, *Society and Education*. See also Richard Breen, "Educational Expansion and Social Mobility in the 20th Century," *Social Forces* (December 2010), pp. 365–388; Richard V. Reeves and Joanna Venator, "The Inheritance of Education," October 27, 2014, posting by the Brookings Institution, available at **www.brookings.edu**; Richard V. Reeves, Joanna Venator, and Kimberly Howard, "The Character Factor," October 22, 2014, posting by the Brookings Institution, available at **www.brookings.edu**; and Rhonda Rosenberg, "Drive, Prudence Factors in Achievement," January 8, 2015, posting by the American Federation of Teachers, available at **www.aft.org**.

TECHNOLOGY @ SCHOOL

DEALING WITH THE DIGITAL DIVIDE

Recent years have brought much attention to the extent and implications of the digital divide—the gap between advantaged and disadvantaged Americans in access to digital media. For example, a report titled "Connected to the Future" on children's Internet use stated that 66 percent of high-income children had Internet access at home, compared with only 29 percent of low-income children. The report is available at The White House website. Similarly, federal government data state that 48 percent of black students and 50 percent of Latino students use a computer at home, compared to 81 percent of white students.

As a teacher, you will encounter students who have had extensive computer exposure and other students with little, if any. You will need ways to help all of them become more proficient with computers, just as you address other individual differences. Your school may or may not have widespread and fast access to the Internet, but in either case, you should help all your students use the Internet and other digitized resources to improve their learning.

You'll find discussion and proposals regarding possibilities for narrowing the digital divide in society and schools in a report titled "Bridging the Digital Divide" on the Houghton Mifflin Harcourt website (click on "Classroom").

- Although many working-class students attend predominantly working-class schools that reinforce their initial disadvantages through ineffective instruction, many others attend mixed-status schools with teaching and learning conditions more conducive to high performance. In addition, a growing number of working-class schools appear to be emphasizing higher-order learning.
- Although we cannot pinpoint the exact percentage of working-class students who succeed in the schools or who use their education to advance in social status, the schools do serve as an important route to mobility for many economically disadvantaged children.

11-4e Issues in Measuring and Interpreting Socioeconomic Mobility

Numerous important issues regarding the measurement and interpretation of socioeconomic mobility have been emerging and/or becoming more prominent during the past few decades. Particularly during recent years, there has been growing concern that the United States has become more divided between the very wealthy and the very poor, and that opportunities for children to move upward beyond their parents in social status have been declining. Among the issues involved in assessing such trends toward inequality are the following:[58]

- What is the most useful way to measure social class to improve understanding of mobility? We noted that respected historical measures assess occupation, income, education, and neighborhood, but much research on socioeconomic mobility is limited to income because measures of other components are more difficult to obtain. However, many people have varying income from year to year, often due to a one-time event such as inheritance or bankruptcy. This makes it problematic to interpret a change in income as a change in SES.
- What noncognitive traits should be measured and taken into account in identifying reasons for improvement or decline in status? Research has long indicated that

[58]Richard V. Reeves and Joanna Venator, "Jingle-Jangle Fallacies for Non-Cognitive Factors," December 19, 2014, posting by the Brookings Institution, available at **www.brookings.edu**; and Carol Graham, "Happiness Requires Opportunity, Not Just Contentment," January 5, 2015, posting by the Brookings Institution, available at **www.brookings.edu**.

noncognitive traits such as self-control and perseverance play an important part in determining career and life outcomes, but much research on mobility examines only cognitive variables such as IQ or SAT scores along with socioeconomic data. When this happens, it is difficult if not impossible to determine, for example, whether people become successful based mostly on family advantages or instead on meritocratic considerations such as hard work and planning for the future.

How should we interpret the quality and rewards of socioeconomic origins and outcomes? People may attain the same status as did their parents, but does this necessarily indicate a failure of mobility? Most persons today have considerably more income than their parents did, but even if they have the same income, they also have more reliable and attractive automobiles, more impressive media to enjoy, and often more comfortable housing. (Of course, people today may have longer commutes and much higher costs to educate their children.) In such cases, it is not at all clear that the outcome should be interpreted as a failure in mobility for the individual or the society.

11-4f Reclaiming the Promise of Equal Opportunity for All Students

Historically, educational leaders such as Horace Mann worked to establish and expand the public-school system partly because they believed this would help give all American children an equal chance to succeed in life, regardless of the circumstances of their birth. The data cited in this chapter suggest that the traditional public-school function of providing equal educational opportunity has taken on a more charged meaning, at a time when educational attainment is becoming an increasing prerequisite for success in the economy. Provision of equal opportunity in society now depends on improving the effectiveness of instruction for low-income children and youth—particularly those who attend predominantly poverty schools. In several of the following chapters, we describe major efforts that are underway to accomplish this, including existing and emerging early-childhood programs, projects attempting to bring about comprehensive ecological intervention, charter schools focused on helping big-city students, and the effective-schools movement aimed at improving achievement at high-poverty schools.

FOCUS Where does your position on equality of opportunity best fit—with a traditionalist, revisionist, or intermediate viewpoint? Why?

SUMMING UP

1. Social class relates both to achievement in elementary and secondary schools and to entry into and graduation from college. Students with low SES tend to rank low in educational attainment; middle-class students tend to rank high. Low achievement is particularly a problem in poverty areas of large cities.

2. Low-income minority groups generally are low in educational achievement, but little or no independent relationship exists between race or ethnicity and achievement after taking account of social class.

3. Major reasons for low achievement include the following: (1) students' homes and family environments poorly prepare them for success in the traditional school; (2) genetic considerations (that is, heredity) may interact with environment in some cases to further hamper achievement; and

(3) traditionally organized and operated schools have failed to provide effective education for economically disadvantaged students.

4. Many problems in the schools tend to limit achievement: inappropriate curriculum and instruction, lack of previous success in school, difficult teaching conditions, teacher perceptions of student inadequacy, ineffective homogeneous grouping, delivery-of-service problems, overly large classes, negative peer pressures, differences in teacher and student backgrounds, and incompatibility between classroom expectations and students' behavioral patterns.

5. Research on social class and education has somewhat supported the revisionist view that schools help perpetuate the existing social-class system. This contrasts with the

traditional view that US society and its educational system provide children and youth with equal opportunity to succeed regardless of their social-class background.

6. There are several issues involved in measuring, assessing, and interpreting SES that make it difficult to reach conclusions about the extent of mobility from one generation to another. These issues include the problem of obtaining information on components of status other than income,

the question of what it means to attain higher income and status, and the extent to which the researcher is able to take account of noncognitive traits that help determine school and life outcomes.

7. Because recent research indicates that schools can be much more effective, we may move closer to the ideal of equal educational opportunity in the future.

SUGGESTED RESOURCES

INTERNET RESOURCES

Useful sites to explore regarding topics in this chapter include the home pages of professional organizations such as the American Psychological Association and the National Education Association. Sites sponsored by the Brookings Institution, the Institute for Research on Poverty, and the Rand Organization also provide information on relevant topics.

The Spring 2011 issue of the *American Educator* is devoted to the theme of "Equalizing Opportunity" and includes articles by William J. Wilson on being poor and black, James Heckman on early childhood education, and Charles Payne on demanding and supporting high expectations.

Educational Testing Service (ETS) offers information on equality of educational, economic, and social opportunity at its Policy Information Center.

PUBLICATIONS

Herndon, James. *The Way It Spozed to Be*. New York: Bantam, 1968. *A classic account of the way education works, or doesn't work, in inner-city schools.*

Noguera, Pedro A. *The Trouble with Black Boys: ...And Other Reflections on Race, Equity, and the Future of Public Education*. Thousand Oaks, CA: Jossey-Bass, 2009. An e*xamination of the many facets of race in schools and society and a discussion of what it will take to improve outcomes for all students.*

Payne, Charles M. *So Much Reform, So Little Change*. Cambridge, MA: Harvard Education Press, 2008. *Subtitled "The Persistence of Failure in Urban Schools," this volume examines the intense problems of high-poverty schools but in doing so also suggests how some schools have begun to counteract the roots of failure.*

Tough, Paul. *How Children Succeed*. Boston: Houghton Mifflin, 2013. *Subtitled "Grit, Curiosity, and the Hidden Power of Character," this book examines much of the research on the frequently negative, long-lasting effects of growing up in a difficult environment.* (The Kindle edition is available at no cost from Amazon.)

12

PROVIDING EQUAL EDUCATIONAL OPPORTUNITY

LEARNING OBJECTIVES

12-1 Describe the major obstacles and approaches in desegregating the schools.

12-2 Describe and discuss the major approaches to compensatory education.

12-3 Understand the forms of multicultural education present in elementary and secondary schools, along with their major benefits and dangers.

12-4 Understand what the law says about providing education for students with disabilities, and recognize the major issues in their education.

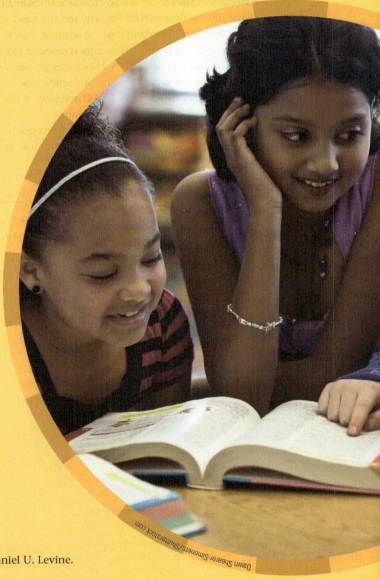

Dawn Shearer-Simonetti/Shutterstock.com

This chapter was revised by Daniel U. Levine.

US SCHOOLS were the world's first to aim at providing all students with educational opportunity through high school and postsecondary levels. Nonetheless, as Chapter 11, Social Class, Race, and School Achievement, indicated, effective education all too rarely extends to economically disadvantaged and minority students. Stimulated by the civil rights movement, many people have recognized the need to improve educational opportunity, not just for disadvantaged students but also for students with disabilities.

In this chapter, we examine desegregation, compensatory education for economically disadvantaged students, multicultural education (including bilingual education), and education for students with disabilities. These topics reflect four significant movements that have attempted to enlarge and equalize educational opportunities for our students. You may agree that our schools should provide equal opportunity but consider this a matter for the government, the school board, and civil rights groups. Equal opportunity may affect you in the classroom in several ways:

- Wherever you teach, you will find yourself professionally and morally obligated to furnish specific help for low-achieving students.
- The increasing racial and ethnic diversity in student populations means that you will probably need to accommodate students from a variety of ethnic groups, cultural backgrounds, and languages.
- More students than ever before are being classified as having disabilities, and increasingly these students are included in regular classrooms. As a teacher, you will be at least partly responsible for addressing their special needs.

12-1 DESEGREGATION

desegregation
Attendance by students of different racial and ethnic backgrounds in the same school and classroom.

integration
The step beyond simple desegregation that includes effective action to develop positive interracial contacts and to improve the performance of low-achieving minority students.

Desegregation of schools is the practice of enrolling students of different racial groups in the same schools. **Integration** generally means that not only are students of different racial groups attending school together but also that effective steps are taken to accomplish two of the underlying purposes of desegregation: (1) overcoming the achievement deficit and other disadvantages of minority students, and (2) developing positive interracial relationships. During the past five decades, attention has turned increasingly from mere desegregation to integration, with the goal of providing equal and effective educational opportunity for students of all backgrounds. However, we have much to do to fully achieve either of these goals.

12-1a A Brief History of Segregation in American Education

Discrimination and oppression by race were deeply embedded in our national institutions from their very beginnings. The US Constitution, for example, provided for representation of the free population but allowed only three-fifths representation for "all other persons," generally meaning slaves. ("Representation" refers to distribution of seats in the US House of Representatives.) In most of the South before the Civil War, it was a crime to teach a slave to read and write.

After the Civil War, the Thirteenth, Fourteenth, and Fifteenth Amendments to the Constitution attempted to extend rights of citizenship irrespective of race. During Reconstruction, African Americans made some gains, but, after 1877, legislative action segregated blacks throughout the South and in other parts of the country. They were required to attend separate schools, were barred from competing with whites for good employment, and were denied the right to vote.[1] Victimized by these so-called

---

[1]In this chapter, the term "whites" refers to non-Hispanic whites, that is, citizens not classified as members of a racial or ethnic minority group for the purposes of school desegregation.

Jim Crow laws, African Americans were required to use separate public services and facilities (for instance, transportation, recreation, restrooms, and drinking fountains) and frequently had no access at all to private facilities such as hotels, restaurants, and theaters. Many were lynched or severely beaten by members of the Ku Klux Klan and other extremist associations.

Asian Americans, Latinos, Native Americans, and some other minority groups experienced similar, though generally less virulent, discriminatory practices. For example, some states excluded Chinese Americans by law from many well-paid jobs and required their children to attend separate schools.[2]

On any measure of equality, schools provided for African Americans seldom equaled schools attended by whites. As an example, in the early 1940s, school officials in Mississippi spent $52.01 annually per student in white schools but only $7.36 per student in black schools. In many cases, African American students had to travel long distances at their own expense to attend the nearest black school, and, in many instances, black senior high schools were a hundred miles or more away from a black student's home.[3]

Legal suits challenged segregation in elementary and secondary schools in the early 1950s. The first to be decided by the US Supreme Court was a case in which lawyers for Linda Brown asked that she be allowed to attend white schools in Topeka, Kansas. Attacking the legal doctrine that schools could be "separate but equal," the plaintiffs argued that segregated schools were inherently inferior, even if they provided equal expenditures because forced attendance at a separate school automatically informed African American students that they were second-class citizens and thus destroyed many students' motivation to succeed in school and in society. In May 1954, in a unanimous decision that forever changed US history, the Supreme Court ruled in *Brown v. Board of Education* that "the doctrine of separate but equal has no place" in public education. Such segregation, the Court said, deprived people of the equal protection of the laws guaranteed by the Fourteenth Amendment.[4]

Effects of the *Brown* decision soon were apparent in many areas of US society, including employment, voting, and all publicly supported services. After Mrs. Rosa Parks refused in December 1955 to sit at the back of a bus in Montgomery, Alabama, protests against segregation were launched in many parts of the country. Dr. Martin Luther King Jr. and other civil rights leaders emerged to challenge deep-seated patterns of racial discrimination. Fierce opposition to civil rights demonstrations made the headlines in the late 1950s and early 1960s as dogs and fire hoses were sometimes used to disperse peaceful demonstrators. After three civil-rights workers were murdered in Mississippi, the US Congress passed the 1964 Civil Rights Act and other legislation that attempted to guarantee equal protection of the laws for minority citizens.[5]

Initial reaction among local government officials to the *Brown* decision was frequently negative. The Supreme Court's 1955 *Brown II* ruling that school desegregation

[2]Greg Barrios, "Walkout in Crystal City," *Teaching Tolerance* (Spring 2009), available at **www.tolerance.org**; Collin Tong, "Lessons from Infamy," 2011 posting by Crosscut, available at **www.crosscut.com**; John Lee, "How Segregation Worked for Asian Americans Back in the Day," September 24, 2014, posting by American Fobs, available at **www.americanfobs.com**; and German Lopez, "Multiracial Coalitions May Be Necessary to Combat Racism," February, 20, 2015, posting by Vox, available at **www.vox.com**.

[3]National Research Council, *Common Destiny* (Washington, DC: National Academy Press, 1989); Peter McCormick, "How a Band of High School Students Influenced Desegregation," *Brown Quarterly* (Winter 2009), available at **www.brownvboard.org**; Richard Rothstein, "Brown v. Board at 60," April 17, 2014, posting by the Economic Policy Institute, available at **www.epi.org**; and Richard Florida, "A Painstaking New Study Reveals the Persistence of US Racial Segregation," February 27, 2015, posting by City Lab, available at **www.citylab.com**.

[4]William L. Taylor, "The Role of Social Science in School Desegregation Efforts," *Journal of Negro Education* (Summer 1998), pp. 196–203; and Beverly D. Tatum, "Reflections on Brown v. Board at 60," May 17, 2014, posting by CNN, available at **www.cnn.com**.

[5]Marian S. Holmes, "The Freedom Riders," *Smithsonian* (February 2009), available at **www.smithsonian.org**; and **Jon N. Hale,** "The Forgotten Story of the Freedom Schools," *Atlantic* (June 26, 2014), available at **www.theatlantic.com**.

Bettmann/Corbis

> **PHOTO 12.1** Since 1957, when the National Guard escorted African American students to a formerly all white public high school in Little Rock, Arkansas, considerable progress has been made in desegregating the country's public schools in medium-sized cities and towns in rural areas.

should proceed with "all deliberate speed" met massive resistance in much of the United States. This resistance took such forms as delaying reassignment of African American students to white schools, opening private schools with tuition paid by public funds, gerrymandering school boundary lines to increase segregation, suspending or repealing compulsory attendance laws, and closing desegregated schools. In 1957, Arkansas governor Orval Faubus refused to allow school officials at Central High in Little Rock to admit five African American students, and President Dwight Eisenhower called out the National Guard to escort the students to school (Photo 12.1). As of 1963, only 2 percent of African American students in the South were attending school with whites.

12-1b The Progress of Desegregation Efforts

After the early 1960s, school districts in medium-sized cities and towns and in rural areas made considerable progress in combating both **de jure segregation** (segregation resulting from laws, government actions, or school policies specifically designed to bring about separation) and **de facto segregation** (segregation resulting from housing patterns rather than from laws or policies). In response to court orders, school officials have reduced African American attendance in racially isolated minority schools (often defined as either 50 percent or more minority, or 90 percent or more minority).[6] As shown in Figure 12.1, the national percentage of African American students attending schools with an enrollment consisting of 90 percent or more minority decreased from 64 percent in 1969 to 33 percent in 1988. (Progress was greatest in the South, where the percentage of African American students in schools 90 percent or more minority decreased from 78 percent in 1969 to less than 35 percent early in the 1980s.) However, this improvement was not entirely sustained: the percentage of African American students in schools with an enrollment consisting of 90 percent or more minorities increased from 33 percent to nearly 40 percent between 1988 and 2014.[7]

de jure segregation Segregation resulting from laws or government action.

de facto segregation Segregation associated with and resulting from housing patterns.

---

[6]The term "minority" in this context refers to African Americans, Asians, Latinos, Native Americans, and several other smaller racial or ethnic groups as defined by the federal government. In 2010, the government began counting students as "multiracial" if they or their parents chose this category when asked to designate race/ethnicity.

[7]Lindsey Cook, "U.S. Education: Still Separate and Unequal," *U.S. News & World Report* (January 28, 2015).

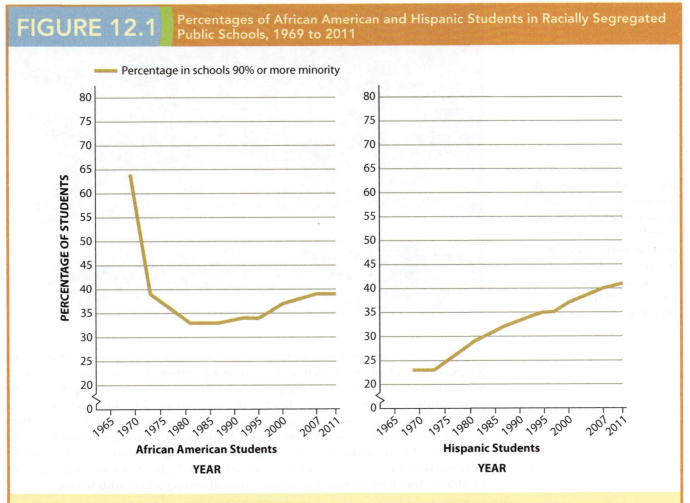

FIGURE 12.1 Percentages of African American and Hispanic Students in Racially Segregated Public Schools, 1969 to 2011

Source: Data adapted from Gary Orfield and Chungmei Lee, "Racial Transformation and the Changing Nature of Segregation," 2006 paper prepared for the Harvard University Civil Rights Project; Gary Orfield, "Reviving the Goal of an Integrated Society," 2009 paper prepared for The Civil Rights Project/*Proyecto Derechos Civiles* at the University of California at Los Angeles, available at **www.civilrightsproject.ucla.edu**; and *Digest of Education Statistics* (Washington, DC: National Center for Education Statistics, 2014).

For Hispanic students, however, the percentage attending predominantly minority schools has increased since 1969 (see Figure 12.1). In that year, 23 percent of Latinos attended schools with an enrollment consisting of more than 90 percent minority; by 2014, more than 40 percent of Latino students attended such schools. This trend reflects the movement of Latino people into inner-city communities in large urban areas, particularly the migration of Mexicans into cities in Arizona, California, and Texas, and of Puerto Ricans into New Jersey, New York, Chicago, and other eastern and midwestern cities.[8]

As some re-segregation has been occurring among African American students, desegregation has been proceeding for non-Hispanic white students, for whom the percentage in schools more than 90 percent white declined from 49 percent in 1990 to about 25 percent in recent years. Both trends have been produced partly by the declining percentage of non-Hispanic whites in public-school enrollment,

---

[8]Gary Orfield and Erica Frankenberg, "The Last Have Become First," 2008 paper prepared for The Civil Rights Project, available at **www.civilrightsproject.ucla.edu**; and John Iceland, Daniel Weinberg, and Lauren Hughes, "The Segregation of Detailed Hispanic and Asian Groups in the United States: 1980–2010," *Demographic Research*, Vol. 32, Art. 20, 2014, available at **www.demographic-research.org**.

who now constitute less than half. Both trends can be expected to continue as the overall percentage of minority students in the public schools continues to rise in the future.[9]

At the same time that small-town and rural districts have significantly desegregated, segregation in large metropolitan regions has increased. A main cause has been increasingly pronounced housing segregation in those areas. Today, the large majority of public-school students in big cities such as Atlanta, Chicago, Detroit, New York, and Philadelphia are minority students, and most attend predominantly minority schools. A major stumbling block to desegregation of schools has been the desire of most whites, and of many minority parents, to maintain neighborhood schools. Highly segregated residential patterns in most metropolitan areas produce highly segregated neighborhood schools.

In many instances, predominantly minority neighborhoods also have high poverty rates and rank extremely low in socioeconomic status. Opposition to desegregation is strong in school districts where a high percentage of minority students are from low-income families. As noted in Chapter 11, Social Class, Race, and School Achievement, schools in these neighborhoods struggle with the effects of concentrated poverty, and most have failed to provide effective education. White parents and middle-class parents generally are quick to withdraw their children from schools in which desegregation has substantially increased the proportion of low-income students. The net result is that city school districts and schools have become increasingly low income and minority in their student composition.[10]

In the 1990s and 2000s, many school districts ceased all or part of the desegregation plans they had introduced in previous decades. They cited various reasons for their decisions:

- Some urban districts had predominantly minority enrollment in all their schools and found it difficult or impossible to maintain desegregated schools even with substantial student busing.
- In some districts, courts ruled that the district had accomplished enough to overcome discriminatory effects attributable to the original constitutional violations.
- In other districts, public and school officials concluded that desegregation efforts did little to actually help minority students.
- In 2007, the Supreme Court ruled that school districts could no longer use race as the sole or major factor in devising a desegregation plan.

12-1c Desegregation Plans

Plans to accomplish desegregation usually involve one or more of the following actions:

- Alter attendance areas to include a more desegregated population.
- Establish **magnet schools**—schools that use specialized programs and personnel to attract students throughout a school district.
- Bus students involuntarily to desegregated schools.
- Pair schools, bringing two schools in adjacent areas together in one larger zone. For example, School A enrolls all students from grades 1 through 4; School B enrolls all students from grades 5 through 8.

magnet school A type of alternative school that attracts voluntary enrollment from more than one neighborhood by offering special instructional programs or curricula; often established in part for purposes of desegregation.

---

[9]Jill Barshay, "Are Schools More Segregated Than in the 50s? What Does the Data Say?" May 22, 2014, posting by Education by the Numbers, available at **http://hechingerreport.org**; and Derek Thompson, "The Curse of Segregation," *Atlantic* (May 5, 2015), available at **www.theatlantic.com**.
[10]Carl Chancellor and Richard D. Kahlenberg, "The New Segregation," *Washington Monthly* (November/December 2014), available at **www.washingtonmonthly.com**; and Sam Pizzigati, "Segregation's Insidious New Look," February 27, 2015, posting by the Stanford Graduate School of Education, available at **https://ed.stanford.edu**.

controlled choice A system in which students can select their school as long as their choices do not result in segregation.

- Allow **controlled choice**, a system in which students may select the school they want to attend as long as such choice does not result in segregation.
- Provide voluntary transfer of city students to suburban schools.

Means such as these at least temporarily led to substantial school desegregation in many small- or medium-sized cities. A good example is Milwaukee. At a time when African American students made up approximately 40 percent of the city's school population, Milwaukee increased the number of its desegregated schools (defined as 25 to 50 percent black) from 14 in 1976 to 101 in 1978. Most of this increase was achieved through (1) establishing magnet schools, (2) implementing a voluntary city-suburban transfer plan, and (3) redrawing school boundaries. The number of desegregated students fell greatly when the city-suburban program ended, but the pattern illustrates what voluntary desegregation might accomplish in all but the largest, most segregated cities. Inter-district magnet schools are being operated in several metropolitan areas.[11]

Large central-city districts—especially those with 50 percent or higher minority enrollment—find desegregated schooling extremely difficult to attain. For example, in a big city with 80 percent minority students, action to eliminate predominantly single-race schools may involve hour-long bus rides and transporting students from one largely minority school to another. For these and similar reasons, desegregation plans in many big cities generally concentrate on trying to improve the quality of instruction.

According to some research, even large and heavily segregated cities can produce more desegregation by expanding magnet schools than through large-scale, involuntary busing that transports students to predominantly minority schools. The most frequently used themes include arts, business, foreign languages, health professions, international studies, Montessori early childhood, science and mathematics, and technology. Districts that operate or have operated a substantial number of magnet schools include Buffalo, Dallas, Houston, Jacksonville, and Minneapolis.[12] The Taking Issue box explores the effectiveness of magnet schools.

12-1d Nonblack Minorities

Another aspect of desegregation that deserves special attention is the status of nonblack minority groups. Depending on regional and local circumstances and court precedents, various racial minority groups may or may not be counted as minority for the purposes of school desegregation. For example, in the 1970s, the courts determined that Mexican American students in the Southwest were victims of the same kinds of discrimination as were African American students. However, in some cities, the courts did not explicitly designate Mexican American and other Latino students to participate as minorities in a desegregation plan, even though many or most attend predominantly minority schools.[13]

---

[11]Robert S. Peterkin, "What's Happening in Milwaukee?" *Educational Leadership* (January 1991), pp. 50–52; Thomas Pettigrew, "Justice Deferred," *American Psychologist* (September 2004), pp. 521–529. See also Dana Goldstein, "Across District Lines," *American Prospect* (June 2009), available at **www.prospect.org**; Aida Tefera et al., *Integrating Suburban Schools* (Los Angeles: Civil Rights Project, 2011), available at **www.civilrightsproject.ucla.edu**; Nicole Hannah-Jones, "Lack of Order," May 1, 2014, posting by Pro Publica, available at **www.propublica.org**; and Richard D. Kahlenberg, "An Opening for Montgomery's Schools to Lead the Way on Opportunity For All," *Washington Post* (April 25, 2014), available at **www.washingtonpost.com**.

[12]Christine H. Rossell, "The Desegregation Efficiency of Magnet Schools," *Urban Affairs Review* (May 2003); and Claire Smrekar and Ngaire Honey, "The Desegregation Aims and Demographic Contexts of Magnet Schools," *Peabody Journal of Education* (January–March 2015).

[13]However, federal data collection activities are standardized and have required that student enrollments be reported separately for the following groups: "Black," "American Indian," "Spanish-Surnamed American," "Portuguese," "Asian," "Alaskan Natives," "Hawaiian Natives," and "Non-Minority."

TAKING ISSUE

Read the brief introduction below, as well as the Question and the pros and cons list that follows. Then, answer the question using *your* own words and position.

MAGNET SCHOOLS AND DESEGREGATION

In recent years, many city school districts have established desegregation plans that rely in part on magnet schools. Magnet schools offer a specialized program in a particular field of interest to attract students from all parts of a city or region, thereby creating a mix of ethnic and racial groups. Critics have argued, however, that magnet schools often cause more problems than they solve.

Question

Are magnet schools an effective means of promoting desegregation and achieving related school-improvement goals? (Think about this question as you read the PRO and CON arguments listed here. What is *your* take on this issue?)

Arguments PRO

1. Research in various cities has shown that a coordinated plan involving magnet schools can lead to substantial gains in desegregation. Milwaukee and Buffalo, for example, are using magnet schools effectively.

2. Magnet schools' specialized, high-level programs attract middle-class and college-bound students to the public-school system, thus helping reverse the white, middle-class exodus that has long plagued desegregation efforts.

3. In addition to attracting various ethnic and racial groups, magnet schools create a mixture of socioeconomic classes. Working-class and middle-class students gather in a setting that encourages beneficial socialization.

4. Concentration of resources allows magnet schools to offer a better education than a system of nonspecialized schools. Most important, they make this high-quality education available to everyone, regardless of racial, social background, or cultural background.

5. As students gain recognition for academic excellence at the magnet schools, community pride will grow. The schools will become a means of promoting community identity, bringing together all races and classes in a common endeavor.

Arguments CON

1. Only limited evidence supports the idea that magnet schools make a significant contribution to desegregation. Because magnets frequently are expensive to develop and maintain, they may well become unjustifiable financial burdens for school districts.

2. Magnets often drain away the best students, leaving other public schools in the district with high concentrations of low achievers. These other schools find it increasingly difficult to maintain teacher and student morale and deliver a good education.

3. Converting a local school into a magnet has sometimes led to increased tension between socioeconomic groups. Local students distrust the "outsiders" (generally of a different social class) who come into the neighborhood to attend the school.

4. Many magnet schools are in fact not for everyone. Instead, they are selective: students must meet certain achievement standards to be admitted. Thus, low-achieving students—the ones most in need of help—are less likely to benefit from magnet schools than are other students.

5. Their elitist nature prevents magnet schools from fostering a sense of community. They are more likely to provoke resentment among parents whose children are excluded—especially when taxes are raised to support the magnet program.

Question Reprise: What Is Your Stand?

Reflect again on the following question by explaining *your* stand about this issue: Are magnet schools an effective means of promoting desegregation and achieving related school-improvement goals?

12-1e Movement to Charter Schools Reinforcing Segregation

As we describe in Chapter 16, School Effectiveness and Reform in the United States, and elsewhere in this book, charter schools are public schools that are released from some state or local regulations regarding teachers' credentials and dismissals, staff unionization, hours of operation, enrollment restrictions, or other matters. They can be authorized by school boards or by outside agencies such as for-profit consulting firms. By 2015, more than 6,400 charter schools had been established, enrolling more than 2.5 million students. A majority of charters have been created in urban areas, often in big cities where achievement is low and officials hope to reform unsuccessful practices. In some big cities, such as Kansas City and New Orleans, there are now more charters than regular public schools.[14]

Elsewhere in this book, we discuss the success (or lack of success) of charter schools in improving student outcomes. Here we should acknowledge that many are small schools that enroll mostly low-income minority students who are potential dropouts; as such, they may be as segregated or even more segregated than the regular schools they came from. Yet there generally has not been as much public concern about their segregated status as there has been for racial and economic isolation in regular public schools.

The situation is further complicated by the relatively large number of Asian American groups in many big cities. With a rapidly growing population of Filipino, Korean, and Vietnamese students added to the many students of Chinese and Japanese ancestry, city school districts face considerable uncertainty in devising multiethnic desegregation plans. The court order for San Francisco, for example, required multiethnic enrollment and busing of four groups: Asian American, African American, Hispanic, and non-Hispanic white.

Questions regarding the desegregation of nonblack minority groups might multiply in the future as more Asian and Latino students move into many localities. Many of these students need bilingual services, which are easiest to deliver to a group of students together. Grouping them together, however, will conflict with desegregation goals that emphasize dispersal and multiethnic enrollment.

12-1f Effects on Student Performance and Attitudes

To what extent do students benefit from integrated schools? The voluminous research on this subject is somewhat contradictory. Some studies show a positive relationship between desegregation and academic achievement, but other studies show little or no relationship. Several analysts have concluded that desegregation seldom detracts from the performance of white students and frequently contributes to achievement among minority students. Achievement among low-income minority students is most likely to improve when they attend schools with middle-income nonminority students. This can only happen, however, when desegregation plans are well implemented and schools take substantial action to improve the effectiveness of instruction.[15]

What about students' attitudes toward people from other racial and ethnic groups? As with achievement, some data show that desegregation has positive effects on interracial attitudes, while other studies indicate no effect or even a negative effect. Positive intergroup relationships develop only if desegregation is implemented well and if educators promote equal-status contact between minority and nonminority students.

[14]Corey G. Johnson, "Charter Schools Perpetuating Racial Segregation," 2011 posting by California Watch, available at **www.californiawatch.org**; "Charter School Enrollment Up 13 Percent This Year," February 12, 2014, posting by the National Alliance for Public Charter Schools; and Christopher Bonastia, "The Racist History of the Charter School Movement," January 5, 2015, posting by Alternet, available at **www.alternet.org**.

[15]Ronald A. Krol, "A Meta Analysis of the Effects of Desegregation on Academic Achievement," *Urban Review* (December 1980), pp. 211–224; Daniel U. Levine, "Desegregation," in Torsten Husen and T. Neville Postlethwaite, eds., *International Encyclopedia of Education,* 3rd ed. (Oxford: Pergamon, 1994), pp. 1483–1486; Richard Rothstein, "The Racial Achievement Gap, Segregated Schools, And Segregated Neighborhoods—A Constitutional Insult," November 12, 2014, posting by the Economic Policy Institute, available at **www.epi.org**; and Richard Kahlenberg and Halley Potter, "Smarter Charters," *Educational Leadership* (February 2015).

Studies on students' aspirations are much more consistent, indicating that desegregation frequently improves the educational aspirations and college enrollment of minority students by making those aspirations more realistic and better informed. Several studies also indicate that desegregated schooling helps minority students enter the mainstream network of social and cultural contacts useful for success in later life.[16]

The complexities of desegregation and its effects on achievement and attitudes leave many people perplexed: What does desegregation imply for minority students who attend predominantly minority, low-achieving schools in low-income neighborhoods? Assigning such students to a desegregated school with a substantially higher percentage of high-achieving students places them in a potentially much less dysfunctional educational environment. Provided that they receive appropriate support and teaching, their academic performance can substantially improve. We emphasize elsewhere—particularly in Chapter 16, School Effectiveness and Reform in the United States—that some high-poverty schools are unusually successful and that many more should be equally successful. Until that happens, effective instruction at desegregated schools is an important alternative for helping low-achieving minority students.

Unfortunately, only a few studies focus on schools in which desegregation seems to have worked. One of the most comprehensive of such studies evaluated the Emergency School Aid Act, which provided hundreds of millions of dollars between 1972 and 1982 to facilitate desegregation. This study indicated that desegregation aided African American students' achievement in schools in which (1) resources were focused on attaining goals, (2) administrative leadership was outstanding, (3) parents were more heavily involved in the classroom, and (4) staff systematically promoted positive interracial attitudes.[17]

Despite the mixed evidence, perhaps the most compelling reasons for integration are moral and political. Morally, our national education policy must reflect a commitment to American ideals of equality. Politically, two separate societies, separately educated, cannot continue to exist in America without serious harm to the body politic.

FOCUS Were the schools you attended well integrated, or did one racial or ethnic group predominate? Do you want to teach in a school with enrollment similar to that where you attended or one with differing enrollment? Why?

12-2 COMPENSATORY EDUCATION

compensatory education
An attempt to remedy the effects of environmental disadvantages through educational enrichment programs.

Another aspect of our nation's commitment to equal educational opportunity is the **compensatory education** movement, which has sought to overcome (that is, compensate for) disadvantaged background and thereby improve the performance of low-achieving students, particularly those from low-income families. Stimulated in part by the civil rights movement in the 1960s, compensatory education was expanded and institutionalized as part of President Lyndon Johnson's War on Poverty.

The Elementary and Secondary Education Act (ESEA), passed in 1965, among other provisions immediately provided $1 billion to improve the education of economically disadvantaged children. (A disadvantaged student was defined as a student from a family below the government's official poverty line.) The monies are known as

---

[16]Janet Schofield, "School Desegregation and Intergroup Relations," in Gerald Grant, ed., *Review of Research in Education* 17 (Washington, DC: American Education Research Association, 1991), pp. 335–412; Richard D. Kahlenberg, "Back to Class," *American Prospect* (January/February 2007), available at **www.prospect.org**; and Roslyn A. Mickelson, Stephen S. Smith, and Amy H. Nelson, eds., *Yesterday, Today, and Tomorrow* (Cambridge, MA: Harvard University Press, 2014).

[17]J. E. Coulson, *National Evaluation of the Emergency School Aid Act* (Washington, DC: System Development Corporation, 1976). See also Janet W. Schofield and Leslie R. M. Hausmann, "School Desegregation and Social Science Research," *American Psychologist* (September 2004), pp. 536–546; and Rucker C. Johnson, "Long-Run Impacts of School Desegregation and School Quality on Adult Attainments," National Bureau of Economic Research Working Paper 16664, May 2014.

TECHNOLOGY @ SCHOOL

AN INTERNET SITE ABOUT SUCCESSFUL TITLE I SCHOOLS

Go to a study titled "Hope for Urban Education" at the federal government's ERIC site, to read a description of "high-performing, high-poverty" schools. Select a school from the list, and read the description of developments and outcomes at the school. As you read, ask yourself the following questions:

- What seems to have improved achievement the most?
- Are the described practices "transportable," that is, easy to use at other schools?

- How were special education and/or bilingual programs and teachers involved?
- How were Title I funds spent?
- Would you want to teach at this school?

You might also want to share your conclusions and material with classmates who selected other schools.

Title I A portion of the federal Elementary and Secondary Education Act that provides funds to improve the education of economically disadvantaged students.

Title I funds, named after the portion of the ESEA that describes them. The federal government distributes the funds to the states, which, along with school districts, identify schools with sufficient disadvantaged students to receive a share. More than $200 billion were spent on Title I between 1965 and 2012. By 2009, Title I funding of more than $14 billion annually provided assistance to more than five million students, and many additional students participated in other compensatory programs. Schools and districts use the money to establish substantial compensatory education programs that provide tutoring, longer school days, early childhood learning, instructional technology, and many other services and activities. Some of the important services and activities of compensatory education are listed next. The Technology @ School box also tells you how to learn more about successful Title I schools.

1. *Parental involvement and support.* Programs have ranged from helping parents learn to teach their children to improving family functioning and parents' employability.
2. *Early childhood education.* **Head Start** and **Follow Through** have been the largest programs of this kind. Head Start generally attempts to help disadvantaged four- and five-year-olds achieve readiness for the first grade. Follow Through concentrated on improving achievement in the primary grades.
3. *Reading, language, and math instruction.* Most Title I projects have concentrated on improvement in reading, language, and math.
4. *Bilingual education.* Latino children constitute the largest group in bilingual programs, but programs have been provided in more than sixty languages. Bilingual programs are discussed in the following section on multicultural education.
5. *Guidance, counseling, and social services.* Various psychological and social services have been provided for disadvantaged students.
6. *Dropout prevention.* Services that include vocational and career education have aimed at keeping students from dropping out of school.
7. *Personnel training.* Many preservice and in-service training programs have been funded to help teachers improve instruction.
8. *After-school programs.* These provide academic-improvement services, general enrichment activities, or both.
9. *Computer laboratories and networks.* In recent years, compensatory funds have helped many schools establish computer laboratories and in-school networks.

Head Start A federal government program that provides preschool education for economically disadvantaged four- and five-year-old students.

Follow Through A program that concentrated on improving achievement of low-income children in the primary grades.

12-2a Early Childhood Compensatory Education

During the first decade of compensatory education, most interventions appeared to be relatively ineffective in raising student achievement levels and cognitive development.

Despite the expenditure of billions of dollars per year, students generally were not making long-range academic gains.

This discouraging start led to corrections. The federal and state governments improved monitoring procedures, required more adequate evaluation, and sponsored studies to improve compensatory education. Some states also began to provide additional money for compensatory programs. By the early 1980s, research suggested that compensatory education in preschool and the primary grades could indeed improve the cognitive development and performance of disadvantaged students.

In particular, several studies of outstanding early childhood education programs demonstrated that such efforts can have a long-lasting effect if they are well conceived and effectively implemented. Positive long-range achievement results have been reported for disadvantaged students in outstanding preschool programs in Ypsilanti, Michigan; Syracuse, New York; and several other locations. Compared with nonparticipants, students who participate in such programs are less likely to be placed later in special education or to repeat grades (both costly). Participants are also more likely to graduate from high school and to acquire the skills and motivation needed for rewarding employment, thereby increasing tax revenues and reducing reliance on public assistance.[18]

These impressive results, however, usually come from programs that researchers consider exemplary. Most preschool programs have been less well funded or less well implemented and have produced fewer gains. In general, Title I programs still fail to ensure that most low-achieving students will acquire the academic and intellectual skills necessary to obtain good jobs in a modern economy.

12-2b Comprehensive Ecological Intervention

Educators face great difficulty when working to overcome the extreme disadvantages of students who grow up in particularly harmful environments, such as neighborhoods of concentrated poverty. For this reason, policy makers and educators increasingly support **ecological intervention**—comprehensive, multidimensional efforts to improve the home, school, and neighborhood environments of students, particularly young children.

ecological intervention
Comprehensive efforts to improve the environments of young children.

Advocates of ecological intervention point to research on the important cognitive development that occurs during infancy, as well as to the frequently disappointing results of Head Start programs that do not begin until age 3 or 4. Comprehensive psychological, social, and economic support can be successful, research indicates, if it begins when children are younger. Some effective interventions of this type enroll young children in educationally oriented day-care or preschool classes. Successful programs typically include nutrition and health care, as well as counseling for parents. Some particularly comprehensive programs also include assistance in obtaining adequate housing, improvement of neighborhood services involving community centers and public safety, and close coordination with and among educational institutions ranging from preschool to the postsecondary level.[19]

---

[18]W. Steven Barnett and Colette M. Escobar, "The Economics of Early Educational Intervention," *Review of Educational Research* (Winter 1987), pp. 387–414; Douglas Besharov and Craig Ramey, "Preschool Puzzle," *Education Next* (Fall 2008), available at **www.educationnext.org**; Valerie Strauss, "Why Preschool Critics Are Wrong," *Washington Post* (February 28, 2014), available at **www.washingtonpost.com**; and Margaret Talbot, "The Talking Cure," *New Yorker* (January 12, 2015).

[19]Lisbeth Schorr, *Within Our Reach* (New York: Anchor Doubleday, 1989); Paul Tough, "Learning Zone," *Edutopia* (November 19, 2008), available at **www.edutopia.org**; "Unlocking Opportunities," July 31, 2014, posting by the DC Fiscal Policy Institute, available at **www.dcfpi.org**; James J. Heckman, "Reauthorize an Early Start and a Great Finish," February 9, 2015, posting by Roll Call, available at **www.rollcall.com**; and Robyn Tedder, "Want to Close the Achievement Gap? Start Quality Education Well before Children Are 5 Years Old," *Hechinger Report*, January 1, 2015, available at **www.hechingerreport.org**.

12-2c Current Promising Examples of Comprehensive Ecological Intervention

Comprehensive ecological interventions are being inaugurated or expanded in many locations, supported or encouraged in many cases by federal, state, and/or local taxes and by philanthropic foundations and donors. Among some of the best-known and promising projects are the following.[20]

- The Chicago Child-Parent Centers (CPCs) have been established to provide comprehensive educational and family support to low-income families and their children. The program is founded on the belief that providing productive family and school environments during preschool and the first four years of elementary school will result in academic gains. Positive results have been validated over several decades of operation.

- The Harlem Children's Zone (HCZ) serves residents of 97 blocks in New York and provides services such as early education for all children; various forms of family support and counseling; health services beginning in infancy; collaboration with churches, parks, businesses, and schools to develop safe, nurturing environments for children and youth; employment training; establishment and operation of several charter schools; and an after-school program for middle-school students. Impressive results have included the findings that 99 percent of 4-year-olds in a preschool finished with readiness scores of average or above, nearly all students completing third grade at the charter schools were at or above grade level in math, 90 percent were at or above grade level in English-Language Arts, and 92 percent of high school seniors have been accepted into college.

- The Promise Zones project gives communities an advantage in seeking funds for community and institutional development and coordination, and it aims to help communities provide "cradle to career" support with emphasis on schools becoming neighborhood centers where residents can receive prenatal care, mental health services, job training, and other assistance. The project aims to be operating in twenty sites nationwide by 2018.

- An Omaha, Nebraska, Learning Community project involves cooperation among the Omaha Public Schools, ten surrounding school districts, and numerous local and regional institutions in providing home visits for children from birth to age 3, high-quality preschool for 3- and 4-year-olds, and a coordinated and consistent curriculum and support for students in kindergarten through third grade. The program particularly focuses on helping about 4,300 students at twelve schools (four in the city school district) that have the services of twenty-five school-based home visitors, family facilitators, and instructional coaches. Professional development and relevant technical assistance and consultation also are provided to other schools enrolling low-income students in the participating districts. The project is particularly notable because it requires so much cooperation by public-school districts in a sizable metropolitan area.

---

[20]"A National Model for Breaking the Cycle of Poverty with Proven Success," 2014 posting by the Harlem Children's Zone, available at **www.hcz.org**; "Child-Parent Centers," 2014 posting by the Promising Practices Network, available at **www.promisingpractices.net/programs .asp**; "Geoffrey Canada and the New Harlem Renaissance," *Time* (April 9, 2014), available at **www.time.com**; John Gabrieli, "The Promise of the Harlem Children's Zone," *Harvard Political Review* (June 11, 2014), available at **www.harvardpolitics.com**; P. L. Chase-Linsdale and Jeanne Brooks-Gunn, "Two-Generation Programs in the Twenty-First Century," *Future of Children* (Spring 2014), available at **www.futureofchildren.org**; Angela G. Blackwell, "Promise Zones Provide Opportunity and a Pathway to an Equitable Future," *Huffington Post* (January 6, 2015), available at **www.huffingtonpost.com**; Introductory Page, 2015 posting by Purpose Built Communities, available at **www.purposebuiltcommunities.org**; and Joe Dejka, "Learning Community Unveils 'a Game-Changer' for Early Childhood Education," *Omaha World-Herald* (January 30, 2015), available at **www.omaha.com**.

● The Purpose Built Communities (PBC) approach is, in the words of its origina-tors, "working to break the cycle of intergenerational poverty…[by] helping local leaders transform struggling neighborhoods, and bringing together the vital components…high-quality mixed-income housing, an effective cradle-to-college education pipeline, and comprehensive community wellness resources." By 2015, this approach was receiving substantial philanthropic funding to function in ten neighborhoods.

We will discuss comprehensive ecological intervention and its potentially critical role in improving and reforming US schools and society in Chapter 16, School Effec-tiveness and Reform in the United States.

12-2d The No Child Left Behind Act

In 2001, Congress reauthorized the ESEA and Title I but, in so doing, established sweeping new requirements for all elementary and secondary schools. The revised law, known as the **No Child Left Behind Act (NCLB)**, has affected not only schools that receive Title I funding, but nearly all public schools. In addition to policies described in our discussion of rules for teachers in Chapter 1, Motivation, Preparation, and Con-ditions for the Entering Teacher, NCLB includes regulations in the following key areas (see the "Status of NCLB and Movement toward Waivers" section for updates to these original standards):[21]

● *Standards and testing.* States and school districts are required to develop challeng-ing academic content and achievement standards for all students in reading/language arts, mathematics, and science, with the goal of having all students attain proficiency by the 2013–2014 school year. To assess progress toward these stan-dards, states must test students, including annual tests for students in grades 3–8 in reading/language arts and mathematics, and at least two tests for students in grades 9–12. At least 95 percent of students overall and in each special-needs sub-group (see the next listed item) must be tested.

● *Students with special needs.* The performance of different special-needs subgroups of students (including English Language Learner [ELL] students, students with dis-abilities, poverty students, and racial/ethnic minorities) must be *disaggregated,* that is, reported separately from the total for all students at a school.

● *Adequate yearly progress.* A key provision of NCLB is that all schools and dis-tricts must make **adequate yearly progress (AYP)** toward their 2013–2014 goals. Schools and districts that fail to make sufficient progress are designated as "needing improvement." The school is identified as needing improvement if the school as a whole or any disaggregated subgroup has achievement scores below those the state government has determined are required in moving for-ward to meet its 2013–2014 goals. Because many schools compile scores for fifty or more subgroups, it is easy for a school to be identified as needing improvement.

Schools needing improvement are to receive special help from their district or state, such as consultants, professional development, or other additional resources. Students at Title I schools needing improvement also are to receive "supplemental services" such as tutoring, after-school help, or summer school. If, after several years, a school still fails to meet yearly progress goals, its students are eligible to transfer to another public school in the district. Still further failure to make adequate progress subjects schools to "corrective action" or "restructuring," which may include replacing all or part of the faculty and administration, conversion to charter-school status, or

adequate yearly progress (AYP)
The regular increments of achievement gain that schools and districts must register under NCLB to have all students attain academic proficiency.

---

[21]Diane Ravitch and John Chubb, "The Future of No Child Left Behind," *Education Next* (Spring 2009), available at **www.educationnext.org**; and Alyson Klein, "ESEA's 50-Year Legacy a Blend of Idealism, Policy Tensions," *Education Week* (April 1, 2015).

takeover by an outside organization, along with a variety of instructional and curricular innovations selected by a school or district.[22]

States, school districts, teachers, students, and parents have all experienced a great deal of confusion and uncertainty concerning how to implement NCLB requirements. (The NCLB involves nearly seven hundred pages of law and thousands of pages of regulations.) Part of the confusion involves the fact that states create their own definitions of most terms and concepts in the legislation. States not only decide which skills and concepts are tested and which tests are administered but also define what is considered proficient or acceptable achievement. These definitions vary widely from state to state and even within states. For example, one study indicated that eighth graders with the same skills would be at the thirty-sixth percentile in Montana but the eighty-ninth percentile in Wyoming. The same study showed that in Washington, the fourth-grade proficiency level was set at the fifty-third percentile in reading but at the seventy-sixth percentile in mathematics.[23]

The states also determine what type and how much yearly progress is adequate for schools. Some states define acceptable achievement in terms of closing gaps among different subgroups of students; others use terms of absolute performance levels. However, all states were required to specify that all students would be proficient in 2014, and many "back-ended" goals rapidly expanding the percentages of students that would become proficient as 2014 approached. As a result, by 2012, many thousands of schools were classified as not making AYP. Furthermore, officials at the US Department of Education estimated that by 2014, nearly all public schools would be deficient with respect to AYP.[24]

The desire to avoid being viewed as failures and consequently having to impose increasingly drastic interventions induced many school officials to attempt to "game the system," that is, use statistical and organizational manipulations to increase the likelihood that their schools and districts would attain AYP. Many analysts assert that students are hurt by such practices, which include the following:

- Some critics believe that NCLB has frequently resulted in lowering standards and student performance. Several states, for example, have reset scores needed to achieve proficiency at levels lower than before NCLB.
- A subgroup must generally include a minimum of students—say, thirty or fifty—before test scores of those students are counted in determining a school's AYP. This led some school officials to identify fewer students with disabilities to keep this subgroup below the minimum number. Conversely, some districts included students with disabilities in larger subgroups for which their low scores could be masked by the higher scores of nondisabled students. Some schools and districts may be encouraging or facilitating dropouts or transfers among students whose low achievement might detract from AYP status, or the schools/districts may be retaining some students in middle school or the ninth grade if their promotion might damage the high schools' classification on AYP.
- Faculty have been reported to be discouraging gifted students from attending special schools or programs elsewhere because their withdrawal would reduce AYP scores.

[22]Nancy Kober, "The AYP Blues," *American Educator* (Spring 2005), available at **www.aft.org**; Sarah Karp, "Last-Ditch Efforts Aim to Stop School Closings, Turnarounds," *Catalyst Chicago* (February 21, 2012), available at **www.catalyst-chicago.org**; and "More Schools, Districts 'In Need of Assistance' Under NCLB," September 16, 2014, posting by the State of Iowa, available at **www.iowa.gov**.

[23]G. Gage Kingsbury et al., "The State of State Standards," 2003 report published by the Northwest Evaluation Association, summary available at **www.nwea.org/research/national.asp**; and Jennifer L. Jennings and Jonathan M. Bearak, "'Teaching to the Test' in the NCLB Era," *Educational Researcher* (November 2014).

[24]Stan Karp, "Taming the Beast," *Rethinking Schools* (Summer 2004), available at **www.rethinkingschools.org**; VTD Editor, "State: Three-Quarters of Schools Fail to Meet NCLB Standards," August 8, 2012, posting by VTDigger, available at **www.vtdigger.org,** and Nick Sheltrown, "Opinion: The Uneven Legacy of No Child Left Behind," January 22, 2015, posting by edSurge, available at **www.edsurge.com**.

- Many schools and teachers are thought to be concentrating teaching resources on students with scores near the proficient level and thereby neglecting or reducing efforts to help their lowest and highest achievers.
- Many analysts also believe that more teachers and schools are emphasizing low-level skills of the kind likely to be tested on state assessments since the passage of the NCLB.

12-2e Status of NCLB and Movement toward Waivers

One observer has described the NCLB as "an aspirational goal"—all students should succeed—"married to real punishments"—schools can be publicly shamed or even closed or reorganized if even only a few students are unsuccessful. Given this apparent absurdity, states and districts desperately sought to avoid having schools classified as "failing" to make AYP. Before 2012, the US Department of Education made several relatively small modifications in response to complaints about NCLB regulations. For example, it exempted scores of new ELL students from AYP calculations, and it allowed a few states to experimentally use students' growth in achievement rather than a point-in-time snapshot of students' proficiency status in calculating AYP. But critics remained stridently unhappy. The prospect of rapid growth in the number of schools classified as making inadequate AYP raised the possibility that most schools nationally would be required to engage in significant restructuring, even in the case of otherwise high-achieving schools with only one or a few relatively small nonproficient subgroups.[25]

What Will Happen to NCLB? As 2013, approached it became apparent that few schools would be designated as having attained AYP in 2014 and that states and districts would have to greatly escalate their efforts to assist and reform schools, In this context, government officials sought ways to modify and improve NCLB policies and practices. When it became apparent that Congress was unlikely to modify NCLB and in doing so reauthorize the ESEA before 2015, the Department of Education acted to allow states to obtain waivers from NCLB requirements. States receiving waivers were allowed to develop alternate approaches to assess and classify student performance, and also to create systems for evaluating teachers that go beyond one-time proficiency scores each year and instead include such components as student growth in test scores, principal observation, and parent and student feedback. Waiver states must continue to take action to improve the achievement of low performers.

By 2015, most states had obtained these waivers, but there was considerable opposition to the requirement frequently imposed that teachers be evaluated at least partly on the basis of students' performance on standardized tests. Distressing anecdotes were widely circulated about a teacher who had won awards for her work but whose job was in jeopardy because her students could not read the test and therefore showed no progress, and another whose score for student growth was negative because she was given a class much lower in performance than the previous year.[26]

In April of 2015, the major US Senate committee dealing with education unanimously passed an ESEA reauthorization proposal called the Every Child Achieves Act. Some of the major provisions of this proposed legislation are listed here, but it must

---

[25]Quote is from Anya Kamenetz, "It's 2014. All Children Are Supposed to Be Proficient. What Happened?" October 11, 2014, posting by NPR, available at **www.npr.org**. See also Matthew Di Carlo, "The Persistent Misidentification of 'Low Performing Schools'," February 3, 2015, posting by Shanker Blog, available at **www.shankerinstutite.org**.

[26]Amanda A. Fairbanks, "Will Test-Based Teacher Evaluations Derail the Common Core?" *Hechinger Report* (January 8, 2015), available at **www.hechingerreport.org**.

be approved by the full Senate, the House of Representatives, and the President to become law:[27]

- The states would still be required to test annually in mathematics and English/language arts in every grade from 3 through 8, and in one high school grade. The requirement to test annually in science in grade 3, 4, or 5; in grade 6, 7, or 8; and at one high school grade also would be continued.

- The escalating accountability requirements such as the need to make AYP toward all students becoming academically proficient were eliminated; instead, for purposes of acceptable accountability, the states must develop plans to help students attain college and career readiness by high school graduation.

- States and districts would still have to report disaggregated scores for subgroups such as low-income students, minority students, and disabled students.

- School districts would have responsibility for designing evidence-based interventions for low-performing schools, while the federal government would be prohibited from mandating or defining the specific steps districts or states must take to improve these schools, as it did during the implementation of NCLB.

12-2f Questions about Compensatory Education

Although data collected since the 1980s suggest that compensatory education can help disadvantaged students, important questions remain about its nature and effectiveness:

1. *How can we make compensatory education more effective?* Organizational changes such as Response to Intervention (described later in the "The Discrepancy Model, Response to Intervention and Incentives to Mislabel" section of this chapter) are improving achievement in numerous schools; the Effective Schools model (see Chapter 16, School Effectiveness and Reform in the United States) has produced improved performance in many schools; and expanded staff development has helped some teachers learn how to broaden compensatory instruction beyond mechanical subskills. On the other hand, data we cited in Chapter 11, Social Class, Race, and School Achievement, indicate that millions of low-income children continue to achieve at unacceptably low levels.

2. *What type of early instruction should we provide?* Much uncertainty in early compensatory education surrounds whether programs should use a behavioristic direct-instruction approach, which focuses on basic skills such as decoding of words or simple computation in math, or instead should emphasize conceptual development and abstract thinking skills. Some direct-instruction programs have had excellent results through the third grade, but performance levels often fall when participating children enter the middle grades. Results in cognitive-oriented programs stressing independent learning and thinking skills generally have been less successful in terms of mastery of mechanical skills in the primary grades, but some of the best cognitive approaches have resulted in gains that show up later.[28]

3. *What should we do in high schools?* High schools have achieved moderate success in individual classrooms and in "schools within a school," in which a selected group

---

[27]Craig Clough, "No Child Left Behind Reborn as 'Every Child Achieves,'" *Real Clear Education* (April 17, 2015), available at **www.realcleareducation.com**; and Andy Smarick, "The Great Achievements of the Every Child Achieves Act," *Education Next* (April 15, 2015), available at **www.educationnext.org**.

[28]Sharon L. Kagan, "Early Care and Education," *Phi Delta Kappan* (November 1993), pp. 184–187; Katherina Galuschka, et al., "Effectiveness of Treatment Approaches for Children and Adolescents with Reading Disabilities," February 26, 2014, posting by PLOS ONE, available at **www.plosone.org**; Debbie Hepplewhite, "Where Next for Phonics?" *Special Educational Needs* (May 23, 2014); Douglas Fisher and Nancy Frey, "Improve Reading with Complex Texts," *Phi Delta Kappan* (February 2015); and "History and Controversy," undated posting by K12 Academics, available at **www.k12academics.com**.

of teachers work intensively with relatively few low-achieving students. However, researchers still know little about the best compensatory approaches for secondary-school students.[29]

How Much Can the Schools Accomplish in the Absence of Major Social and Economic Reforms?   In view of the low achievement levels still characteristic of many schools and groups of students, some educators question whether compensatory education by itself can significantly improve a student's chances of succeeding in school and in later life—especially a minority student living in a neighborhood of concentrated poverty. As described in Chapter 11, Social Class, Race, and School Achievement, revisionist critics argue that in the absence of fundamental reforms in society as a whole, US public schools will continue to marginalize disadvantaged students. Thus, some observers believe that we may need to improve low-income parents' economic and social circumstances before their children's school achievement will rise significantly on a widespread basis. It remains to be seen whether efforts to improve education for disadvantaged students carried out in isolation from much larger efforts to improve their families and communities can be sufficiently effective to disprove these skeptics' pessimism.[30]

FOCUS Do you think you are or will be well prepared to teach students who receive or should receive compensatory services? What might you do to be better prepared?

12-3 MULTICULTURAL EDUCATION

multicultural education Education that includes the cultures and cultural contributions of all racial, ethnic, language, and gender groups, especially those marginalized in the traditional curriculum. Many multicultural programs also emphasize positive intergroup and interracial attitudes and contacts.

Multicultural education refers to the various ways in which schools can take productive account of cultural differences among students and improve opportunities for students with cultural backgrounds distinct from the US mainstream. Certain aspects of multicultural education focus on improving instruction for students who have not learned Standard English or who have other cultural differences that place them at a disadvantage in traditional classrooms. As a teacher, you should also be concerned with the larger implications of multicultural education that make it valuable for *all* students. By fostering positive intergroup and interracial attitudes and contacts, multicultural education may help all students function in a culturally pluralistic society. (From this point of view, the movement toward desegregation can be considered a part of multicultural education.)

Although the US population always has been pluralistic in composition, the emphasis throughout much of our history, as noted in Chapter 4, Pioneers of Teaching and Learning, has been on assimilating diverse ethnic groups into the national mainstream rather than on maintaining group subcultures. In educating diverse groups of immigrants, the public-school system has stressed the development of an American identity. Students learned how Americans were supposed to talk, look, and behave, sometimes in classes of fifty or sixty pupils representing the first or second generation of immigrants from ten or fifteen countries. Although this approach succeeded in "Americanizing" and allowing social mobility for many immigrants, observers have pointed out that African Americans, Asian Americans, Latinos, Native Americans, and certain European ethnic groups were systematically discriminated against in a manner that revealed the shortcomings of the melting-pot concept.[31]

---

[29]Daniel U. Levine, "Educating Alienated Inner City Youth: Lessons from the Street Academies," *Journal of Negro Education* (Spring 1975), pp. 139–149; Sarah Karp, "Losing Students, Neighborhood High Schools Caught in Downward Spiral," *Catalyst-Chicago* (December 9, 2014), available at **www.catalyst-chicago.org**; and John Buntin, "Changing a Culture Inside and Out of School," *Governing* (January 2015), available at **www.governing.com**.

[30]**Monica** Potts, "Stress, Poverty, and the Childhood Reading Gap," *American Prospect* (February 12, 2014), available at **www.prospect.org**; and Tim Walker, "Shameful Milestone," *NEA Today* (January 16, 2015), available at **www.neatoday.org**.

[31]Min Zhou and Carl L. Bankston III, *Growing Up American* (New York: Russell Sage, 1998); Suzanne Fields, "A Melting Pot Gone Cold," *Real Clear Politics* (April 22, 2011), available at **www.realclearpolitics.com**; and Tasnim Ahmed, "The Melting Pot That Never Was," *Harvard Crimson* (March 5, 2014), available at **www.thecrimson.com**.

cultural pluralism Acceptance and encouragement of cultural, ethnic, language, and religious diversity within a larger society.

In the 1960s, civil rights leaders fought to reduce the exclusion of minority groups and to shift emphasis from assimilation to diversity and cultural pluralism. In place of the melting-pot metaphor, **cultural pluralism** introduced new metaphors such as "tossed salad" or "mosaic" that allow for distinctive group characteristics within a larger whole. According to the American Association of Colleges for Teacher Education (AACTE), "to endorse cultural pluralism is to endorse the principle that there is no one model American." From this viewpoint, the differences among the nation's citizens are a positive force.[32]

Remember, emphasizing cultural pluralism does not mean you support a philosophy aimed at cultural, social, or economic separation. Depending on how we define cultural pluralism, it may or may not stress integration in cultural, social, or economic matters. Generally, it lies somewhere between total assimilation on the one hand and strict separation of ethnic or racial groups on the other hand. Cultural pluralism, particularly in education, is more important than ever before as the United States becomes transformed into what observers call the first "universal nation."

12-3a Multicultural Instruction

One key area in multicultural education concerns instructional approaches for teaching students with differing ethnic and racial backgrounds. Several of the most frequently discussed approaches address student learning styles, recognition of dialect differences, bilingual education, and multiethnic curriculum.

learning styles Distinctively different ways students learn, such as emphasis on oral or visual activities.

Student Learning Styles In Chapter 11, Social Class, Race, and School Achievement, we briefly described behavioral patterns and **learning styles** that appear to correlate with students' socioeconomic status and, perhaps, with their race or ethnicity. We also mentioned attempts to modify instruction to accommodate different learning styles. One good example of research on this subject was provided by Vera John-Steiner and Larry Smith, who worked with Pueblo Indian children in the Southwest. They concluded that schooling for these children would be more successful if it emphasized personal communication in tutorial (face-to-face) situations. Other observers of Native American classrooms have reported that achievement rose substantially when teachers interacted with students in culturally appropriate ways (that is, social control was mostly indirect); integrated tribal culture into the curriculum while emphasizing mastery of state standards; and/or avoided putting students in competitive situations. Similarly, several researchers have reported that cooperative learning arrangements are particularly effective with some Mexican American students whose cultural background deemphasizes competition.[33]

Analysts also have examined research on the performance of Asian American students. Several observers believe that certain subgroups of Asian students (for example, Koreans and Vietnamese) tend to be nonassertive in the classroom and that this reluctance to participate may hinder their academic growth, particularly with respect to verbal skills. (However, research suggests that such behavioral patterns diminish or disappear as Asian American students become more assimilated within US society.) In addition, Asian American students can be harmed by a stereotype

---

[32]"No One Model American: A Statement of Multicultural Education" (Washington, DC: American Association of Colleges for Teacher Education, 1972), p. 9. See also Amy Kiley, "Many Nations under God," *US Catholic* (May 2011), pp. 18–22; and Richard J. Bernstein, "Cultural Pluralism," *Philosophy and Social Criticism* (January 4, 2015).

[33]Vera John-Steiner and Larry Smith, "The Educational Promise of Cultural Pluralism," 1978 paper prepared for the National Conference on Urban Education, St. Louis, Missouri; Paulette Running Wolf and Julie A. Rickard, "Talking Circles," *Journal of Multicultural Counseling & Development* (January 2003), pp. 39–43; Mae Ackerman-Brimberg, "Achieving Equal Educational Opportunities for Native American Youth," *Youth Law News* (January–February 2014); and Celia Llopis-Jepsen, "Native American Education Needs Boost," *Topeka Capital-Journal* (January 11, 2015), available at **www.cjonline.com**.

indicating that they are all part of a model minority who have no serious problems in school.[34]

Recognition of Dialect Differences   Teachers generally have tried to teach so-called proper or Standard English to students who speak nonstandard dialects. Frequently, however, a simplistic insistence on proper English has caused students to reject their own cultural background or else to view the teachers' efforts as demeaning and hostile. In recent years, educators have been particularly concerned with learning problems among students who speak Black English. Some teachers have developed "code-switching" techniques that use students' dialects to provide a bridge to Standard English. But research shows that Black English is not simply a form of slang; it differs systematically from Standard English in grammar and syntax. Because Black English seems to be the basic form of English spoken by many low-income African American students who are floundering academically, educators have proposed that schools use Black English as the language of instruction for these students until they learn to read. Although this approach seems logical, little research has provided support for it.[35]

Analysis of the dialect of many African American students (that is, Black English) frequently is referred to as **Ebonics**. An important controversy regarding Ebonics and its possible use in improving instruction for African American students arose in 1997 after the Oakland, California, school board declared that Black English is a distinctive language. The board requested state and federal bilingual education funds to help teachers use Black English in implementing approaches for improving black students' performance with respect to Standard English and reading. After television sound bites allowed for the interpretation that Oakland schools were abandoning the goal of teaching "good" English, numerous national figures (including Reverend Jesse Jackson) criticized the board for its policies regarding the use of Ebonics in teaching. Although the Linguistic Society of America declared that Oakland's policy was "linguistically and pedagogically sound," the Oakland Board of Education responded by removing terminology involving Ebonics from its policies and setting aside $400,000 for a "Standard English Proficiency" program designed to help teachers understand and build on dialect characteristics in instructing students whose language patterns strongly emphasize Black English.[36]

Bilingual Education   **Bilingual education**, which provides instruction in their native language for students not proficient in English, has been expanding in US public schools as immigration has increased. In 1968, Congress passed the Bilingual Education Act, and, in 1974, the Supreme Court ruled unanimously in *Lau v. Nichols* that the schools must take steps to help students who "are certain to find their classroom experiences wholly incomprehensible" because they do not understand English. Although

Ebonics Frequently used as a synonym for Black English, Ebonics also refers to analysis of a dialect used by many African Americans and of how it might play a part in teaching Standard English.

bilingual education Instruction in their native language provided for students whose first language is not English.

---

[34]Benji Chang and Wayne Au, "You're Asian, How Could You Fail Math?" *Rethinking Schools* (Winter 2007/2008), available at **www.rethinkingschools.org**; Helen Gym, "Tiger Mom and the Model Minority Myth," *Rethinking Schools* (Summer 2011), available at **www.rethinkingschools.org**; Scot Nakagawa, "The Origins of the Asian American Model Minority Myth," February 21, 2014, posting by Race Files, available at **www.racefiles.com**; and Neil Chaudhary, "Dismantling the 'Model Minority' Myth," *Stanford Daily* (January 8, 2015), available at **www.stanford.com**.

[35]J. R. Harber and D. N. Bryan, "Black English and the Teaching of Reading," *Review of Educational Research* (Summer 1976), pp. 397–398; Abha Gupta, "What's Up wif Ebonics, Y'All?" 1999 posting at Reading Online, available at **http://readingonline.org/articles/gupta**; and Sarah D. Sparks, "Students Learn to 'Toggle' Between Languages," *Education Week* (September 9, 2014).

[36]Wayne O'Neill, "If Ebonics Isn't a Language, Then Tell Me, What Is?" *Rethinking Schools* (Fall 1997), available at **www.rethinkingschools.org**; John H. McWhorter, "Throwing Money at an Illusion," *Black Scholar* (January 1997); Mary E. Flannery, "Yo! From Tupac to the Bard," *NEA Today* (November/December 2008), available at **www.neatoday.org**; G. L. "Do It Be Makin' Sense?" 2010 posting by the *Economist*, available at **www.economist.com**; Lex Friedman, "Ain't No Reason," *The Magazine* (March 14, 2013), and Michael T. Ndemanu, "Ebonics, To Be or Not To Be? A Legacy of Trans-Atlantic Slave Trade," *Journal of Black Studies* (January 2015).

OVERVIEW 12.1

COMPARISON OF BILINGUAL EDUCATION AND ENGLISH LANGUAGE INSTRUCTION FOCUS FOR ENGLISH LANGUAGE LEARNERS

Approach	Variations	Pros	Cons
Bilingual Education	First-language maintenance—emphasis on teaching in the native language over a long time	• Might sustain a constructive sense of identity among ethnic or racial minority students. • Can provide a better basis for learning higher-order skills such as reading comprehension while students acquire basic English skills.	• Requires many speakers of native languages as teachers. • Separates groups from one another. • Might discourage students from mastering English well enough to function successfully in the larger society.
	Transitional bilingual education (TBE)—providing intensive English instruction and then proceeding to teach all subjects in English as soon as possible.	• Supported by federal and most state governments. • Moves students relatively quickly into regular classes. • Requires relatively few native language speakers as teachers.	• Students may not sufficiently master English before moving to regular classes, hurting their ability to learn other subjects.
	Universal bilingual education—instruction in two languages for all students, native and nonnative English speakers.	• All students learn more than one language, increasing their competence in a global society.	• Requires many trained staff members. • Expensive to provide adequate materials.
English Language Instruction	Submersion—placing ELL students in regular classrooms with no modifications. Structured immersion—placement in regular classes with special assistance provided inside and outside of class. Sheltered immersion—using principles of second-language learning in regular classrooms.	No or little extra cost to school.	Students generally may fail to learn English or other subjects.

the federal and state governments fund bilingual projects for more than sixty language groups speaking various Asian, Indo-European, and Native American languages, the majority of children served by these projects are native speakers of Spanish. Students for whom English is their second language and therefore are classified as English Language Learners (ELL) now constitute more than 10 percent of public school enrollment. In 2015, several federal agencies reminded school officials that English learners must be taught by qualified teachers and must be integrated as much as possible into mainstream classrooms. Overview 12.1 summarizes several approaches for helping children whose first language is not English.

The Supreme Court's unanimous decision in the *Lau* case, which involved Chinese children in San Francisco, did not focus on bilingual education as the only remedy. Instead, the Court said, "Teaching English to the students of Chinese ancestry is one choice. Giving instruction to this group in Chinese is another. There may be others." In practice, early federal regulations for implementing the *Lau* decision tended to focus on bilingual education as the most common solution for ELL students. The regulations generally suggested that school districts initiate bilingual programs if they enrolled more than twenty students of a given language group at a particular grade. Bilingual programs proliferated accordingly. Since 1983, however, the federal government has accepted, and sometimes even encouraged, English-as-a-second-language (ESL) instruction or other nonbilingual approaches for providing help to ELL students.

Researchers agree that ELL students should be given special help in learning to function in the schools. "Submersion" approaches, which simply place ELL students in regular classrooms without any special assistance or modifications in instruction, frequently result in failure to learn. Data collected by the Council of Chief State School Officers and other organizations indicate, moreover, that significant numbers of ELL students are receiving little specialized assistance to help them learn English and other subjects.[37]

first-language maintenance
Continued teaching in a language while introducing instruction in another language.

transitional bilingual education (TBE) A form of bilingual education in which students are taught in their own language only until they can learn in English.

Controversies over bilingual education have become increasingly embittered. As in the case of teaching through dialect, arguments erupt between those who would immerse children in an English-language environment and those who believe initial instruction will be more effective in the native language. Educators and laypeople concerned with ELL students also argue over whether to emphasize teaching in the native language over a long period of time, called **first-language maintenance**, or provide intensive English instruction and teach all subjects in English as soon as possible, called **transitional bilingual education (TBE)**. Those who favor maintenance believe that this will help sustain a constructive sense of identity among ethnic or racial minority students and provide a better basis for learning higher-order skills, such as reading comprehension, while they acquire basic English skills. Their opponents believe that maintenance programs are harmful because they separate groups from one another or discourage students from mastering English well enough to function successfully in the larger society.[38] TBE has been supported by federal guidelines and by legislation in certain states. Studies indicate that approximately 75 percent of Hispanic students and nearly 90 percent of other groups such as Asian and Russian students exit transitional programs within three years.

Among scholars who believe that bilingual education has produced little if any improvement, several have reviewed the research and concluded that "structured immersion" (placement in regular classes with special assistance provided inside and outside of class) and "sheltered immersion" (using principles of second-language learning in regular classrooms) are more successful than TBE. Other scholars disagree, arguing that well-implemented bilingual programs do improve achievement, and several reviews of research have reported that bilingual education worked significantly better than immersion or other mostly monolingual programs. (Part of the reason for these differences in conclusions involves disagreements about which studies should be reviewed and the criteria for selecting them.)[39]

---

[37]*Meeting the Needs of Students with Limited English Proficiency* (Washington, DC: US Government Accounting Office, 2001); Margarita Calderon, Robert Slavin, and Marta Sanchez, "Effective Instruction for English Language Learners," *The Future of Children* (Spring 2011), available at **www.futureofchildren.org**; Dan Alpert, "Our Public and Personal Histories," April 17, 2014, posting by Corwin Connect, available at **www.corwin-connect.com**; and Emma Brown, "New Federal Guidelines Highlight Civil Rights of English Language Learners," *Washington Post* (January 7, 2015), available at **www.washingtonpost.com**.

[38]Rosalie P. Porter, *Forked Tongue* (New York: Basic Books, 1990); Kelly D. Salas, "Defending Bilingual Education," *Rethinking Schools* (Spring 2006), available at **www.rethinkingschools.org**; Herman Badillo, *One Nation One Standard* (New York: Sentinel, 2007); Kenji Hakuta, "Educating Language Minority Students and Affirming Their Equal Rights," *Educational Researcher* (May 2011); and Rosalie P. Porter, "Bill to End Ban on Bilingual Education Hurts Immigrant Kids," *San Francisco Chronicle* (September 17, 2014), available at **www.sfgate.com**.

[39]Ann C. Willig, "A Meta-Analysis of Selected Studies on the Effectiveness of Bilingual Education," *Review of Educational Research* (Fall 1985), pp. 269–317; Stephen Krashen, "Bilingual Education Works," *Rethinking Schools* (Winter 2000/2001), available at **www.rethinkingschools.org**; Angela Pascopella, "Successful Strategies for English Language Learners," *District Administration* (February 2011), available at **www.districtadministration.com**; and Laura Baecher, "Policies and Practices to Promote English Language Learner Academic Success," May 21, 2014, posting by the CUNY Institute for Education Policy, available at **http://ciep.hunter cuny.edu**.

Claude Goldenberg reviewed much of the research and concluded that "...primary-language instruction enhances English-language learners' academic achievement...[but] certain accommodations must be made when ELL students are instructed in English, and these accommodations probably must be in place for several years, until students reach sufficient familiarity with academic English to permit them to be successful in mainstream instruction." He cited a number of important accommodations such as strategic use of the native language, frequent interaction with target language users, ample opportunities to use and practice English, extended explanation, and building on student experiences and familiar content. He also presented the following conclusions that he believes can be drawn from multiple studies on instruction for ELL students:[40]

- *If feasible, children should be taught reading in their primary language....*
- *As needed, students should be helped to transfer what they know in their first language to learning tasks presented in English....*
- *Teaching in the first and second languages can be approached similarly. However, adjustments or modifications will be necessary, probably for several years and at least for some students, until they reach sufficient familiarity with academic English to permit them to be successful in mainstream instruction....*
- *ELLs need intensive oral English language development (ELD), especially vocabulary and academic English instruction....*
- *ELLs also need academic content instruction, just as all students do; although ELD is crucial, it must be in addition to—not instead of—instruction designed to promote content knowledge.*

Many scholars believe that all students, regardless of their ethnic group, should receive bilingual education. In part, this argument stems from the international economic advantages of a nation's citizens knowing more than one language. Programs that provide education in both English and another language for all students at a multiethnic school are sometimes referred to as "two-way" or "dual" bilingual immersion. To make this type of education a positive force in the future, several groups of civic leaders have recommended stressing multilingual competence, rather than just English remediation, as well as insisting on full mastery of English.[41]

Multiethnic Curriculum and Instruction Since the mid-1960s, educators have been striving to take better account of cultural diversity by developing multiethnic curriculum materials and instructional methods. Many textbooks and supplemental reading lists have been revised to include materials and topics relating to diverse racial and ethnic groups. In-service training has helped teachers discover multiethnic source materials and learn to use instructional methods that promote multicultural perspectives and positive intergroup relations.

Efforts to implement multiethnic curricula have been particularly vigorous with respect to Native American students. For example, educators at the Northwest Regional Education Laboratory have prepared an entire Indian Reading Series based on Native American culture. Mathematics instruction for Native American students sometimes uses familiar tribal symbols and artifacts in presenting word and story problems, and local or regional tribal history has become an important part of the social studies curriculum in some schools. Many observers believe that such approaches can help Native

---

[40]Claude Goldenberg, "Teaching English Language Learners," *American Educator* (Summer 2008), p. 42, available at **www.aft.org**; Claude Goldenberg, "Unlocking the Research on English Learners" *American Educator* (Summer 2013), available at **www.aft.org**; and Claude Goldenberg, "Research on the Education of English Learners," *Literate Nation Opinion* (Summer 2014).

[41]"The Benefits of Dual-Immersion Education," 2011 posting by Imagine Learning, available at **www.imaginelearning.com**; Lesli A. Maxwell, "School Successes Inspire N.C. Push for Dual Language," *Education Week* (October 14, 2014); and Conor Williams, "Research on Making Policy Reforms Work for Dual Language Learners," *Washington Monthly* (August 30, 2014), available at **www.washingtonmonthly.com**.

American students establish a positive sense of identity conducive to success in school and society.[42]

However, multiethnic curricula are not intended merely to bolster the self-image and enhance the learning of minority students. A crucial purpose is to ensure that all students acquire knowledge and appreciation of other racial and ethnic groups.

Culturally Responsive Teaching   Advocates and practitioners of this variant of multicultural education generally emphasize its relevance for motivating students, particularly low-income African American students. In a definition offered by Geneva Gay, culturally responsive teaching involves "using the cultural knowledge, prior experience, frames of references, and performance styles of ethnically diverse students to make learning encounters more relevant to and effective for them…[and to] teach to and through the strengths of these students." Teachers implementing culturally responsive teaching typically stress advantages such as the following:[43]

- Acknowledges the legitimacy of the cultural heritages of a variety of ethnic groups and their value when included in the formal curriculum
- Builds bridges between students' home and school experiences
- Allows teachers to pursue a wide variety of instructional strategies appropriate for a range of students
- Allows teachers to incorporate multicultural resources and materials in subjects and skills routinely taught
- Allows teachers to anchor curriculum in the everyday lives of students
- Allows teachers to select participation structures that reflect students' ways of behaving

Afrocentric Initiatives   In recent years, particular attention has been given to ensuring that curriculum and instruction are not overwhelmingly *Eurocentric* (reflecting the culture and history of ethnic groups of European origin) but incorporate the concerns, culture, and history of ethnic and racial groups of different origins. Such approaches not only introduce materials dealing with the history and status of minority groups but also involve activities such as community-service assignments and cooperative learning tasks designed to acquaint students with minority cultures.

Most such curricula include the contributions of many groups; others focus on a single group. For example, *Afrocentric* programs focus on the history and culture of African Americans. Several schools have been established that feature Afrocentric curriculum and instruction to the extent that they are named for their emphasis on this approach. Efforts to introduce Afrocentric and other minority-oriented themes have provoked controversy in California, New York, and other states, as well as in individual school districts. Critics suggest that such programs reject Western culture and history, leaving students lacking knowledge common in US society. Some also suggest that many such curricula include historical inaccuracies. Another concern is that minority-oriented curricula can isolate minority students in separate schools or classes. An additional criticism is that emphasis on minority culture and history sometimes becomes a

---

[42]Lee Little Soldier, "Is There an Indian in Your Classroom?" *Phi Delta Kappan* (April 1997), pp. 650–653; Cindy Long, "Save the Indian, Save the Child," *NEA Today* (November/December 2008), available at **www.neatoday.org**; "Charting a New Course for Native Education," 2010–2011 posting by the National Education Association, available at **www.nea.org**; and Tanya H. Lee, "5 Ways Native American Education Is Getting Better Into 2015," January 1, 2015, posting by Indian Country, available at **www.indiancountrytodaymedianetwork.com**.

[43]Geneva Gay, "Culturally Responsive Pedagogy," 2010 posting by the Saint Paul Public Schools Office of Equity, available at **http://equity.spps.org**; Geneva Gay, *Culturally Responsive Teaching* (New York: Teachers College Press, 2010); and Deborah S. Peterson, "A Culturally Responsive Alternative to 'Drill and Kill' Literacy Strategies," *Multicultural Perspectives* (October–December 2014).

substitute for other difficult actions required to improve minority students' academic performance.

Supporters of Afrocentric and other minority-oriented themes respond by pointing out that few advocates of these approaches want to eliminate Western culture and history from the curriculum. Molefi Asante argues that the Afrocentric movement strives to de-bias the curriculum by adding appropriate Afrocentric materials, not by eliminating Western classics. In addition, they note that few, if any, supporters of Afrocentric or related approaches minimize the importance of academic achievement or advocate its de-emphasis in the curriculum.[44]

12-3b Multiculturalism for the Future

The controversies about multicultural education as a whole follow lines similar to the specific arguments about Afrocentric and other minority-oriented curricula. Critics worry that multicultural education may increase ethnic separatism, fragment the curriculum, and reinforce the tendency to settle for a second-rate education for economically disadvantaged or minority students. To avoid such potential dangers, multiculturalists have provided useful guidelines for you, as a teacher, to use in providing instruction:[45]

- *Find out what positive aspects of Western civilization are being taught.* If students are not learning that constitutional government, the rule of law, and the primacy of individual rights are among the hallmarks of Western civilization, then they are not learning the essential features of their heritage.
- *Find out if students are being taught that racism, sexism, homophobia, and imperialism are characteristics of all cultures and civilizations at some time—not culture-specific evils.* America's failings should not be taught in isolation from the failings of other countries—no double standard.
- *Insist that all students study both Western and non-Western cultures.* Students need solid academic courses in Latin American, African, and Asian history, in addition to European history.

Despite the controversies, most influential educators believe there is an urgent need for multicultural approaches that give attention to minority experiences. "If children are to do well academically," said former New York State Commissioner of Education Thomas Sobol, "the child must experience the school as an extension, not a rejection, of home and community." A central goal, Sobol contends, should be to "develop a shared set of values and a common tradition" while also helping "each child find his or her place within the whole."[46]

[44]Molefi Asante, *The Afrocentric Idea* (Philadelphia, PA: Temple University Press, 1987); Molefi Asante, "Afrocentric Curriculum," *Educational Leadership* (January 1992), pp. 28–31; Dennis Byrne, "Afrocentric Curriculum Divisive, Not Unifying," 2006 essay prepared for Real Clear Politics, available at **www.realclearpolitics.com**; Kim G. Shockley, "Reaching African American Students," *Journal of Black Studies* (March 2011); Krystle Crossman, "At Afro-Centric Schools, Children Thrive," September 3, 2014, posting by Black Youth Project, available at **www .blackyouthproject.com**; and Alison DeNisco, "Pride, History Boost African-American Achievement," *District Administration* (April 2015), available at **www.districtadministration.com**.

[45]Jynotsa Pattnaik, "Learning about the 'Other,'" *Childhood Education* (Summer 2003), pp. 204–211; Cornell Thomas, "Difference Does Not Mean Less Than," *New Directions for Teaching and Learning* (December 2014); and Jamie Gumbrecht, "How to Talk to Kids About Racism," January 19, 2015, posting by CNN, available at **www.cnn.com**.

[46]Thomas Sobol, "Understanding Diversity," *Educational Leadership* (February 1990), pp. 27–30. See also Karen M. Teel and Jennifer E. Obidah, eds., *Building Racial and Cultural Competence in the Classroom* (New York: Teachers College Press, 2008); Christine E. Sleeter, "Are Standards and Multicultural Education Compatible?" *ASCD Express* (No. 15 2011), available at **www.ascd.org**; and Amy S. Wells, "Seeing Past the 'Color Blind' Myth of Education Policy," *Education Digest* (November 2014).

FOCUS In what ways are you preparing to work with students from a variety of cultural and linguistic backgrounds? How might you benefit as a teacher from knowing more about the cultural background of students different from yourself?

12-4 EDUCATION FOR STUDENTS WITH DISABILITIES

Major developments in education in the past thirty years have involved schooling for children with disabilities. (Placement in special education usually means that a disabled student receives separate, specialized instruction for all or part of the day in a self-contained class or a resource room.) Table 12.1 shows the numbers of students with selected disabilities served in or through public education in 2012. Analysis conducted by the US Department of Education indicates that about 60 percent of students with disabilities receive most or all of their education in regular classes, up from 33 percent in 1991; only about 15 percent spent less than 40 percent of their time in regular classes.[47]

Federal requirements for educating students with disabilities have been enumerated through a series of federal laws, including the **Education for All Handicapped Children Act** of 1975 (often known by its public law number, PL 94-142), the **Individuals with Disabilities Education Act (IDEA)** of 1990, and the **Individuals with Disabilities Education Improvement Act (IDEIA)** of 2004. The basic requirements spelled out in these acts, as well as by other laws and judicial interpretations, are as follows:

1. Children cannot be labeled as disabled or placed in special education on the basis of a single criterion such as an IQ score; testing and assessment services must be fair and comprehensive.
2. If a child is identified as disabled, school officials must conduct a functional assessment and develop suitable intervention strategies.

Education for All Handicapped Children Act (Public Law 94–142) A law passed in 1975 which mandated that children with handicaps must have access to a full public education in the least restrictive educational environment.

Individuals with Disabilities Education Act (IDEA) Legislation enacted in 1990.

Individuals with Disabilities Education Improvement Act (IDEIA) A 2004 law which requires that if a child is identified as disabled, school officials must conduct a functional assessment and develop suitable intervention strategies.

TABLE 12.1	Number of Students Receiving Public Special-Education Services in 2012, by Type of Disability
Type of Disability	
Learning disabled	2,698,098
Speech or language impaired	1,032,729
Other health impaired	757,904
Autistic	440,952
Intellectual disability	415,697
Emotional disturbance	359,389
Multiple disabilities	124,722
Developmental delay	122,901
Hearing impaired	68,069
Orthopedically impaired	52,052
Visually impaired	24,987
Traumatic brain injury	25,020
Total	5,693,441

Note: Numbers do not add up to the total because not all categories are shown.
Source: Penny Gould, Andrew Meloche, Anna Brennan-Curry, and Matthew Gianino, *2014 Annual Disability Statistics Compendium* (Durham, NH: Institute on Disability), Tables 11.3a–11.3d.

---

[47]US Department of Education, *To Assure the Free Appropriate Education of All Handicapped Children* (Washington, DC: US Department of Education, 1996); and Grace Kena et. al., *The Condition of Education 2014* (Washington, DC: National Center for Education Statistics, 2014).

> **PHOTO 12.2** Effective mainstreaming of students with disabilities into regular classroom settings requires a variety of special resources, relatively small classes, and educators skilled in and dedicated to creating an effective learning environment and acceptance for all students.

E.D. Torial/Alamy

individualized education program (IEP) Plans including both long- and short-range goals for educating students with disabilities.

least restrictive environment A term used in educating students with disabilities to designate a setting that is as normal or regular as possible. Federal law requires that children with disabilities be placed in special or separate classes only for the amount of time necessary to provide appropriate services.

mainstreaming Placing students with disabilities in regular classes for much or all of the school day, while also providing additional services, programs, and classes as needed.

inclusion Educating students with disabilities in regular classrooms in their neighborhood schools, with collaborative support services as needed.

3. Parents or guardians must have access to information on diagnosis and may protest decisions of school officials.

4. Every student eligible for special-education services must be taught according to an **individualized education program (IEP)** that includes both long-range and short-range goals. Because it is an agreement in writing regarding the resources the school agrees to provide, the IEP is a cornerstone of a school's efforts to help students with disabilities. It must specify special and related services that will be provided in accordance with the needs of the student. Within thirty days of when the child is declared eligible for special services, the IEP must be prepared by a committee that includes the student's teacher, parent or guardian, and an administrator's designee.

5. Educational services must be provided in the **least restrictive environment**, which means that children with disabilities should be in regular classes to the extent possible. They may be placed in special or separate classes only for the amount of time judged necessary to provide appropriate services. If a school district demonstrates that placement in a regular educational setting cannot be achieved satisfactorily, the student must be given adequate instruction elsewhere, paid for by the district.

As a result of these legal mandates, school districts throughout the country have made efforts to accommodate students with disabilities in regular class settings for all or most of the school day. The term *mainstreaming* was originally used to describe such efforts. More recently, the term *inclusion* has been applied. Inclusion usually denotes an even more strenuous effort to include disabled students in regular classrooms as much as is possible and feasible (Photo 12.2). Even if a disability is severe enough that a child needs to spend a substantial amount of time *away* from the regular classroom, he or she can still be encouraged to take part in activities open to other children, such as art or music.

Neither mainstreaming nor inclusion approaches are necessarily intended to eliminate special services or classes for children with exceptional needs. Children in these arrangements may receive a wide range of extra support, from consultation by specialists skilled in working with a particular disability to provision of special equipment.[48]

---

[48]Cindy Long, "Going Mainstream," *NEA Today* (February 2008), available at **www.neatoday .org**; and "Your Child's Right to Inclusion," October 17, 2014, posting by Special Education Law Blog, available at **http://blog.foxspecialedlaw.com**.

Research on mainstreaming and inclusion has produced ambiguous results. Early studies generally failed to find evidence that placement of disabled students in regular classes for most or all of the day consistently improved their academic performance, social acceptance, or self-concept. Few classrooms examined in that early research, however, provided a fair test because too little had been done to train teachers, introduce appropriate teaching methods, provide a range of suitable materials, or otherwise ensure that teachers could work effectively with heterogeneous groups of disabled and nondisabled students. Reflecting such criticism, several studies were conducted that were limited to districts and states considered outstanding in providing mainstreamed or inclusive opportunities for students with disabilities. But mainstreaming/inclusion is very difficult to implement effectively, and, again, relatively few indications emerged that mainstreaming/inclusion has been consistently beneficial for disabled students. In addition, some studies have found an academic decline among regular students in classes with a high percentage of poorly performing disabled students.[49]

On the other hand, several assessments of individual schools have been more promising. In general, these schools have been described as models of restructuring. They made systematic reforms to prepare teachers to work with heterogeneous groups; they provided special resources to assist both students and teachers who need help; they had administrators who promoted collaboration between special-education teachers and regular faculty; and they kept class size relatively small. In addition, teachers were effective at individualizing instruction and introducing cooperative learning. The researchers tend to agree that successful mainstreaming or inclusion on a national basis will require similar effective restructuring of schools throughout the United States.[50] The From Preservice to Practice feature presents concerns that you and others entering the teaching profession might have about inclusion.

The legal requirements for educating students with disabilities create several challenges for teachers and administrators, beginning with determining who qualifies. After an appropriate determination has been made, schools must assess which services children need and how well they can fulfill those needs. We'll explore these challenges, as well as other questions about special education next.

12-4a Classification and Labeling of Students

Educators face many difficulties in identifying students who require special-education services. It is hard to be certain, for example, whether a child with very low achievement is intellectually disabled and could benefit from special services or is simply a slow learner who requires more time and guidance to learn. Similarly, it is difficult to determine whether a child who is working below capacity has a learning disability or is performing inadequately because he or she is poorly motivated, poorly taught, or

---

[49]Andrew R. Brulle, "Appropriate, with Dignity," *Phi Delta Kappan* (February 1991), p. 487; Ann C. Dybvik, "Autism and the Inclusion Mandate," *Education Next* (No. 1 2004), available at **www.educationnext.org**; Michelle Diament, "Educators Support Inclusion But Find Students Ill-Prepared," 2011 posting by Disability Scoop, available at **www.disabilityscoop.com**; and Laura M. Justice et al., "Peer Effects in Early Childhood Education," *Psychological Science* (July 25, 2014).

[50]Allan Gartner and Dorothy Kerzner Lipsky, "Beyond Special Education," *Harvard Educational Review* (November 1987), pp. 367–395; Julie Causton-Theoharris and George Theoharris, "Creating Inclusive Schools for All Students," *School Administrator* (September 2008), available at **www.aasa.org**; Barbara McClanahan, "Help! I Have Kids Who Can't Read in My World History Class!" *Preventing School Failure* (Winter 2009), pp. 105–112; Sherry L. Hicks-Monroe, "A Review of Research on the Educational Benefits of the Inclusive Model of Education for Special Education Students," *Journal of the American Academy of Special Education Professionals* (Winter 2011); "Children with Disabilities Benefit from Classroom Inclusion," *Science Daily* (July 28, 2014), available at **www.sciencedaily.com**; James McLeskey and Nancy L. Waldron, "Effective Leadership Makes Schools Truly Inclusive," *Phi Delta Kappan* (February 2015); and "Does Inclusion Help Students," undated posting by the National Association of Special Education Teachers, available at **www.naset.org**.

FROM PRESERVICE TO PRACTICE

MEETING ALL NEEDS

Josh and Rob are graduating this year and heading for their first year of classroom teaching. Josh looks over at Rob. "I don't know about you, Rob, but I'm pretty overwhelmed by what we're expected to do with and for special-needs students in an inclusion program. I know it's important for special-needs students to spend as much time as possible in the least restrictive environment, but just dealing with the requirements for normal students will be plenty of responsibility for me in my first year of teaching."

Rob nods. "I agree. I suspect that inclusion helps the school district's financial situation. Look at the state formula for funding special education. More money comes to the districts that practice inclusion. But I'm not at all sure that inclusion is the best practice for most students with disabilities. I certainly don't have the training to deal with emotionally disabled students. If a disabled student becomes disruptive, how does a teacher proceed normally?" Rob taps his finger on the table. "I am also really wondering how all of this affects learning for regular students. We'll have to follow Individual Education Plans for all disabled students. Couldn't following the IEP sometimes lead regular students to suspect unfairness? Before I took 'Overview of Special Education' this year, even I kind of thought special-education students could get away with doing almost nothing and call it 'adapting the curriculum.' How can I explain the differences to my class?"

Josh sighs. "I was only worried about meeting the special ed needs. But I can see potential problems in developing or maintaining effective education for regular students, too. In the effort to serve disabled students, I might be tempted to ease up on my preparation for regular students, and vice versa. And behavior problems of just one student can easily distract a whole class, causing all of us to waste valuable time. I wonder how new teachers feel about this after their first year."

Rob makes a note on a notepad. "Let's ask Professor Jackson if we could have a panel discussion. She would know which of last year's graduates are teaching in a school using full inclusion. Then we could ask all our questions about this issue."

Josh looks over at the notepad. "I think we should include teachers who have lots of experience and who have seen how other arrangements work, as well. I remember the old resource rooms where they used to send most of the disabled students. That setup may have worked better for some kids, but I also remember the disruption in class when they gathered up their stuff to go for their special sessions."

"Maybe the working teachers can talk about team teaching," Josh adds. "We don't necessarily have to work alone, you know. I've heard of shared teaching responsibilities, where a special-education teacher teams with the regular teacher. I would definitely like to learn more about that. And there are always aides. Some of them serve as teachers even though they're not certified. Let's ask about all these questions—and more."

CASE QUESTIONS

1. What arrangements do local schools use to provide services to special-education students?

2. What do you see as the most effective way to serve disabled students?

3. Do you have concerns about working with certain classes of disabled students?

4. Arrange to talk to regular and special-education teachers. What arrangements do special-education teachers believe serve special-education students best? How do regular classroom teachers answer the same question?

culturally unprepared for assessment materials. Although "learning disability" is currently the most used label—covering students with deficits in reading, math, writing, listening, or other skills—experts disagree among themselves not only on what constitutes such a disability but also on what services should be provided to ameliorate it. Experts encounter similar problems in distinguishing between severe and mild emotional disturbances or between partial and complete deafness. Children who appear borderline in disability status (a potentially fuzzy borderline) are especially difficult to classify.

The Discrepancy Model, Response to Intervention, and Incentives to Mislabel
Since passage of the IDEIA, students are not to be classified using the Discrepancy Model; that is, they should not be classified as learning disabled on the basis of discrepancies between their achievement scores and their scores on IQ tests, but instead they should receive help with specific problems and then be classified as learning disabled

only if they do not respond satisfactorily to that intervention. This approach is called **Response to Intervention (RTI)**, and dictates leaving a child in the regular school program while providing him or her with suitable interventions; only if that does not work is the child referred for special education or disability services. The RTI approach was developed largely in the 1990s. It has since morphed into an approach to whole-school improvement that we will describe in Chapter 16, School Effectiveness and Reform in the United States.[51]

Many analysts have suggested that the vagueness of the learning disabilities (LD) category has encouraged school districts to use this classification as a way to obtain federal funds to improve educational services for low-achieving students. Because most LD students spend much of their time in regular classes but receive extra assistance in resource rooms, LD services often provide compensatory education for disadvantaged or low-achieving students who do not qualify for Title I services. This may help to explain why the number of US students classified as LD has more than tripled since the 1970s. Research indicates that half or more LD students may not meet criteria commonly accepted by special-education experts. On the other hand, analysts believe that some schools and districts are avoiding classifying students as LD so that their low achievement scores can be obscured among large numbers of regular students rather than counted as part of an NCLB subgroup (see the "The No Child Left Behind Act" section concerning adequate yearly progress earlier in this chapter), where low scores can result in failure to make adequate yearly progress.

Effects of Labeling   Critics also are concerned that classification may become a self-fulfilling prophecy. Students labeled as "disturbed," for example, may be more inclined to misbehave because the label can make unruly behavior acceptable and expected. They may also be prescribed drugs that in some cases can have serious side effects and occasionally may generate dependency. Researchers have tried to determine whether placement in a special class or program has either a positive or a detrimental effect on students. Among the variables they have considered are peer acceptance and effects on self-concept. On the whole, the research is inconclusive. (Difficulties in conducting this type of research include defining terms, measuring program effects, and allowing for students' differing reactions to a given program.) Although some researchers report that special-education classes limit the progress of many students, others have found that special-class placement can be beneficial when instruction is well planned and appropriate.[52]

12-4b Disproportionate Placement of Minority Students

Data on special-education placement show that students from some racial minority groups are much more likely to be designated for programs enrolling students with severe intellectual disabilities than are non-Hispanic white students. African American students, for example, are nearly three times as likely as white students to be in

[51]Perry A. Zirkel, "Sorting Out Which Students Have Learning Disabilities," *Phi Delta Kappan* (April 2001), pp. 639–641; Judy Elliott, "Response to Intervention," *School Administrator* (September 2008), available at **www.aasa.org**; Charles A. Hughes and Douglas D. Dexter, "Response to Intervention," *Theory into Practice* (Issue 1, 2011); and Kimberly A. Turse and Susan F. Albrecht, "The ABCs of RTI," *Preventing School Failure* (Issue 2, 2015), available at **www.tandfonline.com**.

[52]Gaea Leinhardt and Allan Pallay, "Restrictive Educational Settings," *Review of Educational Research* (Winter 1982), pp. 557–578; Douglas Fuchs and Lynn S. Fuchs, "Sometimes Separate Is Better," *Educational Leadership* (December 1994–January 1995), pp. 22–26; Naomi Zigmond, "Where Should Students with Disabilities Receive Special Education Services?" *The Journal of Special Education* (Vol. 37, No. 3, 2003), available at **www.eric.ed.gov**; Susan Baglieri et al., "Disability Studies in Education," *Remedial and Special Education* (July 2011), pp. 267–278; Ruth E. Tkachyk, "Questioning Secondary Inclusive Education," *Interchange* (December 2013), available at **www.eric.ed.gov**; and Michelle Ball, "Special Education," January 13, 2015, posting by Education Law and Student Rights, available at **www.edlaw4students.blogspot.com**.

"educable mentally retarded" classes. In addition, black students in special education are approximately twice as likely to spend significantly more of their time outside regular classrooms than are white students with disabilities. Placement in intellectual-disability categories also correlates highly with students' socioeconomic background and poverty status.

Many analysts believe that placement in classes for the intellectually disabled has been too dependent on intelligence tests, which have been constructed for use with middle-class whites. Some also believe that disproportionate numbers of minority students are shunted into classes for emotionally disturbed or "retarded" children mainly to alleviate teachers' problems in dealing with culturally different children and youth. Furthermore, there are indications that parents of low-income students, many of whom are minority, are reluctant or unable to challenge officials' problematic decisions about where to locate their disabled students. Many educators and parents worry that such placements may constitute a new version of segregation and discrimination, by which minority students are sentenced to special classes with low or nonexistent educational expectations.[53]

12-4c Issues and Dilemmas

We have touched on several issues involved in special education, mainstreaming, and inclusion. In this section, we focus on four issues or dilemmas that may have particular prominence in the next several years. How these issues are resolved will affect your day-to-day life as a teacher.

1. *How will we handle the costs?* Legal rulings that schools must provide an appropriate free education for children with disabilities have often been interpreted to mean that schools must provide the services necessary to help children with special needs derive as much benefit from education as do other students—perhaps establishing an optimal learning environment for every student who requires special assistance. However, providing an optimal learning environment for students with severe disabilities (or, perhaps, for any student) can be expensive. The federal government, while raising academic standards for disabled students under the NCLB, has provided only a fraction of the funds needed to support these services. Upon studying this issue, one legislator confessed that federal failure to fully fund implementation of disability regulations "has to be the mother of all unfunded mandates in this country."[54]

Arguments have arisen between school officials, who claim they cannot afford to provide maximally effective education for all students with disabilities, and parents or other advocates who believe that such students have a constitutional right to whatever services ensure maximum educational gains. Administrators face a series of dilemmas here. Although key court cases have suggested that schools must provide only the level of services that give disabled students "a basic floor of opportunity," federal laws seem to require increasing levels of support. Administrators must not only determine their legal obligations but also decide whether additional services beyond the minimal obligations—and additional costs—are worth the educational payoff for the child. Then they must decide how to pay those costs.

[53]Dara Shifrer, Chandra Muller, and Rebecca Callahan, "Disproportionality and Learning Disabilities," *Journal of Learning Disabilities* (May–June 2011), pp. 246–257; and Shaun Heasley, "In Practice, IDEA Remedies May Not be Available to All," January 14, 2015, posting by Disability Scoop, available at **www.disabilityscoop.com**.

[54]Charles K. Trainor, "Special Education Plans," *American School Board Journal* (January 2011), pp. 63–64; Alison DeNisco, "Navigating Special Education Disputes in Schools," *District Administration* (October 2013), available at **www.districtadministration.com**; and Michael Reilly, "Crucial Education Issues the City Will Tackle 2015," September 23, 2014, posting available at **www.silive.com**.

One possible response is to divert local funds. Another is to classify more students as LD to receive additional federal funding. Still another possibility involves including disabled students in regular classes *without* providing costly additional services there or undertaking systematic restructuring. Although any of these approaches can compromise education for both students with disabilities and without, such responses have been common in many school districts.[55]

2. *What standards should be established for disabled students, and how should disabled students be assessed?* The NCLB legislation required that disabled students be held to the same standards as other students, but it allowed them to have accommodations such as increased time and assistance (for example, visual aids for students with limited vision) in accordance with their needs. There also have been possibilities for modifications in testing requirements and arrangements, such as classifying students as proficient or not in relation to their IEP targets, and administering equivalent, alternate assessments approved by the state. These provisions generated numerous issues involving the extent to which the performance of severely disabled students affected Adequate Yearly Progress classification required by NCLB, whether students with little reading ability could be given "out-of-level" tests they actually could read, and related matters. In some cases, there were even reports of disturbing incidents such as when test material was read out loud to deaf students based on the premise that this would be a useful accommodation. Some of the policies and practices involved in testing of disabled students frequently had a destructive effect on the morale of disabled students and their teachers.[56]

As it became clear in 2015 that NCLB would not be reauthorized as previously constituted, government officials had to consider not only whether general testing requirements should be revised but also how disabled students should be assessed given the federal government's increasing emphasis on higher-level skills and college readiness as part of the Common Core movement. In this context, Secretary of Education Arne Duncan stated that standards for disabled students should be based on "high expectations" that reflect a "robust curriculum." While that prescription can be viewed as making sense for many or most disabled students, even under the expiring NCLB regime, many analysts had serious doubts whether it makes sense for those with severe mental, physical, and/or emotional disabilities. Although the future policies and practices for teaching and testing disabled students remain to be clarified, clearly there is some tension between efforts to raise standards and the practicality of doing so for many disabled students.[57]

3. *To what extent do arrangements and services for educating disabled students detract from the education of nondisabled students?* If school officials divert substantial amounts of money from regular budgets to pay for separate placements or special services for disabled students, or if school officials assign students with severe disabilities to regular classes where teachers cannot or do not address

---

[55]Jordan Cross, "25 Years without Paying the Bills," *School Administrator* (November 2000), available at **www.aasa.org**; Patrick Wall, "Special-Education Overhaul Leaves Students Less Isolated, But Schools Struggle to Keep Up," August 11, 2014, posting by Chalkbeat, available at **www.ny.chalkbeat.org**; and J. Maloni, "Special Education Providers Shortchanging Special Needs Children," *Niagra Frontier Publications* (January 12, 2015).

[56]Cindy Long, "A System 'Gone Horribly Wrong'," *NEA Today*, March 5, 2014, available at **www.neatoday.org**; Candace Cortiella, "Determining Appropriate Assessment Accommodations for Students with Disabilities," 2015 posting by Reading Rockets, available at **www.readingrockets.org**; and "Fact Sheet on Assessment of Students With Disabilities," 2015 posting by the American-Speech-Language-Hearing Association, available at **www.asha.org**.

[57]Anya Kamenetz, "Asking Kids with Special Needs to Clear the Same Bar," July 1, 2014, posting by NPR, available at **www.npr.org**; and Bianca Tanis, "Pushing Back Against High Stakes for Students with Disabilities," *American Educator* (Winter 2014/2015), available at **www.aft.org**.

their problems efficiently, will classroom conditions for nondisabled students suffer? Observers disagree. In addition, serving disabled students in regular classes and then including them in test averages can reduce a school's status on accountability rankings even if the support provided is clearly helping the disabled students. Some believe that mainstreaming and inclusion have not substantially detracted from opportunities and outcomes for nondisabled students. Other observers believe that because regular classroom teachers often receive little or no help in dealing with students who have severe mental or emotional problems, some now have more difficulty delivering effective instruction for all students.[58]

4. *What services should we provide for which students, where, when, and how?* Posing this omnibus question indicates that many issues we have discussed remain unresolved. For example, to what extent should we make differing arrangements for severely and mildly disabled students, or for differing students within either category? To what extent should schools implement "full inclusion" arrangements for all or most of the day, as contrasted with "partial inclusion" that assigns students to resource rooms or separate schools for significant amounts of time? To what extent should such decisions rest with parents, who may have little understanding of their school-wide effects, or with professionals, who may lack sensitivity to the particular problems of an individual student? To what extent is it desirable—and feasible—to provide regular classroom support services, such as a sign language interpreter for deaf students or a nurse to assist incontinent students? Does using resource rooms complicate and disrupt the operation of the school as a whole—or is it more disruptive to bring a range of support services into the regular classroom? Will school-wide restructuring carried out partly to accommodate full inclusion result in substantially improved schooling for all students, or is it unreasonable and unrealistic to expect effective widespread restructuring in the foreseeable future? These are a few of the questions for which educators still need good answers.

School officials struggling with the uncertainties of providing equal opportunity for students with disabilities could benefit from policies and guidelines for deciding what to do. Many informed observers believe that successfully educating students with disabilities will require changes at all levels of the US educational system, including the following:

- Congress should provide more funds to help schools implement its mandates.
- Legislation should require that teachers receive adequate training.
- States and school districts should find ways to quickly identify classrooms or schools where full inclusion or other arrangements are not working well.
- States should pass legislation to expedite quick removal from regular classes of disabled students who are violent or extremely disruptive.
- Schools opting to pursue full inclusion should receive whatever technical help is necessary.
- Teachers and staff in inclusive classrooms should receive training and support in using appropriate instructional strategies that will help all of their students master basic and advanced learning skills, including peer-mediated instruction, mastery learning, differentiated instruction, and cooperative teaching.

FOCUS What aspects of working with inclusion students do you believe will be most challenging for you as a teacher? What are you doing now to prepare for the challenges?

---

[58]Naomi Dillon, "Lost in Translation," *American School Board Journal* (March 2007); Joanne Jacobs, "It's Time to Debate 'Mainstreaming'" August 6, 2013, posting by Joanne Jacobs, available at **www.joannejacobs.com**; Jonathan Glazzard, "Paying the Price for Inclusive Education," *Support for Education* (February 2014); and Tom Sherrington, "Inclusion and Exclusion in a Community School," January 4, 2015, posting by Head Guru Teacher, available at **www.headguruteacher.com**.

SUMMING UP

1. Concern for equal educational opportunity has been expanding to emphasize issues involving racial and ethnic desegregation, achievement levels of students from low-income families, introduction of bilingual education and other aspects of multicultural education, and inclusion of students with disabilities in regular classrooms. Each of these and related sets of issues involve sizable expenditures to enlarge opportunities and ensure that the benefits of education are realistically available to all students. As you enter the education field in the next decade, you will play an important role in determining the extent to which such efforts succeed or fail.

2. Although much desegregation has occurred in smaller school districts, big-city districts, with their concentration of minority students and economically disadvantaged students, have found stable desegregation difficult.

3. Compensatory education seemed unsuccessful until evidence accumulating in the 1980s began to justify a more positive conclusion. However, many serious questions remain concerning the degree to which compensatory

education can have large-scale, substantial, and lasting results. The No Child Left Behind Act (NCLB) has caused sweeping changes not only in compensatory education but also in public schooling for all students.

4. Efforts toward constructive cultural pluralism through education include multicultural education approaches that take account of student learning styles, recognize differences in dialect, provide for bilingual education, and introduce methods and materials involving multiethnic curriculum and instruction. These approaches can help improve the performance of economically disadvantaged minority students and otherwise promote a productive pluralistic society.

5. Legislative and court mandates have led to large expansions in education for students with disabilities. As part of this process, educators are trying to mainstream these students as much as possible to avoid the damaging effects of labeling and separation. Research, however, is unclear concerning the overall gains and losses associated with mainstreaming or inclusion, and many questions remain.

SUGGESTED RESOURCES

INTERNET RESOURCES

In addition to federal government sites, ERIC sites, and other more specialized Internet locations identified elsewhere in this text, you can research the important policy issues introduced in this chapter at the websites of organizations that conduct public-policy analysis. These include the Brookings Institution, Education Sector, the Heritage Foundation, and the Rand Corporation. Electronic journals such as *Educational Policy Analysis Archives* also address issues reviewed in this chapter. You can also visit many sites related to specific chapter topics.

Desegregation

The Century Foundation's *Equality & Education* site provides information about desegregation, school choice, unequal resources, and related topics.

Compensatory Education and Comprehensive Ecological Intervention

The Spring 2014 issue of *The Future of Children* is devoted to Two-Generation Programs.

The website of the Harlem Children's Zone offers much detail on the programs in operation and the impressive results.

MULTICULTURAL EDUCATION

Much of the Fall 2000 issue of *Rethinking Schools*, available on the Rethinking Schools website, is devoted to multicultural education. *Education Week's* Research Center provides a summary of issues involving English Language Learners.

The theme of the Spring 2011 issue of *The Future of Children* is "Immigrant Children."

Materials and practices involving multicultural education are described at the National Center for Culturally Responsive Educational Systems site.

Materials and methods for providing culturally responsive instruction for African American students are available at the Successful Urban Teachers website.

Special Education

The September 2008 issue of *The School Administrator* (see the American Association of School Administrators website) focuses on "Inclusion and Intervention" involving special education.

PUBLICATIONS

Banks, James A., and Cheryl A. M. Banks, eds. *Handbook of Research on Multicultural Education,* 7th ed. New York: Allyn & Bacon, 2009. *A wide variety of research-based chapters deal with cultural diversity and learning, effective instruction for low-income students, desegregation, the history and performance of minority groups, multicultural instruction, and related topics.*

Buntin, John. *A series of instructive 2014 and 2015 articles in the journal* governing *describe a significant effort to reform an inner-city high school.*

Gibson, Margaret A., and John U. Ogbu, eds. *Minority Status and Schools.* New York: Garland, 1991. *In addition to analyzing the experience of minority students in several countries, this book deals specifically with African American, Korean, Latino, Sikh, Ute Indian, and West Indian students in the United States.*

Kahlenberg, Richard D. *Rescuing Brown v. Board of Education.* New York: Century Foundation, 2007. *Profiles and analyzes developments in twelve school districts that have been trying to bring about or maintain socioeconomic integration.*

Kirp, David L. *Improbable Scholars.* Oxford: Oxford University Press, 2013. *Subtitled "The Rebirth of a Great American School System," this volume describes and explains how the Union City school district was able to substantially raise achievement in predominantly low-income schools.*

CHAPTER **13**

THE CHANGING PURPOSES OF AMERICAN EDUCATION

LEARNING OBJECTIVES

13-1 Examine the relationship among educational goals, standards, and objectives.

13-2 Describe how educational goals shifted throughout American history since the end of the nineteenth century.

13-3 Compare and contrast the themes of major policy reports on education and federal legislation over the past thirty-five years.

Lisa F. Young/Shutterstock.com

This chapter was revised by Dr. David E. Vocke, Towson University.

CONTEMPORARY SOCIETY is constantly changing and evolving. As it changes, we must adapt to meet the challenges of new times and circumstances. Throughout our history, Americans have looked to the schools to help cope with the ebb and flow of change. As a society, we react to change and social pressures by revising our educational purposes and demanding that schools respond by changing their instructional programs.

As a nation, what goals do we have for our education system? As teachers and educators, what are our real purposes, how are these influenced by established educational philosophies and theories, and how should they be guiding our work? As critical stakeholders in the education system you, as a future educator, should reflect on the role that the education system plays in responding to and affecting societal change.

As society has changed in response to world events, scientific innovations, political shifts, and social movements, the philosophies and theories examined in Chapter 6, Philosophical Roots of Education, have held varying degrees of influence on the goals for America's schools and ultimately classroom instruction. Certain eras in American education have been dominated by particular philosophical approaches. As times change, the dominant philosophy or theory often changes, and the impact is felt in classrooms across the country—classrooms like those you are about to enter. As a new teacher, you will be entering schools that are influenced by current social conditions, and you will need to look for a fit between your personal philosophy of education and the educational values of the school district and school in which you teach. Examine your school district's goals as well as those of your school. How do these goals translate into curriculum and teaching methods, and, most importantly, how comfortable are you philosophically with the answers to these questions?

This chapter describes the relationship between the philosophies and theories of education and the purposes that have prevailed at different times in the history of American education. We then examine the important changes in educational goals of recent years that have been promoted by influential policy reports and significant legislative acts. First, however, the chapter shows how we define educational purposes in terms of goals, standards, and objectives.

13-1 ESTABLISHING GOALS AND OBJECTIVES

goals Broad statements of educational purpose.

standards Focused statements on the purposes of education.

objectives Specific statements of educational purpose, usually written for a particular subject, grade, unit, or lesson; commonly defined in behavioral terms so that student experiences and performance can be observed and measured.

When we talk about the purposes of education, we may be referring to purposes at one or more of the following levels: nation, state, school district, school, subject/grade, unit plan, or individual lesson plan. Despite mixed opinions, most educators use the terms **goals**, **standards**, and **objectives** to distinguish among levels of purpose, with goals being the broadest statements of intent, standards being more focused statements, and objectives being more specific guides to daily classroom instruction. These terms describe a direction—what we are seeking to accomplish. Educators often refer to these terms as "ends" or "endpoints" of education.

All endpoints, however, reflect the influences of social forces and prevailing philosophies or theories of education. Social forces and philosophies combine to shape the goals adopted at the national or state level; these goals in turn affect the standards and objectives that guide school districts, schools, and classrooms. Over time, changes in social forces can also lead to modifications in prevailing philosophies and theories. The three main types of influential forces are (1) society in general, (2) developments in knowledge, and (3) beliefs about the nature of the learner.[1]

---

[1]The concept of three sources of change is rooted in the ideas of Boyd Bode and John Dewey, who wrote approximately eighty-five years ago. These ideas, popularized by Ralph Tyler in 1949, have been developed by contemporary curriculum theorists such as Allan Ornstein, J. Galen Saylor, and Robert Zais.

Changes in *society* include shifts in emphasis among the various influences examined in Chapter 10, Culture, Socialization, and Education, and in Chapter 11, Social Class, Race, and School Achievement, such as the family, peer groups, social class, and the economy. Changes in *knowledge* include new developments in science and technology, new methods of processing and storing information, and new methods of defining or organizing fields of study. Finally, changes in beliefs about the nature of the *learner,* such as new discoveries in cognitive science or child development, may also produce changes in educational theories and purposes.

13-1a Goals

Although goals are important guides in education, we cannot directly observe them; rather, they are broad statements of intent that denote a desired and valued competency, a theme or concern that applies to education in general. The most general goals are often called *aims.*

Goals or aims are formulated at national and state levels, often by prestigious commissions or task forces. An example of a goal at the national level that has been influential in directing current educational reform states, "Every student should graduate from high school ready for college or a career."[2] Another national or state goal present throughout our history is to prepare students for democratic citizenship. Although these are admirable goals, it is unclear how local school districts or individual schools might achieve them. They merely suggest a general direction to follow.

Goals at the school district level begin to become more focused. For example, a Maryland school district's goal related to the national goals for citizenship and readiness for postsecondary school life is the following: "Every student will experience high academic achievement and continuous growth by participating in a rigorous instructional program designed to raise the academic bar and close achievement gaps so that every student will become a globally competitive citizen in a culturally diverse world."[3] This goal helps to point teachers, principals, and superintendents toward certain general ends.

Goals at the school level usually narrow in focus even more, translating national, state, and district goals into statements that coincide more closely with the philosophy and priorities of the local school community.[4] School-level goal statements often appear in documents known as *school improvement plans,* which are usually developed by school improvement teams. These goal statements flow from an overall school *mission statement,* which articulates the school's role in educating the community's youth.[5]

In the late 1940s, Ralph Tyler developed an outline for the development and implementation of school goals that remains useful today. Tyler identified four fundamental questions to consider:

1. What educational purposes should the school seek to attain?
2. What educational experiences can be provided to help attain these purposes?
3. How can these educational experiences be effectively organized?
4. How can we determine whether [and to what extent] the purposes have been attained?[6]

---

[2] US Department of Education, *College- and Career-Ready Students,* available at **www2.ed.gov/policy/elsec/leg/blueprint/college-career-ready.pdf** (February 16, 2015).

[3] Baltimore County Public Schools, *Blueprint 2.0: Our Way Forward,* available at **http://bcps.org/blueprint/goalOne.htm** (February 16, 2015).

[4] Allan C. Ornstein and Francis P. Hunkins, *Curriculum: Foundations, Principles, and Issues,* 5th ed. (Boston: Allyn and Bacon, 2008); and Hugh Burkett, *The School Improvement Planning Process* (Washington, DC: The Center for Comprehensive School Reform and Improvement, January 2006).

[5] "School Mission Statements: Where Is Your School Going?" *Education World* (2011), available at **www.educationworld.com/a_admin/admin/admin229.shtml** (February 17, 2015); and Susan Black, "Mission Critical," *American School Board Journal* (July 2011), pp. 34–35.

[6] Ralph W. Tyler, *Basic Principles of Curriculum and Instruction* (Chicago: University of Chicago Press, 1949).

FROM PRESERVICE TO PRACTICE

STANDARDS AND OBJECTIVES

"What did your students learn from the lesson I just observed, Joanne?" Professor Yates asked.

"In this case, Dr. Yates, I would like to have all students learn to appreciate the many different ways that birds adapt to various environments," Joanne replied. "Then I would like them to apply the concept of adaptation to one or more of our local birds. If they can do that, they ought to be able to understand adaptation as an important concept in science."

"I am not sure the students learned what you just described. What came across to me is that birds are found in many sizes, colors, and places. Adaptation didn't seem to be a main point. It would be helpful if you would project your objective for the lesson on the smart-board at the start of the lesson. What skills and attitudes did you want to link with this knowledge?"

"Well," Joanne said. "I want them to learn to observe, to reflect on what they observe, and to appreciate nature's remarkable variety of adaptations, particularly in birds. I can start tomorrow's lesson with a review and ask some pointed questions about today's lesson. That should tell me pretty quickly if the kids didn't understand the concept of adaptation in birds. What do you think of that, Professor Yates?"

Professor Yates nodded. "That might be one strategy to try. I would also like you to talk with your mentor teacher here at the school. Ms. Butler may have ideas to help you. You need to develop specific objectives when preparing a lesson. If you

know what learning you expect from students, it will help guide your lesson. And, you'll be sure the class is following your thought pattern as you teach the lesson if you ask questions as you go along that relate back to the objective. Now I have some more questions for you to consider about your lesson. With which state science standard does this objective align? I would also like to know which literacy standard from the Common Core State Standards science and technical subjects you could incorporate into the lesson."

"Gosh, I didn't even think about that," Joanne said, a little disconcerted. "I thought it was enough to try to prepare the lesson with the specifics on the birds. I guess I need to expand my vision about how all of this ties together. This semester of interning has really been tough for me, but I can see that having a vision of how everything fits together might help me keep on target. I want to rethink my lesson for tomorrow. Can you give me some leads, Professor Yates?"

"I could, but I won't," Dr. Yates replied. "I want you to work with Ms. Butler and think out these things for yourself. Your students' responses will tell you if you are successful or not. Be sure that you know the standards that will structure the organization of your curriculum objectives and the specific lesson objectives. I'll be back to observe another lesson next week. Meanwhile, concentrate on developing specific objectives as you prepare your lessons."

CASE QUESTIONS

1. Why is Professor Yates pushing Joanne to consider specific objectives as well as links to the state standards in science?

2. If Joanne were teaching in your state, what resources could Joanne take advantage of to find the state standards for her teaching area?

3. If schools are particularly concerned with helping students adapt to changing life conditions, how might Joanne expand her lesson beyond biology?

The process of developing goals for a school district or individual school should permit citizens, parents, and students to give meaningful input. Working in partnership with professional educators who understand child development and the learning process, citizens can provide a valuable perspective in helping to decide the emphasis of the public school's direction.[7]

Whether formulated at the national, state, school district, or school level, goals are usually written in nonbehavioral terms as general statements of intent. They are intended to be long-lasting guides. Goals provide a direction by describing what schooling is intended to accomplish, but they are too broad and long term for teachers and students to apply them directly in classroom lessons.

---

[7]"School Boards and Student Achievement: A Comparison of Governance in High- and Low-Achieving Districts," *ERS Spectrum* (Winter 2001), pp. 38–40; and Ronald S. Brant and Ralph W. Tyler, "Goals and Objectives," cited in Allan C. Ornstein, Edward F. Pajak, and Stacey B. Ornstein, *Contemporary Issues in Curriculum*, 5th ed. (Upper Saddle River, NJ: Pearson, 2011).

13-1b Standards

In recent years, standards have been developed as intermediate steps in translating goals or aims into more specific direction for classroom instruction. Standards define what students should know and be able to do as a result of studying academic content at specific points in their schooling. Academic or content standards emphasize the facts, ideas, concepts, and information of the disciplines and the skills needed to apply that knowledge.[8] They are designed to provide a description of the organizational structure of the subject and aid educators in developing curriculum, classroom experiences, and assessments that enable learners to gain a deep understanding of subject matter.[9] Because they have a more narrow focus than goals, standards provide direction for the development of a rigorous curriculum and priorities for what should be taught in individual subjects at each grade level.

Common Core State Standards (CCSS) Standards released by the National Governors Association Center for Best Practices (NGA Center) and the Council of Chief State School Officers (CCSSO) in 2010 to define the knowledge and skills students should know by their graduation from high school.

The most influential set of standards are the **Common Core State Standards (CCSS)**, which were developed by the National Governors Association and the Council of Chief State School Officers in 2010. As of 2015, forty-three states were employing the CCSS as the framework for developing state curriculum in math and English/language arts. "The standards define the knowledge and skills students should gain throughout their K–12 education in order to graduate high school prepared to succeed in entry-level careers, introductory academic college courses, and workforce training programs."[10]

One of the primary motivations for the development of standards can be linked to Tyler's fundamental questions listed earlier in the chapter—standards provide specific (more so than goals or aims) "educational purposes that the school seeks to attain." Because the standards list the content and skills necessary to master each subject, it becomes possible to develop assessments to measure student progress, thus determining "whether the purposes have been attained." This idea of assessment-based accountability, whereby the standards are linked to assessments that measure student and school level of success mastering the content standards, has driven school reform efforts for the past twenty-five years.[11] This effort has recently evolved from each state having its own assessment that measured its individual state standards to the current practice where many states are guided by the CCSS in math and English/language arts and then assessed by a common assessment instrument. Currently, twelve states and the District of Columbia are implementing the assessment known as the Partnership for Assessment of Readiness for College and Career (PARCC), and another seventeen states and one territory utilized the Smarter Balanced assessment system in 2014–2015; both assessments are designed to measure success on mastering the CCSS.[12]

Professional organizations such as the National Council of Teachers of Mathematics and the National Science Teachers Association initially developed content standards beginning in the late 1980s as a result of the reform reports that will be discussed later in the chapter. As a result of subsequent federal statutes, states created standards that guided the development of curriculum within each state.

13-1c Objectives

Objectives are the tools that make goals and standards operational in classroom instruction. Although objectives are more specific than goals and standards, educators

---

[8]US Department of Education, *College and Career Ready Standards* (n.d.), available at **www .ed.gov/k-12reforms/standards** (February 16, 2015).

[9]AFT, "The American Federation of Teachers' Criteria for Setting Academic Standards," *Setting Strong Standards* (Washington, DC: American Federation of Teachers, 2003), available at **www .aft.org/sites/default/files/settingstrongstandards0603.pdf** (February 17, 2015).

[10]"About the Standards," *Common Core State Standards Initiative* (n.d.), available at **www .corestandards.org/about-the-standards/** (February 21, 2015).

[11]Lorrie Shepard, Jane Hannaway, and Eva Baker, eds. *Standards, Assessments, and Accountability— Education Policy White Paper* (Washington, DC: National Academy of Education, 2009).

[12]"PARCC States," *PARCC* (n.d.), available at **www.parcconline.org/parcc-states** (February 21, 2015); and "Member States," *Smarter Balanced Assessment Consortium,* (n.d.), available at **www .smarterbalanced.org/about/member-states/** (February 21, 2015).

OVERVIEW 13.1

GOALS AND OBJECTIVES OF EDUCATION

Ends	Level of Direction	Developed By	Example(s)
National and state goals	Nation, state	Commissions, task force groups, US Department of Education, state departments of education, professional associations of the disciplines	Improving basic literacy skills
Standards	Nation, state	State departments of education, professional associations of the disciplines/educators, nonprofit educational organizations, political organizations	"Construct viable arguments and critique the reasoning of others." (**www.corestandards .org/Math/Practice/**)
Local goals	School district, school	Groups of administrators, teachers, and/or community members; professional associations	Acquiring information and meaning through reading, writing, speaking, and mathematical symbols
General objectives	Subject/grade	Subject-centered professional associations; curriculum departments or committees of state departments of education; large school districts' curriculum specialists	Improving reading comprehension; appreciating the reading of whole books
	Unit plan	Textbook authors; teams of teachers of specific subjects or grade levels, individual teachers	Developing word-recognition skills; listening to stories read
Specific objectives	Lesson plan	Teachers; textbook authors	Identifying the thesis statement in the essay; describing the characteristics of a leader

disagree about how detailed they ought to be. Some prefer fairly general objectives; others advocate objectives precise enough to be measured in behavioral or performance terms—that is, by an observable student behavior.

In practice at the classroom level, you will most likely organize instruction with a combination of general and specific objectives in mind. General objectives are characterized by "end" terms such as to *know, learn, understand, comprehend,* and *appreciate.* Such objectives will help you develop a sequenced curriculum for a grade level or a unit.

At the level of the individual lesson plan, objectives usually become specific, as recommended by Robert Mager. They use precise wording (often action words) such as *describe in writing, state orally, compare, list, identify, evaluate,* and *solve.* Sometimes called *behavioral* or *performance* objectives, these statements are content or skill specific, require particular student behavior or performance, and are observable and measurable.[13] Both teacher and learner can evaluate the amount or degree of learning because the objective establishes the task the students will perform to demonstrate their learning.[14] The From Preservice to Practice box on page 380 gives one example of how teachers and their students can benefit from preparing clear objectives.

---

[13]Robert F. Mager, *Preparing Instructional Objectives,* 3rd ed. (Atlanta, GA: Center for Effective Performance, 1997).

[14]Anne R. Reeves, *Where Great Teaching Begins: Planning for Student Thinking and Learning,* (Alexandria, VA: Association for Supervision and Curriculum Development, 2011).

As a prospective teacher, you have likely been introduced to the curriculum standards for your state. The local school districts and teachers have aligned their curricula, and thus their objectives, with these state standards.[15]

An example of a general unit objective might be that "students will understand why American colonists wanted to separate from Great Britain in the 1770s." Transposing this general objective into a specific lesson objective, we might get the following: "Students will describe in writing three reasons American colonists gave in favor of separation from Great Britain." This objective refers to a specific kind of knowledge, states what is expected of students, and gives a precise criterion of three reasons.

Overview 13.1 summarizes the differences among the various levels of goals, standards, and objectives. As we move from national goals to lesson objectives, the examples become more specific, that is, easier to observe and/or measure.

FOCUS Can you identify state standards for your discipline and the influence these have on your school district's curriculum when you, as a teacher, plan your lesson objectives?

13-2 HISTORICAL PERSPECTIVE

As an educator, you will discover that policy makers and the public at large are continually questioning the purposes of American education. What should our schools be trying to do? The answers are varied, and the debate has often been heated. To understand this debate, we need to know how educational aims have developed and changed over the years. As the following sections illustrate, the goals of American education have undergone many transformations.

Before the twentieth century, the perennialist theory generally dominated American education. Subject matter was organized and presented as an accounting of information. Proponents of the **mental discipline** approach believed that the mind is strengthened through mental activities, just as the body is strengthened by exercising. Traditional subjects, such as languages (Latin, Greek, French, and German), mathematics, history, English, physics, chemistry rhetoric, and logic, were valued for their cultivation of the intellect; the more difficult the subject and the more the student had to exercise the mind, the greater the value of the subject.[16]

mental discipline Strengthening the mind through mental activities, just as the body is strengthened through exercise.

Gradually, demands were made for various changes in schooling to meet the needs of a changing social order. The accelerated pace of immigration and industrial development led a growing number of educators to question the classical curriculum and the emphasis on mental discipline and repetitive drill. Adherents of the new pedagogy represented the progressive voice in education. They emphasized school subjects designed to meet the needs of everyday life for all children in the contemporary world. By the early twentieth century, the effort to reform the schools along more progressive lines was well under way.

In contrast to the perennialist philosophy and mental discipline approach that prevailed before World War I, the period from World War I to post–World War II was dominated by the philosophy of progressivism and the science of child psychology. These philosophies emphasized the **whole-child concept** and life adjustment. The prevailing view held that schools must be concerned with the growth and development of the entire child, not just with certain selected mental aspects. The life-adjustment movement, which expanded its influence in the 1940s, was concerned with addressing the needs of all students, especially the students in the middle, that is, those not in

whole-child concept The view that schools must concern themselves with all aspects of students' growth and development, not merely with cognitive skills or academic learning.

[15]National Center for Educational Evaluation and Regional Assistance, "State Standards and Assessment Systems," in *What States Can Learn about State Standards & Assessment Systems from No Child Left Behind Documents & Interviews* (March 2008), pp. 2–5, available at **http://ies .ed.gov/ncee/edlabs/regions/central/pdf/REL_2008036.pdf**; Matthew Tungate, "Standard Bearers," *Kentucky Teacher* (March 2010), pp. 4–5; and Wangui Njuguna, "Teachers Extol Planning with Standards as Best Practice," *Education Daily* (November 16, 2010), pp. 1–3.

[16]Ellwood P. Cubberley, *Public Education in the United States,* rev. ed. (Boston: Houghton Mifflin, 1947); and Arthur K. Ellis, *Exemplars of Curriculum Theory* (New York: Taylor and Francis, 2004).

TABLE 13.1	Goals of Education: Two Major Statements of the Progressive Approach

Cardinal Principles of Secondary Education (1918)

1. *Health:* provide health instruction and a program of physical activities; cooperate with home and community in promoting health.

2. *Command of fundamental processes:* develop fundamental thought processes to meet needs of modern life.

3. *Worthy home membership:* develop qualities that make the individual a worthy member of a family.

4. *Vocation:* equip students to earn a living, to serve society well through a vocation, and to achieve personal development through that vocation.

5. *Civic education:* foster qualities that help a person play a part in the community and understand international problems.

6. *Worthy use of leisure:* equip people to find "recreation of body, mind, and spirit" that will enrich their personalities.

7. *Ethical character:* develop ethical *character* both through instructional methods and through social contacts among students and teachers.

Ten Imperative Needs of Youth (1944)

Develop skills and/or attitudes that enhance the following:

1. Productive work experiences and occupational success

2. Good health and physical fitness

3. Rights and duties of a democratic citizenry

4. Conditions for successful family life

5. Wise consumer behavior

6. Understanding of science and the nature of man

7. Appreciation of arts, music, and literature

8. Wise use of leisure time

9. Respect for ethical values

10. The ability to think rationally and communicate thoughts clearly

Source: Commission on the Reorganization of Secondary Education, *Cardinal Principles of Secondary Education,* Bulletin No. 35 (Washington, DC: US Government Printing Office, 1918), pp. 11–15; and Educational Policies Commission, *Education for All American Youth* (Washington, DC: National Education Association, 1944).

the college track or the vocational track.[17] Goals related to cognitive or mental growth had to share the stage with other important purposes of education involving areas of social living such as hygiene, family living, driver's education, and social relations with peers. The goal was to present students with a meaningful and relevant curriculum.[18] Table 13.1 describes the two most important statements of goals of this era. The whole-child concept and the corresponding growth of child psychology had a tremendous impact on schools that we still feel today (Photo 13.1).

During the era of the Cold War and the Soviet *Sputnik* flight (1957), international events gave major impetus to challenge the life-adjustment curriculum and to reexamine academic disciplines as the focus of schooling. The country was appalled at the notion of losing technological superiority to the Soviets; national pride was challenged, and national goals were perceived as threatened.

---

[17]"Challenge to Schools—Factors Involved in Curriculum Changes," *Congressional Digest* 37, (August 1958), pp. 199–224; and Sister Mary Janet, "Life Adjustment Opens New Doors to Youth," *Educational Leadership* (December 1954), pp. 137–141.

[18]Robert V. Bullough and Craig Kridel, "Adolescent Needs, Curriculum and the Eight-Year Study," *Journal of Curriculum Studies* (March 2003), pp. 151–169; and Thomas D. Fallace, "The Effects of Life Adjustment Education on the US History Curriculum, 1948–1957," *History Teacher* (August 2011), pp. 569–589.

> **PHOTO 13.1** Educational approaches influenced by progressive philosophies emphasize focusing on educating the "whole child," rather than strictly on imparting academic content. Which approach is closer to your personal philosophy of education?

Steve Debenport /iStockphoto.com

Influenced by the perennialist and essentialist theories of education, critics called for a return to academic essentials, intellectual rigor, and mental discipline. Thus, hard on the heels of *Sputnik* came national legislation to support training and programs in fields considered vital to defense. The National Defense Education Act of 1958 targeted science, mathematics, modern languages, and guidance (often considered a way to steer youth into the three former fields and into college). The scientific community, university scholars, and curriculum specialists were called upon to reconstruct subject-matter content, especially on the high school level, while government and philanthropic foundations provided the funds.[19] The new educational climate also included an increasing emphasis on providing enriched educational opportunities for the academically talented child.

The 1960s saw a shift in focus as increased concern about poverty, racial discrimination, and civil rights brought new educational priorities, often related to the progressive and social reconstructionist theories of education. Educators noted that most students did not go on to college and that many failed to graduate or graduated as functional illiterates. Under those circumstances, serious problems could be anticipated if educational goals continued to be narrowly directed toward the most able students, thus equal educational opportunity became a goal of newly expanding federal education programs that were embodied in the Elementary and Secondary Education Act of 1965.[20]

The focus on students who were then characterized as "disadvantaged" extended into the 1980s and expanded to include limited English proficient (LEP) students and students with disabilities. The nation's expanding multicultural and bilingual efforts were characterized by increased federal funding for Hispanic, Asian American, and Native American students, and by legal support for students with limited English skills (*Lau v. Nichols,* US Supreme Court, 1974).[21]

---

[19]Kathleen Anderson Steeves, Philip Evan Bernhardt, James P. Burns, and Michele K. Lombard. "Transforming American Educational Identity after Sputnik," *American Educational History Journal* (Spring 2009), pp. 71–87; and Erwin V. Johanningmeier, "A Nation at Risk and Sputnik: Compared and Reconsidered," *American Educational History Journal* (2010), pp. 347–365.

[20]John W. Gardner, *Excellence: Can We Be Equal and Excellent Too?* (New York: Harper and Row, 1961), pp. 28–29, 77; and Virginia R. L. Plunkett, "From Title I to Chapter 1: The Evolution of Compensatory Education," *Phi Delta Kappan* (April 1985), pp. 533–537.

[21]Maria E. Brisk, *Bilingual Education: From Compensatory to Quality Schooling* (Mahwah, NJ: Lawrence Earlbaum, 2005); and "ELLs and the Law: Statutes, Precedents," *Education Week* (January 8, 2009), pp. 8–9.

From the 1970s through the 1990s, much concern also surfaced for special education, especially for students with learning disabilities or other special needs. Two landmark pieces of legislation, the Education for All Handicapped Children Act (PL 94-142, 1975) and the Individuals with Disabilities Education Act (IDEA, 1990), detailed policies and procedures for including students with disabilities in regular classrooms, to the extent possible.[22] This approach came to be known as "inclusion" (see Chapter 12, Providing Equal Educational Opportunity, for more on this topic).

In the 1990s, however, conservative reactions against these trends continued to surface. As noted in Chapter 11, Social Class, Race, and School Achievement, multicultural and bilingual programs were heavily criticized as contributing to fragmentation and separatism rather than cultural unity. Several states approved statutes signifying English as the official state language, leading some to attack funding of bilingual programs. Educators also split into factions over the most effective way to conduct special education. Some wanted full inclusion (elimination of self-contained classrooms for special-education students and assignment of special-education teachers to co-teach regular classrooms). Others supported partial inclusion (whereby students with learning disabilities are placed in general-education classrooms as much as possible). Still others favored maintaining mostly separate, or self-contained, classes for special-education students.[23]

The end of the twentieth century also brought increased demands for educational accountability (demands expressed by elected officials and business leaders as well as by laypeople). Many argued that education should focus more clearly on *outcomes* or outputs—that is, measurable academic results—rather than on inputs such as money, programs, efforts, and intentions. According to some of these critics, a high school diploma means little if students cannot use their education in real-life contexts. As a result of this focus, a majority of states developed an **outcomes-based education (OBE)** approach to curriculum development. Although many educators believed the focus on student outcomes was a sensible way to look at educational goals, OBE was not without its critics. Some feared that it emphasized affective outcomes (that is, values) and critical-thinking processes to the detriment of religious faith and family values. Others claimed that OBE promoted vague, minimal academic standards, dumbing down the curriculum because of the focus on process rather than content. Still other critics claimed that OBE involved higher costs without corresponding results.[24]

While some educators focused on student performance outcomes, the first decade of the twenty-first century found other educators and policy makers calling for clear **state standards** focusing on content to which all students would be taught. Advocates for state standards wanted to assess student proficiency. As part of the federal 2001 **No Child Left Behind Act (NCLB),** each state was required to establish its own standards in school subjects and then assess progress to hold students, teachers, schools, and school districts accountable for learning by every student. Schools where students were not successful in reaching proficiency levels on the yearly assessments were said to not meet adequate yearly progress (AYP) and faced sanctions.[25]

Many educators expressed concern that the assessments were linked to such high-stakes outcomes that they became intimidating for those taking the tests. Another critique was that each state developed its own tests and set its own

outcomes-based education (OBE) Education guided by the principle that success should be judged by student "outcomes" (generally seen in terms of abilities to function in real-life contexts) rather than by "inputs" such as programs, courses, or funding. Many proponents would revise traditional curricula that fail to produce desired outcomes.

state standards Performance indicators showing students have achieved academic mastery at levels set by state boards of education.

No Child Left Behind Act (NCLB) The federal Elementary and Secondary Education Act passed in 2001, which requires states and school districts that receive federal funding to show adequate yearly progress, as measured by standardized tests of students in grades 3–8, and to provide all students with "highly qualified" teachers.

---

[22]"Special Education Milestones," *Congressional Digest* 84 (January 2005), p. 9.

[23]Devery R. Mock and James M. Kauffman, "Preparing Teachers for Full Inclusion: Is It Possible?" *Teacher Educator* (Winter 2002), pp. 202–215; Myrna Mandlawitz, *What Every Teacher Should Know about IDEA 2004 Laws and Regulations* (Boston: Allyn and Bacon, 2007); and Patricia Gándara, "The Impact of English-Only Instructional Policies on English Learners," *Colorín Colorado* (2012), available at **www.colorincolorado.org/article/50832/** (February 16, 2015).

[24]Bill Zlatos, "Outcomes-Based Outrage Runs Both Ways," *Education Digest* (January 1994), pp. 26–27; and Bruno V. Manno, "Outcome-Based Education," *Current* (July 1995), p. 3.

[25]PBS, "The New Rules," *Frontline* (March 2002), available at **www.pbs.org/wgbh/pages/frontline/shows/schools/nochild/nclb.html**.

TECHNOLOGY @ SCHOOL

Teachers, both new and experienced, must be well informed about national, state, and local educational goals and how these goals will affect their work in the classroom. For state curriculum standards, you can visit your state department of education website. A number of sites provide access to the appropriate pages of the various departments of education, but two are especially helpful. The first is the "National Standards" page at the Education World website. In addition to access to the state standards by subject, it also provides easy accessibility to each state's entire set of standards and to links for the CCSS in English/language arts and mathematics. Also provided are links to the voluntary National Education Standards for most subject areas; these were developed by the respective professional organizations of each discipline and preceded the development of the state standards.

A second site that provides access to the curriculum standards of each of the fifty states is the Pattern-Based Writing website. Provided are links to each state's content standards page and their "Common Core State Standards" page. As an aspiring teacher, you can examine these two resources to get an idea of what states across the nation have developed as standards to guide the K–12 curriculum. What similarities might be found among a random sample of state standards in the same subject area? What impact would these findings have for schools in the United States?

You can follow news about the Common Core State Standards implementation in states across the nation and examine various resources with information about the standards at the Common Core State Standards Initiative website.

"cut-scores" to determine proficiency; thus there was no reliable way to determine how the nation as a whole was progressing in meeting standards. Even so, in many states, test results helped support decisions about promotion, graduation, and school curriculum, and they were related to a range of consequences for the school districts and professionals preparing students for those exams, including school sanctions, pay raises, and bonuses.[26]

In spite of the critics, NCLB advocates maintained that standards were worth sustaining. They claimed that for the first time in the history of American public education, rigorous goals were established for all children, and schools were paying more attention to the achievement gap and learning needs of children who had historically been left behind.[27]

As mentioned in the previous section, one of the major criticisms of the NCLB accountability measures targeted the fragmented system that exists because each state has its own set of standards and corresponding assessments. In an effort to reform this situation, in 2010, the National Governors Association Center for Best Practices (NGA Center) and the Council of Chief State School Officers (CCSSO) released the Common Core State Standards (CCSS) in English/language arts and mathematics for grades K–12.[28] Developing the CCSS has been a voluntary, state-led effort, and by the beginning of 2015, forty-three states and the District of Columbia had formally adopted them for use. These standards are intended to define the knowledge and skills students should gain during their climb of the educational ladder so that by the time they graduate high school, they will be able to succeed in academic college courses and in future career training programs.[29]

---

[26]James W. Popham, "Content Standards: The Unindicted Co-Conspirator," *Educational Leadership* (September 2006), pp. 87–88; and Sandra Myers, "High-Stakes Testing," *Research Starters* (Toledo, OH: Great Neck Publishing, 2008).

[27]Paul Parkison, "Political Economy and the NCLB Regime: Accountability, Standards, and High-Stakes Testing," *Educational Forum* (Winter 2009), pp. 44–57; and Mark Groen, "NCLB—The Educational Accountability Paradigm in Historical Perspective," *American Educational History Journal* (March 2012), pp. 1–14.

[28]David T. Conley, Kathryn V. Drummond, Alicia de Gonzalez, Jennifer Rooseboom, and Odile Stout, *Reaching the Goal: The Applicability and Importance of the Common Core State Standards to College and Career Readiness* (Eugene, OR: Educational Policy Improvement Center, 2011).

[29]"About the Standards," *Common Core Standards Initiative* (n.d.), available at **www.corestandards.org/about-the-standards** (February 17, 2015); and "In the States," *Common Core Standards Initiative* (n.d.), available at **www.corestandards.org/standards-in-your-state/** (February 17, 2015).

FOCUS Over the decades, educational goals have targeted different groups of students, such as the academically talented or special-needs students. Which group of students now appears to be the target of most educational goals?

Those promoting a common set of standards for schools across the country that are internationally benchmarked with other top-performing countries on international assessments contend that this will make education in America more competitive in the global economy. They say more rigorous standards that require deeper understanding and better alignment of content and skills have to be an improvement over the diverse system of standards and assessments that existed under NCLB.[30]

The CCSS are intended to ensure consistency in the quality of education from state to state and school to school. Some educators are concerned, however, that the standards will simply encourage the development of a college-preparatory curriculum for all students, and the common assessments that are being implemented to accompany the standards will be especially costly to implement.[31]

13-3 THE CALL FOR EXCELLENCE

Keeping in mind how American educational goals have changed over time, we can look back over the past thirty-five years at the recent history of the demand for reform in the schools. How have the various proposals from the past decades reflected important changes in American educational purposes that we see in education policy today? How well do particular reforms fit your own ideas about the purpose of education?

13-3a Overview of Policy Reports

In the early 1980s, national attention was focused on the need for educational excellence and higher academic standards for all students—particularly the neglected average student—and not just the needy or the talented. Subsequent national policy reports, most of which reflected a so-called neoessentialist perspective, urged reforms to improve the quality of education in the United States. Six of the most influential were as follows:

● *Action for Excellence* (1983)
● *Educating Americans for the 21st Century* (1983)
● *High School* (1983)
● *A Nation at Risk* (1983)
● *First Lessons: A Report on Elementary Education in America* (1986)
● *The National Education Goals* (1990, 1994, 1997)

To support their proposals, the reports presented discouraging details and statistics indicating a serious decline in American education. For example:

1. Average achievement scores on the Scholastic Aptitude Test (SAT) declined steadily from 1963 to 1980. Average verbal scores fell more than 50 points, and mathematics scores dropped almost 40 points.[32]
2. *Educating Americans for the 21st Century* bemoaned the low level of student participation in math and science courses, which had been on the decline for twenty years. The need for improved professional development for math and science teachers was also noted.[33]

---

[30]"Myths vs. Facts," *Common Core Standards Initiative, available* at **www.corestandards.org /about-the-standards/myths-vs-facts/** (February 17, 2015); and Matthew Tungate, "Standard Bearers," *Kentucky Teacher* (March 2010), pp. 4–5.

[31]"Are You Ready to Implement Common Core Standards," *District Administration* (March 2011), p. 16; and Daniel Orlich, "Educational Standards—Caveat Emptor," *Kappa Delta Pi Record* (Winter 2011), pp. 52–57; and Anne Whitney and Patrick Shannon, "Metaphors, Frames, and Fact (Checks) about the Common Core," *English Journal* (November 2014), pp. 61–71.

[32]National Commission on Excellence in Education, *A Nation at Risk: The Imperative for Educational Reform* (Washington, DC: US Department of Education, 1983).

[33]Katherine K. Merseth, "From the Rhetoric of Reports to the Clarity of Classrooms," *Educational Leadership* (December 1983), pp. 38–42.

> **PHOTO 13.2** Recent shifts in educational goals have brought a new emphasis on assessment and accountability for students, teachers, and schools, including the use of controversial "high-stakes" testing used to make decisions about outcomes such as graduation and promotion.

Bill Freeman/Alamy Limited

3. As the nation looked toward 2000, US 15-year-olds still performed below their peers in twenty (math) and fifteen (science) other industrialized nations (out of a total of twenty-eight countries)—hardly the performance at "world-class standards" called for in the *National Education Goals*.[34] (See Chapter 15, International Education, for further discussion of international comparisons.)

4. According to *A Nation at Risk*, "Some 23 million American adults are [in 1983] functionally illiterate by the simplest test of everyday reading, writing, and comprehension."[35]

5. It was reported that many 17-year-olds did not possess the critical-thinking skills that should be expected of them, nearly 40 percent could not draw inferences from written material, and only 20 percent could write a persuasive essay. Forty percent of 17-year-olds lacked the intermediate reading skills they needed to be successful in lessons at the seventh- or eighth-grade levels.[36]

The reports emphasized the need to strengthen the curriculum in the core subjects of English, math, science, foreign language, and social studies. Technology and computer courses were mentioned often, and at the beginning of the twenty-first century, the need to improve students' technology skills and to upgrade schools technologically was almost a mantra. High-level cognitive and thinking skills were also stressed.

The reports further emphasized rigorous standards and tougher courses, and a majority proposed that colleges raise their admission requirements. Most of the reports also proposed increasing homework, time for learning, and time in school, as well as instituting more demanding grading, testing, homework, and discipline (Photo 13.2). They mentioned upgrading teacher certification, increasing teacher salaries, increasing the number of science and math teachers and paying them higher salaries, and providing merit pay for outstanding teachers. Overall, the reports stressed academic achievement, not the whole child, and increased productivity, not relevancy or humanism.

---

[34]Mariann Lemke and Patrick Gonzales, "Special Analysis: US Student and Adult Performance on International Assessments of Educational Achievement," *The Condition of Education—2006* (Washington, DC: National Center for Education Statistics, 2006).

[35]National Commission on Excellence in Education, *A Nation at Risk: The Imperative for Educational Reform* (Washington, DC: US Department of Education, 1983).

[36]Ibid.; and William J. Bennett, *First Lessons: A Report on Elementary Education in America*, (Washington, DC: US Department of Education, 1986).

Most of the reports expressed a popular concern that the schools are pressed to play too many social roles; that the schools cannot meet all these expectations; and that the schools are in danger of losing sight of their key purpose—teaching academic skills and core subjects, new skills for computer use, and higher-level cognitive skills for the world of work and technology. Many of the reports, concerned not only with academic productivity but also with national productivity, linked human capital with economic capital. Investment in schools would be an investment in the economy and in the nation's future stability. If education failed, so would our workforce and the nation in the global marketplace. Hence business, labor, and government pledged to work with educators to help educate and train the US population.[37]

In the following sections, we will look more closely at the two most popularized and influential reports: *A Nation at Risk*, published in 1983, and *The National Education Goals*, a 1994 revision of a report first published in 1990. Note the connections these works have with the reform efforts of today.

A Nation at Risk A landmark national report critical of public education in the United States that resulted in raising high school graduation requirements in most states.

National Education Goals, The A 1990 National Governors' Conference report on education in America that delineated six educational guidelines for state and local education agencies; revised in 1994.

A Nation at Risk

The report by the National Commission on Excellence in Education, compiled by a panel appointed by the US Department of Education, indicated that a "rising tide of mediocrity" was eroding the well-being of the nation.[38] This mediocrity was linked to the foundations of our educational institutions and was spilling over into the workplace and other sectors of society. The report listed several aspects of educational decline that were evident to educators and citizens alike in the late 1970s and early 1980s: lower achievement scores, lower testing requirements, lower graduation requirements, lower teacher expectations, fewer academic courses, more remedial courses, too many electives, and higher illiteracy rates. It stated that the United States compromised its commitment to educational quality as a result of conflicting demands placed on the nation's schools and concluded that the schools attempted to tackle too many social problems that the home and other agencies of society either would not or could not resolve.

The report initiated the call for tougher standards for graduation, including more courses in science, mathematics, foreign language, and the "new basics" such as computer skills. It also argued for a longer school day and school year; far more homework; improved and updated textbooks; more rigorous, measurable, and higher expectations for student achievement; higher teacher salaries based on performance and career ladders that distinguish among the beginning, experienced, and master teacher; demonstrated entry competencies and more rigorous certification standards for teachers; accountability from educators and policy makers; and greater fiscal support from citizens.[39]

Reports such as *A Nation at Risk* often spring from a broad-based concern about the quality of public education in changing times. The goal of such reports is to make what are perceived as practical recommendations for educational improvement and, as such, provide guidance to state and local boards of education, school districts, and ultimately teachers as they plan for instruction. The changes that took place during the 1980s and 1990s—increases in high school graduation requirements, increases in required mathematics and science courses, a return to academic basics, more emphasis on technology, and increased college entrance requirements—have been attributed to the recommendations made in *A Nation at Risk*.[40] It has also been suggested that the

---

[37]G. T. Sewall, "Against Anomie and Amnesia: What Basic Education Means in the Eighties," *Phi Delta Kappan* (May 1982), pp. 603–606; and Erwin V. Johanningmeier, "A Nation at Risk and Sputnik: Compared and Reconsidered," *American Educational History Journal* (2010), pp. 347–365.

[38]National Commission on Excellence in Education, *A Nation at Risk: The Imperative for Educational Reform* (Washington, DC: US Department of Education, 1983); Gerald W. Bracey, "April Foolishness: The 20th Anniversary of *A Nation at Risk*," *Phi Delta Kappan* (April 2003), pp. 16–21; and Jennifer Borek, "A Nation at Risk at 25," *Phi Delta Kappan* (April 2008), pp. 572–574.

[39]Thomas A. Kessinger, "Efforts toward National Educational Reform: An Essentialist Political Agenda," *Mid-Western Educational Researcher* (Spring 2007), pp. 16–23.

[40]James W. Guthrie and Matthew G. Springer, "A Nation at Risk Revisited: Did 'Wrong' Reasoning Result in 'Right' Results? At What Cost?" *Peabody Journal of Education* (January 2004), pp. 7–35.

TAKING ISSUE

Read the brief introduction below, as well as the Question and the pros and cons list that follows. Then, answer the question using *your* own words and position.

COMMON CORE STATE STANDARDS

The FAQ section of the CCSS website answers the question, "What do the Common Core State Standards mean for students?" as follows:

> "Today's students are preparing to enter a world in which colleges and businesses are demanding more than ever before. To ensure all students are prepared for success after graduation, the Common Core establishes a set of clear, consistent guidelines for what students should know and be able to do at each grade level in math and English language arts."

Question

Are the CCSS improving American education? (Think about this question as you read the PRO and CON arguments listed here. What is *your* take on this issue?)

Arguments PRO

1. A common set of standards will benefit a highly mobile society where children move from state to state. Students will be more likely to experience the same curriculum regardless of their state of residence under the common standards.

2. If students from the United States are to compete with their peers from around the world on international assessments, only common standards that are internationally benchmarked will transform our education system to be competitive.

3. It is less expensive and more efficient to develop assessments that measure performance on the common standards than it has been to assess the fifty separate sets of assessments (that tend to be weak and disjointed) developed under NCLB mandates.

4. With common standards in place, it is more economical to align digital media and textbooks to address the standards and thus support instruction.

Arguments CON

1. A common set of standards for the United States cannot address the educational needs of students in the fifty individual states that have such diverse economic, demographic, political, and social characteristics.

2. Not all countries that do well on international assessments operate under one set of common standards; more comprehensive educational reforms must be considered if we are to become competitive on the global stage.

3. The federal government has become too involved in the direction of the standards-driven reform and is co-opting the idea of state and local control of schooling by overstepping its legal authority.

4. Although much effort and collaboration has gone into developing the common standards in English/language arts and math, no evidence supports the claim that these efforts will improve the quality of education in the United States.

Question Reprise: What Is Your Stand? Reflect again on the following question by explaining *your* stand about this issue:
Are the CCSS likely to improve American education?

"standards movement" that has resulted in the Common Core State Standards was sparked by the report's criticism of low expectations for student performance.[41]

Goals 2000: Educate America Act
The 1994 revision of the *National Educational Goals* that added two additional goals and updated states' progress on the *National Educational Goals* while providing additional services, programs, and classes as needed.

The National Education Goals In 1994, Congress passed the **Goals 2000: Educate America Act**. The complete set of goals, published as *The National Education Goals* and often referred to simply as Goals 2000, is listed in Table 13.2. The overriding theme

---

[41]Sally Blake, "A Nation at Risk and the Blind Men," *Phi Delta Kappan* (April 2008), pp. 601–602; and Mark Lavenia, Lora Cohen-Vogel, and Laura B. Lang, "The Common Core State Standards Initiative: An Event History Analysis of State Adoption," *American Journal of Education* (February 2015), pp. 145–182.

TABLE 13.2	The National Education Goals

Goal 1 School Readiness
By the year 2000, all children in America will start school ready to learn.

Goal 2 School Completion
By the year 2000, the high school graduation rate will increase to at least 90 percent.

Goal 3 Student Achievement and Citizenship
By the year 2000, all students will leave grades 4, 8, and 12 having demonstrated competency over challenging subject matter, including English, mathematics, science, foreign languages, civics and government, economics, arts, history, and geography, and every school in America will ensure that all students learn to use their minds well, so they may be prepared for responsible citizenship, further learning, and productive employment in our nation's modern economy.

Goal 4 Teacher Education and Professional Development
By the year 2000, the nation's teaching force will have access to programs for the continued improvement of their professional skills and the opportunity to acquire the knowledge and skills needed to instruct and prepare all American students for the next century.

Goal 5 Mathematics and Science
By the year 2000, US students will be first in the world in mathematics and science achievement.

Goal 6 Adult Literacy and Lifelong Learning
By the year 2000, every adult American will be literate and will possess the knowledge and skills necessary to compete in a global economy and exercise the rights and responsibilities of citizenship.

Goal 7 Safe, Disciplined, and Alcohol- and Drug-Free Schools
By the year 2000, every school in the United States will be free of drugs, violence, and the unauthorized presence of firearms and alcohol and will offer a disciplined environment conducive to learning.

Goal 8 Parental Participation
By the year 2000, every school will promote partnerships that will increase parental involvement and participation in promoting the social, emotional, and academic growth of children.

Source: Goals 2000: Educate America Act (March 31, 1994); *The National Education Goals* (Washington, DC: US Department of Education, 1994).

of those goals was the push for an educated citizenry, well trained and responsible, capable of adapting to a changing world, knowledgeable about its cultural heritage and the world community, and willing to accept and maintain America's leadership position in the twenty-first century. The Goals Panel stated that educators must be given greater flexibility to devise teaching and learning strategies that serve all students, regardless of abilities or interests; at the same time, they should be held responsible for their teaching. Parents must become involved in their children's education, especially during the preschool years. Community, civic, and business groups all have a vital role to play in reforming education. Finally, students must accept responsibility for their education, and this means they must work hard in school.[42]

In 2001, the National Education Goals Panel made its final major report on the progress on the eight goals and twenty-six indicators in Goals 2000. Although the

---

[42]*HR 1804—Goals 2000: Educate America Act* (January 24, 1994), available at **www2.ed.gov /legislation/GOALS2000/TheAct/index.html** (February 17, 2015).

nation as a whole did not meet the national goals by the year 2000, many states were said to make progress, especially in improving opportunities in early childhood education and in the use of student data in instructional decision making. It has been noted that the work of the Goals Panel led to forty-nine states developing their own content standards by 2000; again, this has been seen as another step in the march to establish the standards that exist across the country today.[43] With the suspension of the National Educational Goals Panel in 2002 and the advent of NCLB, America's educational expectations changed to a more specific focus on improved student performance in reading and math, having highly qualified teachers in every classroom, and identifying and improving schools where students were not meeting these standards.

FOCUS The national reports of the 1980s emphasized core curriculum subjects, tougher standards, and accountability. Which of these do you believe has most affected your career as a student? Which will be of most importance to you as a teacher?

13-3b Swings of the Pendulum

In examining educational goals from the turn of the twentieth century until today, we see considerable change but also old ideas reemerging in updated versions. For example, a stress on rigorous intellectual training, evident in the early twentieth century, reappeared in the 1950s during the Cold War, and again from the 1980s through the early twenty-first century, as a result of concern over economic competition with foreign countries. Similarly, as the social ferment of the 1960s and 1970s brought increasing concern for the rights and aspirations of low-income and minority groups, the ideas of the early progressive educators resurfaced, and a renewed stress was placed on educating the disenfranchised. In an era that has stressed accountability, assessment, and core standards, can you decide where the pendulum is swinging at this point in time?

In looking at the broad sweep of American educational purposes, you might ask yourself whether schools are expected to do more than is feasible. The schools are often seen as ideal agencies to solve the nation's problems, but can they do so? Many people throughout society refuse to admit their own responsibility for helping children develop and learn. Similarly, parents and policy makers often expect teachers and school administrators to be solely responsible for school reform. In fact, without significant cooperation from parents and community members, schools are likely to struggle, and reform efforts are likely to be frustrated.

Unquestionably, the goals of education must be relevant to the times. If the schools cannot adapt to changing conditions and social forces, how can they expect to produce people who do? Today, we live in a highly technical and bureaucratic society, and we are faced with pressing social and economic problems—aging cities, deteriorating schools and educational infrastructures, the effects of centuries of discrimination, an aging population, economic dislocations, terrorism, and the pollution of the physical environment. Whether we allow the times to engulf us, or whether we can cope with our persistent problems will depend to a large extent on what kinds of skills are taught to our present-day students—and on the development of appropriate priorities for education.[44]

FOCUS What is your primary goal as a teacher? Ask this same question of several other educators and prospective educators. Compare and contrast your answer with theirs.

---

[43]*National Education Goals Panel—Building on the Momentum (1999)*, *available* at **http://govinfo .library.unt.edu/negp/reports/essays.pdf** (February 17, 2015); David J. Hoff, "Mission Imponderable: Goals Panel to Disband," *Education Week* (January 9, 2002), p. 21; and Jack Campbell, "Goals 2000: A Modest Proposal for Reform," *Research for Educational Reform* (June 2003), pp. 40–45.

[44]Charles Nevi, "Saving Standards," *Phi Delta Kappan* (February 2001), pp. 460–461.

SUMMING UP

1. The purposes of education are influenced by changing social forces as well as by educational philosophies and theories.

2. Broad statements of educational purpose, generated at the national or state level, are usually translated into more specific goals by the school district or individual school. These goals, in turn, are developed into standards and even more specific objectives at the subject, grade, unit plan, and lesson plan levels.

3. Since the turn of the past century, the goals of American education have gone through numerous shifts in emphasis: academic rigor and mental discipline; the whole child; academically talented students, students in poverty, minority students, and children with disabilities; tougher academic

requirements for all students; and holding schools accountable for all students meeting standards.

4. Most of the major reports released since 1983 have emphasized the need for educational excellence and higher standards. Although educators disagree about many of the recommendations, most states implemented changes based on these reports.

5. We must learn to live with some disagreement about the purposes of schooling. Various groups of people need to work together in formulating future educational priorities.

6. We often expect schools to be a key instrument for solving our technological or social problems and preparing our workforce for the future. The years ahead will severely test these expectations.

SUGGESTED RESOURCES

INTERNET RESOURCES

As explained in this chapter, *A Nation at Risk* was a seminal report that influenced school reform throughout the close of the twentieth century. Take some time to analyze the actual report that is archived at the Department of Education website. Closely examine its analysis of schools in the 1980s and its recommendations for remedying the shortcomings. As you look at schools from your personal experiences, how have they changed based on what is portrayed in the report?

Examine the websites of contemporary reform-minded groups. Based on your review of their websites, create a list of goals that these groups have for schools in the second decade of the twenty-first century. Some of the websites to review include Achieve, created by the nation's governors and corporate leaders as an independent, bipartisan, nonprofit education reform organization; The Education Trust, established by the American Association for Higher Education to encourage colleges and universities to support K–12 reform efforts; and The Alliance for Excellent Education, which promotes high school transformation to facilitate that every child graduates prepared for postsecondary education and success in life.

PUBLICATIONS

Conant, James B. *The American High School Today*. New York: McGraw-Hill, 1959. *A classic written during the Sputnik era, this book offers many recommendations for upgrading the high school curriculum.*

Darling-Hammond, Linda. *The Flat World and Education: How America's Commitment to Equity Will Determine Our Future.* New York: Teachers College Press, 2010. *Offers remedies for what schools must do to respond to the learning needs of the twenty-first century.*

Gardner, John W. *Excellence: Can We Be Equal and Excellent Too?* New York: Harper and Row, 1961. *Another classic text, this book remains relevant today. The questions and issues it raises are still of deep concern in American schools and society.*

Goodlad, John I., Roger Soder, and Bonnie McDaniel, eds. *Education and the Making of a Democratic People*. Boulder, CO: Paradigm Publishers, 2008. *Claims we must refocus on the ultimate mission of public schooling—education for democratic citizenship.*

National Commission on Excellence in Education. *A Nation at Risk: The Imperative for Educational Reform*. Washington, DC: US Department of Education, 1983. *Among reports on American education, this one had the most significant impact.*

Spring, Joel. *American Education*. 16th ed. Columbus, OH: McGraw-Hill, 2013. *A concise look at the purposes of public schooling and current issues that shape education.*

Spring, Joel. *Political Agendas for Education: From Race to the Top to Saving the Planet*. New York: Routledge, 2014. *Examines the political influences that shape education policy and goals in contemporary times and how this influences the public schools.*

Tufte, John Elling. *The Wrong Emphasis: Kids Learn What Adults Teach*. Lanham, MD: Rowman & Littlefield Publishers, 2014. *An examination of the current status of American public education and the various influences aimed at improving test scores.*

CURRICULUM AND INSTRUCTION

LEARNING OBJECTIVES

14-1 Identify where subject-centered and student-centered curricula can be found in today's schools.

14-2 Examine issues that influence the development of curriculum.

14-3 Describe how the use of direct instruction, social and emotional learning, differentiated instruction, and technology influence your work as a teacher.

14-4 Identify trends that are likely to affect curriculum and instruction in the immediate future.

Kablonk! RF/Golden Pixels LLC/Alamy

This chapter was revised by Dr. David Vocke,
Towson University.

THROUGHOUT THE CHAPTERS of this textbook, it is clear that Americans demand the utmost from their schools. We ask the schools to teach children to think, to socialize them, to alleviate poverty and inequality, to reduce crime, to perpetuate our cultural heritage, and to produce intelligent, democratic citizens in a complex global society. Inevitably, American schools struggle to meet these obligations. Nonetheless, the demands persist, and the resulting impact ultimately focuses on the *curriculum*—the planned experiences provided through instruction—which is continuously modified as education goals are revised, new innovations are developed, social issues are debated, and new interest groups emerge.

In Chapter 13, The Changing Purposes of American Education, we described how the goals of education often shift with changing national priorities and social pressures. In this chapter, we will look at several major curricular approaches used in recent decades to help meet our changing national goals. You will see that the curriculum approaches also relate closely to the philosophies and theories discussed in Chapter 6, Philosophical Roots of Education.[1] Reflect on how these curricular approaches relate to your own emerging philosophy of education.

As we examine various topics related to curriculum, we will also examine recent instructional approaches and curricular trends that relate to it.

14-1 CURRICULUM ORGANIZATION

curriculum Planned experiences provided via instruction through which the school meets its goals and objectives.

We can view the various types of curriculum organization in American schools from two perspectives. One emphasizes the subject to be taught; the other perspective emphasizes the student. The first perspective views **curriculum** as a body of content, or subject matter, that leads to certain achievement outcomes or products. The second defines curriculum in terms of student needs and interests; it is most concerned with process—in other words, how the student develops her ability to acquire knowledge. Few schools employ pure subject-centered or pure student-centered approaches in the development of school curriculum and the teaching–learning process. You will find that even though most teachers tend to emphasize one approach over the other, they incorporate both choices in their professional decision making about what goes on in the classroom.

14-1a Subject-Centered Curricula

Subject matter is both the oldest and most commonly practiced framework of curriculum organization. It is a deeply ingrained approach primarily because it is convenient, as you can tell from the departmental structure of secondary schools and colleges. Even in elementary schools, where self-contained classrooms force the teachers to be generalists, curricula are usually organized by the various subjects or academic disciplines.

subject-centered curricula Curricula defined in terms of bodies of content or subject matter. Achievement is judged according to defined outcomes such as test scores, correct answers, or appropriate responses.

Proponents of **subject-centered curricula** argue that subjects present a logical basis for organizing and interpreting information, that teachers are trained as subject matter specialists, and that textbooks and other teaching materials are usually organized by subjects. Critics claim that subject-centered curricula often are a mass of facts and concepts learned in isolation. They see this kind of curriculum as de-emphasizing contemporary life experiences and failing to consider the needs and interests of students. In subject-centered curricula, the critics argue, the teacher is the authority and dominates classroom discourse, allowing little student input.

---

[1]See R. Freeman Butts, *The Revival of Civic Learning* (Bloomington, IN: Phi Delta Kappa, 1980); Lawrence A. Cremin, *American Education: The National Experience* (New York: Harper and Row, 1980); and Lawrence A. Cremin, *The Transformation of the School* (New York: Random House, 1964).

The following sections discuss several variations of subject-centered approaches to curricula, such as the subject-area approach, back-to-basics, and the core curriculum. These represent neither the only possible variations nor hard-and-fast categories. Many schools and teachers mix these approaches, drawing from more than one of them.

Subject-Area Approach to Curriculum The subject-area approach is the most widely used form of curriculum organization.[2] This long-standing approach has its roots in the seven liberal arts of classical Greece and Rome: grammar, rhetoric, dialectic, arithmetic, geometry, astronomy, and music. Advocates of the modern subject-area curricula trace its origins to the work of William Harris, superintendent of the St. Louis school system in the 1870s and US Commissioner of Education at the end of the 1800s.[3] Steeped in the classical tradition, Harris established a subject orientation that has virtually dominated US curricula from his day to the present. As a student, you were most likely introduced to "algebra" and "English grammar," "reading" and "writing," as well as "geography" and "history" in one form or another.

The modern **subject-area curriculum** treats each subject as a specialized and largely autonomous body of knowledge. Subjects referred to as the "basics" are considered essential for all students; these usually include the three Rs at the elementary level, and English, history, science, and mathematics at the secondary level. Other specialized subjects develop knowledge and skills for particular vocations or professions—for example, business mathematics and physics. Finally, elective content affords the student optional offerings, often tailored to student interests and needs.

Exploratory subjects refer to subjects that students may choose from a list of courses designed to suit a wide range of learning styles, abilities, and interests. These courses, which can include such subjects as dance, technology, creative writing, career exploration, and drama, allow the school to diversify its offerings and allow students the opportunity to explore topics that might stimulate their interests outside of the realm of the traditional subjects. They appear most often in middle-school and late elementary-school curricula.[4] Schools that include exploratory subjects in the curriculum tend to be more progressive in outlook than schools that solely favor the traditional academic subjects.

Perennialist and Essentialist Influence on Curriculum Two of the educational theories described in Chapter 6, Philosophical Roots of Education, are fundamentally subject centered: perennialism and essentialism.[5] Believing that the main purpose of education is the cultivation of the intellect, the perennialists concentrate their curriculum on Latin, grammar, rhetoric, and logic at the elementary level, adding study of the classics at the secondary level. The assumption of the **perennialist-influenced curriculum**, according to Robert M. Hutchins, is that the best of the past—the so-called permanent studies, or classics—remains equally valid for the present because they deal with fundamental questions that are relevant throughout time.[6]

Essentialists believe that the elementary curriculum should consist of the three Rs, and the high school curriculum should consist of five or six major disciplines: English (grammar, literature, and writing), mathematics, the sciences, history, foreign languages,

subject-area curriculum A type of subject-centered curriculum in which each subject is treated as a largely autonomous body of knowledge. The curriculum emphasizes traditional subjects that have dominated US education since the late nineteenth century, including English, history, science, and mathematics.

perennialist-influenced curriculum A fundamentally subject-centered educational theory that the main purpose of education is the cultivation of the best of the past, the classics.

---

[2]Peter F. Oliva and William R. Gordon II, *Developing the Curriculum*, 8th ed. (Boston: Pearson Education, 2012).

[3]Henry Warren Button, "Committee of Fifteen," *History of Education Quarterly* (December 1965), pp. 253–263.

[4]Allan C. Ornstein, Thomas Lasley, and Gail Mindes, *Secondary and Middle School Methods* (New York: Allyn and Bacon, 2005); Steven Scarpa, "A Shift in Middle School," *District Administration* (April 2005), p. 19; and Patrick Akos, Pajarita Charles, Dennis Orthner, and Valerie Cooley, "Teacher Perspectives on Career-Relevant Curriculum in Middle School," *Research in Middle Level Education Online* (January 2011), pp. 1–9.

[5]Theodore Brameld, *Patterns of Educational Philosophy* (New York: Holt, 1950).

[6]Robert M. Hutchins, *The Higher Learning in America* (New Haven, CT: Yale University Press, 1936); and Robert M. Hutchins, "The Organization and Subject Matter of General Education," in Forrest W. Parkay, Eric J. Anctil, and Glen Hass, *Curriculum Planning: A Contemporary Approach* (Boston: Pearson Education, 2006), pp. 31–34.

essentialist-influenced curriculum A subject-centered educational theory based on six major disciplines: English, mathematics, the sciences, history, foreign languages, and geography. Contemporary essentialists also add computer literacy.

and geography.[7] Adherents of the **essentialist-influenced curriculum** believe these subjects constitute the best way of organizing information and keeping up with today's explosion of knowledge. They argue that there is essential information that adults have learned over time that must be passed on to society's young. Students need an academic knowledge base—"essential knowledge"—to deal with new ideas and challenges that will confront them in the future.[8] Teachers should be held accountable for teaching the essentials of the curriculum through a systematic program of study and assessment.[9]

Essentialism shares with perennialism the notion that curriculum should focus on rigorous intellectual training, training that is possible only through the study of certain subjects. Both perennialists and essentialists advocate educational meritocracy. They favor high academic standards and a stringent system of grading and testing to help schools sort students by ability. Today, many parochial schools and academically oriented public schools stress various aspects of the perennialist and essentialist curricula.

back-to-basics curriculum A type of subject-centered curriculum that emphasizes the three Rs at the elementary level and academic subjects at the secondary level; also includes a defined minimum level of academic standards.

Back-to-Basics Approach to Curriculum   In the early 1980s, many educators and laypeople called for a **back-to-basics curriculum**.[10] Like the essentialist curriculum influence, "back-to-basics" connotes a heavy emphasis on reading, writing, and mathematics. So-called solid subjects—English, history, science, and mathematics—are required in all grades, and the back-to-basics proponents are even more suspicious than the essentialists of attempts to expand the curriculum beyond this solid foundation; electives or exploratory subjects are not encouraged. Critics of this approach worry that a focus on basics will suppress students' creativity and shortchange other domains of learning, encouraging conformity and dependence on authority.[11]

Back-to-basics proponents insisted on the need to maintain minimum standards, and much of the state school reform legislation enacted from the late 1970s through the 1990s reflects this popular position. As a major component of the back-to-basics movement, minimum competency tests (MCT) were implemented in a majority of states during this time. These statewide tests to demonstrate mastery of minimum skills were required of students to graduate from high school. Advocates claimed such tests validated the high school diploma; high school graduates would be seen as having a useful set of minimum skills needed to enter the world of work. The MCT would serve as the precursor to the school-wide assessment programs required after the turn of the twentieth century by the No Child Left Behind Act (NCLB) and the high-stakes exit exams implemented in many states—twenty-four in 2014—for high school students. Today, the rigorous PARCC and Smarter Balanced assessments continue this trend.[12] For more on high-stakes exit exams, see the Taking Issue box.

---

[7]Arthur Bestor, *The Restoration of Learning* (New York: Knopf, 1956); and James B. Conant, *The American High School Today* (New York: McGraw-Hill, 1959).

[8]William C. Bagley, "The Case for Essentialism in Education," *Today's Education: Journal of the National Education Association* (October 1941), pp. 201–202; and G. T. Sewall, "Against Anomie and Amnesia: What Basic Education Means in the Eighties," *Phi Delta Kappan* (May 1982), pp. 603–606.

[9]Wesley J. Null, "William C. Bagley and the Founding of Essentialism: An Untold Story in American Educational History," *Teachers College Record* (April 2007), pp. 1013–1055.

[10]"Back-to-Basics Stifling Creativity?" *Newsweek* (January 27, 1986), p. 59; and Anne Wescott Dodd, "Curriculum Mood Swings," *Education Week* (June 9, 1993), pp. 26, 46.

[11]Elliot W. Eisner, "What Really Counts in School," *Educational Leadership* (February 1991), pp. 10–17; and David W. Jardina, "Back to Basics: Rethinking What Is Basic to Education," *Alberta Journal of Educational Research* (Summer 2001), pp. 187–190.

[12]James S. Catterall, "Standards and School Dropouts: A National Study of Tests Required for High School Graduation," *American Journal of Education* (November 1989), pp. 1–34; Allan C. Ornstein, "National Reform and Instructional Accountability," *High School Journal* (October–November 1990), pp. 51–56; Marie Gould, "Minimum Competencies," *Research Starters Education* (June 2008), pp. 1–7; "Smarter Balanced Assessments," *Smarter Balanced Assessment Consortium* (n.d.), available at **www.smarterbalanced.org/smarter-balanced-assessments/** (April 17, 2015); Caralee Adams, "Report Calls for States to Rethink High School Exit Exams," *Education Week* (July 15, 2014) at **http://blogs.edweek.org/edweek/college_bound/2014/07/report_calls_for_states_to_rethink.html** (April 18, 2015); and "The PARCC Assessment," *PARCC* (2015) at **www.parcconline.org/parcc-assessment** (April 17, 2015).

TAKING ISSUE

Read the brief introduction below, as well as the Question and the pros and cons list that follows. Then, answer the question using *your* own words and position.

HIGH-STAKES EXIT EXAMS FOR GRADUATION

Many states use high-stakes exit exams as a high school graduation requirement. To obtain a high school diploma, students must pass a battery of tests aligned with state content standards. Failure to achieve a passing score on the assessment can mean denial of the high school diploma. With the implementation of the Common Core State Standards (CCSS) and the more rigorous assessments that are associated with them, some states are considering eliminating the exit exam requirement.

Question

Are high-stakes exit exams beneficial to students and schools? (Think about this question as you read the PRO and CON arguments listed here. What is *your* take on this issue?)

Arguments PRO

1. When the tests are aligned to the state curriculum standards, the exit exams focus the curriculum and ensure that classroom instruction covers key content deemed appropriate for high school graduates.

2. The rise in requirements for graduation brought about by exit exams is especially important for students from schools that are economically disadvantaged. To break the cycle of poverty and joblessness, these students must be given the skills needed for productive employment ensured by the exit exam.

3. Testing for graduation shows the public that schools are being held accountable for their performance. The test results help to identify schools that are not doing their jobs properly.

4. With the increased rigor that accompanies the CCSS, students will be provided a quality education that prepares them to pass the test. For the few who have difficulty, alternative pathways to graduation can be implemented, such as alternative assignments or waivers.

5. Using the data provided by the exit exams, educators can discover where the overall problems lie. Policies can be modified accordingly, and curricula can be designed to address the problem areas.

Arguments CON

1. Statewide exit exams are cumbersome, costly, and might not lead to much improvement in the quality of education. The effort must come from the local level, where educators know the strengths and weaknesses of their own schools.

2. Exit exams unfairly penalize students from low-income, underperforming schools. These students fail the tests in disproportionate numbers, which stigmatizes them unjustly and further damages their prospects for employment.

3. For systems with exit exams, there is a decrease in the flexibility of curriculum offerings during high school. Students are required to focus on those courses or subjects that are included in the requirements for graduation, which may entail taking numerous remedial courses.

4. Exit exams place one more hurdle for students to clear prior to graduation, and, for some, this may prove to be too formidable. As a result, more students are likely to drop out prior to their senior year.

5. Most teachers already know where the problems lie with student performance. Moreover, soon after an exit exam is established, many teachers begin to teach the test. Thus, the data obtained from such examinations become meaningless and misleading.

Question Reprise: What Is Your Stand?

Reflect again on the following question by explaining *your* stand about this issue: Are high-stakes exit exams beneficial to students and schools?

Core Approach to Curriculum   The importance of basic subjects in the curriculum is also expressed by the term *core curriculum*. Unfortunately, in the post–World War II era, this term has been used to describe two different approaches to organizing curricula.

The first approach, which we will call *core curriculum*, gained popularity in the 1930s and 1940s and had its greatest influence at the junior high school level. In this approach, students study subject matter in an integrated fashion, usually through the study of social-personal issues or themes that cut across subjects (for example, an interdisciplinary examination of a local environmental problem). The teachers organize instructional units in an interdisciplinary manner, showing how diverse subjects relate to one another. This approach, often organized in extended blocks of time, sometimes consisting of two or three periods of the school day, uses problem solving as the primary method of instruction and is tied to a progressive theory of education.[13]

new core curriculum (core subjects approach) A curriculum of common courses that all students are required to take. Emphasis is usually on academic achievement and traditional subject matter.

The second approach, in contrast, was born out of the 1980s educational reform movement and reflects the more conservative theory of essentialism. In this version, which we will call the **new core curriculum (core subjects approach)**, students experience a common body of required subjects—subjects that advocates consider central to the education of all students.[14] As described in Chapter 13, The Changing Purposes of American Education, the impetus for this new core curriculum was the reform report, *A Nation at Risk*. Students were seen as being inadequately prepared for life beyond high school, whether college or the world of work. The report criticized the cafeteria-style curriculum, where students favored desserts and appetizers (that is, less rigorous elective courses) rather than the solid, core subjects. The remedy for this deficiency was an increase in course requirements for graduation; the recommendation for the minimum requirements for high school included four years of English, three years of math, three years of science, three years of social studies, and one-half year of computer science.[15]

The proponents of this new core curriculum helped make subject-matter requirement changes in states and districts nationwide that have certainly impacted you as a student.[16] Those changes are summarized in Figure 14.1. From 1982, just prior to publication of the *At Risk* report, until 2009, the percentage of high school graduates who completed a basic curriculum in the core subjects (that is, four credits of English; three credits each of social studies, science, and math; and two credits of foreign language) recommended in the report increased from 9.5 percent to nearly 62 percent.[17] The testing group ACT has consistently found that students who take the recommended core curriculum are more likely to be ready for college or career than those who take fewer of the recommended core courses.[18]

Critics argue that the core curriculum, by focusing only on courses and content, ignores an important component of the education equation—the student. The next section will examine approaches and theories that place considerations about the student at the center of the curriculum.

14-2b Student-Centered Curricula

student-centered curricula Curricula that focus on the needs and attitudes of the individual student. Emphasis is on self-expression and the student's intrinsic motivation.

In direct contrast to subject-centered curricula, **student-centered curricula** of various types emphasize student interests and needs, including the affective aspects of learning. At its extreme, the student-centered approach is rooted in the philosophy of Jean Jacques Rousseau, who encouraged childhood self-expression. Implicit in Rousseau's

[13]Miki M. Caskey, "The Evidence for the Core Curriculum—Past and Present," *Middle School Journal* (January 2006), pp. 48–54; and Peter F. Oliva and William R. Gordon II, *Developing the Curriculum*, 8th ed. (Boston: Pearson Education, 2012).

[14]John I. Goodlad, "A New Look at an Old Idea: Core Curriculum," *Educational Leadership* (December 1986–January 1987), pp. 8–16; and Richard W. Riley, "World Class Standards: The Key to Educational Reform" (Washington, DC: Department of Education, 1993).

[15]National Commission on Excellence in Education, *A Nation at Risk: The Imperative for Educational Reform* (Washington, DC: US Government Printing Office, 1983); and ACT, *Rigor at Risk: Reaffirming Quality in the High School Core Curriculum* (Iowa City, IA: ACT, 2007).

[16]*Digest of Education Statistics, 2013* (Washington, DC: US Government Printing Office, 2013), Table 225.10 at **http://nces.ed.gov/programs/digest/d13/tables/dt13_225.10.asp?current=yes** (April 17, 2015).

[17]*Digest of Education Statistics: 2013*, Table 225.50 at **http://nces.ed.gov/programs/digest/d13/tables/dt13_225.50.asp?current=yes** (April 17, 2015).

[18]*The Condition of College & Career Readiness 2014* (Iowa City, IA: ACT, 2014) at **www.act.org/research/policymakers/cccr14/index.html**.

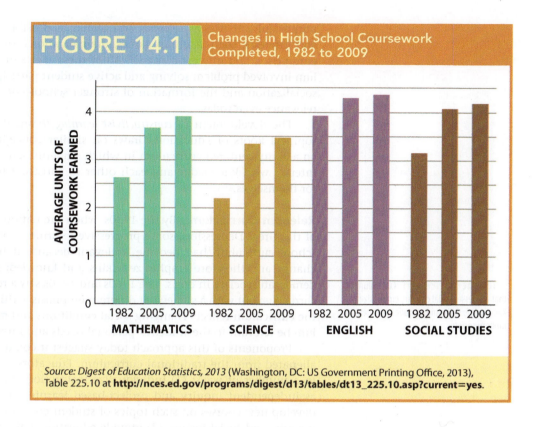

FIGURE 14.1   Changes in High School Coursework Completed, 1982 to 2009

Source: Digest of Education Statistics, 2013 (Washington, DC: US Government Printing Office, 2013), Table 225.10 at **http://nces.ed.gov/programs/digest/d13/tables/dt13_225.10.asp?current=yes**.

philosophy is the necessity of leaving the children to their own devices, allowing them the creativity and freedom essential for growth.

Progressive education of the early 1900s gave impetus to the modern student-centered curricula. Progressive educators believed that when the interests and needs of learners were incorporated into the curriculum, students would be intrinsically motivated, and learning would be more successful. This does not mean that students' whims or passing fads should dictate the curriculum. However, one criticism of student-centered curricula is that proponents sometimes overlook important academic content.

John Dewey, a champion of student-centered curricula, attempted to establish a curriculum that balanced subject matter with student interests and needs. As early as 1902, he pointed out the fallacies of either extreme. The learner was neither "a docile recipient of facts" nor "the starting point, the center, and the end" of school activity.[19] Dewey tried to emphasize the need for balance while creating a curriculum that would prepare children for the modern, democratic world.

Over time, at least five major approaches to organizing student-centered curricula have been identified: activity-centered approaches, relevant curriculum, the humanistic approach, alternative or free schools, and values-centered curricula.

activity-centered curriculum
A type of student-centered curriculum that emphasizes purposeful and real-life experiences and, more recently, student participation in school and community activities.

Activity-Centered Approaches   The movement for an **activity-centered curriculum** has strongly affected the public elementary schools. William Kilpatrick, one of Dewey's colleagues, was an early leader of this movement. In contrast to Dewey, Kilpatrick believed that teachers could not anticipate the interests and needs of children, which made any preplanned curriculum impossible. Thus, he attacked the traditional school curriculum as detached and unrelated to the problems of real life. Instead, he advocated

---

[19]John Dewey, *The Child and the Curriculum* (Chicago: University of Chicago Press, 1902), pp. 8–9; and William J. Reese, "The Origins of Progressive Education," *History of Education Quarterly* (Spring 2001), pp. 1–24.

purposeful activities as relevant and lifelike as possible and tied to a student's needs and interests, such as group games, dramatizations, story projects, field trips, social enterprises, and interest centers.[20] All of these facets of the activity-centered curriculum involved problem solving and active student participation. They also emphasized socialization and the formation of stronger school–community ties. Thus, they have relevance even today.

The development of *constructivist learning theory*, described in Chapter 6, Philosophical Roots of Education, draws on similar concepts. Constructivists might use an activity-centered curriculum in which students actively (mentally and physically) interact with knowledge and each other to construct meaning and new knowledge for themselves.[21]

relevant curriculum Curriculum that addresses social change, emphasizing knowledge, skills, and attitudes pertinent to modern society.

Relevant Curriculum By the 1930s, when the nation was consumed by the tumult of the Great Depression, some progressive reformers complained that the traditional school curriculum had become irrelevant because it had failed to adjust to social change and therefore emphasized skills and knowledge not pertinent to a modern democratic society in crisis. The 1960s and 1970s saw a renewed concern for a **relevant curriculum** but with a somewhat different emphasis. Critics expressed less concern that the curriculum reflects changing social conditions and more concern that the curriculum be relevant to the students' personal needs and interests.

Proponents of this approach today suggest it could best benefit students who are alienated from the traditional curriculum. Educators could implement the approach in a number of ways: (1) individualize instruction through such teaching methods as independent inquiry and project-based learning; (2) revise existing courses and develop new courses on such topics of student concern as environmental protection, poverty, and social justice; (3) provide educational alternatives (such as electives and open classrooms) that allow more freedom of choice and meet the needs of students in special circumstances, such as those from homeless families; and (4) extend the curriculum beyond the school's walls, through such means as community service projects and field trips.[22]

humanistic approach to curriculum A student-centered curriculum approach that stresses the personal and social aspects of the student's growth and development. Emphasis is on self-actualizing processes and moral, aesthetic, and higher domains of thinking.

Humanistic Approach to Curriculum A **humanistic approach to curriculum** emphasizes affective outcomes, those that address attitudes or emotions, in addition to cognitive outcomes. Such a curriculum draws heavily on the work of humanistic psychologists Abraham Maslow, Carl Rogers, and Arthur Combs.[23] Advocates of humanistic education contend that the contemporary school curriculum has failed miserably and that teachers and schools are determined to stress academic achievement and to control students, *not* for students' good but for the benefit of adults. Humanistic educators emphasize more than affective processes; they seek higher domains of spirit, consciousness, aesthetics, and morality. They stress more meaningful relationships between students and teachers, student independence and self-direction, and greater acceptance of self and others. The teacher's role from a humanistic approach is to help learners cope

---

[20]William H. Kilpatrick, "The Project Method," *Teachers College Record* (September 1918), pp. 319–335; Leonard J. Waks, "The Project Method in Postindustrial Education," *Journal of Curriculum Studies* (July 1997), pp. 391–406.

[21]Lois T. Stover, Gloria A. Neubert, and James C. Lawlor, *Creating Interactive Environments in the Secondary School* (Washington, DC: National Education Association, 1993), pp. 20–23; and William J. Matthews, "Constructivism in the Classroom: Epistemology, History, and Empirical Evidence," *Teacher Education Quarterly* (Summer 2003), p. 51.

[22]Velma Menchase, "Providing a Culturally Relevant Curriculum for Hispanic Children," *Multicultural Education* (Spring 2001), pp. 18–20; Julie Landsman, "Bearers of Hope," *Educational Leadership* (February 2006), pp. 26–32; and John Larmer and John R. Mergendoller, "Seven Essentials for Project-Based Learning," *Educational Leadership* (September 2010), pp. 34–37.

[23]Abraham H. Maslow, *Toward a Psychology of Being* (New York: Van Nostrand Reinhold, 1962); Arthur W. Combs, *A Personal Approach to Teaching: Beliefs That Make a Difference* (Boston: Allyn and Bacon, 1982); and Carl Rogers, *Freedom to Learn*, 2nd ed. (Columbus, OH: Merrill, 1983).

with their psychological needs, to develop a positive classroom environment that fosters positive self-esteem, and to facilitate self-understanding among students to make more effective learning possible.[24] According to humanists, when students are secure and stable in their own being, they are better able to be effective learners.

Alternative or Free Schools Programs   You are likely to find student-centered curriculum programs in **alternative** or **free schools**, which are often private, experimental institutions. Some have been organized by parents and teachers who were dissatisfied with the public schools. These schools typically feature much student freedom, noisy classrooms, and an often-unstructured learning environment where students are free to explore their interests. Most are considered radical and antiestablishment, even though many of their ideas are rooted in the well-known student-centered doctrines of progressivism.

Paulo Freire, Ivan Illich, Herbert Kohl, and John Holt have stressed the need for and, in many cases, have established student-centered alternative or free schools.[25] Critics, however, condemn these schools as places where little cognitive learning takes place and little discipline and order are instilled. Proponents counter that children do learn in student-centered alternative schools, which—instead of stressing conformity—are made to fit the students and address their needs.

A second type of alternative school is that which public-school systems run for students who experience persistent behavioral problems or exhibit at-risk behaviors. In a national survey, 64 percent of school districts reported having at least one alternative school or program for at-risk students. These schools start from the premise that school systems must change to provide a more flexible approach to learning. They generally stress greater collaboration among staff members and between staff and students in terms of both innovative curriculum and varied instructional methods. Students are generally reassigned to these schools until their behavior improves, at which time they are likely to return to their traditional school.[26]

Values-Centered Curriculum   In the 1970s, *values clarification* was a popular values-centered curriculum approach that gained favor among many student-centered theorists. In values clarification exercises, students carefully studied a specific dilemma and investigated relevant facts; considered the alternative actions, values, and consequences involved; and then chose the value that would guide further actions, rather than being "told the right answer" by an adult. As might be expected, this approach fell out of favor as more conservative forces influenced schools in the 1980s.[27]

A more recent **values-centered curriculum**—more popularly known as *character education*—places special emphasis on moral and ethical development. Character-education

alternative (free) school A public or private school that provides learning opportunities different from those in local public schools. Some such schools follow a student-centered curriculum characterized by a great deal of freedom for students and a relative lack of structure.

values-centered curriculum Places special emphasis on moral and ethical issues; more popularly known as *character education*.

---

[24]Carol Witherell and Nel Noddings, *The Challenge to Care in Schools* (New York: Teachers College Press, 1992); Elliot Eisner, *The Educational Imagination*, 3rd ed. (New York: Macmillan, 1993); Vincent A. Anfara Jr., "Advisor-Advisee Programs: Important But Problematic," *Middle School Journal* (September 2006), pp. 54–60; and Allan C. Ornstein, "Critical Issues in Teaching," in Allan C. Ornstein, Edward F. Pajak, and Stacey B. Ornstein, eds., *Contemporary Issues in Curriculum*, 4th ed. (Boston: Pearson Education, 2007).

[25]See, for instance, Paulo Freire, *Pedagogy of the Oppressed* (New York: Herder and Herder, 1970); Ivan Illich, *Deschooling Society* (New York: Harper and Row, 1971); Henry A. Giroux, *Teachers as Intellectuals* (Granby, MA: Bergin and Garvey, 1988); Ron Miller, "John Holt: His Prophetic Voice," *Education Revolution* (Autumn 2002), pp. 28–33; and Camilla A. Lehr and Cheryl M. Lange, "Alternative Schools Serving Students with and without Disabilities: What Are the Current Issues and Challenges?" *Preventing School Failure* (Winter 2003), pp. 59–65.

[26]Lionel H. Brown and Kelvin S. Beckett, "Chapter 1: Alternative Schools: Portraits in Black and White," in *Building Community in an Alternative School: The Perspective of an African American Principal* (New York: Peter Lang Publishing, 2007), pp. 1–16; and Allan Porowski, Rosemarie O'Conner, and Jia Lisa Luo, *How Do States Define Alternative Education?* (Washington, DC: US Department of Education, Institute of Education Sciences, National Center for Education Evaluation and Regional Assistance, Regional Educational Laboratory Mid-Atlantic 2014) at **http://ies.ed.gov/ncee/edlabs/regions/midatlantic/pdf/REL_2014038.pdf** (April 17, 2015).

[27]Bonnidell Clouse, "Character Education: Borrowing from the Past to Advance the Future," *Contemporary Education* (January 2001), pp. 23–28.

> **PHOTO 14.1** Character education programs are now common in many states and include building a sense of community and respect for others, bullying prevention programs, and visually displaying positive virtues throughout the school.

Robin Nelson/PhotoEdit

advocates contend that because a growing number of children are exhibiting problematic behaviors and attitudes, programs to instill a climate of respect within the classroom are necessary.[28] A much broader view of the purpose of character education recognizes the character-related problems that exist in contemporary society—corporate greed, apathy, corrupt politicians—and calls for character education to develop active citizens who act in ethical ways. To this end, at least thirty-five states have passed legislation encouraging or mandating character education.[29]

School practices that are incorporated into character-education programs include building a sense of community and respect for other students in the development of bullying-prevention programs.[30] Some character-education programs visually display positive virtues throughout the school, such as self-discipline, respect, or honesty (Photo 14.1).[31]

One concern about efforts to infuse character education into the curriculum is that such programs developed for schools might simply be attempts at indoctrination. Students are drilled in how to act ethically rather than engaging in analytical thought about what goes into being ethical. Often, school character programs are grounded in incentives that critics claim encourage students to perform for the reward instead of investigating the process for making conscious decisions about ethically appropriate actions.[32] An additional criticism is that attempts at incorporating character education in the curriculum are ineffective and divert time from the academic mission of the school.[33]

---

[28]Diana Brannon, "Character Education: It's a Joint Responsibility," *Kappa Delta Pi Record* (Winter 2008), pp. 62–65.

[29]Sanford N. McDonnell, "America's Crisis of Character—And What to Do about It," *Education Week* (October 08, 2008), p. 25. "Character Education—What States Are Doing," (n.d.) at **www .character.org/wp-content/uploads/What-States-Are-Doing.pdf** (April 17, 2015).

[30]Eric Schaps, "Creating Caring School Communities," *Leadership* (March 2009), pp. 8–11.

[31]Sara Efron and Pamela Joseph, "Seven Worlds of Moral Education," *Phi Delta Kappan* (March 2005), pp. 525–533.

[32]Alfie Kohn, "A Critical Examination of Character Education," in Allan C. Ornstein, Edward F. Pajak, and Stacey B. Ornstein, *Contemporary Issues in Curriculum*, 5th ed. (Boston: Pearson Education, 2011), pp. 164–181; and David Light Shields, "Character as the Aim of Education," *Phi Delta Kappan* (May 2011), pp. 40–53.

[33]Kenneth Godwin, Carrie Ausbrooks, and Valerie Martinez, "Teaching Tolerance in Public and Private Schools," *Phi Delta Kappan* (March 2001), pp. 542–546; and Debra Viadero, "Proof of Positive Effect Found for Only a Few Character Programs," *Education Week* (June 20, 2007), p. 20.

FROM PRESERVICE TO PRACTICE

CURRICULUM CHOICES

Sandra Helenski, Bobby Owens, and Laura Rittilini are new to Frederick Douglass Middle School and the teaching profession. All are on the team assigned to teach seventh-grade students. Sandra teaches English, Bobby teaches life science, and Laura teaches band. All would say they teach students first and the subject second.

Discussion in the teachers' lounge is warming up today as they debate a few of their concerns with the most experienced teachers at Frederick Douglass.

Mrs. Middendorf, one of the veterans in the profession, says, "I don't see how you can take the time to teach 'character' if you want them to pass the Smarter Balance assessments in March. You have to stay focused on the math and reading standards—the assessment content. If you want to last a few years here, I think you should stick to making sure your students can write correctly, read well, and do rigorous math. Also, you have to be very careful: Are you sure you know the values of the community or of the parents? If you teach tolerance of diversity that includes gays and lesbians, many conservative religious parents won't be happy. It's all too easy to be misunderstood and to step on someone's toes."

"But, when I have a perfectly good opportunity to use student needs and interests in teaching concepts in the state curricula that relate to values, perhaps through special projects or book assignments, why shouldn't I do that?" responds Sandra. "For example, why can't students learn to search for and evaluate authors' statements about respect for all individuals just as easily as they can learn to search for and evaluate metaphors?"

"I'm including some activities that emphasize care for the environment," said Bobby. "Students will test water and take air samples near the county landfill. They'll analyze their lab results in teams and send reports to the county commissioners. Certainly we can include values with this approach." He turned to the veterans. "What do you think?"

A more experienced teacher responded. "Well, I would be sure that my time was used wisely. That sort of activity can get away from you, and before you know it, March is here, and your students aren't ready for the assessments. So, just be careful in how you plan and implement your objectives."

Laura chimed in with her observation that the skills, knowledge, and dispositions of each band member were important to her. She wanted to be sure that each student valued being part of a team and also valued the discipline and hard work it took from all members to form a championship band. "Certainly," she said, "each of us in our own way is teaching values anyway. Perhaps we need to reflect on what values we teach just doing everyday things."

CASE QUESTIONS

1. What do all three new teachers hold in common? What kinds of curriculum organization are really under discussion here?

2. What is your reaction to the experienced teachers' comments to Sandra? How would you reply?

3. What curriculum approach do you favor? Why?

4. Do you agree with Laura's comment that all teachers teach values? How do you expect the experienced teachers to react to Laura's comment?

Despite these criticisms, many educators contend that it is possible—even with our diverse society—to incorporate character-education programs into our schools and establish a set of values that represent an American consensus. Table 14.1, for example, lists "character objectives" included by the school system in Baltimore County, Maryland, in its student handbook. Many educators believe that developing such character traits is an urgent responsibility of American schools.

14-1c Curriculum Contrasts: An Overview

As we noted earlier, subject-centered and student-centered curricula represent the opposite ends of a continuum. You will find that most schooling in the United States falls somewhere between the two—keeping a tenuous balance between subject matter and student needs, as well as between the cognitive and affective dimensions of students' development.

TABLE 14.1	"Character Objectives," as Identified by the Baltimore County (Md.) Public Schools

1. To develop the wisdom and good judgment to make reasoned decisions.

2. To develop a sense of justice that is informed by fairness, honesty, and civility.

3. To develop and demonstrate respect for self, respect for others, and respect for property.

4. To demonstrate tolerance and understanding of others regardless of race, gender, ethnicity, disability, national origin, religion, creed, socioeconomic status, marital status, pregnancy, personal record, sexual orientation, or political belief.

5. To demonstrate compassion for others through the development of empathy, kindness, and service.

6. To demonstrate discipline and responsibility by exhibiting self-control and the willingness to admit mistakes and correct them.

7. To develop a positive attitude that reflects hope, enthusiasm, flexibility, and appreciation.

8. To demonstrate pride in oneself and others by doing the best for self, family, school, and community and by respecting the achievement of others.

9. To exhibit personal and academic integrity through honesty, expressing beliefs in appropriate ways, and working to one's full potential.

Questions

1. Which of the character objectives in Table 14.1 do you consider most important and why?

2. What character objectives would you add to this table?

Source: The Baltimore County Public Schools Student Handbook 2014–2015 (Towson, MD: Baltimore County Public Schools, 2014).

Decisions about what you should teach and how your teaching curriculum is organized will be influenced by the philosophical orientation of your school system or school. More traditional schools that subscribe to a perennialist or essentialist philosophy lean toward a subject-centered curriculum. Schools oriented more toward progressive education tend to use a student-centered approach. Overview 14.1 summarizes the various subject-centered and student-centered approaches to curricula and their corresponding philosophies, content emphases, and instructional emphases. As you begin to think seriously about in which district and school you want to teach, consider asking interviewers questions about curricular organization to ensure a fit between your philosophy and that of the district or school. In the next section, we move on to the curriculum development process and the main issues it raises.

FOCUS Which approach do you believe has been most important in driving curriculum emphases at the schools you visit? In your opinion, which approach *should* be most important? Why?

14-2 ISSUES IN CURRICULUM DEVELOPMENT

Whether the curriculum is subject centered or student centered, the process of developing it involves (1) assessing the needs and capabilities of all learners and (2) selecting or creating the instructional materials and activities that will address those needs.

At the national level, curriculum making has taken on a more influential role due to the recent emphasis on the CCSS. Curriculum development at the state level has intensified over the past two decades, starting with the requirement by NCLB to develop state standards, assessments, and, by implication, corresponding curriculum realignment. The new state curricula were prepared by professional staff in the states'

OVERVIEW 14.1

CURRICULUM ORGANIZATION APPROACHES

Curriculum Approach	Corresponding Philosophy or Theory	Content Emphasis	Instructional Emphasis
Subject-Centered			
Subject-area	Perennialism, essentialism	Three Rs; academic, vocational, and elective subjects	Knowledge, concepts, and principles; specialized knowledge
Perennialist	Perennialism	Three Rs; liberal arts; classics; timeless values; academic rigor	Rote memorization; specialized knowledge; mental discipline
Essentialist	Essentialism	Three Rs; liberal arts and science; academic disciplines; academic excellence	Concepts and principles; problem solving; essential skills
Back-to-basics	Essentialism	Three Rs; academic subjects	Specific knowledge and skills; drill; attainment of measurable ends or competencies
New core curriculum (core subjects)	Perennialism, essentialism	Common curriculum for all students; focus on academics	Common knowledge; intellectual skills and concepts; values and moral issues
Student-Centered			
Activity-centered	Progressivism	Student needs and interests; student activities; school–community activities	Active, experimental environment; project methods; effective living
Relevant	Progressivism, social reconstructionism	Student experiences and activities; felt needs	Social and personal problems; reflective thinking
Humanistic	Progressivism, social reconstructionism, existentialism	Introspection; choice; affective processes	Individual and group learning; flexible, artistic, psychological methods; self-realization
Alternative or free schools	Progressivism	Student needs and interests; student experiences	Play oriented; creative expression; free learning environment
Values-centered (character education)	Social reconstructionism, existentialism	Democratic values; ethical and moral values; cross-cultural and universal values; choice and freedom	Feelings, attitudes, and emotions; existentialist thinking; decision making

departments of education, assisted by curriculum consultants and experts in the disciplines. The curriculum guidelines became prescriptive, including lists of "core learning goals" or "state learning outcomes" and instructional materials, either mandated or recommended, that were aligned with state-developed standards.[34]

---

[34]James W. Popham, "Curriculum Matters," *American School Board Journal* (November 2004), pp. 30–33; and Barbara Reys and Glenda Lappan, "Consensus or Confusion?" *Phi Delta Kappan* (May 2007), pp. 676–680.

The greatest responsibility for curriculum development still falls on the local school district—or on the schools themselves. Large school districts have the resources to employ personnel who specialize in curriculum development, including subject-matter specialists and assessment coordinators. Smaller school districts generally assign curriculum development to a group of teachers organized by subject or grade level; sometimes parents, administrators, and even students participate.

Historically, college admission standards have exerted a strong influence on curriculum choices for high schools. Efforts have been made to align the curriculum from preschool through the four years of college. This has been referred to as P–16 alignment, and it envisions a seamless, articulated curriculum in which what is learned in primary, elementary, and secondary schools builds to prepare students to be ready for college or career upon graduation from high school. This concept is consistent with the emphasis of the federal initiatives of the Obama administration to graduate students who are "college and career ready."[35]

For decades, a major influence on curriculum—one whose importance is now in a state of flux—has been the textbook. Textbooks have long been the most frequently used instructional medium at all levels beyond the primary grades. As such, they have dominated the nature and sequence of courses and profoundly affected students' learning experiences. Because courses often are aligned with the topics addressed in the textbook, especially in small districts that lack curriculum specialists, they play an important role in influencing what is taught in the classroom.

To be appealing to school districts, and thus a large potential market, textbooks have been criticized as being generic, noncontroversial, and bland. Because they are usually written for the largest book markets, they tend to disregard many local or regional issues. Aiming for the greatest number of average students, they may fail to meet the needs and interests of any particular group or individual. In the recent past, in an attempt to address the standards that were established by the various state departments of education, publishers included a wide range of topics and volumes of facts that left little room for conceptual thinking, critical analysis, and evaluation. Because they are expensive, textbooks have made up a large portion of a district's discretionary spending. Also, although the life cycle of the typical textbook is five to seven years, they are often used well after they should be retired because they are expensive.[36]

In 2015, the influence of the textbook is evident by the size of the market its sales generate. An estimated $7–9 billion is spent annually on textbooks in K–12 schools in the United States. Now we are witnessing a shift in the textbook world as publishers can advertise their texts as being aligned with CCSS. Thus, they are able to reach a broader market made up of the forty-three states that have adopted CCSS, as opposed to just a few years earlier when they had to be concerned about aligning with the standards of the fifty different state systems of standards.[37]

---

[35]John R. Hoyle and Timothy M. Kutka, "Maintaining America's Egalitarian Edge in the 21st Century: Unifying K–12 and Postsecondary Education for the Success of All Students," *Theory into Practice* (Fall 2008), pp. 353–362; Shepherd Siegel, "A Meaningful High School Diploma," *Phi Delta Kappan* (June 2009), pp. 740–744; Education Commission of the States, P–16, at **www.ecs.org/html/issue.asp?issueid=76** (April 17, 2015); and Todd Bloom, *College and Career Readiness: A Systemic P-20 Response* (Arlington, VA: Naviance, 2010).

[36]Gilbert T. Sewall, "Textbook Publishing," *Phi Delta Kappan* (March 2005), pp. 498–502; and Lee Wilson, "A SaaS Content Pricing Model Emerges," *The Education Business Blog* (March 27, 2014) at **www.educationbusinessblog.com/2014/03/saas-educational-content-pricing-model-emerges.html** (March 4, 2015).

[37]Sarah Garland, "Common Core Standards Shake Up the Education Business," *The Hechinger Report* (October 15, 2013) at **www.hechingerreport.org/common-core-standards-shake-up-the-education-business** (March 5, 2015); Lelani Cauthen, "How Big Is the K–12 Digital Curriculum Market?" *The Learning Counsel* (January 2014) at **http://thelearningcounsel.com/archives/k12-digital-market** (March 5, 2015); and Diane Ravitch, "Researcher: Most 'Common Core-Aligned' Textbooks Are Shams," Diane Ravitch's blog (March 8, 2014) at **http://dianeravitch.net/2014/03/08/researcher-most-common-core-ligned-textbooks-are-shams/** (March 5, 2015).

Another transformation that is underway that will impact what is taught in school is the transition from physical textbooks to digital content, especially cloud-based content.[38] While the actual textbook market is dominated by three giant publishers, the digital market is described as "fractured" with numerous products coming from small nonprofits, ed-tech start-ups, and other new ventures. They are creating new learning apps and online curricular materials that can supplement or replace textbooks.[39] That is clearly the future for the state of Florida whose legislature approved a statute that requires school districts to spend half of their instructional materials budget on digital content by the 2015–2016 school year.[40]

censorship The suppression of ideas and information that certain persons—individuals, groups, or government officials—find objectionable or dangerous.

Another issue in curriculum development is the question of **censorship**. The American Library Association (ALA) defines censorship as "the suppression of ideas and information that certain persons—individuals, groups or government officials—find objectionable or dangerous."[41] In states that prepare approved lists of instructional materials for their schools, the trend is growing to "limit what students shall read." The list of objectionable works has recently included such works as *Captain Underpants,* by Dav Pilkey, and *The Bluest Eye,* by Toni Morrison. Today, almost any instructional material that contains political or economic messages, obscenity, sex, nudity, profanity, slang or questionable English, ethnic or racially sensitive material, or any material that could be interpreted as antifamily, antireligious, or anti-American is subject to possible censorship.[42] Additionally, students' online access to various websites and social networks, as discussed in the Technology @ School box, is of much concern to teachers and parents. In an attempt to protect students from objectionable sites, over-blocking of Internet resources through school-wide filtering systems restricts access so severely that intellectual freedom questions arise.[43]

Although censorship is often overt, it can operate in subtle ways as well. Curriculum developers may quietly steer away from issues and materials that would cause controversy in the community. Moreover, textbooks and instructional materials might omit topics that could potentially upset specific audiences or interest groups. Even pictures are important; some organizations count the number of pictures of one ethnic group versus another group, of boys versus girls, and of business versus labor. School boards can also exert a type of censorship when they recommend certain topics or points of view in subject content and implicitly discourage other approaches. You must be sensitive to censorship because it is an issue you will likely encounter during your career as an educator. In dealing with such issues, we often find that Herbert Spencer's fundamental question, "What knowledge is of most worth?" becomes "*Whose* knowledge is of most worth?"[44]

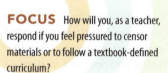

FOCUS How will you, as a teacher, respond if you feel pressured to censor materials or to follow a textbook-defined curriculum?

---

[38]Lee Wilson, "A SaaS Content Pricing Model Emerges," *The Education Business Blog* (March 27, 2014) at **www.educationbusinessblog.com/2014/03/saas-educational-content-pricing-model-emerges.html** (March 4, 2015).

[39]Sarah Garland, "Common Core Standards Shake Up the Education Business," *The Hechinger Report* (October 15, 2013) at **http://hechingerreport.org/common-core-standards-shake-up-the-education-business** (March 5, 2015); Lelani Cauthen, "How Big is the K–12 Digital Curriculum Market?" *The Learning Counsel* (January 2014) at **http://thelearningcounsel.com/archives/k12-digital-market** (March 5, 2015).

[40]Michelle R. Davis, "Digital Shift: 'Big Three' Publishers Rethink K–12 Strategies," *Education Week* (February 6, 2013), pp. 22, 42–44.

[41]American Library Association, "Intellectual Freedom and Censorship Q and A" (ALA, n.d.) at **www.ala.org/advocacy/intfreedom/censorshipfirstamendmentissues/ifcensorshipqanda** (April 17, 2015).

[42]Fran Falk-Ross and Jeannetta Caplan, "The Challenge of Censorship," *Reading Today* (April 2008), p. 20; and American Library Association, "Frequently Challenged Books of the 21st Century," (n.d.) at **www.ala.org/bbooks/frequentlychallengedbooks/top10** (March 4, 2015).

[43]Mike Nantais and Glenn Cockerline, "Internet Filtering in Schools: Protection or Censorship?" *Journal of Curriculum & Pedagogy* (Winter 2010), pp. 51–53; and Doug Johnson, "Filtering Fallacies," *Educational Leadership* (December 2012/January 2013), pp. 86–87.

[44]Kenneth Kidd, "Not Censorship But Selection: Censorship and/as Prizing," *Children's Literature In Education* (September 2009), pp. 197–216; *National Coalition Against Censorship, The First Amendment in Schools: Censorship* (n.d.) at **http://ncac.org/resource/the-first-amendment-in-schools-censorship/** (March 4, 2015); and Jack Healy, "After Uproar, School Board in Colorado Scraps Anti-Protest Curriculum," *The New York Times,* (October 4, 2014), p. A11.

TECHNOLOGY @ SCHOOL

SAFETY ISSUES AND SOCIAL MEDIA

Educators and parents alike agree that adult supervision of students' Internet use, both at home and at school (a form of censorship), is critical. As a teacher, you need to educate your students about responsible online behavior and safety issues. An excellent website for this is Media Smarts. This site alerts teachers and students to safety issues associated with websites, social networking/virtual environments, texting, and e-mail. It includes information on the benefits and risks of these activities and offers practical advice on how you can ensure that your students have safe and rewarding online experiences. The site also includes a link for parents with much the same information. Additionally, the Federal Trade Commission provides advice for the responsible use of social networking sites at OnGuardOnline.gov.

An important issue that deserves attention and that has perhaps been facilitated by social networks is **cyberbullying**, a form of online taunting meant to intimidate a particular child. The National Crime Prevention Council website includes audio messages and videocasts about combating cyberbullying and creating safe environments for students.

A site with resources for teachers interested in appropriately incorporating flipped learning in their classroom instruction is the Flipped Learning Network. This site provides information on all things flipped, including numerous ongoing blogs, opportunities to participate in helpful webinars, podcasts, and an online Professional Learning Community. Even the most technology-savvy educator could browse for hours on this site.

cyberbullying Actions that involve the use of electronic means to torment, threaten, harass, humiliate, embarrass, or otherwise target another person.

As teaching becomes more professionalized, teachers are increasingly expected to make curriculum choices and deal with the complex and controversial issues they present. To preserve your academic freedom to make decisions that best address the learning needs of your students, you will need a full understanding of community concerns, statewide standards, and school policies to exercise your professional judgement.[45]

14-3 INSTRUCTIONAL APPROACHES

Although educators recognize there are multiple definitions of curriculum, most agree that curriculum and instruction are interrelated. To carry out the curriculum, one must rely on instruction—the strategies, materials, and methods used to teach students. Even more than with curriculum approaches, most teachers incorporate a variety of instructional strategies in their classes. The search for new programs and methods of instruction is continual. The past four decades, in particular, have witnessed a major effort to improve learning outcomes and have students become more efficient and effective learners.

Although we cannot survey all of the major instructional innovations, the following sections describe a few that have influenced classrooms. Chapter 16, School Effectiveness and Reform in the United States, treats the subject of instructional approaches in the context of school reform and school effectiveness.

14-3a Differentiated Instruction

differentiated instruction A type of instruction based on the premise that all students differ in how they learn, their personal strengths and weaknesses, their backgrounds, and their interests.

Differentiated instruction describes an approach to designing lessons that addresses the wide range of differences that exist among students in today's classrooms.[46] Differentiated instruction is a form of personalized instruction with the goal of maximizing each

---

[45]American Library Association, "Strategies and Tips for Dealing with Challenges to Library Materials," (n.d.) at **www.ala.org/bbooks/challengedmaterials/support /strategies#schoollibraries**.

[46]Donald C. Orlich, Robert J. Harder, Richard C. Callahan, Michael S. Trevisan, Abbie H. Brown, and Darcy E. Miller, *Teaching Strategies: A Guide to Effective Instruction*, 10th ed. (Belmont, CA: Wadsworth Cengage Learning, 2013), pp. 57–58.

learner's potential and giving meaning to students' learning. It has also been described as matching teaching to the needs of individual learners.[47]

A key component of differentiated instruction is through a conceptually based curriculum focus that emphasizes constructing understanding rather than accumulating facts and regurgitating information. The teacher must be able to establish what students should know and understand, as well as the skills that are necessary to develop the learning. She then plans classroom experiences that are engaging and challenging for students; incorporating a variety of media likely to appeal to the learners, providing students with choices for assignments to complete, and drawing upon an array of instructional methods. It is common that options also be provided for the grouping of students when completing instructional tasks. In other words, students are offered multiple paths to reach a lesson's preset learning objectives. This method of instruction is designed to be engaging because it shows students the connections between their experiences and the authentic curriculum they are studying. Ultimately, the teacher uses various forms of assessment to discover each learner's knowledge and skill level to differentiate instruction to meet the objectives of the planned curriculum.[48]

Proponents suggest that differentiated instruction is a particularly appropriate strategy for classrooms in the twenty-first century. Where classrooms are increasingly becoming more diverse in multiple ways, students who may have been sorted into lower tracked classes in the past are now likely to be mixed into more advanced classes to be prepared to attain higher academic standards. Additionally, classrooms are likely to be more diverse as schools continue to incorporate the inclusion of students with special needs, those from families in poverty, and the number of English Language Learners (ELLs) increases. Based on the varying needs of learners as they strive to master the curriculum, instruction needs to be differentiated to address their varied achievement levels, learning styles, and interests. The goal through such instruction is that all students should reach mastery of the intended outcomes.[49]

Critics of differentiated instruction contend that it is too time-consuming and impossible to implement on top of the other requirements that teachers face. Additional objections include that there are too many standards to be covered, the standardized tests are not differentiated, and class sizes are just too large. Some parents have complained that their children might be neglected while the teacher works with different groups of students during classroom instruction.[50]

14-3b Social and Emotional Learning

While the ability to learn in classrooms is dependent on factors such as teachers, instructional strategies, materials, and the implementation of technologies, a school environment where students feel safe and comfortable and have positive relationships with adults and peers is also critical. Conversely, high-stress environments where students feel chronically unsafe and uncared for make it harder to learn and more likely for students to act out or drop out.[51]

[47]Carol Ann Tomlinson, "Mapping a Route toward a Differentiated Instruction," *Educational Leadership* (September 1999), pp. 12–16; and Julie Anna Hartwell, "ABCs of Differentiating Instruction," *New Teacher Advocate* (Winter 2006), pp. 6–7, 12.

[48]Lori Tukey, "Differentiation," *Phi Delta Kappan* (September 2002), pp. 63–65; and Jennifer Carolan and Abigail Guinn, "Differentiation: Lessons from Master Teachers," *Educational Leadership* (February 2007), pp. 44–47.

[49]James H. VanSciver, "Motherhood, Apple Pie, and Differentiated Instruction," *Phi Delta Kappan* (March 2005), pp. 534–535; and Carol Tomlinson, "This Issue," *Theory into Practice* (Summer 2005), pp. 183–184.

[50]Jennifer Carolan and Abigail Guinn, "Differentiation: Lessons from Master Teachers," *Educational Leadership* (February 2007), pp. 44–47; and Douglas B. Reeves, "From Differentiated Instruction to Differentiated Assessment," *ASCD Express* (July 2011) at **www.ascd.org/ascd-express/vol6/620-reeves.aspx** (May 2015).

[51]Sarah D. Sparks, "Students' Social, Emotional Needs Entwined with Learning, Security," *Education Week* (January 10, 2013), pp. 16–21.

social and emotional learning (SEL) Involves the process of children developing the skills, attitudes, and values necessary to acquire social and emotional competence (that is, managing emotions, achieving positive goals, showing empathy for others, maintaining positive relationships, and making responsible decisions).

To create a balanced environment that optimizes school success, a growing number of educators are promoting the idea that the best schools are those that foster students' academic, social, and emotional competencies, thus the adoption of **social and emotional learning (SEL)** programs are expanding throughout districts in the United States.[52] Although predominantly found at the preschool and elementary levels, the recognition that social and emotional factors can positively affect academic engagement, achievement, and attainment has many secondary schools exploring implementation strategies for SEL programs as well.[53]

Social and emotional learning is aligned to a set of skills that individuals need to succeed in school, the workplace, relationships, and as citizens.[54] It is defined as a process through which children "acquire and effectively apply the knowledge, attitudes and skills necessary to understand and manage emotions, set and achieve positive goals, feel and show empathy for others, establish and maintain positive relationships, and make responsible decisions." The five core competencies are identified as self-awareness, self-management, social awareness, relationship management, and responsible decision making.[55] Advocates suggest that individuals with social and emotional competence are most likely to succeed academically. They claim that if schools can improve students' attitudes and beliefs about self, others, and school, there is a foundation for better adjustment and academic performance.[56]

Children need skills such as managing negative emotions, being calm and focused, following directions, and maintaining healthy relationships with peers and adults. To do this, schools have adopted SEL programs. Most programs to date have been found primarily in pre-K and elementary schools, but SEL educators contend social and emotional skills have been identified as critical to success in college and the workplace, therefore, social competence is necessary for success across all grade levels. This view has been supported by The Gates Foundation and the National Association of Colleges and Employers.[57]

Initially, SEL programs were justified as a way to foster better relationships among pre-K students who were entering a school setting for the first time. Additionally, social and emotional skills were critical components of successful antibullying programs.[58] Research supported the claims that when appropriately implemented, SEL programs improved social and emotional skill, bonding to school, and classroom behavior. There were also fewer delinquent acts, less bullying, and reduced emotional distress.[59]

---

[52]Stephanie M. Jones and Suzanne M. Bouffard, "Social and Emotional Learning in Schools: From Programs to Strategies," *Social Policy Report* (2012) at **www.acknowledgealliance.org /wp-content/uploads/srcd-policy-brief-sel-in-schools.pdf** (April 13, 2015); and Roger P. Weissberg and Jason Cascarino, "Academic Learning + Social-Emotional Learning = National Priority," *Phi Delta Kappan* (October 2013), pp. 8–13.

[53]Barbara Cervone and Kathleen Cushman, "Integrating Social-Emotional Learning into High School," *Education Week* (May 20, 2014), pp. 24, 28.

[54]Stephanie M. Jones and Suzanne M. Bouffard, "Social and Emotional Learning in Schools: From Programs to Strategies," *Social Policy Report* (2012) at **www.acknowledgealliance.org /wp-content/uploads/srcd-policy-brief-sel-in-schools.pdf** (April 13, 2015).

[55]"What Is Social and Emotional Learning?" *Collaborative for Academic, Social and Emotional Learning (CASEL)* (n.d.) at **www.casel.org/social-and-emotional-learning** (April 15, 2015).

[56]Roger P. Weissberg and Jason Cascarino, "Academic Learning + Social-Emotional Learning = National Priority," *Phi Delta Kappan* (October 2013), pp. 8–13; Suzanne Bouffard, "Making School a Calmer Place to Learn," *Education Digest* (May 2014), pp. 12–17; and "What Is Social and Emotional Learning?" *Project EXSEL* (May 14, 2014) at **http://pd.ilt.columbia.edu /projects/exsel/aboutsel/** (April 15, 2015).

[57]"21st Century Skills Vital for the Future Workforce," *Committee for Children* (n.d.) at **www .cfchildren.org/second-step/social-emotional-learning/21st-century-skills-vital-for -future-workforce www.cfchildren.org/second-step/social-emotional-learning** (April 13, 2015); and Stephanie M. Jones and Suzanne M. Bouffard, "Social and Emotional Learning in Schools: From Programs to Strategies," *Social Policy Report* (2012) at **www.acknowledgealliance .org/wp-content/uploads/srcd-policy-brief-sel-in-schools.pdf** (April 13, 2015).

[58]Brian H. Smith and Sabina Low, "The Role of Social-Emotional Learning in Bullying Prevention Efforts," *Theory into Practice* (October 2013), pp. 280–287.

[59]Roger P. Weissberg and Jason Cascarino, "Academic Learning + Social-Emotional Learning = National Priority," *Phi Delta Kappan* (October 2013), pp. 8–13

Polls show that the public is in favor of schools addressing social and emotional competencies in addition to cognitive skills. All fifty states have established preschool SEL standards, and three states—Illinois, Kansas, and Pennsylvania—have stand-alone SEL standards across the K–12 curriculum. Many educators are advocating for a broader adoption of SEL standards because classroom activities that are needed to meet Common Core standards, such as effective communication, project collaboration, and interdisciplinary thinking, necessitate strong social and emotional competence.[60]

14-3c Direct Instruction

direct instruction A systematic method of teaching that emphasizes teacher-directed instruction proceeding in small steps, usually in accordance with a six- to eight-part lesson sequence.

The **direct instruction** model has been incorporated in classrooms, especially at the elementary level. According to its advocates, direct instruction "emphasizes well-developed and carefully planned lessons designed around small learning increments and clearly defined and prescribed teaching tasks."[61] Information is conveyed by the teacher in a way that is explicit and extremely scaffolded in highly organized presentations, and in some cases, through scripted lessons. It is teacher directed, and lessons are systematically sequenced with guided student practice and teacher feedback. Instruction is deliberately guided and precisely explicit for the learner to know the content and skills that need to be learned and performed.[62]

Use of direct instruction was incorporated into President George W. Bush's plan to improve education, the No Child Left Behind Act (NCLB). NCLB, which focused on improving all students' scores on standardized tests, initially targeted underperforming schools in which students fell below expectations; a number of direct-instruction programs targeted a similar audience. School districts, eager to comply with NCLB requirements, incorporated direct-instruction programs that were developed by commercial publishers for a wide array of subjects in the school curriculum, including reading, mathematics, language, science, social science, and handwriting, as well as for special-education programs.[63] The common denominator of these programs is the teacher-directed curriculum, which is highly explicit, scripted, and includes intense teacher–student interaction.

Direct instruction gained recognition for increasing the standardized reading scores of students, especially those in low-income settings. Programs using the model were endorsed by the National Reading Panel in 2000 and the US Department of Education, often linking the term "evidence-based reading instruction" to direct instruction because of the documented improvement in students' test scores. Other proponents have suggested that direct instruction is the optimal way to teach and learn science and other subjects. Claims have also been made that affective behaviors such as self-esteem, a sense of responsibility, and positive attitudes toward school have been enhanced as a result of direct-instruction implementation.[64]

Critics aligned with a more student-centered approach have challenged direct instruction and the studies that suggest its effectiveness. Generally, direct-instruction reading programs incorporate systematic and explicit phonics instruction that is

---

[60]Ibid.

[61]"Basic Philosophy of Direct Instruction (DI)," *National Institute for Direct Instruction* (n.d.) at **www.nifdi.org/what-is-di/basic-philosophy** (April 12, 2015).

[62]Fiona McMullen and Alison Madelaine, "Why is There So Much Resistance to Direct Instruction?" *Australian Journal of Learning Difficulties* (December 2014), pp. 137–151.

[63]"About the Programs," *National Institute for Direct Instruction* (n.d.) at **www.nifdi.org /programs/about-the-programs** (April 12, 2015); Rebecca Harris, "Reading Fundamentals," *Catalyst Chicago* (Summer 2011), pp. 16–19; and "National Reading Panel," *National Institute of Child Health and Human Development* (October 29, 2013) at **www.nichd.nih.gov/research /supported/Pages/nrp.aspx/** (April 12, 2015).

[64]Elaine Bukowiecki, "Teaching Children How to Read," *Kappa Delta Pi Record* (Winter 2007), pp. 58–65; Tricia Smith, "Direct Instruction," *Research Starters—Education* (Toledo, OH: Great Neck Publishing, 2008), pp. 1–7; and *Writings on Direct Instruction* (Eugene, OR: National Institute for Direct Instruction, Winter 2015).

heavily scripted. This approach has been criticized for being overly prescriptive and focusing on isolated skills that might help children become "word readers" but does little to develop comprehension or the ability to read for meaning. Additionally, critics claim that it is too focused on rote learning, too teacher directed, and students are too passive; this seems counter to the type of teaching aligned with CCSS where teachers are to act as facilitators or coaches, and students are to be active, collaborative conversationalists in the classroom.[65]

14-3d Twenty-First-Century Skills

Secretary of Education Arne Duncan suggests that schools in the United States need to dramatically improve teaching, learning, and assessment to prepare students for the twenty-first century.[66] The advocacy group, P21, is representative of educators who are promoting a more comprehensive curriculum and instruction effort to prepare students to be successful in a globally and digitally interconnected world.[67] To master the recommended twenty-first-century set of student outcomes, classroom instruction will have to become more interactive and engaging than it currently is.

The following skills are deemed necessary for students in the modern interdependent global society:

- Learning and innovation skills (creativity and innovation, critical thinking and problem solving, communication and collaboration)
- Core subjects and twenty-first-century themes (global awareness; financial, economic, business, and entrepreneurial literacy; civic literacy; health literacy; environmental literacy)
- Information, media, and technology skills
- Life and career skills (for example, initiative and self-direction, flexibility and adaptability)[68]

In contrast to traditional practice, these recommendations tend to focus more on process rather than content, and as a result, skill development will have to be emphasized along with rigorous curriculum and classroom instruction.

For example, an elementary school implementing twenty-first-century learning incorporated a project-based learning model as the cornerstone of the instructional program. This provided the opportunity for more student engagement as students collaborated on authentic creation of knowledge rather than worksheets. Technology was also integrated into the program as laptops and iPads were provided for student use. They used the technology for research and multimedia presentations and to manage their online portfolios that documented progress toward meeting their learning goals. Students were even able to assist staff in the design of projects that incorporated the technology they were using.[69] Instruction to foster **twenty-first-century skills** attainment must take place in engaging, flexible, and active environments such as this.

twenty-first-century skills Instruction fostering student success in the global job market and problem solving in the modern democratic society that takes place in engaging, flexible, and active environments.

[65]Pat G. Wilson, Prisca Martens, Poonam Arya, and Bess Altwerger, "Readers, Instruction, and the NRP," *Phi Delta Kappan* (November 2004), pp. 242–246; pp. 8–10; Barak Rosenshine, *Five Meanings of Direct Instruction* (Lincoln, IL: Center on Innovation & Improvement, 2008); Fiona McMullen and Alison Madelaine, "Why Is There So Much Resistance to Direct Instruction?" *Australian Journal of Learning Difficulties* (December 2014), pp. 137–151; and Laurie Udesky, "Classroom Coaches Critical as Teachers Shift to Common Core," *EdSource* (February 4, 2015) at **http://edsource.org/2015/classroom-coaches-critical-as-teachers-shift-to-common-core/73730#**.

[66]NEA, *Preparing 21ˢᵗ Century Students for a Global Society* (Washington, DC: National Education Association, May 31, 2012) at **www.nea.org/assets/docs/A-Guide-to-Four-Cs.pdf**.

[67]"FAQ," *P21: Partnership for 21ˢᵗ Century Learning* (n.d.) at **www.p21.org/about-us/p21-faq** (April 11, 2015).

[68]"Framework for 21st Century Learning," *Partnership for 21ˢᵗ Century Learning* (n.d.) at **www.p21.org/about-us/p21-framework** (April 11, 2015).

[69]"Case Study: Katherine Smith Elementary School," *Partnership for 21ˢᵗ Century Learning* (n.d.) at **www.p21.org/exemplar-program-case-studies/1623** (April 11, 2015).

Nineteen states have made a commitment to infusing the twenty-first-century skills mentioned above into their schools along with the core subjects that include the interdisciplinary themes.[70] Although advocates see this as progress for the evolution of curriculum and instruction as we move toward a more competitive global society, critics of the approach contend it is just a fad that is being recycled from the past. They maintain that the cross-disciplinary skills emphasized in this approach water down the academic content and will result in lowered academic performance on required assessments.[71]

14-3e Technology-Enhanced Instruction

Incorporating technology in classroom instruction is pervasive throughout America's schools. As recently as the mid-1990s this was not the case, as only 35 percent of the nation's schools and 3 percent of classrooms were connected to the Internet. Today, virtually every school has at least one instructional computer with Internet access, and students, by a ratio of 3 to 1, have access to computers connected to the Internet.[72] A 2013 nationwide survey of teachers found that 90 percent have access to at least one PC or laptop for their classroom, and nearly 60 percent have access to an interactive whiteboard. More than one-third has access to tablets or eReaders for their classrooms, which is up from 20 percent the previous year. Teachers surveyed indicated that education technology allows them to "do much more than ever before" for their students.[73]

technology-enhanced learning Instructional strategies that draw upon technology in a variety of ways.

Teachers are also aware that infusing CCSS into classroom instruction can be facilitated by student-centered, **technology-enhanced instruction**.[74] Many educators are experimenting with and implementing blended learning to facilitate such classrooms. Blended learning combines face-to-face instruction with personalized online delivery of content and learning using adaptive courseware that gives students control over their time, place, path, and pace of instruction along with continuous assessment of progress.[75] Rather than replacing traditional teaching methods, blended learning complements them.

Advocates for blended learning cite research which suggests that it is more effective than online learning or face-to-face learning as stand-alone options.[76] Teachers also find the approach beneficial because they become facilitators who can tailor lessons to the needs of small groups or individual students.[77]

[70]"Overview of State Leadership Initiative," *Partnership for 21ˢᵗ Century Learning* (n.d.) at **www.p21.org\\members-states\\partner-states** (April 11, 2015).

[71]"21ˢᵗ Century Skills," *Glossary of Education Reform* (September 15, 2014) at **http://edglossary.org/21st-century-skills/** (April 11, 2015).

[72]"Percent of All Public Schools and Instructional Rooms Having Internet Access: Fall 1994 to Fall 2001—Figure 31," *Digest of Education Statistics, 2002,* at **http://nces.ed.gov/programs/digest/d02/fig_31.asp** (April 18, 2015); and Nick Pandolfo, "Education Technology: As Schools Plunge In, Poor Schools Are Left Behind," *The Hechinger Report* (March 25, 2012) at **www.huffingtonpost.com/2012/01/24/education-technology-as-s_n_1228072.html** (April 10, 2015).

[73]PBS Learning Media, *PBS Survey Finds Teachers Are Embracing Digital Resources to Propel Student Learning* (February 4, 2013) at **www.pbs.org/about/news/archive/2013/teacher-tech-survey/** (April 10, 2015).

[74]Caitlin R. Tucker, "The Basics of Blended Instruction," *Educational Leadership* (March 2013), pp. 57–60.

[75]Heather Staker and Michael B. Horn, *Classifying K–12 Blended Learning* (San Mateo, CA: Innosight Institute, April 2013), available at **www.christenseninstitute.org/wp-content/uploads/2013/04/Classifying-K-12-blended-learning.pdf** (April 10, 2015); and Lucille Renwick, "Where Blended Meets Personalized Learning—and Gets Results," *eSchool News* (February 24, 2015) at **www.eschoolnews.com/2015/02/24/blended-learning-change-393/** (April 10, 2015).

[76]Eric Werth, Lori Werth, and Eric Kellerer, *Transforming K–12 Rural Education through Blended Learning: Barriers and Promising Practices* (Vienna, VA: iNACOL, October 2013).

[77]Jordan Money, "In California District, Blended-Learning Approach Turns Teachers into Facilitators," *Education Week* (February 18, 2015).

The Washington, DC, school district has been noted for its implementation of blended learning as part of its school reform effort to enhance student achievement. The district's blended learning initiative in elementary math began in 2012–2013, and the result after two years showed significant academic gains on district assessments.[78] An example of a blended learning math lesson might find students rotating through stations in groups where they spend a portion of the lesson learning online with a self-grading, interactive program and the other part of the lesson with the teacher in small groups that have been assessed to have similar needs or strengths. The teacher uses the data generated through the online lesson to differentiate instruction and tailor her lessons to address student concerns.[79] Teachers note that there is more engagement between students and teachers, and, as a result, there seem to be fewer discipline problems.

flipped classroom A classroom in which students are introduced to lesson content at home, typically through an online video of the teacher's lecture, and practice demonstrating mastery of the content in the classroom with the teacher acting as a facilitator, assisting students who need help.

A specific model of blended learning that has gained favor among a growing number of educators is the **flipped classroom**. Two Colorado high school teachers are credited with developing the approach that involves moving the delivery of basic content instruction—the teacher's lecture—online, usually in the form of a video, so that students have the opportunity to review the material at their own pace.[80] The class is "flipped" because the recorded lecture is viewed by the student at home and the class time is used similar to a workshop where students work with and demonstrate understanding of the information presented in the recorded lecture. The lectures are now viewed as homework, and the work that was formerly done at home is now the focus of the in-class lesson.

The rationale for having the student view the video of the teacher's lecture at home is that the student can control the pace of the lecture to meet his or her needs.[81] The lectures generally contain lower-level cognitive information or basic skill instruction that the students can consume on their own. If they miss something while viewing, they can rewind the video and view it again. If they already know the information, they can fast forward; it is not one pace fits all as it is in a classroom of twenty-five to thirty-five students. The student has ownership of the information.[82] With the information in hand, class time becomes a time where students complete practice problems, discuss issues, or work on projects. Teachers take on roles as coaches or advisors because there is greater potential to provide feedback that bolsters student learning.[83]

Teachers who successfully employ flipped learning note the lessons require careful preparation. Lectures need to be recorded and checked to ensure they clearly present the material. In-class activities must be carefully integrated if students are to be motivated to prepare for class; this requires that learning be based on the results of student assessments.[84] "Flipped" teachers claim multiple benefits associated with the

---

[78]David Rose and John Rice, "Blended Learning: How the Nation's Capital Is Reinventing Its Classrooms for the Future," *District Administration* (April 2015) at **www.districtadministration .com/article/0415-dc-rose** (April 10, 2015).

[79]Lucille Renwick, "Where Blended Meets Personalized Learning—and Gets Results," *eSchool News* (February 24, 2015) at **www.eschoolnews.com/2015/02/24/blended-learning -change-393/** (April 10, 2015).

[80] Hani Morgan, "Flip Your Classroom to Increase Academic Achievement," *Childhood Education* (May/June 2014), pp. 239–241.

[81]Bryan Goodwin and Kirsten Miller, "Research Says/Evidence on Flipped Classrooms Is Still Coming In," *Educational Leadership* (March 2013), pp. 78–80.

[82]Benjamin Levy, "Three Reasons the Flipped Classroom Is Here to Stay," *Education Week* (December 30, 2014).

[83]EDUCAUSE, "7 Things You Should Know About . . . . Flipped Classrooms," *ELI* (February 7, 2012) at **https://net.educause.edu/ir/library/pdf/eli7081.pdf**; and Michael Horn, "The Transformational Potential of Flipped Classrooms," *Education Next* (Summer 2013), pp. 78–79.

[84] EDUCAUSE, "7 Things You Should Know About . . . . Flipped Classrooms," *ELI* (February 7, 2012) at **https://net.educause.edu/ir/library/pdf/eli7081.pdf**; and Hani Morgan, "Flip Your Classroom to Increase Academic Achievement," *Childhood Education* (May/June 2014), pp. 239–241.

approach. They have more opportunities to interact with all students and especially to help struggling students focus on parts of the lecture they did not understand. There is more student engagement with the content and higher levels of thinking. Because there is more one-to-one time to interact with students, relations between students and teachers improve as well. Teachers also indicate that students' academic performance increases.[85]

Although only a small research base supports the use of flipped classrooms, it is spreading to involve more teachers and schools. One study finds that 30 percent more teachers adopted the method between 2012 and 2014, and an online community of teachers engaged in flipped learning grew from 2,500 to 20,000 members during the same period.[86] In another survey, 40 percent of administrators stated they were interested in trying flipped learning, and 25 percent of principals and superintendents agreed that flipped learning had a significant impact on transforming teaching and learning.[87]

Online Instruction and Virtual Schools   As technology continues to infiltrate the K–12 classroom, another platform for delivery of instruction that continues to experience growth is the virtual school. It has been estimated that 315,000 students in 2013–2014 took all of their courses online, an increase of 6.2 percent from the previous year; a decade earlier, only 50,000 students were enrolled.[88] Thirty-one states have statewide, full-time online virtual schools.[89] Arizona, California, Ohio, and Pennsylvania enroll more than 35,000 in their fully online schools.[90]

In addition to those students who attend virtual school full time, it has been conservatively estimated that another 2 million students across the country take individual courses through virtual schools. Several states, among them Florida, Virginia, Alabama, Idaho, and Michigan, have legislation that requires students to take at least one course online to graduate.[91]

Proponents contend that this approach is student-centered, highly personalized, and more efficient than the brick-and-mortar school. Taking classes online enables students to be self-directed learners and may be especially beneficial to those who have

[85]Bryan Goodwin and Kirsten Miller, "Research Says/Evidence on Flipped Classrooms Is Still Coming In," *Educational Leadership* (March 2013), pp. 78–80; and Hani Morgan, "Flip Your Classroom to Increase Academic Achievement," *Childhood Education* (May/June 2014), pp. 239–241.

[86]D. Frank Smith, "How Flipped Classrooms Are Growing and Changing," *EdTech* (June 2014) at **www.edtechmagazine.com/k12/article/2014/06/how-flipped-classrooms-are -growing-and-changing** (April 10, 2015); and Jessia Yarbro, Kari M. Arfstrom, Katherine McKnight, and Patrick McKnight, *Extension of a Review of Flipped Learning* (New York: Pearson, June 2014) at **www.flippedlearning.org/cms/lib07/VA01923112/Centricity /Domain/41/Extension%20of%20FLipped%20Learning%20LIt%20Review%20 June%202014.pdf** (April 10, 2015).

[87]Jessia Yarbro, Kari M. Arfstrom, Katherine McKnight, and Patrick McKnight, *Extension of a Review of Flipped Learning* (New York: Pearson, June 2014) at **www.flippedlearning.org/cms /lib07/VA01923112/Centricity/Domain/41/Extension%20of%20FLipped% 20Learning%20LIt%20Review%20June%202014.pdf** (April 10, 2015).

[88]Suzi Parker, "Would You Send Your Seven-Year-Old to an Online Elementary School?" *Takepart* (April 10, 2014) at **www.takepart.com/article/2014/04/10/virtual-elementary -schools** (April 11, 2015); and John Watson, Larry Pape, Amy Murin, Butch Gemin, and Lauren Vashaw, *Keeping Pace with K–12 Digital Learning 2014* (Durango, Co: Evergreen Education Group, 2014).

[89]Matthew M. Chingos, "Questioning the Quality of Virtual Schools," *Education Next* (Spring 2013) at **http://educationnext.org/questioning-the-quality-of-virtual-schools/** (April 11, 2015).

[90]*States with Statewide Fully Online Schools* (Durango, Co: Evergreen Education Group, 2014) at **www.kpk12.com/wp-content/uploads/KP2014_fully_online_map.png** (April 11, 2015).

[91]Yinying Wang and Janet R. Decker, "Can Virtual Schools Thrive in the Real World?" *TechTrends* (November/December 2014), pp. 57–62; and Jen Karentnick, "Virtual Education: Genuine Benefits or Real-Time Demerits?" *The Atlantic* (February 2015) at **www.theatlantic.com/education /archive/2015/02/virtual-education-genuine-benefits-or-real-time-demerits/385674/**.

FOCUS Which of the instructional methods listed in this section (differentiated instruction, social and emotional learning, twenty-first-century skills, and various methods of electronic instruction) do you feel most comfortable with as a teacher? Why? How can you prepare to make effective use of methods with which you are not yet comfortable?

difficulty in the traditional school setting.[92] Critics contend that results are at best mixed when it comes to evaluating virtual school performance. There are those virtual schools that are cited as effective for the students they serve, such as the Florida Virtual School, but in many cases, due to lack of oversight and follow through, virtual schools have been outperformed by traditional schools on various school performance measures.[93]

To some educators, our rapid technological advances spell the eventual demise of pencil technology. Experts do agree, however, that technological knowledge and skills will be essential components in the preparation and repertoire of all teachers. The role of technology in school reform is discussed further in Chapter 16, School Effectiveness and Reform in the United States, with an emphasis on teacher training when introducing technology.

14-4 SIGNIFICANT CURRICULUM TRENDS

In discussing instructional technology, we have already begun to look into the future. Student learning will increase through interaction with expanding technologies. Not all learning will be centered in the school or classroom, and use of technology, both in school and at home, will greatly expand how you and your students access information and, just as importantly, what information you access. What other trends will continue to develop and influence American classrooms? In the next section, we describe several that are emerging as important issues.

14-4a The Importance of the Arts

The arts, visual arts, music, dance, and drama, have long been part of the PK–12 school curriculum. Over the past decade and a half, however, the emphasis on statewide testing in math and reading have led to cutbacks in arts education offerings as schools have had to find time in the instructional schedule to offer low-performing students remedial classes in the tested subjects. The recent economic downturn also made it difficult to increase arts' offerings as tight school budgets saw the reordering of priorities to enhance the core academic program at the expense of the arts. This has been more pronounced in low-income schools where offerings in music and the visual arts have been less frequent than those in high-income schools.[94]

The evidence continues to mount that the arts deserve to be included in the day-to-day PK–12 curriculum. Secretary of Education Arne Duncan has often stated that the arts "can no longer be treated as a frill" and must be included in the everyday school curriculum.[95] Arts advocates contend that exposing young people to art and culture has a positive impact on their development in a number of ways.[96]

---

[92]Elizabeth Kanna and Lisa Gillis, "Discussing the Pros and Cons of High School Online Learning," *iVirtualschool* (n.d.) at **www.ivirtualschool.com/hscodiscussing-the-pros-and -cons-of-high-school-online-learning** (April 11, 2015); Jen Karentnick, "Virtual Education: Genuine Benefits or Real-Time Demerits?" *The Atlantic* (February 2015) at **www.theatlantic .com/education/archive/2015/02/virtual-education-genuine-benefits-or-real-time -demerits/385674/** (April 11, 2015).

[93]Jen Karentnick, "Virtual Education: Genuine Benefits or Real-Time Demerits?" *The Atlantic* (February 2015) at **www.theatlantic.com/education/archive/2015/02/virtual -education-genuine-benefits-or-real-time-demerits/385674/** (April 11, 2015).

[94]Alison DeNisco, "Students will Dance, Act and Design with Core Art Standards," *District Administration* (March 2015) at **www.districtadministration.com/article/students-will -dance-act-and-design-core-arts-standards**; and Alison DeNisco, "Low-Income Students Benefit from Arts," *District Administration* (March 2015) at **www.districtadministration .com/article/students-will-dance-act-and-design-core-arts-standards**.

[95]Heather Noonan, "Understanding the Big Picture, Claiming a Seat at the Table," *TRIAD* (October/November 2010), pp. 66–69.

[96]Jay P. Greene, Brian Kisida, Carl A Bogulski, Anne Kraybill, Collin Hitt, and Daniel H. Bowen, "Arts Education Matters: We Know, We Measured It," *Education Week* (December 3, 2014) at **www.edweek.org/ew/articles/2014/12/03/13greene.h34.html**.

Longitudinal studies have highlighted the benefits for students who have been engaged in the arts, especially those who are at-risk or attending schools in low-income areas. The findings from one recent study suggests that engagement in the arts leads to better academic performance, higher grades, higher rates of college enrollment, better workforce opportunities, and more civic engagement.[97] Another finds that low-income students who are highly engaged in the arts are more likely to earn an associate's or bachelor's degree than their peers who experience low arts involvement.[98] It is also suggested that having arts instruction leads to better school attendance and behavior and improved reading and math scores.[99]

Interestingly, studies from the National Institutes of Health utilizing magnetic resonance imaging (MRI) have been cited in support of music education. By studying changes in the brain of children who learn to play a musical instrument, the researchers concluded that children could reduce feelings of anxiety, gain control of emotions, improve memory, and give stronger focus to their attention.[100]

For many art educators, the above studies support their concern that schools should continue to support a strong arts curriculum, but they contend that the findings from a large-scale study should be more convincing to policy makers considering cutting the arts. The findings from this study suggest that exposure to the arts improves knowledge about the arts and increases children's desire to be cultural consumers in the future. Arts exposure also encourages more tolerance and empathy, boosts critical thinking, and encourages more careful observations of one's surroundings.[101] These findings suggest that involvement in the arts can lead to the development of the whole child.

14-4b Education of English Language Learners

The number of ELLs (national-origin minority students who are limited in English proficiency) enrolled in US public schools continues to grow, and the projection for the future sees this trend continuing. Nationally, almost 61 million residents, or 21 percent of the population, speaks a language other than English at home—up from just under 18 percent in 2000—and 62 percent of non-English speakers speak Spanish at home.[102] Across the United States, more than one in five of the school-age population speaks a language other than English at home; for California it's 44 percent, and in Texas, Nevada, New Jersey, and New York, it's roughly one in three.

[97]"New NEA Research Report Shows Potential Benefits of Arts Education for At-Risk Youth," *States News Service* (March 30, 2012).

[98]"Increased Arts Involvement Among Disadvantaged Students Leads to: Finding a Better Job, Earning a College Degree and Volunteering," *Americans for the Arts* (March 2014) at **www.AmericansfortheArts.org**.

[99]James S. Catterall, "The Consequences of Curtailing Music Education," *Tavis Smiley Reports* (March 27, 2014) at **www.pbs.org/wnet/tavissmiley/tsr/dudamel-conducting-a-life/the-consequences-of-curtailing-music-education/**; and Alison DeNisco, "Low-Income Students Benefit from Arts," *District Administration* (March 2015) at **www.districtadministration.com/article/students-will-dance-act-and-design-core-arts-standards**.

[100]A. Collins, "Music Education and the Brain: What Does It Take to Make a Change," *Update: Applications of Research in Music Education* (May 2014) pp. 4–10; and James McIntosh, "Learning a Musical Instrument Boosts Kids' Brains," *Medical News Today* (December 31, 2014) at **www.medicalnewstoday.com/articles/287458.php**.

[101]Jay P. Greene, Brian Kisida, Carl A Bogulski, Anne Kraybill, Collin Hitt, and Daniel H. Bowen, "Arts Education Matters: We Know, We Measured It," *Education Week* (December 3, 2014) at **www.edweek.org/ew/articles/2014/12/03/13greene.h34.html**.

[102] US Census Bureau, "New Census Bureau Data Reveal More Older Workers, Homeowners, Non-English Speakers," *US Census Bureau News* (Washington, DC: US Department of Commerce, September 12, 2007); Steven A. Camarota and Karen Zeigler, "One in Five US Residents Speaks Foreign Language at Home, Record 61.8 Million," Center for Immigration Studies (October 2014) at **http://cis.org/record-one-in-five-us-residents-speaks-language-other-than-english-at-home**; and Patricia C. Gandara and Ursula S. Aldana, "Who's Segregated Now? Latinos, Language, and the Future of Integrated Schools," *Educational Administration Quarterly* (2014), pp. 735–748.

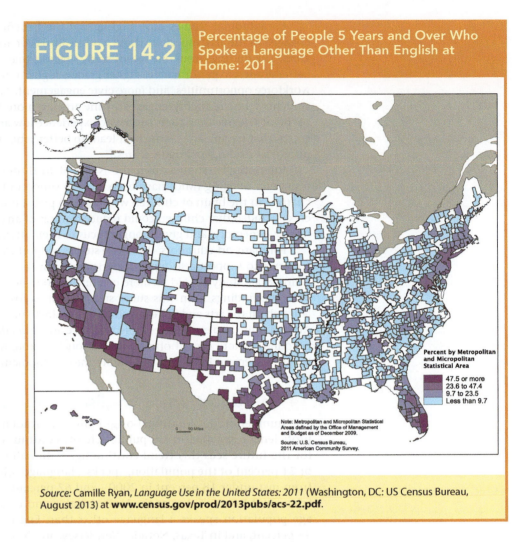

FIGURE 14.2 Percentage of People 5 Years and Over Who Spoke a Language Other Than English at Home: 2011

Percent by Metropolitan and Micropolitan Statistical Area

- 47.5 or more
- 23.6 to 47.4
- 9.7 to 23.5
- Less than 9.7

Note: Metropolitan and Micropolitan Statistical Areas defined by the Office of Management and Budget as of December 2009.

Source: U.S. Census Bureau, 2011 American Community Survey.

Source: Camille Ryan, *Language Use in the United States: 2011* (Washington, DC: US Census Bureau, August 2013) at **www.census.gov/prod/2013pubs/acs-22.pdf**.

It is estimated that 4.4 million students in the United States are enrolled in programs for ELLs.[103] Collectively, more than four hundred different home languages are spoken by ELL students in America's schools.[104]

Almost 56 percent of those who speak a language other than English at home are immigrants representing a wide range of cultures and ethnic backgrounds (Figure 14.2).[105] In addition to Spanish, the most common languages spoken by students are Chinese, French, Vietnamese, Tagalog, Korean, and Arabic.[106] Even school districts that may not be thought of as traditional locations for new immigrants have been impacted. In the St. Paul, Minnesota, school district, 45 percent of students are ELLs. The largest of this group are students who are Hmong speakers followed by those

---

[103]"Table 204.20. Number and Percentage of Public School Students Participating in Programs for English Language Learners, by State: Selected Years, 2002–03 through 2011–12," *Digest of Education Statistics – 2013* (Washington, DC: National Center for Education Statistics, 2013) at **https://nces.ed.gov/programs/digest/d13/tables/dt13_204.20.asp**; and "English Language Learners," *The Condition of Education* (Washington, DC: National Center for Education Statistics, May 2014) at **https://nces.ed.gov/programs/coe/indicator_cgf.asp**.

[104]Margarita Calderón, Robert Slavin, and Marta Sánchez, "Effective Instruction for English Learners," *Future Of Children* (Spring 2011), pp. 103–127.

[105]Steven A. Camarota and Karen Zeigler, "One in Five US Residents Speaks Foreign Language at Home, Record 61.8 Million," *Center for Immigration Studies* (October 2014) at **http://cis.org/record-one-in-five-us-residents-speaks-language-other-than-english-at-home**.

[106]Camille Ryan, *Language Use in the United States: 2011* (Washington, DC: United States Census Bureau, August 2013).

who speak Spanish. The district is implementing intensive co-teaching strategies that team English for Speakers of Other Languages (ESOL) teachers and general education teachers to meet the needs of the students.[107]

In recent years, there has been an increase in students emigrating from environments that provided little opportunity for formal schooling, or their schooling was interrupted by political and social unrest. The unaccompanied minors who flooded across the southwest border in the 2014 surge were often traumatized by gang violence, war, and poverty. Many children had substantial gaps in their formal education and have been identified as Students with Interrupted Formal Education (SIFE). It is, however, a difficult task to prepare such students to meet rigorous graduation requirements when they have had limited experience with the school environment. In many cases, students who are not proficient English speakers may feel alienated from their school and community.[108]

A number of concerns face school officials who provide services for ELL students, especially those who have recently immigrated. The fundamental question is how can schools effectively help students learn academic content when they do not speak English? This basic question is confounded by a number of factors: What is the appropriate program for serving ELL students; how do we assess these students on rigorous, standardized tests; and how can we find highly qualified teachers for a diverse ELL population?[109]

The major concern among educators is the impact that the standards and assessment mandates are having on ELL students and their schools. In most cases, ELLs are required to take the same assessments of content as those taken by native speakers. In those states where the CCSS have been adopted, this means they must take the rigorous PARCC or Smarter Balanced assessments.[110] Educators understand that ELLs perform better academically and achieve greater language proficiency when they have high-quality English language instruction, but such programs are more costly. Fortunately, since the end of the Great Recession, many states have been able to increase funding for programs that target ELLs. A 2015 report states that forty-six states provide additional funding for ELLs beyond what is provided by the federal government. California is one state that has revamped its K–12 funding formula to concentrate more funds in schools with high numbers of ELLs.[111] Because the ELL population is projected to grow, school officials will continue to grapple with this issue for the foreseeable future.

14-4c Pre-K Education

Across the country, there has been a growing chorus to increase opportunities for young children, especially those living in low-income neighborhoods, to attend high-quality pre-Kindergarten (pre-K) programs. Such programs typically include a maximum class

---

[107]Lesli A. Maxwell, "English-Learner Education: Valeria Silva," *Education Week* (February 6, 2013), pp. S6–S7.

[108]Jennifer Medina, "In School for the First Time, Teenage Immigrants Struggle," *The New York Times* (January 25, 2009) at **http://nytimes.com/2009/01/25/education/25ellis.html** (April 7, 2015); and Susan Zimmerman-Orozco, "Border Kids in the Home of the Brave," *Educational Leadership* (March 2015), pp. 48–53.

[109]"Research Center: English Language Learners," *Education Week* (June 16, 2011) at **http:// edweek.org/ew/issues/english-language-learners**.

[110]Margaret Ramirez, "Can the Common Core Raise Graduation Rate for English Learners?" *Hechinger Report* (February 20, 2015) at **http://hechingerreport.org/can-common-core -raise-graduation-rate-english-learners/**.

[111]Maria Millard, "State Funding Mechanisms for English Language Learners," Trends in State Laws – ELL Funding (January 2015) at **www.ecs.org/html/Document.asp?chouseid =11694**; Madeline Will, "Richard A. Carranza: A One-Time English-Language Learner Puts Premium on Bilingual, Bicultural Education," *Education Week* (February 24, 2015) at **http:// leaders.edweek.org/profile/richard-a-carranza-superintendent-english -language-learner-education/print/**.

size of fifteen students, certified teachers, assistant teachers in every classroom, support services for children and their families, and developmentally appropriate curriculum aligned with state standards.[112]

Numerous studies have shown that when provided with such high-quality programs, program participants benefit from a number of academic and social gains. Longitudinal studies conducted in North Carolina and New Jersey suggest that children enrolled in high-quality preschool programs gain lifelong benefits such as better jobs and higher wages. They are also less likely to be involved with the criminal justice system or have the need to receive social services.[113] For those students who attended high-quality pre-K in low-income schools, by fifth grade, they have had fewer special-education placements and fewer grade retentions. They also are more likely to enter kindergarten ready to learn with their more affluent peers.[114]

A number of governors and policy leaders at the federal level have promoted expanded pre-K school as an investment in the future.[115] Currently, only six states do not provide funding for preschool, and for those that do, from 2013–2014 to 2014–2015, there was a 12 percent increase in funding for these programs; this follows a 6.9 percent increase in funding from the previous year. For the most recent year, twenty-eight states increased funding while eleven states maintained the same level of funding.[116]

In addition to governors promoting preschool as a way to reduce the achievement gap and ensure long-term student success, the federal Department of Education is also encouraging the expansion of funding for high-quality early education programs. Secretary of Education Arne Duncan points out that the United States ranks twenty-fifth in the world in early learning enrollment and falls behind such countries as Mexico, France, and Singapore.[117] The Obama administration has proposed more than $750 million in new federal grants for states to expand their pre-K programs. The White House suggests that universal preschool for all 4-year-olds would be a highly beneficial policy—only 30 percent now have access to state-funded programs—but that is not a policy that can be imposed by the federal government.[118]

14-4d Career and Technical Education (CTE)

With the pronouncements that students must be college and career ready to compete in the global economy, the focus on **career and technical education (CTE)** has grown as a critical component of the school curriculum. In response to headlines shouting that US employers are having difficulty filling openings for skilled trade positions, engineers, IT staff, and nurses, and the recent studies showing that 50 percent of all STEM jobs are open to workers with less than a bachelor's degree, CTE has been touted as

career and technical education (CTE) Provides students with the academic and technical skills, knowledge, and training necessary to succeed in future careers and to become lifelong learners. CTE prepares learners for the world of work by introducing them to the workplace environment, and makes academic content accessible by providing it in a hands-on context.

---

[112]W. Steven Barnett, Kwanghee Jung, Min-Jong Youn, and Ellen C. Frede, *Abbott Preschool Program Longitudinal Effects Study: Fifth Grade Follow-Up* (Piscataway, NJ: National Institute for Early Education Research – Rutgers, March 20, 2013).

[113]Lyndsey Layton, "Study: High-Quality Early Education Could Reduce Costs," *The Washington Post* (February 3, 2015).

[114]Steven Barnett, Kwanghee Jung, Min-Jong Youn, and Ellen C. Frede, *Abbott Preschool Program Longitudinal Effects Study: Fifth Grade Follow-Up* (Piscataway, NJ: National Institute for Early Education Research – Rutgers, March 20, 2013); and Lyndsey Layton, "Study: High-Quality Early Education Could Reduce Costs," *The Washington Post* (February 3, 2015).

[115]Stepanie Aragon and Julie Rowland, "Governors' Top Education Issues: 2015 State of the State Addresses," *ECS Education Trends* (February 2015).

[116]Bruce Atchison and Emily Workman, "State Pre-K Funding: 2014-15 Fiscal Year," *ECS – Early Learning* (Denver, CO: Education Commission of the States, January 2015).

[117]US Department of Education, *Early Learning: America's Middle Class Promise Begins Early* (Washington, DC: US Department of Education, n.d.) at **www.ed.gov/early-learning** (March 5, 2015).

[118]Justin Sink, "Obama to Unveil $1B Early Childhood Education Funding," *The Hill* (December 10, 2014).

a way to address this need for skilled workers.[119] For years, students have been encouraged to focus on going to college to enter the competitive job market, but it is now recognized that not everyone is suited for college, and not all jobs require a four-year academic degree. Advocates for CTE suggest that "career ready" indicates a need for highly skilled technicians in many fields and that the compensation and prestige in these fields may surpass four-year college graduates.[120]

CTE is an education strategy that provides young people with academic, technical, and employability skills, as well as knowledge to pursue postsecondary training, higher education, or enter a career field prepared for ongoing learning.[121] Students can choose from a range of career options, known as career clusters, such as health science; information technology; hospitality and tourism; and agriculture, food, and natural resources.[122] CTE incorporates courses that focus on the various career options with academic subjects in a rigorous and relevant curriculum. CTE is no longer characterized by low-level courses that were associated with its predecessor, vocational education. Integrated and sequenced programs of study that align with and can lead to postsecondary education help students persist in and complete their high school careers; more than 70 percent of secondary CTE concentrators pursued postsecondary education shortly after high school.[123]

While CTE is seen as a remedy for the lack of appropriate education and training for new jobs that the expanding economy has created, it is also promoted as a solution for keeping disengaged students engrossed in their schooling. Studies show that 81 percent of dropouts indicate that relevant, real-world learning opportunities would have kept them in school.[124] This is a strength of CTE, as high-risk students are eight to ten time less likely to drop out in the eleventh and twelfth grades if they are enrolled in a CTE program rather than a general education program.[125] Additionally, students attending CTE high schools have higher rates of on-time graduation and credit accumulation.[126]

CTE programs can be found in stand-alone technical high schools, school-within-a-school career academies, and small learning communities in comprehensive high schools.[127] Components of the programs often include internships, work experience, mentoring, and project-based instruction. CTE students report developing problem solving, project completion, research, math, college application, work-related communication, time management, and critical thinking skills during high school. Many programs lead to industry-recognized credentials.[128]

---

[119]*CTE Works!* (Alexandria, VA: Association for Career and Technical Education) at **www .acteonline.org/factsheets/#** (April 9, 2015).

[120]Benny L. Gooden, "College and Career Readiness: Synonymous or Separate?" *School Administrator* (May 2013), p. 47.

[121]Betsy Brand, Andrew Valent, and Andrea Browning, *How Career and Technical Education Can Help Students Be College and Career Ready: A Primer* (Washington, DC: American Institutes for Research, March 2013).

[122]*What Is CTE?* Association for Career and Technical Education (n.d.) at **www.acteonline .org/cte/#**. (April 9, 2015).

[123]*What Is CTE?* Association for Career and Technical Education (n.d.) at **www.acteonline .org/cte/#** (April 9, 2015); and Betsy Brand, Andrew Valent, and Andrea Browning, *How Career and Technical Education Can Help Students Be College and Career Ready: A Primer* (Washington, DC: American Institutes for Research, March 2013).

[124]*CTE Today!* (Alexandria, VA: Association for Career and Technical Education, October 2014) at **www.acteonline.org/CTETodayOct14** (April 9, 2015).

[125]ACTE, "Career and Technical Education's Role in Dropout Prevention," *Issue Sheet* (February 2009) at **www.acteonline.org/search.aspx?q=dropout prevention** (April 8, 2015).

[126]*CTE Works!* (Alexandria, VA: Association for Career and Technical Education) at **www .acteonline.org/factsheets/#** (April 9, 2015).

[127]Betsy Brand, Andrew Valent, and Andrea Browning, *How Career and Technical Education Can Help Students Be College and Career Ready: A Primer* (Washington, DC: American Institutes for Research, March 2013).

[128]ACTE, "Career and Technical Education's Role in Dropout Prevention," *Issue Sheet* (February 2009) at **www.acteonline.org/search.aspx?q=dropout prevention** (April 8, 2015); and *CTE Today!* (Alexandria, VA: Association for Career and Technical Education, October 2014) at **www.acteonline.org/CTETodayOct14** (April 9, 2015).

Forty-six states and the District of Columbia have approved more that 150 new policies for promoting CTE programs; thirty-six states have increased funding due to concerns about closing the workforce skills gap and meeting the needs of employers.[129] California has significantly increased funding for promoting CTE programs that encourage partnerships among school districts, colleges, and businesses to increase the number of students receiving industry credentials and certificates.[130] A Florida State Board of Education policy requires that a student not enrolled in an advanced placement (AP) or honors course will take CTE for at least three years and earn an industry certification. Kansas's Excel in CTE initiative provides high school students a chance to qualify for free college tuition in technical courses at the state's community colleges.[131]

Throughout your teaching career, you can expect that the curriculum will continue to evolve to serve a changing society. It also seems certain that the pull from the ends of the curriculum continuum—subject-centered on one side and student-centered on the other—will continue to influence the innovations that are likely to infiltrate the classrooms of the future. As you move forward in your career, consider your own position on this continuum and how your orientation will impact your reaction to new ideas and instructional strategies. Regardless of the approach that influences you most, remember that the ultimate goal of the curriculum is to develop learners willing to participate in a democratic society.

FOCUS Which of the trends in this section do you believe will have the strongest influence on your career as a teacher? Why? In what ways will you be affected?

SUMMING UP

1. In organizing the curriculum, most educators hold to the traditional concept of curriculum as the body of subjects, or subject matter. Nevertheless, progressive educators who are more concerned with the learner's experiences regard the student as the focus of curriculum.

2. Examples of a subject-centered approach include the following types of curriculum: (1) subject area, (2) perennialist and essentialist, (3) back-to-basics, and (4) new core.

3. Examples of a student-centered approach include the following types of curriculum: (1) activity-centered approaches, (2) relevant curriculum, (3) the humanistic approach,

(4) alternative or free schools programs, and (5) values-centered curriculum.

4. A number of instructional innovations have influenced education over the years, including (1) differentiated instruction, (2) social and emotional learning, (3) direct instruction, (4) twenty-first-century skills, and (5) technology-enhanced instruction.

5. Developing curricular trends include the following: (1) the importance of the arts, (2) education of ELLs, (3) expanding pre-K education, and (4) career and technical education (CTE).

SUGGESTED RESOURCES

INTERNET RESOURCES

The Internet has exponentially expanded teacher access to curriculum resources that will supplement classroom lessons. The P21 site provides tools and resources for educators to infuse

the framework for twenty-first-century learning into a school's program. Toolkits, Twitter feeds, webinars, blogs, YouTube videos, and downloadable files assist educators in integrating this forwarding-looking approach into teaching and learning.

---

[129]Emily Ann Brown, "Report Shows Increased Interest in CTE at State Level," *Education Daily* (February 13, 2015).

[130]Michelle Maitre, "Governor Proposes Boost for Career Education," *EdSource* (January 28, 2015) at **http://edsource.org/2015/governor-proposes-boost-for-career-education/73624#** (April 8, 2015).

[131]*Beating the Odds: Keeping Kids in School with Career Technical Education and Adobe Certifications, Adobe Career and Technical Education* white paper, (n.d.) at **www.ncacinc.com/sites/default /files/media/research/edu-k12-cte-beating-the-odds-whitepaper.pdf** (April 8, 2015); and Emily Ann Brown, "Report Shows Increased Interest in CTE at State Level," *Education Daily* (February 13, 2015).

Curriki is another resource that not only provides curriculum materials for the classroom but also encourages contributions and the development of networks. Its blogs, Twitter feeds, and Facebook sites are dedicated to sharing innovative ideas with other teachers.

Edutopia also serves as a vast resource for enhancing the curriculum as you create lessons for the classroom. It has videos, blogs, content resource sites, and information about field-tested teaching strategies.

The Association for Supervision and Curriculum Development (ASCD) website is an invaluable resource for any educator concerned about effective curriculum development. Membership in the organization allows full access to the site, which provides archived articles from the many publications of the organization, access to blogs from educators around the world, and podcasts and webinars of discussions with experts on curriculum-related topics.

The Common Core State Standards Initiative website is the source for all things related to the standards. Because these will be influencing curriculum and assessment reform in many states for the foreseeable future, you should explore the resources at this site.

PUBLICATIONS

Bellanca, James, ed. *Deeper Learning: Beyond 21st Century Skills.* Bloomington, IN: Solution Tree Press, 2015. *Education experts offer ideas for teaching students the deeper thinking skills to succeed in the twenty-first century.*

Fleming, Michael. *The Arts in Education: An Introduction to Aesthetics, Theory and Pedagogy.* New York: Routledge, 2012. *Introduces the key theoretical questions that face arts education and explains how these are related to practice.*

García Coll, Cynthia T., and Amy Kerivan Mark, eds. *Immigrant Stories: Ethnicity and Academics in Middle Childhood.* New York: Oxford University Press, 2009. *Examines second-generation immigrant children's emerging cultural attitudes and identities, academic engagement, and academic achievement.*

Giordano, Gerard. *Twentieth-Century Textbook Wars: A History of Advocacy and Opposition.* New York: Peter Lang Publishing, 2003. *Takes a historical look at the textbook industry and its evolution from the nineteenth century through the end of the twentieth century. Provides a thorough review of the controversies surrounding the industry.*

Gordon, Howard R. D., *The History and Growth of Career and Technical Education in America,* 4th ed. Long Grove, IL: Waveland Press, Inc., 2014. *A history of career and technology education that incorporates current research and statistics, the participation of women and minorities, gender-equity issues, and closing the achievement gap and the skills gap.*

Horn, Michael B., and Heather Staker. *Blended: Using Disruptive Innovation to Improve Schools.* San Francisco, CA: Jossey Bass, 2015. *This book serves as a practical guide for implementing blended learning in K–12 classrooms.*

Humphrey, Neil. *Social and Emotional Learning: A Critical Appraisal.* Thousand Oaks, CA: Sage Publications, 2013. *Examines the international research literature on SEL and highlights strengths and flaws in the theory and research.*

Magana, Sonny, and Robert J. Marzano. *Enhancing the Art and Science of Teaching with Technology.* Bloomington, IN: Marzano Research Lab, 2014. *Provides advice on incorporating technology into classroom practice, and includes strategies to help teachers use educational technology effectively.*

Noddings, Nel. *Education and Democracy in the 21st Century.* New York: Teachers College Press, 2013. *Looks at education and raises critical questions about standardization, the search for "one-best-way" solutions, and the tradition of maintaining separation between the disciplines.*

Tomlinson, Carol Ann, and Marcia B. Imbeau. *A Differentiated Approach to the Common Core: How Do I Help a Broad Range of Learners Succeed with Challenging Curriculum?* Alexandria, VA: Association for Supervision and Curriculum Development, 2014. *Provides practical strategies for implementing differentiated instruction to meet the challenges of teaching students in diverse classrooms with the requirements of the Common Core.*

CHAPTER **15**

INTERNATIONAL EDUCATION

LEARNING OBJECTIVES

15-1 Describe several characteristics that educational systems in various countries have in common.

15-2 Describe how educational systems differ with respect to the resources they devote to education, student–teacher and enrollment ratios, teaching conditions reported by US teachers compared with teachers elsewhere, the extent of centralization, vocational vs. academic education, enrollment in higher education, size of the nonpublic sector, and achievement levels among students and young adults.

15-3 Identify several countries that provide examples of outstanding educational activities that may be worth emulating elsewhere.

15-4 Summarize how the purposes and attainments of US schools compare with those of other countries.

Monkey Business Images/Shutterstock.com

This chapter was revised by Daniel U. Levine.

MANY EDUCATIONAL REFORMERS have suggested that the United States could improve its educational system by emulating other countries. Japanese education has received particular attention because it appears to have contributed in large measure to Japan's economic success during the past fifty years. But imitating educational practices from other countries raises questions. Would they work in an American context? Do they mesh with American beliefs and values?

Before beginning to answer such questions, we need to understand the varieties of educational systems other countries employ: how they resemble one another, how they differ, and which particular features are most effective in which contexts. In this chapter, we offer an introduction to that kind of analysis. We then consider education in developing countries and international studies of school improvement. Finally, we offer a brief comment on the accomplishments of US schools in an international context.

15-1 COMMONALITIES IN EDUCATIONAL SYSTEMS

At first glance, classrooms around the world may seem to have little in common. Consider a classroom in a rural Sudanese village and one in contemporary Japan, for example. In Sudan, the building has no electricity, and the earthen floor is uncovered. The students are all boys. Few of the teachers have a high school diploma; the curriculum and teaching, which rely heavily on memorization and recitation, are determined by the country's ministry of education. In highly developed Japan, by way of contrast, modern school buildings house classes of boys and girls, almost all of whom will complete high school. Teachers are highly respected professionals with college degrees. They are given considerable latitude in devising activities and adapting materials that satisfy the national guidelines, which emphasize development of children's thinking and problem-solving skills, as well as social, moral, and physical instruction that benefits the whole person.

Despite the great variety in educational systems worldwide, however, certain commonalities exist. The following sections describe widespread characteristics and problems: the strong relationships between students' social-class origins and their success in school, and the educational challenges posed by multicultural populations. Overview 15.1 summarizes commonalities and differences among educational systems.

15-1a Social-Class Origins and School Outcomes

As we noted in Chapter 11, Social Class, Race, and School Achievement, various national and international studies have illustrated the strong relationships between students' socioeconomic background and their success in school and in the economic system. For example, World Bank studies have reported that family socioeconomic background is a salient predictor of students' achievement in both industrialized and developing countries. Similarly, Donald Treiman and others have found that individuals' social-class origins and background relate to their educational and occupational attainment regardless of whether their society is rich or poor, politically liberal or conservative.[1]

---

[1]Donald J. Treiman, *Occupational Prestige in Comparative Perspective* (New York: Academic Press, 1977); and Marlaine E. Lockheed, Bruce Fuller, and Ronald Nyirongo, *Family Background and School Achievement* (New York: World Bank, 1988). See also Richard Wilkinson and Kate Pickett, "Greater Equality," *American Educator* (Spring 2011), available at **www.aft.org**; Eric A. Hanushek, Paul E. Peterson, and Ludger Woessmann, "US Students from Educated Families Lag in International Tests," *Education Next* (Fall 2014), available at **www.educationnext.org**; and Tori DeAngelis, "Class Differences," February 2015 posting by the American Psychological Association, available at **www.apa.org**.

OVERVIEW 15.1

AREAS OF SIMILARITIES AND DIFFERENCES AMONG EDUCATIONAL SYSTEMS OF THE WORLD

Commonalities—Many educational systems in the world face the same challenges.

Social Class Origins and School Outcomes	Throughout most of the world, lower-income students are at an educational disadvantage.
Multicultural Populations	Nearly every nation must find ways to effectively educate diverse student populations.

Differences—Many areas of distinction define individual countries' educational systems.

Resources Devoted to Education	The percentage of gross domestic income spent on education varies due to countries' incomes and the priority they give to education. Larger expenditures allow for more student enrollment and a higher level of educational services.
Extent of Centralization	Nations vary widely in how much educational decision making occurs at local and national government levels.
Vocational versus Academic Education	After the first few years of common schooling, some nations more commonly separate students into academic or vocational educational tracks for further education.
Enrollment in Higher Education	Emphasis on academics in earlier schools, resources devoted to education, and occupational requirements in different countries contribute to wide variations in enrollment and completion of college and university studies.
Nonpublic Schools	Differences in culture and governmental structure contribute to variations in the size and functioning of nonpublic education.
Achievement Levels	US students rank toward the middle on most international achievement tests, which leads many to conclude that US schools need improvement.

A multitude of studies such as these also demonstrate that the family and home environments of low-income students generate the same kinds of educational disadvantages in other countries as in the United States.[2]

15-1b Multicultural Populations

Except in a few homogeneous countries, nationwide systems of education enroll diverse groups of students who differ significantly with respect to race, ethnicity, religion, native language, and/or cultural practices. (Its geographic isolation and cultural insularity make Japan one of the exceptions to this generalization.) Most large nations historically have included numerous racial/ethnic and cultural subgroups, but the twentieth and twenty-first centuries seem to have greatly accelerated the mixture of diverse groups across and within national boundaries. World and regional wars, global depressions and recessions, migration and immigration to large urban centers that offer expanded economic opportunity, and other destabilizing forces have led some historians to see recent decades as the era of the migrant and the refugee. These forces more or less ensure that you, as a teacher, will have students from other nations in your classes. As the From Preservice to Practice box describes, you might consider using

---

[2]Alan C. Purves and Daniel U. Levine, eds., *Educational Policy and International Assessment* (Berkeley, CA: McCutchan, 1975); Emily Beller and Michael Hout, "Intergenerational Social Mobility," *The Future of Children* (Fall 2006), available at **www.futureofchildren.org**; and Ludger Woessmann, "An International Look at the Single-Parent Family," *Education Next* (Spring 2015), available at **www.educationnext.org**.

FROM PRESERVICE TO PRACTICE

NEW PERSPECTIVES

Dr. Harris introduced his main topic for the day's discussion to a classroom of education majors: "I'm wondering if any of you know how many languages are spoken in Minneapolis schools, in New York City schools, Houston schools, or Los Angeles schools. Right here in Minneapolis, we have students speaking more than ninety different languages.

"How many of you speak more than one language? How many of you have traveled to other countries to see how children are educated in various parts of the world? Whether or not you have traveled, whether or not you are bilingual, you will be working with students from different cultures and with parents who have differing expectations from educators.

"We have a responsibility to serve all our children well," he continued. "What do you think we can do to help you preservice teachers prepare to deal effectively with students from other countries?"

"One obvious way is to have us read about the different types of schooling and the different approaches to teaching used around the world," suggested Michael Ervin.

"We could research countries on the Internet to get a sense of how their schools are organized and run," commented Sally Newman.

"Why don't we use on-campus resources?" Bob Barrett said. "We could interview international students who we are familiar with about their countries' educational processes."

Tanghe Yu added, "I think the best way to gain an appreciation of the different perspectives would be to actually visit the school site. That way, whether we're students or student teachers, we could immerse ourselves in the educational experiences of the students. I moved here from Taiwan when I was 8 years old. I can tell you that my schooling there and here, even in the early years, differed substantially."

Dr. Harris nodded. "Yes, those are all great suggestions. Tanghe, I think your idea has special merit. Since the 9/11 attacks, I have been thinking that we really need to help build more understanding between and among different groups. Who might be interested in traveling and learning about schools in other countries?" About half of the people in the class raised a hand. "Right now, we don't have the funds, but perhaps we can start by looking at grant opportunities that may help us."

CASE QUESTIONS

1. How are you, as a preservice teacher, preparing yourself to deal with the students and families who come to public schools with languages and cultural backgrounds different from your own?

2. How have the schools you observed in your own community worked with students and families with varying cultural backgrounds? What strategies do you consider most effective?

3. Would you want to participate in a program such as the one suggested by Dr. Harris? If so, to which country would you travel, and why? If not, why not?

the ease of global travel to your advantage now, to help you prepare for the opportunities and challenges of teaching international students.

Not surprisingly, then, other countries encounter challenges in multicultural education similar to those of the United States: ineffective traditional instruction, providing bilingual education, and desegregating minority students. This is partly because minority racial, ethnic, and religious groups in many nations, as in the United States, frequently are low in socioeconomic status. England, France, the Netherlands, and other European countries, for example, have many lower-income students from Africa, Asia, the Caribbean, the Middle East, and other distant locations. Germany is struggling to provide effective education for the children of Romany (Gypsy), Slavic, and Turkish migrants, and most West African nations include students from numerous disadvantaged tribal and minority-language groups.[3]

FOCUS How do you think US schools would be affected if the country devoted a greater percentage of its resources to education and children's well-being? What if the United States began to devote fewer resources to these concerns?

---

[3]Nigel Grant, "Some Problems of Identity and Education," *Comparative Education* (March 1997), pp. 9–28; and Fred Dervin, "Towards Post-Intercultural Teacher Education," *European Journal of Teacher Education* (February 2015).

15-2 DIFFERENCES IN EDUCATIONAL SYSTEMS AND OUTCOMES

Each nation's educational system also differs in important ways from other systems. In this section, we will discuss some of the most significant differences, including the following: resources devoted to education; student–teacher and enrollment ratios; teaching conditions reported by US teachers compared with teachers elsewhere; the extent of centralization; vocational vs. academic education; enrollment in higher education; size of the nonpublic sector; and achievement levels among students and young adults.

15-2a Resources Devoted to Education

One fundamental way in which nations differ is in the percentage of resources they devote to education rather than to priorities such as highways, health care, and military forces. As a percentage of gross domestic product (wealth produced annually), public expenditures on K–12 and higher education range from 2 percent in nations low in average income and/or that place relatively little priority on education, to more than 6 percent in nations with high average income and/or that emphasize education. In some of the world's poorest countries, average per capita expenditures on military forces are nearly one-third greater than per capita spending for education.[4]

15-2b Student–Teacher Ratios at the Primary Level

Relatively wealthy nations, as well as nations that allocate many of their resources to education, can provide a higher level of services than poor nations that mobilize relatively few resources for their schools. For example, average primary-level student–teacher ratios tend to be much higher in poorer regions than in wealthier regions. Many African nations report an average student–teacher ratio of more than forty to one, whereas most European and North American nations average twenty to one or fewer. Large differences also emerge, however, when we compare wealthy countries with each other, and when we compare poor countries with other poor countries.[5]

15-2c Enrollment Ratios

The resources devoted to education also help determine whether most children and youth attend school and whether they obtain diplomas or degrees. Data collected by UNESCO indicate that in their category of "more developed regions" (Australia, Japan, New Zealand, North America, and most of Western Europe), nearly all children attend elementary schools. In less-developed countries in the bottom fifth on wealth, about 30 percent of primary-school-age students are not enrolled in school. Discrepancies in enrollment between developed and less developed nations become even greater at the secondary- and higher-education levels.[6]

---

[4]*EFA Global Monitoring Report 2013/14* (Paris: United Nations Educational, Social and Cultural Organization, 2014), available at **www.unesco.org**.

[5]"Worldwide Teacher Shortage," January 30, 2013, posting by Childhood Education International, available at **www.acei.org**; *Education for All 2000–2015* (Paris: United Nations Educational, Social and Cultural Organization, 2015), available at **www.unesco.org**; and "Pupil-Teacher Ratio, Primary," undated posting by The World Bank, available at **http://data .worldbank.org**.

[6]"Rapid Acceleration of Progress Is Needed to Achieve Universal Primary Education by 2015," November 2014 posting by UNICEF, available at **www.data.unicef.org/education /primary**; *Fixing the Broken Promise of Education for All* (Montreal: UNESCO Institute for Statistics, 2015); and numerous other materials available at **www.unesco.org**.

> **PHOTO 15.1** Classrooms, schools, and school systems around the world differ in many ways, some obvious as in this picture, others less obvious. Schools also share commonalities, such as the joys most teachers find in working with their students.

15-2d Male and Female Enrollments

We noted in Chapter 10, Culture, Socialization, and Education, that US girls have higher reading scores than boys and that females have become a majority in higher-education institutions. The same pattern has appeared in other developed nations. With a few exceptions, such as Japan and Turkey, female enrollment in colleges and universities in wealthy nations has been growing to the extent that more women than men obtain first degrees. However, the pattern is different in developing nations, where males frequently outnumber females in higher education, secondary schools, and, sometimes, even elementary schools. Many analysts believe that the low enrollment ratio for girls compared to boys in many low-income countries in Africa and Asia is both a cause and an effect of economic development problems.[7]

15-2e The United States among Industrial Nations

For certain purposes, it is instructive to compare wealthy or highly industrialized nations with each other rather than with poor or economically underdeveloped nations. Other factors remaining equal, nations with less wealth and fewer resources have a much harder time supporting education or other government services than do those with a strong economic base (Photo 15.1). Thus, to analyze how well the United States provides education, we should compare it with other developed countries.[8]

Several controversies have erupted about this subject. Although public-school critics have claimed that American education expenditures are unsurpassed, many researchers disagree. When we subtract funding for higher education, the United States

---

[7]"Out-of-School Children and Adolescents," June 30, 2014, posting by Friedrich Huebler, available at **www.huebler.blogspot.com**; and "Ratio of Female to Male Tertiary Enrollment (%)," undated posting by The World Bank, available at **http://data.worldbank.org**.

[8]"Developed" nations as classified by the United Nations Educational, Scientific, and Cultural Organization (UNESCO) include Australia, Canada, most of Europe, Israel, Japan, South Africa, the former USSR, the United States, and New Zealand. All others are classified as "developing" nations.

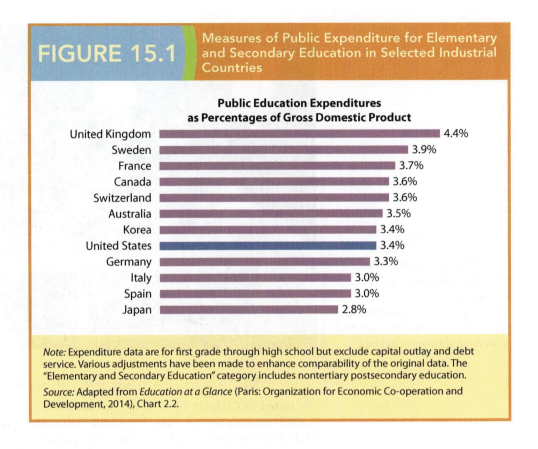

FIGURE 15.1 Measures of Public Expenditure for Elementary and Secondary Education in Selected Industrial Countries

Public Education Expenditures as Percentages of Gross Domestic Product

Country	Percentage
United Kingdom	4.4%
Sweden	3.9%
France	3.7%
Canada	3.6%
Switzerland	3.6%
Australia	3.5%
Korea	3.4%
United States	3.4%
Germany	3.3%
Italy	3.0%
Spain	3.0%
Japan	2.8%

Note: Expenditure data are for first grade through high school but exclude capital outlay and debt service. Various adjustments have been made to enhance comparability of the original data. The "Elementary and Secondary Education" category includes nontertiary postsecondary education.

Source: Adapted from *Education at a Glance* (Paris: Organization for Economic Co-operation and Development, 2014), Chart 2.2.

ranks below the top on education expenditures. Figure 15.1 shows such a comparison in graphic form. In terms of public-education expenditures for grades 1 through 12 as a percentage of gross domestic product, the United States tied for seventh among twelve industrial countries.[9]

Analysts also debate whether US teacher salaries are high or low in comparison with those of other industrial countries. Data on teacher salary averages indicate that for both beginning and experienced teachers, average salaries in countries such as Ireland and Norway are a good deal lower than in the United States, but in some other countries, they are generally higher.[10]

Sometimes, the comparisons expand to other types of considerations that support children's well-being and development. For example, Timothy Smeeding, comparing the United States with Australia, Canada, Germany, Sweden, and the United Kingdom, found that these five countries average about the same for government expenditures on children's education and health services as a percentage of gross domestic product. However, he also found that US government expenditures to help provide income security for children's families are less than half the average for these countries. Smeeding concluded that high rates of divorce, out-of-wedlock births, and other social forces are creating a larger urban and rural underclass, making it "increasingly hard to argue that all US children have equal life chances." A later study by the United Nations

---

[9]Ludger Woessman, "Why Students in Some Countries Do Better," *Education Next* (Summer 2001), pp. 67–74, available at **www.educationnext.org**; and *Education at a Glance* (Paris: Organization for Economic Co-operation and Development, 2014).

[10]Daniel U. Levine, "Educational Spending: International Comparisons," *Theory into Practice* (Spring 1994), pp. 126–131; Liao Maozhong and Shen Hua, "Educational Inequality Analysis," *International Journal of Business and Social Science* (September 2011), available at **www.ijbssnet .com**; and "How Much Are Teachers Paid and How Much Does It Matter," *Education Indicators in Focus* (April 2014).

Children's Fund (UNICEF) supported these conclusions in reporting that the United States stood very near the bottom among twenty-four industrialized nations ranked on various measures of childhood well-being.[11]

15-2f US Teachers in the TALIS Survey

The Organization for Economic Co-operation and Development (OECD) surveyed more than 100,000 teachers at 140 schools in 34 nations as part of the Teaching and Learning International Survey (TALIS).[12] Among the respondents were more than 2,000 US teachers of grades 7, 8, or 9, whose answers were compared with those of lower-secondary teachers in other nations. Findings and conclusions included the following:

- Almost two-thirds of US middle-school teachers work in schools where more than 30 percent of students are below the poverty line, nearly triple the average TALIS rate.
- US teachers reported spending forty-five hours per week on work-related activities, compared with an average of thirty-eight hours for the other thirty-three nations.
- There was an average ratio of 14.9 students to teachers in US schools, compared with an average of 12.4 for the other thirty-three nations.
- Among US teachers, 87 percent agreed with the statement that "The advantages of being a teacher clearly outweigh the disadvantages," 84 percent agreed that "If I could decide again, I would still choose to work as a teacher," 91 percent agreed that "I enjoy working at this school," and 89 percent agreed that "All in all, I am satisfied with my job." Teachers in most other nations responded with similarly positive responses.

Some of the analysts who examined the preceding and related data concluded that the information about concentrated poverty and teacher loads helps to explain the relatively low achievement levels sometimes reported for US students on international tests. For example, Linda Darling-Hammond discussed the results and expressed the belief that "It is time for the United States finally to equalize school funding, address childhood poverty . . . , institute universal early care and learning programs, and provide the wraparound services—health care, before- and after-school care, and social services—that ensure children are supported to learn."

15-2g Extent of Centralization

All governments must decide whether to emphasize decentralized decision making, which allows for planning and delivering instruction in accordance with local circumstances, or centralized decision making, which builds accountability up and down a national or regional chain of command. Examples go far in either direction. In the United States, most important decisions are decentralized across thousands of diverse public-school districts. At the other extreme, France, Greece, and Japan, for example, all have highly centralized educational systems and decisions, following nationwide standards concerning acceptable class size and what will be taught in a given subject at a particular grade and time. In some countries, centralization has led to long lines

---

[11]Timothy M. Smeeding, "Social Thought and Poor Children," *Focus* (Spring 1990), p. 14. See also Lee Rainwater and Timothy M. Smeeding, *Rich Kids in a Poor Country* (New York: Russell Sage, 2003); Wiemer Salverda et al., eds., *Changing Inequalities in Rich Countries* (New York: Oxford University Press, 2014); and "School Performance in Context," 2015 posting by the Horace Mann League, available at **www.hmleague.org/fullreport**.

[12]"An International Study on Teaching and Learning," 2014 posting by the Organisation for Economic Co-operation and Development, available at **www.oecd.org**; Gregory A. Strizek, Ebru Erberber, and Patrick Gonzales, "(TALIS) 2013: US Technical Report," December 2014 posting by the National Center for Education Statistics, available at **www.nces.ed.gov**; and Linda Darling-Hammond, "Want to Close the Achievement Gap?" *American Educator* (Winter 2014/2015), available at **www.aft.org**.

TAKING ISSUE

Read the following brief introduction, as well as the Question and the pros and cons list that follows. Then, answer the question using *your* own words and position.

ESTABLISHMENT OF A NATIONAL CURRICULUM

Countries with highly centralized public education generally expect teachers to follow a national curriculum that specifies the topics to be taught and the objectives and materials to be emphasized in each subject and grade level. Countries that follow a decentralized pattern primarily relegate decisions about subject matter and materials to a regional group of schools (such as a school district) or individual faculties or teachers. Government officials in some highly decentralized nations such as the United States are considering whether a national curriculum should be established to provide for a more standardized approach in planning and delivering instruction.

Question
Would a US national curriculum be preferable to decentralized policies that allow individual school districts, schools, or teachers to select instructional objectives and materials?

Arguments PRO

1. Availability of a national curriculum is partly responsible for the high achievement levels in Japan, Korea, and other countries.

2. A national curriculum based on the careful deliberation of subject-area specialists and experienced teachers makes it easier to achieve in-depth teaching of well-sequenced objectives and materials.

3. Uniformity in objectives and materials reduces the inefficiencies and learning problems that occur when students move from one classroom, school, or district to another.

4. A national curriculum will improve teacher education because preparation programs can concentrate on objectives and materials that trainees will teach when they obtain jobs.

5. Because it draws on a large base of resources, national curriculum planning can incorporate the best current thinking in each subject area and help prepare technically excellent tests.

Arguments CON

1. Establishment of a national curriculum runs counter to promising trends toward school-based management and professional autonomy for teachers.

2. A national curriculum is undesirable because its objectives and materials will be too difficult for many students and too easy for others.

3. Particularly in large and diverse countries such as the United States, the standardized materials that form the basis for a national curriculum will be uninteresting and unmotivating for many students.

4. Even if the national curriculum allows flexibility in objectives and materials, teachers will be pressured to follow the same path as everyone else, and most likely funds will be unavailable for alternative materials. Therefore, students and classes that might benefit from alternatives will suffer.

5. The extreme difficulty in preparing challenging national curriculum materials appropriate to use across a wide range of classrooms will reinforce tendencies to emphasize low-level skills and uncreative materials.

Question Reprise: What Is Your Stand?
Reflect again on the following question by explaining *your* stand on this issue: Should the federal government encourage or even pressure the states and school districts to adopt national/centralized goals and related practices for the schools?

of citizens from all parts of the nation waiting outside the ministry of education for appointments with central school officials who determine what schools children will attend and how students will be treated.[13] We consider centralized versus decentralized systems in the Taking Issue box.

---

[13]Jenn Hatfield, "Here's How Different the US Educational System Is vs. Other Nations," February 23, 2015, posting by the American Enterprise Institute, available at **www.aei.org**.

15-2h Vocational versus Academic Education

School systems around the world also differ greatly in how they are organized to provide education through the postsecondary level. Although most nations now provide at least four years of first-level education during which all students attend primary or elementary schools, above that level, systems diverge widely. Most students continue in common first-level schools for several more years, but, in many countries, students are divided between academic-track schools and vocational schools after four to eight years of first-level education. This arrangement, which corresponds to the traditional European dual-track pattern described in Chapter 3, The World Origins of American Education, is often known as a **bipartite system**.

bipartite system A dual-track system consisting of academic schools and vocational schools.

The proportion of secondary students enrolled in primarily vocational programs varies from less than one-tenth in industrial countries such as Denmark and the United States to more than one-fifth in others such as Germany. Similar variation appears in academic tracks. Some countries, beginning at the secondary level and extending into postsecondary education, enroll large proportions of students in academic schools designed to produce an elite corps of high school or college graduates. In others, including Canada and the United States, most secondary students continue to attend common or comprehensive schools, and many enroll in colleges that are relatively nonselective.[14]

15-2i Enrollment in Higher Education

Countries that channel students into vocational programs tend to have low percentages of youth attending institutions of higher education. By contrast, more youth go on to higher education in countries that provide general academic studies for most high school students. Other factors that help determine enrollment in higher education include a nation's investment of resources in higher education, emphasis on postsecondary learning rather than job-market entry, traditions regarding the use of higher education to equalize educational opportunities, and the extent to which colleges and universities admit only high-achieving students.

Developing countries with relatively little funding available for higher education and problems in increasing elementary and secondary enrollment levels predictably have low proportions of youth participating in higher education. Thus, Afghanistan, Ethiopia, Ghana, and many other developing nations enroll less than 20 percent of their young people in higher education. Most industrial countries provide postsecondary education for more than 40 percent of their young adults.

After high school graduates are enrolled in postsecondary institutions, numerous considerations determine whether they will stay enrolled and eventually gain their degrees: curriculum difficulty, financial aid opportunities, motivation levels, and access to preferred institutions and courses. Industrial nations differ greatly in the proportion of young people who obtain postsecondary degrees. As shown in Table 15.1, for example, the percentage of young adults who complete postsecondary education in industrial nations varies from 23 percent in Italy to more than 50 in Canada and South Korea.

Decline in US Ranking for College Participation Until the 1990s, the United States generally had higher percentages of young people attending and completing higher-education institutions than any other nation. Only Canada came close. The data

---

[14]Michael McVey, "The Role of Vocational Education and Training in Promoting Lifelong Learning in Germany and England," *International Review of Education* (May 2007), pp. 325–327; Anita Ratam, "Traditional Occupations in a Modern World," *International Journal for Educational and Vocational Guidance* (No. 2, 2011), pp. 92–109; and "Global Monitoring Report 2014/2015," 2015 posting by The World Bank, available at **http://openknowledge.worldbank.org**.

TABLE 15.1		Percentage of Twenty-Five- to Thirty-Four-Year-Olds Who Have Attained Postsecondary (Tertiary) Education, Selected Countries	
Australia	46	Italy	23
Belgium	43	Korea (South)	67
Canada	58	Netherlands	43
Denmark	41	Norway	47
Finland	40	Spain	41
France	44	Sweden	45
Germany	27	United Kingdom	48
Iceland	40	United States	45
Ireland	51		

Note: Data are for 2013.

Source: Adapted from Rodrigo C. Valle, Simon Normandeau, and Gara R. Gonzalez, *Education at a Glance Interim Report* (Paris: Organisation for Economic Co-operation and Development, 2015).

in Table 15.1 indicate that this pattern no longer holds. Several nations now surpass the United States in postsecondary participation, and others are gaining rapidly. This change led the author of a study conducted for the Educational Commission of the States to conclude that "if current trends persist and students in the United States continue to enroll in college at the rate they do now, America is likely to slip further behind the growing number of developed nations that have stepped up their efforts over the last decade to increase educational attainment." She further warned of a serious risk "that competing public priorities and shrinking resources will put access to an affordable and high-quality college education further out of reach for more and more Americans."[15]

15-2j Nonpublic Schools

Depending on their histories, political structures, religious composition, legal frameworks, and other factors, nations differ greatly in the size and functions of their nonpublic education sectors. In a few countries, such as the Netherlands, more than half of elementary and secondary students attend private schools. At the other extreme, governments in Cuba, North Korea, and other nations have prohibited nonpublic schools to suppress ideologies different from those supported by the state. In most countries, private-school students constitute less than 20 percent of total enrollment.[16]

Nations also vary widely in the extent to which they provide public support for nonpublic schools or students. They differ as to government regulation of nonpublic systems, people's perceptions of public and nonpublic schools, and the role that private schools are expected to play in national development. In some countries, nonpublic schools enroll a relatively small, elite group of students who later enter the most prestigious colleges; in others, they serve a more representative sample of the nation's

---

[15]Sandra S. Ruppert, "Closing the College Participation Gap," 2003 paper prepared for the Education Commission of the States, pp. 6–7. See also Daniel Gross, "The Education Factor," *Education Next* (Spring 2009), available at **www.educationnext.org**; and Rodrigo C. Valle, Simon Normandeau, and Gara R. Gonzalez, *Education at a Glance Interim Report* (Paris: Organisation for Economic Co-operation and Development, 2015).

[16]Rafak Piwowarski, "The Role of Non-Public Schools in Modern Education Systems," *International Review of Education* (September 2006), pp. 397–407; Michael Omolewa, "Private Schooling in Less Economically Developed Countries," *International Review of Education* (January 2008); and "School Enrollment, Secondary, Private (% of Total Secondary)" 2014 posting by The World Bank, available at **http://data.worldbank.org**.

children and youth. In some countries, many private schools are small shoestring operations enrolling poor students in urban slums. Given this variety, it is not possible to cross-nationally define a private school or generalize about policies that encourage or discourage nonpublic schools. Clearly, productive national policies on nonpublic schools must reflect each country's unique mix of circumstances and challenges.[17]

15-2k Achievement Levels of Elementary and Secondary Students

International Association for the Evaluation of Educational Achievement (IEA) A research group that began conducting cross-national studies in the 1960s.

Differences in school achievement among nations have received considerable attention since the **International Association for the Evaluation of Educational Achievement (IEA)** began conducting cross-national studies in the 1960s. One of the first major IEA projects collected and analyzed data on the achievement of 258,000 students from nineteen countries in civic education, foreign languages, literature, reading comprehension, and science. This study showed a wide range in average achievement levels across nations. In general, the United States ranked close to the middle among the nations included in the study. Later studies, such as the **Program for International Student Assessment (PISA)**, the **Progress in International Reading Literacy Study (PIRLS)**, and the **Third International Mathematics and Science Study (TIMSS)**, also have found that our students generally rank near the international average among developed nations (see Table 15.2). (These assessments, depending on the test, generally examined the performance of fourth graders, eighth graders, and/or 15-year-olds.) Companion analysis also has concluded that the United States trails some other nations, such as Finland, Japan, and Korea, in producing outstanding achievement that includes relatively high scores among low-income students and relatively low cost.[18]

Program for International Student Assessment (PISA) Numerous documents published by the Organisation for Economic Co-operation and Development providing information and analysis based on data regarding student performance in reading, mathematics, and other subjects collected in more than seventy nations.

Progress in International Reading Literacy Study (PIRLS) An international comparative study of the reading literacy of students at the fourth-grade level. It has been administered periodically since 2001.

Third International Mathematics and Science Study (TIMSS) A research group that has conducted cross-national research since 1996.

Analyzing data from these international studies, scholars have reached conclusions that include the following:[19]

- National scores in subjects such as reading, math, and science tend to be highly correlated. For example, seven of the eight nations with the highest reading scores in data collected by PISA also were in the highest eight nations with respect to math and science scores.

- As shown in Table 15.2, US students' reading scores were well below those of students in the highest-scoring nations. Some nations, including the United States, have a much greater spread between the performances of low- and high-achieving students than do others such as Finland, Japan, and Korea. The performance of high-achieving American students, however, sometimes is comparable to that of the highest performers in other nations. Furthermore, students in US schools with a low percentage of poverty students score as high as students in high-scoring nations. Conversely, US students in high-poverty schools score about as low as the average student in the lowest-achieving industrialized countries.

---

[17]Karen Evans and Anna Robinson-Pant, "Public-Private Strategies, Regulatory Regimes and Education Systems," *Compare* (February 2009), pp. 1–4; Lily Tsai, "Friends or Foes?" *Studies in Comparative International Development* (March 2011), pp. 46–69; and "In What Ways Do Public and Private Schools/Institutions Differ?" 2014 posting by the Organisation for Economic Co-operation and Development, available at **www.oecd.org**.

[18]Purves and Levine, *Educational Policy and International Assessment;* Justin Baer et al., *The Reading Literacy of Fourth-Grade Students in an International Context* (Washington, DC: National Center for Education Statistics, 2007); *Education at a Glance 2013* (Paris: Organisation for Economic Co-operation and Development, 2013), available at **www.oecd.org**; Tim Walker, "What Do the 2012 PISA Scores Tell Us about US Schools?" *NEA Today* (December 3, 2013), available at **www .neatoday.org**; and Jennifer Craw, "Education Performance, Equity and Efficiency," January 30, 2015 posting by the Center on International Education Benchmarking, available at **www.ncee.org**.

[19]Cynthia McCabe, "The Economics behind International Education Rankings," *NEA Today* (December 10, 2010), available at **www.neatoday.org**; and J. T. Blakely, "The Effectiveness of International Exams as a Policy Tool," December 26, 2014, posting by Glimpse from the Globe, available at **www.glimpsefromtheglobe.com**.

TABLE 15.2	Reading and Math Scores of Fifteen-Year-Olds in Twenty-Three Nations				
Nation	**Reading**	**Math**	**Nation**	**Reading**	**Math**
Japan	538	536	Denmark	496	500
Korea	536	554	Italy	490	485
Finland	524	519	Portugal	488	487
Canada	523	518	Spain	488	487
Poland	518	518	Iceland	483	493
New Zealand	512	500	Sweden	483	478
Belgium	509	515	Greece	477	453
Germany	508	514	Russian Federation	475	482
France	505	495	Mexico	424	413
Australia	504	512	Brazil	410	391
United Kingdom	499	494	Argentina	396	388
United States	498	481			
			Average	**496**	**494**

Note: The average score is for OECD nations.

Source: Adapted from "What 15-Year-Olds Know and What They Can Do with What They Know" (Paris: Organisation for Economic Co-operation and Development, 2014).

- Whereas US students generally have reading and science scores near the average for industrialized nations, their mathematics scores are significantly lower.

- Social class correlates strongly with achievement test scores in nearly all nations. However, the spread between working-class and middle-class students is much greater in nations such as the United States than in others such as Finland and Japan that have high average scores and relatively low spread between high and low achievers.

- Instructional characteristics (including class size, amount of time allocated to instruction, teachers' experience, and amount of homework) generally do not correlate with achievement test scores. For example, many countries studied, including the United States, frequently implement mathematics instruction based on "tell and show" approaches that emphasize passive, rote learning. Because some of these countries had scores considerably higher than US scores, however, such approaches could not account for mediocre US performance levels except in interaction with other variables.

- Some analysts have concluded that US curricula and instruction, particularly in mathematics, generally are a mile wide and an inch deep and that the mediocre performance resulting from this superficial teaching poses a serious threat to our international competitiveness. Several scholars studying the US math curriculum in an international context concluded that it is *unfocused*, with too many topics in too little depth; *highly repetitive; incoherent,* with little logical order to topics; and *undemanding,* particularly at the middle-school level. In addition, US mathematics curricula, in contrast to many other nations, are highly differentiated. That is, our middle-level students tend to be sorted into mathematics tracks that stress algebra and other advanced topics for high-achieving students and simple arithmetic for low achievers. Thus, many students with low- or medium-achievement levels have little opportunity to proceed beyond basic skills. This is in marked contrast to Finland, Japan, and some other locations where most students are challenged to perform at a higher level. Most analysts who have reviewed these patterns believe that action must be taken to reduce this kind of curriculum differentiation.[20]

- Improvement in US student performance will require systemic change involving setting of standards, assessment of students, teacher preparation, instructional methods, and other aspects of our educational system.

Publication of the PIRLS, PISA, and TIMSS studies has helped ignite emotional controversies. On one side, observers claim that our educational system is more satisfactory than it is often portrayed. While usually admitting that it needs major improvements, these observers point to such factors as the following:[21]

- Our students generally perform at a relatively high reading level through the fourth grade.
- Cultural factors, not deficiencies in the schools, may be causing much of the relatively low student performance. For example, the high levels of mathematics achievement reported for Hungary, Japan, and Korea may be attributable significantly to the great value their cultures attach to mathematics performance and to strong family support for achievement.
- Contrary to critics' statements, achievement in US schools has improved during the past few decades, particularly considering the increased enrollment of minority students from low-income families. These improvements may be attributable in part to the positive effects of compensatory education and school desegregation (see our Chapter 11, Social Class, Race, and School Achievement) and to efforts at educational reform.

Critics of US performance have been unappeased by such arguments. Frequently pointing to the particularly low scores that our students register on tests assessing higher-order skills such as math problem solving, they reiterate the importance of improving students' skills in comprehension, geography, math, science, and other subjects. They conclude that the rankings of US students in numerous international achievement studies represent a deplorable performance level that cannot be corrected without radical efforts to reform or even replace our current system of education.[22]

15-2l US Achievement among Young Adults

We noted in an earlier section of this chapter that some other nations have caught up with and surpassed the United States in enrolling young people in higher education.

---

[20]William H. Schmidt, Chi W. Hsing, and Curtis C. McKnight, "Curriculum Coherence," *Journal of Curriculum Studies* (September 2005), pp. 525–559; Xiaoxia Newton, "Reflections on Math Reform in the US," *Phi Delta Kappan* (May 2007), pp. 681–685; William H. Schmidt, "What's Missing from Math Standards?" *American Educator* (Spring 2008), available at **www.aft.org**; William H. Schmidt et al., "Content Coverage Differences across Districts/States," *American Journal of Education* (May 2011); Stephen Tung, "How the Finnish School System Outshines US Education," 2012 posting at Physorg.com, available at **www.physorg.com**; "The Common Core Faq," May 27, 2014, posting by NPRED, available at **www.npr.org**; and Gary Phillips and Alicia N. Garcia, "Setting Performance Standards for Student Success," February 2015 posting by the American Institutes for Research, available at **www.air.org**.

[21]Purves and Levine, *Educational Policy and International Assessment;* Erling E. Boe and Sujie Shin, "Is the United States Really Losing the International Horse Race in Academic Achievement?" *Phi Delta Kappan* (September 2005), pp. 688–695; Gerald W. Bracey, "US School Performance, Through a Glass Darkly (Again)," *Phi Delta Kappan* (January 2009), pp. 386–387; Ziyi Mai, "The Myth of US Student Performance," January 8, 2014, posting by Technician Online, available at **www.technicianonline.com**; and Sarah D. Sparks, "Broader Picture of International Education Progress Unveiled in Study," *Education Week* (January 20, 2015).

[22]William H. Schmidt, Richard Houang, and Leonard Cogan, "A Coherent Curriculum," *American Educator* (Summer 2002), available at **www.aft.org**; Eric Hanushek et al., "Education and Economic Growth," *Education Next* (Spring 2008), available at **www.educationnext.org**; William H. Schmidt, Leland S. Cogan, and Curtis C. McKnight, "Equality of Educational Opportunity," *American Educator* (Winter 2010–2011), available at **www.aft.org**; and Drew Desilver, "US Students Improving—Slowly—in Math and Science, But Still Lagging Internationally," February 2, 2015, posting by the Pew Research Center, available at **www.pewresearch.org**.

Reinforcement of this pattern has been provided by data collected as part the Programme for the International Assessment of Adult Competencies (PIAAC) that was initiated by the Organization for Economic Co-operation and Development (OECD). Its reports include information on the literacy numeracy, and problem-solving skills of 16- to 34-year-olds in developed nations. Among the findings of this research are the following:[23]

- Regarding literacy, US participants scored fifth from the bottom among the twenty-two nations for which data were available.
- Regarding numeracy, US participants scored last.
- Regarding problem solving (when using digital technology), US participants scored next to last.
- Economic and social background has a stronger impact on literacy skills in the United States than in other countries. Low-income African Americans and Hispanics are overrepresented in the low-skills category.

Analysts at the Educational Testing Service examined the PIAAC data and pointed out that both the highest and lowest segments of the US sample performed poorly compared with their counterparts in most other nations, thus indicating that the "skills challenge is systemic." They further concluded that too many of our youth and adults are "graduating high school and completing postsecondary educational programs without receiving adequate skills." In addition, these analysts reported that the gap between our highest and lowest scorers was among the largest among the participating nations. Finally, they concluded that because the skills assessed are necessary for success in modern economies, these patterns will function to limit US international competitiveness and to perpetuate inequalities in our society.

The PIAAC methodology also identified "minimum levels of proficiency" at which OECD policy makers consider that students begin to "demonstrate the skills that will enable them to participate effectively and productively in life." PIAAC data showed that 50 percent of US young adults were below the minimum on literacy, 64 percent were below the minimum on numeracy, and 54 percent were below the minimum on problem solving. These percentages led the Educational Testing Service analysts to conclude that our national future is bleak if it depends on the skills of the young-adult cohort in our population.

15-2m Sex Differences in Achievement in the United States and Internationally

In Chapter 10, Culture, Socialization, and Education, we described how girls in the United States traditionally scored higher in reading than boys but lower in mathematics, although the differences in math have become small in recent years. Recent PISA studies have found a somewhat different pattern internationally. Analysts examined the scores of more than 1.5 million 15-year-olds in seventy-four nations and other jurisdictions (regions and cities within nations) and reported the following:[24]

- In 70 percent of the locations studied, girls outperformed boys in reading, mathematics, and science literacy except among students with the best scores, where

---

[23]"Time for the US to Reskill?" 2013 posting by the Organization for Economic Co-operation and Development, available at **www.oecd.org**; Madeline J Goodman, Anita M. Sands, and Richard J. Coley, "America's Skills Challenge," 2015 posting by the Educational Testing Service, available at **www.ets.org**; and Robert Pondiscio, "Overeducated and Unprepared," February 25, 2015, posting by Flypaper, available at **www.edexcellence.net**.

[24]The quotation is from Hannah Richardson, "'Girls Outperform Boys at School' Despite Inequality," January 22, 2015, posting by the BBC, available at **www.bbc.com**. See also Eduardo Porter, "Gender Gap in Education Cuts Both Ways," *New York Times* (March 10, 2015); "Girls Lead Boys in Academic Achievement Globally," *Science Daily* (January 26, 2015), available at **www .sciencedaily.com**; and "The ABC of Gender Equality in Education," 2015 posting by the Organisation for Economic Co-Operation and Development, 2011), available at **www.oecd.org**.

boys had higher performance. Gijsbert Stoet described the pattern as indicating that "with the exception of high achievers, boys have poorer educational outcomes than girls around the world."

● In many nations, including the United States, the percentage of boys who are below proficient in all three subjects is higher than the percentage for girls.

● The gaps between the scores of girls and boys generally were smallest in nations with the highest PISA scores, such as Finland, Japan, and South Korea.

The Organisation for Economic Co-operation and Development, sponsor of the PISA program, summarized some of the implications suggested by sex differences in achievement as indicating that many boys are "trapped in a cycle of poor performance, low motivation, disengagement from school, and lack of ambition," and consequently will have limited chance to succeed in the job markets of the future.

FOCUS How might your work as a teacher be affected by international comparisons of achievement? How should it be affected?

15-3 EXEMPLARY REFORMS: A SELECTION

effective schools Schools that are unusually successful in producing high student performance, compared with other schools that enroll students of similar background; sometimes defined as schools in which working-class students achieve as well as middle-class students.

As in the United States, educators in other parts of the world are introducing reforms to make schools more effective. Some of these reforms are based on studies of unusually successful schools and how they function. Most research on these **effective schools** occurred in the United States, but important studies have also taken place in Australia, Canada, the Netherlands, the United Kingdom, and other countries. In this chapter, we consider substantial reforms many nations have introduced in their educational systems.[25] Some countries have been respected for many decades for the quality and effectiveness with which they provide early childhood opportunities, mathematics instruction, vocational schooling, or other important educational experiences. In the next chapter, we'll explore in detail characteristics of effective schools, as well as research indicating that systematic change and long-term commitment are the keys to successful school reform.

15-3a Early Childhood Education in France

Recognizing the critical importance of the preschool years in a child's social, physical, and educational development, many countries have taken steps to provide stimulating learning opportunities and positive day-care arrangements for most or all young children. For example, more than 90 percent of 3- to 5-year-olds in Belgium, Hong Kong, and Italy are enrolled in early childhood education programs, compared with little more than half in the United States. Outstanding child-care arrangements for infants are easily accessible to families throughout Scandinavia. The mix of preschool and day-care programs varies considerably from one country to another, as does the extent to which early childhood educators work with parents and families. Overall, however, early childhood education has become a topic of urgent interest throughout much of the world.

France has what many observers consider a model approach to preschool services. Nearly all 3- to 5-year-olds are enrolled in preschool programs, and average salaries of preschool teachers are considerably higher than in the United States or most other countries. Participating children pursue stimulating activities before and after school, during vacation, and at other times when school is out. Equally important, parents have financial incentives to enroll their children in high-quality programs that provide pediatric and other preventive health services. Child-care specialists and civic leaders

---

[25]David Reynolds, "World Class Schools," *Educational Research & Evaluation* (December 2006), pp. 535–560; Chris James et al., "High Attainment Schools in Disadvantaged Settings," *International Studies in Educational Administration* (No. 2, 2008), pp. 66–79; "Against the Odds," 2011 report prepared for PISA, abstract available at **www.oecd.org/pisa/**; and Roelande H. Hofman, W. H. A. Hofman, and John M. Gray, "Three Conjectures about School Effectiveness," *Cogent Education* (January 2015), available at **www.tandfonline.com**.

who examined the French system have reported the following aspects of French programs as worth considering in the United States:[26]

- Virtually all children have access to a coordinated system linking early education, day care, and health services.
- Paid parental leave from jobs after childbirth or adoption helps to nurture positive parent–child relationships.
- Good salaries and training for early childhood teachers help to keep turnover low and program quality high.
- Nearly all young children are enrolled in preschool programs.
- The government provides additional resources to ensure high quality at locations enrolling low-income children.

15-3b Finnish Achievement and Teacher Preparation

The education system in Finland has become known for high achievement and attainment at all levels from preschool through higher education. Various observers have cited features they believe help account for this success: a national core curriculum that emphasizes thinking and students' active role in learning, school-level (not national) requirements that students perform at high levels, some flexible grouping rather than rigid streaming or tracking, a highly qualified teaching force (see the next paragraph) that has high status and good pay, nearly universal public preschool, significant time in the school day set aside for teacher planning and assessment of students, provision and updating of science laboratory equipment and materials and of computer hardware and software, provision of funds so that schools enrolling many immigrant students can afford such interventions as resource teachers and special-needs classes, various other interventions to help struggling students in elementary and secondary schools, and a national culture highly supportive of literacy and learning.[27]

As noted in the previous paragraph, observers believe that the quality of teaching and of the teacher workforce helps account for high achievement levels in Finnish schools. Analysts have described notable aspects of Finland's strong teacher preparation as including the following:[28]

- Entry into teacher-training programs is highly selective. Few applicants are accepted initially, and candidates must then do well in a clinical situation before gaining entry.
- Candidates then must earn at least a two-year master's degree at one of eight well-respected universities.
- Candidates must spend a significant amount of time in clinical practice in a model classroom associated with the university.
- Candidates to teach at the elementary level must take at least two subject-area minors in arts or science departments. Candidates for higher grades must participate in a subject-area master's degree program.
- Candidates who receive a degree in the subject they will teach must receive another master's degree in teaching.

---

[26]Conn-Powers et al., "The Universal Design of Early Education," *Young Children* (September 2006); Moncrieff Cochran, "International Perspectives on Early Childhood Education," *Educational Policy* (Issue 1, 2011), pp. 65–91; and "Gettin 'Em Young," *Economist* (January 24, 2015).

[27]LynNell Hancock, "Why Are Finland's Schools Successful?" *Smithsonian* (September 2011), available at **www.smithsonianmag.com**; Alain Jehlen, "How Finland Reached the Top of the Educational Rankings," *NEA Today* (March 4, 2011), available at **www.neatoday.org**; Pasi Sahlberg, "Lessons from Finland," *American Educator* (Summer 2011), available at **www.aft.org**; Hani Morgan, "The Education System in Finland," *Childhood Education* (November/December 2014); Pasi Sahlberg, *Finnish Lessons 2.0* (New York: Teachers College Press, 2014); and "A Tool for Peace and Development," January 27, 2015, posting by Education International, available at **www.ei-ie.org**.

[28]Linda Darling-Hammond, "Soaring Systems," *American Educator* (Winter 2010–2011), available at **www.aft.org**; Valerie Strauss, "Teach for Finland? Why It Won't Happen," *Washington Post* (February 12, 2015), available at **www.washingtonpost.com**.

TECHNOLOGY @ SCHOOL

AN INTERNET SITE DEALING WITH ACHIEVEMENT AND WHAT INFLUENCES ACHIEVEMENT AROUND THE WORLD

The Organisation for Economic Co-operation and Development has been publishing numerous documents providing information and analysis based on data regarding student performance in reading, mathematics, and other subjects collected in more than seventy nations as part of the Program for International Student Assessment (PISA). Most of these publications can be downloaded for free from the Programme for International School Assessment website. For example, reports highlighted in 2015 included the following: "How Has Student Performance Evolved Over Time?" and "Do Countries with High Mean Performance in PISA Maintain Their Lead as Students Age?" You probably will find that several of the reports are of particular interest to you.

The publication titled "Improving Performance: Leading from the Bottom" (found by using the search box at the upper right of the home page) has information about thirteen countries that registered reading gains among 15-year-olds between 2000 and 2009. Analysis by PISA staff concluded that success in these countries was due at least in part to the establishment of clear, ambitious policy goals, monitoring of student performance, granting more autonomy to schools, offering the same curriculum to all 15-year-olds, and providing support for low-performing schools and students. Some questions relevant to educators who read this report include the following:

1. To what extent are policies and actions identified in this report transferable to other countries?

2. Where policies and actions are transferable, how might they need to be modified?

3. What kinds of additional support for low-performing students and schools are feasible and desirable?

Several analysts also emphasize that Finland and other high-performing nations exemplify systemic arrangements involving such coordinated components as a focus on higher-order learning, a well-trained teaching force, collaborative planning and assessment of lessons, and high coordination and articulation of curriculum and instruction across grade levels. Although high-quality teaching seems to be a hallmark of all these nations, student performance also is dependent on correlated arrangements that appear to vary from nation to nation. Analysts also point out that Finland is a small, relatively homogeneous nation; some practices that help account for its success in education may not work in much larger and more heterogeneous nations such as the United States. In addition, Tom Loveless of the Brookings Institution has pointed out that the gap between the very high reading achievement of girls in Finland and the lower achievement of boys is the largest of any PISA nation, and that Finnish boys' reading achievement is close to the average for economically developed nations.[29]

15-3c Mathematics and Science Education in Japan

International achievement studies indicate that Japanese students consistently attain high scores in mathematics, science, and other subject areas. For example, the second International Study of Achievement in Mathematics reported that eighth graders in Japan on average answered 62 percent of the test items correctly, compared with 45 percent in the United States and 47 percent across the eighteen countries included in the study. With respect to science achievement among eighth graders, Japanese students attained an average score of 554, compared with an average of 500 for other nations included in the fourth assessment. As shown in Table 15.2, Japanese students score very high in the PISA studies.[30]

---

[29]"The Finland Phenomenon," December 17, 2014, posting by *The Daily Riff*, available at **www.thedailyriff.com**; and Tom Loveless, "2015 Brown Center Report on American Education," March 24, 2015, posting by The Brookings Institution, available at **www.brookings.edu**.

[30]Barbara J. Reyes and Robert E. Reyes, "Japanese Mathematics Education," *Teaching Children Mathematics* (April 1995), pp. 474–475; and Robert Fish, "Recent Trends in Education Reform," 2015 posting by the Asia Society, available at **www.asiasociety.org**.

Indeed/Getty Images

> **PHOTO 15.2** Japanese students consistently attain high scores in mathematics, science, and other subject areas.

Certain aspects of Japanese education and society may help account for high achievement levels among Japanese youth (Photo 15.2). Most of the following characteristics apply to Japanese education in general, not merely to math and science programs. The list of pertinent factors is long, and researchers remain unsure which are important. Perhaps they all are.[31]

- Outstanding day care helps prepare children for school success. In addition, socialization practices in the family and in early childhood education help students learn to adapt to classroom situations and demands. US schools, in contrast, tend to attain good discipline by making instruction attractive and by bargaining with students to obtain compliance (see Chapter 10, Culture, Socialization, and Education), at great cost to academic standards and rigor.
- Intense parental involvement is expected. In particular, mothers feel great responsibility for children's success in school. Families provide much continuing support and motivation, ranging from elaborate celebration of entry into first grade to widespread enrollment of children in supplementary private cram schools (*juku*), which students attend after school and on weekends. Compared with US parents, Japanese parents emphasize effort over ability when asked to identify causes of success or failure in school.
- Students attend school 240 days a year (compared with less than 200 in the United States).
- Beginning at an early age, students are given much responsibility for schoolwork and learning.
- Large amounts of homework correlated with classroom lessons contribute to high student performance.
- Careful planning and delivery of a national curriculum help students acquire important concepts within a sequential and comprehensive framework.
- Compared with elementary-school practices in the United States and in many other countries, lessons de-emphasize rote learning.

---

[31]Thomas P. Rohlen, "Differences That Make a Difference," *Educational Policy* (June 1995), pp. 129–151; Elizabeth Green, "Why Do Americans Stink at Math?" *New York Times* (July 23, 2014); "Japan Overview," 2015 posting by the Center on International Education Benchmarking, available at **www.ncee.org**; and Harold W. Stevenson and Roberta Nerison-Low, "To Sum It Up," undated paper prepared for the US Department of Education, available at **www.ed.gov/pubs/SumItUp**.

- The schools emphasize the development of students' character and sense of responsibility through such practices as assigning students chores and having them help each other in learning.
- Educators tend to take responsibility for students' learning. For example, many teachers contact parents to recommend homework schedules and curfews.
- Prospective teachers must pass rigorous examinations and are intensely supervised when they enter the profession.
- Japanese educators have relatively high social status, which enhances their authority in working with students and parents. Partly for this reason, there are numerous applicants for teaching positions, thus allowing administrators to select highly qualified candidates.
- School schedules provide considerable time for counseling students, planning instruction, and engaging in other activities that make teachers more effective.
- Generous time and support available to slower students help produce less variability in achievement than in the United States and most other countries. Japanese schools have relatively few extremely low achievers.

Those familiar with the Japanese educational system also point out some apparently negative characteristics:[32]

- Emphasis appears relatively slight on divergent thinking. Some observers believe that insufficient emphasis on creativity may severely hamper future social and economic development in Japan.
- Opportunities for working-class students and women to attend postsecondary institutions and gain high occupational status appear severely limited. For example, one study found that only 11 percent of students in college-prep high schools had fathers who had not completed high school, compared with 32 percent of students in less academic high schools.
- Partly because of restricted higher-education opportunities, secondary education is exam driven—instruction covers immense quantities of factual information likely to be tested on entrance examinations. In turn, examination pressures further stifle divergent thinking and frequently lead to mental distress and even suicide.
- In accordance with the old Japanese proverb, "The nail that sticks out gets hammered down," behavioral standards and expectations in many Japanese schools are so narrow and rigid that some educators believe they generate too much conformity.
- More than ever before, young people in Japan seem to be rejecting the traditional customs and values on which the educational system is founded.
- Many students with disabilities receive little help.
- Bullying appears to be a widespread problem in Japanese schools.
- Japanese schools have done relatively little to introduce computers and other aspects of modern technology.

In reviewing its various strengths and weaknesses, several thoughtful observers have concluded that we have much to learn from the Japanese educational system, but they add that we should make sure that promising practices from elsewhere are workable and appropriately adapted to our own situation. Likewise, government commissions in Japan have been considering reform proposals that incorporate the more positive aspects of education in the United States (for example, to reduce the emphasis on conformity). A professor of Japanese studies at Harvard University has summarized the situation in this way: "As a mirror showing us our weakness and as a yardstick against which to measure our efforts," Japanese education has great value for us.

FOCUS What are the potential benefits of using other nations' educational reforms as models for improving our own schools? What are the drawbacks? What cautions should educators observe in adopting school reforms from other countries?

---

[32]Ken Schoolland, *Shogun's Ghost* (New York: Bergin and Garvey, 1990); Maso Miyamoto, *Straitjacket Society* (Tokyo: Kodansha, 1994); "Japanese Education Reforms to Further Prepare Students for Globalised World," February 4, 2014, posting by ICEF Monitor, available at **http://monitor.icef .com**; and Chris Forlin and Norimune Kawai, "Educational Reform in Japan towards Inclusion," *International Journal of Inclusive Education* (March 2015).

We should not, however, "allow ourselves either to ignore or to imitate" its approach. Instead, we should "look periodically into the 'Japanese mirror' while we quite independently set out to straighten our schools and our system within our own cultural and social context."[33]

15-4 THE INTERNATIONAL CONTEXT AND THE CHALLENGES FACING US SCHOOLS

Some observers believe that international study of education is becoming increasingly useful because developed societies are growing more alike. Throughout the world, more citizens are becoming middle class, and school systems and other institutions are emphasizing preparation for dealing with advanced technology and rapid social change. Mass media and other technologies exert a common influence across national borders. Even so, no two societies ever will be exactly alike, nor will cultural and social differences disappear entirely. Still, characteristics of social institutions (including the family and the school) will likely converge. For example, Kenichi Ohmae has remarked that Japan's "Nintendo Kids"—youngsters who have grown up with computers, video games, and global media—"have more in common with similar youngsters outside Japan than with other generations within Japan."[34]

If that is true, we have much to learn from studying effective education in other nations. Likewise, other nations can learn from the United States. Despite its many shortcomings described in this book, the United States was long an international leader in striving to educate all students regardless of their social background or previous achievement. Richard Kahlenberg and Bernard Wasow examined educational systems and achievement patterns internationally and reached the following conclusions with respect to implications for the United States: "American public schools have helped make Americans out of wave after wave of immigrants. . . . That said, the public-school system fails a substantial segment of the population, and this failure aligns sharply with class and race." As we noted in this chapter, the achievement of our students is mediocre, and we have fallen behind some other developed nations in college attendance and completion. Recognizing these shortcomings, US Secretary of Education Arne Duncan said soon after taking office that "we used to lead the world, and we have sort of lost our way in the last couple of decades." Aspects of reform that might help us return to world leadership and equality will be considered in the next chapter.[35]

FOCUS Do you believe that increasing similarities between developed nations will eventually lead to increasingly similar educational systems?

---

[33]Thomas P. Rohlen, "Japanese Education: If They Can Do It, Should We?" *American Scholar* (Winter 1985–1986), p. 43. See also Jackyung Lee, "School Reform Initiatives," *Education Policy Analysis Archives* (April 24, 2001), available at **http://epaa.asu.edu/ojs**; William Jeynes, "What We Should and Should Not Learn from the Japanese and Other East Asian Education Systems," *Educational Policy* (November 2008), pp. 900–927; Heidi Knipprath, "What PISA Tells Us about the Quality and Inequality of Japanese Education in Mathematics and Science," *International Journal of Science and Mathematics Education* (June 2010), pp. 389–408; and Tom Loveless, "Six Myths in the New York Times Article by Elizabeth Green," August 7, 2014, posting by Brookings, available at **www.brookings.edu**.

[34]Kenichi Ohmae, "China's 600,000 Avon Ladies," *New Perspectives Quarterly* (Winter 1995), p. 15. See also Iris C. Rotberg, "US Education in a Global Context," *Education Week* (February 9, 2005); Craig C. Wiekzorek, "Comparative Analysis of Educational Systems of American and Japanese Schools," *Educational Horizons* (Winter 2008), pp. 99–111; *Lessons from PISA for the United States* (Paris: Organisation for Economic Co-Operation and Development, 2011), available at **www.oecd.org**; and "Transforming Teacher Work Around the World," 2014 posting by Advance Illinois, available at **www.advanceillinois.org**.

[35]Richard D. Kahlenberg and Bernard Wasow, "What Makes Schools Work?" *Boston Review* (October–November 2003); Yong Zhao, "The Best and Worst of the East and West," *Phi Delta Kappan* (November 2005), pp. 219–222; Amanda Ripley, *The Smartest Kids in the World and How They Got That Way* (New York: Simon and Schuster, 2013); Luke Towler, "Time for the US to Learn the Right Lessons from High-Performing Nations," *NEA Today* (October 21, 2014), available at **www.neatoday.org**; and C. K. Jackson, Rucker C. Johnson, and Claudia Persico, "The Effects of School Spending on Educational and Economic Outcomes," January 2015 posting by the National Bureau of Economic Research , available at **www.nber.org**.

SUMMING UP

1. Although educational systems differ considerably between nations, they tend to confront the similar problem of providing effective instruction for large numbers of students whose opportunities and performance relate to their social and cultural background.

2. School systems around the world differ greatly in the resources they devote to education, enrollments, student–teacher ratios, male–female student ratios, the extent of centralization or decentralization, curriculum content and instructional emphasis, approaches to teacher preparation, higher-education and vocational-education opportunities, nonpublic-school availability and roles, teacher responsibilities for low-income students, and student achievement.

3. Educational services or practices appear exemplary in several countries: early childhood education in France, general achievement in Finland, and mathematics and science education in Japan. Arrangements for attaining high achievement in Finland include a national core curriculum that emphasizes thinking and students' active role in learning, school-level requirements for high levels of student performance, some flexible grouping rather than rigid streaming or tracking, a highly qualified teaching force, nearly universal public preschool, significant time in the school day set aside for teacher planning and assessment of students, and various interventions to help struggling students in elementary and secondary schools. Efforts to provide an effective teaching force include emphasis on preparing highly qualified new teachers.

4. Researchers can learn much from studying educational systems in other countries, but it is not always easy to identify the reasons for a system's success or failure or its implications for different societies.

5. The United States has been an international leader in the effort to provide equal and effective educational opportunities for all groups of students, but it has been slipping in this regard in comparison with other nations.

SUGGESTED RESOURCES

INTERNET RESOURCES

The posting, "Great Expectations: Girls in Schools Today," on the Organization for Economic Co-Operation and Development website provides links to international analysis and research involving girls and women and education.

PUBLICATIONS

Comparative Education Review. This journal emphasizes such topics as the development of national school systems, education and economic development, comparisons across nations, and international aspects of multicultural education.

International Journal of Educational Research. Recent theme issues have dealt with equal opportunity, giftedness, private education, science education, and other topics of worldwide concern.

Sahlberg, Pasi. *Finnish Lessons 2.0*. New York: Teachers College Press, 2014. *Subtitled "What Can the World Learn from Educational Change in Finland?"* this book concludes that systematically focusing on teacher and leader professionalism, building of trust between the society and its schools, and investing in equity rather than competition and choice is responsible for reaching very high levels of achievement in the Finnish educational system.

Ripley, Amanda. *The Smartest Kids in the World and How They Got That Way*. New York: Simon and Schuster, 2013. *Ripley interviewed US teenagers who studied in Finland, South Korea, and Poland, respectively, as well as other students in those nations and exchange students who studied in the United States. She analyzes and compares educational systems and cultures in trying to determine why students in high-achieving nations perform much better than American students.*

SCHOOL EFFECTIVENESS AND REFORM IN THE UNITED STATES

LEARNING OBJECTIVES

16-1 Describe several fundamental reasons why the educational system should be improved and reformed.

16-2 Understand the characteristics of effective teaching and instruction to improve higher-order learning.

16-3 Describe what research says about unusually effective schools.

16-4 Discuss some keys to implementing successful school reforms.

16-5 Describe how we can improve instruction across classrooms and at the school level.

16-6 Describe and discuss the potential of technology for improving education and some of the ways in which technology is being introduced to improve achievement.

16-7 Describe ways in which schools are cooperating with other institutions, the status of rural education and education for gifted and talented students, and efforts to increase teaching and learning time.

16-8 Discuss whether and how expansion of school-choice plans may be improving education.

16-9 Determine what systemic reforms may be accomplishing in some states and school districts.

16-10 Identify and discuss some of the school reform efforts that may help improve the functioning of the educational system.

Monkey Business Images/Shutterstock.com

This chapter was revised by Daniel U. Levine.

MUCH OF THIS book is concerned with problems and trends in the reform of elementary and secondary schools. The material in this chapter deals even more explicitly with key selected issues in school effectiveness and reform. After highlighting several major challenges that confront the US educational system, we will examine arguments about and research into the characteristics of effective instruction and effective schools. We will also look at the process of school improvement and reform and other important topics often discussed under the headings of school effectiveness and reform.

Debates about school reform can be resolved partly by analyzing actual research evidence. This chapter cannot discuss or provide comprehensive information about every possible change but instead will examine some of the proposals that seem to hold particular promise or that have received widespread attention. As you read, consider which ideas have solid evidence to support them. Investigate some of the sources in the footnotes to determine whether they report or take account of research, not just provide arguments for or against a particular point of view. Think also about the prerequisites for success, the underlying conditions that may help make each suggested reform appropriate or inappropriate, and how they may affect your career as a teacher.

16-1 IMPERATIVES TO IMPROVE THE SCHOOLS

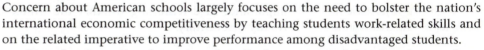

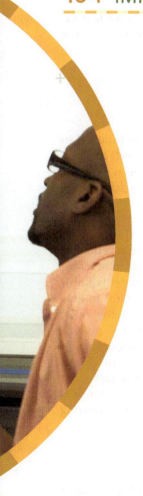

Concern about American schools largely focuses on the need to bolster the nation's international economic competitiveness by teaching students work-related skills and on the related imperative to improve performance among disadvantaged students.

Several major national reports and studies have suggested that American students are leaving school unprepared to participate effectively in jobs that will, in an increasingly sophisticated and technology-based world economy, require them to carry out complicated tasks at a high level. Echoing these reports, President Barack Obama prefaced his proposals for education reform by stating, "The future belongs to the nation that best educates its citizens. . . . We have everything we need to be that nation . . . and yet, despite resources that are unmatched anywhere in the world, we have let our grades slip, our schools crumble, our teacher quality fall short, and other nations outpace us."[1]

Nearly all of the recent reports and studies dealing with educational reform also call for improving the performance of economically disadvantaged students to make educational outcomes more equitable. In addition to the desire for fairness, educational equity has also been related to the need for economic competitiveness. Thus, the Forum of Educational Organizational Leaders concluded that "if we wish to maintain or improve our standard of living, we must work smarter . . . [but] it is not possible to succeed if only middle-class people from stable families work smarter. . . . [This capacity] must—for the first time in human history—be characteristic of the mass of our population."

Specific areas of concern for educators working to reform educational opportunities for disadvantaged students include the following:

- *At-risk students and schools.* Social and economic opportunities have declined rapidly for low-achieving students and those without good postsecondary credentials. Perhaps the farthest-reaching set of proposals for helping at-risk and disadvantaged

[1] Daniel Gross, "The Education Factor," *Education Next* (Spring 2009), available at **www .educationnext.org**; "States Announce Actions to Close Skills Gaps for All Students," December 1, 2014, posting by the Council of Chief State School Officers, available at **www.ccsso.org**; and James Rosenbaum et al., "The New Forgotten Half and Research Directions to Support Them," January 2015 posting by the William T. Grant Foundation, available at **www.wtgrantfoundation.org**.

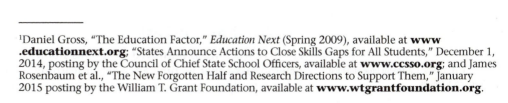

students is in the policy statements of the Council of Chief State School Officers (CCSSO). CCSSO's statements argue that state laws should guarantee educational programs and other services "reasonably calculated to enable all persons to graduate from high school."

- *Inner-city poverty.* As we pointed out in Chapter 11, Social Class, Race, and School Achievement, and elsewhere in this book, educational problems are particularly severe in inner-city minority neighborhoods of concentrated poverty. A total response to the problems in these neighborhoods will involve improvement of employment, transportation, housing, affirmative action, and social welfare supports; desegregation and deconcentration of poverty populations; reduction of crime and delinquency; and other efforts—in which elementary and secondary education must play a pivotal part.

- *Concentrated rural poverty.* Some rural areas have communities of concentrated poverty similar in many respects to those in big cities. Among these are the Appalachian region in the eastern United States and the Ozarks region in the South. Although many poor rural communities have mostly nonminority populations, indicators of social disorganization—high teenage-pregnancy rates, widespread juvenile delinquency, extremely low school achievement, and pervasive feelings of hopelessness—run as high or nearly as high as those in poor minority urban neighborhoods. For the US economy as a whole to work smarter, these rural students, like their inner-city counterparts, need effective education.

Many observers believe that our response to these challenges will be of historic importance in determining whether the United States prospers or declines in the twenty-first century.

FOCUS What do you believe is the most urgent reason for educational reform?

16-2 CHARACTERISTICS OF EFFECTIVE CLASSROOMS

The push for greater educational effectiveness became a national growth industry in 1983, and since then, it has generated hundreds of research studies as well as thousands of discussion papers and improvement plans. Many studies have been designed to identify the characteristics of effective classroom teaching and **effective schools**.

effective schools Schools that are unusually successful in producing high student performance, compared with other schools that enroll students of similar background; sometimes defined as schools in which working-class students achieve as well as middle-class students.

16-2a Classroom Management

Research on classroom management indicates that effective teachers use a variety of techniques to develop productive climates and to motivate students. Effective teachers emphasize practices such as the following: (1) making sure that students know what the teacher expects; (2) letting students know how to obtain help; (3) following through with reminders between activities and rewards to enforce the rules; (4) providing a smooth transition between activities; (5) giving students assignments of sufficient variety to maintain interest; (6) monitoring the class for signs of confusion or inattention; (7) being careful to avoid embarrassing students in front of their classmates; (8) responding flexibly to unexpected developments; (9) designing tasks that draw on students' prior knowledge and experience; (10) helping students develop self-management skills; (11) attending to students' cultural backgrounds; and (12) ensuring that all students are part of a classroom learning community.

16-2b Time-on-Task

time-on-task Classroom time engaged in learning activities.

Effective teaching as portrayed in various studies brings about relatively high student **time-on-task**—that is, time engaged in learning activities. As you might expect, students actively engaged in relevant activities learn more than students who are not so

> **PHOTO 16.1** Questioning skills—such as ensuring long "wait times" and asking "higher-order" questions—are an important aspect of effective teaching.

Hero Images/Getty Images

engaged. Time-on-task studies have pointed out that classrooms can be managed to increase the time students spend on actual learning activities. The school day and the school year can be extended to support academic learning. However, student learning involves more than time spent on academic work. Other variables, such as the suitability of the activities, the students' success or failure in the tasks attempted, and the motivating characteristics of methods and materials, are also important.[2]

16-2c Questioning

One way to stimulate student engagement in learning is to ask appropriate questions in a manner that ensures participation and facilitates mastery of academic content. Several studies have identified questioning skills as an important aspect of effective teaching (Photo 16.1). In particular, research indicates that longer "wait time" (the interval between the posing of a question and selecting or encouraging a student to answer it) significantly improves student participation and learning. Research also indicates that "higher-order" questioning that requires students to mentally manipulate ideas and information is more effective than "lower cognitive" questioning that focuses on verbatim recall of facts.[3]

16-2d Direct Instruction and Explicit Teaching

The terms **direct instruction** and **explicit teaching** (frequently used as synonyms) usually refer to teacher-directed instruction that proceeds in small steps. (Direct instruction also is sometimes referred to as "active teaching.") Research has shown a link between this method, properly implemented, and high levels of student achievement. Barak

direct instruction A systematic method of teaching that emphasizes teacher-directed instruction proceeding in small steps, usually in accordance with a six- to eight-part lesson sequence.

explicit teaching A systematic method of teaching that emphasizes teacher-directed instruction proceeding in small steps, usually in accordance with a six- to eight-part lesson sequence.

[2]Elena Silva, "On the Clock," 2007 paper prepared for Education Sector, available at **www.educationsector.org**; "Increased Time on Task," April 22, 2014, posting by Ed Management Services, available at **www.nysed.gov**; and Jennifer Davis, "More Quality Time," April 23, 2015, posting by the Hechinger Report, available at **www.hechingerreport.org**.
[3]Sophie Wrobel, "The Question Game," January 9, 2015, posting by te@chthought, available at **www.teachthought.com**.

Rosenshine identified the following six teaching steps or functions as central to direct instruction:[4]

1. Begin with a review of previous learning and a preview and goal statement.
2. Present new material in steps, with clear explanations and active student practice after each step.
3. Guide students in initial practice; ask questions and check for understanding.
4. Provide systematic feedback and corrections.
5. Supervise independent practice; monitor and assist seatwork.
6. Provide weekly and monthly review and testing.

16-2e Explicit Comprehension Instruction

Direct instruction has often been criticized for its tendency to neglect important higher-order learning (reasoning, critical thinking, comprehension of concepts) in favor of small-step learning of factual material. In many schools where teachers have been told to follow a prescribed sequence of this kind, the practice emphasizes low-level learning and mindless regurgitation of facts that leaves little room for creativity and analytical thinking.[5]

However, direct instruction need not concentrate on low-level learning. Educators have been refining classroom techniques for explicitly teaching comprehension in all subject areas. David Pearson and his colleagues refer to many such approaches as **explicit comprehension instruction**. Barak Rosenshine has characterized the development of this approach since 1970 as an enormous accomplishment in which educators should take great pride.[6]

Like explicit teaching, explicit comprehension instruction emphasizes review and preview, feedback and correctives, and guided as well as independent practice, but experts suggest that teachers also systematically model conceptual learning, help students link new knowledge to their prior learning, monitor students' comprehension, and train students in summarizing, drawing inferences, and other learning strategies. Techniques and strategies associated with explicit comprehension instruction include the following:[7]

- Prediction activities in which students infer what will be found in the text based on their prior knowledge

explicit comprehension instruction Classroom techniques specifically for teaching comprehension.

---

[4]Barak Rosenshine, "Explicit Teaching and Teacher Training," *Journal of Teacher Education* (May–June 1987), pp. 34–36. See also Barak Rosenshine, "Principles of Instruction," *American Educator* (Spring 2012), available at **www.aft.org**; Brian Christian, "Small Steps and Frequent Feedback," October 20, 2014, posting available at **www.bst.ac.jp/principalsblog/tag/barak -rosenshine**; and Silvia Ybarra, "Explicit Direct Instruction (EDI) vs. Direct Instruction (DI)," July 25, 2014, posting by Data Works, available at **www.dataworks-ed.com**.

[5]Linda M. McNeil, *Contradictions of School Reform* (New York: Routledge, 2000); Sandra Mathison and Melissa Freeman, "Constraining Elementary Teachers' Work," *Education Policy Analysis Archives* (September 24, 2003), available at **http://epaa.asu.edu/ojs/article/view/262**; and Douglas Fisher and Nancy Frey, "Improve Reading with Complex Texts," *Phi Delta Kappan* (February 2015).

[6]P. David Pearson and Janice A. Dole, "Explicit Comprehension Instruction," *Elementary School Journal* (November 1987), pp. 151–165; Shepard Barbash, *Clear Teaching*, 2011 electronic book published by the Education Consumers Foundation, available free at **www.education -consumers.org**; "Explicit Instruction for Implicit Meaning," June 19, 2014, posting by the William and Mary School of Education, available at **https://education.wm.edu**; and Barak Rosenshine, personal communication, January 26, 2015.

[7]Barak Rosenshine and Carla Meister, "Reciprocal Teaching," *Review of Educational Research* (Winter 1994), pp. 479–530; "Interview with Educational Psychologist/Researcher Barak Rosenshine," *Class Notes* (December 2005/January 2006), available at **www.baltimorecp.org**: click on "Newsletter"; Bob Kizlik, "Information about Strategic Teaching, Strategic Learning and Thinking Skills," 2014 posting, available at **www.adprima.com/strategi.htm**; and Iftakhar Shabnum, "The Importance of Metacognitive Strategies to Enhance Reading Comprehension Skills of Learners," *Journal of English Language and Literature* (Vol. 2, No. 3, 2015).

- Reciprocal teaching, student team learning, and other approaches to cooperative learning through which students learn to take more responsibility for helping each other comprehend material
- Semantic maps and thinking maps that organize information
- Computer simulations designed to develop concepts and thinking skills
- Metacognitive learning strategies through which students monitor and assess their own learning processes

16-2f Cognitive Instruction for Low-Achieving Students

Emphasis on passive learning of low-level skills seems particularly pervasive in schools with concentrations of working-class students and low achievers. A change in this pattern will require new approaches for delivering cognitive instruction, as well as fundamental improvements in programming throughout the educational system.[8]

Specific programs aimed at improving the thinking skills of low achievers include the Higher-Order Thinking Skills Program (discussed later in this chapter), the Thinking Foundation's programs to help teachers use Thinking Maps, and the Staircase Curriculum developed by Kathryn Au and Taffy Raphael. Research suggests that such approaches have indeed improved performance. However, specific obstacles must be addressed, including the preference many students have developed for low-level learning, teachers' low expectations for low achievers, and the high financial cost of effective instruction that emphasizes cognitive development.[9]

In summary, research on effective teaching and instruction suggests that successful reform projects should include several changes, including improving teachers' classroom management and questioning skills, increasing time-on-task, expanding the use of direct instruction and explicit comprehension instruction, and introducing cognitive instruction for low-achieving students.

FOCUS Which of the characteristics of effective teaching are you most confident about demonstrating? Which will you need to work hard to develop?

16-3 EFFECTIVE SCHOOLS RESEARCH

The preceding sections addressed effective teaching and instruction at the classroom level. However, reformers must also pay attention to the school as an institution and, in the final analysis, to the larger context of the school district and the environment in which schools operate. The effectiveness of schools and entire districts helps determine what happens in each classroom.

16-3a Elementary Schools

Most of the research on effective schools focuses on elementary education. Researchers usually define effectiveness at least partly in terms of outstanding student achievement.

---

[8]Daniel U. Levine, "Teaching Thinking to At-Risk Students," in Barbara Z. Presseisen, ed., *At-Risk Students and Thinking* (Washington, DC: National Education Association and Research for Better Schools, 1988); Eric J. Cooper and Daniel U. Levine, "Teaching for Intelligence," in Barbara Presseisen, ed., *Teaching for Intelligence*, 2nd ed. (Thousand Oaks, CA: Corwin, 2007); and Shannon Brandner, "How This Principal Connected Teachers to Common Core," May 15, 2015, posting by Education Post, available at **www.educationpost.org**.

[9]Stanley Pogrow, "Challenging At-Risk Students," *Phi Delta Kappan* (January 1990), pp. 389–397; Stanley Pogrow, "Accelerate the Learning of 4th and 5th Graders Born into Poverty," *Phi Delta Kappan* (February 2009), pp. 408–412; Kathryn Au and Taffy Raphael, "The Staircase Curriculum," 2011 posting by School Rise, available at **www.schoolriseusa.com**, click on "Research"; and "How We Know Kids Living in Poverty Can Meet the Common Core Standards," January 30, 2014, posting by The Whole Child, available at **www.wholechildeducation.org**.

For example, Ronald Edmonds and others described an effective school as having characteristics such as the following:[10]

1. A *safe and orderly environment* conducive to teaching and learning and not oppressive
2. A *clear school mission* through which the staff shares a commitment to instructional priorities, assessment procedures, and accountability
3. *Instructional leadership* by a principal who understands the characteristics of instructional effectiveness
4. A climate of *high expectations* in which the staff demonstrates that all students can master challenging skills
5. High *time-on-task* brought about when students spend a large percentage of time engaged in planned activities to master basic skills
6. Frequent *monitoring of student progress,* using the results to improve both individual performance and the instructional program
7. Positive *home–school relations* in which parents support the school's basic mission and play an important part in helping to achieve it

curriculum alignment Coordination of instructional planning, methods, materials, and testing to accomplish important learning objectives.

Another characteristic that contributes to school effectiveness is **curriculum alignment**—the coordination of instructional planning, methods, materials, and testing. When staff development focuses on such coordination, teachers are less likely to rely solely on textbooks and more likely to select or create materials that are most appropriate for teaching a specific skill to a particular group of students.[11]

According to several research reports, other key features of unusually effective schools are (1) attention to goals involving cultural pluralism and multicultural education; (2) emphasis on responding to students' personal problems and developing their social skills; (3) faculty who strive to improve students' sense of efficacy; (4) continuous concern for making teaching tasks realistic and manageable; (5) targeting interventions on low-performing students; and (6) collaborative problem solving by the entire faculty. Researchers at the Northwest Regional Educational Laboratory have identified more than 100 specific practices, grouped in 18 categories, that contribute to school effectiveness.[12]

16-3b High Schools

Relatively few studies have concentrated solely on the characteristics of unusually effective senior high schools. Because high school goals and programs are so diverse and complex, it is difficult to conclude that one is more effective than another, particularly when the social class of the student body is taken into account. In addition, hardly any high schools enrolling mostly working-class students stand out as being relatively high in achievement.[13]

---

[10]Joan Shoemaker, "Effective Schools," *Pre-Post Press* (1982), p. 241. See also Ronald Edmonds, "Effective Schools for the Urban Poor," *Educational Leadership* (October 1979), pp. 15–24; Daniel U. Levine, *Unusually Effective Schools* (Bloomington, IN: Phi Delta Kappa, 2004); and "Successful Title 1 Schools," 2015 posting by Realize the Dream, available at **www.realizethedream.org**.

[11]Daniel U. Levine and Joyce Stark, "Instructional and Organizational Arrangements That Improve Achievement in Inner-City Schools," *Educational Leadership* (December 1982), pp. 41–48. See also Douglas B. Reeves, "School Improvement," *American School Board Journal* (May 2011), pp. 38–39; and Karen Chenoweth, "How Do We Get There from Here?" *Educational Leadership* (February 2015).

[12]Daniel U. Levine, "Update on Effective Schools," *Journal of Negro Education* (Fall 1990), pp. 577–584; "New Approaches to Performance Management and Value-Added in Urban Schools," 2011 posting by the Wisconsin Center for Education Research, available at **www.wcer.wisc.edu**; Greg Anrig, "How We Know Collaboration Works," *Educational Leadership* (February 2015), and descriptions in " Success Stories", available at **www.learningfirst.org**, click on "Resources."

[13]Daniel U. Levine and Eugene E. Eubanks, "Organizational Arrangements in Effective Secondary Schools," in John J. Lane and Herbert J. Walberg, eds., *Organizing for Learning* (Reston, VA: National Association of Secondary School Principals, 1988); Amy Buffenbarger, "Creating a Safe Learning Environment," 2011 posting by the Learning First Alliance, available at **www.learningfirst.org/creating-safe-learning-environment**; and John Buntin, "Changing a Culture Inside and Out of School," *Governing* (January 2015), available at **www.governing.com**.

However, in recent years, researchers have identified and described some high schools that appear unusually effective in educating a broad range of students. In general, these schools heavily emphasize helping low achievers in the entry grade (that is, ninth or tenth grade) and on providing additional support in later grades. They also strive to personalize instruction and avoid rigid grouping into permanent, separate tracks for low-, medium-, and high achievers. In addition, the following approaches have frequently been successful:[14]

1. *Schools-within-a-school for low achievers.* Students who read more than two or three years below grade level are assigned to a special unit of 80–100 students at the entry grade. If their teachers are selected for ability and willingness to work with low achievers, participating students can make large gains in basic skills and transfer to regular courses.

2. *Career academies.* Functioning as schools-within-a-school that enroll students of abilities across several grades, career academies focus on such fields as computers, biology or other science, humanities or the arts, or occupational studies such as law enforcement or journalism. Positive data have been reported regarding student engagement and achievement at career academies.

3. *Smaller high school units in general.* High schools that have low enrollment or have been divided into smaller units such as schools-within-a-school have more student engagement and higher achievement than traditional large high schools with similar students. Assigning students to these smaller schools or units can create a more personalized environment in which the staff members provide individual help to students.

4. *Career/technical high schools.* In recent years, several apparently successful high schools have been established that incorporate a consistent focus on preparing students for challenging careers involving vocational and technical skills and understandings. Many of the students they enroll are from low-income families.

16-3c Evaluation of Effective Schools Research

Keep the following points in mind as we evaluate research on effective schools. First, we should recognize the widespread confusion about definitions. There are nearly as many definitions of effective schools as there are people discussing them. Whereas some people have in mind a school with high academic achievement (taking account of social class), others are thinking about a self-renewing school that can identify and solve internal problems, a school that promotes students' personal growth, a school that has shown improvement in achievement, or a school that concentrates on developing independent study skills and love for learning.

Second, many rigorous studies have focused on high-poverty elementary schools in which academic achievement is higher than at most other schools with similarly disadvantaged students. It is more difficult to identify unusually effective high schools and schools outside the inner city, where high achievement is more common. In addition, the key components of effectiveness outside the inner city may differ somewhat from those at poverty schools.[15]

---

[14]Susan Black, "The Pivotal Year," *American School Board Journal* (February 2004); Howard S. Bloom et al., "Transforming the High School Experience" (Washington, DC: Manpower Demonstration Research Corporation, 2010), available at **www.mdrc.org**; Amy E. Schwartz, Leanna Stiefel, and Matthew Wiswall, "Do Small Schools Improve Performance in Large, Urban Districts? Causal Evidence from New York City," September 8, 2014, posting by Social Science Research Network, available at **http://papers.ssrn.com**; and Kathy K. Demarest and Victoria C. Gehrt, "Get College- and Career-Ready at a Vo-Tech High School," *Phi Delta Kappan* (March 2015).

[15]Daniel U. Levine and Robert S. Stephenson, "Are Effective or Meritorious Schools Meretricious?" *Urban Review* (No. 1, 1987), pp. 25–34; Barry Newstead, Amy Saxton, and Susan J. Colby, "Going for the Gold," *Education Next* (Spring 2008), available at **www.educationnext.org**; and Martin R. West et al., "What Effective Schools Do," *Education Next* (Fall 2014), available at **www.educationnext.org**.

Third, some schools that have been designated or viewed as unusually effective incorporate aspects of selectivity that call into question their allegedly impressive student performance. For example, numerous magnet schools and charter schools in big cities admit only students who meet academic qualifications and/or admit by lottery. In the latter case, students who apply frequently may be low-income but are from unusually motivated families. Several studies have shown that high student performance in these situations is predictable based on students' backgrounds.[16]

Fourth, the literature often tends to beg the question of what teachers and principals should do in the schools. For example, the isolated claim that a school requires good leadership and a productive climate fails to specify what these are or ways to accomplish them.

FOCUS What steps can you take during your teacher-preparation program to help you develop the skills of effective teachers described so far?

16-4 CHARACTERISTICS OF SUCCESSFUL SCHOOL REFORMS

From analysis of past school improvement efforts, we have some understanding of the steps that will ensure reform efforts of significant and lasting impact. The following list describes lessons learned from past efforts:

1. *Adaptive problem solving.* An innovation frequently has little or no effect on students' performance because a host of problems arise to stifle practical application. For example, experts may devise a wonderful new science curriculum for fourth graders, and school districts may purchase large quantities of the new curriculum materials, but teachers may either choose not to use them or not know how to use them. Innovations usually fail unless the organization introducing them is adaptive in the sense that it can identify and solve day-to-day problems.[17]

2. *School-level focus, with external support.* Because the innovating organization must solve day-to-day problems, it must focus at the individual school level, where many problems occur. Conversely, however, a school seeking to improve requires various kinds of guidance and support from central administrators and/or other external agents.[18]

3. *Potential for implementation.* Successful school reform also depends on whether changes can feasibly be implemented in typical schools. Three characteristics that make successful implementation more likely are an innovation's *compatibility* with the context of potential users, its *accessibility* to those who do not already understand the underlying ideas, and its *"doability"* in terms of demands on teachers' time and energy. Levine and Levine have pointed out that many approaches have high "potential for mischief" because they are so difficult to implement.[19]

[16]David Garcia, "Academic and Racial Segregation in Charter Schools," *Education and Urban Society* (July 2008); Patrick Baude, "The Evolution of Charter School Quality," December 16, 2014, posting by the Cato Institute, available at **www.cato.org**; and P. L. Thomas, "Charter Scam Week 2015," *The Progressive* (May 5, 2015), available at **www.progressive.org**.

[17]Emily A. Hassel and Bryan C. Hassel, "The Big U-Turn," *Education Next* (Winter 2009), available at **www.educationnext.org**; Michael Fullan, *The Six Secrets of Leadership* (Thousand Oaks, CA: Jossey-Bass, 2011); and Kristina Brizicha, Ulrika Bergmark, and Dana L. Mitra, "One Size Does Not Fit All," *Educational Administration Quarterly* (February 2015).

[18]Daniel U. Levine, "Creating Effective Schools through Site-Level Staff Development, Planning and Improvement of Organizational Cultures," in David H. Hargreaves and David Hopkins, eds., *Development Planning for School Improvement* (London: Cassell, 1994), pp. 37–48; Michael Fullan, *The New Meaning of Educational Change*, 4th ed. (New York: Teachers College Press, 2007); David Kirp, "Audacity in Harlem," *American Prospect* (September 22, 2008), available at **www.prospect.org**; Tim Goral, "Author Chronicles 'Rebirth of a Great American School System'," *District Administration* (October 2013), available at **www.districtadministration.com**; and Richard D. Kahlenberg and Halley Potter, "Why Teacher Voice Matters," *American Educator* (December 2014–January 2015), available at **www.aft.org**.

[19]Daniel U. Levine and Rayna F. Levine, "Considerations in Introducing Instructional Interventions," in Barbara Presseisen, ed., *Teaching for Intelligence*, 2nd ed. (Thousand Oaks, CA: Corwin, 2007); Michael J. Petrilli, "Education Reform's Most Urgent Task," August 6, 2014, posting by Flypaper, available at **www.edexcellence.net**; and William W. Wayson, "How We Failed to Fix Syracuse Schools for Our Neglected Children (Commentary)," February 1, 2015, posting available at **www.syracuse.com**.

4. *Leadership and shared agreements.* Meaningful innovation requires change in many institutional arrangements, including scheduling of staff and student time, selection and use of instructional methods and materials, and mechanisms for making decisions. The building principal usually is the key person in making these arrangements, but the faculty also must have a shared vision of and must be involved in possible necessary changes. Otherwise, staff members will likely discount proposals that ask them to make significant changes.[20]

5. *Staff training.* Staff development is a core activity in the school improvement process. In an elementary school, the entire staff should participate; in secondary schools, departments may be the appropriate unit for certain activities. Staff development should be an interactive process in which teachers and administrators work together at every stage. Much of the staff development at unusually effective schools is provided by instructional coaches.[21]

6. *Coherence.* Coherence in school reform efforts has at least two major dimensions. The first refers to coherence across grade levels: teachers in each grade must be willing to help students master the curriculum and standards established for their grade, or students will lack the skills required for success in the next grade. *Coherence* also refers to consistency and compatibility across the instructional programs and approaches used in the school. For example, some students probably will struggle to master reading if their teachers use differing materials that introduce key skills at different times and thus conflict with rather than reinforce each other. Some students will not master social skills if their teachers establish greatly different rules of behavior from one class to another.[22]

7. *Professional community.* Schools can ensure that all students learn only if teachers work together, trust their colleagues, and challenge each other to take responsibility for the difficult task of helping low achievers master increasingly challenging material. Analysts refer to this aspect of reform as development of a "professional community."[23]

FOCUS How might you, as a teacher, participate in implementing reforms at your school? What do you believe teachers can do to best help with successful reform implementations?

The From Preservice to Practice box describes a school improvement plan that features many hallmarks of effectiveness. As you read through it and the rest of this chapter, note which reform programs described seem to exemplify each of these best practices.

16-5 IMPROVEMENT APPROACHES ACROSS CLASSROOMS AND GRADE LEVELS

The effective teaching practices cited earlier in this chapter work in individual classrooms, but numerous instructional approaches are designed for use at several or all grade levels in a school. For example, many reading improvement programs often

---

[20]Barbara O. Taylor, "The Effective Schools Process," *Phi Delta Kappan* (January 2002), pp. 375–378; and Michael Fullan, *The Principal* (Thousand Oaks, CA: Jossey-Bass, 2014).

[21]Brian Sims, "Teacher Development Is Key to Closing the Achievement Gap," *Edutopia* (July 22, 2011), available at **www.edutopia.org**; John Rosales, "Oak Hill," 2011 report prepared for the NEA Priority Schools Campaign, available at **www.nea.org**; "Fullan: Systemic Change for Breakthrough Learning," November 4, 2014, posting by Partnership for 21st Century Skills, available at **www.p21.org**; and David C. Berliner and Gene V. Glass, "Trust, But Verify," *Educational Leadership* (February 2015).

[22]BetsAnn Smith et al., "Instructional Program Coherence," *Educational Research Reports* (May 2003); William H. Schmidt, "What's Missing from Math Standards?" *American Educator* (Spring 2008), available at **www.aft.org**; Linda Heitin, "Under Common Core, Teachers Band Together to Build 'Math Coherence,'" *Education Week*, November 10, 2014; and "Key Shifts in Mathematics," 2015 posting by Common Core State Standards Initiative, available at **www.corestandards.org**.

[23]Donna Ford, "Powerful School Change," *Phi Delta Kappan* (December 2008), pp. 281–284; Kimberly K. Hewitt and Daniel K. Weckstein, "Administrative Synergy," *School Administrator* (January 2012), available at **www.aasa.org**; and "Examining the Impact of Professional Learning Communities," 2015 posting by the Stanford Graduate School of Education, available at **http://ed.stanford.edu**.

FROM PRESERVICE TO PRACTICE

SCHOOL REFORM

Paul and Jorge are classmates in the college of education at their university and are studying at the library. Paul shares an email on his laptop. "Jorge, you have to hear about this! My sister Melanie started teaching in this small rural school system last year. You ought to hear some of her stories about how the teachers come together to make things happen for those kids. They don't have much, compared to some of the suburban schools around here, but they do have fine student achievement. I'm thinking that when I graduate, I might want to go that route, too—if they have a teaching position open."

Jorge looks up from his notes. "How do you know that the student achievement is so good, Paul?"

"My sister sent me the results of the statewide exams," says Paul. "Not only is the district rated exemplary, but each of the three schools is rated exemplary, as well. That means that all schools showed 90 percent or more mastery in all the subjects tested. Larger schools have a hard time getting ratings like those. Melanie keeps saying smaller is better."

"You said that they don't have much. What do you mean by that?" Jorge asks.

"Basically, they don't have all the equipment that most schools have," Paul replies. "They don't have extra staff to help with daily routines. The superintendent drives a bus, and each principal drives a bus, too.

"The school libraries have limited books and magazines. The high school has only fifteen computers, all located in the library for instructional purposes. Administrators have computers on their desks, but teachers have to go to the library to use a computer. The other schools have even fewer computers, all in the libraries, too."

"Amazing!" says Jorge. "I don't know what I would do without my laptop! How do they account for the top ratings? Are they still working on the achievement levels?"

"I visited Melanie over the holidays, and actually ended up interviewing her and a friend who teaches with her," Paul answers. "They say the community is close-knit, that faculty members feel like family. It's like moving back in time because everyone knows everyone else. All the students understand that the teachers know their parents, and even grandparents. Melanie says the superintendent and the principals really care. They see each student as a responsible individual. They expect the teachers to pitch in and help each other, to help the students, and yes, to help administrators when they need it. On the other hand, the administrators stand by the teachers, too. It's a team process on each campus. Every teacher who needs training gets it. When they work, they all work hard. When they play, they have fun and enjoy each other's company.

"And, yes," Paul continued. "They are still working to increase achievement levels. Melanie writes that their vision is 100 percent mastery of the statewide tests. They're continually looking for ways to help students."

"Is there any downside to all this?" Jorge laughs.

"Well, the pay is pretty low," Paul admits. Then he brightens. "But there's not much to spend it on around there, either."

CASE QUESTIONS

1. What characteristics of effective schools does this school district exemplify?
2. How does this district seem to support the process of school improvement and reform?
3. In addition to lower pay, what else might a new teacher consider deterrents to signing on as a team member in this small district?
4. Would you be willing to work in a school such as this? Why or why not?

target students in kindergarten and the primary grades. We'll discuss several such improvement efforts in this section.

16-5a Higher-Order Thinking Skills (HOTS) Program

Developed by Stanley Pogrow and his colleagues, the HOTS program is specifically designed to replace remedial-reading activities in grades 4 through 6. The HOTS approach has four major components: (1) use of computers for problem solving; (2) emphasis on dramatization techniques that require students to verbalize, thereby stimulating language development; (3) Socratic questioning; and (4) a thinking-skills curriculum that stresses metacognitive learning, learning-to-learn, and other comprehension-enhancement techniques of the kinds described earlier. Now used in more than a thousand schools, HOTS frequently has brought about extensive improvements in student performance in both reading and math. According to Pogrow, results of the HOTS program show that at-risk students have "tremendous levels of intellectual and academic potential" but that many do not "understand 'understanding.'" This "fundamental learning problem can be eliminated if enough time and enough resources are made available."[24]

16-5b Success for All

As possibly the most comprehensive intervention for improving the reading achievement of disadvantaged students, Success for All provides intensive instructional support for students in elementary schools. It also emphasizes cooperative learning and mastery instruction, with technical support and staff development provided by full-time coordinators and resource persons assigned to participating schools. Measurable improvements in student achievement have been documented at numerous low-income schools in both urban and rural districts. According to its developers, Success for All demonstrates that neither exceptional nor extraordinary schools can routinely ensure success for disadvantaged students. However, the program does require a serious commitment to restructure elementary schools and to reconfigure the use of available funds.[25]

16-5c Degrees of Reading Power Comprehension Development Approach

Based in part on the Degrees of Reading Power (DRP) test originally developed by the College Board, the DRP approach is being implemented successfully at several urban schools. The test is unlike most other standardized reading measures in that it assesses how well a student actually can comprehend written prose he or she encounters in or out of school, not just whether the student is above or below an abstract grade level. After using the DRP to determine their students' comprehension levels, teachers in all subject areas align their instruction accordingly. For homework and other independent assignments, they select materials that challenge but do not frustrate students; they use classwork materials slightly beyond students' comprehension to help them improve.[26]

16-5d Comer School Development Program

Developed by James Comer and his colleagues at Yale University, the School Development Program aims to improve achievement at inner-city elementary schools through enhanced social and psychological services for students, emphasis on parent involvement, and encouragement and support for active learning. Participating faculties involve parents in all aspects of school operation (including governance), and teachers, parents, psychologists, social workers, and other specialists form "Mental Health Teams" that design and supervise individualized learning arrangements for students

---

[24]Stanley Pogrow, "Supermath," *Phi Delta Kappan* (December 2004), pp. 297–303; and Bronwyn Cole and Margit McGuire, "Real-World Problems," *Social Studies and the Young Learner* (March–April 2012). Information about the HOTS Program is available at **www.hots.org**.

[25]Robert E. Slavin, "Shame Indeed," *Phi Delta Kappan* (April 2006), pp. 621–623; Betty Chambers, "Technology Infusion in Success for All," *Elementary School Journal* (September 2008), pp. 1–15; and Robert E. Slavin, *Proven Programs in Education* (Thousand Oaks, CA: Sage, 2014).

[26]Daniel U. Levine, "Instructional Approaches and Interventions That Can Improve the Academic Performance of African American Students," *Journal of Negro Education* (Winter 1994), pp. 46–63; Daniel U. Levine, Eric J. Cooper, and Asa Hilliard III, "National Urban Alliance for Professional Development," *Journal of Negro Education* (Fall 2000), pp. 305–322; and "DRP Overview," 2014 posting by DRP, available at **www.questarai.com**.

with particular problems. Curriculum and instruction are coordinated across subject areas to emphasize language learning and social skills. Schools in various districts have produced improvements in student achievement and behavior after implementing the School Development Program along with other innovations.[27]

16-5e The Algebra Project

The Algebra Project involves curriculum interventions that use disadvantaged students' personal experiences and intuitions to help them shift from arithmetic to algebraic thinking. Data collected at multiple sites suggest that students frequently register large gains in mathematics performance and that many are succeeding in algebra and other advanced math courses they otherwise would not be taking.[28]

16-5f Knowledge Is Power Program (KIPP)

KIPP promotional information describes its schools as "open-enrollment public schools where underserved students develop the knowledge, skills, and character traits needed to succeed in top quality high schools, colleges, and the competitive world beyond." Among the central operational themes is more time for learning: KIPP schools typically function from 7:30 a.m. to 5:30 p.m. on weekdays, and students also attend every other Saturday and for three weeks during the summer. KIPP further describes its approach as emphasizing rigorous "college-preparatory instruction . . . balanced with extracurricular activities, experiential field lessons, and character development."[29]

Since its first school was opened in 1994, KIPP has expanded to include more than 140 schools, mostly middle schools and high schools but also several elementary schools. Nearly all are charter schools in big cities. Of the more than 50,000 students, 95 percent are African American or Hispanic, 88 percent are low-income, 10 percent receive special-education services, and 15 percent are English Language Learners. The creators of this model are carefully implementing plans to obtain dedicated staff willing to work long hours with struggling students, and to train and evaluate administrators and teachers, develop networks of supportive KIPP schools nearby, and articulate an effective program ranging from kindergarten through high school graduation.

Results to date have been impressive. More than 90 percent are graduating from high school, and more than 80 percent enroll in a four-year college, compared with 45 percent of low-income students nationally. KIPP's largely inner-city population of students generally is making good progress academically. For example, 59 percent

---

[27]James P. Comer, "Educating Poor Minority Children," *Scientific American* (November 1988), pp. 42–48; Thomas D. Cook and Paul J. Hirschfield, "Comer's School Development in Chicago," *American Educational Research Journal* (March 2008), pp. 38–67; "When We Know What Works, Why Don't We Do It?" 2011 posting by the Yale Child Study Center, available at **www.childstudycenter.yale.edu**; "Comer Overview," 2014 posting by the Teach Foundation, available at **www.teachfoundation.org/4**; and "Theory of Change," 2015 posting by the School Development program, available at **www.schooldevelopmentprogram.org**.

[28]Tom Loveless, "The Misplaced Math Student," Brown Center Report on American Education (February 2009), available at **www.brookings.edu**; Ed Dubinsky and Robert P. Moses, "Philosophy, Math Research, Math Ed Research, K–16 Education, and the Civil Rights Movement," 2011 posting by the American Mathematical Society, available at **www.ams.org**; and "NSF Research Shows High School Math Cohorts Promising," 2014 posting by The Algebra Project, available at **www.algebra.org**.

[29]Jay Matthews, *Work Hard. Be Nice* (Chapel Hill, NC: Algonquin, 2009); Jay Mathews, "Does KIPP Shed Too Many Low Performers?" *Washington Post*, January 10, 2011; Ira Nichols-Barrer et al., "Does Student Attrition Explain KIPP's Success?" *Education Next* (Fall 2014), available at **www.educationnext.org**; Anna North, "Should Schools Teach Personality?" *New York Times*, January 10, 2015; and information available at **www.kipp.org**.

of eighth graders were at or above the national average in reading in 2013, and 65 percent were above this level in math—both percentages far above those at nearby public schools.

However, some analysts caution that such results might be hard to replicate with other inner-city populations because KIPP students volunteer to attend. In addition, dropping out among the weakest students appears to be significant, leading some critics to argue that this attrition accounts for the relatively high achievement of KIPP students. Research on this possibility is limited, but available studies indicate that dropping out of KIPP by low achievers accounts for only a small part of the progress of its students.

16-5g The Harlem Children's Zone (HCZ) and Purpose Built Communities (PBC)

As noted previously, KIPP appears to be registering important gains in poverty neighborhoods in big cities, but it does not reach the many students who do not enter or win in the lottery for admission or who leave before completing its difficult curriculum and rigorous schedule. Several projects are trying more comprehensive ecological reforms of the kind advocated in Chapter 12, Providing Equal Educational Opportunity. One of the reform approaches that attempts to improve performance throughout an inner-city community is the Harlem Children's Zone initiated by Geoffrey Canada and his colleagues in New York City. The HCZ approach serves residents of ninety-seven blocks and exemplifies the kind of comprehensive ecological intervention we described in Chapter 12, Providing Equal Educational Opportunity. It includes the following components, among others:[30]

- Early childhood education for all children
- Various forms of family support and counseling
- Health services for children beginning in infancy
- Collaboration with churches, parks, local businesses, and schools to develop a safe, nurturing environment for children and youth
- A variety of services such as employment training and assistance for residents
- Systems for providing psychological support for students
- Establishment of two charter elementary schools, a charter middle school, and a charter high school, all with longer-than-regular school days and school years
- An after-school program for students in regular middle schools
- A fifth-grade institute to help prepare students for middle school
- Coordination of services between charter schools and regular schools
- Best practices for teaching disadvantaged students
- Hiring and supporting talented teachers

Analysts have been reporting impressive outcomes from the first few years of implementation. For example:

- All of the 4-year-olds who participated in the Harlem Gems preschool in 2012–2013 finished with a school-readiness classification of average or above.

---

[30]Paul Tough, *Whatever It Takes* (Boston: Houghton Mifflin Harcourt, 2008); Grover J. Whitehurst and Michelle Croft, "The Harlem Children's Zone, Promise Neighborhoods, and the Bolder, Broader Approach to Education," 2010 report prepared for the Brookings Institution, available at **www.brookings.edu**; Will Dobbie and Roland G. Fryer, Jr., "Are High-Quality Schools Enough to Close the Achievement Gap?" 2011 report published by Harvard, available at **www.economics.harvard.edu/faculty/fryer**; "Helping 12,000+ Children Succeed— One at a Time," 2014 posting by the Harlem Children's Zone, available at **www.hcz.org**, click "Documents and Publications" at the bottom; "Geoffrey Canada and the New Harlem Renaissance," *Time* (April 9, 2014), available at **www.time.com**; John Gabrieli, "The Promise of the Harlem Children's Zone," *Harvard Political Review* (June 11, 2014), available at **www.harvardpolitics.com**; and "Whatever It Takes," 2015 posting by Education Dive, available at **www.educationdive.com**.

- All students completing third grade at the charter schools in 2012–2013 were at or above grade level in math, and about 90 percent were at or above grade level in English language arts. At the charter middle school, almost 90 percent of eighth graders were at or above grade level in math.
- For the 2013 school year, 92 percent of high school seniors were accepted for entry into postsecondary institutions.
- By 2015, more than 100 HCZ-participating students had graduated from colleges.

16-5h Advancement via Individual Determination Program (AVID)

AVID is a support program for grades 3–12 that prepares students for college eligibility and success. Aimed particularly at middle- to low-performing students at schools with significant proportions of disadvantaged students, AVID provides many kinds of support, including help in mastering study skills and learning strategies, personal and career counseling and mentoring, and assistance in enrolling in and completing advanced courses. First developed in San Diego in 1980, AVID is now functioning in almost 5,000 schools internationally and has compiled an impressive record in helping participating students graduate from high school and enter postsecondary institutions. In fact, most AVID students graduate from high school, 75 percent of 2013 AVID graduates were accepted by a four-year college, and almost 60 percent of recent AVID eighth graders enrolled in and passed algebra (compared with 34 percent nationally).[31]

16-5i Response to Intervention with Tiered Instruction

Response to Intervention (RTI) An approach that dictates leaving a child in the regular school program while providing him or her with suitable interventions; only if that does not work is the child referred for special-education or disability services.

As we noted in Chapter 12, Providing Equal Educational Opportunity, **Response to Intervention (RTI)** began as an approach to avoid mistaken labeling and placement of students into special education, but it soon evolved to become a broader approach. Many implementations have involved the identification of three tiers of instruction. The first tier generally consists of 75 or 80 percent of students who are progressing satisfactorily following the school's arrangements for delivering instruction; often these incorporate flexible grouping (see Chapter 11, Social Class, Race, and School Achievement, and Chapter 12, Providing Equal Educational Opportunity), uninterrupted blocks of time for instruction, explicit comprehension instruction, and other improvement strategies we have described elsewhere.

A key element of this approach involves careful monitoring of all students' status and progress, along with assessment of the problems of perhaps 20 or 25 percent of students who are not progressing adequately, resulting in selection and delivery of appropriate additional interventions (for example, tutoring of individuals and providing students with materials at their functional reading levels) for this second tier of students. Only if these more-intensive interventions still fail to help a student meet standards is he or she referred for further help through special education, considered as a third tier.

Most tiered-instruction implementations have aimed to improve reading in elementary schools, but some schools have begun to adapt RTI for other subjects and for high schools and preschools. Many schools also are adapting the approach to address students' behavioral problems, with the first tier involving school-wide policies and

---

[31]Jennifer Jacobson, "Focusing on the Forgotten," *American Educator* (Fall 2007), available at **www.aft.org**; "National Research Study Confirms Minority and Low Socioeconomic Students Outpace Peers into Second Year in College," January 27, 2014, posting by PR Newswire, available at **www.prnewswire.com**; Lisa Klein, "Education—AVID Program Provides Access and Opportunity," January 27, 2015, posting by News8000, available at **www.news8000.com**; and information available at **www.avid.org**.

practices; then individual or small-group interventions are provided for students whose behavior is still unacceptable.[32]

We noted in Chapter 12, Providing Equal Educational Opportunity, that some or many efforts toward inclusion in regular classrooms have failed because the challenge of doing so is very difficult and much must be done to train teachers, introduce appropriate teaching methods, provide a range of suitable materials, or otherwise ensure that teachers can work effectively with heterogeneous groups of students. The same or even greater challenge is present for RTI approaches that aim to provide effective instruction for several tiers of students. Analysts have identified the following components, among others, that should be implemented well for RTI to succeed:[33]

- Monitor students' progress with technically adequate assessments.
- Choose and implement proven interventions to address students' problems.
- Ensure that the interventions are implemented effectively.
- Limit competing initiatives that consume time and resources.
- Follow explicit rules to identify students not making sufficient progress.
- Monitor student outcomes with at least biweekly assessments.
- Determine the intensity of the support needed for student success.
- Convince parents of children with disabilities that RTI is more effective than traditional special education.

FOCUS Have you visited any schools that use programs described in this section? Which programs appeal most to you as a teacher? Why?

16-6 TECHNOLOGY AND SCHOOL REFORM

We described the fundamental role technology has attained in instructional practice in Chapter 14, Curriculum and Instruction. In this chapter, we emphasize some of the ways in which technology has been involved as a means to improving the functioning of schools and the effectiveness of education. Educators confront many questions and challenges with respect to the introduction of new and emerging technologies as part of school reform efforts. We will consider several aspects, including the effective introduction of new technologies in schools and classrooms, equity in technology use, and cautions regarding developments that have occurred during recent decades.

16-6a Effective Introduction of Computers and Other Technologies

Analysts have identified many considerations that determine whether the introduction of computer-based technologies will produce substantial improvements in the performance of elementary and secondary students. State and district decision

---

[32]Laura B. Casey et al., "A Much Delayed Response to *A Nation at Risk*," *Phi Delta Kappan* (April 2008), pp. 593–596; W. David Tilly et al., "Three Tiers of Intervention," *School Administrator* (September 2008), available at **www.aasa.org**; and Kimberly A. Turse and Susan F. Albrecht, "The ABCs of RTI," *Preventing School Failure* (Issue 2, 2015), available at **www.tandfonline .com**.

[33]Charles R. Greenwood et al., "The Response to Intervention (RTI) Approach in Early Childhood," *Focus on Exceptional Children* (May 2011), pp. 1–22; John J. Hoover and Emily Love, "Supporting School-Based Response to Intervention," *Teaching Exceptional Children* (January–February 2011), pp. 40–48; Maurice McInerney and Amy Elledge, "Using a Response to Intervention Framework to Improve Student Learning," May 2013 posting by the American Institutes for Research, available at **www.rti4success.org**; Evan Levsky, "The Power to Transform Schools and Districts," April 10, 2014, posting by the RTI Action Network, available at **www.rtinetwork.org**; "Response to Intervention-RTI Resources," 2015 posting at Intervention Central, available at **www.interventioncentral.org**; and material available from the National Center on Response to Intervention, **www .rti4success.org**.

makers have been considering and often acting on recommendations such as the following:[34]

- Teachers must receive ongoing training and technical support in how to use technologies effectively. Technical support staff should be available at both the district and school levels.
- Teacher licensing standards should include assessment of knowledge and skills involving incorporation of technology in classroom lessons.
- Computers must be sufficiently concentrated to make a difference. For example, one study found that placing one computer in a classroom did not change student achievement but that providing classrooms with three or more computers did produce better outcomes.
- Training must be sufficiently intensive to make a difference. For example, several studies found that providing teachers with more than ten hours of training results in much more change in instruction than shorter training periods.
- Unsurprisingly, how teachers use computers helps determine student outcomes. For example, one major study using data from hundreds of schools supported the conclusion that eighth graders whose teachers emphasized problem solving and learning of concepts using computers learned significantly more than did those whose teachers emphasized low-level "drill and kill" exercises.
- Plans for computer use must coordinate with arrangements for scheduling, testing, class size, and other aspects of instruction. If class periods are too short or classes are too large to allow the teacher to deliver a lesson effectively, or if teachers are preoccupied with preparing students for tests or with other urgent tasks, computer availability may make little or no difference.
- Teachers who use technology heavily should not neglect motivational and affective aspects of their instruction.

One predominant theme throughout our preceding review of computer-based technologies and successful school reform is that substantial, appropriate teacher training is definitely a prerequisite. The federal government has recognized this imperative in provisions of federal legislation that require states to develop plans to ensure that teachers can use new technologies effectively. Many of these plans focus on training teachers to implement improved technologies in the classroom.[35]

16-6b Research on Technology Achievement Effects

Over many decades, thousands of studies have examined one or another effect of a multitude of technologies on a wide variety of aspects of achievement. Given that implementations vary wildly from fragmentary to comprehensive, achievement changes are very difficult to measure, outcomes will be diverse for differing groups of students, and there are numerous other obstacles to valid assessment, it is no surprise that analysts who generalize across many studies report that technology has not been found to substantially boost student achievement across the board. However, some studies of individual projects report large achievement gains when goals are clearly

---

[34]Suzie Boss, "Overcoming Technology Barriers," *Edutopia* (August 8, 2008), available at **www
.edutopia.org**; Chris Riedel, "The 4 Keys to a Successful Online School," *THE Journal* (January
27, 2012), available at **www.thejournal.com**; Leila Meyer, "Interoperability, Accessibility
Top ConnectED Framework Priorities," *THE Journal* (January 26, 2015), available at **www
.thejournal.com**; and Mandy Zatynski, "What Does Online Learning Look Like?" *Education
Next* (January 22, 2015), available at **www.educationnext.org.**

[35]Doug Johnson, "Stretching Your Technology Dollar," *Educational Leadership* (December 2011/
January 2012); Alison De Nisco, "Creating Tech-Savvier Teachers," *District Administration* (May
2014), available at **www.districtadministration.com**; and Carla Winer, "The Importance of
Teacher Training," January 7, 2015, posting by The Linkage, available at **www.everyoneon
.org/2015/01/07/the-importance-of-teacher-training**.

defined and implementation addresses key issues such as meaningful training for teachers and adequate funding.[36]

16-6c Full-Time Virtual Schools

Numerous projects have involved establishment and operation of virtual schools at which all or almost all of the instruction is delivered by computers and other electronic media. In many cases, these schools are charter schools operated by private organizations, frequently for profit. Students acquiring all or most of their education at virtual schools include those who were unsuccessful at or expelled from regular schools, homeschoolers, and advanced students hoping to proceed at a rapid pace. With the variety of student clients and the range of quality in the hardware/software that is used, it is particularly difficult to assess gains and losses. In addition, because attention is frequently lacking regarding the implementation of, and the fact that sponsors may not be required to report much in the way of achievement and other outcomes, analysts disagree among themselves as to the value and success of virtual schools. Thus, at the present time, online schools should be viewed as a potentially important generator of school reform in the future rather than a demonstrated success in practice.[37]

16-6d Blended Learning Grab Bag

The term "Blended Learning" refers to approaches that combine computer-mediated activities with noncomputerized classroom instruction to form an integrated set of activities. In general, students in blended programs learn in supervised school settings at least some of the time. In some cases, the noncomputer segment of instruction involves a teacher/coach who provides assistance and guidance; in other implementations, companion lessons are taught in a traditional manner. Software used in the computer curriculum frequently allows for much individualization and considerable opportunity to draw on students' interests and correct their recurrent learning problems; however, this is very hard to do for students who start far behind grade level and have many problems outside of school.

Regarding assessment of blended learning, there are so many possible components (for example, computers, video, social media, online community, tablet-based) and mixtures of components in blended approaches that it is difficult to study much less draw conclusions about learning outcomes. On the other hand, some schools that appear to have implemented blended approaches effectively have reported promising results. An analysis funded by the federal government reported that although there was too little research of K–12 results to support firm conclusions, it appears that blended approaches may produce somewhat better achievement than either totally online instruction or traditional teacher-oriented classrooms.[38]

---

[36]Rana M. Tamin et al., "What Forty Years of Research Says about the Impact of Technology on Learning," *Review of Educational Research* (March 2011), pp. 4–28; Kathy Boccella, "In Spring City, Hybrid Learning Sends Test Scores Soaring," February 8, 2015, posting by *The Inquirer*, available at **www.philly.com**; and Tim Walker, "Technology in the Classroom: Don't Believe the Hype," *NEA Today* (January 8, 2015), available at **www.neatoday.org**.

[37]Alex Molnar et al., "Virtual Schools in the US 2014," 2014 posting by the National Education Policy Center, available at **www.nepc.colorado.edu/publication/virtual-schools-annual-2014**; Gene G. Glass, Kevin G. Welner, and Justin Bathon, "Online K–12 Schooling in the United States," *NEPC Policy Briefs* (October 25, 2011), available at **www.nepc.colorado.edu/publications/policy-briefs**; and Anya Kamenetz, "Virtual Schools Bring Real Concerns about Quality," February 2, 2015, posting by NPRED, available at **www.npr.org**.

[38]Susan McLester, "Building a Blended Learning Program," *District Administration* (October 2011), available at **www.districtadministration.com**; "Blended Learning 2015," August 14, 2014, posting by Interactive Services, available at **www.interactiveservices.com**; and Thomas Arnett, "Why Teachers Can't Deliver Real Personalized Learning in Today's Schools," January 30, 2015, posting by the Clayton Christensen Institute, available at **www.christenseninstitute.org**.

16-6e Flipped Classrooms

A particular form of blended learning that is receiving considerable attention and support is sometimes referred to as "flipped instruction" or the "flipped classroom." The most fundamental definition of this approach has postulated that initial instruction is provided by videos or other electronic media studied at home or elsewhere out of class, and class time is devoted to such activities as guided practice, explication of key concepts, and assistance in carrying out what used to be follow-up homework. But numerous variations have been developed or envisioned that involve most students viewing the media while the teacher works with individuals; students viewing the media as an introductory, intermediate, or culminating part of a lesson or unit; or other alternatives.

Practitioners and other proponents of flipping argue that it can enhance inquiry learning, address critical thinking and other higher-order learning objectives, reduce or eliminate problems involving absence and truancy, personalize students' education, and help satisfy other important goals. Numerous elaborations on these possibilities are available in files at The Daily Riff website. Several proponents of this approach are developing curricula built around the popular Khan Academy videos, but other video-oriented materials used for initial instruction also are being explored.[39]

16-6f One-to-One Provision of Computers or Other Devices to Students

Some years ago, many enthusiasts argued that widespread use of computers in schools would revolutionize instruction and vastly improve achievement. (Before that, some reformers said that instructional videos would accomplish this result, and before that, several visionaries pointed to instructional television as the agent-to-be of enormous improvement.) Exploring the possibilities, numerous schools provided computers for every student in select grades to determine whether major improvements could be registered. The largest efforts involved provision of laptops as part of systematic experiments in Maine and several other states.[40]

Unfortunately, the results of these innovative efforts have tended to be disappointing. Some schools have reported gains in some subjects, particularly mathematics, but these gains tended to be small and inconsistent. Even when substantial professional development has been provided and capable leadership has been present, the massive task of incorporating appropriate computerized instruction throughout a curriculum aligned with other materials and assessment has proven to be very difficult. This has left computers in some classrooms functioning as little more than what one analyst termed "glorified pencils."

16-6g Mobile Learning and Bring-Your-Own-Devices (BYOD)

One definition for Mobile Learning (or M-Learning) is that it is "any educational technology delivered through mobile technology." M-Learning hardware can include smartphones, handheld PCs, netbooks, tablets, E-book readers, and other

---

[39]Bill Tucker, "The Flipped Classroom," *Education Next* (Winter 2012), available at **www.educationnext.org**; Jon Bergmann, Jerry Overmyer, and Brett Willie, "The Flipped Class," 2013 posting by The Daily Riff, available at **www.thedailyriff.com**; Microsoft Education Team, "Flipped Learning," January 28, 2015, posting available at **www.flippedclass.com**; and Abigail G. Scheg, *Implementation and Critical Assessment of the Flipped Classroom Experience* (Hershey, PA: IGI Global, 2015).

[40]Bryan Goodwin, "One-to-One Laptop Programs Are No Silver Bullet," *Educational Leadership* (February 2011), available at **www.ascd.org**; Bridget McCrea, "Measuring 1:1 Results," *The Journal* (November 16, 2011), available at **www.thejournal.com**; Susan McLester, "Lesson Learned from One-to-One," *District Administration* (June 2011), available at **www.districtadministration.com**; and Gretchen Logue, "Is the Pen Mightier Than the Laptop? The Research Might Surprise You," January 6, 2015, posting by Missouri Education Watchdog, available at **www.missourieducationwatchdog.com**.

devices able to run mobile applications. Software can include virtually anything that can be "mobilized" to induce or assist learning. Analysts have identified numerous potential advantages of M-Learning such as capacity for authentic learning, users' easy access to their mobile devices, possibilities for individualizing instruction and drawing on multimedia resources, and ease in updating or otherwise modifying curriculum.[41]

There also are serious difficulties and potential disadvantages in designing and delivering M-Learning, such as incompatibilities between mobile devices, providing access to unsavory sources, lack of sufficient broadband and other carrying capacity, tendencies to be distracted when pursuing learning objectives, and technical complexity of hardware and software. In view of such difficulties, it seems apparent that effective M-Learning may be even more challenging to bring about than other technological approaches discussed in the preceding sections.

The pursuit of M-Learning beginning to take place in some schools varies from projects at one extreme that allow students to use whatever mobile devices are normally available to them (the BYOD or Bring-Your-Own-Device approach), to provision of the same device for all students at the other extreme. Although the latter approach clearly is much more expensive, both seem to have what Levine and Levine termed high "Potential for Mischief," which, in this case, is the temptation for educators to advertise their introduction of the latest innovation without facing up to the grave difficulties involved in effective implementation.

16-6h Gaming to Learn

In Chapter 10, Culture, Socialization, and Education, we pointed out that video games and other media may be having negative effects on children and youth, although the research is not always clear-cut, and researchers frequently disagree on its interpretation. In any case, gaming of various kinds is being introduced into curriculum and instruction, and many teachers are positive and even enthusiastic about its advantages and results. Among the benefits some educators and analysts cite are that it can improve student engagement; widen opportunities for self-directed learning and problem solving; bolster reading, writing, and spatial skills; develop better digital citizenship; support career development; sharpen attention spans and cognition; and reinforce social skills such as empathy and cooperation with other individuals.[42]

Without doubt, teachers who introduce gaming can increase engagement and other positive behaviors, but those who have made serious efforts to integrate games into lessons or make them a basis for the curriculum report that a tremendous amount of planning and hard work is necessary to produce the intended results. Whether the

---

[41]The quote is from "7 Things You Should Know about Mobile Apps for Learning," 2010 Brief posted by Educause, available at **www.educause.edu**. See also Daniel U. Levine and Rayna F. Levine, "Considerations in Introducing Instructional Interventions," op. cit.; Patricia Wallace, "M-Learning," *New Horizons* (Winter 2011), available at **www.education.jhu.edu**; Katie K. Remis, "How Schools Are Bringing Mobile Under Control," *District Administration* (December 2014), available at **www.districtadministration.com**; and Don Soifer, "Transforming Education Through Digital and Blended Learning," February 4, 2015, posting by the Lexington Institute, available at **www.lexingtoninstitute.org**.

[42]"Game-Based Learning," October 6, 2014, posting by Edutopia, available at **www.edutopia .org**; Mark Griffiths, "Evidence Continues to Mount on Learning Benefits of All Video Games," November 13, 2014, posting by Games and Learning, available at **www.gamesandlearning .org**; "Using Technology to Support At-Risk Students' Learning," September 10, 2014, posting by the Alliance for Excellent Education, available at **www.all4ed.org**; Alexandra Ossola, "Teaching in the Age of Minecraft," February 6, 2015, posting by *The Atlantic,* available at **www.theatlantic .com**; Mary Talbot, "Playing Games in School," January 9, 2015, posting by the Hechinger Report, available at **www.hechingerreport.org**; and "Video Game Play May Provide Learning, Health, Social Benefits, Review Finds," February 2015 posting by the American Psychological Association, available at **www.apa.org**.

games are digital or traditional board games, teachers in experimental projects investigated by Mary Talbot reported that their participation was a labor-intensive process requiring exhaustive collaboration.

16-6i Equity and the Use of Technology

Another key issue, particularly at the national and state levels, is ensuring equal opportunity for all students to access the benefits of technology improvements. Whether in their schools or homes, low-income students generally have less access to certain computer-based learning opportunities than do middle-income students. Until recently, many low-income families have been unable to afford computers. Schools enrolling high percentages of low-income students usually have computers available, but, in recent years, increasing reliance on Internet and multimedia usage in US schools has bypassed numerous high-poverty schools in big cities.[43]

16-6j Cautions Regarding Computer-Based Technologies in Education

As implied previously, not everyone is optimistic about the likelihood that technology will produce productive reforms and widespread improvement in the educational system. Skeptics abound, and their ranks include some of the most knowledgeable analysts of recent developments in the schools and of the evolution of computers in general. For example, Clifford Stoll, widely known for his contributions to Internet development, has written a book titled *Silicon Snake Oil* in which he points out that although computers may be fun to use in the classroom, entertainment is not synonymous with learning. Stoll sees computers as potentially equivalent to the grainy films and the disjointed filmstrips that teachers used years ago mainly to keep their students occupied.[44]

Similarly, Jane Healy had become well known as an enthusiast about the computer's potential for opening new worlds to students and then shocked many of her readers with a book in which she questioned the effects of new technologies on children both inside and outside the schools. After two years spent visiting classrooms, she concluded that computers in many classrooms are supervised by ill-prepared teachers whose students engage mostly in mindless drills, games unrelated to coherent learning objectives, "silly surfing," and/or "idle clicking." Other analysts, also on the basis of visits to numerous classrooms, have reached the conclusion that expensive multimedia setups frequently serve more as a medium for classroom control and public relations than as a learning tool. In reaching such conclusions about computer-based technologies in the schools, Healy and other skeptics typically offer the following cautions and criticisms:[45]

- Research indicating that computers are producing widespread gains in student performance frequently is poorly designed or otherwise invalid.

[43]Tina Barseghian, "For High-Risk Youth, Is Learning Digital Media a Luxury?" 2011 posting by Mind Shift, available at **ww2.kqed.org/mindshift**; Alison DeNisco, "School Librarian Cutbacks Widen Digital Divide," *District Administration* (August 2014), available at **www.districtadministration.com**; and Susan Magsamen, "Bridging the Digital Divide," February 5, 2015, posting by Houghton Mifflin Harcourt, available at **www.hmhco.com/media-center**.

[44]Clifford Stoll, *Silicon Snake Oil* (New York: Doubleday, 1995). See also Todd Oppenheimer, "The Computer Delusion," *Atlantic* (July 1997), available at **www.theatlantic.com**; Todd Oppenheimer, *The Flickering Mind* (New York: Random House, 2003); Mark Bauerlein, *The Dumbest Generation* (New York: Tarcher, 2008); and Larry Cuban, "The Lack of Evidence-Based Practice," February 12, 2015, posting by Larry Cuban, available at **www.larrycuban.wordpress.com/2015/02**.

[45]Jane M. Healy, *Failure to Connect* (New York: Simon and Schuster, 1998); Paul Saffo, "Neo-Toys," *Civilization* (November 1998); Michael B. Horn, "Is There a K–12 Online Learning 'Bubble'?" *Education Next* (April 7, 2011), available at **www.educationnext.org**; and Jin-Soo Huh, "Five Edtech Takeaways from an Administrator who Returned to Teaching," January 29, 2015, posting by edSurge, available at **www.edsurge.com**.

- Computers too often detract from students' creativity by constraining them within prescribed boundaries of thought and action.
- Schools respond to perceived or real public demands and expectations that classrooms should be loaded with advanced technologies by buying expensive equipment that soon becomes obsolete. This may be happening now with iPads and other tablets.
- Fantasy worlds and other imaginary digitized environments are distorting children's sense of reality.

In reviewing these cautions, we should keep in mind the preceding parts of this section as well as earlier parts of this chapter that identified actions associated with the successful implementation of computer-based technologies and other substantial efforts to reform the schools. Will schools and districts provide large-scale and ongoing training and the meaningful technical support required for teachers to use technology effectively? Will educators carefully align the introduction of such technologies and coordinate them with curriculum objectives, testing, and school climate improvements? Fortunately, many educators are working to make this happen.

FOCUS Have you had significant experience with any of the technology approaches described in the preceding sections? If yes, to what extent did they assist you in learning?

16-7 RELATED EFFORTS AND ASPECTS INVOLVING EDUCATIONAL EFFECTIVENESS

We lack space to describe all of the many activities and proposals related to the topics discussed so far, but we'll mention several of the more important efforts in the following pages and summarize them in Overview 16.1.

16-7a Cooperation and Participation with Business, Community, and Other Institutions

Many schools and school districts are attempting to improve the quality of education by cooperating with other institutions, particularly those in business and industry (Photo 16.2). Promising efforts include the following:[46]

- Partnership or adopt-a-school programs in which a business, church, university, or other community institution works closely with an individual school, providing assistance such as tutors or lecturers, funds or equipment for vocational studies, computer education, or help in curriculum development
- Provision of expert help and financial assistance that helps charter schools deal with start-up problems and operating challenges such as evaluation and accounting
- Funding of student awards for reading books or other positive behaviors
- Donations of equipment and supplies
- Substantial financial support for reform efforts such as the Harlem Children's Zone project
- Financial support, such as Intel's $300 million, for K–12 education in Science, Technology, Engineering, and Mathematics (STEM)

A far-reaching example of cooperation with public schools is the Boston Compact. In forming the Compact in 1982, business leaders agreed to recruit at least two hundred companies that would hire graduates of the Boston public schools, as well as providing employment opportunities for students. In return, school officials agreed to establish competency requirements for graduation, increase placement rates of graduates into

---

[46]Kathleen D. Marais et al., "Critical Contributions," 2011 report posted by the University of Georgia and Kromley and Associates, available at **www.giarts.org**; and Michal Lev-Ram, "The Business Case for STEM," *Fortune* (February 1, 2015), available at **www.fortune.com**.

OVERVIEW 16.1

EXAMPLES AND TRENDS INVOLVING EFFORTS AT SCHOOL REFORM OR IMPROVEMENT

Area of Reform or Improvement	Examples and Trends
Business and Community Participation	• Community and business volunteers, donations, awards for schools. • Boston Compact.
Technology	• Extensive introduction of computers, increases in Internet access. • Research that guides effective technology use. • Schools' efforts to improve equity in technology use. • Researchers and educators offer cautions and concerns about ineffective use of technology.
Rural Education	• Research to determine effective improvement programs for rural areas emphasizes that unique approaches are needed because rural areas are diverse. • Distance learning may help rural students.
Gifted and Talented Students	• Many possible approaches make it hard to determine ways to meet the potential of gifted and talented students. • Most programs emphasize acceleration through curriculum, enriching curriculum, or a blend of both. • Schools must expand efforts to identify disadvantaged and minority gifted and talented students.
Increasing Time for Teaching and Learning	• Longer school years and year-round schools. • Longer school days. • After-school and summer learning programs. • 21st Century Community Learning Centers.

> **PHOTO 16.2** Many school districts are cooperating with business and industry to improve education quality in their schools. Business partners supply schools with mentors, supplies, funds, and apprenticeship opportunities or guaranteed postsecondary school funding for students.

Peter Cade/Iconica/Getty Images

higher education as well as into full-time employment, and reduce dropout and absenteeism rates. City students got the message: "If you stay in school, work hard, and master the basics, you will be helped to find a job."[47]

By the early 2000s, more than four hundred companies were participating in the Compact. Activities had expanded to include more than twenty local colleges and universities, and tens of thousands of Boston students had been placed in summer jobs programs or had received help in obtaining full-time jobs after graduation. Data collected by Compact officials indicate that high proportions of high school graduates in Boston either enter college or are employed full-time, and most college entrants are persisting to graduation.

The apparent success of the Boston Compact has helped stimulate major corporate and foundation efforts to help improve education. For example, the MacArthur Foundation provided $40 million to support reform efforts in the Chicago public schools, and the Bill and Melinda Gates Foundation and the Annenberg Foundation each have provided hundreds of millions of dollars to improve schools in Chicago, Los Angeles, New York, and many other school districts.[48]

16-7b Rural Education

About 20 percent of students and 30 percent of schools are located in rural areas, and about one-half of school districts are rural. In trying to improve rural education, educators must confront the extreme diversity of rural locations, which makes it difficult to generalize across communities. One group of observers defined rural school districts as those that have fewer than one hundred fifty residents per square mile and are located in counties in which at least 60 percent of the population resides in communities with populations under five thousand. Even within this fairly restricted definition, rural communities exemplify hundreds of subcultures that differ in racial and ethnic composition, extent of remoteness, economic structure, and other characteristics.[49]

This diversity is partly why the particular problems of rural schools have received relatively little attention during the past fifty years. Recently, however, a small group of scholars has been trying to determine how to provide high-quality education in a rural setting. They have reached several major conclusions:[50]

1. The tremendous diversity in rural America requires similarly diverse school-improvement efforts that also address multicultural education goals.
2. The small scale of rural schools offers advantages. Teachers can know students and parents personally, and schools can work closely with community agencies.
3. Teachers in rural schools frequently require substantial technical support. In some cases, they also require financial or other help in obtaining suitable housing.
4. Many rural schools can benefit from distance learning and other advanced technology.

---

[47]Diana Lam, "Charters, Private, and Public Schools Work Together in Boston," *Phi Delta Kappan* (February 2014); Dale Russakoff, "Schooled," *New Yorker* (May 19, 2014); and "About the Compact," 2015 posting by the Boston Compact, available at **www.bostoncompact.org**.

[48]See information at **www.gatesfoundation.org**.

[49]David Monk, "Recruiting and Retaining High-Quality Teachers in Rural Areas," *The Future of Children* (Spring 2007), available at **www.princeton.edu/futureofchildren**; "Persistent Poverty Dynamics," July 22, 2014, posting by the Rural Policy Research Institute, available at **www.rupri.org**; "Poverty Rates Unchanged for Rural Children," *Rural Policy Matters* (September 24, 2014); and Douglas J. Gagnon and Marybeth J. Mattingly, "Half of Rural Schools Have No AP Classes," *Daily Yonder* (February 16, 2015), available at **www.dailyyonder.com**.

[50]Carrie Aguas, "Rural Elementary School Achieves Gains across All Grades," 2005 description prepared for Houghton Mifflin Beyond the Book site, available at **www.beyond-the-book.com**, click on "Success Stories"; Dan Gordon, "Off the Beaten Path," *THE Journal* (October 4, 2011), available at **www.thejournal.com**; and "Schools in Rural West Virginia Aim to Improve Students' Prospects," February 3, 2015, posting by PBS Newshour, available at **www.pbs.org**.

Many rural schools face serious problems in attracting specialized and qualified teachers. States have increased certification requirements and reduced the flexibility to employ teachers without proper certification, which has left many rural districts unable either to find or to afford sufficient teaching personnel, particularly in science, math, and foreign languages. But school systems can overcome this problem, in part, by using television, interactive computers, and other forms of **distance education** that deliver cost-effective instruction.[51]

distance education Instruction by people or materials distant from the learner in space or time; many distance-education projects use interactive television, the Internet, and other modern communication technologies.

16-7c Gifted and Talented Students

Widespread program trends in gifted education include radical acceleration of learning opportunities for gifted and talented students; special mentoring assistance; increased emphasis on independent study and investigative learning; use of individualized education programs (IEPs), as with students with disabilities; opportunities to engage in advanced-level projects; instruction delivery in accordance with students' learning styles; special schools, Saturday programs, and summer schools; increased community resource use; varied instructional approaches to match student interests and abilities; and compacting curriculum to streamline content that students already know and replace it with more challenging material.[52]

A major issue involving gifted and talented students is the selection of effective approaches to curriculum and instruction. In general, educators have tended to emphasize either acceleration through the regular curriculum or enrichment that provides for greater depth of learning, but some have argued for a confluent approach that combines both. Developing this idea, analysts have advocated combining elements: (1) a "content" model, which emphasizes accelerated study; (2) a "process-product" model, which emphasizes enrichment through independent study and investigation; and (3) an "epistemological" model, which emphasizes understanding and appreciation of systems of knowledge. In general, analysts believe that open-ended, problem-solving approaches should be emphasized for gifted students in any of these or other models.[53]

In recent years, special attention has been given to the situation of "twice exceptional" students who have high intellectual potential but also have difficulties paying attention, regulating their emotions, or controlling related tendencies that limit their performance. Educators interested in this group of students have devised challenging activities that can generate successful experiences in school.[54]

Much concern has been expressed about the low participation of minority students and economically disadvantaged students in gifted education. Evidence indicates that selection criteria frequently fail to identify disadvantaged students who might benefit

[51]Wallace H. Hannum et al., "Distance Education Use in Rural Schools," *Journal of Research in Rural Education* (No. 3, 2009), available at **www.jrre.psu.edu**; Alison DeNisco, "4G Offers Options for Rural Education," *District Administration* (August 2014), available at **www.districtadministration.com**; and information available at **www.jrre.psu.edu**.

[52]Sally M. Reis, "No Child Left Bored," *School Administrator* (February 2007), available at **www.aasa.org**; Joseph S. Renzulli, "What Makes Giftedness?" *Phi Delta Kappan* (May 2011), pp. 81–88; David Y. Dai, *Paradigms of Gifted Education* (Waco, TX: Prufrock Press, 2013); Joan Brasher, "Are Gifted Students Getting Lost in the Shuffle?" January 6, 2014, posting by Vanderbilt University, available at **www.vanderbilt.edu**; Carolyn M. Callahan et al., "What Works in Gifted Education," *American Educational Research Journal* (February 2015); and "Gifted Education Practices," undated posting by the National Association for Gifted Children, available at **www.nagc.org**.

[53]Joyce Van Tassel-Baska, "Effective Curriculum and Instructional Models for Talented Students," *Gifted Child Quarterly* (Fall 1980), pp. 162–168. See also Jane Clarenbach, "All Gifted Is Local" and "Defying the Ripple Effects," both in the *School Administrator* (February 2007), available at **www.aasa.org**; and Jonathan A. Plucker and Carolyn M. Callahan, "Research on Giftedness and Gifted Education," *Exceptional Children* (Summer 2014).

[54]Susan Baum, "Authentic Opportunities and Talent Development," *Gifted Education Communicator* (Winter 2015), available at **www.giftededucationcommunicator.com**.

TAKING ISSUE

Read the brief introduction below, as well as the Question and the pros and cons list that follows. Then, answer the question using *your* own words and position.

MORE TIME IN SCHOOL

One suggestion for improving student achievement has been to increase the amount of time students spend in school by lengthening the school day, school year, or both. This idea is based in part on observations of countries such as Japan, where students spend considerably more time in school than do American students. It also reflects research indicating that time-on-task is an important determinant of students' performance.

Question

Should the United States extend the amount of time students spend in school? (Think about this question as you read the PRO and CON arguments listed below. What is *your* take on this issue?)

Arguments PRO

1. Extending the school year or school day will give teachers more contact time and an opportunity to teach students in depth. This is particularly vital for at-risk students, who need special services and remedial work.

2. Experience in countries such as Japan indicates that increased time spent in school can assist in raising achievement scores. Many national task-force reports have also recommended extending time in school.

3. Extending school time can help to solve the problems of latchkey children, who must look after themselves while their parents work. In this way, schools can benefit the family as well as improve education.

4. Lengthening students' time in school will indicate to taxpayers that schools are serious about raising educational standards. Taxpayers will therefore be more willing to support the schools.

5. The present system of school attendance originated in an agrarian period when families needed children's help with farm tasks. In an industrial society, the best use of students' time is to give them additional schooling that prepares them for the world of the twenty-first century.

Arguments CON

1. Extending time in school will not compensate for the poor teaching that takes place in too many schools. The problem is not quantity but quality of schooling, and longer hours could well *reduce* quality.

2. So many social and cultural differences exist between Japan and the United States that simple comparisons are not valid. Little hard evidence indicates that increasing students' time in school will raise achievement levels in the United States.

3. Extending the time children spend in school will add to the growing institutional interference with basic family life. Such interference, however well intentioned, contributes to the fragmentation of the modern family.

4. Extending school time will require major new expenditures to increase salaries and refurbish buildings. Taxpayers will not willingly pay for these expenses.

5. We know too little about the effects of lengthening the school day or year. Do children in our culture need ample breaks from school? Do their originality and creativity suffer when they are kept too long in classes? Until we have answers, we should not make students spend more time in school.

Question Reprise: What Is Your Stand?

Reflect again on the following question by explaining *your* stand about this issue: Should the United States extend the amount of time students spend in school?

---

from participation. For this reason, many efforts are under way to broaden definitions of giftedness to include indicators such as very strong problem-solving skills, high creativity, high verbal or nonverbal fluency, and unusual artistic accomplishments and abilities.[55]

---

[55]Julie D. Swanson, "Breaking through Assumptions about Low-Income, Minority Gifted Students," *Gifted Child Quarterly* (Winter 2006), pp. 11–25; Eric Smith, "Weaving the Gifted into the Full Fabric," *School Administrator* (February 2007), available at **www.aasa.org**; David Card and Laura Giuliano, "Does Gifted Education Work? For Which Students?" September 2014 posting by the National Bureau of Economic Research, available at **www.nber.org**; and Donna Y. Ford, "Segregation and the Underrepresentation of Blacks and Hispanics in Gifted Education," *Roeper Review* (July–September 2014).

16-7d Increasing Teaching and Learning Time

Several national reports, including *A Nation at Risk* and *Prisoners of Time,* have recommended providing more time for teaching and learning. Possible approaches include extending the school year, lengthening the school day, or offering after-school and summer learning programs.

Longer School Years or School Days Numerous school districts have lengthened the school day or the school year. Some offer **year-round schools** that run on rotating schedules so that three-quarters of students attend for nine weeks while the remaining quarter are on vacation for three weeks. Year-round schools have usually been established where schools are seriously overcrowded.

Such moves usually provoke controversy because they require a significant increase in staff costs and may disrupt parents' child-care arrangements. Action to extend time for learning also requires substantial changes in curriculum and instruction in order to improve student achievement. Massachusetts has begun an effort to help districts and schools restructure their instructional practices and their daily, weekly, and annual schedules to provide students with more time for learning.[56] For a debate on this topic, see the Taking Issue box.

After-School and Summer Programs Rather than increase the school year or school day for all students, many districts have been initiating or expanding after-school and summer learning programs. After-school and summer programs can provide struggling students with more time for learning or offer safe and educational opportunities for latchkey and other children (see Chapter 10, Culture, Socialization, and Education). These programs have grown rapidly in recent years as the No Child Left Behind Act (NCLB) resulted in the identification of thousands of schools not making adequate yearly progress (AYP). The federal government now provides millions of dollars annually to support them under the **21st Century Community Learning Centers** legislation, and state and local sources provide still more support. The 21st Century Community Learning Centers provide tutoring, after-school classes, summer school, and other academic-enrichment activities for students attending low-performing schools. Analysts and evaluators who have studied the centers and similar efforts have reached several conclusions:[57]

- After-school and summer programs can improve academic performance if implemented well.
- Implementation considerations include selecting and training staff, providing appropriate materials, and making sufficient resources available.
- Progress is difficult to measure because students typically make relatively small gains on tests that assess regular schooling. Therefore, officials should assess

year-round school Rotating schedules that allow students to attend school for three out of four quarters during a chronological year.

21st Century Community Learning Centers These centers, supported through the No Child Left Behind Act, provide tutoring, after-school classes, summer school, and other academic-enrichment activities for students attending low-performing schools.

[56]National Education Commission on Time and Learning, *Prisoners of Time* (Washington, DC: US Department of Education, 1994); Hilary Pennington, "The Massachusetts Expanding Learning Time to Support Student Success Initiative," 2007 paper prepared for the Center for American Progress, available at **www.americanprogress.org**; Robert M. Stonehill et al., "Enhancing School Reform through Expanded Learning," 2009 paper prepared for Learning Point Associates, available at **www.learningpt.org**; David Farbman, "Breaking from the Norm—Expanded-Time Schools Are Doable," February 2, 2015, posting by the National Center on Time & Learning, available at **www.timeandlearning.org**; and postings at the Summer Matters site, available at **www.summermatters.com**.

[57]Beth Frerking, "A New Learning Day," *Edutopia* (February 2007), available at **www.edutopia .org**; Chris Gabrieli, "Time—It's Not Always Money," *Educational Leadership* (December 2011/January 2012); Soumya Bhat, "Using Afterschool and Summer programs to Help Low-Income Children Succeed," October 17, 2014, posting by the DC Fiscal Policy Institute, available at **www.dcfpi .org**; "Inspiring Students with a Connected Learning Approach," January 2015 posting by the Afterschool Alliance, available at **www.afterschoolalliance.org/documents/Afterschool _and_Connected_Learning.pdf**; and information available at **www.mass2020.org**.

attendance, parent support, student effort, and other possible correlates of improved attitudes.

- Nonacademic goals such as providing a safe environment, expanding students' interests, and developing social skills are worthwhile and should be addressed in implementing after-school and summer programs.

16-8 SCHOOL CHOICE

school choice A system that allows students or their parents to choose the schools they attend.

In recent years, **school choice** plans have been advocated as a way to introduce greater flexibility and accountability into education. The basic idea is to enhance students' opportunities to choose where they will enroll and what they will study. School choice is a broad goal, and various programs offer students and their families varying levels of choices. Many alternative schools have been established to provide education for students who have been failing in regular public schools. Advocates of school choice point out that parents typically find only one model of education in any given public-school neighborhood. Some advocates argue for creating choices within the public-school system; others contend that the only true alternatives are outside the system. Efforts to increase school choice include the following:[58]

magnet schools A type of alternative school that attracts voluntary enrollment from more than one neighborhood by offering special instructional programs or curricula; often established in part for purposes of desegregation.

alternative schools A public or private school that provides learning opportunities different from those in local public schools. Some such schools follow a student-centered curriculum characterized by a great deal of freedom for students and a relative lack of structure.

- *Magnet and alternative schools.* Many school districts offer their students the opportunity to choose magnet schools or alternative schools within the district. **Magnet schools**, as described in Chapter 12, Providing Equal Educational Opportunity, are designed to attract voluntary enrollment by offering special programs or curricula that appeal to students from more than one neighborhood. They are often part of a reform effort aimed at decreasing segregation and providing students with opportunities to participate in instructional programs not available in their local schools. More than one thousand magnet schools are now functioning in public-school districts. **Alternative schools** provide learning opportunities unavailable in the average public school. From this point of view, magnet schools are a type of alternative school. So, too, are many parochial and other nonpublic schools and institutions such as street academies, storefront schools, and high school "outposts" designed to make education more relevant for inner-city students. Studies of alternative schools have indicated that they frequently enroll students who have not succeeded in traditional schools. Compared to traditional schools, alternative schools allow for greater individualization, more independent study, and more openness to the outside community. They tend to offer small class size, high staff morale, freedom from external control, and strong concern for noncognitive goals of education.[59]

charter schools A public school governed by a community group granted a special contract (charter) by the state or the local school board. Charter schools often form to offer educational alternatives unavailable in regular public schools.

- *Charter schools.* As is discussed in Chapter 8, Financing Public Education, charter schools funded by public sources also frequently provide opportunities for parents and students to choose among schools. Charter schools can be established by school districts or by other chartering authorities. Some are managed by

[58]Christine Rossell, "Magnet Schools," *Education Next*, (No. 2 2005), available at **www.educationnext.org**; "Alternative Schooling," 2015 posting, available at **http://education.stateuniversity.com**; and Claire Smrekar and Ngaire Honey, The Desegregation Aims and Demographic Contexts of Magnet Schools," *Peabody Journal of Education* (January–March 2015).

[59]Daniel U. Levine, "Educating Alienated Inner City Youth: Lessons from the Street Academies," *Journal of Negro Education* (Spring 1975), pp. 139–148; "Best Practices in Alternative Education," 2012 posting by the Kentucky Center for School Safety," available at **www.kycss.org**; Rebecca Leech, "Rethinking High School Pathways," *Educational Leadership* (September 2014); and "The Public Charter Schools Dashboard," 2015 posting by the National Alliance for Public Charter Schools, available at **www.publiccharters.org**.

private profit-making corporations. Charter schools typically have more leeway in spending funds, utilizing faculty, and carrying on other operations than do regular public schools. They also can have their charter revoked if they are not successful. More than forty states now allow for establishment of charter schools, and more than six thousand charter schools are operating nationally, enrolling more than two million students. About a third of charter schools have 75 percent or more low-income students, compared with about one-fifth of other public schools. Many are attended largely by students who have been low achievers susceptible to dropping out of school. In several urban districts, such as Kansas City and Washington, DC, charter schools enroll 30 percent or more of public-school students. The New Orleans school district was reorganized after Hurricane Katrina, and now more than 90 percent of students there attend charter schools. President Obama has recognized that many charter schools are functioning successfully and has called on states to "reform their charter rules and lift caps on the number of allowable charter schools, wherever such caps are in place."[60]

- *Open enrollment attendance options.* Several states have also created plans that allow all students the option to transfer to their choice of public schools within, or sometimes outside their local school district. Colorado laws, for example, require that all districts allow students to transfer freely within their boundaries. Washington's legislation provides students who experience a "special hardship or detrimental condition" with the right to enroll in another school district that has available space; it also requires districts to accept students who transfer to locations close to their parents' place of work or child-care site.

- *Privately funded school choice vouchers.* Philanthropists in numerous locations have provided vouchers to enable students to attend nonpublic schools. After a group of business executives funded scholarships that helped 2,200 New York City students (out of more than 40,000 applicants) to attend nonpublic schools in 1998 and 1999, a larger group raised millions of dollars for a national program to provide inner-city students with similar scholarships. Thousands of students have received such scholarships.

- *Tuition tax credits.* Initiated in 1997, Arizona's universal tax credit approach allows any taxpayer who pays tuition for a child attending a public or nonpublic school to take a dollar-for-dollar deduction (up to half what the local public schools would have spent) in state tax liability. In addition, taxpayers can receive a credit for donations to "private tuition" charities that spend at least 90 percent of this income for tuition assistance to low-income students. Several other states also have begun to provide this type of assistance. After the US Supreme Court approved Arizona's arrangements in 2011, the state government increased donation limits by 50 percent.

- *Taxpayer-funded scholarships.* Choice in Arizona received a further boost in 2006 when the state began paying nonpublic-school tuition for disabled students and foster-care children. Several other states also provide scholarships to help some students attend private elementary or secondary schools.

- *Publicly funded school choice vouchers.* Although small government-funded voucher programs have been implemented in Colorado, Florida, Maine, Ohio, and Vermont, the best-known voucher project is the sizable program funded by the Wisconsin legislature for low-income students in Milwaukee. Originally initiated

---

[60]Joe Williams, "Games Charter Opponents Play," *Education Next* (No. 1, 2007), available at **www.educationnext.org**; Lisa M. Stulberg, *Race, Schools, and Hope* (New York: Teachers College Press, 2008); "Arizona Moves to Increase Tuition Tax Credits," April 2011 posting by the Mackinac Center for Public Policy, available at **www.mackinac.org**; Steve Drummond and Anya Kamenetz, "The End of Neighborhood Schools," September 2, 2014, posting by NPR, available at **www.npr.org**; and Jandel Crutchfield, "What Does Charter School Mean to You," *Educational Leadership* (February 2015).

to help students attend nonreligious private schools, the Milwaukee program expanded in 1998 to include attendance at religious schools.[61]

16-8a Controversy about School Choice

As programs have been implemented to expand school choice, numerous recommendations for and against additional action are being put forward. Those who support choice recommend policies such as enrollment across school district boundaries, vouchers to attend both public and nonpublic schools, magnetization and/or "charterization" of entire school districts and regions, and creation of alternative-school networks. Supporters of choice emphasize the following arguments:[62]

● Providing choice for disadvantaged students will enable them to escape from poorly functioning schools.
● Achievement, aspirations, and other outcomes will improve for many students because they will be more motivated to succeed at schools they select.
● Both existing public schools and alternative learning institutions (whether public or nonpublic) will provide improved education because their staffs will be competing to attract students.
● Increased opportunities will be available to match school programs and services with students' needs.
● Parents will be empowered to play a larger role in their children's education.

Critics of school choice plans question these arguments, particularly in cases that involve public financing of nonpublic schools. The critics maintain the following:[63]

● Choice plans will reinforce stratification and segregation because highly motivated or high-achieving white and minority students will be disproportionately likely to transfer out of schools that have a substantial percentage of students with low achievement or low social status.
● Public financial support for nonpublic schools is unconstitutional.
● The opening and closing of numerous schools based on their competitive attractiveness will disrupt the operation of the entire educational system.
● There is little or no reason to believe that most schools presently enrolling relatively few disadvantaged students will be more successful with such students than are their present schools.

---

[61]Barbara Miner, "A Brief History of Milwaukee's Voucher Program," *Rethinking Schools* (Spring 2006), available at **www.rethinkingschools.org**; Jason Bedrick, "School Tax Credits Are Good for Parents, Taxpayers," *New Hampshire Business Review* (October 8, 2014), available at **www.cato.org**; and "Walker's Budget Expands School Vouchers, Holds Line on Taxes," February 3, 2015, posting by the *Milwaukee Journal Sentinel*, available at **www.jsonline.com**.

[62]Matthew J. Brouillette, "The Case for Choice in Schooling," 2001 paper posted at the Mackinac Center for Public Policy site, available at **www.mackinac.org**; John E. Chubb, "Ignoring the Market," *Education Next* (No. 2, Spring 2003), available at **www.educationnext.org**; Nelson Smith, "Charters as a Solution?" *Education Next* (No. 1, 2007), available at **www.educationnext .org**; Kathleen Porter-Magee, "Democracy, Community, and School Choice," June 11, 2014, posting by Flypaper, available at **www.edexcellence.net**; and Chad Miller, "Providing Equality of Opportunities," January 27, 2015, posting by the American Action Forum, available at **www.americanactionforum.org**.

[63]Herbert J. Grover, "Private School Choice Is Wrong," *Educational Leadership* (January 1991), p. 51; Jay Mathews, "Charter Schools Lag, Study Finds," *Washington Post* (August 23, 2006); Dennis Epple and Richard Romano, "Educational Vouchers and Cream Skimming," *International Economics Review* (November 2008), pp. 1395–1435; Barbara Miner, "Public Studies Puncture the Privatization Bubble," *Rethinking Schools* (Winter 2007/2008), available at **www.rethinkingschools .org**; James Harvey, "Privatization," *Educational Leadership* (December 2011/January 2012); and Spencer C. Weiler and Linda R. Vogel, "Charter School Barriers," *Equity and Excellence in Education* (February 2015).

- Even if one assumes that schools capable of substantially improving the performance of low achievers are widely available in a choice plan, many students and parents lack the knowledge necessary to select them, and these outstanding schools may not accept many low achievers.
- Although accountability may increase in the sense that unattractive schools will lose students and may even be closed, overall accountability will be reduced because nonpublic schools receiving public funds frequently are not subject to government standards and requirements, such as obligations to enroll special-education students and to administer state tests.
- Public financing of nonpublic institutions will result in the establishment of "cult" schools based on divisive racist or religious ideologies.

These worries about school choice are shared even by people who have supported proposals to expand student options. For example, John Leo thinks that school choice is "reform's best choice" but also is education's "600-pound gorilla." He believes it may harm education by funding schools that encourage social, racial, and economic separatism. In this context, many analysts have been trying to identify policies that could make choice plans as constructive as possible. They have suggested policies including the following:[64]

- Ensure that students and parents receive adequate counseling and information.
- Provide free transportation, scholarships, and other support to make sure that choices are fully available, and do not depend on social status.
- Include guidelines to avoid segregation and resegregation.
- Include provisions to release government-operated schools from regulations not imposed on nonpublic schools.
- Do not ignore other reform necessities and possibilities; instead, treat choice as part of a comprehensive reform agenda that involves systemic reform of the kind described elsewhere in this chapter.

Research to date has not conclusively established whether or not students exercising school choice generally achieve at a significantly higher level than comparable students in regular public schools. With some exceptions (such as the KIPP approach described earlier) that either favor schools of choice or report no differences, evaluations of voucher programs, charter schools, and other choice initiatives have tended to conclude that achievement gains generally were small and inconsistent. However, many charter schools enroll primarily low-income students in urban districts and when these schools are compared with comparable nearby schools, many of the charters have impressive achievement and graduation rates. On the other hand, many charter schools are being criticized for not replacing low achievers who withdraw, so it is frequently difficult to attribute gains to those schools' instructional policies and practices.[65]

FOCUS Are you interested in teaching at a charter school? What do you think would be some of the advantages and disadvantages? Do you think you would do well in a charter environment?

---

[64]John Leo, "School Reform's Best Choice," *US News and World Report* (January 14, 1991), p. 17; Sol Stern, "School Choice Isn't Enough," *City Journal* (Winter 2008), available at **www.city-journal.org**; Leigh Dingerson et al., "Prophet Motives," *Rethinking Schools* (Summer 2008), available at **www.rethinkingschools.org**; Robin Lake, "Time to Take Stock on Charter Authorizing," October 28, 2014, posting by the Center on Reinventing Public Education, available at **www.crpe.org**; and Richard Whitmire, "Inside Successful District-Charter Compacts," *Education Digest* (January 2015).

[65]John Fensterwald, "Mixed Results for Charter Schools Statewide in New Study," March 24, 2014, posting available at **www.edsource.org**; Haley Ferretti, "Fla. League of Women Voters Releases Startling Charter School Study," May 29, 2014, posting by the Jackson Free Press, available at **www.jacksonfreepress.com**; Anya Kamenetz and Claudio Sanchez, "Charter Schools, Money and Test Scores," July 22, 2014, posting by NPRED, available at **www.npr.org**; "CREDO Study Finds Urban Charter Schools Outperform Traditional School Peers," March 18, 2015, posting by the Center for Research on Student Outcomes, available at **http://urbancharter.stanford.edu/news.php**; and James Vaznis, "Boston Public-School Grads Exceed Charter-School Peers," *Boston Globe* (January 20, 2015), available at **www.bostonglobe.com**.

16-9 SYSTEMIC RESTRUCTURING AND STANDARDS-BASED REFORM

restructuring Multiple changes to bring about systemic improvement in a school or group of schools.

systemic improvement Reform efforts that simultaneously address all or most major components in the overall educational system.

In recent years, many reform efforts have been discussed in terms of **restructuring** all or part of the educational system. Although this term has been interpreted in many different ways, it increasingly is used to indicate the need for **systemic improvement**—that is, reform that simultaneously addresses all or most major components in the overall system. For example, officials of the Education Commission of the States have stated that all parts of the educational system from "schoolhouse to statehouse" must be restructured to bring about systematic improvement in teaching and learning. Systemic restructuring deals with instructional methods; professional development; assessment of student, teacher, and/or school performance; curriculum and materials; school finance; governance; course requirements; and other aspects of education.[66]

When many changes are introduced simultaneously, restructuring and reform activities must be coherent; they must be compatible with and reinforce each other, rather than becoming isolated fragments that divert time and energy from priority goals. Because systemic reforms work for coherence by identifying student performance standards and then aligning testing, instructional methods and materials, professional development, and other aspects of education, they frequently are referred to as "standards-based" reforms.

16-9a State-Level Systemic Reform

One of the best examples of state-level systemic reform is in Kentucky, where in 1989, the state supreme court declared the state's system of common schools unconstitutional on the grounds that it was ineffective and inequitable. The court then instructed the legislative and executive branches to improve the "entire sweep of the system—all its parts and parcels." As a result, the following changes, among others, have been phased in as part of the Kentucky Education Reform Act (KERA):[67]

- Curriculum, instruction, and student assessment are performance-based, emphasizing mastery-oriented learning and criterion-referenced testing.
- Parents can transfer their children out of schools they consider unsatisfactory.
- Faculty members at unsuccessful schools receive help from state-appointed specialists.
- Youth and family service centers have been established in communities where 20 percent or more of students are from low-income families.
- All districts offer preschool programs for disadvantaged 4-year-olds.
- Taxes have been increased by billions of dollars to pay for the changes.

16-9b District-Level Systemic Reform

Clear examples of gains in student performance on state assessments and other tests have been particularly evident in Baltimore. In the Baltimore City Schools, students improved both their reading and math scores at every grade tested by the state after 2003, and elementary students also made major progress on nationally normed tests.

---

[66]"What Is Systemic Reform?" 2005 posting at the National Academies Internet site, available at **www.nas.edu/rise/backg3.htm**; Ledyard McFadden, "District Learning Tied to Student Learning," *Phi Delta Kappan* (April 2009), pp. 545–553; Mariana Haynes, "Meeting the Challenge," *Alliance for Excellent Education Policy Brief* (January 2011), available at **www.all4ed.org**; and Edith Lai, "Enacting Principal Leadership," *Research Papers in Education* (February 2015).

[67]Thomas R. Guskey and Kent Peterson, "The Road to Classroom Change," *Educational Leadership* (December 1995–January 1996), pp. 10–15; "Governor, Education Commissioner Present Strong Progress Report for Kentucky Schools, Students," 2013 posting by the Kentucky Department of Education, available at **www.education.ky.gov**; and "Kentucky's P–12 Achievements," May 15, 2015, posting by the Kentucky Department of Education, available at **www.education .ky.gov/comm/p12**.

The percentages of fifth graders reading at or above the proficient level increased from 44 percent in 2003 to 76 percent in 2011, and comparable scores for third graders improved from 39 percent to 69 percent. Observers have attributed these gains to such coordinated reform initiatives as professional development dealing with balanced literacy; standards-based teaching in reading, writing, and math; increased early childhood, after-school, and summer learning opportunities; and requirements for student promotion from one grade to the next. However, reading and math scores declined greatly in 2014 after the district introduced Common Core curricula, but continued to administer Maryland's assessment that was no longer aligned with curriculum and instruction. Many educators in the district are expecting that student performance will rebound in future years.[68]

Another district that has registered impressive gains is in Union City, New Jersey. As described by David Kirp in his book *Improbable Scholars,* some of the key developments and interventions included full-day preschool beginning at age 3; curriculum-wide emphasis on language development; students who start with little or no English are taught to fluency in their native language and then in English; a high degree of alignment in a challenging curriculum; reaching out to parents to enlist as partners in their children's education; and strong efforts to maintain a culture of caring. After years of steady work toward improvement, Union City reports that its heavily low-income enrollment now generally approximates statewide achievement scores, and about 90 percent of students graduate from high school.[69]

Some other districts throughout the nation also have initiated outstanding reform approaches that are producing gains on their states' standards-based assessments of student performance. In addition, we are learning much about what districts should do to make their reform plans successful. For example, a study conducted for the Educational Research Service reported that the following practices were characteristic of six districts rated high in performance, based on having brought about substantial achievement improvements while enrolling significant proportions of low-income students:[70]

- The superintendent and other leaders developed widely shared beliefs about the necessity for high expectations.
- Extensive work was done to align curriculum with state tests.
- Regular assessments of student performance helped ensure tutoring for students falling behind.

16-9c The Sad Situation of Many Big City Districts

Despite significant progress in some city districts, achievement and other outcomes in big city districts remain disappointing for the most part, particularly in those districts with a very high percentage of low-income students. For example, the National Assessment of Educational Progress found that only 27 percent of eighth-grade students scored proficient or above in mathematics and only 34 percent scored at this level in reading

[68]"Baltimore Builds for Success," *American Teacher* (December 2003–January 2004), available at **www.aft.org**; Judy Lightfoot, "What Can We Learn from the Struggles of Baltimore Public Schools?" *Crosscut* (January 24, 2011), available at **www.crosscut.com**; and Hilary Tone, "Fox News Figures Blame Baltimore's 'Awful,' 'Worst Schools on Earth' for Riots," April 29, 2015, posting by Media Matters For America, available at **www.mediamatters.org**.

[69]"Academic Success in Low-Income New Jersey School District Offers National Model," December 3, 2014, posting by The Annie E. Casey Foundation, available at **www.aecf.org**; Chris Thelen, "Urban Students Can Get a Great Public Education, Too," September 4, 2014, posting by Where's My Eraser?, available at **www.wheresmyeraser.com**; and David L. Kirp, *Improbable Scholars* (New York: Oxford, 2015).

[70]Gordon Cawelti and Nancy Protheroe, *How Six School Districts Changed into High-Performance Systems* (Arlington, VA: Educational Research Service, 2001). See also Jason C. Snipes, Fred Doolittle, and Corinne Herlihy, *Case Studies of How Urban School Systems Improve Student Achievement* (New York: MDRC, 2002), available at **www.mdrc.org**; Ellen Foley, "Contradictions and Control in Systemic Reform," 2011 report prepared for the Consortium for Policy Research in Education, available at **www.cpre.org**; and Robert Pondiscio, "The Year of Curriculum Based Reform?" January 7, 2015, posting by the Thomas B. Fordham Institute, available at **www.edexcellence.net**.

FOCUS What do you think are the most serious problems that have prevented big city districts from bringing about adequate improvements in student achievement?

in 2013 testing carried out in twenty-one urban districts with a population of 250,000 or more. About 70 percent of students enrolled in public schools in these districts were low-income students eligible for federal lunch subsidies. Among this subgroup, only 18 percent attained a rating of proficient or above in math, and only 17 percent in reading. In several of the largest districts, the percentages of low-income students scoring proficient or above were below 10 percent. It is no surprise that the graduation rates at some high schools in these cities are less than 50 or 60 percent.[71]

16-10 CONCLUSION: THE CHALLENGE FOR EDUCATION

We began this chapter by recognizing the need for improved performance on the part of students in our educational systems. This is particularly true with respect to the development of higher-order skills in all segments of the student population and specifically among disadvantaged students. In Chapter 13, The Changing Purposes of American Education, we described how attention increasingly has focused on national goals. In our chapters dealing with teachers and the teaching profession, we described how emphasis is being placed on preparing and hiring qualified teachers who can function effectively throughout our school systems. In several other chapters, including this one, we have cited successful instructional interventions that can be incorporated into large-scale reform plans. All of these efforts are currently receiving attention in federal and state governments' educational improvement plans. Among other activities, governments are providing billions of dollars to improve teacher preparation and functioning, encourage and facilitate higher standards that can be implemented on a widespread basis, and identify and support successful reforms to help disadvantaged students.

With regard to the more specific need to reduce or eliminate achievement gaps by social class and by race and ethnicity, we have described numerous aspects of an overall effort that can help make this goal a reality. Chapter 12, Providing Equal Educational Opportunity, and material in this chapter indicated that comprehensive ecological interventions addressing school, family, and home environments during infancy and early childhood; school arrangements responsive to the particular problems of low-achieving students; and alleviation of disadvantages arising from segregation and concentrated poverty should play important roles in addressing this challenge. Reforms considered in this chapter, such as effective introduction of technology, charter schools specifically serving low-income students in big cities, and systemic plans to implement these or similar components throughout a school district, can generate large performance gains that substantially reduce or eliminate achievement gaps.[72]

Here, too, our school systems and governments are initiating action to meet the challenge. Our federal and state governments are doing much to increase and disseminate research on instructional approaches that work, on procedures to assess higher-order skills, on programs to prepare teachers for urban schools, and on a multitude of other topics involving school reform. We already have learned much about improving educational effectiveness at the district, school, and classroom levels. However, using this knowledge to fundamentally improve the schools is a difficult and complex task. As a teacher, you will face this task because you will play an important part in determining whether the reform effort is successful.

---

[71]Andy Smarick, "End. The Broad Prize. Now," September 24, 2013, posting by Flypaper, available at **www.edexcellence.net**; Tim Goral, "Confronting a Low-Income Crisis in US Schools," *District Administration* (April 2015), available at **www.districtadministration.com**; and data available at **www.nationsreportcard.gov**.

[72]"Diane Ravitch, "Schools We Can Envy," *New York Review of Books* (March 8, 2012), available at **www.nybooks.com**; Monica R. Almond and Tiffany D. Miller, "Linked Learning," October 7, 2014, posting by the Center for American Progress, available at **www.americanprogress.org**; and Matthew Lynch, "Implementing and Sustaining School Reform," February 3, 2015, posting by The Edvocate, available at **www.theedadvocate.org**.

SUMMING UP

1. The educational system is being challenged to improve achievement to keep the United States internationally competitive and to provide equity for disadvantaged and other at-risk students.

2. Research on effective teaching and instruction provides support for appropriate emphasis on efficient classroom management, direct instruction, high time-on-task, skillful questioning of students, explicit comprehension instruction, and other methods that promote achievement.

3. Research indicates that schools unusually effective in improving student achievement have a clear mission, outstanding leadership, high expectations for students, positive home–school relations, high time-on-task, frequent monitoring of students' achievement, and an orderly, humane climate. Research also has identified somewhat more specific characteristics such as curriculum alignment and school-wide emphasis on higher-order skills. Regarding high schools, researchers have found that schools-within-a-school, career academies, and smaller units sometimes are effective.

4. It now is possible to create more effective schools, provided educators use what we have learned about the school improvement process.

5. Many efforts, such as the Higher-Order Thinking Skills Program, seek to improve instruction across grade levels. An approach called Response to Intervention is growing in popularity, but it is difficult to implement effectively.

6. Research efforts designed to improve whole schools stem from research indicating that the individual school level is crucial in bringing about reform.

7. Many school districts and states have undertaken improvement efforts involving cooperation with businesses and other institutions, year-round schooling, and improving rural education and education for gifted and talented students.

8. Emerging technologies offer great potential for improving elementary and secondary education, but effective use of technologies will require considerable planning, effort, and resources.

9. Many possibilities exist for improving education through expanding school choice, but many potential dangers also exist.

10. Promising efforts are now under way to bring about systemic, coherent restructuring and reform. Systemic reforms can do much to meet the challenge of reducing or eliminating achievement gaps by social class and race/ethnicity.

SUGGESTED RESOURCES

INTERNET RESOURCES

The Internet is a treasure trove of places where you can read descriptions and analyses of successful schools and instructional practices as well as other reform topics discussed in this chapter. The following list provides a brief sampling:

The Education Gadfly is available biweekly through a free subscription.

The October 2011 issue of *Educational Leadership* includes several articles on how coaches help improve teaching and schools. The February 2015 issue focuses on the theme "Improving Schools: What Works?"

Studies opposing school choice approaches are emphasized in analyses at the American Federation of Teachers "Vouchers Home Page." Studies supporting school choice approaches are emphasized in *School Reform News*.

The National Association for Gifted Children provides research-based materials for teachers of gifted students.

Material regarding Response to Intervention is available from the National Center on Response to Intervention.

The Thinking Foundation provides information about metacognitive strategies in general and thinking maps in particular, as well as case studies of schools that have greatly improved instruction using these strategies.

Thoughtful articles dealing with school reform are presented in the online journals *Education Next* and *Education Policy Analysis Archives*.

PUBLICATIONS

Fullan, Michael. *The New Meaning of Educational Change*, 4th ed. New York: Teachers College Press, 2007. *Analysis of both the theoretical basis and the practical implications of research on the school change process.*

Gradillas, Henry, and Jerry Jessness. *Standing and Delivering*. Lanham, MD: Rowman & Littlefield Education, 2010. *A fascinating account of how startling improvements were brought about by improving climate, instruction, and other effective-schools considerations at an inner-city high school in Los Angeles.*

Kirp, David, L. *Improbable Scholars,* New York: Oxford, 2015. *Subtitled "The Rebirth of a Great American School System and a Strategy for America's Schools," this inspiring book recounts what was done in Union City, New Jersey, to substantially improve achievement and other indicators of effective education.*

Stulberg, Lisa M. *Race, Schools, and Hope: African Americans and School Choice after Brown*. New York: Teachers College Press, 2008. *This book explains why some African American leaders have been strong advocates of school choice.*

GLOSSARY

21st Century Learning Centers These centers, supported through the No Child Left Behind Act, provide tutoring, after-school classes, summer school, and other academic-enrichment activities for students attending low-performing schools.

A

Abrahamic tradition Monotheism, the belief in one God, which originated with Abraham in Judaism and has shaped Christianity and Islam.

academic freedom A protection permitting teachers to teach subject matter and choose instructional materials relevant to the course without restriction from administrators or other persons outside the classroom.

academy A type of private or semipublic secondary school dominant in the United States from 1830 to 1870 that was the high school's institutional predecessor. Today, some secondary schools, often private institutions, are called academies.

accountability Holding teachers, administrators, and/or school board members responsible for student performance or for wise use of educational funds.

activity-centered curriculum A type of student-centered curriculum that emphasizes purposeful and real-life experiences and, more recently, student participation in school and community activities.

adequate yearly progress The regular increments of achievement gain that schools and districts must register under NCLB to have all students attain academic proficiency.

aesthetics The subdivision of axiology that establishes criteria for judging that something—such as literature, music, and art—is beautiful or not.

alternative certification Teacher certification obtained without completing a traditional teacher-education program at a school or college of education.

alternative school A public or private school that provides learning opportunities different from those in local public schools. Some such schools follow a student-centered curriculum characterized by a great deal of freedom for students and a relative lack of structure.

American Federation of Teachers (AFT) The second largest organization that represents teachers in America. Affiliated with the AFL-CIO, it often is associated with union representation.

Americanization The dominant ideology in public schools imposed on immigrant and minority group children in the nineteenth and early twentieth centuries.

a priori ideas Ideas deduced from self-evident first principles that are conclusions based on reason alone. Associated with realism, Thomism, and perennialism, Dewey and the pragmatists argue that the epistemology of *a priori* ideas is not based on verifiable experience.

assimilation The strategy that immigrant children should be schooled into the dominant "American" culture by learning to speak and read the English language, the values of hard work and punctuality prescribed by the Protestant ethic, and respect for the laws of the United States.

axiology The area of philosophy that examines value issues, especially in morality, ethics, and aesthetics.

B

back-to-basics curriculum A type of subject-centered curriculum that emphasizes the three Rs at the elementary level and academic subjects at the secondary level; also includes a defined minimum level of academic standards.

basic-skills testing Testing that examines preservice teachers' basic skills with respect to subjects such as reading, mathematics, and communications.

bilingual education Instruction in their native language provided for students whose first language is not English.

bipartite system A dual-track system consisting of academic schools and vocational schools.

block grants General-purpose funding from the federal government, allowing each state considerable freedom to choose specific programs on which to spend the funds.

boarding schools Residential institutions where students live and attend school.

breach of contract What occurs when one side fails to perform as agreed in a contract.

C

career and technical education (CTE) Provides students with the academic and technical skills, knowledge, and training necessary to succeed in future careers and to become lifelong learners. CTE prepares learners for the world of work by introducing them to the workplace environment, and makes academic content accessible by providing it in a hands-on context.

catechistic method of instruction Catechisms—religious textbooks—were organized into questions and answers that summarized the particular denomination's doctrines and practices.

categorical grants Funds designated for specific groups and purposes; the standard method of federal education funding before the 1980s and again more recently.

censorship The suppression of ideas and information that certain persons—individuals, groups, or government officials—find objectionable or dangerous.

central office staff A cadre of supervisors and specialists who work closely with the superintendent to carry out school board policy.

certification State government review and approval that permits a teaching candidate to teach.

charter school A public school governed by a community group granted a special contract (charter) by the state or the local school board. Charter schools often form to offer educational alternatives unavailable in regular public schools.

chief state school officer The chief executive of the state board of education; sometimes called the state superintendent or commissioner of education.

child benefit theory A theory that government aid directly benefits the child rather than a nonpublic institution he or she attends.

child depravity theory A theory that children, because of their sinful nature, tend to be disorderly and lazy and need strict discipline to develop a personal sense of order and civility.

Children's Internet Protection Act (CIPA) An act providing that schools and libraries receiving discounts on electronic equipment and media are required to install a "technology protection measure" preventing minors from using computers to access "visual depictions that are obscene, child pornography, or harmful to minors."

classical humanists The leading theory and general method of education during the Renaissance; the study of the classical Greek and Roman texts with an emphasis on their humanistic (human-centered) meaning.

collective bargaining A procedure for reaching agreements and resolving disagreements between employers and employees through negotiation.

Commission on the Reorganization of Secondary Education A National Education Association commission that shaped the high school curriculum through its recommendations in *The Cardinal Principles of Secondary Education* (1918).

Committee of Ten A committee of the National Education Association chaired by Charles Eliot, which shaped the high school curriculum through its recommendations of a four-year program and a curriculum that included academic subjects for all students.

Common Core State Standards Standards released by the National Governors Association Center for Best Practices (NGA Center) and the Council of Chief State School Officers (CCSSO) in 2010 to define the knowledge and skills students should know by their graduation from high school.

common school A publicly supported and locally controlled elementary school.

community control An elected community council or board that shares decision-making power with the local school board.

community participation Citizen advisory committees at either the local school or school board level.

community schools When the school is seen as only one of the educational agencies within the community, and the school serves as a partner, or coordinating agency, in providing educational, health, social, family support, recreational, and cultural activities to the community.

compensatory education An attempt to remedy the effects of environmental disadvantages through educational enrichment programs.

concrete-operational period A stage of human development identified by Jean Piaget that occurs from ages 7 to 11 years, when children organize their concepts in performing increasingly complex mental operations.

Confucius (551–478 BCE) Chinese philosopher, government official, and educator who devised an ethical system still observed in China and other countries in Asia.

consolidation The combining of small or rural school districts into larger ones.

constructivism A theory of learning which argues that children learn most effectively and readily by constructing ideas based on direct explorations of the environment.

continuing contract An employment contract that is automatically renewed from year to year without need for the teacher's signature.

controlled choice A system in which students can select their school as long as their choices do not result in segregation.

Council for the Accreditation of Educator Preparation The national accrediting body for educator preparation programs that uses peer review and evidence-based accreditation.

critical theory (critical pedagogy) A theory of education which contends that some public-school systems limit educational opportunities for students marginalized due to race, class, and gender biases. Proponents argue that teachers should be "transformative intellectuals" who work to change the system. Also known as "critical discourse."

cultural pluralism Acceptance and encouragement of cultural, ethnic, language, and religious diversity within a larger society.

culture Patterns of acquired behavior and attitudes transmitted among the members of society.

curriculum Planned experiences provided via instruction through which the school meets its goals and objectives.

curriculum alignment Coordination of instructional planning, methods, materials, and testing to accomplish important learning objectives.

cyberbullying Actions that involve the use of electronic means to torment, threaten, harass, humiliate, embarrass, or otherwise target another person.

D

deconstruction Critical examination and dissection of texts or canons to determine the power relationships embedded in their creation and use. Often used by educators who follow a postmodernist philosophy.

deductive logic The process of thinking by which consequences or applications are drawn out of general principles or assumptions; the process of thought in which conclusions follow from premises.

de facto segregation Segregation associated with and resulting from housing patterns.

de jure segregation Segregation resulting from laws or government action.

desegregation Attendance by students of different racial and ethnic backgrounds in the same school.

differentiated instruction A type of instruction based on the premise that all students differ in how they learn, their personal strengths and weaknesses, their backgrounds, and their interests.

direct instruction A systematic method of teaching that emphasizes teacher-directed instruction proceeding in small steps, usually in accordance with a six- to eight-part lesson sequence.

distance education Instruction by people or materials distant from the learner in space or time; many distance-education projects use interactive television, the Internet, and other modern communication technologies.

dual-track school system The traditional European pattern of separate primary schools for the masses and preparatory and secondary schools for males in the upper socioeconomic classes.

due process A formalized legal procedure with specific and detailed rules and principles designed to protect the rights of individuals.

due process clause A Fourteenth Amendment statement that government shall not deprive any person of life, liberty, or property without due process of law.

E

Ebonics Frequently used as a synonym for Black English, Ebonics also refers to analysis of a dialect used by many African Americans and of how it might play a part in teaching Standard English.

ecological intervention Comprehensive efforts to improve the environments of young children.

Education for All Handicapped Children Act (Public Law 94–142) A law passed in 1975 which mandated that children with handicaps must have access to a full public education in the least restrictive educational environment.

educational ladder The system of public schooling developed in the United States that begins with kindergarten, proceeds through elementary school, continues through middle and high school, and leads to attendance at a community college, state college, or university.

educational voucher A flat grant or payment representing a child's estimated school cost or portion of the cost. Under a typical voucher plan, the parent or child may choose any school, public or private, and the school is paid for accepting the child.

effective schools Schools that are unusually successful in producing high student performance, compared with other schools that enroll students of similar background; sometimes defined as schools in which working-class students achieve as well as middle-class students.

enculturation A process of cultural transmission by which children learn their group's language, customs, and values.

environmentalist view of intelligence The belief that intelligence is mostly determined by environment.

epistemology The area of philosophy that examines knowing and theories of knowledge.

equal protection clause A Fourteenth Amendment statement that government shall not deny any person the equal protection of the law.

essentialism An educational theory that emphasizes basic skills and subject-matter disciplines. Proponents favor a curriculum consisting of reading, writing, and arithmetic at the elementary level and five major disciplines (English, math, science, history, and foreign language) at the secondary level. Emphasis is on academic competition and excellence.

essentialist-influenced curriculum A subject-centered educational theory based on six major disciplines: English, mathematics, the sciences, history, foreign languages, and geography. Contemporary essentialists also add computer literacy.

establishment clause A constitutional provision that prohibits the establishment of a government-sanctioned religion.

ethical relativism Asserting that ideas and values are constructed by specific cultural groups during a particular historical period, they depend on the place, time, circumstances, and situations in which they arise. Ethical relativism denies the existence of universal and eternal truths and values. It is associated with pragmatism, progressivism, social reconstructionism, and critical theory.

ethics The subdivision of axiology that examines questions of right and wrong and good and bad.

ethnic group A group of people with a distinctive history, culture, and language.

ethnicity A shared cultural background based on identification and membership with an ethnic group.

exclusive product rights Special privileges whereby commercial enterprises pay a fee for the exclusive right to market their product (for example, Pepsi Cola) in the school district.

existentialism A philosophy that encourages individuals to define themselves by making significant personal choices.

experience As defined by John Dewey, the interaction of a person with his or her environment.

explicit comprehension instruction Classroom techniques specifically for teaching comprehension.

explicit teaching A systematic method of teaching that emphasizes teacher-directed instruction proceeding in small steps, usually in accordance with a six- to eight-part lesson sequence.

F

fair use A principle allowing use of copyrighted material without permission of the author under specific, limited conditions.

Family Educational Rights and Privacy Act (Buckley Amendment) A law passed in 1974 to curb possible abuses at institutions receiving federal funds.

flipped classroom A classroom in which students are introduced to lesson content at home, typically through an online video of the teacher's lecture, and practice demonstrating mastery of the content in the classroom with the teacher acting as a facilitator, assisting students who need help.

first-language maintenance Continued teaching in a language while introducing instruction in another language.

Follow Through A program that concentrated on improving achievement of low-income children in the primary grades.

formal-operational period A stage of child development identified by Jean Piaget that occurs from age 11 through early adulthood, when individuals formulate abstract generalizations and learn how to perform complex problem-solving processes.

free exercise clause A constitutional provision that protects rights of free speech and expression.

G

gender roles Socially expected behavior patterns for girls and boys, and men and women.

goals Broad statements of educational purpose.

Goals 2000 The 1994 revision of the *National Educational Goals* that added two additional goals and updated states' progress on the *National Educational Goals* while providing additional services, programs, and classes as needed.

H

Head Start A federal government program that provides preschool education for economically disadvantaged four- and five-year-old students.

hereditarian view of intelligence The belief that intelligence is mostly determined by heredity.

"hidden" curriculum What students learn, other than academic content, from the school milieu or environment.

high school A secondary school for students that typically includes grades 9 or 10 through 12.

highly qualified teacher An aspect of the No Child Left Behind Act, which specifies that teachers should have (1) a bachelor's degree; (2) full state certification and licensure as defined by the state; and (3) demonstrated competency as defined by the state in each core academic subject he or she teaches.

homogeneous grouping Involves the sorting of students into groups or subgroups based on their ability and/or previous achievement, following the assumption or belief that this makes it easier to provide effective instruction.

hornbook A single sheet of parchment containing the Lord's Prayer, letters of the alphabet, and vowels, which is covered by the translucent, flattened horn of a cow and fastened to a flat wooden board. It was used in colonial primary schools.

humanistic approach to curriculum A student-centered curriculum approach that stresses the personal and social aspects of the student's growth and development. Emphasis is on self-actualizing processes and moral, aesthetic, and higher domains of thinking.

hurried children Children highly pressured to excel at an early age.

I

idealism A philosophy which asserts that reality is spiritual, intellectual, and nonmaterial.

inclusion Educating students with disabilities in regular classrooms in their neighborhood schools, with collaborative support services as needed.

individualized education program (IEP) Plans including both long- and short-range goals for educating students with disabilities.

Individuals with Disabilities Education Act (IDEA) Legislation enacted in 1990.

Individuals with Disabilities Education Improvement Act (IDEIA) A 2004 law which requires that if a child is identified as disabled, school officials must conduct a functional assessment and develop suitable intervention strategies.

induction Providing a supportive environment for novice teachers so they may experience a more methodical entry into the teaching profession.

inductive logic The process of reasoning from particulars to generalities, from the parts to the whole, and from the individual to the general. It is the basis of the scientific method, emphasized by Dewey and the pragmatists.

in loco parentis The idea that schools should act "in place of the parent."

integration The step beyond simple desegregation that includes effective action to develop positive interracial contacts and to improve the performance of low-achieving minority students.

intelligent design The argument that life is too complex to be formed through natural selection as portrayed by Darwin; therefore, it must be directed by an "intelligent designer."

intermediate unit or regional educational service agency (RESA) An educational unit or agency in the middle position between the state department of education and the local school district; usually created by the state to provide supplementary services and support staff to local school districts.

International Association for the Evaluation of Educational Achievement (IEA) A research group that began conducting cross-national studies in the 1960s.

Islam Religion founded by Mohammed (569–632 CE); currently practiced in many Middle Eastern and other countries.

J

Judeo-Christian tradition The Western cultural tradition that has been shaped by Judaism and Christianity.

junior high school A two- or three-year transitional school between elementary and high school, commonly for grades 7–9.

L

land grant A grant in which the income from a section of federal land is used to support education.

land-grant college A state college or university offering agricultural and mechanical curricula, funded originally by the Morrill Act of 1862. Today, many institutions originally established as land-grant colleges are large multipurpose state universities.

latchkey children Children unsupervised after school.

Latin grammar school A preparatory school of the colonial era that emphasized Latin and Greek languages and studies required for college admission.

learning styles Distinctively different ways students learn, such as emphasis on oral or visual activities.

least restrictive environment A term used in educating students with disabilities to designate a setting that is as normal or regular as possible. Federal law requires that children with disabilities be placed in special or separate classes only for the amount of time necessary to provide appropriate services.

liberation pedagogy Paulo Freire's educational theory that encourages teachers and their students to develop a critical consciousness of the conditions that oppress them and to free themselves from this oppression.

litigants Parties in a lawsuit.

local school board A body of citizens, either appointed or elected, who set policy regarding schools in a local school district.

M

macrocosm The universal whole or entirety. In idealism, it is the most universal, complete, and abstract idea from which all subordinate ideas are derived.

magnet school A type of alternative school that attracts voluntary enrollment from more than one neighborhood by offering special instructional programs or curricula; often established in part for purposes of desegregation.

mainstreaming Placing students with disabilities in regular classes for much or all of the school day, while also providing additional services, programs, and classes as needed.

mediated entry The practice of inducting persons into a profession through carefully supervised stages.

mental discipline Strengthening the mind through mental activities, just as the body is strengthened through exercise.

merit pay A plan that rewards teachers partially or primarily on the basis of performance or objective standards.

metaphysics The area of philosophy that examines issues of a speculative nature dealing with ultimate reality.

microcosm A smaller part of the greater whole, the macrocosm, from which it is derived.

middle class Professionals and small-business owners, as well as technicians and sales and clerical workers.

middle school A two- to four-year transitional school between elementary and high school, commonly for grades 6–8.

mill A unit of the local tax rate representing one-thousandth of a dollar.

monitorial method A method of instruction, also known as mutual instruction, developed by the English educators Andrew Bell and Joseph Lancaster, which was popular in the early nineteenth century.

Montessori schools Early childhood institutions that follow Maria Montessori's philosophy and method of instruction. They emphasize that children learn by developing sensory, motor, and intellectual skills by using didactic materials in a structured environment.

multicultural education Education that includes the cultures and cultural contributions of all racial, ethnic, language, and gender groups, especially those marginalized in the traditional curriculum. Many multicultural programs also emphasize positive intergroup and interracial attitudes and contacts.

municipal overburden Severe financial crunch caused by population density and a high proportion of disadvantaged and low-income groups.

N

National Assessment of Educational Progress (NAEP) A periodic assessment of educational achievement under the jurisdiction of the Educational Testing Service, using nationally representative samples of elementary and secondary students.

National Board for Professional Teaching Standards (NBPTS) A national nonprofit organization that issues certificates to teachers who meet its standards for professional ability and knowledge.

National Education Association (NEA) The largest organization that represents teachers in the United States.

National Education Goals, The A 1990 National Governors' Conference report on education in America that delineated six educational guidelines for state and local education agencies; revised in 1994.

Nation at Risk, A A landmark national report critical of public education in the United States that resulted in raising high school graduation requirements in most states.

naturalistic theory The educational rationale that education and instruction should be based on the natural stages of human growth and development.

Neolithic Age The "new stone age" in human development characterized by the making of tools, domestication of plants and animals, and settlement in small villages, which began around 10,000 BCE.

new core curriculum (core subjects approach) A curriculum of common courses that all students are required to take. Emphasis is usually on academic achievement and traditional subject matter.

No Child Left Behind Act (NCLB) The federal Elementary and Secondary Education Act passed in 2001, which requires states and school districts that receive federal funding to show adequate yearly progress, as measured by standardized tests of students in grades 3–8 and in high school, and to provide all students with "highly qualified" teachers.

normal school A two-year teacher-education institution used to prepare elementary teachers in the nineteenth and early twentieth centuries.

nuclear family Mother and father living with their children.

O

object lesson A method developed by Johann Heinrich Pestalozzi, who used concrete objects as the basis of form, number, and name lessons.

objectives Specific statements of educational purpose, usually written for a particular subject, grade, unit, or lesson; commonly defined in behavioral terms so that student experiences and performance can be observed and measured.

occupational prestige The special status accorded to certain occupations and not to others.

oral tradition The use of the spoken, rather than the written language, to transmit the cultural heritage through songs, stories, and myths.

outcomes-based education (OBE) Education guided by the principle that success should be judged by student "outcomes" (generally seen in terms of abilities to function in real-life contexts) rather than by "inputs" such as programs, courses, or funding. Many proponents would revise traditional curricula that fail to produce desired outcomes.

overloaded schools Schools with a high incidence of serious problems that make it difficult for educators to function effectively.

P

Paideia Proposal, The Mortimer J. Adler's educational proposal that uses the Greek term *paideia*, the total educational formation, or upbringing of a child in the cultural heritage, to assert that all students should pursue the same curriculum consisting of intellectual skills and organized knowledge in language, literature, the arts, sciences, and social studies. It is a modern form of perennialism.

Paleolithic period The prehistoric "old stone age," which lasted for 2.6 million years to about 10,000 BCE), when small, nomadic bands of people searched for food.

Parent-Teacher Association (PTA) A national organization of parents, teachers, and students to promote the welfare of children and youth that has affiliated local groups in school communities.

parent-teacher group An organization of parents and teachers in a local school community.

peer culture Behaviors and attitudes of similar-age children or youth in an institution or society.

perennialism An educational theory that emphasizes rationality as the major purpose of education, asserting that the essential truths are recurring and universally true. Proponents generally favor a curriculum consisting of the language arts, literature, and mathematics at the elementary level, followed by the classics, especially the "great books," at the secondary and higher levels.

perennialist-influenced curriculum A fundamentally subject-centered educational theory that the main purpose of education is the cultivation of the best of the past, the classics.

performance pay A compensation plan that offers financial incentives for teachers who can demonstrate that their performance enhances student academic achievement.

personal income tax A tax based on a percentage of personal income.

philosophies Systematic developed bodies of thought, each representing a generalized worldview about reality, logic, and values.

plaintiffs Persons who sue.

Plato's *Republic* Plato's most systematic philosophical statement on politics and education. Using the format of dialogues, it portrays a perfect city ruled by philosopher-kings according to the principle of justice.

postmodernism A philosophy that is highly skeptical of the truth of meta-narratives, the canons that purport to be authoritative statements of universal or objective truth. Rather, postmodernists regard these canons as historical statements that rationalize one group's domination of another.

pragmatism A philosophy that assesses the validity of ideas by acting on and testing them; the consequences of such action determines an idea's viability.

preoperational stage A stage of human development identified by Jean Piaget that occurs from age two to seven years, when children create categories, classify, add to, and reconstruct their conceptions of reality through systematic environmental explorations.

principal The chief administrative officer of the school who is responsible for school operation.

profession An occupation that rates high in prestige and requires extensive formal education and mastery of a defined body of knowledge beyond the grasp of laypersons.

professional development Continued education or training of a school district's teaching staff.

Professional Learning Community (PLC) In collaborative groups, teachers and other colleagues work together to improve instruction for their students.

professional practice board A state or national commission that permits educators to set professional standards and minimal requirements of competency.

Program for International Student Assessment (PISA) Numerous documents published by the Organisation for Economic Co-operation and Development providing information and analysis based on data regarding student performance in reading, mathematics, and other subjects collected in more than seventy nations.

Progress in International Reading Literacy Study (PIRLS) An international comparative study of the reading literacy of students at the fourth-grade level. It has been administered periodically since 2001.

progressive taxes Taxes based on the taxpayer's ability to pay, for example, income taxes.

progressivism An antitraditionalist theory in American education associated with child-centered learning through activities, problem solving, and projects. The Progressive Education Association promoted progressivism as an educational movement.

property tax The main source of revenues for local school districts, based on the value of real property (land and improvements on land).

R

race Groups of people with common ancestry and physical characteristics.

Race to the Top (RTTT) A federal program that between 2009 and 2015 provided competitive grants to support educational innovations and reforms in states and districts.

realism A philosophy which asserts that reality consists of an objective order of objects that, though they are external, can be known by humans through their senses and power of abstraction.

reflective teaching A style of teaching that emphasizes reflective inquiry and self-awareness.

regressive taxes Taxes that require lower-income groups to pay relatively more of their income than higher-income groups.

relevant curriculum Curriculum that addresses social change, emphasizing knowledge, skills, and attitudes pertinent to modern society.

reminiscence The recalling or remembering of ideas that Plato asserted were latently present in the mind. Through skilled questioning, the teacher stimulates students to bring these ideas to the conscious mind.

resistance theory The view that working-class students resist the school in part because a hegemonic traditional curriculum marginalizes their everyday knowledge.

Response to Intervention An approach that dictates leaving a child in the regular school program while providing him or her with suitable interventions; only if that does not work is the child referred for special-education or disability services.

restructuring Multiple changes to bring about systemic improvement in a school or group of schools.

revisionist view of schools The belief that elite groups have channeled disadvantaged students into second-rate schools and inferior jobs.

rhetoric The theory and practice of public speaking, declamation, and oratory in ancient Greece. During the Middle Ages, it tended to emphasize written discourse as well as speaking. Along with grammar and logic, rhetoric was part of the *trivium* of the liberal arts.

S

sales tax A tax based on purchase of taxable goods (generally not food or services).

Scholasticism A method of theological and philosophical scholarship and teaching used in medieval higher education which argued that the Christian scriptures and doctrines, and human reasoning, especially Aristotle's philosophy, were complementary sources of truth.

school choice A system that allows students or their parents to choose the schools they attend.

school infrastructure The basic physical facilities of the school plant (plumbing, sewer, heat, electric, roof, windows, and so on).

scientific method A systematic approach to inquiry in which hypotheses are tested by replicable empirical verification.

sensorimotor stage A stage of child development identified by Jean Piaget that occurs from birth to two years, when children develop their earliest concepts by environmental exploration.

sexting The act of using a smartphone or comparable electronic device to transmit sexually explicit images of oneself to individuals known to or in contact with the sender.

social and emotional learning (SEL) Involves the process of children developing the skills, attitudes, and values necessary to acquire social and emotional competence (that is, managing emotions, achieving positive goals, showing empathy for others, maintaining positive relationships, and making responsible decisions).

social Darwinism Spencer's ideology applied Darwin's biological principles of the "survival of the fittest" and competition to individuals in society.

social reconstructionism The theory developed by a group of progressive educators who believe schools should deliberately work for social reform and change.

socialization The process of preparing persons for a social environment.

socialized education Jane Addams's educational philosophy in which the school curriculum includes units on multiculturalism, urbanization, industrialization, technology, and the peaceful resolution of international conflicts.

socioeconomic status (SES) Relative ranking of individuals according to economic, social, and occupational prestige and power; usually measured in terms of occupation, education, and income, and generally viewed in terms of social-class categories ranging from working class to upper class.

Socratic method The method of inquiry named for the ancient Greek philosopher, Socrates, who asked probing questions about truth, goodness, and beauty that caused his students to examine their beliefs and values.

Sophists Members of a group of itinerant educators in ancient Greece during the period from 470 to 370 BCE who emphasized rhetoric, public speaking, and other practical skills. Their approach contrasts with that of the speculative philosophers Plato and Aristotle.

standards Focused statements on the purposes of education.

state board of education An influential state education agency that advises the state legislature and establishes policies for implementing legislative acts related to education.

state department of education An agency that operates under the direction of the state board of education. Its functions include accrediting schools, certifying teachers, apportioning state school funds, conducting research, issuing reports, and coordinating state education policies with local school districts.

state school code A collection of state laws that establish ways and means of operating schools and conducting education.

state standards Performance indicators showing students have achieved academic mastery at levels set by state boards of education.

student-centered curricula Curricula that focus on the needs and attitudes of the individual student. Emphasis is on self-expression and the student's intrinsic motivation.

subject-area curriculum A type of subject-centered curriculum in which each subject is treated as a largely autonomous body of knowledge. The curriculum emphasizes traditional subjects that have dominated US education since the late nineteenth century, including English, history, science, and mathematics.

subject-centered curricula Curricula defined in terms of bodies of content or subject matter. Achievement is judged according to defined outcomes such as test scores, correct answers, or appropriate responses.

superintendent of schools The chief executive officer of the local school district who implements policies adopted by the school board.

supply and demand Market conditions that affect salaries such that pay decreases when there is a large supply of teachers and rises when supply is low and teachers are in high demand.

synthesizers' view of intelligence The belief that intelligence is determined by interaction of environment and heredity.

systemic improvement Reform efforts that simultaneously address all or most major components in the overall educational system.

T

tax base Basis upon which taxes to support public schools are assessed at state and local levels—for example, property tax, sales tax, or income tax.

taxpayer resistance When taxpayers show reluctance to continue paying increased taxes to support public schools.

technology-enhanced learning Instructional strategies that draw upon technology in a variety of ways.

tenure Permanence of position granted to educators after a probationary period, which prevents their dismissal except for legally specified causes and through formalized due-process procedures.

theories Sets of related ideas or beliefs, often based on research findings or generalizations from practice, that guide educational policies or procedures.

Third International Mathematics and Science Study (TIMSS) A research group that has conducted cross-national research since 1996.

time-on-task Classroom time engaged in learning activities.

Title 1 A portion of the federal Elementary and Secondary Education Act that provides funds to improve the education of economically disadvantaged students.

Torah The first five Books of Moses that form the foundation of Hebraic religion, culture, and education.

torts Civil wrongs.

town school The eighteenth- and early-nineteenth-century New England elementary school that educated children living in a designated area and was the common school's predecessor.

traditional view of schools The belief that the educational system provides students, including economically disadvantaged ones, with meaningful opportunities. Also, the historically based perception that schools should teach basic skills such as reading, writing, spelling, arithmetic, and academic subjects.

transitional bilingual education (TBE) A form of bilingual education in which students are taught in their own language only until they can learn in English.

tuition tax credits Tax reductions offered to parents or guardians of children to offset part of their school tuition payments.

twenty-first-century skills Instruction fostering student success in the global job market and problem solving in the modern democratic society that takes place in engaging, flexible, and active environments.

U

underclass Section of the lower working class subject to intergenerational transmission of poverty.

upper class Wealthy persons with substantial property and investments.

US Department of Education A cabinet-level department in the executive branch of the federal government that is in charge of federal educational policy and the promotion of educational programs.

user fees Special fees charged specifically to those who use a facility or service (for example, recreational facilities, bus service, or after-school centers).

utilitarian education The teaching of skills and subjects applicable to daily life, work, and society. Herbert Spencer argued that the subject of most use, or utility, was science.

values-centered curriculum Places special emphasis on moral and ethical issues; more popularly known as *character education*.

Vergara v. California A state-court ruling that tenure unconstitutionally deprives students at low-achieving schools of equal educational opportunity.

vernacular schools Primary institutions that provided instruction in students' common language, in contrast to schools that instructed in classical languages such as Greek or Latin.

W

whole-child concept The view that schools must concern themselves with all aspects of students' growth and development, not merely with cognitive skills or academic learning.

working class Skilled crafts workers and unskilled manual workers.

Y

year-round schools Rotating schedules that allow students to attend school for three out of four quarters during a chronological year.

INDEX

Note: Figures and tables are indicated by *f* or *t* following page numbers.